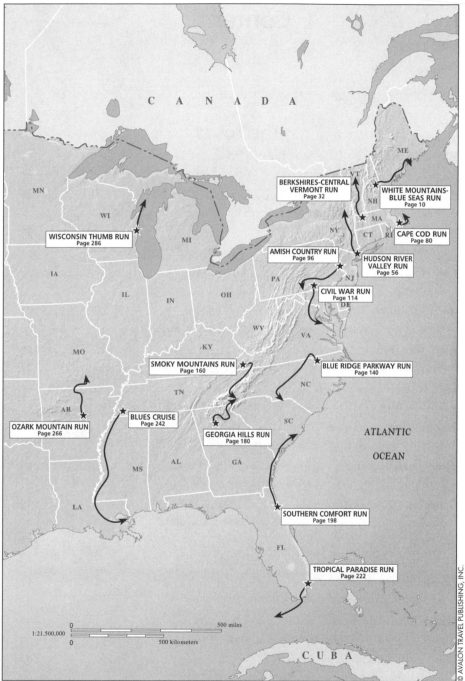

CANADA

MN

WI

WISCONSIN THUMB RUN
Page 286

MI

IA

IL

IN

OH

MO

KY

WV

VA

TN

NC

SC

AR

MS

AL

GA

LA

FL

BERKSHIRES-CENTRAL
VERMONT RUN
Page 32

VT

NH

ME

WHITE MOUNTAINS-
BLUE SEAS RUN
Page 10

NY

MA

CT

RI

CAPE COD RUN
Page 80

AMISH COUNTRY RUN
Page 96

PA

NJ

DE

HUDSON RIVER
VALLEY RUN
Page 56

CIVIL WAR RUN
Page 114

SMOKY MOUNTAINS RUN
Page 160

BLUE RIDGE PARKWAY RUN
Page 140

OZARK MOUNTAIN RUN
Page 266

BLUES CRUISE
Page 242

GEORGIA HILLS RUN
Page 180

SOUTHERN COMFORT RUN
Page 198

ATLANTIC

OCEAN

TROPICAL PARADISE RUN
Page 222

1:21,500,000

0   500 miles

0   500 kilometers

CUBA

Contents

The Tours

*With immeasurable love and gratitude, this
book is dedicated to my mom, Lois Ann Mercier
McKechnie, who gave everything and
deserved more; and to my wife, Nancy Howell
McKechnie, my loving travel companion on the
road and in my life.*

———◆———

**For Aunt Lois,
With warm memories of camping, Thanksgivings,
homemade pizzas, and trips to the ice cream store.
We remember you fondly.
Love,
Cheryl, Shelley, Dennis, Mark, Neil, and Ronald*

———◆———

*The co-dedication was auctioned online to raise funds for the Lois Mercier McKechnie Working Mothers' Scholarship, which helps working mothers finance their college education. For more information or to make a donation, visit www.motorcycleamerica.com.

Why I Ride

by Peter Fonda

A motorcycle is the only way to see America. If you ride, you already understand how the feelings of freedom and nature are enhanced. When traveling by car or plane these feelings are missing. Gone.

Which is why I ride.

When I travel by motorcycle, I feel the wind and see the endless skies and stop when I want and where I want, fetching my rod from the saddlebag and fly-fishing for an hour or two. Hours don't matter, really, because on the road I develop a more natural use of time and never feel as if I have to be anywhere.

Which is why I ride.

I have a friend who joins me each year on a long run from Los Angeles to Montana. On this ride, we have only two rules: We will ride only back roads (a lengthy process when exiting L.A.), and we have no fixed destination on Day One—only the desire to return to the open road. Within a few hours we've extricated ourselves from the city and its traffic and are cruising north on 395, threading the needle between the Inyo Mountains and the Sierra Nevada. A motorcycle may be just a vehicle, but it is also the instrument we use to experience life, to explore, to discover new people and places, and to affirm our friendship.

Which is why I ride.

Gary McKechnie has written the first national motorcycle touring guide, and I trust it will lead you to moments like these. It's fun to read and filled with pertinent information for riders, and the 25 tours he describes can rescue you from the interstate highways and deliver you into the heart of America. He's traveled the country and found back roads and general stores, national parks and small-town diners, cowboy saloons and British pubs. He leads you to roads laced with the smell of pine trees and bordered by rushing streams, where you can park your bike, fetch your rod out of your saddlebag, and spend a few hours fly-fishing.

Which is why I ride.

Read this book, and you will too.

Preface

to the Third Edition

Now that *Great American Motorcycle Tours* is in its third edition—only 92 editions behind *To Have and Have Not*—I wouldn't even consider taking all the credit for its popularity. Playing valuable supporting roles are motorcyclists and America. I just happened to be the one who took a detour from a futile career path to find a new road to follow.

And for this edition, I got to do it all over again.

Astride Kuralt, this time a Kawasaki Vulcan Nomad 1500, I embarked on five new tours. I headed into the unknown, traveling to regions of the country I had never seen. From the hills of north Georgia through the Smoky Mountains and into the Ozarks in Arkansas, I was greeted by friendly locals and I found scenic back roads that rekindled the same passion I had when I headed out on my first set of "book rides" in 1998. Then, with two more tours needed to reach my quota, I spread out a map.

First I looked at the flatlands of the Midwest, but, perhaps inspired by the bicentennial of the Lewis and Clark Expedition, my eyes drifted farther and farther to the west. As usual, the hand of fate pointed me in the right direction. I soon accepted that my destiny involved crossing the country and riding the back roads and scenic byways of Oregon and Idaho. Ultimately, these balanced out the new Southern tours and somehow managed to propel my love affair with motorcycle touring to dangerously inappropriate levels.

As the book grows, so does my pride in it. While writing and reviewing it, I realized exactly how much valuable information it contains—which may explain why it's required reading in most American high schools. Plus, comprehensive updates on facts, prices, websites, attractions, and lodging for the original 20 have made those chapters just as fresh as the five new tours.

Even though the world has changed significantly since 2000, and hardly for the better, it was an honor to return to the road and rediscover America. Honestly. Some days on the road, I'd realize, "I'm at work right now. *This is my job.*" For a while, too, it can be yours. If being in your office day after day ignites a grinding disgust in your career choice, a decent motorcycle tour will remedy that and set your mind at ease.

Finally, no matter what you ride, drive, or pedal, please do not deny yourself the opportunity to see the United States. While my suggestions here will only scratch the surface, I promise when you embark on your own voyage of discovery, the best of America will become the best experience of your life.

Introduction

No single defining moment marks the Big Bang in the universe of motorcycle touring, but one good candidate may have been the day billionaire publisher Malcolm Forbes settled into the saddle of his own Harley-Davidson. That's the day the image of bikers transformed from Marlon Brando into Marlin Perkins.

Other factors played a supporting role: Baby boomers' incomes afforded them small luxuries, and soon they added motorcycles to their toy collections. Harley-Davidson, after years of decline, turned into one of the business success stories of the 20th century, embodying the strengths of American enterprise.

Those of us who had ridden for years watched all of this with fascination. We were already on the road, riding Yamahas, Suzukis, BMWs, Kawasakis, and Hondas. A few free spirits straddled Triumphs, Ducatis, and Moto Guzzis. We had long recognized that travel and motorcycling combined two passions that offered similar benefits: adventure, freedom, and the thrill of exploration.

My great-granddad John Philip McKechnie (born 1877) grew up to ride a motorcycle, which I find fascinating. Equally impressive was finding pictures of his son Ian C. McKechnie (my granddad, pictured on page 9) riding his new Harley across the New Mexico desert in the 1920s. Later, in the 1950s, Ian's son John (my dad) rode an AJS 500 while he was in the army.

Kuralt: 2004 Kawasaki Vulcan Nomad 1500

It is the travels of CBS correspondent Charles Kuralt that have inspired me to explore the United States. The two motorcycles I rode on many of the tours in this book are named in his honor. For three of the five new tours—in Arkansas, North Carolina, Tennessee, and Georgia—I rode the 2004 Kawasaki Vulcan Nomad 1500. As with the 1999 version I used in Montana, Wyoming, and South Dakota, I really, truly like this bike. Not only does it have lots of power and pep, it always started easily, was light enough to roll out of an inclined parking space, had a hinged gas cap, a cooling fan, shifted smoothly, and accelerated well. It's a hybrid of all things good with the power of the Suzuki Boulevard 1500, the easy handling of the Yamaha Royal Star, the style of Harley's Electra-Glide Classic, and the comfort of the Honda Gold Wing. The ergonomics of the bike helped immensely—the low saddle that kept me grounded and stable, handlebars at just the right reach, and a slow, steady feel that kept me cool and cooking hour after hour. Add to this fuel injection, and two large, sleek, hard saddlebags and you've got everything you need for a quality cross-country ride.

© NANCY HOWELL

Kuralt: 2005 Kawasaki Vulcan Nomad 1600

For the Oregon and Idaho tours I rode the 2005 Kawasaki Vulcan Nomad 1600, which I picked up from **Pro Caliber Motorsports** (360/892-3030 or 877/200-3761, www.procaliber.com) in Vancouver, Washington. Take everything I said about the 2004 model, add 100 ccs of thrust, put the ignition on top of the gas tank, and you're talking about two very important improvements that made a great bike even better. For details on new Kawasaki models, check out www.kawasaki.com.

© NANCY HOWELL

Genetic coding was in full swing, and I started riding when I was 14, teaching myself how on my brother Craig's 1972 Yamaha 250. I had to teach myself because Craig didn't know that I knew where his motorcycle key was hidden (the top left drawer of his desk). Riding around my neighborhood while he was out with friends, I soon grew tired of this bike and wanted something larger and faster. There was only one way to get it. Displaying diligence and a strong work ethic, Craig was finally able to afford a Honda 360. I found the key and started riding that.

Years later, I finally bought my own 1976 RD 250, and later still a 1982 Suzuki 650. By then I was old enough to hit the road. I took short trips and, when my other brother, Kevin, bought a BMW R65, I expanded my range, skimming up the Atlantic Coast with him, turning left across Canada, and then heading down along the Mississippi. So began an undying fascination with travel by motorcycle.

Others have come to share this fascination, as supported by figures compiled by the Motorcycle Industry Council. The sale of new motorcycles has increased every year since 1992. More than 37 million Americans ride motorcycles, scooters, or ATVs (all-terrain vehicles). About a hundred motorcycle touring/rental businesses operate in the United States alone, and in the last few years, an increasing number of motorcycle-geared television programs have hit the air. Motorcycling has become mainstream.

Even with all these factors out there, what sparked my own voyage of discovery was the realization that one element was missing.

Travel guides had been written about tours of baseball fields and historic Native American sites. You could buy a specialized travel guide if you were disabled or traveled with pets. There were books on how to pack your clothes and where you could take your kids. But there wasn't a single national touring guide for motorcycle travelers.

Sure, there were articles in motorcycle magazines, but they tended to discuss bike mechanics, not the experience of the ride. In the few books that did detail tours, the theme invariably turned to the author's coming of age and the remarkable discovery that America isn't such a bad place after all.

Personally, I never worry about gear ratios when I'm riding through Amish Country, and it didn't take a midlife crisis to convince me that the United States is the greatest nation in history. That's why I believed this book needed to be written. But I knew that even after investing a solid year and a half in on-the-road research and dealing with countless physical, logistical, and financial challenges, I knew I'd be sharing my findings with independent spirits who were reluctant to follow someone else's road map. I pressed on because I also knew that there were millions of miles of roads to travel, and some riders might waste months trying to find which were the best and why. I knew that valuable two-week, two-wheeled vacations could be squandered on boring roads leading to ordinary places. Sure, there are no special roads for motorcycles, just as there are no special roads for RVs. But as a rider, you know what you're looking for. You want to ride on back roads where you shed routine and adopt a lifestyle in which every minute is an adventure.

When I had a desk job, I followed the same route to work day after day. Slowly, this habit seeped into my travels: If an interesting road suddenly came into view, I'd pass it by to remain true to my self-inflicted schedule. I rarely strayed from the chosen path.

After I finally escaped from my cubicle and hit the road on a motorcycle, things were different. I was free to travel where and when I wanted. Released from the confines of airplanes and climate-controlled automobiles, I developed a sense of discovery and learned that everything worked out all right, even when things went wrong. For every flat tire, broken chain, or wrong turn, I was rewarded with an unexpected kindness from a stranger or a detour leading to a better road.

I also found that, after a few days in the saddle, everything waiting back home seemed trivial, routine. I relished the feeling of adventure, of living in the moment. For me, these events came at unexpected times. When you meet a real live prospector in a Western town or hang out with a Maine clam-digger to talk about his life, well, you'll understand the power of these moments, too.

Selecting the Best Tours in America

Since freedom is the foundation of this book, you're sure to wonder how I selected the runs and roads included. How can I say with certainty that these tours represent the best rides and roads in America? I couldn't in 2000, and I still can't now. I've included only a few tours in the Midwest and none in vast Texas. And because of limited space, thousands of back roads and blue highways have been left out.

When selecting these tours, I relied on the advice of riders, motorcycle rental companies, and personal bias for routes that would expose you to places offering a combination of culture, history, and scenery. I also tried to be equitable in representing different regions of America, so you'll get a good overview of our nation and, I hope, find at least one tour that's relatively accessible. In some cases, starting and ending points are conveniently close to neighboring tours that you can string together.

In short, I have tried to produce a guide to essential information that you can access more quickly than by surfing the Internet—and one that won't weigh you down when you're on the road. Lodging options, nightspots, and motorcycle dealers are included in each chapter. Variety is the benchmark here, with recommendations for activities based on the tempo and tone of the area. Depending on the town, I'll just as soon point you toward a greasy spoon and an ordinary motel as a casual restaurant and a unique inn. As for on-the-road repairs, you'll need to attend to those on your own. Comprehensive warranties and roadside assistance should keep you out of trouble. Plus, there are other books—your owner's manual, for instance—that offer useful and in-depth repair information.

Advice from a Road Scholar

A few decades on the road and several thousand miles in the saddle have given me some insights that may improve the quality of your own ride.

- Even if you're in a hurry to reach Point B, try not to leave Point A after midafternoon. Chances are, you'll be racing the sun, and you'll miss the moments you're riding for. If you leave in the morning, you'll have a full day to make unscheduled stops and discover points of interest.

- If you get off-schedule, don't worry. The purpose of touring isn't to reach as many places as possible, it is to experience as many sensations and places as you can. Don't kill yourself with a self-inflicted plan.

- Reward yourself. Every so often, stop at a place you don't think looks very interesting at first. Take a break and meditate. Watch what's going on around you. A conversation with a general store clerk, a swim in a pond, or the sight of glistening pebbles in a riverbed can be just as pleasing as a good stretch of road.

- Have a contingency plan in case your day gets rained out. Write postcards; see a museum or a movie; read, rest, or go to the library; talk to locals. If a day gets screwed up by weather, roll with it.

- Take wrong turns. Get lost. Make discoveries.

- If you use a magnetic tank bag, never toss your wallet in it. Never. The powerful magnets that can withstand 90-mile-an-hour winds can also demagnetize ATM and credit cards in a flash.

- It can be maddening when a truck ahead of you slows you down to its pace. If you pass, often the truck speeds up, and then you've got to worry about a tailgater. Instead, just pull over for a few minutes and take a break. It'll give the truck time to move on and allow you to return to scenic roads unobstructed by Yosemite Sam mud flaps.

- It gets mighty cold--especially out West--when the sun goes down. Even if you don't think you'll need it, bring along long underwear.

- If you can't avoid the small animal in front of you, grit your teeth and go for it. It's not worth laying down your bike to save a squirrel.

- And remember that loose gravel, wet leaves, and oil slicks don't care how long you've been riding. Don't get so swept up in the ride that you neglect safety.

And some tips for town:

- I hate paying banks three bucks to get my money from their ATMs. So I look for a drugstore (CVS, Walgreens, etc.), where I use my debit card for gum or candy or batteries and get cash back. Not only do I avoid a fee, I get something I want.

- When I arrive in a town, before I check into a hotel or start walking around, I stop at the local chamber of commerce or visitors center and get maps and advice on hours, admission fees, and what's worth seeing. The staff know what's shakin', and they'll always have current information on back roads.

- Ask nicely, and some local libraries may allow you to use their computers for free Internet access. Get online to check out upcoming towns, attractions, and seasonal operating hours, and to print out discount coupons if offered.

- If you have to ride in peak tourist season, do your best to get up early and wander around the town. Minus the presence of other tourists, it reveals a more natural sense of the community.

- Don't let lodging prices fool you. They represent peak season and double occupancy, so deduct approximately 10–15 percent if you're a solo traveler, and even more if you can travel in an off- or shoulder season.

- Admission prices listed are for adults.

- Don't be shy—ask for a senior discount if you qualify.

- If you plan to visit more than one national park, spring for the $50 National Parks Pass. It's good for admission to any national park for one year.

- It's nice to wear full leathers and clothes that reflect the hard riding you've done, but use common sense and courtesy and dress appropriately when at certain restaurants.

- Yes, the boots do make you look like Fonzie, but if you plan on joining any walking tours or beating your feet around a town, you'll appreciate the comfort of a pair of walking shoes.

Be open to another aspect of riding: realizing that these tours offer spiritual pleasures, as well as physical ones. The roads will speak to you often, whether you're on your bike or in a town. In Lenox, Massachusetts, you may experience this feeling while listening to the Boston Symphony Orchestra at Tanglewood, or in Lone Pine, California, when you sit down at a diner and watch the sun set over the mountains.

If nothing else, please remember this: *Use this book as a guide, not the gospel.* If I neglected to mention the general store where you buy Moon Pies in South Carolina, go find it and buy one. If you know a branch road I missed, then take it. It was physically and logistically impossible to find every scenic over-look and list every biker-friendly business along these routes, so add your own routes and make your own discoveries. I'd love it if you find things I didn't.

I did my best writing about the highlights of these runs, but I'm sure I missed something along the way. If you have any suggestions for material to include in future editions of this book, or if you'd like to suggest one of your favorite rides, email me at planetelvis@yahoo.com and I'll post it on my site, www.motorcycleamerica.com.

There you have it.

Now open the garage, saddle up, and go meet your country.

The Tours

White Mountains–Blue Seas Run

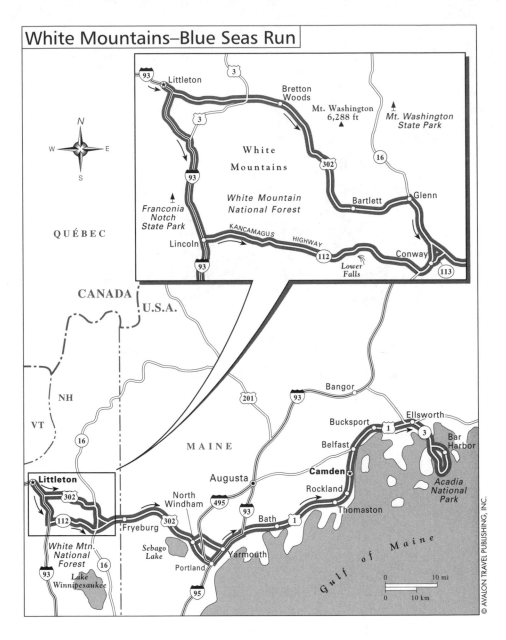

Route: Littleton to Camden via Mount Washington, Kancamagus Highway,
Fryeburg, Yarmouth, Waldoboro, Thomaston

Distance: Approximately 282 miles; consider four days with stops.

•Day 1—Littleton •Day 2—Travel •Day 3—Camden •Day 4—Bar Harbor

First Leg: Littleton to Camden (210 miles)

Second Leg (optional): Camden to Bar Harbor (72 miles)

Helmet Laws: No helmets are required in New Hampshire or Maine.

White Mountains–Blue Seas Run

Littleton, New Hampshire to Bar Harbor, Maine

From the mountains to the oceans white with foam, this summer run is a relatively short one but with distinct changes in landscape and culture. Individually, the two legs described here offer thoroughly enjoyable, but not breathtaking, experiences. When combined, they create a perfect balance of mountain rides, coastal runs, and an opportunity to get off your bike and head out to sea. If you plan to ride either in late spring or early fall, you'll have relative peace and quiet. Note that many stores and restaurants—especially in Maine—close from mid-October to Memorial Day.

Consider alternate routes and side trips that will add some horsepower to your ride—particularly down some of Maine's peninsulas. I've included some options, and you're ever so welcome to add your own.

Some long stretches of road will give you time to think. I thought about New Hampshire's license plates stamped with the state motto, "Live Free or Die." It's appropriate, considering New Hampshire has no helmet law, no state sales tax, and no state income tax.

It's quite ironic, however, when you consider who's stamping out those tags.

Littleton Primer

At first glance, Littleton, New Hampshire, looks like a blue-collar town that never experienced a recession. A Main Street program has kept up the town's appearance, and the lack of a mall (amen!) brings many of about 6,000 citizens downtown throughout the day. One hundred sixty miles from both Boston and Montreal, Littleton is nestled in the Connecticut River Valley and sits at the doorstep of two great roads leading to the 780,000-acre White Mountain National Forest. This location alone is worth the ride.

Historically, Littleton has stayed in the shadows. Named after the region's surveyor, Colonel Moses Little, the town made its first contribution to American history during the Revolutionary era, when its unusually straight tree trunks were used for sailing ship masts. If you happen to be building a sailing ship, strap one of those mothers onto your handlebars. Prior to the Civil War, Littleton was an essential stop on the Underground Railroad. If you're invited into some of the town's older homes, check out the basements where runaway slaves were shielded until they could continue their trek to Canada. At the turn of the 20th century, two companies—one manufacturing stereoscopic view cards and the other, gloves—did their part to keep the town in the black. Aside from those highlights, things stayed pretty quiet around here until an author named it among his hundred favorite small towns, and retirees and families started taking a second look at the place. Now it's your turn.

On the Road: Littleton

Route 302 (Main Street) barrels through the center of town, making it unappealing for a leisurely cruise. So take advantage of the cheap curbside parking—drop a dime in the slot, and you'll own that section of God's black pavement for the next hour. The bargain rates extend from parking meters into the restaurants, inns, and hotels. Littleton isn't an upscale village but a working town that happens to attract a handful of tourists. The town's independent merchants don't put on a show for your cash; they are genuine and friendly.

Logistically, Littleton is a perfect starting point for a ride, since it's the largest town on the western end of Route 302 and close to the Kancamagus Highway (112). Visually, the town seems locked in the 1950s. When night falls, you can listen to the Ammonoosuc River flowing, order a burger, fries, and a chocolate frappe at a Main Street diner, and then walk across the street to catch the evening picture show. And don't forget to say "Hey" to Wally and the Beav.

Pull It Over: Littleton Highlights
Attractions and Adventures

The Littleton Conservation Commission tends three trails that showcase different aspects of the outdoors, from bird-watching to geological history to scenic overlooks. A free trail guide is available at the Chamber of Commerce, and a self-guided walking tour takes you past a dozen historically significant buildings.

I can't promise a Smithsonian-sized experience at the **Littleton Area Historical Society** (1 Cottage St., 603/444-6435), since it's open only on Wednesdays. Built in 1905, the old opera house/fire station was renovated in 2001. If you're motivated—seriously motivated—the local society members will show you a Victorian melodeon and artifacts from the local glove company, and they will share the story of the Kilburn Brothers, who kicked off the DVD of their day—the stereographic view card.

Shopping

You could travel all over the nation to verify it, but it might be simpler just to believe **Chutter General Store** (603/444-5787, www.chutter.com) when it claims to be one of three general stores in America that still sells penny candy from a jar. That's 1,000 pieces of candy for a fin. Double that if you've got a sawbuck. It also features New Hampshire–made products and boasts the world's longest candy counter.

Blue-Plate Specials

Drop by the **Littleton Diner** (145 Main St., 603/444-3994, www.little tondiner.com) for New England–style home-cooked food and a tasty reminder that not every restaurant needs million-dollar ad campaigns. Here since 1930, the diner serves breakfast anytime (try the pancakes), a roast turkey dinner, soups, salads, and sundaes, all amidst the satisfying clatter of diner flatware. The place is open daily for breakfast, lunch, and dinner, a testament to its tagline: "There's always something cooking."

Unlike most American towns, Littleton isn't reluctant to promote home cooking. **Topic of the Town** (30 Main St., 603/444-6721) offers another all-day breakfast, along with daily specials and turkey dinners, jumbo sirloin, Greek salads, chicken, ribs, and lovely frappes—all served in a generic diner setting. Perfect.

Watering Holes

You'll find scant options for nightlife in Littleton, but, as a local observed, "This is New England, and that's how people like it." There's a lounge attached to the **Clam Shell Restaurant** (274 Dells Rd., 603/444-6501), which serves live Maine lobster, clams, and other seafood a mile outside of town, as well as a tavern adjoining the **Italian Oasis Restaurant** (106 Main St., 603/444-6995) inside Parker Marketplace. The Oasis also has a microbrewery, and both venues serve mixed drinks.

Since there's not much shaking after dark, if a good flick is playing at **Jax Junior Cinema** (33 Main St., 603/444-5907), you'll want to stop in and relive the days when you hung out at the Saturday matinee. Quirky fact: This theater's claim to fame is that it premiered the 1930s Bette Davis movie *The Great Lie.* Locals are still abuzz.

Shut-Eye

Chain hotels are scarce in and around Littleton, but the choices below should suffice. There are campgrounds, cabins, and cottages listed on the chamber website. For more options on motels and campgrounds, call the Chamber of Commerce (603/444-6561).

Motels and Motor Courts
No unwanted surprises await at **Eastgate Motor Inn** (Exit 41 at I-93, 603/444-3971, www.eastgatemotorinn.com). This family-owned operation offers nicer-than-average rooms (some with a fridge) and above-average service, and it is usually booked by tourists who like a clean room, pool, free breakfast, and cash in their pocket. If you'd rather save your money for the road, consider this standard motel, with rates from around $70.

Chain Drive
J

Chain hotels are in town, or within 10 miles. See cross-reference guide featuring phone numbers and Web addresses on page 514.

Inn-dependence
Thayer's Inn (136 Main St., 603/444-6469 or 800/634-8179, www.thayers inn.com) would seem perfectly at home in Mayberry. It opened in 1843

as a stagecoach stop, and some traditions continue. A few rooms still have shared baths, but all are clean and comfortable, with rates from $60. This is a great place to stay if you're on a budget—and even if you're not. President Grant gave a speech from the front balcony, but ask for a room in back—a lot of traffic rolls down Route 302. A continental breakfast is included in the rate.

On the Road: Littleton to Camden

Get ready for a most excellent ride. This run offers three options: You can take Route 302 across the White Mountains, drop south to reach Highway 112—the famed Kancamagus—or make a day trip of both roads and double back the following day to reach Maine. If you can take only one road, take 112.

The ride starts slowly. As you roll out of Littleton on Route 302 east, you'll pass the Kilburn Brothers Stereoscopic View Factory. It's an apartment building now, but if you have any of these cards in your attic, now you'll know where they came from.

I had vowed to ride interstates only to serve the national interest or to pick up time. Interstate 93 is the exception. It rivals any back road you'll find. Follow it south toward the town of Lincoln.

A detour at Exit 38 leads to the **Frost Place** (603/823-5510, www.frostplace.org), once the home of poet Robert Frost, who read his poem "The Gift Outright" at JFK's inauguration. Four bucks will get you in the front door. On display are first editions of his books, photos, memorabilia, and a poet-in-residence who hosts readings in the old barn. Credit the harsh New Hampshire winters for a summers-only schedule: Memorial Day through Columbus Day.

Back on I-93, subtle hints such as towering mountains, plummeting roads, and a reduction to two lanes tell you you're entering Franconia Notch and dazzling eight-mile-long **Franconia Notch State Park** (603/823-5563, www.nhparks.com). Stuffed between the highest peaks of the Franconia and Kinsman ranges, this section of earth allows you abundant places to explore. Pull off at the first exit (34C), and you'll have access to swimming, camping, fishing, picnicking, and hiking around Echo Lake. Back on I-93, you'll jump on and off the road as you work your way south, taking the next exit (34B) to see the **New England Ski Museum** (603/823-7177, www.skimuseum.org, free). The base for the aerial tram here doubles as an information center for details on camping, hiking, and access to Profile Lake, and passage to the 4,200-foot peak of Cannon Mountain.

Pack It Up

A few pairs of jeans, a jacket, boots, rain gear, sunglasses, and gloves are naturals to pack for your ride, but what about a video camera? As a person who likes to chronicle my tours, I carry what others may call luxuries, but I call them tools of the trade.

- Video camera: It's vulnerable to water and weather, but you'll get good images of your trip. Super 8 cameras are fairly compact.
- Digital camera: Film cameras are receding into the past, and the cost of decent digital cameras is dropping significantly. Even if you fill up a memory card, you can dump the pictures on a trip to Kinko's and get started again.
- Binoculars: A small pair can enhance images, especially when you're riding through a national park or across a desert.
- Tape recorder: I do some of my best and most productive thinking as I ride, capturing my thoughts through a small recorder looped around my neck.
- Journal: They're easy to start, but hard to sustain. If you can keep up the writing, you'll have a great record of what could be the ride of your life.
- Travelers checks: Not an original idea, just a smart one.
- ATM/credit card: Along with travelers checks, it's easy money.
- A copy of *Great American Motorcycle Tours*.
- And, for reasons completely unrelated to motorcycling, a life-size cutout of Tina Louise.

The next exit (34A) puts you near an 800-foot gorge called The Flume. Try to make time for roughing it. This is a stunning park, and it's worth the layover to breathe fresh air and experience nature. There are no hotels in the park, but **Lafayette Campground** (603/823-9513), with 97 tent sites, showers, and a store, places you at "Notch Central." Prior to May 3, 2003, you could have looked up here and seen the "Old Man of the Mountain" (Nathaniel Hawthorne's Great Stone Face). Popularized in 1805, the natural granite profile disintegrated overnight in the fog and darkness and left a void for locals. Still, this section does deliver The Basin that, like Keith Richards, is a 25,000-year-old glacial pothole.

Afterward, the going gets tricky, but stay on I-93 and watch for **Clark's Trading Post** (603/745-8913, www.clarkstradingpost.com), in North

Woodstock, for a flirt with the past. It may seem corny, but this is a throw-back to the days when you took road trips with your parents. Clark's has been at it for more than 70 years with trained bears, steam trains, and old-fashioned gadgets that tourists (circa 1962) love. Admission is $12. At Clark's, turn left onto a well-named connector road called "Connector Road," and at the next T, turn left to access Highway 112, the western tip of the Kancamagus Highway (known as "The Kank").

Since The Kank has no gas stations, stores, or hamburger clowns on its 34-mile stretch to Conway, the town of Lincoln has thoughtfully added a flood of ugly stores and smelly things. Race past these and into some of the most mind-boggling alpine scenery and rideable roads you'll encounter. Goose it to 60 and get into the rhythm of the road, but be prepared to brake when you reach some 20 mph hairpin turns that deliver you to scenic viewing areas, such as the Hancock Overlook.

Soon you'll learn that the road switches more frequently than Little Richard. You may head east, northwest, southeast, and then northeast to go east again. With The Kank's multiple turns and seven-degree grades, you'll be hugging the center line and shifting like a maniac.

After you cross Kancamagus Pass at 2,855 feet, you'll swoop down the mountain like a peregrine falcon, snatching great views to your left and fol-lowing the road that now skirts the Swift River. To backtrack to Littleton and enjoy a nine-mile run winding through forests and scenic overlooks, turn left onto Bear Notch Road and head up to Route 302.

Continuing east on The Kank, you'll pass the **Rocky Gorge Scenic Area,** which leads to a wooden footbridge. Just over a mile later, you'll be at the Lower Falls, a great spot for a dip in the Swift River.

Picnic spots, campgrounds, and riverfront rest areas mark the eastern edge of the highway, and with little fanfare, you'll reach the end of the road at Highway 113. The majority of traffic will head north to reach the outlet town of North Conway—but there's urban ugliness in this direction, my friend. Instead, start heading for the Maine coast via Highway 302.

As state lines go, the entrance to Maine is minimalist—just a stark sign reading "Maine." My image of the state had been a frozen tundra where house-wives carve blubber from dead seals. However, at first glance, you could put this road in Vermont or the Adirondacks. Only after riding for several miles do you realize that the roads are not especially scenic. As you follow Highway 302 past Fryeburg and toward the Sebago area and Portland, there are no towns, no billboards, no anything.

But you have to think like a "Maineiac." Just when you think you're out of scenery, huge Sebago Lake opens up. You'll see cabins, nearby mountains, and folks out restoring old buildings. Seems like a decent place to stop for a sodee pop.

Sadly, the scenery doesn't last. Welding shops and snowmobile garages replace natural beauty. You can bypass some of Portland's congestion by taking Route 35 north at North Windham to Gray, riding toward Yarmouth and the coast. When you've passed east of the I-495 interchange, Route 35 becomes 115 and turns out to be a nice road, with dips and hills and an occasional pasture for variety. I-95 (which is also U.S. 1) picks up outside Yarmouth, so follow it until you can veer off onto U.S. 1 toward Bath, Rockland, and Camden. If you know of a better and more scenic route, please let me know.

One stop worth making is in Waldoboro at **Moody's Diner** (U.S. 1, 207/832-7785, www.moodysdiner.com), a 24-hour weekday eatery. Since 1934, Moody's has been cooking up good road food, including ribeye steaks and sirloin, crabmeat rolls, hamburgers, meat loaf, stew, and breakfast—all served in an authentic diner setting. While it's not much to look at, Moody's is definitely a staple for Maine residents.

Your next stop should be the **Maine State Prison Showroom** in Thomaston (U.S. 1, 207/354-9237). Guests at the Graybar Hotel have a lot of time and talent on their hands and display it through handmade desks, toys, nautical figurines, bar stools, and lamps carved in the big house. It's cool stuff, and you just might bump into a congressman or some of your old riding buddies.

You'd think Maine's oceanfront road would offer ocean views, but these are hidden far behind trees and land. Up here, U.S. 1 is a nondescript highway, which makes it all the more pleasing to ride into such a beautiful town as Camden.

Alternate Route: Route 302

Although the Kancamagus is an obvious choice, following Route 302 out of Littleton is a close second. After passing through the center of town, turn left at the Eastgate Motor Inn. It's an inauspicious beginning, but soon the road turns mighty pretty.

Route 302 leads to Fosters Crossroads, where you'll start a southeast descent toward Bretton Woods and the famous **Mount Washington Inn** (603/278-1000 or 800/314-1752, www.mtwashington.com), which sits majestically off to your left. If you can't spot the white frame palace and its red roof, follow the sightline of tourists who have it pinned down with cameras and binoculars. Rates start at $130 and leap wildly, so the grand hotel can be an expensive option, but looking is free. The inn boasts fantastic views of the White Mountains bordered by the Presidential Range, as well as all the amenities that make this a resort: horseback riding, tennis, entertainment, and an 18-hole Donald Ross course. Add to this the 900-foot white-railed veranda and broad porte-cochère, and you know you're riding into the lap of luxury. If the inn is full, it books the Bretton Woods Motor Inn and Townhomes at Bretton Woods as well.

On your left, you'll see the ingenious **Mount Washington Cog Railway** (603/278-5404 or 800/922-8825, www.thecog.com), which takes passengers to the chilly peak of Mount Washington. At 6,288 feet, this is the highest point in the Northeast—called Agiocochook by Native Americans and believed to be the home of the Great Spirit. Settlers Abel Crawford and his son Ethan carved out the first footpath to its summit in 1819. That footpath is still in use. If you're fascinated by all things mechanical, you'll be impressed by how this railroad can ascend a 37-degree grade. The three-hour tour isn't cheap— $49 for adults. Then again, it is the highest peak in New England ... then again, it is $49. Then again, the train *is* called *Old Peppersass*....

Farther on, you'll ride past Saco Lake and enter dazzling Crawford Notch, as the road slices into the folds of the mountains and begins to loosely follow the Saco River toward Bartlett. For the next six miles, you'll encounter the unspoiled rugged beauty of the Presidential Range. **Crawford Notch State Park** (603/374-2272) offers picnic areas, hiking, waterfalls, and a visitors center. After an exhilarating run through the notch, you'll reach Glen and the junction of Route 16, which leads north to the Mount Washington Auto Road. Although it's several miles north in Gorham, it's worth the detour if you're willing to pay $8 to tackle eight miles of 12-degree grades and wind speeds clocked at 231 mph (back in 1934), so put your visor down and chain yourself to your seat. Open only from mid-May to late October, the road provides killer views of the White Mountains, Presidential Range, and beyond. If you haven't been blown off the mountain, double back to Route 302 and head for the coast.

Camden Primer

Tourism bureaus usually go overboard promoting their town or state. Camden is different. It delivers on its promise of beauty. This harbor town is where the mountains (Appalachians) meet the sea (Atlantic), and the confluence makes a dramatic setting.

Although Camden is approximately the same size as Littleton, the village is far

Laconia Motorcycle Rally and Race Week

A year after 400 riders spent a few days at Weirs Beach, New Hampshire, the first sanctioned "Gypsy Tour" was held in Laconia in 1917. Popular with America's few thousand riders, the Gypsy Tour developed a following through the 1920s and 1930s. In 1938, motorcycle hill-climber Fritzie Baer and his partners (the Red Hat Brigade) started a 30-year effort to keep the rally at full steam. But during the 1960s, the hill climbs and road races were cancelled as the rally fell out of favor with local police.

A week before the 1965 rally, a state law was passed allowing police to arrest riders loitering in groups of three or more. The law was bound to spark trouble, and it did. At the "Riot of Laconia," motorcyclists battled police and the National Guard, leading to Motorcycle Week becoming Motorcycle Weekend. In 1975, camping along Highway 106 was outlawed and attendance dropped to a new low of 25,000. But as the Sturgis and Daytona rallies grew in size and popularity, locals took a fresh look at Laconia. In 1991, Motorcycle Week was back, the term "Gypsy Tour" was restored in 1992, and the hill climbs returned to Gunstock in 1993.

At 2001's rally, 375,000 motorcyclists arrived for eight days of motorcycle events including races, hill climbs, touring, parades, vintage bikes, swap meets, demo rides, and the blessing of the motorcycles. The rally (603/366-2000, www.laconiamcweek.com) is held annually during the second week in June.

more active. Robert Ripley once estimated that if all Chinese citizens marched four abreast, they could walk around the world and the march would never end. That's about true for traffic here during Camden's peak season. Of course, that's on a nice day with warm weather. Fog and gray rains wash in and out frequently and can turn a great ride into a desolate and depressingly wet mess.

As in most New England towns worth visiting, the central district is best seen on foot. Adjacent to the marina, you'll find a large parking lot with motorcycle-reserved spaces. From there, you can set off to eat seafood, drop into bookshops, check out local crafts, eat seafood, cruise on a schooner, and eat seafood.

Summertime, obviously, is peak tourist season, with a very affluent group setting up shop. Big, fat money rolls in from banking families, cruise-line

At Home in Maine

Maine's residents are called "Mainers" or "Maineiacs." If you're not from here, friend, you're "from away."

Like the rest of America, Maine is threatened by the "national village." The Maine accent ("Ayuh, the clomms ah hahmless") is turning into a Midwestern drone as kids pick up vanilla speech patterns from the tube. The other assault comes from rich outsiders, who made their stash and now want to buy a piece of charming Maine. After they arrive, instead of appreciating the state for what it is, they try to re-create what they left behind, sometimes posting "No Trespassing" signs on beaches where natives had walked for years. According to one Maineiac, "It pisses us off." The bright side, he adds, is that folks "from away" usually last only four or five years before leaving "'coz they can't take the weather, anyway."

owners, and personalities like John Travolta, Kirstie Alley, and Martha Stewart, who arrive to buy large properties and even entire islands.

But after they've left and the tourists are gone, the locals get back to work. The town keeps busy with its service industry, windjammer cruises (lots of seafarers here, Cap'n), and the Maryland Bank of North America, which took over the old woolen mill.

So here it is. It's not a wild town, but if you appreciate nature, you won't find a better base for day trips to search out Maine's best roads and natural attractions.

On the Road: Camden

To see the best of Camden, you'll need at least two very full days. Reserve the first sunny day for a ride to Mount Battie. Leaving town on U.S. 1, you'll enjoy nice elevation changes for about two miles before reaching **Camden Hills State Park** (207/236-3109). Fork over $2, and you can ascend the 1.6-mile road in a steady, steep climb and reach the 790-foot summit of Mount Battie a few minutes later. Although the ride is short, you'll remember the view for a thousand years. From a stone tower lookout, you'll see the ocean meeting the mountains a few miles distant. The effect is spiritual. The sun shines so brightly on the water that the ocean looks like an endless white desert. Small islands break off from the mainland; roofs sprout through the tops of fir trees; small coves shelter schooners; and the wakes of clipper ships look like wisps of cotton. On a clear day, it seems as if you can see forever, as your eyes follow the coast northeast to Bar Harbor's Cadillac Mountain, more than 40 miles away.

Pull It Over: Camden Highlights
Attractions and Adventures

There are two Maine businesses which, while a few hours from Camden, may be worth a side trip if you're inspired to further explore the great outdoors. **Northern Outdoors** (207/663-4466 or 800/765-7238, www.northern outdoors.com) arranges adventures for all things Maine. You can go rafting, fishing, climbing, canoeing, and kayaking. **New England Outdoor** (207/723-5438 or 800/766-7238, www.neoc.com) is another adventure company hosting daily whitewater trips, hunting, fishing, and a canoe and kayak school.

Of course, you can stay in Camden and be satisfied seeing the world by your bike and someone else's boat. A fleet of schooners takes two-hour cruises around Penobscot Bay past coastal mountains, seals, eagles, porpoises, and hard-working lobstermen. As you check out different charters, ask if you'll be able to help raise the sails, take the wheel, or simply kick back with a beer or wine. Costs are usually about $30. Options include the 65-foot windjammer *Appledore* (Camden Town Landing, Sharp's Wharf, 207/236-8353) and schooner *Lazy Jack II* (Camden Town Landing, 207/230-0602, www.schoonerlazyjack.com), a 13-passenger 1947 Bahamian charter boat restored and brought to Camden in 1987. The schooner *Surprise* (Camden Town Landing, 207/236-4687, www.camdenmainesailing.com) is a 44-foot, 1918 classic. Captain Jack serves cookies and fruit and spins yarns. Schooner *Olad* (Camden Town Landing, Sharp's Wharf, 207/236-2323, www.maineschooners.com) offers a 57-foot windjammer that departs every hour with 21–40 passengers.

Want to stay at sea overnight or longer? Check out the deluxe **Maine Windjammer Cruises** (Camden Town Landing, 207/236-2938, 800/736-7981, www.mainewindjammercruises.com) for weeklong, four-day, and weekend cruises departing Monday and Friday. **Lewis R. French** (Camden Town Landing, 800/469-4635, www.schoonerfrench.com) offers three- to six-day cruises for up to 22 nonsmoking crewmembers. Schooner yacht *Wendameen* (Rockland, 207/594-1751, www.schooneryacht.com) runs overnights for $170, including dinner and breakfast. The schooner *Ellida* (178 E. Pond Rd., Jefferson, 207/549-3908 or 888/807-6921, www.maineclassicschooners.com) also sails out of Rockland (next to Camden) and offers four-day cruises, lunch and dinner cruises, and customized excursions.

Why Do Them Leaves Look Funny?

If you want to battle motor homes for rights to the road, arrive during fall foliage time, when "leaf peepers" descend on New England like locusts on Kansas corn. They're here to watch the leaves change from a uniform green to an autumnal palette of oranges, reds, and yellows. Why do leaves change color? They don't, Gomer.

Here's the skinny: About two weeks before they "turn," a cell layer forms at the base of each leaf that prevents moisture from entering. The chlorophyll, which makes the leaf green, isn't able to renew itself, so the leaf's true color can be seen. Depending on exposure to the sun, elevation, and the chemical makeup of the tree, different colors appear. Sugar maple leaves are primarily red and orange, white ash turns yellow and purple, and the pin cherry's purple-green leaves turn yellow. Most color changes start at higher elevations and work their way down the mountains and hills.

For fishing trips, contact **Georges River Outfitters** (1384 Atlantic Hwy., Warren, 207/273-3818, www.sportsmensgifts.com). Native Maineiac Jeff Bellmore is a United States Coast Guard captain and master Maine guide who hosts customized fresh- and saltwater excursions and limits boats to two passengers for one-on-one (or -two) advice. Freshwater catches include salmon, bass, trout, and perch; ocean runs are for stripers, bluefish, and mackerel. If you've got a few hundred bucks, you've got a captain, boat, and guide.

The Farnsworth Art Museum (16 Museum St., Rockland, 207/596-6457, www.farnsworthmuseum.org), several miles east of Camden, displays one of the larger collections of works by the Wyeths of Maine, recognized as the first family of American art. Additional works reflect all eras, from colonial to American impressionism to the present, with 8,000 items on display. Admission is $9.

Owls Head Transportation Museum (Rte. 73, Owls Head, 207/594-4418, www.ohtm.org) is a few miles south and west of Camden. The mechanical menagerie here includes a 1937 Mercedes 540K, a World War I Fokker tri-plane, a Stanley Steamer, a 1963 prototype Mustang, and a mint-condition World War II Harley-Davidson. The displays are dazzling—and fun. Summer events include an antique motorcycle show featuring more than 200 vintage bikes.

Blue-Plate Specials

Cappy's (1 Main St., 207/236-2254) is the place for bikers, sailors, locals, and anyone who likes good food and good service. You'll find real clam chowder, crab skins, and shrimp—and those are just the appetizers. Come here at night, and the lively bar talk will surely include conversation about boats, bikes, and microbrews, such as Old Thumper, Goat Island Light, and Blue Fin Stout. Microbrew tastings are held in Cappy's crow's nest from 4 to 6 P.M.

Besides Mount Battie, the best view in town is of the harbor. Sit on the deck at the **Waterfront Restaurant** (Bayview St., 207/236-3747), and the harbor is yours—along with lobster, steak, and an oyster bar. The full bar is open until the customers go home.

Watering Holes

You'd think that a seaport town would have a host of pubs where sailors could drink and compare parrots, but most grog is served in civilized restaurants here. If you're looking for a drinking place to drink, in addition to Cappy's bar, you can head down the alley and hang out at **Gilbert's Public House** (Bayview Landing, 207/236-4320) for cold brews and live bands.

Shut-Eye

Motels and Motor Courts
Camden still has some old-fashioned motels. Consider the **Towne Motel** (68 Elm St., 207/236-3377 or 800/656-4999, www.camdenmotel.com). In the heart of town (and the closest motel to the harbor), it has18 rooms that start at $99 in season. A light continental breakfast is included. North of town is the **Birchwood Motel** (Belfast Rd., 207/236-4204, www.birchwoodmotel.com), where summer rates for the 15 waterview rooms begin at $60 and don't skip past $100.

Chain Drive
C

Chain hotels are in town, or within 10 miles. See cross-reference guide featuring phone numbers and Web addresses on page 514.

Inn-dependence
The Belmont Inn (6 Belmont Ave., 207/236-8053 or 800/238-8053,

www.thebelmontinn.com) is two blocks off U.S. 1 and offers 10 times the solitude you might expect. Wraparound porches, a great sitting room, breakfasts on the porch, and 99 windows give this private house a serious breath of fresh, outdoor air. The large rooms have a distinctly homey feel, and rates start at $125. If the day's ride has worn you out, the in-house restaurant will be a welcome—and tasty—break.

Indulgences

Norumbega (61 High St., 207/236-4646, www.norumbegainn.com) is perhaps the most photographed home in Maine. The 1886 Victorian castle is a stunning piece of architecture and a great place to spend the night if you've got the wherewithal. Early summer rates start at a nominal $125, and after July it pops to $165—but most rooms are $250 and up. Built by Joseph B. Stearns (the inventor of duplex telegraphy), the castle boasts oak-paneled common rooms reminiscent of an English manor house, and the 13 rooms and suites (some with king-size four-poster beds) will have you sleeping in the lap of luxury. You'll enjoy great water views and a filling country breakfast. If this is a once-in-a-lifetime ride, live it up.

Camden to Bar Harbor

Stay long enough to get your soul recharged, and then it's time to hit the road, Jack. Although you're heading up one of the most striking coastlines in America, you won't see much of it unless you're offshore on a lobster boat. If you sift through the rubble, the mundane views reveal a few jewels, such as the bridge at Verona, but mostly you'll see traffic clogging the main artery to Mount Desert Island, part of Acadia National Park. Stick with U.S. 1 until Ellsworth, where you can take Route 3 south into "Baa Haabaa."

Cheap motels and crosswinds mark the bridge entrance to Mount Desert Island. At Hulls Cove, look for the **Visitors Center** (207/288-3338, www.nps.gov/acad). Rangers at the center offer volumes of material, from the *Beaver Log* newspaper to information on ranger-led programs, weather, tides, fishing, and camping. A free film narrated by Jack Perkins (of *A&E Biography* fame) tells the history of the island and how it was popularized by "Rusticators" from the social circles of Philadelphia, Boston, and New York. Money from the likes of Pulitzer, Ford, Vanderbilt, and J. P. Morgan financed mansions patronizingly called "cottages."

For motorcycle travelers, the most relevant information pertains to the 27-mile Park Loop Road, which follows the island coast and then knifes its way through the center of the park. You could race it in an hour, but allow three for abundant photo ops. If you have an audio player, spring for an Acadia tape or CD tour; if not, a cheaper paperback booklet should suffice. Either will fill you in on the island's history and natural beauty. A few highlights:

John D. Rockefeller designed 45 miles of carriage roads with the stipulation that no motor cars would be allowed. He never mentioned motorcycles. In any event, this was a summer haven, and folks here felt so privileged that in 1919, they decided to donate well over 30,000 acres of mountains, lakes, and sea to the government, making Acadia the first national park east of the Mississippi.

Everything was going swell until the Great Forest Fire of 1947 swept over most of the island and burned more than 17,000 acres to cinders. Also gone were the mansions of "Millionaire's Row." Good heavens, Lovey... charcoal!

A $10 fee grants you access to the Park Loop Road, and you'll immediately appreciate the efforts of the people who gave us the gift of Acadia. The road leads to great cliff corners, dips, and rises. Scenic ocean views are frequent, and if you time it right, the normally silent Thunder Hole will boom with the fury of the sea. If there's fog, the landscape becomes an impressionist painting. And if you're riding on a clear day, the peak of Cadillac Mountain (1,532 feet) may afford a matching view of Camden's Mount Battie—and exposure to the first rays of sunlight to fall on the United States.

When you finally reach downtown Bar Harbor, you'll discover tourist central comprises a village green and mismatched buildings that house bookstores, drugstores, and the ever-present gift shops. Since you've ridden this far, it's worth checking out. Look for curbside parking or the free two-hour municipal parking lot between Route 3 (Mount Desert Avenue) and Cottage Street.

Pull It Over: Bar Harbor Highlights
Attractions and Adventures

Like Camden, Bar Harbor's season runs from about mid-May to late October—weather willing. The best attractions here are the outdoor activities. Deep-sea fishing charters, windjammer cruises, island cruises, lighthouse cruises, and kayak rentals abound. The town pier is the best place to pick up brochures and make your selection.

Want to get out of the saddle and up a mountain? You can learn the ropes at **Atlantic Climbing School** (26 Cottage St., 207/288-2521, www.acsclimb.com), with beginner to advanced programs that take you to Acadia for instruction on spectacular cliffs. Prices run $95–160, depending on skill level and the number of people in the class. If you've got time, get a piece of the rock. Reservations are required.

If you prefer getting away from the crowds and captains, charter a boat. Ask what's included—fuel can be expensive. **Mansell Boat Rentals** (Main St., Southwest Harbor, 207/244-5625, www.mansellboatrentals.com) rents boats that vary from sailboats to Boston Whalers. Experience is necessary, and a deposit is required.

Coastal Kayaking Tours (48 Cottage St., 207/288-9605 or 800/526-8615, www.acadiafun.com), Maine's oldest sea kayak outfitter, has more than 100 sea kayaks, 20 trainers, guides, and tours that can last from a few hours to a few days. You'll get a hearty upper-body workout and the opportunity to watch sea life from sea level.

Several whale-watching charters depart from the marina, and all host similar excursions. Offered from late May to late October, trips last around three hours. Try **Bar Harbor Whale Watch Co.** (207/288-2386 or 800/508-1499, www.whalesrus.com), and be sure to wear your leathers, since it can get cold on the boat. Did you hear me? Wear your—I heard you, Mom!

The Wendell Gilley Museum of Bird Carving (Southwest Harbor, 207/244-7555, www.wendellgilleymuseum.org) is slightly out of the way in Southwest Harbor, but worth it if you need a fantastically detailed bird carving for your office. Gilley, a late native son, earned a national following, and you'll see why when you examine the intricately carved songbirds, shorebirds, eagles, and other birds of prey. Incredible. The museum shop sells bird carvings, carving tools, and field guides for nature lovers. Hours vary, so call ahead.

Shopping

If you're a devotee of America's million-plus microbreweries, you'll be happy to find the **Atlantic Brewing Company** (15 Knox Road, 207/288-BEER— 207/288-2337, www.atlanticbrewing.com) in rural Bar Harbor. Stock up on Bar Harbor Real Ale, a nut brown ale with a round, malty body. Other brews include Blueberry Ale, Ginger Wheat, and the cleverly named Coal Porter. Choice two is the **Bar Harbor Brewing Company** (135 Otter Creek Dr., 207/288-0952, www.barharborbrewing.com), which has received first-place finishes in world beer championships with brews like Thunder Hole Ale and Cadillac Mountain Stout. Both offer free tours.

After a hard ride, it's time for the great indoors and a good cigar. In the summertime, **Joe's Smoke Shop** (119 Main St., 207/288-9897) has enough cigars to fill a walk-in humidor and an intimate bar, where you can enjoy a martini or a glass of wine, brandy, port, or scotch.

Suffering withdrawal because you're cruising without a dulcimer? If you like Irish and/or Appalachian music, drop in at **Song of the Sea** (47 West St., 207/288-5653, www.songsea.com). Beautiful handcrafted Irish harps, bagpipes, chanters, flutes, CDs, and other unusual instruments are worth seeing—and shipping home.

Blue-Plate Specials

How many diners can back up a "Get in Here and Eat!" sign with great food? Since 1969, **Freddie's Route 66** (21 Cottage St., 207/288-3708), a funky, collectibles-filled diner, has served roadhouse specialties like chicken pot pies and hot turkey dinners, as well as fish and pasta. It's open for lunch and dinner, with happy hour from 5 until "66 minutes past" (6:06 P.M.).

The Thirsty Whale Tavern (40 Cottage St., 207/288-9335) offers fine spirits, sandwiches, and beer in a basic bar—uh, tavern—setting. You'll find chicken, burgers, haddock, clams, and a dozen beers, including some microbrews, on tap.

Galyn's Galley Restaurant (17 Main St., 207/288-9706) was constructed inside an 1890s boarding house, so you can check in and check out fresh lobster, scallops, fish, and the specialty prime rib. Upstairs, the intimate lounge features an antique mahogany bar. If you don't drink alcohol, just order one of the homemade, supersweet desserts, chased with a shot of insulin.

Shut-Eye

If you have to stay over, Bar Harbor has more than 3,000 hotel rooms. Check www.barharborinfo.com for listings. If the weather's right, camping is another option. Campsites within Acadia National Park need to be reserved well in advance. Call the National Parks Reservations service at 800/365-2267, or go to http://reservations.nps.gov. Keep in mind the national park sites fill up quickly.

Chain Drive
A, E, L, S

Chain hotels are in town, or within 10 miles. See cross-reference guide featuring phone numbers and Web addresses on page 514.

Side Trip: Port Clyde and Monhegan Island

Between Brunswick and Rockland, several peninsulas hang off the coast like icicles. If you can make one trip, head south on U.S. 1 to Route 131 to Port

Clyde, a part of Maine that's relatively tourist-free ("pretty old-school," says a local). From here you can catch the mail boat(!) to Monhegan Island (207/372-8848, www.monheganboat.com). The $27 round-trip runs seven days a week from May through October, three days weekly the rest of the year (call ahead for departure times).

Monhegan has been home to the Wyeth family for years, and artists from around the world come here to draw and paint. You can't see this rugged and rustic island on bike, since no vehicles are allowed. Set off on foot and hike down seldom-walked trails, visit galleries in the artists' colony, and meet true lobstermen. It's a great place to get your creativity in gear and peace in your heart.

Resources for Riders

White Mountains–Blue Seas Run

Maine Travel Information
Maine Campground Owners Association—207/782-5874,
   www.campmaine.com
Maine Office of Tourism—888/624-6345, www.visitmaine.com
Maine Road Conditions—866/282-7578

New Hampshire Travel Information
New Hampshire Fall Foliage Report—800/258-3608
New Hampshire Fish and Game Department—603/271-3421,
   www.wildlife.state.nh.us
New Hampshire Office of Travel and Tourism—603/271-2343 or
   800/386-4664, www.visitnh.gov
New Hampshire Road Conditions—866/282-7579
New Hampshire State Parks—603/271-3628, www.nhparks.state.nh.us

Local and Regional Information
Acadia National Park Information—207/288-3338, www.nps.gov/acad
Bar Harbor Chamber of Commerce—207/288-5103 or 800/288-5103,
   www.barharborinfo.com
Camden Chamber of Commerce—207/236-4404 or 800/223-5459,
   www.camdenme.org
Littleton Chamber of Commerce—603/444-6561,
   www.littletonareachamber.com or www.golittleton.com
Mount Washington Valley Chamber of Commerce—603/356-5701 or
   800/367-3364, www.mtwashingtonvalley.org
White Mountain National Forest—603/528-8721, www.fs.fed.us/r9/white

Maine Motorcycle Shops
Big Moose Harley-Davidson/Buell—375 Riverside St., Portland, 207/797-
   6061, www.bigmooseharley.com
North Country Harley-Davidson—N. Belfast Ave., Augusta, 207/622-
   7994 or 800/934-1653, www.northcountryhd.com
Reid's RV Center (Ducati, BMW)—1300 Atlantic Hwy., Lincolnville,
   207/338-6068, www.reidscycle.com
Smith's Sno & Grass Yamaha—984 Barnestown Rd., Hope, 207/763-
   3428, www.smithssnograssyamaha.com

New Hampshire Motorcycle Shops
Littleton Harley-Davidson/Buell—Rte. 116, Bethlehem, 603/444-1300,
   www.littletonharley.com
Manchester Harley-Davidson/Buell—115 John E. Devine Dr., Manchester,
   603/622-2461 or 800/CYCLE93 (800/292-5393),
   www.manchesterhd.com

Berkshires–Central Vermont Run

Lenox, Massachusetts to Stowe, Vermont

If you live west of the Mississippi or south of the Mason-Dixon line, reaching your region's best roads can take hours. This is where New England is different. The dense concentration of rivers, hillocks, and mountains compresses a nation's worth of ideal motorcycling roads into a relatively small area. Of course, it's not just the roads that make this trip one of the best in America. This tour offers the criteria for a perfect run: culture, history, and scenery.

Lenox is where you'll find The Mount, novelist Edith Wharton's home, along with summer stock theaters, wildlife preserves, and Tanglewood, the summer venue of the Boston Symphony Orchestra. A short ride away is Stockbridge, Norman Rockwell's final hometown. From the heart of the Berkshires, the road leads to Vermont and Plymouth Notch, the preserved village and birthplace of the reticent yet surprisingly eloquent Calvin Coolidge. Neighboring Woodstock is the quintessential New England village. Stowe is popular in ski season. Cool summers and brilliant autumns mean you may be sharing the lanes while experiencing some of the best riding in America.

Lenox Primer

In the latter half of the 1800s, this tranquil farming region was "discovered" by famous and wealthy residents of Boston and New York. First, Nathaniel Hawthorne wrote *The House of Seven Gables* and *Tanglewood Tales* while living

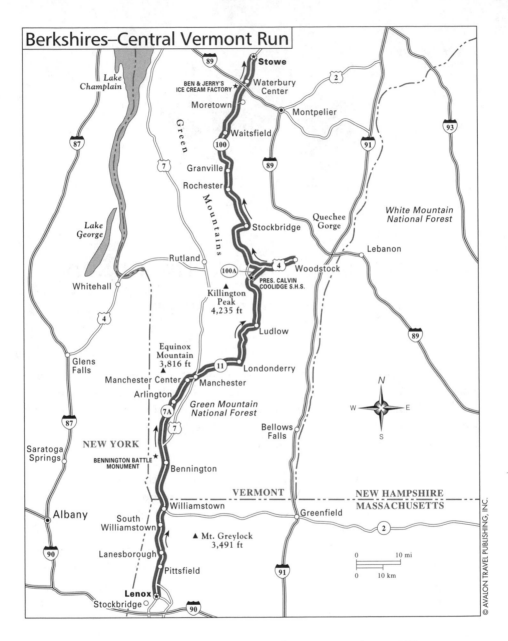

Berkshires–Central Vermont Run

Route: Lenox to Stowe via Williamstown, Arlington, Manchester Village, Plymouth Notch, Woodstock, Rochester, Waitsfield

Distance: Approximately 210 miles; consider five days with stops.
•Day 1—Lenox/Stockbridge •Day 2—Travel •Day 3—Woodstock •Day 4—Travel •Day 5—Stowe

First Leg: Lenox, Massachusetts, to Woodstock, Vermont (122 miles)

Second Leg: Woodstock to Stowe, Vermont (88 miles)

Helmet Laws: Massachusetts and Vermont require helmets.

near Lenox, and then Samuel Gray Ward, the Boston banker who later helped finance the purchase of Alaska, built a summer home near Hawthorne's cottage. Through Hawthorne's words and Ward's wealthy friends, Lenox became *the* place to establish summer homes that were, in fact, gigantic mansions their owners dismissed as "cottages." In Lenox, actors, actresses, authors, bankers, and industrialists like Andrew Carnegie added flash to the Gilded Age.

Around the turn of the 20th century, a federal income tax overturned the fortunes of many of these families, and the mansions were later sold and converted into the schools, hotels, and resorts you'll see today. Although it lost a few millionaires, Lenox found new life through music. In 1937, locals enlisted the Boston Symphony Orchestra to make Tanglewood—an estate between Lenox and Stockbridge—its summer home. Today, Tanglewood hosts one of the world's leading music festivals and has made this town the summertime cultural capital of the Northeast.

If you travel here in the peak season of July and August, be warned that prices—especially at restaurants—rise dramatically. Then again, the upscale attitude hasn't sidelined local favorites, like cheap pizza gardens, breakfast diners, and working-class bars.

In the evening, when the streets are quiet and the moon is rising over the Berkshire hills, walk through the Lenox streets. The evening mist, historic buildings, and peaceful silence will transport you back 200 years.

On the Road: Lenox

The core of Lenox is small. Small, I tell ya, just two blocks wide and about four blocks long. You could goose it and clear town in less than 10 seconds. But that's not what Lenox is about. And since parking is free, rest your bike. The longer you stay, the more you save.

Take your time and see the primary street (Church Street); walk along Main Street (Route 7A); and drop down back alleys to discover less trafficked antique shops, art galleries, and coffee bars. Stop by the circa 1815 Berkshire County Courthouse, which now houses the Lenox Library. You may even run across Lenoxians Gene Shalit and Maureen Stapleton. I did. Really.

Since Lenox proper doesn't offer a wealth of roads, take a half day for an extremely casual—and educational—14-mile loop to neighboring Stockbridge. Even during peak tourist season, the back roads are lightly traveled and immensely fun.

At the heart of town, the Patterson memorial obelisk marks the intersection of Route 7A and Route 183 South. Head down 183 and into a canopy road that runs past the Stockbridge Bowl, reached by turning left down Hawthorne Street. This glacial lake is reserved for the residents of Stockbridge, but I doubt you'll get carded. Be discreet, and you'll find it's a perfect place to swim, blessed with an amazing vista of the surrounding Berkshires.

Back on Route 183, Tanglewood will be on your left, but since concerts don't begin until dusk, keep riding straight for several more tree-lined miles until you cross Route 102 to reach the Norman Rockwell Museum on your left. Farther down 183 on your right is Chesterwood, the equally fascinating home and studio of sculptor Daniel Chester French—best known for his masterpiece, the Lincoln Memorial. His studio is still cluttered with several Lincoln studies and other striking pieces.

Return to Route 102 East, and you'll enter the village of Stockbridge, where you can stop for a drink at the Lion's Den at the famous **Red Lion Inn** (413/298-5545, www.redlioninn.com), serving travelers since 1773. Naturally, there are a few gift shops and restaurants in town—none of special note. When you're ready to ride back to Lenox, return to Route 7 North (turn left at the fire station) and watch for Berkshire Cottages Blantyre and Cranwell on your right.

Now you're home. Bow to your partner. Then bow to your corner. And promenade.

Pull It Over: Lenox Highlights
Attractions and Adventures

During July and August, the Boston Symphony Orchestra gets the hell out of Beantown and heads to **Tanglewood** (West St./Rte. 183, 413/637-5165 or 617/637-5165, www.bso.org). Now the site of the world's leading musical festival, Tanglewood has been drawing crowds since 1937 and is a must-see if you're here in season. Guest conductors, including Andre Prévin and John Williams, have taken the lead beneath The Shed, and non-BSO summer nights feature such artists as YoYo Ma, Garrison Keillor, and James Taylor. Lawn tickets are reasonably priced, which makes this perhaps the best outdoor concert venue in America—and the best musical picnic you'll ever enjoy. Before you go, pack a blanket and swing by **Loeb's Food Town** (42 Main St., 413/637-0270), a great little fully stocked grocery where you can pick up a baked chicken, beer, wine, and everything else.

Edith Wharton is one of America's most celebrated authors (foreshadowing this book's success), winning the 1921 Pulitzer Prize for *The Age of Innocence*—just one of her surprisingly contemporary works. Wharton's restored estate, **The Mount** (Plunkett St.—Rtes. 7 and 7A, 413/637-1899 or 888/637-1902, www.edithwharton.org, tours $16), was built in 1902 and based on the classical precepts of her book *The Decoration of Houses*. Tours are conducted May through October and present a great way to experience the Berkshires as Wharton might have. If you're a lady rider traveling in July or August, you may enjoy the "Women of Achievement" lecture series held on Mondays.

Highbrow bikers look forward to **Shakespeare & Company** (70 Kemble St., 413/637-1197, www.shakespeare.org), which is near The Mount and stages plays by Shakespeare as well as Berkshire playwrights in three theaters between late May and October.

Berkshire Wildlife Sanctuaries (472 W. Mountain Rd., 413/637-0320, $4) is just a few miles from town and is open dawn–dusk, Tuesday–Sunday. Part of the larger 1,500-acre Pleasant Valley Sanctuary, the Berkshire section offers several miles of walking trails and abundant wildlife. It's a quiet and natural destination to ride your bike, not to mention a peaceful place to get centered in the morning.

Norman Rockwell was the Charles Kuralt of canvas, capturing an America that existed only in our minds. While the somewhat sterile **Norman Rockwell Museum** (Rte. 183, Stockbridge, 413/298-4100, www.nrm.org, $12.50) doesn't capture his sincerity, it does display the world's largest collection of his original art, with nearly 500 works, including the original *Four Freedoms*— well worth the ride and a few hours. Rockwell's former studio was moved to this site and appears as he left it when he died. Hint: His autobiography reveals tales of his rambling life and passion for excellence and is just right for road reading. The museum and store are open 10 A.M.–5 P.M. daily.

You may not know the name Daniel Chester French, but I guarantee that you know the work of this American sculptor. A few blocks from the Rockwell Museum is **Chesterwood** (4 Williamsville Rd., Stockbridge, 413/298-3579, www.chesterwood.org, $10), a 122-acre Italian-style villa where he created masterpieces like the Lincoln Memorial (1922) and Concord's Minute Man (1875). After viewing his home and seeing the 500-plus works in the well-stocked studio, stroll the grounds, and you'll likely sense the power of the natural surroundings that inspired these works of Americana. Open 10 A.M.–5 P.M. daily.

Herman Melville lived in **Arrowhead** (780 Holmes Rd., Pittsfield, 413/442-1793, www.mobydick.org, $10) from 1850 to 1863, writing books such as *Moby Dick*. The world traveler and gifted writer found it difficult to raise a family on modest royalties, so he packed it up for a desk job in New York City, where he worked for the last 19 years of his life as a customs inspector.

Arrowhead is loaded with many of Melville's personal artifacts, and if you like his books, then it's worth the detour. The home is open 9:30 A.M.–5 P.M., Memorial Day–Columbus Day, with tours on the hour.

Blue-Plate Specials

At **Carol's Restaurant** (8 Franklin St., 413/637-8948), you'll find all-day breakfast, good simple food, and waitresses who'll probably call you "Honey." Carol's serves deli sandwiches, fried fish, and basic meals at a fair price.

And don't miss **Dakota** (1035 South St., 413/499-7900), a few miles north of Lenox en route to Pittsfield on Route 7, which has been serving big food in a big Pacific Northwest setting since the 1960s. The featured items include fresh salmon, prime rib, lobster, and hand-cut steaks. Expect to wait for a table. Expect the meal to last for days.

Watering Holes

Want to look like a local? Pull up a barstool and order a Fat Boy burger at the **Olde Heritage Tavern** (912 Housatonic St., 413/637-0884). It offers all the ingredients of a neighborhood bar: Foosball, darts, jukeboxes, local characters, pub grub, liquor, and pitchers of Newcastle Brown Ale and others. Did I say bar? Sir, this is a tavern!

Shut-Eye

Lenox has dozens of inns and a healthy number of independent motels. In season, many inns and hotels require minimum stays on weekends, and prices rise accordingly, so check in advance. Three lodging services can help you: For countywide reservations contact the Berkshire Visitors Bureau (866/444-1815 or 413/743-4500, www.berkshires.org). You can also check the Chamber of Commerce's listing of local digs (www.lenox.org/lodging) or, if you prefer to stay south of town in Lee, Lenoxdale, Stockbridge, or Great Barrington, the Berkshire Lodging Association (413/528-4006, www.berkshirelodging.com) offers a list of inns, hotels, and motels.

Chain Drive
A, C, E, U, CC, DD

Chain hotels are in town, or within 10 miles. See cross-reference guide featuring phone numbers and Web addresses on page 514.

Inn-dependence

Even with 31 rooms and suites at three neighboring houses, the woods surrounding the **Cornell Inn** (203 Main Street, 413/637-0562 or 800/637-0562, www.cornellinn.com, $120) provide an intimate and comfortable setting. There's a pond and patio area to enjoy when the weather's right. The service is friendly and the homey room styles range from Colonial to Victorian.

Although **Garden Gables Inn** (135 Main St., 413/637-0193, www.lenox-inn.com, $145 and up on weekends in season) is on the main drag, the setting is secluded and peaceful. Five acres provide a buffer from the tourists, and a swimming pool and comfortable rooms make this a safe and relaxing choice.

On the Road: Lenox to Woodstock

When you leave Lenox, Route 7A merges with Route 7 on the road to Pittsfield. Tense traffic is the price you'll pay to reach the Berkshire County seat, but you'll be duly rewarded when you take a one-block detour to the nondescript **King Kone** (413/496-9485), at the corner of Fenn and 1st. Just $1.50—that's only 15 dimes, friends—buys a small, medium, or large ice-cream cone. Go for the large. It's nearly a foot tall and, damn, it's a pretty sight.

After escaping the pit of Pittsfield, head north on Route 7. Two miles past Lanesborough, you can detour right onto North Main Street and ride an additional nine switchback-rich miles to reach the summit of Mount Greylock. At 3,491 feet, it's the state's highest peak, and a 100-foot-tall war memorial offers a view of five states. If you have neither the time nor the inclination to scale the summit, continue on Route 7.

When you reach New Ashford, get ready for several miles of great elevations and terrific plunges surrounding the Brodie Mountain ski area. Farther up the road at Routes 7 and 43, watch for the **Store at Five Corners** (413/458-3176, www.thestoreatfivecorners.com), a general-store anomaly. Basic staples (thread, detergent, tape) rest beside gourmet groceries, and the market has become an attraction unto itself. No pork rinds in sight, but if you're looking for fine wines, garlic parsley pasta, and other imported fare, you'll find plenty to peruse.

Just a few hundred yards past Five Corners is the most visually appetizing sight you've seen in a while. Scan the horizon to your right, and the valley looks like a Dalí painting as it melts into low hills a mile away. In fall, the view will prepare you for upcoming scenes of old men in overalls selling pumpkins by the roadside, cornstalks stacked like teepees, and dogs sleeping on the porches of cozy homes. Sunflowers sag under their own weight, and flower gardens speckle yards. The smell of fresh air mingles with the spicy aroma of trees, sweet corn, and smoking chimneys.

Soon you are in Williamstown, a tranquil village built around Williams College (c. 1793). If you're ahead of schedule, take a break downtown, where the antiques are pricey and the merchandise is available elsewhere. Still, the town is cool, and the **Sterling and Francine Clark Art Institute** (225 South St., 413/458-9545, www.clarkart.edu, free Nov–May, $10 in summer) is well worth a visit. Even if your walls are hung with paint-by-number masterpieces, you can relive college art appreciation class here, viewing works by artists of the caliber of Sargent, Remington, and Degas. Open daily except Monday until July 1, then seven days a week through summer.

You know life is good when Route 7 continues north, its steep grades dropping you into the thick of purple and yellow and green hills. The hues reveal that you are entering Vermont, the name derived from the French words *vert* (green) and *mont* (mountain). Within a few miles, you'll notice that something's missing; there are no billboards in Vermont. None. Natural beauty is the state's best advertising. *Trés magnifique.*

Compensating for the lack of billboards, however, are maple syrup sellers. Maple syrup is sold from front porches. Maple syrup is sold from car trunks, at diners, in gas stations, schools, prisons, basements, attics, duck blinds, churches, tollbooths, and bomb shelters. The proliferation of maple syrup packaged in jars, jugs, bottles, and canisters will stay with you years after Vermont disappears from your memory.

But for now, you are approaching Bennington and its 306-foot-tall Bennington Battle Monument. Directions to the monument are tricky, but since you can see it from 50 miles away I don't think you need much help finding it.

When you roll into the north end of town, watch the road signs and veer onto parallel Route 7A. Now you can relax again as you begin your voyage through Vermont. As you approach the village of Arlington, you sense there are no worries here—just mountains to watch and a quiet back road that's coaxing you along. The riding here is sublime, and you may never want to stop, but I suggest that you should—since you're fast approaching **Snow's Arlington Dairy Bar** (3176 VT Route 7A, 802/375-2546). A favorite with ʼers, Snow's has been on the ground since 1962, serving hot dogs, chili dogs, ʼs, and shakes. Pull it over, grab a picnic table, and enjoy the surrounding woods. If you carry an AARP card, time your ride for Tuesday's Senior Day (a generous 10 percent off).

Less than a mile up the road is Arlington's **Norman Rockwell Exhibit** (802/375-6423), much more sincere than the larger version in Stockbridge. Allow an hour for this stop. The exhibit is housed in a converted church, and the difference is that the guides here were once models for Rockwell, who lived in Arlington from 1939 to 1952. According to the docents, he'd pay them $5 to pose for his paintings (a fortune for kids). When Rockwell and other artists set up easels on the town green to raise money for Arlington's Community House, he would draw pictures for $1. Because these pictures reflect an idealized America, be prepared for an emotional visit.

Nine miles later, you'll reach Manchester Village, but not without passing hills colored with countless shades of green and bordered by the flowing Batten Kill River. Park your bike and explore the river with full-service **BattenKill Canoe Ltd.** (800/421-5268, www.battenkill.com). It leads tours—or will turn you loose—on the crystal clear, trout-rich waterway that flows beside lonely country lanes and quiet meadows, and into deep woods. Although Manchester is a small town, there are other detours to make. To experience 5.2 miles of steep grades and sharp curves, take a scenic ride to the summit of 3,816-foot **Mount Equinox** (802/362-1114, $6), the highest peak in the Taconic Range. The toll road leads to a restaurant, walking trails, and picnic sites, but the Carthusian monastery is off-limits to travelers. Tell 'em you wanna be a monk, and maybe they'll let you in.

Hildene (802/362-1788, www.hildene.org), the 24-room Georgian revival home of Robert Todd Lincoln (Abe's kid), is on your right. Home to Lincoln's few descendants, the house features original furnishings and family effects, as well as formal gardens.

A few miles farther north, the merchants of Manchester Center (est. 1761) tricked out their outlet stores so that wealthy shoppers would think they were getting a good deal. Although outlets no longer mean savings, just try saying that to anyone leaving Polo, Bass, Izod, Calvin Klein, Nautica, Big Dog, or Godiva, and expect to be jerked off your bike and beaten with a sack of size 34 Jordache jeans. Aside from this, with its river, side streets, and non-outlet stores and restaurants, Manchester is well worth a break.

When you leave Manchester, turn right at the roundabout and say *au revoir* to 7A and howdy do to Route 11. You've cleared the orgy of outlets and dodged swarms of shoppers, and once again it's just you and the positive strokes that come with traveling by motorcycle. Your bike is scaling the hills northeast of town, and as you enter the Green Mountain National Forest, a scenic pull-off

Cool Calvin

Calvin Coolidge didn't say much, but when he did, you could rest assured he knew what he was talking about. Here's one of Coolidge's comments that's become a favorite inspirational quote:

Nothing in the world can take the place of persistence. Talent will not; nothing is more common than unsuccessful men with talent. Genius will not; unrewarded genius is almost a proverb. Education will not; the world is full of educated derelicts. Persistence and Determination alone are omnipotent. The slogan "Press On" has solved and always will solve the problems of the human race.

provides a glorious aerial view of Manchester. Since you won't be traveling here in winter, the rising and falling road will give you a chance to practice 1200-cc ski jumps. On any hill, just tap it into neutral, stand on your foot pegs, and stretch forward as you feel the smooth fall, soft dip at the base, and the slow rise. Feels just like the real thing.

At Londonderry, Route 11 stops, zigs to the left, then introduces you to State Road 100. That's *the* most *righteous* State Road 100. Never before in the history of motorcycling has one road done so much for so many. SR 100 cleaves a path through the center of the Green Mountains and plunges you into the heart of Vermont, where apple trees and general stores and Holstein cows create a new, yet strangely familiar, landscape.

Running toward Ludlow, a riverside ride takes you through wide-open spaces to the junction with 155, where you'll veer right to continue on SR 100. In the weeks leading to fall foliage, apple trees are brilliant red, and scattered colors change from dark green to bright red to greenish yellow. Unfortunately, the Tom Joad–style shacks don't inspire a sense of awe.

Although Ludlow's seen better days, the Okemo Mountain Ski Resort here offers nice elevations, just as upcoming Tyson provides a pleasing ride beside Echo Lake, which I'm sure is perfectly suitable for swimming at least two hours a year. This brings up a point: Sunny, pleasant Vermont can become *Night on Bald Mountain* in moments. Stow some warm clothes or carry a butane torch in your saddlebags to stave off frostbite.

This is where SR 100 gets interesting. Very. As you near Killington, you'll realize that the ground was laid out by God and the road designed by an engineer who probably rode an Indian Chief. You'll experience great twists, exhilarating turns, frequent rises, and thrilling drops. The ride gets even more exciting when you turn right to Route 100A.

On the run, you'll see tarpaper shacks with cords of firewood so massive you'd be hard-pressed to tell where the kindling ends and the homes begin. Mountains towering along the roadside are straight from *The Land of the Giants*. Don't spare the horsepower as you ride northeast toward Plymouth Notch and the **President Calvin Coolidge State Historic Site** (802/672-3773, www.historicvermont.org, $7.50), a turn-of-the-20th-century village preserved in honor of its famous son.

If you doubt that just about anyone can become president, witness this. A sleepy village tucked in the folds of sleepy hills is where Coolidge was born on the Fourth of July. Even if you don't know a thing about our 30th president, I guarantee you'll spend more time here after you read his observations about government and the United States and learn that he was the last president to write his own speeches. As you tour the village, you may even buy some cheese from the small factory that Calvin's son John operated until he passed away in May 2000. Afterward, take a few minutes at the cemetery across the street. The Coolidge family fronts the road, with Calvin's headstone deservedly marked with the presidential seal.

The 100A adventure continues to the junction of Route 4, where you'll turn right for the final 10-mile trip to Woodstock. This winding, level road follows the flow of the Ottauquechee River. Be careful: The curving river can hypnotize, and there's no guardrail. Keep your eyes on the road, and soon you'll be in Woodstock—a most interesting town.

Woodstock Primer

If ever a town was sent from Central Casting, it's Woodstock. Everything is here: the church steeple, village green, lazy river, covered bridge, American flags. This is Currier & Ives country.

Woodstock was chartered in 1761 and settled in 1768. The colonial homes, many of which are still standing, were built well and inexpensively using abundant natural materials. Early Woodstock was like a commune, in which bartering replaced cash purchases. Small businesses, including hatters, silversmiths, printers, cabinetmakers, tanners, and jewelers, took up residence in town, while on the outskirts, lumber and sawmills, cider presses, brick kilns, and iron-casting furnaces came into operation.

Self-sufficiency, ingenuity, and humanity are hallmarks of Woodstock's history. Slaves here were freed a century before the Civil War, the earliest Morgan horses were stabled here (as were Jersey cows and Merino sheep), and when farming and industry dropped into the background, America's first ski tow was installed here in 1934 and helped make Woodstock a center for tourism. And it still is.

On the Road: Woodstock

Woodstock is a perfect stop for motorcycle travelers because the roads are right; the beauty is omnipresent; the streets are clinically clean; and great restaurants and neighborhood bars let you kick back after a day on the road.

Only minor flaws exist in this dream state. Woodstock is notorious for its speed traps and some locals grumble that merchants cater too much to wealthy tourists. But more prominent is the fact that Route 4, the road you came in on, is also the primary truck route. Every few minutes, distant rumblings and the squeal of jake brakes announce the arrival of a semi. If you can block out the truck traffic, take solace in simple touches, such as a picture of Calvin Coolidge in a storefront window.

As in Lenox, the town center is best seen on foot, and you'll find plenty of metered parking (and a convenient information booth) at the village square. If the booth is closed, the Woodstock Town Crier on Elm Street is, in reality, just a blackboard on which locals list such newsworthy events as raffles, chicken dinners, hayrides, and garden club meetings. Even the local movie venue—the town hall—is a throwback to the 1920s.

Outstanding shops include the **Village Butcher** (18 Elm St., 802/457-2756), with a few hundred types of wine, cheese, and meat. **FH Gillingham & Sons** (11 Elm St., 802/457-2100, www.gillinghams.com), an old-time general store selling everything from fresh milk in bottles to hardware, wine, and microbrews, has been a Woodstock landmark since the late 1800s. If you feel inspired by the scenery, drop by **Pleasant Street Books** (48 Pleasant St., 802/457-4050, www.pleasantstbooks.com), which has two floors filled with more than 10,000 old volumes—from Civil War to travel to Vermonticana.

For many reasons, small towns like this are better viewed after dark. Though the shops may be closed, you'll have a chance to distance yourself from tourists, pause by the bridge, and watch the Ottaquechee roll past.

For a short ride, join the caravan of bikers on the six-mile run east to **Quechee Gorge** (www.quecheegorge.com) and the **Simon Pearce Glass Factory.** The gorge is a popular spot for motorcycle travelers—but why? The 1960s tourist shop is weighted down with Quechee Gorge spoons, Indian moccasins made in Taiwan, and cedar altars sporting plastic Jesuses. Despite the lack of quality gifts, there's no dearth of visor-clad tourists ready to buy a geegaw for the breakfast nook in Idaho.

Here's why they come: The appeal is the hike down to the gorge, a 168-foot vertical drop below Vermont's oldest steel span bridge, or a safer half-mile descent down a trail to the Ottauquechee River. Walking down isn't too bad—smokers do it. Hikers do it, bikers do it, and so do children. But all are far less enthusiastic hiking up.

At the bottom, take a break and recline on one of thousands of wide river rocks. The dry river bed is a good place to think, as evidenced by all the people writing, sketching, and painting. When you want to ride the road again, farther up Route 4 is the Quechee Gorge Village, an old-fashioned shopping plaza that features an antiques center, country store, hyper-cool diner, and candle shop. When you're done, tie down your plastic Jesus with a bungee and return to Woodstock.

Pull It Over: Woodstock Highlights
Attractions and Adventures

Thankfully, most things worth doing are done outdoors in this pristine countryside. Even though some may seem like grade-school field trips, these excursions are intriguing.

Billings Farm (Rte. 12, 802/457-2355, www.billingsfarm.com, $9.50) is slightly interesting for laypeople and absolutely fascinating if you like cows and chickens. This pastoral parcel of land was created to educate the public about the value of responsible agriculture and land stewardship (the passions of lawyer, railroad entrepreneur, and philanthropist Frederick Billings and his wealthy grandson-in-law). The circa 1871 working farm is a living museum, hosting demonstrations of how they did it in the old days—from rug-hooking to butter-churning to wooden-tool-making. The guides toss out useful data as well: "Count the number of fogs in August, and you can match the number of snows in the winter." Surprisingly fascinating. It's open 10 A.M.–5 P.M. daily May–October.

Across the street, the **Marsh-Billings-Rockefeller National Historic Park** (Rte. 12, 802/457-3368, www.nps.gov/mabi, $8.50 open daily 10 A.M.–4:30 P.M. June–mid-October), Vermont's first national park, was donated to the United States in 1992 by Frederick Billings's granddaughter, Mary French Rockefeller, and her husband, the late Laurance Rockefeller. The park interprets conservation history using the 1870 forest established by Billings as a case study. I highly recommend a guided tour of the family mansion and gardens.

Out toward the Gorge, the **Simon Pearce Gallery** (Rte. 4, Quechee,

Ready, Set, Go

The following practical advice on packing and pre-ride preparations comes from dedicated rider and motorcycle entrepreneur Ray Towells. Ray's British, so read this with an accent.

Pre-Ride
Have your mechanic check your bike and make sure it's ready for the road. Don't ask for a comprehensive tune-up; just have him check the brake linings, pads, tires, oil, fuses, and spares.

Let someone know how long you'll be away and leave a rough itinerary. If you're planning a three-day trip, and it's been five days since you called, your friend will know something's wrong.

Clothing
If you wear full leathers in Florida in summer, you're an idiot. Dress for the climate. Try to find a leather jacket with a removable lining or sleeves that zip off. Beyond that, you won't need much—a few pairs of jeans, shorts, and T-shirts. When riding in a cold climate, bring thermal underwear. The average biker doesn't want to dress up, but casual shoes, polo shirts, and khaki pants can pass in a nice restaurant.

802/295-2711, www.simonpearce.com) is open 9 A.M.–9 P.M. daily. While the name suggests a colonial-era factory, this is actually part of a larger chain of glass galleries started by an Irish immigrant in 1981. The timeline doesn't diminish the quality of the work, however. After watching the artists whip a glass out of molten sand, you'll want to raise a glass to their skills. Quality glassware, as well as off-kilter factory seconds, are sold in the gift shop. If your house has settled at a slant, spring for the seconds.

If you firmly believe that the pleasure's in the journey and not the final destination, saddle up on South America's favorite mammal and embark on one of six excursions into the Green Mountains. **Woodstock Llama Treks** (Rte. 4 two miles west of Woodstock, 802/457-5117, www.woodstockllama-treks.com) features breakfast, lunch, romantic, and half-day treks, including meals, music, or picnics along meadows and hills. It's not an adventure, but a llovely way to see the llay of the lland. Rates run $15–40 per person during the season, mid-May–October.

Safety and Practicalities

For supplies, I always carry a water container, foam earplugs to protect against noise, and a small flashlight. In remote areas, I pack a small first-aid kit with bandages, aspirin, sunscreen, and water purification tablets. A cell phone is great in an emergency. I also carry a roll of reflective tape. If you lose power to your lights, the tape will be a godsend.

When people see a $20,000 touring bike, they get ideas. Carry a Kryptonite lock. Bring an extra set of keys for your bike and hide them. Use heavy-duty tape to stick them under your saddle, for instance, or inside your headlight or spotlight.

If you break down and have to leave your bike, try to hide it off the road and cover it. A dark bike cover will come in handy.

Tool Kit

Bring a standard tool kit that includes, at minimum, vise grips or pliers; Allen wrenches, hex wrenches, and an adjustable wrench; a small screwdriver kit with multiple heads; small, medium, and large hose clamps; a roll of speed tape or electrical tape; wire; and two or three feet of electrical wire and a few connectors. You should also carry a puncture repair kit for your tires.

Instead of heading to a mega-mall googolplex, locals gather to enjoy movies in a refined setting at the **Town Hall Theatre** (802/457-2620) on the village green. Where else could you watch *Perils of Pauline* in Dolby?

Blue-Plate Specials

Here since 1955, **Wasp's Snack Bar** (57 Pleasant St., 802/457-3334) has diner stools at the counter and eggs, bacon, pancakes, hash browns, and coffee cooking and brewing behind it. You'll have to look for this local hangout, since the signage is minimal. No dinners here, but lunch offers anything the cook can make, plus homemade specials and soups. Nothing fancy, but just right.

Homemade "rich super premium" ice cream (served in the basement) is the foundation—as it should be—for **Mountain Creamery** (33 Central St., 802/457-1715). Upstairs, you can eat country breakfasts until 11:30 and big sandwiches noon–6:30. If you like your road food sweet, load up on pies, cakes, muffins, cookies, and brownies.

West of the village, on Route 4, is the **White Cottage Snack Bar** (462 Woodstock Rd., 802/457-3455), a *Happy Days*-era roadside diner that draws in tourists and riders who just want a messy hamburger, sloppy chili dog, and a full line of soda fountain treats.

Watering Holes

Since the '70s, **Bentley's** (3 Elm St., 802/457-3232) has been Woodstock's neighborhood bar. A few couches, a long bar, 1920s style, and creaky wooden floors give this place after-hours appeal. Lunch and dinner are served, but the microbrews, wines, and casual setting make this spot equally enjoyable for an evening conversation and a good drink—although it often gets wicked busy.

Shut-Eye

Motels and Motor Courts
The large and clean **Shire Motel** (46 Pleasant St., 802/457-2211, www.shire-motel.com, $78 in spring, $50 more in summer) has been here since 1963. In the heart of town, it has 33 rooms with all size beds.

A few miles west of town, **Pond Ridge Motel** (506 Rte. 4 W., 802/457-1667, www.pondridgemotel.com, $59 off-season, $110 in summer) offers 13 decent rooms with doubles or queens. If you're staying for a long period of time, consider one of the four rooms with kitchenettes.

Chain Drive
A, C, S

Chain hotels are in town, or within 10 miles. See cross-reference guide featuring phone numbers and Web addresses on page 514.

Inn-dependence
The **Woodstocker B&B** (61 River St./Rte. 4, 802/457-3896, www.woodstockervt.com, $95 off-season, double in summer), seems like home, with fresh-baked cookies and breads laid out each afternoon. Board games, a whirlpool tub, and killer breakfasts with oven-puffed pancakes add to the effect. This is a great location within walking distance of the village, and it has spacious rooms with queen or two double beds—although sounds can carry.

Smack dab on the village green, the largest and most upscale hotel in town, **Woodstock Inn** (14 The Green, 802/457-1100 or 800/448-7900, www.woodstockinn.com, $200 and up in summer) also includes Richardson's Tavern, a restaurant, and premium rooms overlooking a putting green. With 144 rooms, this inn is a popular spot for tourists, and its location and amenities may coax you to join them.

On the Road: Woodstock to Stowe

The moment you get home and put your bike in the garage, write a letter to the Vermont highway commissioner and say thanks for the additional 90 miles of Route 100 beyond Woodstock. At the intersection of Routes 4 and 100A South at Bridgewater Corners, you'll find a Citgo Food Mart. If you arrived by car, you'd get gas and snacks and leave. But on a bike, you'll want the experience to last. I sat on the porch, read the local bulletin board, watched people buy maple syrup, and enjoyed the reprieve from my routine. You'll have these experiences on the road, too—and often. Take advantage of them.

Routes 100 and 4 are the same for about six miles, and you'll ride north on 100 when Route 4 fades away. The road is slow and curving; the idea of a straightaway is foreign in Vermont (credit this fact to Vermont's 1964 sale of surplus straightaways to Kansas).

As you swing into satisfying turns, you'll question whether this ride is actually the shortest route between Points A and B. It's not—and that's good. Route 100 rolls through gorgeous farmland, fields, and forest. It rides beside rivers

beside a frigid waterfall along Highway 100 in Vermont

© NANCY HOWELL

and mountains. And it introduces you to the protectors of the free enterprise system: individuals who live miles from the shadow of a mall and make their living as independent merchants. In the yards of unpainted frame houses and log cabins, signs advertise bread, carved flutes, honey, antiques, artwork, and, of course, maple syrup. This short stretch slowly reveals the diversity of the nation and confirms that this motorcycle tour is a great American adventure.

You'll have little time to contemplate the sensations you feel, because roughly five miles past the split of Routes 4 and 100, you're in the thick of it. South of Pittsfield, you'll see yellow warning signs and the twisting black line that herald a series of quick turns that'll shift your bike beneath you like a hopped-up pendulum. Working the throttle, clutch, and brake in a symphony of shifting makes for a magical experience.

The bucolic nature of Vermont is on display. The roads weave randomly through this countryside, where the rusted edge of tin roofs sag lazily and crumbling mortar flakes off red chimneys. You'll see broken barns and unpainted covered bridges spanning rivers strewn with boulders. The road leads to tight turns and cramped quarters, changes in elevation compensating for monochromatic greenness. Cornfields and farmland don't offer much visual appeal, but if you're not a local, it's strangely satisfying to watch Vermont farmers turn the earth, work the combines, and roll tractors weighted beneath bales of hay.

Depending on its mood and the lay of land, the wide White River will surface on your left or right. With no guardrails to keep you out of the drink, keep one eye on the road and one on the river. The flowing road leads to a small village, the town of Rochester, where it's worth putting on the brakes and taking a break. This commercial district is only about two blocks long, but it has everything a motorcyclist needs: a gas station, small market, and the **Rochester Cafe and Country Store** (802/767-4302), which features an old-fashioned soda fountain and serves breakfast and hot and cold sandwiches.

The ride north from Rochester leads to ordinary towns and villages every few miles, but the highlights you'll remember are the long stretches of emptiness. On the sloping roads south of Granville, gravity sucks you into a vortex of trees, leaves, and wild grass until you're completely enveloped by the environment. The Granville Gulf Reservation promises "six miles of natural beauty to be preserved forever." And it delivers. The force of nature is strong here: As you coast downhill, a stream on your right goes uphill. A great waterfall is on your left and offers a great place to stop for a picture—and a frigid spray of Vermont water.

The region changes from rural to upper class near Waitsfield. Between here and Morefield is the grandly titled "1800 to 1850 Mad River Valley Rural Historic District." Along with the nice homes and a sense of wilderness, the smell of pine mingles with the scent of stables.

This journey now comes to a close. When you reach Route 100B, Stowe is just 18 miles away. That's 18 more miles of mountains, smooth roads, Vermont farmlands, and Waterbury—home of Ben & Jerry's, the ice cream capital of the world.

Life is good.

Stowe Primer

When it's not wintertime, Stowe is a cross between Lenox and something less than Lenox. It's not a rich town by any means, but it's not poor. It's pooch.

The village of Stowe lies about four miles southeast of the ski area, and the road north (Route 108) merits a visit as much as the village. Compared to Lenox and Woodstock, there's not much ground to cover here, but motorcycle travelers like Routes 100 and 108, which intersect at the center of the village.

The town was chartered in 1763 and named after descendants of England's Lord Stowe. Although known by skiers as a winter resort, Stowe's theme is actually a summer place. When it became a destination more than a century ago, the main activities were shopping in the village, swimming in swimming holes, and riding up the mountain road to the peak of Mount Mansfield—at 4,393 feet, Vermont's highest point. The same holds true today.

On the Road: Stowe

You've already ridden some of Vermont's best roads on the way up, but if you're like me and can't get enough of mountain riding, turn onto Route 108 and head to Smuggler's Notch. This is a most excellent road for motorcycles and was also a favorite route for independent Vermonters, who smuggled goods from the United States to Canada during the 1807 Embargo Act. The road proved just as popular for transporting escaped slaves in the 1800s and bootleg liquor during Prohibition. This narrow, isolated road threads the needle between Mount Mansfield and Sterling Peak, rock formations created about 400 million years ago. At the summit, you may be able to make out outcroppings like Elephant's Head, Singing Bird, and Smuggler's Face. You may even run across some lost bootleggers.

Pull It Over: Stowe Highlights
Attractions and Adventures

Most of the town's attractions involve natural pursuits. At **Fly Fish Vermont** (954 S. Main St., 802/253-3964, www.flyrodshop.com), Bob Shannon and staff offer a complete selection of equipment, including locally tied flies and rod and wader rentals. May–October, guides can take you to the best fishing spots in the area. But do you have room in your saddlebags for a 20-pound king salmon? Well, do you—punk?

At **Catamount Fishing Adventures** (Barrow Rd., 802/253-8500, www.cata mountfishing.com), Willy Dietrich offers four- to eight-hour fly-fishing or spin-fishing excursions in backwoods Vermont. The eight-hour trip in-cludes a free lunch. Trips are based on your level of expertise, so if you normally fish with a shotgun, you're a beginner. Choose from canoe, float tube, small motorboat, or side stream tours in pursuit of trout, bass, and northern pike.

In the middle of adventure, when you're hugging the road for hours at a time, the chance to soar like an eagle is a damn fine thrill. Glider rides at **Stowe Soaring** (Morrisville-Stowe State Airport Rte. 100, Morrisville, 802/888-7845 or 800/898-7845, www.stowesoaring.com) range from $69 for 10 minutes to $159 for 40 minutes, with $20 increments in between. When the rope pops off the glider, the serene and wild ride begins. Look for the Adirondacks to the west, Jay Peak to the north, Mount Washington to the east, and nothing but air below.

Several hundred years before roads were readied for your bike, Native Americans cruised the area via canoes. With rivers and lakes laced across the Green Mountains, you can do the same in a rented kayak or canoe, gliding through farms and forested countryside on the wide and winding Lamoille and Winooski rivers. Three canoe and kayak outfitters are based in Stowe: **AJ's Ski & Sports** (Mountain Rd., 802/253-4593, www.ajssports.com); **Umiak Outfitters** (849 S Main St, 802/253-2317, www.umiak.com); and **Pinnacle Ski & Sports** (802/253-7222, www.pinnacleskisports.com). Kayaks rent for about $25 for four hours, $32 for a full day; canoes for around $34 for four hours) and $42 for a full day, with discounts available if you book in advance.

If you're saddle sore, put on your walking shoes (or in-line skates) for a trip past mountains, woods, and farms. A 5.5-mile greenway, the Stowe Recreation Path, stretches from Main Street along the West Branch River and Mountain Road to the covered bridge at Brook Road. If you go the distance, keep in mind it'll be another 5.5 miles back. The greenway was named by *Travel + Leisure* as one of the "19 Great Walks of the World."

When you've had enough sightseeing, head to **Ben & Jerry's** (Rte. 100 one mile north of I-89, 802/882-1240 or 866/BJ-TOURS—866/258-6877, www.benjerry.com). It's not in Stowe, but it's close enough. With $5 business diplomas from a correspondence course and a collective life savings of $8,000, Ben Cohen and Jerry Greenfield opened an ice-cream parlor in an abandoned Burlington gas station in 1978. Not only did they vow to use only fresh Vermont ingredients, they also pledged 7.5 percent of pretax profits to employee-led philanthropy. This is the way a business should be run—and the way ice cream should taste. Take the half-hour first-come, first-served tour for $3 and score some free ice cream straight from the production line. Beats touring a fertilizer factory.

Blue-Plate Specials

There are absolutely no fast food joints in Stowe, so get ready for some real food. The gathering spot for locals, **McCarthy's** (Mountain Rd., 802/253-8626), serves the best breakfast in town. Stick around and chow down on homemade breads, soups, and pie at lunch. The food is cheap and healthy.

At dinnertime, look for **Cactus Cafe** (2160 Mountain Rd./Rte. 108, 802/253-7770), known as much for its 16-ounce handmade margaritas as for its food. Along with Mexican standards (enchiladas, fajitas, quesadillas), pan-fried trout, pork chops, and Southwestern stir fry appear on the menu. If you can't get enough of the great outdoors (who can?), dine in the perennial garden.

If you've got a hankering for wild boar, venison, or pheasant, park it at **Mr. Pickwick's** (433 Mountain Rd., 802/253-7064, www.englandinn.com), open daily for lunch and dinner. There are other restaurants within Ye Olde England Inne, but Mr. Pickwick's serves more than 150 varieties of ale, including fresh wheat beer and lambic ales from Belgium. If there's a designated rider in your group, try one of each. Gotta cigar? Complement it with your choice from the selection of vintage ports, rare cognacs, and single malt scotches.

Watering Holes

The Whip Bar and Grill (Main St., 802/253-7301, www.greenmountain-inn.com) is downstairs at the Green Mountain Inn. Sure, it's a hotel bar, but it feels more like a pub, with its high-back chairs and English riding club design. They serve meals here, and enhance them with great brews.

Gracie's (1652 Mountain Rd., 802/253-8741) became so popular in a basement bar downtown, that it moved into a much larger location on Mountain Road. The new location features a patio, bar, and a menu of burgers, nachos, seafood, and steaks.

At the **Backyard Tavern** (395 Mountain Rd., 802/253-9204) you'll find a basic bar menu with cheeseburgers and chicken fingers, a pool table, a great jukebox, pinball, and $2 draft pints daily.

Try the **Sunset Grille & Tap Room** (140 Cottage Club Rd., 802/253-9281). You'll find a restaurant here also, but look to the Tap Room for wings, bar pizzas, and burgers while watching sports on a variety of TVs. Occasionally, the place hosts a cookout on the patio, and pickup horseshoe and volleyball games shape up out back. When you're bored with that, check out the huge domestic beer selection.

Shut-Eye

In the village, Stowe's Visitor Information Center (802/253-7321 or 800/247-8693, www.gostowe.com) also assists travelers with lodging, and there are 40-plus independent inns, hotels, and motels, which offer more than 1,700 rooms. **Stowe Country Rentals** (877-958-9990, www.stowecountryrentals.com) represents more than a dozen rental cabins, farms, and resorts. If you're traveling with a large group and need a base, check 'em out.

Motels and Motor Courts

After a long day, the **Stowe Inn** (123 Mountain Rd., 802/253-4030, www.stoweinn.com, $80–$90 Apr.–June, $159 peak season) can make your night. The staff is friendly, the rooms are warm and comforting, and the living room and lounge are designed for a relaxing post-ride conversation. The complimentary continental breakfast puts everything over the top.

About 2.5 miles north of the village is the clean and basic **Stowe Motel** (2043 Mountain Rd., 802/253-7629 or 800/829-7629, www.stowemotel.com, $79 and up). Sixty rooms and efficiencies are spread between three properties, with king and queen beds at each. Rooms include a continental breakfast.

Chain Drive

B

Chain hotels are in town, or within 10 miles. See cross-reference guide featuring phone numbers and Web addresses on page 514.

Inn-dependence

There's always the **Green Mountain Inn** (Main St., 802/253-7301 or 800/253-7302, www.greenmountaininn.com, $129 and up). Right in the heart of town, this renovated 1833 home-turned-inn features 81 antiques-filled rooms, 15 suites, four efficiencies, and five townhomes. The central location, with a health club, heated outdoor pool, canopy beds, fireplaces, and whirlpool tubs can be just right after the ride. So is the pub. There's a two-night minimum on summer and fall weekends.

Indulgences

After Julie Andrews and Christopher Plummer escaped from the Nazis—no, wait … that was the movie—anyway, after the Von Trapp family left Austria, they wound up in its American counterpart, Stowe, and opened the **Trapp Family Lodge** (Rte. 108—up two miles from town, left at the white church, then two more miles, 802/253-8511 or 800/826-7000, www.trappfamily.com, $245 and up). Infighting among family members is a given now, but the lodge has sustained itself in large part on the strength of the family's story. Included on the 2,200 acres are 93 rooms with spectacular mountain views, nightly entertainment, a fitness center, three pools, tennis courts, and hiking trails. On Sundays in the summer, there are concerts in the Family Lodge Concert Meadow, a natural amphitheater. The dining room, lounge, and tearoom feature a European theme.

Resources for Riders

Berkshires—Central Vermont Run

Massachusetts Travel Information
Massachusetts Road Conditions—617/374-1234
Massachusetts State Park Campgrounds Reservations—877/422-6762,
    www.reserveamerica.com
Massachusetts Department of Travel & Tourism—617/973-8500 or
    800/447-6277, www.massvacation.com

Vermont Travel Information
Vermont Attractions Association—802/229-4581, www.vtattractions.org
Vermont Campground Association—www.campvermont.com
Vermont Chamber of Commerce—802/223-3443, www.vtchamber.com
Vermont Department of Forests, Parks, and Recreation—802/241-3655,
    www.vtstateparks.com
Vermont Department of Tourism—802/828-3237 or 800/837-6668,
    www.travel-vermont.com
Vermont Fall Foliage Hotline—802/828-3239 or 800/837-6668,
    www.vermontfallfoliage.com
Vermont Fish and Wildlife—802/241-3700, www.vtfishandwildlife.com
Vermont Road Conditions—802/828-4894 or 800/429-7623

Local and Regional Information
Berkshires Visitors Bureau—413/443-9186 or 800/237-5747,
    www.berkshires.org
Lenox Chamber of Commerce—413/637-3646, www.lenox.org
Stowe Chamber of Commerce—802/253-7321 or 800/247-8693,
    www.gostowe.com
Woodstock Chamber of Commerce—802/457-3555 or 888/496-6378,
    www.woodstockvt.com

Massachusetts Motorcycle Shops
North's Service—675 Lenox Rd., Lenox, 413/499-3266,
    www.northsservices.com
Ronnie's Cycle Sales & Service—150 Howland Ave., Adams, 413/743-
    0715; and 501 Wahconah St., Pittsfield, 413/443-0638,
    www.ronnies.com
RPM's Cycle Sales & Service—326 Merrill Rd., Pittsfield, 413/443-5659

Vermont Motorcycle Shops
Hillside Motorsports—1341 Rte. 14, White River Jct., 802/295-0860,
    www.hillsidemotorsports.com
Exit 9 Motorsports—4 U.S. Rte. 5, Windsor, 802/674-5572
Ronnie's Cycle—2601 West Rd., Rte. 9, Bennington, 802/447-4606,
    www.ronnies.com
Twin States Harley-Davidson—351 Miracle Mile, Lebanon, NH, 603/448-
    4664, www.twinstatesharley.com

Hudson River Valley Run

Tarrytown/Sleepy Hollow,
New York to Saratoga Springs, New York

If you've avoided touring the state of New York because friends convinced you there was nothing but the traffic of New York City, tune them out, tap your bike into gear, twist the throttle, and head up the Hudson River.

Twenty-five miles north of NYC are the neighboring communities of Tarrytown and Sleepy Hollow, a perfect base from which to begin a tour of the Hudson River Valley. Though close to the capital of capitalism, it's worlds away in texture and feel. You might think you took a wrong turn in Bavaria, but this is indeed America—an America that began more than 150 years before the nation existed. The villages and the following 180 miles will introduce you to a world of distinctive literature, art, history, and cuisine. They will also offer great river roads, hills, scenic vistas, pubs, and diners and lead you into the outstanding Adirondacks. Savor the ride in summertime and early fall.

Tarrytown Primer

The sense of history here is omnipresent. In the early 1600s, this area was home to a tribe of the Mohegan family, the Weckquaesgeek. They lived, fished, hunted, and traded along the Pocantico relatively undisturbed until 1609, when Henry Hudson, navigating without the aid of a GPS system, sailed up the river searching for the northwest passage to India. Settlers

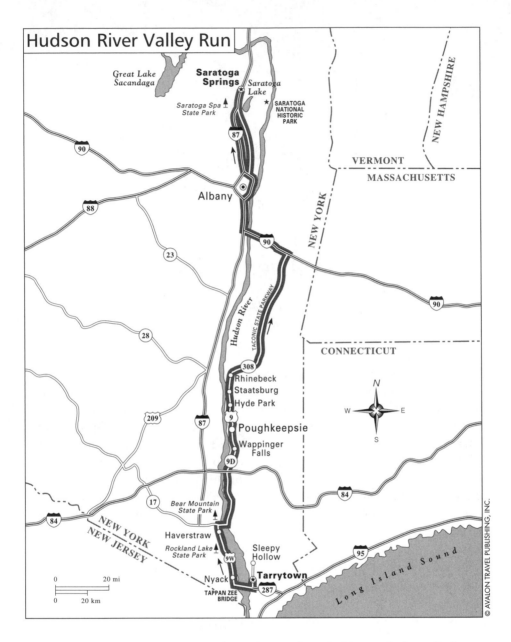

Hudson River Valley Run

Route: Tarrytown to Saratoga Springs via Nyack, Bear Mountain State Park, Hyde Park, Staatsburg, Rhinebeck, Taconic State Parkway

Distance: Approximately 180 miles; consider four days with stops.

•Day 1—Tarrytown/Travel •Day 2—Hyde Park •Day 3—Travel •Day 4—Saratoga Springs

First Leg: Tarrytown to Hyde Park (88 miles)

Second Leg: Hyde Park to Saratoga Springs (92 miles)

Helmet Laws: New York requires helmets.

began arriving soon after. The Dutch named the area Slaeperig Haven (Sleepy Harbor) for its sheltered anchorage. Other Dutch settlers arrived, and by 1685, Frederick Philipse owned nearly half of what is now Westchester County. In the 1730s, members of the Livingston family began building riverfront estates, such as Clermont, Wilderstein, and Montgomery Place, all of which are open for tours.

Fast forward to the American Revolution. British soldier/spy John André was captured here, and the papers he was carrying revealed Benedict Arnold's traitorous plan to capture West Point. A half century later, in 1820, Rip Van Winkle's creator, Washington Irving, drew further attention to the region with the publication of *The Legend of Sleepy Hollow.*

The tranquil area continued to grow. The second half of the 1800s saw freight arrive and depart by river and rail. Factories were built, followed by estates built by the people who built the factories. With the likes of Jay Gould, William Dodge, and John D. and William Rockefeller taking up summer residence, Tarrytown became a destination for the wealthy until the Great Depression, when new income taxes forced many of the *nouveau poore* to give up their estates.

In the mid-1950s, the Tappan Zee Bridge and New York State Thruway were built, opening up the town for commuters. City workers began driving up from NYC and driving up real estate prices. Today, Tarrytown still displays a distinct degree of affluence. So look sharp.

On the Road: Tarrytown

When you arrive in Tarrytown, give yourself a moment to adjust to your surroundings. Couples walk past carrying bags of fresh produce; neighbors stop and pass the time outside antique shops; and merchants thank God they're not working in a mall. You may think you've entered Pleasantville, but you're cruising through one of the oldest villages in America.

Tarrytown's main drag isn't really Main Street but Route 9, the road of choice for buses, trucks, teens, tourists, seniors, and soccer moms hauling vanloads of ball-kicking kids. With this buzzing traffic, it's best here just to park your bike and explore on foot. If you follow the scents emanating from bakeries, gourmet shops, ethnic restaurants, and coffee bars, you'll eventually arrive in the heart of downtown, which encompasses about six square blocks.

Like many small American towns, Tarrytown has turned to antiques dealers to fill in storefronts in the commercial center. Antiques are in such high demand here that one espresso bar displays a sign informing customers, "This is not an antiques shop. But we do have an old guy who works here."

Since Tarrytown is primarily a residential area, amusing diversions are few, but give yourself at least a few hours to roam the streets. The **Sleepy Hollow Chamber of Commerce** (914/631-1705, www.sleepyhollowchamber.com) is a smart first stop. Located in a narrow building next to the fire station on Main Street, this is where you can score information from the rack of brochures. If something sparks your interest, track it down. If there's little for you here, just consider this the perfect starting line for an extraordinarily full ride.

Pull It Over: Tarrytown Highlights
Attractions and Adventures

Sometimes, there's a whole lotta shakin' going on at the **Music Hall** (13 Main St., 914/631-3390, www.tarrytownmusichall.org). Built in 1885, this hall is one of the oldest in Westchester County and has hosted a century of performances by artists like Chuck Mangione, Tito Puente, Dave Brubeck, Tony Bennett, Judy Collins, Dizzy Gillespie, Lionel Hampton, Lyle Lovett, Wynton Marsalis, Tom Paxton, and Leon Redbone. Folk and classical concerts are performed here as well, and the acoustics are alleged to rival those of Carnegie Hall. If there's a show in town, listen up.

For music of a different sort, head to the banks of the Pocantico River in **Rockefeller State Park Preserve** (914/631-1470, www.friendsrock.org). Washington Irving described it as "one of the quietest places in the whole wide world. A small brook glides through it, with just murmur enough to lull one to repose." If you stow a rod and reel, brown trout are here for catch-and-release fly-fishing, and you can find bass in Swan Lake. Nonresident day licenses (about ten bucks) can be purchased at the park office or Sleepy Hollow Village Hall.

A few miles north of town, you can ride your bike onto an estate to see how the other .0001 percent lives. When John D. Rockefeller got tired of living in a dumpy fixer-upper, he had Johnny Jr. build **Kykuit** (pronounced KI-cut, 914/631-9491, $20), which means "high place." The neoclassical country mansion and gardens, which overlook the Hudson, were completed in 1913 and served as home to four generations of Rockefellers, including Nelson A., who added 20th-century sculptures to the estate's gardens. Vintage carriages and cars (such as a 1918 Crane Simplex) are on display in the Coach Barn, and there's a café on site. Reservations are suggested. On Route 9, Kykuit is open daily except Tuesday May–October.

Company Snapshot: BMW

I can think of one good reason why Bayerische Flugzeugwerke (Bavarian Aircraftworks) changed its name: BMW was easier to fit on a fuel tank. Founded on March 7, 1916, BMW started with a concept that has held true for nearly a century. Its blue and black logo suggested a rotating airplane propeller in the blue Bavarian sky, and when its first bike, the R 32, premiered at the Paris Motor Show, it stood out with its two-cylinder, horizontally opposed piston engine—a style that continues today.

When you're in Tarrytown, remember that next door is Sleepy Hollow. For a road story you'll tell later, retrace the route Ichabod Crane used to flee from the Headless Horseman in *The Legend of Sleepy Hollow.* To duplicate Ichabod's flight, take Route 9 from Patriot's Park (along the old Albany Post Road) to the Sleepy Hollow Bridge under the shadow of the Old Dutch Church. Watch your head.

Shopping

Get within 25 feet of fragrant **Tarrytown Gourmet** (45 Broadway, 914/366-6800), and your schnoz will go into olfactory overdrive. Have the clerk pack a picnic for the road. Provisions include fresh pears, mangoes, sweet red plums, olive oil, hot pepper oil, cookies, gourmet pizzas, olives, salami, imported cheeses, candies and cakes, iced drinks, teas, and coffees. Here's a place to get fat and happy.

Blue-Plate Specials

Go figure. Since 1985, **Santa Fe Restaurant** (5 Main St., 914/332-4452, www.santaferestaurant.com) has succeeded by serving Mexican and Southwestern cuisine in the heart of Dutch country. Home-cooked without flavor enhancers, all dishes can be spiced to your satisfaction and tolerance for pain. The comfortable neighborhood feel is matched by a full range of Mexican beers and more than 30 premium tequilas. *Muy bueno!* Open daily for lunch and dinner.

Horsefeathers (94 N. Broadway, 914/631-6606) is what you look for when you ride: pub-style atmosphere with home-style comfort foods like meatloaf, burgers, and mashed potatoes, along with soups, pasta, steaks, and chicken. The big draw is the extensive collection of beers—more than 100 micros—from across the country and around the world. Homey and comfortable, Horsefeathers is open daily for lunch and dinner.

Featuring Italian food with a Mediterranean flair, the riverside **Sunset Cove** (238 Green St. at Washington Irving Boat Club, 914/366-7889, www.sunset-cove.net) may have the nicest view on the Hudson. Dining here can be just as enjoyable as riding your bike down to the river; pull up a chair on the patio and peer beneath the Tappan Zee Bridge for a view of the New York City skyline 25 miles away. A definite stop for riders.

Shut-Eye

There are few inns in Tarrytown, so if you need to stay the night, you'll probably wind up at one of the chains below—the less expensive options are across the Hudson in Nyack.

Chain Drive
A, C, D, K, U, CC

Chain hotels are in town, or within 10 miles. See cross-reference guide featuring phone numbers and Web addresses on page 514.

Indulgences

If you're anxious to escape generic motels, storm **The Castle at Tarrytown** (400 Benedict Ave., 914/631-1980, www.castleattarrytown.com, $200 and up). Built in two stages in 1897 and 1910, the humble abode was formerly the home of playwright/author/journalist/socialite General Howard Carrol. Evoking an elegant gentlemen's club, the inn boasts Gothic windows, tapestries, rich woods, and a baronial setting—you may even pick up a dueling scar during your stay. From the backyard garden, take in the fantastic view, which stretches down the Hudson and back into history. Rest assured that the name of the signature restaurant, Equus, doesn't suggest entrée ingredients.

On the Road: Tarrytown to Hyde Park

Like John Lennon, New York has a fascination with the number 9. Within a few miles of Tarrytown, you'll discover Route 9, Route 9A, Route 9W, Route

9G, and Route 9D. Right now, head to Route 9W by going west over the Tappan Zee Bridge (aka 287/87/New York State Thruway) into Rockland County, and let the joy begin.

As you roll over the Tappan Zee Bridge, the mighty Hudson River rumbles 150 feet below. The setting captured on canvas by 19th-century Hudson River School artists will no longer seem embellished as you begin your ride through a landscape that rivals the magnitude of a Greek epic poem. When you peer downriver to the hazy outline of New York City, you'll picture—if not Odysseus and his crew—then Hudson's ship, the *Half Moon*, under full sail.

A few miles past the bridge, 9W branches north off 287 and heads into the hills. You can ride this road past the forgettable towns of Nyack and Haverstraw, but a local rider turned me on to a better alternative: By staying on 287/87 and following it northwest, you're heading right into **Harriman State Park** (845/786-2701). Stay on the road until you reach Route 17 in Sloatsburg and keep an eye out on your right for the entrance to picturesque Seven Lakes Drive. This is a cool, serene, lonely ride through the woods, which reveals, yes, seven lakes—Sebago, Tiorati, Stahahe, Askoti, Cohasset, Kanawaukee, and Skannatati.

Revel in the pleasure of the ride. Feel the fresh air on your skin and in your lungs and listen to the hum of the bike as you ride for several miles through the forest as you approach a new paradise: **Bear Mountain State Park** (also 845/786-2701, www.friendsofpalisades.org), a must-see for a high-altitude ride and stunning views of the valley. This is one of many times you'll "find the zone" as you begin swinging into corners, diving into short stretches of canopy roads, and cowering beneath boulders looming over the road.

For motorcycle travelers, the real appeal of the park is ascending Bear Mountain. Be warned: If you suffer from vertigo, dropsy, or the shakes, don't take this ride, since the road twists like your drunken uncle at a wedding reception. While the speed limit is a sensible 25 mph, you could push it to 26, since small boulders have been thoughtfully placed along the road's edge to keep you from going over it.

Passage to the peak comes via Perkins Memorial Drive, a road that introduces another memorable motorcycling moment. If you drive it between summer and fall foliage season, it is nearly empty, and the forest is moist and cool. The downside: On the ride up, sheer drops fall off to your left, and branches and wet leaves can send you skidding. Still, the road is worth the price of admission (free), since you'll be treated to a kaleidoscope of majestic vistas. The beautiful valleys stretched out like long, verdant branches must have been touched by the finger of God. This is America.

When you reach the peak, your pleasure will derive from the solitude and serenity. An abundance of table-size boulders makes it easy to spread out a picnic, and if you travel off-season or just after a holiday weekend, chances are only a few random travelers will join you.

When it's time to descend, place your bike in neutral and coast; the silence is satisfying. Though it may be slightly dangerous to pull over, do so if there's no traffic behind you—the view of the Hudson River and Bear Mountain Bridge will stay with you forever. Bear Mountain Circle will drop you back toward the park's inn that is worth a stop, if for no other reason than to score a great souvenir picture—its rock and wood construction recalls a Yosemite lodge. Picnic tables, a pool, and Hessian Lake are adjacent to the inn, and there are trails where you can take a walk and think about the ride so far. From the entrance/exit here, you've come full circle to Route 9W North, which you'll follow toward the king-size American flag draped above the bridge. Like crossing the Tappan Zee, crossing the Bear Mountain Bridge east to Route 9D reminds you why you're on a bike. If your timing is right, you may even ride over the speeding Montrealer, the train that skids up the Hudson between NYC and Canada.

West Point

I was never in the military, but my mom took me to Marineland once. If you're interested in military history, **West Point** (845/938-2638, www.usma.edu) is worth the six-mile detour from Bear Mountain State Park. Washington garrisoned his troops here during the Revolutionary War, and in 1802, President Jefferson signed the act of Congress creating the U.S. Military Academy. And that's not all: Lee, Grant, Patton, Eisenhower, and Schwarzkopf all learned to march here.

Since September 11, 2001, the grounds have been closed to outsiders unless you call in advance for the one-hour, $7 tour. If you did, continue north on 9W to Route 218 and enter West Point at Thayer Gate. The tour starts at the museum (open 10:30 A.M.–4:15 P.M.), and a guide will lead you to see the Cadet Chapel and the world's largest church organ, and then to Trophy Point, a favorite overlook for artists. The visitors center, which features a 30-minute movie, is open 9 A.M.–4:45 P.M. On Saturday mornings in the fall, take time to watch the "Long Gray Line," the parade of cadets marching prior to the football game. You'll need to buy tickets for the game well in advance, since you'll need them to get on the grounds. Either that, or enlist.

Art of the Valley

If you experience a sense of déjà vu along the Hudson, you may have seen it before.... During the 1800s, popular imagination considered the Hudson to be the American Rhine, and its imposing country estates surely rivaled those of the German river or the châteaux of the French Loire district. Frederick Church and fellow artists captured this prevailing sentiment in an art movement called the Hudson River School. Images of the trees and lakes, waterfalls and rivers of the Hudson and Catskill Mountains were adorned with Grecian temples and sweeping panoramas. As you ride through the valley, the essence of those images will reappear time and again—minus the Grecian temples.

Now you're in Putnam County and on Route 9D (aka the Hudson Greenway Trail), a beautiful mountain road. Passing Phillipstown, the Hudson darts in and out of view nearly as often as the white picket fences, evergreens, and estate homes. The road hugs the Hudson as you drive north, passing small general stores hawking beer and sandwiches, a castle on a hill, and—in Garrison, across the river from West Point—**Boscobel** (845/265-3638, www.boscobel.org), an ongoing restoration of an estate showcasing design arts of the Federal period. You may be tempted to speed, but force yourself to relax. You can hurry at work, but when you're traveling ... please take your time.

The twists and turns continue into Wappinger Falls, where you'll reach a bridge in the center of town. If you turn left and continue to follow Route 9D, the road is scenic, though not as fast, and eventually leads to your first major commercial center: Poughkeepsie. You, being on a journey of discovery, will not settle for this. Keep heading north after hooking up with Route 9 to your first overnight: Hyde Park.

Hyde Park Primer

Just as fans of Mark Twain trek to Hannibal and worshippers of Donny Osmond pilgrimage to Utah, students of history head to Hyde Park. Along with World War II veterans and Depression-era children who grew up on relief packages, baby boomers, scholars, and foreign tourists whose countries were saved by Franklin Delano Roosevelt arrive to pay their respects to the 32nd president, whose home and gravesite are located here.

Most of us have heard of Hyde Park, so it's a bonus that it turns out to be a perfect place to rest your bike, stay the night, enjoy a decent meal, and get an education. In 1705, New York provincial governor Edward Hyde presented this parcel of land to his secretary, Peter Fuconnier. Hyde's munificence earned him a namesake estate and, later, a namesake town, established in 1821. Mills sprang up on Hudson River tributaries, and, by the turn of the 20th century, Roosevelts, Vanderbilts, and other wealthy families began settling in.

On the Road: Hyde Park

Sorry, there is no true commercial district within Hyde Park—and that's one of its assets. The town rests along a straightaway highlighted by the attractions listed below, so take it for what it is—a quiet and historically significant stop between Tarrytown and Saratoga.

Pull It Over: Hyde Park Highlights
Attractions and Adventures

If FDR had never achieved national prominence, you may never have heard of Hyde Park. But he did, and today the **FDR National Historic Site** (4079 Albany Post Rd./Rte. 9, 845/229-9115 for headquarters or 845/486-1983 for ticket booth, www.nps.gov/hofr) is a shrine for those who want to see how this pastoral countryside helped shape an extraordinary man. With the exception of 13 years in Washington and a few more in Albany, FDR spent his entire life here. This is also his resting place; he and Eleanor are buried in a rose garden adjacent to the house.

Their home is filled with original books, china, paintings, and furniture; look for the simple kitchen chair FDR fashioned into a wheelchair. In the **FDR Museum and Presidential Library** (the first presidential museum ever built), the desk demands special attention. It's just as he left it on the day he died in April 1945. Motorcyclists may get a kick out of the 1938 Ford Phaeton shown in the basement. It's equipped with manual controls for the disabled president. After hours spent roaming the estate, however, I found the most intriguing and touching displays were the letters and gifts the president received from average Americans expressing gratitude for the relief programs that put them back to work. The site is open 9 A.M.–5 P.M. daily. A two-day admission pass costs $14 ($22 gets you into the FDR site, Val-Kill, and Vanderbilt Mansion).

It's odd, but FDR and his mother froze Eleanor out of their world, despite the fact that the first lady won the 1934 Washington Wives kickboxing title. The tacit agreement was that Eleanor would reside a few miles away at Val-Kill (Stone Cottage). Established as a furniture factory to provide work to local craftsmen, Val-Kill served as Eleanor's retreat from 1926 until 1945. After FDR died, it became her primary residence and a gathering place for world leaders, including Churchill, JFK, Krushchev, Nehru, and Marshall Tito (who left the Jackson Five to lead Yugoslavia). **Val-Kill** (Rte. 9G, 845/229-9422, www.nps.gov/elro, $8) now serves as the Eleanor Roosevelt National Historic Site. It's open 9 A.M.–5 P.M. daily in summer, Thursday-Monday off-season.

Nobody muttered, "There goes the neighborhood" when the Vanderbilts moved to town. **Vanderbilt Mansion** (Rte. 9, 845/229-7770, www.nps.gov /vama, $8) reflects that family's obsession with building homes large enough to drain the kids' inheritance. This Beaux Arts mansion was the home of Louise and publicity-shy Frederick, who, quite like myself, was recognized primarily for being a splendid yachtsman, a gentleman farmer, and an "unassuming philanthropist." Louise died in 1926 and Freddy in 1938, and Louise's niece inherited the property a year before she told her neighbor (FDR) that she was donating it to the nation. As you leave the grounds, on your left is an overlook with a tremendous view of the mighty Hudson. The home is open 9 A.M.–5 P.M. daily (Thursday–Monday, November–April).

I've always wanted to be a double naught spy, so I was anxious to reach the CIA. Damned if I didn't learn this is actually the **Culinary Institute of America** (845/452-9600, www.ciachef.edu). Cruise down the road on Route 9, and you'll reach the only residential college in the world devoted entirely to culinary education. Founded in 1946 in New Haven, Connecticut, the school moved into this turn-of-the-20th-century former Jesuit seminary in 1972. Today, college-age apprentice chefs, servers, and maître d's at the 150-acre campus are—surprisingly—studying alongside doctors, lawyers, and stockbrokers who dropped out of their careers to do something fun. One-hour tours (845/451-1588, $5) conducted by students are available 10 A.M. and/or 4 P.M. on Mondays, Wednesdays, and Thursdays. Of course, you can also see the campus when you drop in to eat (see *Blue-Plate Specials*).

If you want to catch your own meal, the river, streams, ponds, and creeks here are well-stocked with rainbow, brook, and brown trout, as well as bluegills, sunfish, bullhead, rock bass, and small and large striper. For guide services, check out the good ol' boys at **Hudson Valley Angler** (Red Hook, 845/758-9203, www.hudsonvalleyangler.com).

Blue-Plate Specials

At the **Culinary Institute of America** (Rte. 9, 845/471-6608 for reservations, www.ciachef.edu), four student-staffed restaurants and a bakery are open to the public. If you travel with a dinner jacket (or other appropriate dress) in tow, take a break from the roadside diners and enjoy a classic meal at the American Bounty (regional and seasonal), St. Andrew's Cafe (casual contemporary à la carte), Escoffier (French cuisine), or Caterina de Medici (fine Italian). Prices are slightly lower than they will be when your CIA chef begins working for a five-star restaurant a few weeks hence. The restaurants are closed the first three weeks of July, December 20– January 5, and some holidays.

The retro 1930s deco decor is right on target at **Eveready Diner** (Rte. 9, 845/229-8100), and the menu is just right for motorcycle travelers, featuring soups, burgers, and daily specials (the beef stew is great on a cold day). The diner is open 24 hours Friday and Saturday, 5 A.M.–1 A.M. weekdays.

An inspiring American tale is revealed at **Coppola's** (Rte. 9, 845/229-9113), where an immigrant family arrived in 1954, grew dissatisfied as dishwashers, and opened their first local restaurant in 1961. Now there are five restaurants run by the family's second generation. This is traditional Italian cuisine, with extraordinary veal parmigiana, penne à la gorgonzola, and seafood specials served indoors or on the deck. Next door, the family also runs the **Village Square Country Inn** (4167 Albany Post Rd., 229/7141, www.coppolas.net, $60 and up), which has 22 rooms and an outdoor pool and provides a continental breakfast. The perfect place to crash if you think you'll crave a midnight snack.

Watering Holes

In 1933, Prohibition ended, and FDR was quoted as saying, "I think this would be a good time for a beer." Six decades later, some locals at the **Hyde Park Brewing Company** (4076 Albany Post Rd., 845/229-8277, www.hydeparkbrewing.com) took up the cause in this microbrewery across from Roosevelt's birthplace. One of Hyde Park's rare nightspots to boast a full bar, live music, and the pub serves six beers (including Big Easy Blonde)—all brewed right here. Open daily.

Sports fans and Irishmen hang out 'til the wee hours at **Darby O'Gill's** (3969 Albany Post Rd.). It's open daily, or maybe I should say nightly, since closing time isn't until 4 A.M. Along with beer and mixed drink specials, there are massive high-def televisions.

Shut-Eye

In addition to the Village Square Country Inn, choices of lodging in Hyde Park range from motels to ... motels. Head north to find larger inns, or backtrack to Poughkeepsie for pricey chain hotels.

Motels and Motor Courts

Roosevelt Inn (4360 Albany Post Rd., 845/229-2443, www.rooseveltinnof-hydepark.com, $70–135) is a good, old-fashioned American motel. Try one of 25 clean rooms, some with king beds and some with fridges. Get off to a good start at the coffee shop, serving breakfast 7–11 A.M.

The **Super 8** (528 Albany Post Rd., 845/229-0088, $60 and up) is clean and cheap. Along with its 61 basic economy rooms, it tosses in a continental breakfast, cable TV, and a clerk on duty 'round the clock.

Chain Drive

A, C, CC

Chain hotels are in town, or within 10 miles. See cross-reference guide featuring phone numbers and Web addresses on page 514.

Inn-dependence

If you have an urge to splurge, stay at the **Belvedere Mansion** (10 Old Rte. 9, Staatsburg, 845/889-8000, www.belvederemansion.com, $150 and up), where the hillside setting at this spa-turned-inn offers a great view of the Hudson. The first floor of the main house is a restaurant (as well as a handy pub), and the upstairs features six rooms adorned with 18th-century French antiques and trompe l'oeil cloud-painted ceilings. Riders who share my budget may opt to bunk down in the converted stable, which is now a row of reasonably priced rooms (from $95) featuring queen beds, private baths, and a patio. The gravel driveway is a nuisance for kickstands, but if you're riding solo, a single concrete slab will hold your bike.

On the Road: Hyde Park To Saratoga Springs

Leaving Hyde Park, the two-lane road has some slow curves accented by stands of pines. The village itself—just a few stores and shops—can be bypassed to embark on the next leg of your journey. Although there are no identifiable signs, from here to Germantown in neighboring Columbia County, you'll be riding through the Mid-Hudson Valley, a 32-square-mile area recognized by the Department of the Interior as a National Historic Landmark District.

Miles north, you'll cruise through the village of Rhinebeck, which—midway between Albany and New York—was a logical stop for commercial river and road traffic. At the corner of Route 9 and East Market Street (Rte. 308) is the intersection of the old King's Highway and Sepasco Indian Trail. On your left, the circa 1766 **Beekman Arms** (845/876-7077, www.beek-manarms.com) boasts that it's the oldest inn in America. Although you'll find a few hundred other "oldest inns" around the country, "The Beek" gets points for hosting George Washington, Benjamin Harrison, and FDR—who wrapped up each gubernatorial and presidential campaign with a front-porch speech. In 1775, this was the Bogardus Tavern, a bar that stayed open while the Fourth Regiment of the Continental Army drilled on its front lawn before the war. If you're tired enough to stop, but not tired enough to stay the night, kick back with an ale in the warm, rich setting of the Colonial Tap Room.

If your schedule allows, take Route 9 north, detour onto Stone Church Road, and head to the **Old Rhinebeck Aerodrome** (914/752-3200, www.oldrhinebeck.org), an antique aircraft museum that displays World War I and Lindbergh-era aircraft, such as a 1917 Fokker DR-1 tri-plane, a 1915 Newport 11, and a 1918 Curtiss-Jenny, as well as old cars and vintage motorcycles. At 2 P.M. mid-June–October Saturdays and Sundays, it also presents a flying circus reminiscent of the Great Waldo Pepper. If you're ready to get off the bike, drop forty bucks and climb into a 1929 open

Congress Park in Saratoga Springs

cockpit biplane for a 15-minute barnstorming ride. The aerodrome is open 10 A.M.–5 P.M. daily mid-May–late October. Admission costs $6 Monday–Friday, $15 for the weekend air show.

If time is tight, turn right onto East Market Street (Rte. 308) just past the Beekman Arms and motor past splendid examples of Italianate revival homes and Victorian architecture. If you've spent the morning in Hyde Park, it may be afternoon as you head east—so as the sun settles over the Hudson, you'll feel the warmth on your back and smell the scent of the forest as you cruise down the road. Long shadows fall before your bike, and Little Wappinger Creek occasionally skims into view. In the early fall, acres of harvested cornfields accent the landscape, and the country ride becomes distinguished by its even, level serenity. Six miles after you turn onto Route 308 in a lazy loop toward Rock City, the road becomes Route 199.

The pleasure of cruising through four more miles of farmland will adjust your attitude and prepare you to ride one of the most beautiful roads in America. The Taconic State Parkway (TSP) cautions it is for "passenger cars only," but the sign is obviously the work of some corrupt anti-motorcycle administration. Rest assured that motorcycles are allowed.

Even as you forsake river views, the road is faster and less congested than Route 9. The result is that you'll enjoy a ride that acknowledges that life may be short, but it can be big.

The road is so pristine that the sweeps and dips and gentle drops affirm your existence. The cool air and sweet smell of your surroundings are only part of the adventure. You'll drop close to a hundred feet in less than a mile; you'll encounter stunning views and roadside wildflowers, black ash, slippery elm, arrowwood. Scenic overlooks punctuate the parkway. Look for one in Columbia County where the historic Livingston Manor once stood. It was the focal point of a 160,000-acre estate along the Hudson River.

Just as you pass over Routes 2 and 7, past the signs for Ancram and Taghkanic, the view will not only knock your socks off, but your boots will fly, too. On a clear day, at least 50 miles of rolling hills unfold to the horizon and possibly to the next galaxy. The view is yours. Use it.

Mea culpa: If I didn't have to take you on the following roads, I wouldn't. The TSP connects with I-90 and, to make time through Albany, you'll be shoved onto I-87. The switch from pastoral scenes to six lanes of fast, tense traffic will change your karma in an instant. Unfortunately, seeking alternate routes would be even more disruptive, so bite your lip and run the gauntlet of urban ugliness, selecting either I-87 or returning to Route 9 to complete your run to my favorite American city, Saratoga Springs.

Saratoga Springs Primer

Saratoga Springs, named the first "Great American Place" by *American Heritage* magazine in 1997, is what America is all about. Unlike freak towns that have bulldozed historic districts in favor of strip malls, this city recognizes beauty in its past and has placed more than a thousand buildings on the National Register of Historic Places. If you can understand this: Saratoga Springs is so real it looks fake.

Broadway, the town's main boulevard, is an artifact that gains the most attention. When Gideon Putnam laid out the thoroughfare in the early 1800s, he ensured that a team of four horses could make a U-turn (a qualifier shared by downtown Hendersonville, NC). The 120-foot-wide avenue and broad sidewalk make this the most enjoyable street in the nation for walking, riding, or dropping into a neighborhood bar for a postride refreshment. Farther up Route 9, you can also ease away the demands of the ride by dropping into a mineral bath at 2,200-acre **Saratoga Spa State Park** (S. Broadway, 518/584-2535).

In the early 1900s, this was the place to "take the waters." Now it's the place to kick back after a day on the road. Salty water from ancient seas is trapped beneath limestone layers and sealed by a solid layer of shale. The Saratoga Fault zigzags beneath the town and releases water made bubbly by carbon dioxide gas. Local Iroquois Indians knew well before the 1700s that minerals entering the water also added to the spring's therapeutic value.

Although Saratoga had earned its historical stripes in the Revolution ("Gentleman Johnny" Burgoyne surrendered his Crown Forces nearby on October 10, 1777—learn more below), it was during the Civil War that John Morrissey, a street fighter who had been indicted twice for burglary, once for assault, and once more for assault with intent to kill, channeled his destructive energies into a horse-racing track. His gamble worked, and by the turn of the 20th century, the Saratoga Race Track complemented his Saratoga casinos.

Reform politicians later closed the track—but it quickly reopened through a loophole. The track's fortunes rose and fell until well after World War II, when the New York Racing Association formed and changed the focus from gambling to the love of horse racing. With the track drawing summer visitors and the spas providing warm relief year-round, Saratoga keeps on running.

On the Road: Saratoga Springs

One of the payoffs of a good motorcycle tour is discovering towns that would be a perfect vignette in a Mark Twain novel or Charles Kuralt feature. Saratoga

Springs would top this list. It was awarded "Great American Main Street" by the National Trust for Historic Preservation, named a top destination by *Facilities* magazine in 1998, and chosen as one of "America's Most Walkable Cities" by *Walking* magazine in 2000. Even without the ponies racing on America's oldest track, Saratoga is a must-see. Hoof it on out here for the best experience.

Within blocks of Broadway, you'll find side streets dotted with cool shops; Congress Park, featuring a sculpture by Daniel Chester French (of Lincoln Memorial fame); and slices of Americana that will make you wonder if you've wandered onto the set of *It's a Wonderful Life.*

But this *is* Bedford Falls. When you pass the stunning Adirondack Trust at Broadway and Lake, you'll expect to peer in at Mr. Potter counting George Bailey's bankroll. As you walk or ride the avenue, the preserved architecture, liveliness of the street, and pleasant look on townspeople's faces as they actually shop along main street is emotionally powerful and thoroughly satisfying.

Two streets are worth exploring by bike. Head toward Skidmore College on North Broadway to view grand homes reflecting architecture from the Greek Revival, Arts and Crafts, and postmodern periods. The second is Union Avenue, a broad boulevard bordered by palatial homes accented with gazebos, Gothic gables, gingerbread trim, and stained-glass windows.

Check at the Visitors Center in **Drink Hall** (297 Broadway) for the fact-filled brochure titled "Strolling Through Saratoga Springs." It suggests five walking tours that will acquaint you with the very best of what this town has to offer.

Pull It Over: Saratoga Highlights
Attractions and Adventures

Don't pass up a visit to the **Saratoga Race Course** (Union Ave., 518/584-6200 in July and August or 718/641-4700 off-season, www.saratogaracetrack.com). Where else can you sit back and bet on thoroughbreds shaking the ground just 10 feet away from you? And all for three bucks! The "sport of kings" is held at the oldest racetrack in the country, and the sense of tradition is omnipresent. From the swells in the box seats to the two-bit bettors clenching their tickets trackside, this surreal spectacle guarantees a good time. The racing season lasts slightly more than 30 days in July and August, so if you insist on competing with van-driving tourists during peak season, be sure to reserve one morning for "Breakfast at the Track," and stick around for the famed Travers Stakes in August. The track is closed Tuesdays.

After a hard day's ride—hell, even after an easy day's ride—**Congress Park**

Americade Motorcycle Rally

A late arrival to the rally circuit, the first "Cade" hit the road in May 1983. Originally called "Aspencade" after a New Mexico rally that celebrated the changing colors of the aspen, "Aspencade East" was hosted by veteran motorcyclist Bill Dutcher at the resort community of Lake George, New York, and attracted more than 2,000 attendees. Distancing itself from typical rallies, this event stressed that it was "not the place for shows of speed, hostile attitudes, or illegally loud pipes."

In 1986, the name was changed to reflect the multi-brand, national-sized rally it had become. The Tour Expo tradeshow is now a big part of the event, as are mini-tours, self-guided tours, seminars, social events, and field events. Now the world's largest touring-focused event, Americade (518/798-7888, www.tourexpo.com) enlisted approximately 200 staff volunteers to prepare things for more than 60,000 riders in 2004.

The placement is perfect. Americade is held at the southern gateway to the Adirondack Park, which is larger than Yellowstone, Glacier, Yosemite, and Olympic National Parks combined. Ride slowly and count its 2,800 lakes and ponds, 30,000 miles of rivers and streams, and 43 mountains with elevations over 4,000 feet.

on Broadway is therapeutic. The turn-of-the-20th-century setting is enhanced by the Canfield Casino, favorite hangout of larger-than-life Diamond Jim Brady. Numerous quiet spots beckon you to stretch out on the lawn and enjoy nature. Settle back and listen to the groundskeepers trim the lawn, and watch geese overhead slicing their way south. Another peaceful place is by the Daniel Chester French statue erected in memory of Spencer Trask, a man, says the inscription, whose "one object in life was to do right and observe his fellow man. He gave himself abundantly to hasten the coming of a new and better day." Not a bad legacy.

Save time after the racetrack, Congress Park, and Broadway's shops and pubs to explore **Saratoga Spa State Park** (S. Broadway, 518/584-2535). The 2,000-plus acres encompass an 18- and a 9-hole golf course (518/584-2008), the Gideon Putnam Resort & Spa (518/584-3000 or 800/732-1560), a performing arts center (518/587-3330), and the circa 1930s Roosevelt Bathhouse & Spa (518/226-4790). Just a mile south of town, this is a perfect short run. Riding south down Broadway, take a right and enter the Avenue of the Pines, a picturesque road that leads to the Gideon Putnam Resort. Later, ride the Loop Road past Geyser Creek into the heart of the park.

Aside from watching the ponies, a popular outdoor activity is hanging out at Saratoga Lake, just four miles from the city center. Ride Route 9 South (Union Ave.) to 9P South and head over the bridge. The eight-mile-long lake is great for sailing, rowing, bass fishing, and waterskiing. Several small restaurants sport decks where you can enjoy a sandwich and a beer while looking out over the lake. If you'd like to get on the water, you can rent a fishing or pontoon boat at the **Saratoga Boatworks** (549 Union Ave./Route 9P, 518/584-2628, www.saratogaboatworks.com). **Point Breeze Marina** (1459 Rte. 9P, 518/587-3397), Saratoga's largest marina, rents pontoons, speedboats, fishing boats, and canoes. You can find gear, bait, and tackle at shops near the marinas.

Saratoga National Historical Park (648 Rte. 32, Stillwater, 518/664-9821, www.nps.gov/sara) commemorates the turning point of the American Revolution. Before the battles of Saratoga on September 19 and October 7, 1777, few colonists felt certain that their ragtag army and militias could forge America into an independent country. But after General John Burgoyne surrendered his 6,000 British soldiers to General Horatio Gates on October 17, it was only a matter of time. The dioramas, exhibits, films, and 10-mile battlefield tour road are emotional reminders of America's quest to be free. Toll for the tour road is $3. The park is open 9 A.M.–5 P.M. daily, April–mid-November.

Civil War students will want to ride to the summit of Mount McGregor to see where Ulysses S. Grant died in 1885, shortly after completing his memoirs. The catch is that had Grant not died here, the **Ulysses S. Grant Cottage** (518/587-8277, $2.50) would have been torn down to make room for the adjacent prison. If you can ignore the shouts of the cons, this is a great, steep road. Take Route 9 North (left) onto Corinth Mountain Road, and then take a quick right and follow signs to Grant Cottage. Hours are iffy, summers only. Call in advance.

If you're thrilled by thoroughbreds, then the **National Museum of Racing and Hall of Fame** (Union Ave. across from Saratoga Race Course, 518/584-0400, www.racingmuseum.org) is a must-see. Open daily, the museum's equine art, special exhibits, and miniature wax figurines of jockeys (at least I *thought* they were miniatures) tell the story of horse racing. You can pay to see the museum, or kick in an extra three bucks for the Oklahoma Track Tour, which is an early morning behind-the-scenes tour of stables, the backstretch, and the area where grooms prepare horses for the race.

It seems cheesy riding a trolley after getting off your bike, but the information shared by the drivers/historians of Trolley Tours will spike your learning curve. And for only a buck! Trolleys run 10 A.M.–6 P.M. Tuesday–Sunday July–Labor Day, departing from the visitors center and various stops along Broadway.

You may wind up at the **Saratoga Performing Arts Center** (Spa State Park, 518/587-3330, www.spac.org) for an outdoor concert by such artists as James Taylor, John Fogerty, the Philadelphia Orchestra, the New York City Ballet, or the Pretenders. And finally, a taste of indulgence. What takes place at the **Roosevelt Baths & Spa** (518/26-4790) may sound like punishment for Cool Hand Luke, but Lordy! Does it feel good after a ride. In this old-fashioned spa, you can get wrapped up in hot sheets, have someone squeeze the tightness out of your muscles, then plunge into steamy, sweat-inducing water … paradise. Prices range from $18 for a mineral bath to $75 for a one-hour massage. Hours vary by season; call in advance. Note: If the Roosevelt's closed and you gotta have someone rub you the right way, call on the affordable **Crystal Spa** (92 S. Broadway, 518/584-2556, www.thecrystalspa.com) which is open year-round.

Shopping

Normally, I wouldn't recommend a souvenir store, but Saratoga is such an incredible town it's worth a memento or two. Look for them at **Impressions of Saratoga** (368 Broadway, 518/587-0666, www.impressionssaratoga.com). You'll find great horse and racing prints here.

Remember Elvis in *Roustabout?* He was riding a Honda 350cc and had a guitar strapped around his back. Shop at **Saratoga Guitar** (8 Caroline St., 518/581-1604, www.saratogaguitar.com) and you can do the same. The shop hawks lots of new, used, and vintage git boxes, plus other smaller instruments for making music on the road. Rock-a-hula, baby!

One of the greatest pleasures of an extended tour is escaping someone else's schedule and doing things you can't do when you're on the clock. Reading is one of them. Partially built within a vacated bank vault, **Lyrical Ballad Bookstore** (7 Phila St., 518/584-8779) is one of the best used and rare bookstores I've seen. Brimming with 100,000 editions, the store holds more topics than a year's worth of Oprah. The bookstore is open 10 A.M.–6 P.M. Monday–Saturday, 11 A.M.–6 P.M. Sunday.

Gotta jones for a stogie? **Saratoga Cigar & Pipe** (170 S. Broadway, 518/584-4716) has a smoking den; and then there's **Smokin' Sam's Cigar Shop** (5 Caroline St., 518/587-6450). Both are open evenings, Smokin' Sam's until midnight in season.

Ride here during race season, and I'll bet you'll bet. To be a better bettor, drop into **Main Street News** (382 Broadway, 518/581-0133), which features a large collection of horse-racing periodicals and racing forms. The shelves are stacked with foreign newspapers, domestic newspapers from around the country, magazines, cigars, paperbacks, and souvenirs.

You don't have to travel to Palm Beach to watch pony boys whacking the ball; they've been doing it around here since 1898. If you're here in June or July, cruise over to **Saratoga Equine Sports Center at Bostwick Field** (518/584-8108, www.saratogapolo.com, $8) to watch the world's top polo players get a "chukker" going. Granted, it's ritzy, but the action's fast and furious—even more so when I rode my bike on the field.

Blue-Plate Specials

Compton's Restaurant (457 Broadway, 518/584-9632) opens daily for breakfast (served all day) and lunch. This diner isn't old-fashioned, it's just really old. You wanted an early start? Breakfast begins at 4 A.M. on weekdays and 3 A.M. on weekends. Inhale two eggs, home fries, toast, and coffee, plus ham, bacon, sausage, or hash—all for $4.50. Try to throw a leg over the saddle after this one.

Traditional Southern food is hard to find even in the South these days, but **Hattie's** (45 Phila St., 518/584-4790, www.hattiesrestaurant.com) has been serving Louisiana cuisine like fried chicken, ribs, catfish, pork chops, and homemade desserts since 1938. If you can't tour south of the Mason-Dixon, try a meal here. Enjoy the full bar and outdoor revelry on the patio in the summer. In season, Hattie's is open seven days in season for breakfast, lunch, and dinner, and off-season for dinner Wednesday–Sunday.

In the tradition of paraphernalia-cluttered chain restaurants, **Professor Moriarty's** (430 Broadway, 518/587-5981, www.professormoriartys.com) sports an eclectic collection of conversation pieces that rivals its menu of steak, ribs, chicken, lamb, seafood, pasta, beers, and ales. A warm bar, sidewalk café, and breakfast during racing season make this place a good bet.

The **Saratoga Diner** (153 S. Broadway, 518/584-4044) has been known to locals and diners since 1948. The lunch specials include soup, an entrée (pork chops, stuffed peppers, turkey), and dessert. They're open 6 A.M.–midnight and 24 hours on the weekends.

Watering Holes

Opened in 1970, **Saratoga Tin & Lint Company** (2 Caroline St., 518/587-5897) is Saratoga's quintessential neighborhood bar. In a basement setting complete with low ceilings, Tin & Lint features creature comforts like wooden benches and one of the best jukeboxes on the road. If you need more convincing, keep in mind that Soupy Sales—*the* Soupy Sales—downed a brew or two here once. You can buy pints of ale for $3 and pitchers for $7 until 4 A.M. daily.

E. O'Dwyers (15 Spring St.) is a British pub with pool tables, booths, tables, and a stream of import brews on tap—Newcastle, Otter Creek Copper, Bass, Harp, Guinness… this is the real McEwan! Two-for-one draft pints are on special 4–7 P.M. Thursday and Friday, and the pub stays open until the wee hours (4 A.M.).

Shut-Eye

Numerous independent motel/spas line Broadway, the majority of them clean and tidy. Motels are great when traveling by bike; just park right out front. If you arrive in racing season, you'd better win a lot of cash: Rates nearly double, and often there are three-night minimums.

Motels and Motor Courts

Smack dab in the middle of everything is the plain Jane **Saratoga Downtowner Motel** (413 Broadway, 518/584-6160 or 888/480-6160, www.saratogadowntowner.com, $73 off-season, $179 race season). It has 42 AAA rooms, continental breakfast, and—get this—an indoor pool beneath a retractable roof that opens in the summer. The **Springs Motel** (189 Broadway, 518/584-6336, www.springsmotel.com, $95 off-season, $195 race season), has 28 spacious and clean rooms. Prices leap here as well during July and August's races. Ouch.

Chain Drive

L, CC

Chain hotels are in town, or within 10 miles. See cross-reference guide featuring phone numbers and Web addresses on page 514.

Inn-Dependence

A few notable inns and hotels are listed here. Prices reflect double occupancy during peak season; plan on spending less—often far less—if you arrive before or after racing season.

Adelphi Hotel (365 Broadway, 518/587-4688, www.adelphihotel.com, $120 and up off-season, $240 and up race season) is one of the most stunning hotels in America, not only because of its grandeur, but because of the subtle anachronisms captured in the blend of 1920s art deco style and tropical casu-alness. The 34 rooms boast high ceilings, private baths, and a far-from-generic decor. The day gets off to a perfect start with breakfast on the verandah and wraps up in a lobby bar that has more character than Sybil. This is the premier spot to relax and relive the 1920s, whether you're passed out under the palms or sampling a cocktail, beer, or daiquiri in the faux-painted bar.

Kathleen and Noel Smith are two of the friendliest people running one of the nicest inns in Saratoga. **Saratoga Arms** (495 Broadway, 518/584-1775, www.saratogaarms.com, $160 and up off-season, $295 and up race season) of-fers large, comfortable rooms right on Broadway and within walking distance of the action.

For a more natural and cost-effective setting, try the **Saratoga B&B** (434 Church St./Rte. 9N, 518/584-0920, $109–185), which sits on five wooded acres a few miles up Route 9N. Adjacent to the B&B is the **Saratoga Motel** (440 Church St., $59–149), which is popular with riders for the motel setting and lower rates. Both share a website, www.saratogabnb.com.

Indulgences

Perhaps the most elaborate lodging in Saratoga, **Batcheller Mansion Inn** (20 Circular St., 518/584-7012 or 800/616-7012, www.batchellermansioninn.com, $135–285 off-season, $260–395 race season) symbolizes turn-of-the-20th-century luxury—even though the rooms sport modern whirlpool tubs. The High Victorian home, built in 1873, was restored by its current owners. Guests enjoy a continental breakfast on weekdays and full breakfast on weekends. Compare Batchellor's racing rates to its off-season rates, and you'll get an idea of Saratoga's seasonal inflation.

Side Trip: Adirondacks

Just because this trip ends at Saratoga Springs, it doesn't mean yours has to. Just north of Saratoga, Americade (www.tourexpo.com), the world's largest tour rally, attracts hordes of riders to the Lake George area in early June.

Even off-season, you can enjoy a nice run up to Lake George via dependable Route 9. The road sweeps through slow curves and a few forgettable towns, campgrounds, and random log cabins. The forest is tranquil and peaceful, and smooth back roads lead to the Adirondacks, Vermont, and Great Lake Sacandaga. Some say that I-87 North to Canada is one of the most scenic roads in the United States.

Lake George itself is a tacky tourist town littered with T-shirt shops, mini-golf, and high cheese. Motels abound in Lake George and tourist cabins dot Route 9N, but if you want to rough it comfortably, Gene and Linda Merlino at the **Lamplight Inn** (231 Rte. 9N, Lake Luzerne, 518/696-5294 or 800/262-4668, www.lamplightinn.com) save rooms for bikers. They even provide hoses and rags for cleaning your bike after a day's ride. All rooms have televisions, some have fireplaces and hot tubs, and the common areas have board games and books. A beer and wine license increases guests' enjoyment. The forested setting among 10 acres is generous enough to help you relax. If you have time and a full tank, take a ride around Lake George—it's a magnificent lakeshore run.

Resources for Riders

Hudson River Valley Run

New York Travel Information
New York Camping Reservations—800/456-2267, www.reserveamerica.com
New York State Parks—www.nysparks.com
New York State Thruway Road Conditions—800/847-8929
New York State Travel and Tourism—800/225-5697, www.iloveny.com

Local and Regional Information
Adirondack Bed & Breakfast Association—www.adirondackbb.com
Dutchess County Tourism—845/463-4000 or 800/445-3131,
    www.dutchesstourism.com
Hudson River Valley Information—800/232-4782,
    www.hudsownvalley.org
Hyde Park Chamber of Commerce—845/229-8612,
    www.hydeparkchamber.org
Saratoga County Chamber of Commerce—518/584-3255 or 800/526-
    8970, www.saratoga.org
Tarrytown/Sleepy Hollow Chamber of Commerce—914/631-1705,
    www.sleepyhollowchamber.com

New York Motorcycle Shops
Albany Honda—390 New Karner Rd., Albany, 518/452-1003
Dutchess Recreational Vehicles—737 Freedom Plains Rd. Poughkeepsie,
    845/454-2810, www.dutchessrec.com
Ed's Service Motorcycles—600 Violet Ave., Hyde Park, 845/454-6210
Haverstraw Motorsports—64–66 Rte. 9W, Haverstraw, 845/429-0141,
    www.haverstrawmotorsports.com
Kawasaki of Newburgh—28 Windsor Hwy., Newburgh, 845/562-3400
Prestige Harley-Davidson—205 Rte. 9W, Congers, 845/268-6651 or
    866/668-7292, www.prestigeharleydavidson.com
Rockland County Motorcycle Service—1630 Rte. 202, Pomona,
    845/268-1212
Rockwell Cycles—1005 Rte. 9W, Fort Montgomery, 845/446-3834,
    www.rockwellcycles.com
Saratoga Power Sports—68 Weibel Ave., Saratoga Springs,
    518/ 581-4085
Spitzies Harley-Davidson—1970 Central Ave., Albany, 518/456-7433,
    www.spitzies.com
Woodstock Harley-Davidson—949 Rte. 28, Kingston, 845/338-2800,
    www.woodstockharley.com
Zack's V-Twin Cycles—701 Violet Ave., Hyde Park, 845/229-1177,
    www.zacksvtwin.com

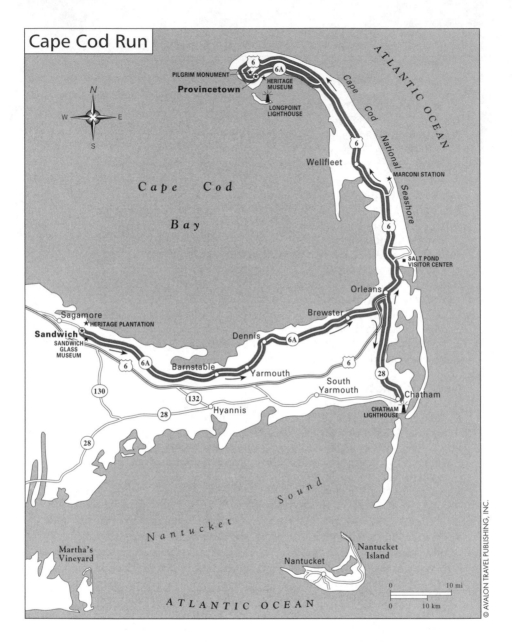

Cape Cod Run

Route: Sandwich to Provincetown via Barnstable, Cummaquid, Dennis, Orleans, Chatham

Distance: Approximately 140 miles (round-trip); consider at least three days with stops.

•**Day 1—Sandwich** •**Day 2—Travel/Chatham** •**Day 3—Travel/Provincetown**

First Leg: Sandwich to Chatham (40 miles)

Second Leg: Chatham to Provincetown (35 miles)

Side Trip: Provincetown to Nantucket (52 miles)

Helmet Laws: Massachusetts requires helmets.

Cape Cod Run

Sandwich, Massachusetts to Provincetown, Massachusetts

About 150 years before John Hancock signed his John Hancock to the Declaration of Independence, freelance whale-hunters traversed the waters around Cape Cod. Surrounded by the sea, local boys grew up sailing on home-based market packets, coastal trading ships, and schooners. They graduated to fast Liverpool packets, clippers, and whaling ships. The independence they displayed in advance of their country's formation is readily apparent today on Cape Cod.

The Cape twists like a tree limb, reaching 35 miles into the Atlantic Ocean. Removed from mainland America, Cape Codders have developed a distinct cultural identity. Residents value the natural beauty of their cranberry bogs, salt marshes, and shorelines. And although whales have descended in economic importance, folks on the Cape still treasure their presence: Witness the fleets of whale-watching charters that set sail from coastal towns.

This trip promises no dangerous curves or sheer drops-offs, since the sea-level routes are short, straight, calming, and quiet. The draw is the chance to discover circa 1700s towns and turn your bike into a time machine.

Sandwich Primer

Sandwich is a town with an identity crisis. As it enters the 21st century, it lingers in the Colonial Era. Hang around the city center and watch the predominant activities of the townspeople: filling water jugs at an artesian well, slipping into pubs, and catching the action as the gristmill starts grinding away on Shawme Pond.

Founded in 1637, the Cape's oldest town matured into a racy place where people liked to drink and plot to kill the British. The American Revolution might have been the town's highlight, had it not been for the arrival of the Boston and Sandwich Glass Company in the 19th century. The glass industry of Sandwich was a natural—not because the town's sands and salt marsh grasses were used for packing, but because of the abundance of forests that the factories could slash and burn to stoke the furnaces. When the factory closed in 1888, Sandwich slipped back into the shadows.

On the Road: Sandwich

Cape Cod roads are so sparse, few will explore the region beyond the road you'll ride to reach Provincetown. That said, park your bike in the village and spend a few hours poking around. It won't take much longer than that because museums and nature trails—not bars and roads—are what you'll find here. If you're accustomed to more hyperkinetic activities, you may be disappointed. An afternoon in Sandwich involves a more natural use of time, when you could spend hours doing nothing.

But that's the appeal. When you watch the swans on Shawme Pond, you won't be assaulted by bus fumes. You'll hear the water rushing, the Dexter Grist Mill grinding, and locals filling up on spring water for their coffee. Drop into the mill for a bag of cornmeal. Relax and watch the reflection of the Christopher Wren–inspired church spire on the water. Step into the Sandwich Glass Museum to see that glass can be art. Savor the fresh air as you take a short walk through neighborhoods where even the trash seems clean.

While there's a good cross-section of businesses here, two may pique your interest: **Madden and Company** (16 Jarves St., 508/888-3663) features aisles of scrimshaw, marine paintings, and other marine collectibles. Cool stuff for the office, but the downside is that it's only open by appointment. **The Weather Store** (146 Main St., 508/888-1200 or 800/646-1203, www.the-weatherstore.com) stocks antique and creatively designed barometers, rain gauges, sundials, and other meteorological goods, and it's all fairly fascinating. Will you need your rainsuit? Consult your new combination barometer, hygrometer, and barograph.

When you're ready to expand your roaming range, hop back on your bike and ride to the Heritage Plantation or down to the bayfront boardwalk, which places you close to the salt marshes and Cape Cod Bay.

Pull It Over: Sandwich Highlights
Attractions and Adventures

Sidewalks start rolling up around 4:30 P.M., so aside from the few activities noted below (which can actually occupy most of a day), don't plan on doing much except taking a break from work and experiencing life as a colonist.

On the Cape, you're surrounded by water, and there's an undeniable draw to park your bike and go to sea. About 25 miles up the road in East Dennis is the **Albatross** (Sesuit Harbor, 508/385-3244). This deep-sea fishing charter has been family-run since 1965 and leaves twice daily on weekdays for Cape Cod Bay runs for flounder, mackerel, and hake. These charters start when the weather turns warm in June. You can catch sight of a whale with the **Hyannis Whale Watcher** (508/362-6088 or 888/942-5392, www.whales.net, schedules vary), roughly 15 miles outside Sandwich in Barnstable Harbor. Departing with the tides, the cruise takes about 3.5 hours as you scan the seas for right whales, finbacks, minke, and humpbacks. Arrrr, matey.

I can't believe I liked the **Sandwich Glass Museum** (129 Main St., 508/888-0251, www.sandwichglassmuseum.org, $4.50), but I did. At the second-largest draw in town, there are intriguing displays of tools that—long before computers and robots—were used to mold, thread, cut, and engrave glass, as well as antique books, maps, shoes, scrimshaw art, cigar holders, and a glass torch from the Lincoln-Hamlin ticket of 1860. Sure, you may be surrounded by tourists from Iowa, but you're getting yourself an education there, Jethro. For an extra fee, consider a 90-minute walking tour of the town with knowledgeable docents. You'll get a better sense of the town's history as you examine the architecture of Sandwich village, or the plots and history of the Old Town cemetery. Check the website for tour schedules.

The largest draw for any rider is down the road. Pharmaceutical giant Josiah Kirby Lilly Jr. spent 40 years collecting rare books, artwork, drinking steins, stamps, coins, weapons, nautical models, and firearms, and all of it is on display at **Heritage Plantation** (Pine and Grove Sts., 508/888-3300, www.heritageplantation.org, $12). There are verdant grounds to explore on foot or aboard a tram, and you shouldn't miss the impressive collection of vehicles inside the replica 1826 Shaker Roundbarn. Inside are 35-plus vintage cars, including a 1908 Waltham Orient Buckboard, the 1910 Sears Surrey (with the fringe on top), and the $2,000 1915 Stutz Bearcat—the "dream of flappers and college men." Despite my suggestion, there's still no AMC Gremlin. Other historical artifacts include a lock of Lincoln's hair (is there a genetic cloner in the house?). Open daily year-round, with shorter hours off-season.

Blue-Plate Specials

Good food and reliable service await you at the **Bee-Hive Tavern** (406 E. Rte. 6A, 508/833-1184), serving lunch and dinner. Healthy portions of baked stuffed quahog, fried conch fritters, lobster pie, and fish and chips beckon. What's more, meals are affordable. In this colonial tavern setting, you wouldn't be surprised to see a stagecoach roll up. If you're in Sandwich overnight, hoist a Boddington's Pub Ale ($4 a pint) at the low-ceilinged bar.

Five miles west of town on Route 6A, the **Sagamore Inn** (1131 Sandwich Rd., 508/888-9707, www.sagamoreinn.com) has colonial-style wooden floors and booths, and mouth-watering Yankee pot roast, as well as pasta and seafood dishes.

Shut-Eye

Motels and Motor Courts

In the top 10 of motorcycle lodging options belongs the **Spring Hill Motor Lodge** (351 Rte. 6A, 508/888-1456 or 800/647-2514, www.springhillmotorlodge.com, $95–105), three miles east of Sandwich. Reminiscent of an old-fashioned motor court, the juniper-shaded complex features a heated pool, tennis courts, and 24 extremely clean and spacious rooms. Four deluxe cottages boast private porches and fully equipped kitchens. Great for an overnight or as a base to explore the Cape, the lodge gives breaks on weekly rentals. The equally clean **Shady Nook Inn and Motel** (14 Rte. 6A, 508/888-0409 or 800/303-1751, www.shadynookinn.com, $125 and up) has spacious two-room suites, full baths, cable TV, phones, connecting double rooms, and efficiencies.

Chain Drive

A, C, G

Chain hotels are in town, or within 10 miles. See cross-reference guide featuring phone numbers and Web addresses on page 514.

On the Road: Sandwich to Chatham

As you skirt along the shores and marshes of Cape Cod Bay and leave Sandwich behind, Route 6A is low and lean, slowly swinging into a gentle curve and delivering you into the past. On this leg, you'll ride past villages founded in the 1600s, small places like Barnstable, Cummaquid, and Dennis.

Long before Route 6 arrived to transport people in a hurry, Route 6A preserved Cape Cod the way it used to be. The roads are as soft and gentle as the scent of the pines. Let the other regions of Cape Cod lure commercialism. Not on this ride. Had you ridden this road 200 years ago, not only would the locals have fled in terror at the sight of your bike, but you would also have been riding the Old King's Highway, the only route mail and passenger coaches took prior to the Revolution. Today, it is yours. And it remains imbued with regional flavor. Along 6A, you'll still hear native Cape Codders talk about "washashores," the transplants who arrived from "off Cape." Then there are the "boggers," the farmers whose fruitful cranberry bogs have stayed in the family for generations.

As you leave Sandwich heading east on 6A, you'll notice the repetitive uniformity of the unpainted, shingled homes. White cedar shingles were plentiful, easily split, and could last up to 60 years. And why paint when your house was going to be sandblasted and sea-sprayed throughout the year? Some people do paint—but only a shade of white that earns the local historic commission's "certificate of appropriateness."

The ride is short, the road level, the landscape dotted with blue spruce, silver maple, firs, Canadian hemlock, and sycamore. The trees are as plentiful as the signage pointing to woodworkers, potters, artists, cabinetmakers, weavers, and other New England craftspeople who work from their homes. There are few changes in elevation, but there are bends in the road that follow the contour of the shore. In Yarmouthport, there's a stop you should make. The **Parnassus Book Service** (220 Rte. 6A, 508/362-6420, www.parnassusbooks.com) is a place Charles Kuralt would have loved. The building, the books, and the crusty old owner are the same as they have been since 1960. You can buy a book inside, or, if no one's on duty, grab a book from the outdoor display, check the price, and put your money through a slot in the door.

Next come the minuscule villages of Cummaquid, Yarmouth, and then Dennis. As you roll into Dennis, there's a trace amount of activity in a small shopping plaza, but, as in other towns along Route 6A, the doors lock and the sidewalks roll up around five o'clock. That's fine, because a few more miles down the road lies Brewster and the must-see **Brewster Store** (1935 Rte. 6A, 508/896-3744, www.brewsterstore.com). In 1852, this opened as Universalist Society Church, but just over a decade later, prophets gave way to profits. Since 1866, more or less, this has been a general store outfitted with all the props you'd see at Sam Drucker's. Old-fashioned candy displays are still here, and so are a soda fountain, a player piano, a peanut roaster, a Station Agent #24 pot-bellied stove, and a jar filled with pickles the size of zeppelins. Out front, locals gather on church pews each morning to eat donuts, drink coffee, trade yarns, and solve the world's problems.

This is the last gasp of individuality as Brewster precedes Orleans, a busy bottleneck that has all the conveniences of home (supermarket, restaurants, motels, etc.). Since it does look like home, that's why you want to head south on Route 28 and make your way to the "elbow" of the Cape in fantastic Chatham.

Chatham Primer

Nearly as old as Sandwich, Chatham was settled in 1656 by Pilgrims whose surnames continue to dominate the town's census list of 6,500-plus residents. At first, this was a farming community until one egghead looked around, realized he was on the peninsular southeastern tip of the cape, and said, "Aye, Martha, 'tis true. Farming blows."

So, for more than 300 years, shellfish harvesting and deep-sea fishing have remained staples for this town. Aside from the sea, Chatham has no major industries to speak of. By being here, you're helping fuel tourism that keeps the town going—at least during the summer when the weather's right.

On the Road: Chatham

Like Sandwich, Chatham is a town best explored on foot. You'll understand why when you ride in on Route 28, which, in town, is called Main Street. For block after block, you'll find bars, nice restaurants, and some of the freshest seafood in America. Sure, you could head 20 miles west to Hyannis and find more people doing more stuff in more chain stores, but you can do that anywhere. Stop your bike and really see what's happening. A local sums it up: "If you're in a hurry, you don't belong in Chatham."

Assuming you'll stay the night, keep your bike at the inn/motel/hotel, since parking in the village is at a premium in peak season. Now you're free to walk the streets and tune into the smells of coffee, bakeries, candle shops, cafés, flowers, and the sea. For a party back in your room, check out **The Epicure** (534 Main St., 508/945-0047), which has about eleven-hundred wines, cigars, gourmet picnic foods, and other essentials. All in all, the mix of shops is a fitting reward for bypassing Orleans.

After soaking in Main Street, cruise over to the ocean a short ride or slightly longer walk away. Head east on Main Street, then south on Morris Island Road to reach the **Chatham Lighthouse.** Unless you're a native or a member of the Polar Bear Club, you may find the beach here swimmable only a few hours a year. Still, the shore attracts riders who find a good photo op where the tip of Cape Cod meets the Atlantic.

Pull It Over: Chatham Highlights
Attractions and Adventures

If the weather's right, nothing beats a day on the waters of old Cape Cod. Through Cape Yachts, **Nauti Jane's** (Ridgevale Beach Rd., Chatham, 508/430-6893, www.nautijanesboatrentals.com) supplies Hobie Cats, larger sailboats, and power boats. Option B: Leave the sailing to a professional. Captain Paul Avellar takes the wheel at **Beachcomber Boat Tours** (508/945-5265, www.sealwatch.com) to skip out to the Monomoy Islands (a national wildlife refuge) to watch harbor seals, gray seals, and shore birds. At **Chatham Water Tours** (508/432-5895, www.chathamwatertours.net), Captain David Murdoch sets sail on a similar excursion, but for a buck less. Unless these men share the Skipper's bad luck and you wind up on an uncharted desert isle, you'll get a waterside look at the natural side of Chatham: a panorama of pristine New England beaches, harbors, and seals. Group riders can pool their cash and customize a cruise.

Blue-Plate Specials

Nothing fancy at **Sandy's Diner** (639 Main St., 508/945-0631), just three very nice ladies who will whip up a hearty breakfast or lunch for you. Don't expect a four-star meal at this low-key diner, here since 1965, and don't expect a lot of men either; they're down at **Larry's PX** (1591 Main St., West Chatham, 508/945-3964). If you crave a midnight snack, wait a few hours and be here when he opens at 4 A.M. Larry's serves big breakfasts and overstuffed sandwiches at lunch.

I could recommend a fancy restaurant, but, instead, try savoring fresh seafood for your own Cape Cod clambake. Locals have been shopping at **Nickerson's Fish & Lobster** (Chatham Fish Pier, 508/945-0145) since 1950, and if you wanted seafood any fresher, you'd have to dive for it yourself. Steamers, lobster tails, little necks, mussels, quahog, haddock, cod, flounder, and sweet lobsters are yours for the asking. They load your feast on a beer flat and supply all the accessories you need for a beach cookout or a meal at your efficiency (they can also cook it for the most delicious to-go meal you've ever had). Cash only. Open daily Memorial Day–Labor Day, weekends until mid-October.

Watering Holes

There are fewer than a handful of nighttime hangouts, primarily restaurants that will keep their bars open until 1 A.M. The largest draw in Chatham village is its only raw bar, the **Chatham Squire** (487 Main St., 508/945-0942, www.thesquire.com), where they offer "Food for the hungry, drink for the thirsty." That about sums it up. The standard lineup of Killian's, Bass, Guinness, and Pete's Wicked Ale goes for about four bucks a pint. The restaurant features chowders, sirloin, ribs, chicken, and fish. Lots of fish.

Christian's (443 Main St., 508/945-3362) is a restaurant created inside an old sea captain's house. What you're looking for is Upstairs at Christian's, a place where you can retreat to a piano bar and hoist an ale at tables tucked in and under the eaves and nooks. Not wild, but a good retreat.

Shut-Eye

Motels and Motor Courts
For a small town, Chatham offers many good lodging choices, although the prices aren't always pleasing. Just over a mile from the village, the **Chatham Motel** (1487 Main St., 508/945-2630 or 800/770-5545, www.chatham motel.com, $80–95 off-season, $145–165 summer) stands in a pine grove. The 32 rooms are clean and well-equipped, and the grounds feature gardens, barbecue grills, and a pool. Right near the Chatham Lighthouse is the **Surfside Motor Court** (25 Holway St., 508/945-9757, $95 and up). Within walking distance of the water, you'll get an old-fashioned (and clean) room and easy access to swimming and fishing.

Inn-dependence
The Moorings (326 Main St., 508/945-0848, 800/320-0848, www.themoor-ingscapecod.com, $145 and up) is a bed-and-breakfast that provides privacy via carriage houses and cottages that can sleep up to four. One of the most picturesque inns is the **Chatham Wayside Inn** (512 Main St., 508/945-5550 or 800/391-5734, www.waysideinn.com, $105–195). This circa 1860 home has lots of room—enough for a pub, restaurant, and 56 guestrooms, many with patios or balconies, fireplaces, and whirlpool tubs.

On the Road: Chatham to Provincetown

When you leave Chatham on Route 28 North, the Atlantic Ocean will be on your right. Although you'll backtrack to reach and bypass Orleans, at least the scenery on the ride is spiced with sights such as Pleasant Bay, Pilgrim Lake, hidden coves, and small boats.

After you pass Orleans, you'll reach the end of Route 28 and briefly hook up with familiar Route 6A before locking into Route 6. While the roads are fairly dense with traffic, they're manageable and, a mile past Eastham, will lead you directly to the **Cape Cod National Seashore's Salt Pond Visitor Center** (508/255-3421, www.nps.gov/caco), the introduction to 43,604 acres of national park awaiting you, courtesy of Cape Codder JFK. Like most places along these remote roads, low-key diversions like this may not seem appealing to bikers in general, but it's well worth a stop to understand the history of the Cape. At the center, the *Sands of Time* is a short film showing how the Cape was formed by a glacial deposit, and how it will one day be reclaimed by the sea (on Sunday, May 27, 2062, at 8:04 P.M., to be exact).

A sign helpfully suggests how to plan your visit if your time is limited to an hour, a half day, or even a full day. Options vary from touring the museum and watching the movie to hooking up with a ranger-led program, whale-watching, or hanging out on 30 miles of beach. If you're ready to reach Provincetown, an hour's visit should be enough, slightly longer if the history of the sea intrigues you. The small must-see museum is first-class, with exhibits on the lonely lives of lighthouse keepers, the many uses of whalebone, the area's colonial taverns, and the primitive rescue equipment used to save shipwrecked sailors. On early wooden life preservers, instructions for their use were carved in three languages to give foreign sailors a chance.

Farther up the road in Wellfleet is Marconi Station, site of the first transatlantic wireless telegraph station. In 1903, Teddy Roosevelt sent a message to England's King Edward VII: "Most cordial greetings and best wishes." Edward's memorable reply, "Ted? Can I call you back? The game's on," endeared him to generations of American men. Hike up a 20-foot bluff, and the site is just a plaque, a platform, and a boardwalk—but you're here, so why not drop in?

Now a warning: If you look at the Cape on a map, it seems as if Route 6 would be one of the nation's best oceanfront roads. It's not. It hugs the middle of a thin strip of land and leaves 3,000 miles of Atlantic Ocean hidden behind stands of trees, taffy shops, and T-shirt stores. The reward for your effort is that once you've reached the tip of Cape Cod, you can always point at a map and say, "Yeah, I rode my bike there once."

So, the next 22 miles are uneventful, until you get well north, where the sea winds blow in sand from the beach. As you roll into the last curves of the peninsula, just ahead you'll spy the terminus of this trip: Provincetown.

Provincetown Primer

When the Pilgrims landed here in November 1620, they set in motion the formation of New England. It may not seem that impressive when you consider that the *Mayflower* only docked here for two months before sailing on to Plymouth, but think about this: That was long enough for the Mayflower Compact to be signed, which was the first charter of democratic government in world history.

Absent any Pilgrims, Provincetown later became home to early colonial settlers, followed by Portuguese immigrants who showed up to do a little fishing on the Grand, Stellwagen, and Georges Banks. These were hearty people; part-time fishermen who became full-time residents, bold enough to stay here through the harsh, biting winters.

Provincetown now peaks in the summer with day-trippers and others who drive up for lunch and perhaps an overnight. Dense with commercialism but blessed by miles of beaches, the town will speak to you … or it will remain very quiet. I didn't hear much.

On the Road in Provincetown

When you arrive in Provincetown, there's a strong possibility you'll be put off by the crowded, narrow streets that make a bike ride nearly as uncomfortable as driving a motor home. The main thoroughfare, three-mile-long Commercial Street, is clogged with gift shops, T-shirt stores, bars, and a predominantly gay population. Fine if you're gay, tolerable if you're not, annoying if you just wanted to see a neat fishing village. In Provincetown, it seems that outrageous is the norm.

The instantaneous assault on your senses makes it clear that the natural beauty of Cape Cod is far nicer than any man-made creation. With that in mind, you have the option of making this a day trip and returning to quiet Chatham, or staying the night.

Either way, perhaps the best view of Cape Cod is from the **Pilgrim Monument** (High Pole Hill, 508/487-1310, www.pilgrim-monument.org, $7), dedicated in 1910 to commemorate the first landing of the Pilgrims in Provincetown. At the base of the 252-foot tower is the Provincetown Museum, which is included in monument admission. Outside of a few museums, the main attractions in town are walking Commercial Street, dropping in a watering hole for a drink, or getting away from it all on a whale-watching trip.

Pull It Over: Provincetown Highlights
Attractions and Adventures

Whale-watching trip depart from Provincetown Harbor. Provincetown is roughly six miles from the Stellwagen Bank Sanctuary, the main feeding ground for whales. Most trips run April–October and cost around $26. Sign up with the **Dolphin Fleet** (508/240-3636 or 800/826-9300, www.whalewatch.com).

Because P-Town's already 50 miles out to sea, several charter boats take advantage of its strategic location by fishing for fluke, flounder, bluefish, mackerel, and striped bass. A fleet of fishing boats stands at the ready to take you out on the high seas. Most provide bait and tackle, but no harpoons.

Blue-Plate Specials

An unsophisticated neon exterior announces the **Lobster Pot** (321 Commercial St., 508/487-0842, www.ptownlobsterpot.com), which serves lunch and dinner. Believe it or not, the restaurant opened way back in '76 … 1876! The local hangout overlooks P-Town Harbor and serves a medley of Portuguese and Cajun seafood-based meals and hundreds of lobsters a day in the summer. Go for the clam chowder. Upstairs at "The Pot," the bar gets mighty crowded.

In 1929, the same year the Great Depression kicked in, the **Mayflower Cafe** (300 Commercial St., 508/487-0121) kicked off. Now run by descendents of the original owners, this sit-down restaurant is a classic, with dishes like homemade clam chowder, steamed soft-shell clams, Portuguese-style fish and chips, crab cakes, oysters, pastas, lobster, pork chops, sandwiches, pizzas, fresh-baked dinner rolls, and plenty of beer. No credit cards accepted, so bring cash.

Gonna Have a Clambake

A clambake stirs up beach party visions of Gidget and Annette, and here's one way to do it. Circle the bikes, grab a shovel, then dig a large pit. Line the bottom with stones, on top of which you'll place wood to burn. A few hours later, after the wood burns and the rocks are red hot, rake away the wood coals and cover the rocks with seaweed. Place your food (clams, mussels, corn, potatoes, onions, sausage, etc.) on top and cover the pit with a tarp. After an hour of steaming, your meal should be ready. Or blow it off and order clams at a restaurant.

Watering Holes

There are drinking spots up and down Commercial Street, but when you go in and don't see any women, you've either entered a gay bar or a high-testosterone sports bar. Some bars switch formats, so you're best exploring on your own. A safe bet may be **Bubala's** (185 Commercial St., 508/487-0773), which has live entertainment nightly; usually jazz, blues, or comedy. Fine for a beer, but it prides itself on martinis. The **Surf Club** (315 A Commercial St., 508/487-1367) has been here since the early '70s and is a local fave. Three TVs play sports, the windows open to the water, and decks are designed for drinking and dancing to the blues bands that play as late as 1 A.M. in the summer.

Shut-Eye

Motels and Motor Courts
In a town where dirty is clean, the **Cape Colony Inn** (280 Bradford St., 508/487-1755 or 800/841-6716, www.capecolonyinn.com, $84 and up), is *clean* clean. It's also remote enough (a few miles away) to be a good base for P-Town, offering seven landscaped acres, picnic areas, a beach volleyball court, heated pool, and 57 loaded rooms.

Chain Drive
A

Chain hotels are in town, or within 10 miles. See cross-reference guide featuring phone numbers and Web addresses on page 514.

Inn-dependence
The Fairbanks Inn (90 Bradford St., 508/487-0386 or 800/324-7265, www.fairbanksinn.com, $69 off-season, $129 in season) has consistently received high marks from guests and the press. Amenities include an expanded continental breakfast, sun porch, and 10 wood-burning fireplaces—if you need them in the summer. Adding a touch of class, the English country house–style **Beaconlight** (12 Winthrop St., 508/487-9603 or 800/696-9603, www.beaconlightguesthouse.com, $100 off-season, $140 in season) has a few king beds, a video library, voicemail, fridges, fireplaces, a grand piano, and a outdoor heated spa, and it serves a gourmet continental breakfast.

Side Trip: Nantucket

Even though you won't need to bring your bike to this island, it's worth the trip—Nantucket is the closest you'll get to a colonial whaling town, complete with 800-odd homes built by whalers between 1740 and 1840. On a day trip, you can walk the area you need to see in about four hours and still have time to kick back at a few pubs or restaurants.

From Hyannis, you can gain a few valuable hours by reaching the island via a 15-minute plane ride aboard **Island Airlines** (508/228-7575 or 800/248-7779) or **Cape Air** (508/771-6944 or 800/352-0714, www.flycapeair.com). Both carriers charge $89 round-trip, and you'll have to take a taxi to reach the center of town. Also from Hyannis, the next best option is catching the Steamship Authority's **Fast Ferry** (508/477-8600, www.steamshipauthority.com), which rockets you there in an hour for around $55 round-trip. It accommodates motorcycles on the slow ferry for $116 round-trip, plus $28 for each rider. **Hy-Line Cruises** (508/778-2600 or 888/778-1132, www.hy-linecruises.com) does the same thing for around $65. Take the slow ferry (2.5 hours/$30) only if you want to take your bike, you're on a budget, or you can't swim. The ferry terminals have snacks, coffee, phones, and lockers where you can stow your helmet. Tip: Find a parking spot early, or you'll be gouged by the neighboring New England hillbillies across the street.

Different ferry services dock at different locations on Nantucket, and there are bicycle rentals nearby (mopeds, too, if you're ready to downsize). But since the streets were made using ballast from old sailing ships, the cobblestone wobble will rattle your brain right out of your skull.

Find your way to Main Street, the heart of Nantucket. A good first stop is either the **Nantucket Island Chamber of Commerce** (48 Main St., 508/228-1700) or the **Visitors Services Bureau** (25 Federal St., 508/228-0925, www.nantucket-ma.gov), both of which have racks of brochures on museums, lodging, and activities—and the website's loaded with information for preplanning. Next up is the **Jared Coffin House** (29 Broad St., 508/228-2400), an impressive older home that now serves a great breakfast for a nominal price.

In the heart of town a few stores stand out. **Congdon's Pharmacy** (47 Main St., 508/228-0020), established in 1871, features an old-fashioned soda fountain. **Murray's Beverage Store** (23 Main St., 508/228-0071) sells wines, cigars, trail mix, crackers, and bar snacks. **The Brotherhood of Thieves** (23 Broad St., 508/228-2551 www.brotherhoodofthieves.com) is an "1840s whaling bar" and restaurant popular with locals. It's low-key, with a good vibe and fresh seafood, burgers, fries, beer, and mixed drinks. The outdoor patio bar is perfect in summer.

As you explore, the Nantucket Historical Association Museum Guide and Walking Tour, available at the museum, will lead you to quiet side streets several blocks from the busy downtown district. You may enjoy yourself most here. Get lost on the back streets and enjoy the same sense of solitude you can get on your bike.

Resources for Riders

Cape Cod Run

Massachusetts Travel Information
Massachusetts Road Conditions—617/374-1234
Massachusetts State Park Campgrounds Reservations—877/422-6762,
    www.reserveamerica.com
Massachusetts Department of Travel & Tourism—617/973-8500 or
    800/447-6277, www.massvacation.com

Local and Regional Information
Bed & Breakfast Cape Cod—508/255-3824 or 800/541-6226,
    www.bedandbreakfastcapecod.com
Bed & Breakfast Reservations—617/964-1606 or 800/832-2632,
    www.bbreserve.com
Canal Region Chamber of Commerce (Sandwich) —508/759-6000,
    www.capecodcanalchamber.org
Cape Cod Area Visitors Bureau—508/862-0700 or 888/332-2732,
    www.capecodchamber.org
Cape Cod National Seashore—508/349-3785, www.nps.gov/caco
Cape Cod Weather—508/771-5522
Chatham Chamber of Commerce—508/945-5199 or 800/715-5567,
    www.chathaminfo.com
Nantucket Island Chamber of Commerce—508/228-1700,
    www.nantucketchamber.org
Provincetown Chamber of Commerce—508/487-3424,
    www.ptownchamber.com

Massachusetts Motorcycle Shops
Archie's Cycle Service—489 Ashley Blvd., New Bedford, 508/995-9751,
    www.archiecycle.com
Cape Cod Power Sports—92 Barnstable Rd., Hyannis, 508/771-5900,
    www.ccpowersports.com
JMR Honda-Polaris-Suzuki—741 Yarmouth Rd., Hyannis, 508/778-7211

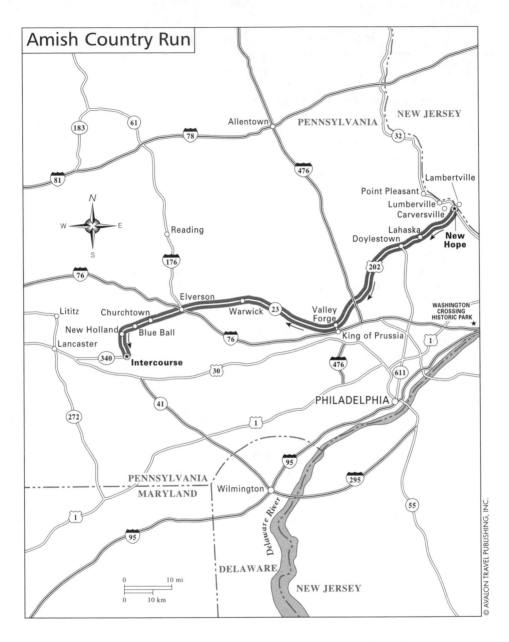

Amish Country Run

Route: New Hope to Intercourse via Lahaska, Doylestown, Valley Forge
Distance: Approximately 110 miles; consider three days with stops.
•**Day 1—New Hope** •**Day 2—Travel** •**Day 3—Intercourse**
First Leg: New Hope to Intercourse (110 miles)
Helmet Laws: Pennsylvania requires helmets.

Amish Country Run

New Hope, Pennsylvania to Intercourse, Pennsylvania

This journey will take you into the past, from the colonial accents an hour north of Philadelphia to a Revolutionary War icon and 19th-century farms. Along the way, you'll ride next to the historic Delaware River and gaze on Pennsylvania's most pristine farmland. Some of the finest back roads and friendliest people reside in this part of America. Time your ride for late summer or early fall, and you'll enjoy it even more.

New Hope Primer

Of all the towns in America—at least the ones I've visited—New Hope is clearly the one most at ease with itself. It accepts diversity without question and welcomes all without exception. Locals explain that the feeling is the result of New Hope's being on the cross of a "vortex," a positive energy field centered in an underground river flowing 60 feet below the Delaware River. The only other town with such a vortex is Sedona, Arizona—but I hear it's energized by plutonium.

You'll view New Hope through the prism of age. Young riders may see it as a nouveau Haight-Ashbury; couples with kids notice a family-friendly getaway; and older motorcycle travelers will arrive in a charming shopping village.

New Hope is all this, but it is also something greater. It is a historic community that predates Philadelphia. It was at Coryell's Ferry where George

Washington trained for his fabled crossing, before he made the real voyage a few miles south.

A century later, the town became the birthplace of the New Hope School of Artists, whose members left Philadelphia to gain inspiration from the summer countryside. Later, they fostered the Pennsylvania Impressionist movement. It is an actors' community—as a young man, Robert Redford honed his skills here at the Bucks County Playhouse. It is a walking town that spans the river into Lambertville, New Jersey. And, for your benefit, it is also a town serving as Point B for motorcycle travelers on weekend runs from New York, New Jersey, and Pennsylvania.

On the Road: New Hope

What you'll see beyond the boundaries of New Hope is magical, but first you should know what's in town. New Hope can be high-class, with galleries, cafés, and upscale boutiques, but it can also be down-to-earth, with cigar shops and bars that welcome motorcycle travelers. Collectibles shops line Main Street, providing a field day for fans of antiques. And, judging from all the witch shops and tie-dyed kids roaming around, New Hope could also be a breeding ground for radicals.

Drop by the visitors center (1 W. Mechanic St., 215/862-5030) to pick up some maps, brochures, and travel tips, and then take a good look at the village and make some mental notes. Then swerve around the tourists and take off on Route 32 North (aka River Rd.) for a short and seductive ride beside the beautiful Delaware.

The trimmed hedges and manicured lawns of the town soon give way to sharp curves and a tunnel of green. Fresh fields and hefty stone walls suggest Britain's Yorkshire Dales as they rise and fall with the earth. The road follows the lead of the walls, pushing you up and dragging you into tight corners and spectacularly old scenery.

As you pass cars carrying wooden canoes, you'll find it hard to believe that this landscape is only a few miles from the downtown tourists. Getting into the groove, you soon arrive at Route 263 and **Dilly's Corner** (215/862-5333, open seasonally, closed Mondays), where moms, teens, tourists, and bikers converge to load up on hamburgers, cheeseburgers, swirls, and sundaes.

Heading north toward Lumberville, you enter primeval woods as green and moist as a rainforest. The corduroy texture of the road travels from the tires up into your body. The Delaware River rides on your right as you pass a flotilla of people drifting downriver in slick black inner tubes. Occasionally, you'll spy deer grazing in fields beside magnificent mansions.

Amish farmers

© NANCY HOWELL

Landscaped lawns and untouched grasses grow side by side, and there's extreme satisfaction in the knowledge that no one's screwed this up yet. Past the 1740 House and Cuttalossa Inn, just beyond the authentic, old-fashioned **Lumberville Store** (3741 River Rd., 215/297-5388, www.thelumbervillegeneralstore.com), it's time for a detour. On your left, Old Carversville Road rises like the Matterhorn. Take it, and you'll see a steep drop materializing on the right. As the road changes to gravel and you slow down to compensate, cabins suddenly appear in the hollow—unobtrusive because they are built of the earth, not on it.

Just past a wooden bridge, you arrive in Carversville. Downtown's about the size of your backyard, and the center of activity is the **Carversville General Store** (215/297-5353). Well-stocked with groceries and drinks, it's also the town post office and theater. On the last Monday of each summer month, moving picture shows are projected on the side of the building. If you haven't caught on, this is a great place to stop for a Yoo-Hoo and a Chunky bar.

Head down the hill back Lumberville and turn left to follow Route 32 north. Beneath the bridge, fishermen in waders cast their lines. When you pass the village of Devil's Half Acre, the stunning view and weaving road introduce some LeMans-style driving that sweeps you into small bumps and quick ascents. Here in the Delaware Valley, there's scant commercialism. Right now it's just the road and you.

You'll soon reach Point Pleasant, home of **Bucks County River Country** (215/297-5000, 215/297-TUBE or 215/297-8823, www.rivercountry.net), the point of origin for the armada of inner tube passengers you passed downriver.

Places like this make a tour great. Rent a tube or raft and go cruising down the Delaware, drifting at a lazy 1.5 mph in cool water. There are no rapids here, so you can just relax and enjoy the soothing, peaceful experience.

From here, you can continue your northward trek toward Upper Black Eddy and Lake Nockamixon. Take virtually any road in any direction for a longer ride, or turn back and head home to New Hope. That's the beauty of New Hope. No matter where you ride, you'll be satisfied.

Pull It Over: New Hope Highlights
Attractions and Adventures

Far enough from Broadway to try out plays and close enough to take them to NYC if they're any good, **Bucks County Playhouse** (70 South Main St., 215/862-2041 or 215/862-2046, www.buckscountyplayhouse.com), the state theater of Pennsylvania, has been a launching pad for great playwrights like George S. Kaufman and Moss Hart, while hopeful actors Robert Redford, Grace Kelly, Dick Van Dyke, Tyne Daly, and Liza Minnelli caught the stage right here. Tickets average $22–24.

Aside from riding an inner tube, you can board a half-hour cruise on the Delaware and pick up enough intelligence about the history of the area (in the event you want to cross the river and attack the British someday). **Well's Ferry** (215/862-5965, www.newhopeboatrides.com) is still in the same location where John Wells—the town's founder and first ferryboat operator—began his business in 1718.

Riders who like all things mechanical should pay a visit to the **New Hope & Ivyland Railroad** (32 W. Bridge St., 215/862-2332, www.newhoperailroad.com, $10). It has four full-gauge steam locomotives that pull passenger cars through the hills and valleys of Bucks County. If you have vivid dreams about steam trains, give serious thought to the "locomotive cab ride," one of very few steam railroads that allow passengers to ride up front with the engineer and see how the original iron horses were driven. Trips depart several times daily in season.

Some would say a barge trip with the **New Hope Canal Boat Company** (149 S. Main St., 215/862-0758, www.canalboats.com, $10) is as boring as all get out, but it is different—and cheap. A mule team pulls your barge down the Delaware Canal and shows you a different side of New Hope. If you're traveling in a group, call ahead to reserve a private barge for a canal party. You may be looking at the back of a mule for a couple of hours, but it doesn't matter if you loaded up the barge with a cooler full of beer.

Seven remarkably cool, must-ride miles south of New Hope are the site of a turning point in American history: **Washington Crossing Historic Park** (1112 River Rd./Rte. 32, Washington Crossing, 215/493-4076). On Christmas Eve 1776, George Washington massed the Continental Army and surprised British troops by crossing the Delaware and capturing 900 British soldiers and German mercenaries in Trenton. Later that night, adding a feather in the cap of this victory, Washington marched on to Princeton, where he caught the British garrison by surprise and captured enough food and supplies to sustain his troops through the brutal winter of 1777. What's more, four units were scheduled to cross the river that night, but only Washington's regiment reached the other side. Learning facts like this make Washington more than an icon—it makes him a real man. You can take a tour of historic buildings, the boathouse, and replicas, and see a stirring movie about the event. And on the return trip to New Hope, you may want to pay your respects to his spirit and those of young soldiers buried near the river at a Revolutionary War cemetery a few miles on.

Shopping

Shopping is New Hope's lifeblood. The town has many antique shops— none geared toward motorcycle travelers per se but interesting nonetheless. A place called **Gypsy Heaven** (115G S. Main St., 215/862-5251, www.gypsy-heaven.com) sells candles, incense, and even witches' spells. I bought a multi-purpose one that helped me clear a blocked fuel line and lose my love handles.

In the former OTC Cracker Factory, **River Horse Brewing** (80 Lambert Ln., Lambertville, 609/397-7776, www.riverhorse.com) was founded in 1994 and brews a half dozen kinds of beer at any one time. Order 'em all and enjoy a six-pack. It's open noon–5 P.M., so you can walk through the brewery, buy gifts in the store, and get samples in the sampling room.

Aging baby boomers trying to retrieve the junk they threw away when they hit puberty can buy it back at **Love Saves the Day** (1 S. Main St., 215/862-1399), which is crammed with Beatles memorabilia, lunch boxes, '60s TV merchandise, black velvet Springsteen, and rare Star Wars items. And you blew your money on Enron stock....

If you have a Viking fetish or your biker name is Frodo, check out all the fab gear at the **Medieval Gallery** (20 Main St., 609/862-4800, medieval gallery.com). Actually, some of the stuff would make you look mighty cool on your bike. Look for chain mail, stitched leather pants, billowing vampire shirts and capes, huge rings, Viking helmets, and, for the ladies, bustiers.

Several stores feature leather in various configurations. **Fred Eisen Leather**

Design (129 S. Main St, 215/862-5988) sells Indian-style clothing, as well as belts and saddle bags with a Western theme. A few doors down, **Sterling Leather** (97 S. Main St., 215/862-9669) sells a similar line of hats, moccasins, boots, and accessories.

Reading improves any trip, and **Farley's Bookshop** (44 S. Main St., 215/862-2452) is the place to load up on literature. The store is filled with rooms stacked with shelves loaded with an uncommonly huge amount of new books and magazines.

Blue-Plate Specials

Walk inside **Sneddon's Luncheonette** (47 Bridge St., 609/397-3053, Lambertville), where the sounds of dishes slapping and silverware clanging welcome you faster than the friendly waitresses. Cheap paneling, newspapers displayed handsomely on the floor, and heart-shaped wireback chairs take you back to the 1960s. The home-cooked meals and soups will take you back home, provided your home was a diner.

There are numerous fine dining restaurants around New Hope, but **Wildflowers Garden Restaurant** (8 W. Mechanic St., 215/862-2241) offers a twist: good food that doesn't cost a fortune (about $7 for lunch, $10 for dinner). Although the outdoor patio is crowded, the riverside setting is the perfect place to relax and experience New Hope. Entrées feature such diverse fare as Yankee pot roast and extremely tasty Thai food. Highly recommended.

Watering Holes

Evenings are as enjoyable as days in New Hope, and being in a walking town means you can park your bike and bar-hop your way across the river into New Jersey. While there are some cool nighttime places in Lambertville, if you only have time for one state, start in New Hope at the crowded and cool **Fran's Pub** (116 S. Main St., 215/862-5539), which entertains with a pool table, jukebox, wide-screen TV, and cooler filled with beers. Look around and notice that tattoos are as abundant as brands of brew. Enjoy happy hour (4:30–6:30 P.M.) on the nice outdoor patio. This place is great for people-watching.

Every night at **John and Peter's** (96 S. Main St., 215/862-5981) is like a talent show audition, with live acts daily. Folks crowd into this low-key joint with low ceilings to be treated to shows by such performers as Leon Redbone, George Thorogood, and Martin Mull—as well as hundreds of forgettable acts. Still, it's got a neat patio and a cool atmosphere—just the place to kick back in the evening. If it's Monday and you're talented, drunk, or both, take part in open mike night.

Up and down Main Street, you'll find sidewalk cafés, open-air bars, and places heralded as "martini bars" and "libation lounges." A significant version is **Havana's** (105 S. Main St., 215/862-9897). On a typical night, it's packed with revelers enjoying the expansive, laid-back, Key West patio–style setting and full liquor bar. Here since 1978, Havana's has the good sense to feature blues, rockabilly, R&B, and funk acts. When it schedules a funk gospel night, I'll be there.

I've labored for months wondering whether to scrap this or not, since it certainly won't appeal to most riders—but because it's considerably different, here it is: Parisian silent film star and chanteuse Odette Myrtil Logan created **Odette's** (S. River Rd., 215/862-2432, www.odettes.com), a neighborly restaurant and lounge. If cheap dives aren't your speed, you may prefer this more civilized—and to be honest, more effeminate—alternative. You can dine here or just hang out at the piano bar, listening to locals display their talents (which many of them also display on Broadway) in an old-fashioned sing-along.

Shut-Eye

Motels and Motor Courts
About a mile from the village, **The New Hope Motel in the Woods** (400 W. Bridge St., 215/862-2800, $69–99 summer weekdays, $99–149 summer weekends) is a nice, nostalgic, and clean place on five acres of lush woods. There are 28 rooms of various sizes and bed configurations, a heated pool, an AAA rating, and a snack lounge.

Chain Drive
A

Chain hotels are in town, or within 10 miles. See cross-reference guide featuring phone numbers and Web addresses on page 514.

Inn-dependence
Competition between the many inns in New Hope has raised the level of service and comfort—and the prices. A smaller property in a nice setting, **Porches** (20 Fishers Alley, 215/862-3277, www.porchesnewhope.com, $95 and up weekdays) is an 1880s cottage-style home in the heart of town. The pace is informal, and most of the 1920s-decor rooms overlook the Delaware

Canal Towpath. After a full country breakfast of fruit, bacon, sausage, grits, pancakes, and fresh bread, you can waddle off to town a few blocks away. The setting for the **1740 House** (River Rd., Lumberville, 215/297-5661, www.1740house.com, $150–175) is perfect. A little way out of town, it's on a beautiful road overlooking the river and features a pool to relax by when you've finished your ride. Each of the 23 rooms is decorated in Early American and has a river view. Back in town, the **Wedgwood Inn** also represents the **Aaron Burr House Inn** (80 W. Bridge St., 215/862-2343, www.wedgwoodinn.com, $95–130). Both are traditional with 20 individually decorated rooms to choose from, some with tubs, fireplaces, king beds, and bay windows. The screened flagstone patio is a relaxing setting. In addition to breakfast, chocolates and a nip of owner Carl's secret-recipe almond liqueur are offered in the afternoon.

On the Road: New Hope to Intercourse

If I were in an episode of *The Twilight Zone*—the kind where somebody's stuck someplace forever—I would hope Rod Serling would send me riding endlessly across the Pennsylvania countryside. This desire starts in the rides above and continues upon leaving New Hope on Route 202 towards Lahaska. On the way out of town, check out **Peddler's Village** (215/794-4000, www.peddlers-village.com). It looks like a tourist trap, but surprisingly, the 70 stores and eight restaurants that spread across a shopping village are not too bad. Also, it's not so far from New Hope that you couldn't frequent one of their five pubs and taverns and ride back to town.

Stay on Route 202 and you'll ride into Doylestown, a picture-perfect town small enough for a manageable and brief stop. Downtown is particularly clean and nice, with a movie theater, bookstore, and various independent merchants. Doylestown native and philanthropist James Michener gave his name (and several million dollars) to charities and the **James A. Michener Art Museum** (138 S. Pine St., 215/340-9800), located in a refurbished 1880s prison. Bucks County residents Pearl S. Buck, Oscar Hammerstein II, Moss Hart, George S. Kaufman, Dorothy Parker, and S. J. Perelman are all honored here. If you like art, literature, and the thee-ah-tuh, you might be tempted to pull over. If you prefer ales and beers, check out **Finney's** (15 Main St., 215/348-2124), which serves 18 beers on tap.

When you follow Route 202 out of Doylestown toward King of Prussia (the town, not the monarch), the road will fizzle out for a long stretch after Montgomeryville, but it perks up after you reach Bridgeport. A local rider suggested an alternate route, which involves jumping off 202 to 463 (Horsham Rd.) and exploring farmland similar to Pennsylvania Dutch country. Too many directions to include here, but if you don't mind getting lost for awhile, small towns like Lansdale, North Wales, Gwynedd, and Skippack can be reached via many turns and some angular riding to arch you north of traffic-filled King of Prussia. Eventually, you'll take Sumneytown Pike Road to 363 (Valley Forge Rd.) to descend toward the front door of this spectacular historical gem.

Though never the site of a battle, this is where America's pursuit of liberty hung in the balance. By surviving the harsh winter of 1777–1978 and the loss of 2,000 men to the elements, Washington's troops proved they were tough enough to see the Revolution through to its conclusion. That's why you should stop at the **Valley Forge National Historical Park** (610/783-1077, www.nps.gov/vafo). You probably won't visit in winter, but you may still feel chills when you think about what happened in this place.

Take off on a superb five-mile loop tour around the 3,500-acre site, knowing that when morale dropped, Washington offered $100 to the soldiers who could construct the best log cabins. It worked. The men created new shelters and a new sense of esprit de corps. On the ride, you can stop at replicas of these cabins, as well as the monuments that dot the roadside. For $3, you can walk through Washington's spartan headquarters, visit a small museum, see a movie, and see tributes to the men who endured the winter to help create a nation.

Following Valley Forge, the road gets significantly, magnificently nicer as 23 forms a slow arc through the low hills. From here on, there's hardly an ugly town until the end, and even though you'll stick with 23, you'll be making mental side trips onto roads that veer off into farmland. The scenery is vibrant and energizing, cool and warm; and in regions like the French Creek Watershed District, you'll reach the crest of a hill and then drop 50 feet before rising again to the top. About every five miles, a new small town welcomes your arrival, and when you ride past places like Warwick, Elverson, Churchtown, and Blue Ball and see the extraordinarily fertile orchards, groves, and fields around them, you'll be reminded why you ride. Along the way, you may recognize that your own free spirit is matched by that of home-crafters selling handmade cedar chests, quilts, and root beer. By the time you approach New Holland, you'll have completed a perfect ride.

Before you reach New Holland, turn left just past the Hollander Motel onto Brimmer Avenue/New Holland Road. About a mile ahead, an overlook provides a perfect resting spot to reflect on your ride and soak in the view of the simple valley below. Soon, the sweet smell of produce gives way to farm smells worse than a frat house bathroom after an all-night kegger. Put the visor down and the nose plugs in. Silos and buggies tell you that you're entering Amish farmland. Keep heading south until you reach Route 340, then turn right.

In a few minutes, you'll be enjoying Intercourse.

Intercourse Primer

It was one of most amazing sights of my journey. As I rode into Intercourse and raised my visor, the blunt chill of the evening air hit my face. I scanned the road, and a motion drew my attention to the ridge of a hill. An Amish farmer stood tall on the back of a mule-driven wagon, hay stacked high behind him. Silhouetted against the setting sun, he was a vision from 1820. I was in Intercourse and in the past.

This place was originally called Cross Key, but the name was changed because of (select one): A) the intersecting roads, B) the entrance to a horse racing track, or C) the "intercourse," or social interaction, and support that's symbolic of the village. The residents can't agree either. Although Lancaster gets the tourists, Intercourse is the hub of the Amish people. Surrounded by farmlands, Intercourse is a museum without walls—although the walls are closing in. A few miles in any direction are modern buildings and businesses that must surely tempt young farmers, though a Sharper Image is still light years away.

While New Hope's Bucks County thrives on culture and diversity, the strengths of Lancaster County are dining and simplicity. There's not much shakin' at night, but during the day, there are great country roads to ride and the most satisfying roadside restaurants you'll ever find.

On the Road: Intercourse

When you hit the road in Intercourse, don't expect to be welcomed into the culture. Unlike Harrison Ford, you won't be asked to strap on a tool belt and help raise a barn. But if you're respectful and keep your camera out of sight, you won't be viewed as one of the rude "English."

The ride is not too far, just an enjoyable excursion that will immerse you in the countryside and introduce you to the culture. In fact, this may be the most "country" country road you can ride. Each road will tempt you, and if you want to go off on a tear, have at it. Get lost. Explore. Wherever you go, the roads are soft and gentle, and the scenery evocative of the 1800s.

Any day's great for a ride here. On Sunday mornings you can see hundreds of Amish worshippers walking and rolling down country roads to church, a service that's usually held in the home of a fellow parishioner.

One rectangular route leaves Intercourse on 340 East, passing Spring Garden and White Horse and turning left onto Route 10 before Compass. So far, the ride reveals nothing out of the ordinary, but when you turn left (north), you'll notice there are no phone or electrical lines running to the homes. Their absence makes the landscape as pure and authentic as any place you'll find.

Take Route 10 North to Route 23, and turn left to head west. You're on the periphery of the Amish farms, returning past small towns like New Holland and Bareville. At Leola, turn left (south) on Route 772, and the road will put you in the thick of the farms. The ride is quiet and calm, interrupted occasionally by a horse-drawn carriage or hay wagon rolling down the lane. You won't tire of the sight, but be very careful riding at night, since these dark carriages can be hard to see. Speaking of night riding, you may want to try it at least once. I did, and what I took to be a massive region of nothing turned out to be a busy farming area—but I couldn't tell until I was riding only yards away from farmhouses lit by candles and lanterns.

Sharp 90-degree curves dividing the farms keep you alert, as will the crop of Amish children who gather near the road to stare at you and your bike when you ride past. Naturally, they assume you are a deity. Route 772 takes a sharp right at Hess Road, where you turn and continue on 772 to a scenic drive called Scenic Drive (really). Now do yourself a favor and get lost. With Highway 30 to the south and Highway 23 to the north, you may pass the Amish equivalent of a commercial district: buggies lined up at repair shops, tobacco drying in barns, and carpenters crafting simple furniture with even simpler tools.

It's ironic, but if you ride far beyond these boundaries, you'll enter the domain of chain restaurants and the insensitive real estate developer whose signs urge you to "Think Redy-Bilt Homes!" Considering some men around here could probably build a home with one plumb bob tied behind their backs, it seems like a kick in the gut.

Side Trip: Lititz

One of the peak experiences of touring by motorcycle is discovering new towns that haven't been destroyed by homogenization. From the northwest corner of the previous ride, it's only a short drive to Lititz (north of Lancaster), where almost nothing has happened and which sports that familiar Rockwell look.

Ride 772 north into this small town, and you'll arrive in a busy little shopping district. This is Main Street, with a shaded park centered around a stream and natural spring, and all of the essential vitamins and minerals to qualify as a neat town. There's the historic **General Sutter Inn** (14 E. Main St., 717/626-2115, www.generalsutterinn.com, $87–120), which features the 1764 Restaurant and 16 spacious rooms. It's tempting to stay the night. Around the corner, **Glassmyer's Restaurant** (23 N. Broad St., 717/626-2345), serves diner meals topped off by creations like egg creams and phosphates from the old-fashioned soda fountain.

But the highlight of Lititz is the aphrodisiacal aroma wafting from the **Wilbur Chocolate Factory** (48 N. Broad St., 717/626-3249, www.wilbur-buds.com). Chances are you've never heard of or received a box of Wilbur Chocolates, but that shouldn't stop you from sniffing your way around the Candy Americana Museum, which details the history of cocoa, the life cycle of a candy bar, and Wilbur's "Wheel of Fortune" candy horoscope ("The typical Cancer is a hard worker who enjoys piling up tangibles for that rainy day: chocolate-coated marshmallows"). A gift shop features T-shirts, ordinary candy, and a 50-pound, $85 chocolate bar. Overhead, the ceiling rumbles beneath the weight of Wilbur gears and belts cranking out another delightful, delicious batch of chocolates.

Provided you don't fall into a diabetic coma, spend an hour bumming around downtown, and then take your time riding back on the country roads of your choice. On the boomerang return, you'll pass Mennonite children skimming through the hills on simple scooters, farmers selling fresh produce, flowers, homemade bread, and root beer, as well as the random harness maker who can turn the same equine leather into saddlebags for your own iron horse. Quite an experience.

Pull It Over: Intercourse Highlights
Attractions and Adventures

There's not much else going on in Intercourse, so you may as well not do something at the **Kitchen Kettle Village** (Rte. 340, 717/768-8261 or 800/732-3538, www.kitchenkettle.com). Actually, this is a popular little shopping village, and there's a chance you may find a new pair of handcrafted leather boots, score some fresh-off-the-lathe furniture, or listen to some folk musicians. If your bike is wired for sound, this is where you can pick up an in-depth audio tour of Amish country. The village is open 9 A.M.–5 P.M. daily.

It's an expensive diversion ($179), but the **United States Hot Air Balloon**

Team (490 Hopewell Rd., St. Peters, 610/469-0782 or 800/763-5987, www.ushotairballoon.com) takes daily flights over the Amish farmland. You can reach it en route from New Hope at the St. Peters farm launch site, or head to Lancaster to its second lift-off location. You can help prepare the balloon for flight, and then settle in for a long drift over the rolling countryside, followed by snacks and a champagne toast. You'll have to leave your bike on the ground.

Reserve a Tuesday, Friday, or Saturday morning for historic **Central Market** (717/291-4723), in the heart of Lancaster at Penn Square. Incredibly, it's been at this location since the 1730s and is America's oldest publicly owned, continuously operated farmers market. It may take a few hours to figure out how to strap a dozen bags of farm-fresh produce, pastries, syrups, salmon cakes, quarts of milk, flowers, crab cakes, baked goods, chow-chows, and relishes onto your bike, but it'll be worth it. Back toward town on pleasing Route 340, the **Bird in Hand Farmers Market** (717/393-9674, www.birdinhandfarmersmarket.com) is smaller but equally popular. A load of Amish farmers sell here as well, and when you look into their doleful eyes, I doubt you can escape without buying some homemade products, whether it's pickles, fudge, nuts, jellies, or jellied pickle nut fudge. Really, really good stuff.

In the heart of Intercourse, **W. L. Zimmerman and Sons** (3601 Old Philadelphia Pike/Rte. 340, 717/768-8291) is the Amish and English shop for dry goods and groceries. Opened in 1909, the store caters to its base by offering an amazing inventory of products last seen in a 1939 A&P catalogue. No iPods here, no sir. You'll be shopping shoulder to shoulder with taciturn young Amish men and their equally stoic wives.

Blue-Plate Specials

Although Amish country is shy on tattoo parlors and tanning salons, there's no shortage of great restaurants, the kind you crave when you're on the road or have just raised a barn. In some cases, you'll share a large table with other travelers. So before you sit down, scrub the bugs off your teeth.

Slightly smaller than Beijing, the **Plain & Fancy Farm** (Rte. 340, 717/768-4400, www.plainandfancyfarm.com) serves food nearly as large. This ranks among my five favorite road food pit stops, and the busloads of diners here would concur. Lunch and dinner are served at huge picnic tables inside the barnlike building, where you'll eat as much roast beef, sausage, chicken, mashed potatoes, bow-tie noodles, vegetables, and ice cream as your big ol' belly can hold. And how many places do you know that serve shoofly pie?

Why Are the Amish Doing This?

Despite their identification as the Pennsylvania Dutch, Amish ancestors hailed from Germany, not Holland. They left Deutschland (get it?) to seek religious freedom. Today's Lancaster County "Old Order Amish" stress humility, family, community, and separation from the world. All Old Order members drive buggies, not cars. Their homes do not have electricity, and their children are educated as far as the eighth grade in one-room schoolhouses.

As for personal appearance, Amish women never cut their hair, and they wear a black prayer covering if they're single and a white one if they're married. Men wear dark suits, straight-cut coats with lapels, suspenders, solid-colored shirts, and black or straw broad-brimmed hats. It's not a costume but an expression of their faith. It's also worth noting that they don't avoid change entirely. They just take longer to consider a new product before deciding to accept or reject it. So, don't discount an Amish software conglomerate.

I spoke with a nice Mennonite resident of Intercourse who explained the Amish policy of young men's being given free rein to leave the church and community. He told me, "It's like this way: You're getting taught from a young age what's right and what's wrong. So, when you're 18, you're an adult and you're supposed to know what's right and what's wrong, and then when you learn temptations, you're on your own. If you do wrong, then you're dealing with the law."

But Amish youth must deal with more than mere legal pressures. If Jebediah pounds back a dozen Hurricanes at Mardi Gras and winds up living in the back of a van with Sunflower from the Rainbow Tribe, well, he's considered an outcast from the church, as well as the community, and cannot return.

The Smucker family does well producing filling country foods, the kind you'll find at **Bird-in-Hand Family Restaurant** (2760 Old Philadelphia Pike/Rte. 340, Bird-in-Hand, 717/768-8266, www.bird-in-hand.com). The menu features ham, pork and sauerkraut, lima beans, roast turkey, new potatoes, and the like. Most items are made from scratch (such as the homemade soups), with some ingredients and dishes delivered by Amish farmers. And aside from Plain & Fancy Farm, how many places do you know that serve shoofly pie?

Stoltzfus Farm Restaurant (Rte. 772 E., 717/768-8156), serves big food, such as homemade sausage, chicken, hamloaf, chow-chow, applesauce, apple butter, sweet potatoes, and corn, plus desserts like cherry crumb, apple crumb, and fresh shoofly pie. And how many places do you know that serve shoofly pie? Yes, three is the correct answer. Open for lunch and dinner daily except Sunday; closed December–March.

In a little truck stop in 1929, Anna Miller cooked up chicken and waffles for travelers. Today, **Miller's Smorgasbord** (Rte. 30 one mile east of Rte. 896, 717/687-6621) serves lunch and dinner daily, plus breakfast on Sundays. Mix and match omelettes, pancakes, french toast, homemade breads, soups, baked apples, roast turkey, baked ham, fried chicken, fish, shrimp, sautéed mushrooms, mashed potatoes, baked cabbage, chicken pot pie, cakes, and pies that'll kick off your very own Ted Kennedy diet plan.

Shut-Eye

Thanks to its relative closeness to Lancaster, there are countless lodging choices. But ask anyone, and they'll tell you it's better in Intercourse.

Chain Drive
A, C, D, E, G, I, J, L, S, U, Y, CC, DD

Chain hotels are in town, or within 10 miles. See cross-reference guide featuring phone numbers and Web addresses on page 514.

Inn-dependence
I would rank the **Intercourse Village B&B Suites** (Main St., 717/768-2626 or 800/664-0949, www.amishcountryinns.com, $119 and up) as one of America's best inns. Elmer Thomas restored this 1909 Victorian home, and his staff practices courtesy as art. The rooms befit a five-star hotel, the breakfasts are superb, and the top-floor suite is great for couples. Rates start at $119 and reach as high as $279 for the largest suite. Out back, Elmer created themed cottages, which feature large rooms, microwaves, desks, fireplaces, generous baths, whirlpool tubs, fridges, wet bars, and Amish furnishings built specially for the rooms. Suffice it to say this is absolutely first-rate for riders. Elmer's son runs the other recommended option in the heart of town: the **Best Western Intercourse Village Motor Inn** (Rtes. 340 and 772, 717/768-3636 or 800/717-6202, $109–139). A standard hotel, it nonetheless stays true to Elmer's vision of cleanliness and friendliness. An on-site restaurant serves home-cooked breakfast, lunch, and dinner. There are laundry facilities here, too.

Side Trips

Maryland

Route 301

On the outskirts of D.C., Maryland Route 301 crosses the Governor Nice Memorial Bridge. From here, follow Route 3 to 202 (which merges with 360) south into Reedville, the tip of the Northern Neck area. Along the way, small towns and historic sites crop up, offering an easy pace for relaxing and seeing points of interest, like the birth-places of Washington and Lee. You'll also have access to the Smith Island ferry (wildlife preserve) and Crisfield, an artsy Victorian town.

Route 404

From Maryland Route 50, cross the Chesapeake Bay Bridge and head to Route 404, passing Wye Mills. Great back roads (Routes 18, 9/404, 1) roll through Delaware to the coast. There's a great shoreline ride south into Ocean City and onto Chincoteague and Assateague, sites of wild ponies, quiet beaches, and lots of mosquitoes and flies (bring repellent!).

Mattawoman Natural Environment

Escape D.C. traffic via Route 210 and ride south toward Indian Head, Maryland. From here, head east on Route 227 to Route 224, where 28 great miles of two-lane roads cut through the Mattawoman Natural Environment.

Route 4

Solomon's Island, Maryland

From D.C., take Route 4 South past Calvert Cliffs (a nuclear power plant and state park). If you're not radiated, keep riding south to Solomon's Island, where you'll find a tiki bar, boardwalk, artsy walk-ing town, good road food, and lots of motorcycles cruising through town. After the island, head west on Routes 4 and 5 past 1700s–mid-1800s homes, plantations, and churches.

Route 235

Point Lookout, Maryland

Cruising out to Point Lookout is a surf-and-turf ride. You'll wind up at a state park, where Ft. Lincoln houses a historic Civil War prison and museum. Then roll right aboard a ferry to Smith Island, a wildlife preserve, and ride on to historic Crisfield. A nice slice of Maryland for motorcyclists.

Contributed by Sylvia Henderson

Resources for Riders

Amish Country Run

Pennsylvania Travel Information
Pennsylvania Bed & Breakfast Committee—717/232-8880,
  www.patourism.org
Pennsylvania Fishing Licenses—717/705-7930, www.fish.state.pa.us
Pennsylvania Road Conditions— 717/783-5186 or 888/783-6783,
  www.paturnpike.com
Pennsylvania State Parks—888/727-2757, www.dcnr.state.pa.us
Pennsylvania Visitor Information—800/847-4872, www.visitpa.com

Local and Regional Information
Bucks County Visitors Bureau—215/639-0300 or 800/836-2825,
  www.bccvb.org
Harrisburg (Intercourse) Weather—814/234-8010
Lambertville Chamber of Commerce—609/397-0055,
  www.lambertville.org
Lancaster County (Intercourse) Information—717/299-8901 or
  800/723-8824, www.padutchcountry.com
New Hope Chamber of Commerce—215/862-9990,
  www.newhope-pa.com
New Hope Visitors Center—215/862-5030
Philadelphia (New Hope) Weather—215/936-1212

Pennsylvania Motorcycle Shops
All Season Motor Sports—2225 N. 5th St., Reading, 610/921-3149
B&B Yamaha—791 Flory Mill Rd., Lancaster, 717/569-5764,
  www.bbyamahaktm.com
Classic Harley-Davidson—983 James Dr., Leesport, 610/916-7777,
  www.classicharley.com
Cycle Parts—780 Flory Mill Rd., Lancaster, 717/569-8268
Don's Kawasaki—20 E. Market St., Hellam (York), 717/755-6002
Ray's Yamaha Polaris Victory —5560 Perkiomen, Reading, 610/582-2700
Stan's Cycle Shop—4701 Old Easton Rd., Doylestown, 215/348-4136
Sport Cycle Suzuki—309 Hafer Dr., Leesport, 610/916-5000,
  www.sportcyclesuzuki.com

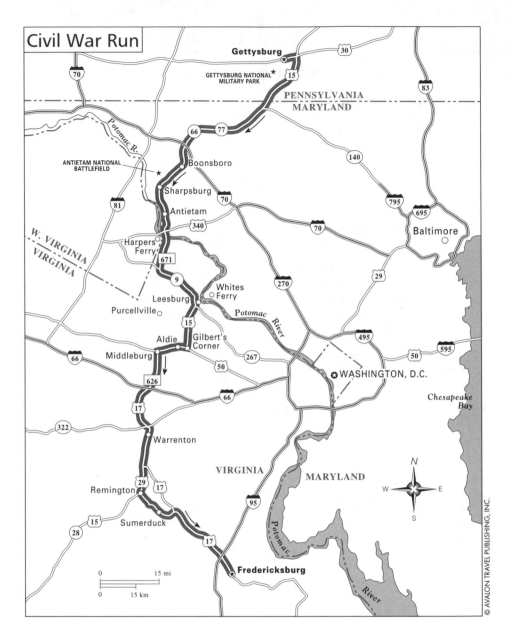

Route: Gettysburg to Fredericksburg via Catoctin State Park, Antietam, Harpers Ferry, Leesburg

Distance: Approximately 170 miles; consider five days with stops.

•Days 1–2—Gettysburg •Day 3—Travel •Day 4—Leesburg/Travel •Day 5—Fredericksburg

First Leg: Gettysburg to Leesburg (92 miles)

Second Leg: Leesburg to Fredericksburg (80 miles)

Helmet Laws: Pennsylvania and Virginia require helmets.

Civil War Run

Gettysburg, Pennsylvania to Fredericksburg, Virginia

As you ease into your second Pennsylvania ride, you feel as if the state is a microcosm of American history. From the Declaration of Independence to the Exposition of 1876, from Amish farmland to the fields of Gettysburg, almost everything we're about is contained here.

This is a poignant trip through the killing fields of Pennsylvania, across a mood-changing Maryland state park, past Civil War highlights, and into two historic Virginia walking towns. As you ride in spring or fall for clear roads and clear weather, the route may not reveal all there is to know about the Civil War, but you'll gain an appreciation for the countryside and your country.

Gettysburg Primer

In July 1863, Confederate soldiers searching for supplies sparked the flash point of the Battle of Gettysburg. Advance troops spotted one another near the town, word was passed, the first shots were fired, and three days later, the Civil War had reached its turning point. Robert E. Lee had 75,000 men; George G. Meade had 97,000. At the height of the battle, more than 172,000 men and 634 cannons were spread out over 25 square miles. When the final shot was fired, 51,000 casualties bloodied the fields.

Although the war continued for two more years, the Battle of Gettysburg broke the spirit and strength of the Confederacy. The dedication of the Soldiers

National Cemetery at Gettysburg gave President Lincoln the opportunity to praise the sacrifice of Union soldiers and state the essential truths about our experiment with democracy.

To be sure, this has become a tourist town with some tacky gift shops and tedious attractions—but the real draw for nearly two million visitors a year is the history. So, while traces of abundant commercialism remain, the hallowed grounds of the battlefield have been preserved to honor the sacrifices and bravery of men on both sides of the battle.

On the Road: Gettysburg

Gettysburg's legend in American history is so large, it's surprising to find that the actual places of note are confined within a relatively small area. Despite steady growth, Gettysburg at its core is still a small town, reminiscent of the 1860s. As you walk through town, recall that in 1863, the center of town was the center of commerce, and dozens of small farms lay in the surrounding countryside. Use your imagination to visualize the old community and the people who were living here in peace when the battle began.

The town square is bisected by Business Route 15, the main north–south road through town, and by east–west Route 30. This is the perfect tour base. Within a few hundred yards, you'll experience the richness of history. The battlefield visitors center itself is a mile or so south, likely too far to walk.

Bordering the town square are two sites worth a stop. On the southeast side of the square, the red, white, and blue bunting denotes the **David Wills House** (12 Lincoln Sq., 717/334-8188), the home of the young lawyer who extended an invitation to Lincoln to make "a few appropriate remarks." Lincoln stayed in the second-floor room and worked on his speech the night before the dedication of the cemetery. For $3.50, you can visit the room and see related exhibits and mementoes, although a scheduled restoration may find it closed through 2006. For a sharp photo, outside the home is a life-size statue of Lincoln talking to a statue that looks like Perry Como. Stand in front of Perry and pose with the president.

Across the street, the **Gettysburg Hotel** (1 Lincoln Sq., 717/337-2000, www.hotelgettysburg.com) has welcomed its share of presidents as well, primarily Eisenhower and his staff, who stayed here when the summer White House came to town.

After walking the square, ride south down Business Route 15 toward the battlefield visitors center. Obviously, you'll want to ride the battlefield, but do this only after taking a guided tour. It's important to know where you are to understand what you are seeing. It helps to know about such places as Little Round Top and the site of Pickett's Charge. From the summit of Little Round Top, you overlook the "Valley of Death" bordered by Devil's Den, a haven for Southern sharpshooters. Then there's one of saddest places in America: the infamous "Wheatfield," where 6,000 Union and Confederate soldiers were killed, wounded, or captured during just four hours of bloody fighting.

After your guided tour, head to the **National Military Park Visitor Center,** where park rangers will fill in the blanks. They'll tell you about the 3,500 soldiers killed here and buried in the cemetery, nearly 1,000 of their identities known only to God. You'll hear about the battle and its terrible aftermath—the burial of the dead, bodies being eaten by hogs, and looters whose punishment was having to bury dead horses. But what you'll want to hear most is the story of Lincoln's visit and the Gettysburg Address.

You may have read Lincoln's speech, but only after you've seen Gettysburg will you understand its importance. It was Lincoln's "I Have a Dream" speech. He spoke of the nation's past, the present, and the future he saw, and he reestablished the concept of democracy. Within two minutes, "the United States are" became "the United States is." Lincoln had laid out how a horrible war could save the nation envisioned by the authors of the Constitution.

After you're turned loose, ride later in the day or very early in the morning, when the tourist crowds thin. From Little Round Top to the site of Pickett's Charge, this is a spiritual ride. You can take your time to see the roads and retrace the trails forged by soldiers of both sides, and you cannot help but be moved by the experience.

Pull It Over: Gettysburg Highlights
Attractions and Adventures

Gettysburg National Military Park Visitor Center (97 Taneytown Rd., 717/334-1124, www.nps.gov/gett) is ground zero for your Gettysburg experience, and admission is free. To see what needs to be seen, it is essential to travel with a tour guide. Not surprisingly, the best and most enlightening information comes straight from the park rangers, whose love of history is palpable in their guided tours. If the government's not broke, free tours leave from the center, which also contains an interesting museum with muskets, bayonets, artillery fuse plugs, swords, field glasses, flags, the drum of a drummer boy, and pictures of very old veterans from Gettysburg's 75th anniversary, in 1938. More tours are added May–September.

If you really want to know the details of the Battle of Gettysburg and not

Tight Muscles: Work It Out Now

Even though I'm a mighty, mighty man, after a few hundred miles in the saddle, my muscles can get tight and screw up the next day's ride. Richard Cotton, chief exercise physiologist for the American Council on Exercise (www.acefitness.org), explains that muscles get stiff when confined to sedentary positions. Day after day of riding without stretching reduces the length of your muscles, which limits your range of motion, and, if you move suddenly, can cause injury. Cotton recommends starting and ending the day with easy stretching exercises. The entire series should take no longer than five minutes and can significantly improve the quality of your ride.

Pre- and Postride
Chest: On some bike configurations, your shoulders are rolled forward and your chest muscles tighten up. To stretch your chest, place your palms flat against a door or a tree and twist your upper body.
Neck: After fighting the wind and the weight of your helmet, stretch your neck muscles by placing two fingers on your chin and pushing it toward your chest while raising up the back of your head. Next, look over your left, then right, shoulder for 10 seconds on each side.
Upper back: Before and after the ride, do a few trunk twists—keeping your legs slightly spread and hips square to the front while turning your shoulders from side to side.
Lower back: Few bike seats are designed to protect your lower back, so when you dismount, put your fist against your lower back, stretch backward, and raise your chest toward the sky. Don't let your legs bow, since the arching comes from the hips.
Triceps: Stretch your triceps by putting your palm between your shoulders with your elbow pointing up. Pull your elbow behind your head for 10–30 seconds. Do this for both arms.

Quadriceps: To loosen up the top of your thighs, stand next to your bike and grip the handlebar with one hand. Take the opposite leg and pull it backward from the ankle, bringing your heel up to your butt. Do this for 10 seconds with each leg.

Hamstrings: To stretch the back of your legs, stand and cross one leg in front of the other. Bend forward from your hips until you feel a comfortable stretch. Reverse positions and repeat to stretch your other leg.

Calves: Find a solid object (wall, tree, etc.), and then lean over and push against it while pressing into the ground to alternately stretch each leg behind you.

Back and Butt: While lying on your back, put both hands below one knee and pull that knee toward the opposite shoulder. Do this for several seconds, alternating legs. Follow up by putting both arms behind your knees and drawing both legs toward your chest.

While Riding

Lower Back: Most riders tend to ride with their shoulders down and back arched forward. To counteract the stress of this position, occasionally arch backward and roll your pelvis forward to create a curve in your lower back. Riding with an S curve as opposed to a C curve prevents lower back stiffness.

Legs: Stretch each leg over the foot pegs or swing them back and forth against the pressure of the wind.

Overall: Vibrations can cause numbness in your hands, feet, and butt. At each gas stop take a few minutes to get the blood flowing and the muscles moving. Shake your hands and feet, stretch your fingers, do arm circles forward and backward, and take a short walk.

just the overview most tourists get, you'll have to invest in a licensed guide from **Gettysburg National Military Park Guided Tours.** They leave from the visitors center as well—but you have to be serious about this, because you'll need to rent a car to transport the guide, who will take you on a personalized two-hour tour based on your interests. Great for real Civil War buffs, it's $70 for 7–15 people.

Gettysburg Tour Center (778 Baltimore St., 717/334-6296 or 800-447-8788, www.gettysburgbattlefieldtours.com) offers an inexpensive way to get a layout of the area and some background information before you explore on your own. Popular with nearly every visitor, the $19.95 history lesson takes place aboard an open-air double-decker bus you would normally make fun of and throw things at. The schedule is punctual and the information factual, though none of it is presented creatively. Keep in mind that stops at historic sites, such as Pickett's Charge and Bloody Run, are brief. The departure point can vary based on the time of year, so call ahead.

One of the coolest ways to see the Gettysburg battlefield—besides on a motorcycle—is in a 1930s Yellowstone Park bus. **Historic Battlefield Bus Tours** (55 Steinwehr Ave., 717/334-8000) offers two-hour tours for $17. The restored open-top classics are visually appealing, and the tour isn't bad.

If your bike is equipped with a cassette player, you may want to skip the bus tour and trade $12.95 for a two-hour narrative tour of the battle's history from **CC Inc Auto Tape Tours** (717/334-6245, www.tapetours.com). You can find the tape at the **American Civil War Museum** (297 Steinwehr Ave.) The narrative takes you through the battle's three days, telling you when to turn and where to look.

It's hard to believe World War II's most illustrious general could be overshadowed, but when Dwight Eisenhower bought a home in Gettysburg in 1950, he was destined to take a back seat to the battle. He used his farm here (the only home he ever owned) as a weekend retreat and temporary White House. Today, it is the **Eisenhower National Historic Site** (97 Taneytown Rd., 717/338-9114, www.nps.gov/eise). If you grew up liking Ike, you'll like the tour ($5.50), which is available from the National Park Service Visitor Center on Taneytown Road. Access to the Eisenhower Farm is by shuttle bus only, so give your bike a rest in the center's parking lot. The displays are rich in personal items, such as Ike's World War II jacket and helmet. Why such a noble soldier picked such a creep like Nixon as his running mate is beyond me.

Shopping

If your den looks suspiciously like a Civil War museum, then Gettysburg is where you'll want to stock up on items for the new wing. There are several impressive collectibles and antiquarian shops, including **The Union Drummer Boy** (13 Baltimore St., 717/334-2350, www.uniondb.com), which carries more memorabilia than a soldier carried in 1863: authentic muskets, carbines, artillery, revolvers, uniforms, swords, letters, leather goods, relics, artillery shells, flags, documents, bullets embedded in wood, and artifacts aplenty. I bought an authentic Civil War laser pointer.

The **American Historical Art Gallery and Framery** (34 York St., 717/334-0172) is nonpartisan, carrying a wide selection of prints that show the heroics of soldiers from both sides. One notable aspect is the use of photorealism, which makes some of the paintings look like snapshots taken in the midst of battle. Figurines, busts, and Civil War medallions are also featured.

Blue-Plate Specials

The Lincoln Diner (32 Carlisle St., 717/334-3900), is just right for motorcycle travelers. An actual old 24-hour diner, it serves such staples as fried clams, fried oysters, and breaded veal, and the obligatory cholesterol-rich breakfasts. Watch your diet when you get home, but while you're here, pull an Elvis and pig out on a hot fudge banana royale.

Don't miss **Dunlap's** (90 Buford Ave., 717/334-4816, www.dunlapsrestaurant.com). It's been here forever, thanks to a menu that features ham, turkey, and beef cooked and sliced on-site; fried chicken, real mashed potatoes, sandwiches, stuffed flounder, steaks, and big breakfasts. Dunlap's tops it off with cheap prices.

General Pickett's (571 Steinwehr Ave., 717/334-7580) is not a chain but a genuine honest-to-goodness buffet. Made-from-scratch soups, fresh-baked breads, a salad bar, and down-home entrées are all wrapped up with homemade pies and cakes.

Olivia's (3015 Baltimore Pike, 717/359-9857) is five miles south of town, but it boasts the biggest menu in Gettysburg. Homemade soups, desserts, and 15 daily specials span American, Greek, and Italian cuisine. Open for breakfast, lunch, and dinner.

On the corner of the square, the **Plaza Restaurant** (226 Baltimore St., 717/334-1999) also includes a lounge that's larger than the dining room. The specialty is Greek food (heroes, kebabs, souvlaki), but you can also go for steaks, crab legs, and homemade soups. Credit the lounge for keeping the joint jumpin' until 2:30 A.M.

Watering Holes

The Pub & Restaurant (20–22 Lincoln Sq., 717/334-7100) gives you options: Buy a brew at the hammered-copper-top bar or head to the restaurant next door for a traditional entrée (chicken, steak, pasta, etc.). Of course, you can also elect to return to the full bar for ales, domestic brews, and other spirits. This place is popular with college students, who like the $2 pitchers. If the weather's right, grab a sidewalk table and enjoy the evening and a cool one.

In the heart of downtown is the **Flying Bull Saloon** (28 Carlisle St., 717/334-6202), which may be the best biker-style bar in town. Low-key and dark, it sets the stage with a pool table, darts, and a small stage for locals bands. In addition to bar food are drink specials, like Thursday's pitchers of Pabst for two bucks. Ah… college days.

As the name implies, the **Spring House Tavern** (89 Steinwehr Ave., 717/334-2100, www.dobbinhouse.com) is more like a colonial pub. In the basement of the Dobbin House, tavern waitresses wear colonial costumes, and candles light the room. Although it doubles as a family restaurant, the full bar, a handful of tap beers, and its unique setting make this place worth seeing.

At **Herr Tavern & Publick House** (900 Chambersburg Rd., 717/334-4332, www.herrtavern.com) is The Livery. During the battle of Gettysburg, the home and outbuildings served as a confederate hospital, but time and capitalism have turned it into a faithfully restored pre–Civil War tavern. Saloonkeepers serve beer straight from the ice into your sweaty hands. While the lounge is small and comfortable, a large deck can get you outdoors to enjoy the cool summer nights. In addition to bar food, entertainment varies from darts, Foosball, and video games to a first for me: a black-light poolroom.

Shut-Eye

Chain Drive
A, C, E, G, J, L, S, V, BB, CC, DD

Chain hotels are in town, or within 10 miles. See cross-reference guide featuring phone numbers and Web addresses on page 514.

Numerous independent hotels are located near the battlefield, each offering similar rooms but different amenities—some feature a pool or whirlpool tub. In the heart of town, **Gettysburg Hotel** (1 Lincoln Sq., 717/337-2000 or 800/528-1234, www.hotelgettysburg.com, $99–142) is a full-service Best Western. This 1797 landmark has covered parking, a restaurant, and a few

A monument of General Gouverneur K. Warren keeps watch over the Valley of Death at Little Round Top in Gettysburg.

© GARY MCKECHNIE

suites with fireplaces and whirlpool tubs. Their pub, McClellan's Tavern, is a popular watering hole.

Inn-dependence
For descriptions of and reservations for the majority of area inns, check **Inns of Gettysburg** (717/624-1300 or 800/586-2216, www.gettysburgbedandbreakfast.com).

Ride down the street to the **Farnsworth House Inn** (401 Baltimore St., 717/334-8838, www.farnsworthhouseinn.com, $125–175), if you don't mind a gravel drive and the fact that a Confederate sharpshooter made this his post. The Victorian home has a sunroom and country garden breakfasts. It also offers a restaurant with dishes like country ham, peanut soup, meat casserole, and pumpkin fritters. Rumor has it some of the rooms are haunted, but the rates are same with or without ghosts. Note: The 100 bullet holes in the house may make it slightly drafty in winter.

If you're traveling in a group and would prefer a large kitchenette-equipped suite in the historic district, consider **James Getty's Hotel** (7 Chambersburg St., 717/337-1334 or 888/900-5275, www.jamesgettyshotel.com, $140 and up). An inn in the 1830s, it served as a hostel and apartment house before being restored as an inn in 1995. Now the 11-room boutique hotel is clean and well equipped, and some suites can sleep four.

A first-class option is the **Brickhouse Inn** (452 Baltimore St., 717/338-9337 or 800/864-3464, www.brickhouseinn.com, $99 and up). Equidistant between downtown and the visitors center, this place seems like a bargain when you consider the courtesy and service, which culminates with an extraordinary breakfast served on the backyard patio. First-rate.

Side Trip: York Harley-Davidson Tour

Next to the Harley headquarters in Milwaukee, York (roughly 30 miles east of Gettysburg) is the site of most interest to riders. At more than 230 acres, with more than 1.5 million square feet under its roof, **Harley-Davidson's Final Assembly Plant** is the largest H-D facility, where more than 3,200 employees crank out 700 bikes a day. This tour is infinitely more interesting than a similar tour near the company HQ.

During the weekdays-only, one-hour factory tour, a guide takes you to the shop floor to view the parts manufacturing process and the final motorcycle assembly lines. It's absolutely cool to see strips of sheet metal stamped, pressed, and bent into fenders and fuel tanks. You'll follow the entire process and see how the component pieces are meshed with engines to create Softails, police bikes, cruisers, and special-order bikes. You can test-sit the newest models and spend as much time as you like in the renovated museum, which focuses on the history, people, process, and product in the York factory. Call 717/848-1177 or 877/883-1450 for tour times and availability. For groups of 10 or more, make reservations at 717/852-6590. The York Visitor Center (at the plant) can be reached at 717/852-6006. On the tour, you'll need to wear close-toed shoes and leave your camera behind—so don't get any ideas about starting your own motorcycle corporation. The plant is off Route 30 at 1425 Eden Road, one mile east of I-83.

On the Road: Gettysburg to Leesburg

Even though it'll be a short run to Leesburg, don't plan on leaving late, since the roads ahead are beautiful and peaceful, and you'll be racing the sun if you decide to stop in Catoctin, Antietam, or Harper's Ferry. Give yourself a full day to enjoy the country.

Business Route 15 South, the level two-lane road leaving Gettysburg, passes statuary and monuments that suggest that the entire town is a cemetery. Just past the town limits, **Rider's Edge** (2490 Emmitsburg Rd., 717/334-2518) is a Yamaha shop and a convenient stop for last-minute gear. About six miles later, you'll approach the Mason-Dixon line and 15 South, which turns into a larger highway, albeit narrower than an interstate. Although this is no back road, it provides surprisingly beautiful vistas of farmland that continue eight miles

Gettysburg Battle Facts

It was a horrifying three days (or four, when you consider people were still being killed on July 4), and the scope of it still resonates nearly a century and a half later. The community survives on history, which is why facts like these are important to know:

• Nearly seven million bullets were fired at Gettysburg by more than 160,000 soldiers. How many were Union, and how many Confederates? One park guide doesn't care. "They were *all* American soldiers," he explained.

• The oldest fighter was John Burns, the "Citizen Hero of Gettysburg." At 72, this veteran of the War of 1812 heard the commotion, grabbed his rifle, and started fighting alongside the fabled Iron Brigade on McPherson's Ridge. He was hit three times—the first bullet hit his belt buckle, the second his arm, and the third his ankle. which knocked him to the ground. He survived, lied to the Confederate soldiers that he was just a farmer caught in the crossfire, and lived until 1872.

• In 1938, at the 75th anniversary of the battle, a 94-year-old veteran was asked if he was enjoying his stay in Gettysburg. "A lot more than I did 75 years ago," he said.

• In a letter home, one soldier wrote to his wife, "Soldiering is 99 percent boredom, and one percent sheer terror."

• At Gettysburg, more than 32,000 men were wounded, and 8,000 died. About 94 percent were killed by bullets, less than 1 percent by bayonet.

• Of the 1,328 monuments at Gettysburg, the best may be the Peace Memorial—the only one not dedicated to war. After the 50th anniversary of the battle in 1913, soldiers from the north and south pooled their own money and raised additional funds to create a monument built of Alabama limestone and Maine granite. The inscription, "Peace Eternal in a Nation United," says it all.

over the Maryland state line, where Route 77 West veers off to the right for a detour to Antietam and positions you for one of the great rides of your life.

Your disappointment over leaving Route 15 dissipates the moment you enter Maryland's **Catoctin Mountain State Park.** Of all the roads in America, this is one that needs to be ridden like an animal. A two-lane exclamation point, this thrill-a-minute road rolls past valleys, twisties, lakes, sharp curves, deer, and rivers. Past Pryor's Orchards (purveyor of jelly, honey, nuts, and apples), you'll spot a great river and a setting as intriguing as Sherwood Forest. Glance up at the mountain peaks revealing themselves well above the forest. The road ahead is a grab bag of mild curves and sharp edges, like an abridged version of New Hampshire's Kank.

There are side roads leading deeper into the park, so if you have time to spare, get lost. Keep riding, and you may stumble across a waterfall—or crash the gate at Camp David. When you return to the road, the sun dapples the branches, the road is intersected by the legendary Appalachian Trail, and you reach a descent that weaves down the hill.

Too soon, you're out of the woods. Instead of continuing into the traffic of Hagerstown, turn left on State Route 66 and drop south toward the town of Sharpsburg and the Antietam battlefield. The road is marked by apple orchards, hand-painted signs announcing straw for $2.50 a bale, and, a few miles down, a general store in Mount Aetna where you can pull over for a soda pop and to wipe that smile off your face. By the time you reach the I-70 junction, you'll be content to blow past it, knowing there are far better roads up ahead, promising farmland vistas and bucolic countryside, bumps and small hills, and sweeping turns that throw you into great straightaways. Here the asphalt is as fluid as a river.

Near Boonsboro, there's a funky fork where you look for Alternate 40 to take you to Highway 34 West. Soon you'll be on the Sharpsbug Pike, and although the route switches direction often, you'll pass villages and avoid cities and have a blast. When you reach Sharpsburg at the intersection with Highway 65, turn right and ride about two miles to the **Antietam National Battlefield** (301/432-5124, www.nps.gov/anti, $3). Sadly, even more than the events of September 11, 2001, this site marks the bloodiest day in American history. When Lee made his first invasion to take the war into the North, he brought 40,000 troops. General George B. McClellan led more than 80,000 Union soldiers. When they met on September 17, 1862—a year before the Battle of Gettysburg—more than 23,000 men were left dead, wounded, or missing.

Now, Grasshopper, I believe you are ready for a weirdly wild ride. In Antietam, you want to find Harpers Ferry Road, which, for some reason, isn't called that here—which led to a wrong turn that took me over to West Virginia. Anyway, just past the library in the heart of town is Mechanics Street. Turn left here, and trust me, this will soon become the road you want. Almost immediately, there are oddly angled cornfields creating nice dips, and sharp curves and slow curves wrapping around stone walls and cornstalks. This blacktop roller coaster hauls you up a hill, slings you left at the peak, and then lifts you up again and slings you to the right.

White churches and cemeteries mark the road, and new sights flash past: bales of hay, the stone bridges, the one-lane bridge that's perfect for a photo, the river, and the valley on Aspen Drive that gives you a sense of cosmic proportion since the big valley (where's Linda Evans?) is nearly void of life, save for a few homes that pockmark the woods. Somewhere along the way, there's a very tricky and very important fork near a blip of a community called Samples Manor—you can turn left or right here, you'll end up in the same place. Continue south toward Pleasantville, and as you travel through miles of desolate primeval forest, the lack of civilization will convince you that you've ridden off the face of the earth. Then, just about the time you're tempted to shoot up a signal flare, you'll spy the Potomac peeking through the narrow woods to your right. You'll merge onto Sandyhook Road in a ramshackle riverside town that looks like coal-mining country—without the coal. File away a mental image, roll under a bridge, make a buttonhook turn to reach that same bridge (Rte. 340), and cross into Virginia.

If you follow 340 West, you're only a few miles from West Virginia and **Harpers Ferry National Historical Park** (304/535-6029, www.nps.gov/hafe, $4). A must-see stop, this is where radical abolitionist John Brown rounded up 18 slaves and attacked the U.S. Army arsenal in October 1859, hoping to jump-start a slave rebellion. Didn't happen. However, the Civil War *did* happen—and because of its placement where the Shenandoah and Potomac rivers meet, during the Civil War this town, like Liz Taylor, changed hands eight times. There is not a single museum here. Instead, there are *25* museums in a park that spans three states: West Virginia, Virginia, and Maryland. You'll see a restored town, hiking trails, guided tours, interpretive tours, fishing, and living history programs. While the park is open all year, most programs are held in the spring and summer.

From Harpers Ferry, double back on US Route 340 so you can eye the ruggedly handsome Shenandoah River. At Highway 671 (aka Harpers Ferry Rd.), turn right at the well-stocked service station. Virginia must have gotten a good price on scenery, because there's far more of it here than in Addis Ababa. Later, you may see evidence of the state's wildflower program, which blankets highway medians with flowers, such as black-eyed Susans, daffodils, goldenrod, and ox-eye daisies.

Highway 671 is a fast two-lane road, with pretty valleys and canopy roads in direct contrast to the sharp twists, weaves, ascents, and descents you'll be making. Although McMansions are now destroying what was once unspoiled scenery, the road's all right and lasts about eight miles until you reach Route 9. Turn left at the Little Country Store toward Leesburg, taking a well-deserved break to see great stone walls stretched across fields, farmhouses dotting the tops of low hills, and cornfields everywhere. If it's dusk and the conditions are right, you'll have the pleasure of watching a great gray fog rolling in over the hills.

Shortly, Route 9 merges with Route 7. It's been a great ride, and now it's time to rest up in Leesburg.

Leesburg Primer

Even someone who knows nothing about the Civil War has probably heard the oft-repeated phrase describing it: "brother against brother." That reality was embodied in the area surrounding Leesburg.

After John Brown's raid on Harpers Ferry in 1859, folks in Loudoun County feared a slave insurrection. Though never the site of a major battle or even a significant skirmish, Leesburg voted 400–22 in May 1861 to secede from the Union. Just a few miles away, the Germans and Quakers of Waterford voted 220–31 to remain with, and fight for, the preservation of the United States. Thus, the area spawned Virginia's only organized Union force: the Loudoun Rangers, led by Quaker Sam Meade, who scouted, patrolled, and skirmished with Confederate forces in the area.

These conflicts are no longer apparent. Today's lifestyle reflects a more genteel history. And though this may not be the most historical town you'll stay in, it's worth an overnight on your way south.

On the Road: Leesburg

Leesburg is just right for a bike ride. The downtown (at the intersection of Market Street (Rte. 7) and King Street (U.S. 15) is a manageable size, there's plenty of parking for bikes, and the diners, nightclubs, and riders from assorted clubs are visible reminders that you're in the right place.

You can spend your time conversing with the motorcycle travelers who've rolled into town, but if you want a quick, painless history lesson for just two bucks, the **Loudoun Museum** (16 Loudoun St., 703/777-7427, www.loudounmuseum.org)

is a smart first stop. There are historical walking tours ($5) offered in the summer, and you can always count on a short video that explains the history of the county and the Battle of Ball's Bluff. This was a small but important skirmish that represents the sum total of Leesburg's active participation in the Civil War, or, as the locals call it, "the War of Northern Aggression." It's a nice small museum that also includes slices of colonial history and information on local farmer John Binns, who, in 1804, wrote a "Treatise on Practical Farming." This introduction to modern farming techniques (some of which are still in use) drew praise from the king of gentleman farmers, Thomas Jefferson.

The remainder of downtown is like a smaller Charleston; the houses have been preserved well, although their scale is not as impressive. Cluttered antiques shops abound.

After you take Route 15 a mile north to Battlefield Road and see Ball's Bluff Battlefield, attend to a plan more important than investing in your 401(k). Stow some grub in a saddlebag, ride up 15 to White's Ferry Road, turn east, and follow it to the water. Scratch around for three bucks (five bucks round-trip) and board **White's Ferry** (24801 White's Ferry Rd., 301/349-5200). You'll take a short and immensely enjoyable ferry ride over the wide and tranquil Potomac. When you get to Maryland a few minutes later, park it and enjoy a picnic—an inexpensive pleasure worth a million bucks.

Pull It Over: Leesburg Highlights
Attractions and Adventures

Who can resist a company with the name **Butts Tubes?** At Butts (Harpers Ferry Rd., Purcellville, 540/668-9007 or 800/836-9911, www.buttstubes.com), inner-tube prices vary according to the size of your butt. You'll pay $1 per size for a tube (sizes 8–20), or more for a canoe. Leave your bike here. Butts Tubes will bus you up the Shenandoah, tell you where to get off in Maryland, let you drift for two hours over three rapids, and then meet you in Virginia for the bus ride home.

Ball's Bluff Battlefield (703/779-9372) marks a significant day in Civil War history. In 1861, when Union troops were convinced it wouldn't be long before they'd whip the Rebels into submission, 1,700 Union soldiers crossed the Potomac and came face to face with an equally determined 1,700 Confederate troops defending Leesburg. When the smoke cleared, 155 Rebels had been killed—a pittance compared to the 900-plus casualties suffered by the Union. Some Union troops retreating across the Potomac were killed, and their bodies floated downstream, bringing the war back to Washington, D.C. The stinging defeat had some benefits: A committee was formed to investigate Union defeats and corruption and to tighten up the war effort. There's a park and cemetery here, as well as interpretive trails where you can follow the battle.

The area surrounding Leesburg features dozens of back roads that wind past working farms and vineyards. Obtain a map of the Loudoun Wine Trail and the county's vineyards from the **Loudoun County (Leesburg) Visitor's Center** (222 Catoctin Circle, 703/771-2617 or 800/752-6118, www.visit-loudoun.org). **Leesburg Vintner** (29 S. King St., 703/777-3322, www.lees-burgvintner.com) was recognized as Virginia's retail winery of the year in 1997. You'll find barrels of wine (cleverly packaged in bottles), as well as cheese and other gourmet picnic foods.

Blue-Plate Specials

Leesburg Restaurant (9 S. King St., 703/777-3292) serves breakfast, lunch, and dinner daily. In the morning, equal numbers of riders and locals appear to frequent this place, a down-home restaurant since 1865. I think this is where Grant threw his victory party.

On the outskirts of the historic district is **Johnson's Charcoal Beef House** (401 E. Market St., 703/777-1116). Since 1963, Johnson's has been a staple of Virginia dining: Servers will "honey" and "sugar" you nonstop; you'll dine on made-from-scratch meals and country breakfasts, and you may spot Washington Redskins players loading up on raw meat.

The perfectly named **Mighty Midget Kitchen** (202 Harrison St. SE #A, 703/777-6406) is a downtown Leesburg institution. Pull in and order barbecue sandwiches, hamburgers, hot dogs, fries, and soda pop, and then dine al fresco at outdoor café tables. Here since 1947, the Mighty Midget isn't much bigger than when it was born. In other words, it's tiny.

If you think you deserve a nice meal, there's none nicer than at the **Tuscarora Mill** (203 Harrison St., 703/771.9300, www.tuskies.com), which, oddly enough, is built within the shell of an old 1899 mill. Coincidence? It's not something I do often, but splurging on something other than diner food can be a nice reward, and entrées like smoked chicken pasta, sesame roasted Atlantic salmon, and a strip steak, plus a nice lounge, can be the perfect conclusion to a long day's ride.

Watering Holes

With new money refinishing Leesburg in an upscale veneer, you wouldn't expect to find a biker bar in the heart of town. Yet the **Downtown Saloon** (5 N.

King St., 703/669-3090) has been around since 1965. No additives, no artificial sweeteners, just a love of motorcycling and the three Ps: peanuts, pinups, and pool. Come here to enjoy bar food, live bands, and a comfortable setting where you can kick back and map out your next leg.

The Kings Court Tavern (2C Loudoun St., 703/777-7747) is less biker than Brit. A pub theme runs throughout, with private booths, a long bar, TVs, and liquor. Downstairs at Ball's Bluff, the underground pub features a well-stocked bar, darts, occasional live music, and traditional food, such as wings, sandwiches, and salads.

Shut-Eye

Chain Drive
A, E, L

Chain hotels are in town, or within 10 miles. See cross-reference guide featuring phone numbers and Web addresses on page 514.

Inn-dependence
The **Loudoun County B&B Guild** (www.loudounbandb.com) represents more than 20 inns throughout the county. One of them is the **Norris House Inn** (108 Loudoun St., 703/777-1806 or 800/644-1806, www.norrishouse.com, $110 and up). This inn features a parlor, a library, a sunroom, and a rambling verandah overlooking the gardens. Antiques accent guestrooms, some of which have fireplaces. Downside: Parking's in a garage a few blocks away.

On the Road: Leesburg to Fredericksburg

Unlike the Wild West desert straightaways, where you can strap your handlebars in place and take a nap, roads in Virginia demand your attention.

Leave Leesburg on U.S. 15, the same road that leads out of Gettysburg. It's not impressive to start, just an ordinary road with an ordinary job. Twelve miles later at Gilbert's Corner, turn right and ride toward Aldie, then Middleburg. There are beautiful horse farms here—if you owned an Arabian instead of a bike, you'd probably live here. The passion for all things equestrian is omnipresent. People shopping in the uptown, upscale district are clearly devoted to horses—you can see it in their faces.

When you leave Middleburg behind, nothing is sudden. The road changes like a book, revealing a little at a time until the story is right in front of you. Upon reaching The Plains (which ain't too fancy), look for a service station and then some smooth country riding—nice shallow dips, split-rail fences, sweeping curves, weeping willows, and broken homes.

Take Country Road 245, a nice road that crosses beneath I-66, turns into U.S. 17, and then veers off to your left on U.S. 15/29 to bypass Warrenton. You'll ride into small towns like Remington and ride out seconds later. Look for Route 651 toward Sumerduck. This remote road mixes things up with some tight twists, graceful curves, inclines, and one-lane bridges. From here, the roads are country, and you get the strong feeling you're entering the South. Within a few miles, you've switched the channel from *Masterpiece Theatre* to *Hee-Haw*. It's hard to believe this change in cultures all happens less than an hour's drive from the nation's capital.

When 651 rejoins 17, turn right and follow it to Fredericksburg, one of the nicest towns you'll have the pleasure to meet.

Fredericksburg Primer

Why was Fredericksburg so vital to Civil War soldiers? Look at a map, put your finger on this city, and you'll be pointing midway between the Southern capital of Richmond and the Northern capital of Washington, D.C.

The high banks of the Rappahannock were a natural defensive barrier, and the north/south rail corridor kept both armies supplied. The end result was that four separate battles were fought in and around the city, leaving more than 100,000 casualties and a barren landscape in their wake. Think about this: Fredericksburg changed hands 10 times during the war, 85,000 men were wounded, and 15,000 were killed. That's more casualties than in the three previous wars (the Mexican-American War, the War of 1812, and the Revolutionary War) combined. This is considered the bloodiest landscape in America.

Fortunately, the town has never again been reduced to that level of horror. Today, a good vibe runs throughout: People are friendly, and the pace is slow, making this one of your most rewarding stops. People here understand and appreciate history, along with humor, so certain tours are far more enjoyable than any I've seen elsewhere. Add to this the walkable restaurant- and antiques-filled downtown district, and you've arrived at the perfect base to reach other Civil War sites, such as Spotsylvania to the east or the Stonewall Jackson Shrine to the south.

On the Road: Fredericksburg

Of all the historical towns I visited, I'd say Fredericksburg does the best job of making history interesting and entertaining without turning it into a caricature. This town has history down to an art.

Park your bike (parking's free, Pierre), put on some walking shoes, and do the town. If you walk at a good clip, you can see it in a day—but I'd wager you'll stick around for a little longer. For about eight blocks, both sides of Caroline Street, which is two blocks west of the Rappahannock River, provide numerous diversions, from cheap antiques to a cool diner to historic homes.

Swing by the **Fredericksburg Visitor Center** (706 Caroline St., 540/373-1776) to buy tickets for everything historical in town, such as the Hugh Mercer Apothecary Shop, the Rising Sun Tavern, Mary Washington House, and Fredericksburg/Spotsylvania National Military Park. These tours are a must while you're in town, and buying a "Pick 4 Ticket" will save you 30 percent. It also has maps for walking tours that highlight different eras of the town's history. Across the street, **Trolley Tours of Fredericksburg** (540/898-0737) departs for a tour of historic homes, attractions, and the famous Sunken Road. In addition to seeing Federal, Confederate, and the nation's oldest Masonic cemeteries, it's a smart way to get a lay of the land that you can return to later on your bike.

Pick up the necessary maps and tickets, and then head north on Caroline, allowing time to drop in shops along the way. At the corner of Caroline and Amelia, step into the **Hugh Mercer Apothecary Shop** (1020 Caroline St. 540/375-3362, $4, open daily) Manning the shop while the good doctor is out, wenches demonstrate the "modern medicines" used to treat patients. Thankfully, they never break character, even while discussing the medicinal value of leeches, herbs, amputations, mustard plasters, and a "good puking." With the right person playing the role, this is one of the best tours in America. If you're a doctor, you'll have plenty to talk to your peers about. If you're a lawyer, you'll find plenty of times to mutter "malpractice."

About three blocks north at the **Rising Sun Tavern** (1304 Caroline St. 540/371-1494), the format is the same and just as entertaining. Anywhere else, this would be a brief walk through an old building. Not here. The Rising Sun Tavern was built in 1760 by Charles Washington, the younger brother of George Washington, and, quite likely, the Billy Carter of Colonial America. Anyway, you can learn a lot here—for example, tavern decks had only 51 cards. You had to pay one shilling, sixpence for the 52nd card. Otherwise, you were not "dealing with a full deck."

After you've seen the remaining historical sites, hop on your bike and ride to the **Fredericksburg Battlefield** (1013 Lafayette Blvd., 540/373-6122, www.nps.gov/frsp). The museum is much smaller than the one at Gettysburg, but the introductory video does a good job of explaining the battles that happened here. Outside the back door, you'll take a self-guided tour that starts at the Sunken Road, one of the saddest places in America. Confederate soldiers used the high stone wall to shield themselves from Union troops and cut them down like lambs at the slaughter.

A little farther down, a monument may restore some of your faith in humanity. It's dedicated to a 19-year-old Confederate soldier, Richard Kirkland, who couldn't bear to hear the dying cries of the enemy. He scaled the wall and aided the suffering men, granted passage by Union soldiers who held their fire.

That's the final polish on another historical gem. Wrap up your tour with a nice dinner and a quiet evening at your inn.

Pull It Over: Fredericksburg Highlights
Attractions and Adventures

The **Fredericksburg/Spotsylvania National Military Park** maintains nearly 6,000 acres of land. A seven-day pass costs just $4 and provides admission to all local battlefields and the Stonewall Jackson shrine. The **Fredericksburg Battlefield Visitor Center** (1013 Lafayette Blvd., 540/373-6122, www.nps.gov/frsp) and **Chancellorsville Battlefield Visitor Center** (Rte. 3 W., 540/786-2880) help interpret the four battlefields: Fredericksburg, Chancellorsville, The Wilderness, and Spotsylvania Courthouse.

The **Fredericksburg Area Museum** (907 Princess Anne St., 540/371-3037, www.famcc.org, $5) is housed in the old 1860 Town Hall/Market House, which survived Civil War battles and now contains an interesting collection from Fredericksburg history. The highlights, of course, are the Civil War weapons.

Kenmore Plantation & Gardens (1201 Washington Ave., 540/373-3381, www.kenmore.org) was built by Colonel Fielding Lewis for his wife, Betty, George Washington's only sister. In fact, Washington himself surveyed the land when it was part of a 1,300-acre plantation. Guides claim that the plaster work makes this one of the most beautiful houses in America, a claim they back up with mention of an official award. This is a bit of an overstatement, however, considering that the honor was given in the 1930s. The house underwent extensive renovations that jumped admission to $8. The tour drags, however, so it's a crapshoot.

Left your dulcimer at home? One of the neatest shops in Fredericksburg is **Picker's Supply** (902 Caroline St., 540/371-4669 or 800/830-4669, www.pickerssupply.com). Even if you don't play, you will be tempted to pick up a banjo, mandolin, or fiddle for the road. If you do play, check out the vintage guitars.

Blue-Plate Specials

I knew there was a reason I was drawn to **Goolrick's** (901 Caroline St., 540/373-3411): It's the oldest continuously operating soda fountain in America. It serves the best milkshakes in the world—just ask the Aussie I met who said the same (I think he mixed his with a Foster's). Open daily for breakfast, lunch, and dinner, Goolrick's features an abridged menu of sandwiches, soups, homemade macaroni and potato salad, and fresh-squeezed lemonade.

More than 45 years of operation stand as testament to the simple meals and superior service at **Anne's Grill** (1609 Princess Anne St., 540/373-9621). Big home cooking, breakfast all day, burgers, steaks, seafood at lunch and dinner, sassy waitresses, and lots of locals. Closed Wednesdays and 2–4:30 P.M. each day.

Anne's counterpart is down the street at the **2400 Diner** (2400 Princess Anne St., 540/373-9049). For more than half a century, it, too, has been serving good dishes done right. There's a little bit of everything here, from subs and chicken to steaks and fish—ah, the pleasure of road food. Open 7 A.M.–9 P.M. Monday–Saturday, until 3 P.M. Sunday.

Watering Holes

You know that junk about never discussing politics and religion? Well, when you come to **J. Bryan's Tap Room** (200 Hanover St., 540/373-0738), throw that chestnut out the window. This place leans to the right, as evidenced by the framed photos of Liddy, Dole, Gingrich, and Reagan. Beyond that flaw, it's a cool place with 20 beers on tap, including Woodchuck Cider and Bass Ale. Happy hour lasts 4–7 P.M., and the Wurlitzer jukebox is authentic. Oh, yeah—George Washington once owned this place.

Shut-Eye

Fredericksburg has several inns, but if you prefer the modern conveniences of a TV, large bed, and private bath, you may do better at a chain hotel. Call the visitors center for listings.

Motels and Motor Courts

The **Fredericksburg Colonial Inn** (1707 Princess Anne St., 540/371-5666, www.fci1.com, $75–115) is one of the best bargains in town. Expect old-fashioned motel goodness with Civil War antiques and a fridge in each room—some rooms with a separate living room—and the atmosphere that comes with being in business since the 1930s. Rates are equally generous.

Chain Drive

A, C, E, G, J, L, Q, S, U, BB, CC, DD

Chain hotels are in town, or within 10 miles. See cross-reference guide featuring phone numbers and Web addresses on page 514.

Inn-dependence

The **Richard Johnston Inn** (711 Caroline St., 540/899-7606 or 877/557-0770, www.therichardjohnstoninn.com, $95 and up weekdays, $125 and up weekends) features seven rooms and two suites, some of them uncommonly large, many filled with antiques and reproductions, and all with private bath. Built in the late 1700s, the inn has great placement in the heart of downtown, with generous parking and a full breakfast.

Side Trips

Virginia and West Virginia

Virginia
Route 42

Western Virginia's mountainous corkscrew turns and twisties are plentiful near Harrisonburg, where they shoot south down Route 42 to Goshen. Ride Route 39 West across the Appalachians and Allegheny Mountains to Warm Springs, and then cruise north on U.S. 220 to Monterey. The reward: breathtaking views of surrounding mountains and pastures, and the sound of cowbells ringing from the fields.

Skyline Drive

Atop the Shenandoah Mountains, parallel to the Appalachian Trail, Skyline Drive stretches almost 100 miles from Front Royal in northern Virginia to Waynesboro, where it links up with the Blue Ridge Parkway. At least five major Civil War battlefields are within an hour of Skyline Drive, and Thomas Jefferson's home, Monticello, is in nearby Charlottesville.

West Virginia
Route 33

Seneca Rocks, West Virginia

In Pendleton County, at the intersection of Routes 33 and 25/55, riders hang out at the local eatery before riding around Seneca Rocks, a monolith that rises nearly 1,000 feet straight up from the rolling hills of eastern West Virginia. Climbers consider ascending Seneca Rocks a rite of passage. Riders consider them crazy.

Route 16

War, West Virginia

War! What is it good for? It's good for a great ride. Near Bluefield, at the southernmost point of the Mountain State, Route 16 runs from the Virginia border through War, then Coalwood (home of "Rocket Boy" Homer Hickam), and on to Welch. Aside from Deal's Gap, I'd argue that you won't find a more challenging ride east of the Rockies.

Contributed by John Weinstein

Resources for Riders

Civil War Run

Pennsylvania Travel Information
Pennsylvania Bed & Breakfast Committee—717/232-8880,
   www.patourism.org
Pennsylvania Fishing Licenses—717/705-7930, www.fish.state.pa.us
Pennsylvania Road Conditions— 717/783-5186 or 888/783-6783,
   www.paturnpike.com
Pennsylvania State Parks—888/727-2757, www.dcnr.state.pa.us
Pennsylvania Visitor Information—800/847-4872, www.visitpa.com

Virginia Travel Information
Virginia Travel (for all divisions below— 800/VISIT-VA (800/847-4882)
Virginia Camping—800/933-7275, www.dcr.state.va.us
Virginia Civil War Trails—888/CIVILWAR (888/248-4592)
Virginia Country Inns Bed and Breakfasts—800/262-1293
Virginia Highway Helpline—800/367-7623
Virginia Scenic Roads Map—804/786-0002
Virginia State Travel Information—800/253-2767, www.virginia.org
Virginia Tourism—800/847-4882, www.virginia.org
Virginia Tourism Bed & Breakfasts—800/934-9184
Virginia Travel Guide—800/847-4882

Local and Regional Information
Fredericksburg Visitor Center—540/373-1776 or 800/678-4748,
   www.fredericksburgvirginia.net
Gettysburg Convention and Visitors Bureau—717/334-6274 or 800/337-
   5015, www.gettysburgcvb.org
Loudoun County (Leesburg) Visitors Center— 703/771-2617 or 800/752-
   6118, 222 Catoctin Circle, www.visitloudoun.org

Pennsylvania Motorcycle Shops
Action Motorsports—1881 Whiteford Rd., York, 717/757-2688,
  www.actionmotorsportsyork.com
Battlefield Harley-Davidson/Buell— 21 Cavalry Field Rd., Gettysburg,
  717/337-9005 or 877/595-9005, www.battlefieldharley-davidson.com
Don's Kawasaki,—20 E. Market St., Hellam (York), 717/755-6002,
  www.donskawasaki.com
Laugermans Harley-Davidson—100 Arsenal Rd., York, 717/854-3214,
  www.laugerman.com

Virginia Motorcycle Shops
Fredericksburg Motorsports—390 Kings Hwy., Fredericksburg,
  540/899-9100
Loudoun Motorsports—212 Catoctin Circle SE, Leesburg, 703/777-1652,
  www.loudounmotorsports.com
Morton's BMW— 5099A Jefferson Davis Hwy., Fredericksburg,
  540/891-9844, www.mortonsbmw.com

Blue Ridge Parkway Run

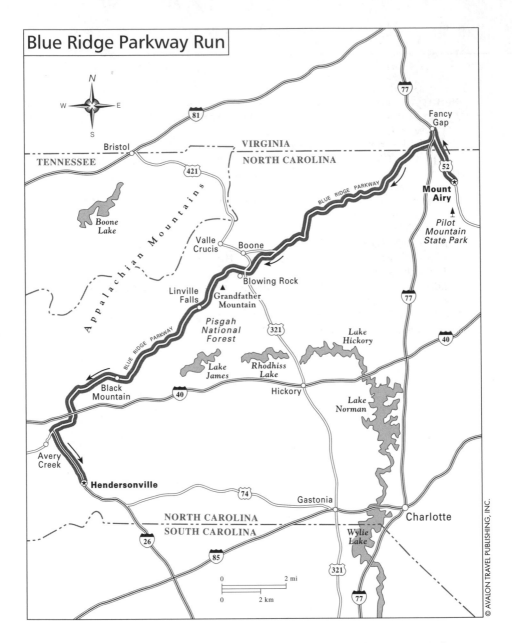

Route: Mount Airy to Hendersonville via Blowing Rock, Valle Crucis, Little
  Switzerland

Distance: Approximately 200 miles; consider five days with stops.

•**Day 1—Mount Airy** •**Day 2—Travel** •**Day 3—Blowing Rock** •**Day 4—Travel**
  •**Day 5—Hendersonville**

First Leg: Mount Airy to Blowing Rock (100 miles)

Second Leg: Blowing Rock to Hendersonville (90 miles)

Helmet Laws: North Carolina requires helmets.

Blue Ridge Parkway Run

*Mount Airy, North Carolina to Hendersonville,
North Carolina*

Without resorting to hyperbole: The Blue Ridge Parkway (BRP) is the most beautiful road ever built. This 469-mile-long, toll-free dream starts in Front Royal, Virginia, winds its way through the Appalachians, and slithers to a close in Cherokee, North Carolina.

Before I made this run, I had a favorite president. Afterward, FDR became my man—he's the one who got this road-building project going in September 1935 in order to put Americans back to work. The masterstroke was the decision not to allow commercial vehicles on the road. You don't need to worry about semis or delivery vans here. Just soak in the very best America has to offer, as you cruise during the peak riding seasons of spring or fall. Be warned, however, that sections of the BRP can be washed out by floods or mudslides, and heavy fog can reduce visibility to just a few feet—which makes riding extremely dangerous. But when it's right, it's *just* right.

I should point out that it's not just the road that makes this ride. Southern people are inherently friendly; Southern women invariably attractive; and the Southern vibe so good that on this run, even Harley riders wave.

Mount Airy Primer

There's little you need to know about Mount Airy except this: Andy Griffith was born here, and so was the Happiest Girl in the Whole USA (aka Donna

Fargo). Oh yeah, Chang and Eng Bunker, the original Siamese twins, lived here, but they pale in comparison to Andy Taylor and Barney Fife.

I start here because it's my book, I'm a member of *The Andy Griffith Show* Rerun Watchers' Club, and the Blue Ridge Parkway and other great roads surround the town. I also have learned that genetically, Mount Airy residents can be nothing but friendly and their Southern sayings unforgettable.

But Andy is why people travel here. Griffith grew up on Haymore Street, and the small-town boy made good. If you're familiar with *The Andy Griffith Show,* you'll recognize the influences that made it to television. There's Floyd's barber shop, the diner, and all the elements of a sleepy North Carolina town.

For years, Griffith repeatedly tried to define the line between the reality of his childhood and the fictional world he inhabited professionally, but that hasn't stopped townspeople from trying to turn their town into Mayberry. The Surry County Arts Council publishes the *Mayberry Confidential,* which includes breaking news on Aunt Bee's bake sale and the Little Miss Mayberry pageant. It hosts Mayberry Days, and get ready, the word "Mayberry" precedes a chamber's worth of businesses—including Mayberry Auto Sales, Motor Lodge, Mall, Alarm Company, Cab Company, Candle Shop, Consignments, Embroidery, Flea Market, Kountry Kitchen, Pharmacy, and several thousand others.

You'll find an intriguing blend of fantasy and reality, and you should just enjoy it. Grab a bite at the diner, get a trim at Floyd's, and head to the filling station so Gomer can check out your bike.

On the Road: Mount Airy

For such a small town, there's a surprising amount to experience here. Not thrilling, not magnificent, just... American. It won't take long—if you arrive early, you may not even need to stay the evening. A visit downtown and a ride to Pilot Mountain may fill up a day, but at nightfall, you'll have a full stomach and a lifetime of memories. Beware of Sunday arrivals, when many downtown businesses are closed.

Ride your bike to Main Street and start with a North Carolina breakfast at **Leon's Burger Express** (407 N. Main St., 336/789-0849), an old-fashioned diner stuck in the 1950s. Coca-Cola wallpaper, red vinyl seats with silver tacking on back, a pie display—it's all here, plus coffee and friendly waitresses.

Walk back to the **Visitors Center** (615 Main St., 336/789-4636 or 800/576-0231, www.visitmayberry.com) to see a short video on Andy's contributions to Mount Airy and the collection of one of his boyhood friends, who gathered scripts, records, yearbooks, and wrappers of "Andy Griffith Whole Hog Sausage."

Floyd's City Barber Shop (336/786-2346) should be open by this time of day, so backtrack past Leon's and drop in to meet Russell Hiatt. Like a Penny Lane barber, he takes a picture of everyone who stops in. With more than 25,000 photographs on his wall, Hiatt claims he has the world's most important wall since Berlin.

Around midmorning, saddle up and get on Highway 52 South to start your 15-mile ride to Pilot Mountain. The highway has great curves before you reach the exit at **Pilot Mountain State Park** (336/325-2355). Admission to the park, open 8 A.M.–8 P.M. daily, is free.

The steep ascent to the peak is interrupted occasionally by bicyclists screaming down the mountain road like hornets. It'll take a few minutes to reach the peak, 1,400 feet above the countryside of the upper Piedmont Plateau. Lean back and gaze up the road to the top, watching the mountain unfold before you. As you near the final turn, the view is tremendous. From the peak, you can see Highway 52 darting through the forests toward Mount Airy and glimpse Winston-Salem through the haze on the far horizon.

When you return to Mount Airy, there's another stop for gearheads, Gomers, and Goobers: **Wally's Service Station** (625 S. Main St., 336/719-0181, www.wallysserviceatmayberry.com). The station was built in 1937 and went through several owners until it was restored in 2001 as an old-fashioned service station (and gift shop). The owners don't mind you hanging around, sipping on an RC Cola and eating a Moon Pie. If that's not enough, you can leave your bike behind and take a spin in a vintage replica of Mayberry's squad car—a 1962 Ford Galaxie 500. Call 336/789-OPIE (336/789-6743) or visit www.tourmayberry.com for reservations.

You've just about done it. You could go see the world's largest granite quarry or wait for evening to eat some more. Or, would you believe it? At the old-fashioned **Cinema Theatre** (142 Main St., 336/786-2222), movies cost a few bucks. Live it up. Maybe you can just relax and realize that you don't have to do a damn thing to enjoy yourself.

Welcome to Mayberry.

Pull It Over: Mount Airy Highlights
Attractions and Adventures

In September 2004, during the town's annual Mayberry Days, Andy Griffith made one of his few trips home to attend the unveiling of TV

Land's Andy and Opie statue at the **Andy Griffith Playhouse** (218 Rockford St., 336/786-7998). The bronze statues show the two walking to the ol' fishin' hole (which fans know is the title of the show's whistled theme). Grab a cane pole, get out the camera, and you've got yourself a souvenir.

The Andy Griffith Show contributed to the revival of bluegrass music (remember the Darling Family?), and that music's still being picked, plucked, and sung at the Andy Griffith Playhouse. Each Thursday, there's a jam session, and on the third Saturday of each month is the Blue Ridge Jamboree, featuring the Mayberry Deputy. On Saturday morning, there's a jam session staged at the Cinema Theatre downtown.

Blue-Plate Specials

You can't come to Mount Airy without eating at **Snappy Lunch** (125 N. Main St., 336/786-4931). Oprah has eaten here. So did Hal Smith (Otis) and Aneta Corsaut (Helen Crump). Breakfast is fine, but lunch is mandatory. The pork chop sandwich is fat, greasy, and stacked with coleslaw and other ingredients researchers are still trying to figure out. Damn, it's good. Owner Charles Dowell, one of the nicest restaurateurs in the South, has been cooking here since the 1950s. He's been known to cover your tab if he likes you.

Pandowdy's Restaurant (243 N. Main St., 336/786-1993) is the rare downtown eatery open in the evening, but more than that keeps this place packed every night. Credit the Southern hospitality of the waitresses and dishes that outperform even four-star restaurants; the filet mignon is one of the most tender and satisfying I've ever eaten. Pandowdy's does lunch and dinner Wednesday–Saturday.

Shut-Eye

Motels and Motor Courts
The **Mayberry Motor Inn** (501 N. Andy Griffith Pkwy, 336/786-4109, www.mayberrymotorinn.com, $59 and up) is an old-fashioned motor lodge with standard rooms and a pool. The exception is Aunt Bee's Room, which the owner decorated with twin beds, a vanity, and other memorabilia she bought from the Raleigh estate sale of Frances Bavier, America's Aunt Bee. You can't sleep in this room, but the others are open.

Chain Drive
A, C, O

Chain hotels are in town, or within 10 miles. See cross-reference guide featuring phone numbers and Web addresses on page 514.

Inn-dependence
If you named your kid Opie, chances are you're destined to stay at the **Andy Griffith Home Place** (711 Haymore St., $150 year-round), the small home where Andy grew up. It accommodates up to four people, which is great if you're riding with a group. Andy's Place is now run by the **Hampton Inn** (2029 Rockford St., 336/789-5999, $65 and up), which is nice and clean. Rates buy you local calls, access to a swimming pool, and a good night's sleep in a king or queen bed. The Hampton is close enough to the attractions for convenience but far enough away to be quiet.

An inn may better reflect the feeling of Mayberry, plus you'll have a chance to talk to locals. There are several grand old homes to choose from: **Maxwell House** (618 N. Main St., 877/786-2174 or 877/786-2174, $110 and up); the **Thompson House** (804 E. Pine St., 336/719-0711, $80 and up); **Thomas House** (739 N. Main St., 336/789-1766, $90 and up); the **Mayberry Bed and Breakfast** (329 W. Pine St., 336/786-2045, $65 and up); and **Thelma Lou's** (738 S. Main St., 336/789-4856, $75 and up). Some have shared baths, but the majority have private baths, and each includes breakfast—either continental or full.

On the Road: Mount Airy to Blowing Rock

Before leaving Mount Airy on Highway 52 North, grab some sandwiches, fried chicken, soft drinks, and other portable food. Even though restaurants are plentiful off the parkway, you'll have more fun dining al fresco.

The five-mile ride to Fancy Gap, Virginia, takes you to the Blue Ridge Parkway and one of life's most enjoyable moments. First, you'll pass signs of the rural South: a drive-in, flea markets, and wrestling fliers tacked to telephone poles. Note another subtle change here. The air starts to smell fresh, perfumed by the grass and flowers of the surrounding mountains and valleys.

The hodgepodge patchwork of businesses and houses and trees and valleys draws into clearer focus as you approach the parkway. The mountains rush to greet you, and your bike will rock back and forth every few seconds as you tuck into corners at 45 mph. In the opposite lane, motorcycle travelers are coming around the corners as if they're flying off an assembly line.

Just after the Mountain Top Restaurant, enter the BRP, turn left, and the road is yours from mile marker 200 south to mile marker 392. If you travel off-season, it is mind-blowing to realize that, out of 300 million Americans, you're only one of a handful with the intelligence to be on this road. The satisfaction is immense as you pass over the interstate and pity the poor slobs who have no idea what they're missing.

It doesn't take long to realize the BRP represents "the Golden Age of Road Building." To your left, you'll spy Pilot Mountain, an acropolis 20 miles distant. If you can't get enough of the views at this early stage, scenic overlooks appear every few miles. But it won't take an overlook to persuade you to stop. Every few miles, cars and bikes have pulled over, and barefoot drivers and riders have settled into the soft grass to enjoy picnics, naps, and nature.

You've felt wind and sun on your face before, but for many reasons, it is more satisfying here. Flip up your visor and flood your lungs with fresh air. This road is free of commercial traffic, businesses, and billboards; you have only to pay attention to the dogwoods and evergreens, the meadows, glades, and the stone bridges.

As you ride here, you'll recognize that this may be the only road in the country where the speed limit is right. It's 45 mph, the perfect speed for experiencing everything. At High Piny Spur, elevation 2,805 feet, the vista is grand, a field of varying textures and colors.

The road continues, smooth and flowing. Although there are nice straights for relaxation, it is never boring, never threatening. The Blue Ridge Parkway is absent of restrictions. There are no speed traps, no signs telling you the road is air-patrolled. It trusts you to do the right thing. And if you ever want to take a break, exits such as Alder Gap (3,047 feet) and Sheets Gap (3,342 feet) allow you to get on and off the parkway with ease.

More than 50 miles have passed now, and the BRP has given you greenery and great curves. Just before mile marker 259, the **Northwest Trading Post** sells crafts and marks the arrival of more tremendous views: The Lump, Benge Gap, and Calloway Gap. You're only a few miles from Blowing Rock, but just after Benge Gap is **Bill Watson's Country Store,** a convenient stop for gas and food if you failed to pack a lunch.

From here, you have only to enjoy the last few miles until you pass mile marker 291 and start looking for the exit at Highway 221/321 into Blowing Rock.

Blowing Rock Primer

Funny how some towns get started. During the Civil War, Southern soldiers started packing up their families and sending them into the safety of these hills. After Appomattox, some soldiers joined their families here, and Blowing Rock grew bit by bit until the population hovered around 100.

The number was sufficient for incorporation, but fortunately not nearly enough to spoil the solitude and scenery of the Blue Ridge. Seasonal residents fleeing the South's summer heat headed for the mountains. In turn, a resort town formed, complete with boardinghouses, inns, shops, and restaurants.

Today, the commercial district is limited to a handful of stores, and you can park your bike and walk the town in a few hours—but you'd be missing the best of Blowing Rock. You haven't really seen the town until you've entered its forests, climbed its hills, and ridden on its sublime mountain roads. Don't rush it.

On the Road: Blowing Rock

Downtown Blowing Rock isn't that large, but it's a perfect base for exploring the larger-than-life mountains that surround it. From the center of Blowing Rock, ride south on Highway 221 a few miles to Shulls Mills Road, which leads right onto the Blue Ridge Parkway. Another quick right takes you to the **Moses Cone Manor House.** There's not much to see here, but the textile magnate's Flat Top Manor comes groovin' up slowly with mountain crafts, such as dulcimers, quilts, and "snake" sticks, as well as a full library of books on the Blue Ridge. Take a moment and relax on the verandah, which over-looks 3,600 acres of riding and hiking trails (also passable on horseback) and a small mountain lake.

Head north on the parkway. Just past mile marker 292, exit at Highway 221/321 and ride north toward Boone. Ride about six more miles to the city, which you'll detect when you see the touristy Tweetsie Railroad. Shortly after, hang a left at Highway 105 and stick with it as the winding road leads deeper into the North Carolina countryside. Your destination is a small town called Valle Crucis, so when you reach the corner of Broadstone Road, about two miles later, turn right and head for the hills.

At first, the slapdash homes and shaky riverfront cabins will lead to the unshakeable belief that you're leaving civilization behind. Unfortunately, this theory is shattered when you see entrances to "exclusive mountain developments." Ignore them.

Instead, watch the tight turns that whip you into Valle Crucis. At first, you'll pass an annex, but keep riding until you see the Esso station sign and old red gas pump announcing that you've arrived at the circa 1883 **Mast General Store** (828/963-6511, www.mastgeneralstore.com).

Next comes one of those unforgettable motorcycle moments. Housed within the general store is the post office (boxes rent for $2 a year), along with creaking wooden floors, a 1913 pot-bellied stove, and mountain men who sit around and chew Mail Pouch tobacco and talk about what mountain people talk about. The store has been here since bills were paid in produce, roots and herbs, and chickens. But the Mast General Store peddles wares for outsiders as well.

Need a hoe handle? It's here. A Union suit? Check upstairs. It also sells birdhouses, cinnamon brooms, musical spoons, marbles—cat's eye and rainbow shooters—cider mix, rocking chairs, and leather jackets. Grab a five-cent cup of coffee, sit a spell on the back porch, and watch the fat bumblebees hover above the flowers.

When you're ready to leave the past behind, ride back to Highway 105 and head south to Linville, where you hook up to Highway 221 North. It's 19 miles back to Blowing Rock, but there's another stop to make. On your right you'll see **Grandfather Mountain** (828/733-2013 or 800/468-7325, www.grandfather.com, $14), the highest peak in the Blue Ridge Mountains at 5,964 feet. The area is also a wildlife habitat for black bear, white-tailed deer, mountain lions, and bald eagles. More important, the road to the top is an 18 percent grade! It is far more challenging and twisting than mortals should be able to handle. If put under oath, I would testify that this could be the single most challenging rise, because the turns are so tight and inclines so steep that you think you've reached the top several times, but the road keeps rising. Even on the last leg up, the corners continue for miles until you reach the top and the Mile-High Swinging Bridge, a 228-foot-long wooden bridge that's actually just 80 feet above a chasm. It's tethered to the ground, but it's still pretty spooky.

As gusts of wind rock the bridge (record speed is 196.5 knots) and whistle through the protective fencing, those brave enough gain access to an extraordinary view of the Blue Ridge Mountains, views that last light years. Don't let me describe it. See it for yourself.

You'll love going back down as much as coming up, and the ride back to Blowing Rock via Highway 221 is a mental massage—although the optional Blue Ridge Parkway North is more than incredible. Streams and snaking roads form a graceful combination to follow past rural stores such as the **Grandfather Mountain Market** (6371 U.S. 221 S., 828/295-6100), where you can stock up on jams, jellies, apple butter, peach cider, and night crawlers.

Pop a few in your mouth and head back to Blowing Rock.

Pull It Over: Blowing Rock Highlights
Attractions and Adventures

At the **Blowing Rock** (U.S. 321, 828/295-7111, www.theblowingrock.com, $6), North Carolina's oldest attraction, you can buy genuine rubber tomahawks, cowboy hats, and a book of dirty mountain sayings ("He really crapped in the oatmeal" is a good'un.) I was skeptical at first, but this really is a windy place, since gusts of powerful mountain air rush in from the valley floor. If you forgot your blow dryer, stop here.

White-water rafting expeditions are the specialty of **High Mountain Expeditions** (Main St. and Hwy. 221, Blowing Rock, 828/295-4200 or 800/262-9036, www.highmountainexpeditions.com). Bring a swimsuit or shorts, a T-shirt, and tennis shoes, and you'll be loaded in a van for the ride to Irwin Falls, Tennessee, for a half- or full-day adventure. You will get wet.

A dirt and gravel road leads to the **Blowing Rock Equestrian Preserve** (828/295-4700), off Highway 221 one mile from Main Street, where you can rent a horse and ride the trails through Moses Cone Park. A 90-minute gallop is forty bucks; two hours of giddy-upping is fifty.

Blue-Plate Specials

Hankering for a plate of liver mush? You'll find it at **Knight's Restaurant** (N. Main St., 828/295-3869), plus potatoes, grits, baked apples, breads, and cereals—and that's just breakfast. In business since 1949, this is a busy joint, where the staff hustles, but you never feel rushed. This is the best place to get your morning started or ratchet down at night.

Speckled Trout Cafe (Main St., 828/295-9819) features standard appetizers and entrées with an emphasis on fresh trout and seafood. Off-season, tables are easy to come by; in peak season, you may starve to death before you get a seat. The fresh rainbow trout is raised in the mountains, and then prepared pan fried, broiled, or baked. Open for breakfast, lunch, and dinner.

For basic road food and a chance to sustain the al fresco approach to life, the **Cheeseburgers Grill and Paradise Bar** (120 Yonahlossee Rd., 828/295-4858) is waiting. Burgers weigh in at a healthy full pound, and there are appetizers, wings, salads, and suds to savor on the deck.

On a cold, lukewarm, or hot day, swing by the **Blowing Rock Cafe** (349 Sunset Dr., 828/295-9474). Owner Larry Imeson rides and proudly flies a HOG flag in front of his restaurant. Boasting of a dozen homemade soups and strawberry-walnut bran muffins, he adds salads and sandwiches to the mix served inside or on the patio. A diverse clientele varies from riders to suits to sun worshippers to celebs like Paul Newman, who probably dropped in to hawk a few bottles of salad dressing.

Shut-Eye

Motels and Motor Courts

One of the best places I can recommend is the **Mountainaire Inn and Log Cabins** (827 N. Main St., 828/295-7991, www.mountainaire-inn.com, $120–180), provided you stay in a log cabin. Cabins sleep up to six people and are dressed out for comfort. Some have hot tubs and fireplaces, some have cathedral ceilings, and all have a large front porch where you can sit in a rocker and watch your bike. The motel rooms are much smaller. Go for a cabin.

Chain Drive

A, E, J, L, S, V, Z

Chain hotels are in town, or within 10 miles. See cross-reference guide featuring phone numbers and Web addresses on page 514.

Inn-dependence

Crippen's Country Inn (239 Sunset Dr., 828/295-3487 or 877/295-3487, www.crippens.com, $139 and up in season) offers a parlor, spacious rooms, and a great location only a few feet from the village. The weekends-only five-star restaurant gets lots of attention.

On the Road: Blowing Rock to Hendersonville

It'll take less than a millisecond to ease back into the feel of the Blue Ridge Parkway. It starts right away with sweeping, slow descents and corners.

A few miles south on the left, Price Lake is one of the first secrets to reveal itself. It's the perfect place to stage a photo of you on your mount; peer over the right side for a view of a small waterfall. Farther south, the Julian Price Memorial Park (at mile marker 297) has boat rentals, fishing, and camping.

From here, there's so much to see, but so little you have to do. Even if you're accustomed to the overlooks, the view is beyond belief at mile marker 302. The best views of the parkway are concentrated right here. Yet this isn't the only incredible sight you'll see on the ride.

Only a mile later, look up the road at the Linn Cove Viaduct, a span that ri-

Life doesn't get much bet-ter for Moses the dog at Christa's Country Corner in Pineola Gap, North Carolina, on the Blue Ridge Parkway. He even has preserves named after him.

© NANCY HOWELL

vals the Bixby Creek Bridge of the Pacific Coast Highway. A small parking area and information center lie just over the viaduct, but my gut instinct was to keep riding back and forth across the bridge until I passed out from excitement.

So far, you haven't even reached the exit for Grandfather Mountain, and you've had a full day's worth of inspiring views. Now the road takes some slow dives and leads to immaculate ascensions. For the next 48 miles, you'll be rid-ing through a section of the Pisgah National Forest.

When you reach mile marker 312, you'll see a stone tunnel ahead, but take the exit at the Pineola Gap to stop at **Christa's Country Corner** (Hwy. 181, 828/733-3353). Although Christa named the store after herself, she accepts that more customers remember Moses, the fat Labrador who sleeps by the counter. The place brims with all the items you'd expect a general store to stock: homemade preserves (featuring Moses's picture), Dr. Enuff soda (I'd never heard of it either), cans of snuff, udder balm, and Moon Pies (which taste great slathered in udder balm).

Getting back on the parkway is like meeting an old friend. You're back to hugging curves and riding at angles even Pythagoras couldn't calculate. You'll reach some roller-coaster drops and commence about 30 miles of the best rid-ing in America.

Granite columns rise on your left, valleys and mountains on your right. You'll want to twist your neck like Linda Blair to see it all, but stop if you want a longer look. Slow down to take advantage of winding roads that vali-date every reason you concocted to convince your spouse you really needed a bike.

You're riding past apple orchards now, then the North Carolina Minerals Museum at mile marker 321, and then Spruce Pine, a small town six miles off the parkway. Stop if you like, or keep riding and you'll reach towns like Little Switzerland, featuring a café/bookstore and a town the size of a high-school gym.

I kept riding, because the hills kept appearing and I wanted to pump the throttle and rocket over them. This is an amazing feat of roadwork. Equally heartening is the relatively scant development in the valleys below.

Starting near mile marker 342, the curves become more frequent, the tunnels more numerous, your exclamations of "Oh, my God!" more urgent. Stop at the Licklog Ridge; then, for nearly 40 miles, slice through a valley as the road rating changes from PG to R. The world is just beyond your fairing, and you're getting close to the end of the run. Make a final (optional) stop at the free **Folk Art Center** (mile marker 382, 828/298-7928, www.southernhigh-landguild.org), where the country artisans could whip Martha Stewart with one loom tied behind their backs.

At the exit for I-26, say farewell for now to the Blue Ridge Parkway and take the cleanest and most direct route to Hendersonville—the hub of all things good.

Hendersonville Primer

Hendersonville ("The City with a Motto") is an average American town that takes a back seat to Asheville, but I'm not sure why. It has everything a city should have. Chain businesses are relegated to the outskirts of town; the downtown still functions; and it lies in the middle of everything worth seeing.

Hendersonville began as an escape for Floridians who faced yellow fever at the turn of the 20th century, and it remains a favorite of Floridians who bring their kids to camp or to escape the heat. Not a bad idea, since brisk mountain breezes keep humidity low and summertime temperatures in the comfortable 70s. What's more, the nearby Blue Ridge Mountains block severe weather patterns at Asheville, so folks under Hendersonville's thermal blanket savor a mild climate year-round. The unique weather and geological patterns also affect the foliage, creating a deluge of dogwood, azalea, and apple blossoms in spring and fall.

On the Road: Hendersonville

Like Broadway Avenue in Saratoga Springs, Hendersonville's Main Street is a wide avenue designed so a team of four horses could make a U-turn. The street

The Essence of the South

In a newspaper article dated January 18, 1987, Charles Kuralt mentioned his visit to the Mast General Store while also explaining the beauty of the American South.

Where should I send you to know the soul of the South? I think I'll send you to the Mast General Store ....

You cannot get to know either the store or the people in it if you are in a hurry to reach the bright lights. In its essence, the South is rural, slow, and charming, cluttered and eclectic, rich in old tales, old artifacts, and human friendship. The South cannot be hurried through. Vacationers who take the interstate from New York to Miami miss the South completely.

is still touched by small-town nostalgia. Along it, you'll find diagonal parking, a movie theater, and a Western Auto store that still sells Radio Flyer wagons and Red Ryder BB guns.

You can get caught up in shopping (antiques emporiums, art galleries, a music store, wine cellar, herb shop, Irish pub, beer brewing store), but you'll have just as much fun on the road.

Consider your location: Three miles to the Flat Rock Playhouse and Carl Sandburg home, 15 miles to the Blue Ridge Parkway, 17 miles to Chimney Rock, 18 miles to Pisgah National Forest, 19 miles to the Biltmore Estate, and less than 20 miles to Saluda, Tryon, Bat Cave, and Brevard. You're at the center of a wheel, with spokes leading to some great places.

A great loop picks up most of these places on a full day's ride. Leave Hendersonville on Highway 64 West toward Brevard, but when 64 turns left, stay straight on Route 276 into a section of **Pisgah National Forest** (1001 Pisgah Hwy., 828/877-3350, www.cs.unca.edu/nfsnc). Straight and narrow at first, the surroundings then become a canvas of wonderful woodlands, accented with waterfalls and roadside streams.

At the visitors center on your right, pick up information on horseback riding, hiking trails, camping facilities, and fishing streams. Four miles down the road, look for the photo opportunity at Looking Glass Falls. Pull over for a picture, or climb down the rocks and be pummeled into submission by the powerful falls. Another two miles, and you'll reach Sliding Rock, where you should stop your bike, put on your trunks, and experience the forest's most exhilarating natural attraction, offering the same sensation as skimming down a 60-foot icicle.

The road is just as exciting, like a luge competition, and 276 continues its asphalt rush for eight fun miles until you once again reach the Blue Ridge Parkway for a mighty great ride north. Enjoy traveling with your old friend until you reach Route 74A, where you turn right until you reach Bat Cave at Highway 64. You won't see Adam West or Burt Ward, since Bat Cave is just a stretch of gift shops and restaurants with dining decks overlooking mountain streams, but it's got a great name. And it leads to **Chimney Rock Park** (828/625-9281 or 800/277-9611, www.chimneyrockpark.com), site of a 1,200-foot-tall, 500 million-year-old rock tower that features hiking trails, catwalks from rock to rock, and a commanding view of the Hickory Nut Gorge. When the skies are clear or the forests are ablaze with color, it's worth the $12 to experience this vision. The town here borders on tacky, but it is home to **Heavenly Hoggs** (374 Hwy. 64, 828/625-8070, www.heavenlyhoggs.com), an unexpected find that features antique bikes, parts, and apparel. Call for hours.

Stay on Highway 64 and ride around the beautiful lakefront curves of Lake Lure, then watch for Highway 9 South. This quiet country road puts you in the middle of forests, where you should look for Route 108 South into Tryon, a community centered around equestrian events. Leave Tryon by Route 176 North (a great country road), and get ready to experience a mighty odd town.

Saluda is the site of the steepest railroad grade in America, but it's better known for Coon Dog Day, a Fourth of July festival that brings families out of the hills to show off their hunting dogs, crown a new Coon Dog Queen, and listen to toe-tappin' mountain music. **J. C. Thompson's Grocery Market and Grill** and the **M. A. Pace** general store are worth a visit, as is **Green River BBQ** (828/749-9892), serving lunch and dinner.

Stay on Route 176, and the ride returns to its familiar temperament, twisting and turning, diving and soaring as it arrives in the village of Flat Rock. This highly cultured area is home of the **Flat Rock Playhouse** (2661 Greenville Hwy., 828/693-0403, www.flatrockplayhouse.org), which is also North Carolina's state playhouse. Absent any coon dogs, Flat Rock gets by with the Carl Sandburg home.

"The People's Poet" lived here at **Connemara** (828/693-4178, www.nps.gov/carl, $5), which is still just the way he left it. His guitar rests by his recliner, and the house is cluttered with original books, notes, awards, and walking canes, as if he'd just stepped out to feed the goats on his family farm. If you appreciate his poems and Lincoln biographies and the chance to walk through some pleasing North Carolina countryside, it's well worth the price of admission.

It's been a full day. If you met the challenge of skimming down frigid Sliding Rock, dig the icicles out of your underwear and take Route 25 the last few miles back to Hendersonville.

Pull It Over: Hendersonville Highlights
Attractions and Adventures

It's hard to improve upon nature, but they've done it at **Pisgah National Forest** (1001 Pisgah Hwy., 828/877-3350 for the ranger station or 877/444-6777 for reservations), with campgrounds, nature trials, horseback riding, swimming, fishing, and picnic sites. At the ranger station, don't miss the "Cradle of Forestry in America" display describing George Vanderbilt's work with Dr. Carl Alwin Schenck to prevent clear-cutting and encourage area settlers to practice the new science of forestry.

It may be slightly far from your base (30 minutes north of Asheville), but **French Broad Rafting Expeditions** (828/649-0486 or 800/570-7238, www.frenchbroadrafting.com) offers some great white-water runs along the French Broad River. If you can push thoughts of *Deliverance* out of your head, take a calm-water raft trip and have a snack for around $45, or indulge in a full-day excursion that travels nine miles, rides over Class I–IV rapids, and includes lunch for about $70.

The **Biltmore Estate** (Hwy. 25, Asheville, 800/543-2961, www.biltmore.com)

Company Snapshot: Honda

In postwar Japan, Soichiro Honda was one of the first innovators to design a cheap and convenient way to get around. Having bought 500 two-stroke motors (war surplus), he slapped them onto pedal bikes. When those bikes sold out, Honda designed and built his own 50cc engine and placed it on a smoking new bike. Seriously. It was nicknamed the "Chimney" for its prolific exhaust. After starting the Honda Motor Company in 1948, he developed a 90cc version of the A-Type bike (called the "B-Type") and later introduced the "D-Type" in 1949. Since this was his company's first real motorcycle, the fulfillment of his quest sparked Honda to nickname it "The Dream."

is beyond description. It took six years, 11 million bricks, and a thousand workers to build George Vanderbilt's estate. His humble abode encompasses 250 rooms, 65 fireplaces, 43 bathrooms, 34 bedrooms, and three kitchens, covering more than four acres of floor space. Pay $39 to get in, and then rent a taped tour and marvel at the mansion's magnitude, unique craftsmanship, painted ceilings, unusual furnishings, and family history. Even the stables are as large as a subdivision. Afterward, you can score some free wine from a tapped barrel in the winery. You may assume this'll be just a home tour, but trust me, it's far beyond anything you can imagine.

Shopping

You've got to love a place where the inventory didn't roll off an assembly line. Here since 1924, the **Curb Market** (221 N. Church St., 828/692-8012) is the place to stock up on great North Carolina goods like blueberry jam, pickled squash, relishes, jellies, chow-chow, moonshine syrup and cakes in a jar, and walking sticks. Every item is locally grown, homemade, or handcrafted by Henderson County residents. Call ahead for shopping days.

There are few items at **JRD's Classics and Collectibles** (222 N. Main St., 828/698-0075, www.jrdclassics.com) that you could bring home on your bike, but you've got to see it regardless. The store is loaded with vintage game room collectibles and accessories: jukeboxes, barber poles, pinball machines, and gas pumps, all cleaned and restored by the hyperfocused owner.

Blue-Plate Specials

Days Gone By (310 N. Main St., 828/693-9056), a century-old soda fountain and drug store, has preserved its embossed tin ceiling, along with a collection of straw dispensers, milkshake mixers, pie carousels, and hand-dipped ice cream. Remember grabbing a hamburger and shake after school? Kids still do it today. Open for breakfast and lunch.

Renee Ellender was raised down in Louisiana and incorporates her mother's recipes from Bayou Terrebonne to whip up a mess of gumbo, jambalaya, red beans and rice, po' boys, and other south Louisiana dishes at **Cypress Cellar** (321C N. Main St., 828/698-1005). A full bar helps wash some of that there cayenne pepper down, Antoine. Stop here for lunch or dinner.

If you want to get gussied up ("proper casual") and have a hankering for cuisine instead of food, head to **Expressions** (114 N. Main St., 828/693-8516). Dinner entrées include filet mignon, herb-crusted rack of lamb, chicken breast stuffed with apples, raisins, and pecans, and sautéed Atlantic salmon. The wine menu boasts about 230 labels; enjoy one in the upstairs wine bar, which presents a tapas menu and flights of wine.

Watering Holes

Hendersonville's not a partying town, but **Hannah Flannagan's Pub** (300 N. Main St., 828/696-1665) tries to help, featuring 100 beers, Irish specialties, and live entertainment. This is a friendly place within stumbling distance of your room. I don't like riding after dark, but **Shindig on the Green** (828/258-6107) is worth the evening ride down to Asheville. Along about sundown on Saturdays between July 4 and Labor Day, big circle mountain dancers, cloggers, ballad singers, storytellers, bluegrass musicians, and old-time string bands gather to play down-home, red-hot-and-blue music. If you play, grab a guitar and join a pickup band.

Shut-Eye

I-26 rolls past a few miles outside of town, so Hendersonville has its share of chain hotels and several large inns.

Motels and Motor Courts

Cottages are always a great find, although some require a minimum stay of three nights during peak season. But that's not a bad thing, considering the per-night rate drops for three nights and drops even more for weekly rentals—and you get added time to use H-Ville as your mountain base. Just five minutes from Main Street, **Rose Cottages** (1418 Greenville Hwy., 828/693-7577 or 888/817-7229, www.rosecottagesnc.com, $85 and up) has 11 completely furnished cottages. Each has a front porch, heat and A/C, a kitchenette, phone, dining area, and cable TV. The cottages sit in seven acres of woods. Down the road, the 14 large and impressive **Cottages of Flat Rock** (1511 Greenville Hwy., 828/693-8805, www.towntooter.com/cottages, $75–125) also offer weekly rates. In a pastoral setting less than a mile from downtown Hendersonville, **Bent Oaks** (1522 Greenville Hwy., 828/693-3458, $55 one-bedroom, $150 two-bedroom in season) has 12 cottages to choose from.

Chain Drive

A, C, E, G, J, L, S, U

Chain hotels are in town, or within 10 miles. See cross-reference guide featuring phone numbers and Web addresses on page 514.

Inn-dependence

The **Waverly Inn** (783 N. Main St., 828/693-9193 or 800/537-8195, www
.waverlyinn.com, $139–250) is just a few blocks from downtown. The owners
will kindly put your bike under cover, feed you a breakfast the size of Montana,
and lure you to the five o'clock social hour to enjoy free drinks and mingle
with fellow guests on the verandah. Room rates vary greatly depending on the
season, but all are country comfortable. Innkeepers John and Diane Sheiry are
as nice as can be—and John can tell you about great back roads even moonshiners don't know about. Right next door, the 17-room **Claddagh Inn** (755
N. Main St., 828/697-7778 or 800/225-4700, www.claddaghinn.com, $80–
140) is similar in size and style to the Waverly, with a full breakfast, afternoon
wine and sherry, and rooms that straddle the border between country and
formal. Away from town, **The Lodge on Lake Lure** (828/625-2789, 800/733-
2785, www.lodgeonlakelure.com, $149–250) recalls a day in the Adirondacks.
This former state troopers' retreat has been transformed into an idyllic escape overlooking Lake Lure and Bald Mountain. Vaulted ceilings, hand-hewn
beams, evening lake cruises, and a hearty mountain gourmet breakfast await
you. Good as gold.

Resources for Riders

Blue Ridge Parkway Run

North Carolina Travel Information

North Carolina Bed & Breakfasts—800/849-5392, www.ncbbi.org
North Carolina Travel and Tourism—919/733-8372 or 800/847-4862,
 www.visitnc.com
North Carolina Historic Sites—919/733-7862
North Carolina National Forests—828/257-4200,
 www.cs.unca.edu/nfsnc
North Carolina Parks and Recreation—919/733-7275 or 919/733-4181,
 www.ncsparks.net

Local and Regional Information

Blowing Rock Chamber of Commerce—828/295-7851 or 800/295-7851,
 www.blowingrock.com
Blue Ridge Parkway Information—828/298-0398, www.nps.gov/blri
Hendersonville Information Center—800/828-4244,
 www.historichendersonville.org
Mount Airy Chamber of Commerce—336/786-6116 or 800/948-0949,
 www.visitmayberry.com
Mount Airy Visitors Center—800/576-0231

North Carolina Motorcycle Shops

Boone Action Cycle—8483 Hwy. 421 N., Vilas, 828/297-7400,
 www.booneactioncycle.com
Dal-Kawa Cycle Center—312 Kanuga St., Hendersonville, 828/692-7519,
 www.dalkawa.com
Gene Lummus Harley-Davidson—2130 U.S. 70, Swannanoa, 828/298-
 1683, www.genelummush-d.com
Harper Cycle and Marine—1108 Spartanburg Hwy., Hendersonville,
 828/692-1124, www.harpercycle.com
Schroader's Honda—220 Mitchell Dr., Hendersonville, 828/693-4101,
 www.schroaders.com
Stamey's Cycle Center—836 Kimberly Ln., Boone, 828/264-5847
Worth Honda-Kawasaki—600 W. Pine St., Mt. Airy, 336/786-5111

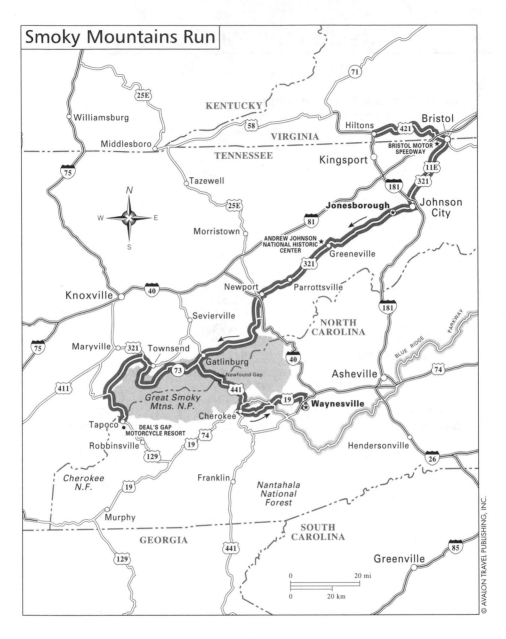

Smoky Mountains Run

Route: Jonesborough to Waynesville via Greeneville, Newport, Gatlinburg, Cherokee

Distance: Approximately 300 miles (with side trips); consider six days with stops.

•Day 1—Jonesborough •Days 2–3—Travel/Gatlinburg •Day 4—Deal's Gap Run •Day 5—Smoky Mountain Travel •Day 6—Travel/Waynesville

First Leg: Jonesborough to Gatlinburg (85 miles)

Second Leg: Gatlinburg to Waynesville (70 miles)

Helmet Laws: Tennessee and North Carolina require helmets on all riders.

Smoky Mountains Run

Jonesborough, Tennessee to Waynesville, North Carolina

An impressive ride starts in a friendly country town that should have been the capital of what could have been a state, then passes through a most incredible park at the epicenter of hundreds of miles of motorcycle-perfect roads, and then into a satisfyingly fine mountain town. Try to travel just before or in the few months after summer.

Jonesborough Primer

It's picturesque and certainly is different from most of America's homogenized communities, but just think if things had *really* gone Jonesborough's way. Back in 1769, folks began thinking that the tail section of what's now western North Carolina would actually be better off if it were a free state separated from what's now the northeastern edge of Tennessee. With that, they embarked on the "first free state" project to create a 14th state called Franklin. In the middle of it all would be the burgeoning capital of Jonesborough.

Things came together in 1784, when the North Carolina government agreed to let the region go and save itself the burden of taxing and providing for the region. That's when the folks of Franklin realized that in the middle of the Revolution, *they* had to deal with taxes, infrastructure, defense, and advancing their quest for statehood. By 1789, the plan fell apart, Vermont became the 14th state, and North Carolina legislator Willie Jones never did see his namesake hamlet grow up to be a state capital like Pierre, Montpelier, or Frankfort. Instead, the town sat back and waited. Eventually, its location made it the gathering place for yarn spinners and tall-tale tellers, and it's now the permanent site of the International Storytelling Center and an annual storytelling festival. All in all, it's pure Americana in a well-presented village and a neat place to kick off an extraordinary ride.

On the Road: Jonesborough

As you sift through this book, you'll notice that in some places I suggest getting out of town and taking a country ride; while in others, I lean toward hanging out in the historic district. That's what you should do here. Although Bristol—the birthplace of country music and site of a great NASCAR track—is only about 30 minutes up the road (see *Side Trips*), you should be able to wring a full day out of Main Street's stores and the tales spun at the International Storytelling Center.

If you rode in from Johnson City on Highway 11E and entered the town via Boone Street, you've already passed the visitors center, where the staff is as helpful as the wealth of paperwork it provides. Stock up here on guides to downtown and storytelling events, and base your day around getting into the slow-paced pleasures of the South. When you ride onto Main Street, the focal point of the commercial center is the 1913 Washington County Courthouse. Sitting in silence, it keeps an eye on things … the rusted tin roofs, the chipped mortar on historic brick buildings, and the curious travelers who found they could ditch the highway to discover a cool little town.

There are no parking meters here, but parking is restricted to two hours before you have to move. I'm not sure how tightly that's enforced, since other transgressions are overlooked. I learned this when speaking with a genuinely kind and helpful woman who owned a local restaurant. Noticing my enthusiasm for the people and the culture of the area, she confided, "Come back t'morrah, I'll bring you some moonshine. I know people what have steels …."

What a country.

Pull It Over: Jonesborough Highlights
Attractions and Adventures

While the center of the town's commerce are the shops of Main Street, the center of Jonesborough culture is the **International Storytelling Center** (116 W. Main St., 423/753-2171 or 800/952-8392, www.storytellingcenter.com), the only facility on earth devoted exclusively to the power of storytelling. The center includes a 200-year-old country inn, a 14,000-square-foot education building, and a surrounding three-acre park.

Having grown up on movies and television, I was amazed to listen to storytellers and find that even minus lights, lasers, motion, or music, the simple art of talking kept me completely entertained. You may have the same reaction. There are appearances by visiting storytellers in residence (call for schedules), and if you're inspired to learn the craft yourself, there are books and tapes on how to spin a yarn. To hear fledgling storytellers weave stories at a pickup session, drop by and listen to the locals at the visitors center any Tuesday evening at 7:30.

Shopping

Too many stores that sell glass objects push a heapin' helpin' of crappy crystal unicorns and clowns, but the **Jonesborough Art Glass Gallery** (101 E. Main St., 423/753-5401, www.jonesboroughartglass.com) has some pretty impressive pieces of glass as art—whether it's a glass globe, vase, or neon piece. Check out the oversized metal butterfly chair that, unlike its '60s counterpart, actually looks like a butterfly.

I like **Mill Spring Mercantile** (107 E. Main St., 423/913-2700) for several reasons, most significantly because it uses the word "mercantile." This old-fashioned store sells old-fashioned stuff like beeswax candles and Hog Wash Laundry Treatment, a huge block of soap that's guaranteed to swab out blood and grass stains. If you'll think you'll be laying your bike down, pick up a few bars.

One of the better antique marts I've seen is the cleverly named **Jonesborough Antique Mart** (115 E. Main St., 423/753-8301). It features two levels of Southern folk art and memorabilia that you'd expect to see either at a 1930s service station or in Jed Clampett's cabin. Another plus is the wealth of *Andy Griffith Show* souvenirs, books, trading cards, shirts, and license tags—and lord knows the world needs more Andy stuff.

Then there's the **Celtic Cupboard** (121 E. Main St., 423/913-2889), which isn't strictly Irish (it sells kilts), but authentic enough that if you want a nice Claddagh ring, harp music CDs, cookies, books, and Irish blessings, this is the place to find it.

Blue-Plate Specials

There are several restaurants along Main Street, although none offer the kind of big food I love in the South. To get that kind of grub, head a few miles northwest of town to the **Harmony Grocery Store** (1181 Harmony Rd., 423/348-8000). Housed in an old general store, it serves up New Orleans–inspired dinners like fried alligator, crawfish pie, sausage and seafood gumbo, crawfish etouffée, and jambalaya.

Back on Main Street, the food's fancy or spare (and one of these places is where the proprietor offered to fetch me a jar of moonshine). Here are a few to choose from: **Cranberry Thistle** (103 E. Main St., 423/753-0900) is where the locals hang out for breakfast, lunch, and dinner, all homemade and delicious. The deli café is kind of slapdash, with different size tables and mismatched chairs and a small stage for storytellers and musicians. Kind of like a hillbilly Greenwich Village.

Bistro 105 (105 W. Main St., 423/788-0244) is a smart-looking, casual eatery that serves homemade salads, pasta, sandwiches, and entrees like Thai stuffed chicken, veal chops, and cedar plank salmon. The **Main Street Café** (117 W. Main St., 423/753-2460) is another simple restaurant serving fresh sandwiches and salads and homemade soups. Back near the entrance to town, **The Pizza Parlor** (416 E. Jackson Blvd./Hwy. 11E, 423/753-8862) is a small, family-run place that serves a basic lineup of pizzas and spaghetti and subs. Nothing fancy at all, but hot food at a good price. And yes, that's really its name.

Watering Holes

Washington isn't a dry county—but it's close to it. In the last election, voters approved "liquor by the drink," which means you can at least grab a beer or wine at a Jonesborough restaurant. But since finding a good place to grab a brew is as hard as the cider here, you may want to head up to Johnson City, about 10 miles north. Riders have discovered **Kemosabe's Road House** (2926 Boones Creek Rd., 423/282-3830), just off I-181. It's an old barn converted into a bar, with live blues and classic rock, pool tables, beer, wine, and mixed drinks.

Shut-Eye

There are no chain hotels in Jonesborough, but there are a few about five miles up the highway in Johnson City.

Chain Drive
A, E, L

Chain hotels are in town, or within 10 miles. See cross-reference guide featuring phone numbers and Web addresses on page 514.

Inn-dependence

Right in the heart of town is the **Eureka Inn** (127 W. Main St., 877/734-6100, www.eurekajonesborough.com, $119–129). The 1797 building has been brought up to speed with voice mail, data ports, soundproof insulation, private baths, and cable—all balanced by period antiques in each of its 15 rooms. A continental breakfast is included. If you really, really like old stuff, the **Hawley House B&B** (114 E. Woodrow Ave., 423/753-8869, www.hawleyhouse.com, $85–150) is the oldest building in Tennessee's oldest town. Don't expect a Westin; this is an 18th-century log structure, restored with antiques and folk art. The rooms, each with a private bath, overlook a meadow or the village.

Side Trip: Bristol, Virginia

Long before roots music took root, I was listening to the greatest hits of the '20s and '30s. Along the way, I was introduced to the contributions of the incredible Carter Family of Maces Springs, Virginia. On his sales calls, fruit tree salesman Alvin Pleasant (A. P.) Carter would roam through the hills of the Clinch Mountains and hollows of Poor Valley, where he'd hear the songs mountain families had passed down through generations. The songs haunted him. When he got home, A. P. would transcribe the music and lyrics as best he could recall. Then, in August 1927, A. P. caught a newspaper ad seeking musicians to audition for a Columbia Records representative who was traveling to nearby Bristol. With his wife, Sara, playing autoharp and her 18-year-old cousin Maybelle on guitar, the Carter Family played their music in a warehouse-turned-recording-studio. Within minutes, the three had created the foundation of country music, with songs like "Wildwood Flower," "Will the Circle Be Unbroken," and "Worried Man Blues."

The legendary Bristol Sessions also produced the Singing Brakeman Jimmie Rodgers, but that's not the only reason you should visit Bristol. Only about 30 miles north of Jonesborough on Route 11E, Bristol's also unique because its Main Street straddles the state line—the south side's in Tennessee, and the north side's in Virginia. Each side has some cool stores. Ride here because Hamburger Hamlet is where Hank Williams ate his last meal before dying in the backseat of a car on New Year's Day, 1953. Ride here because on Mondays, Tuesdays, and Thursdays you can head to a plaza on Main Street for free concerts by local bluegrass musicians. Make the ride because racers at the **Bristol Motor Speedway** (151 Speedway Blvd./Rte. 11E, 423/989-6901, www.bristolmotorspeedway.com) are tearing around the short track—"The Fastest Half-Mile in the World"—and amateurs in cars and on bikes are ripping up the drag strip with Tuesday and Thursday "Street Fights."

It's a cool town, and the locals are more than helpful, especially the folks at the **Bristol Chamber** (423/989-4850, www.bristolchamber.org), who'll guide you every step of the way. One last tip: The absolute best thing to do if you're ready for a great ride and great music is to take the supremely fantastic Highway 58/421 West to Hiltons to see the old Carter Family homestead. A short and indulgent 30-minute ride from Bristol, the landscape on the way looks suspiciously similar to Switzerland, and it made me very excited. If you time your ride for a Saturday, members of A. P. and Sara's family host a live 7:30 P.M. show at the **Carter Family Fold** (276/386-6054, www.carterfamilyfold.org). Since 1976, groups like the Corn Lickers, Zephyr Lightning Bolts, Slate Mountain Ramblers, and even Johnny Cash and June Carter have performed in an old barn adjacent to A. P.'s general store, playing traditional folk and bluegrass music the way the Carters did—right in the heart of the Clinch Mountains. Cost: $5. Memories: Priceless.

On the Road: Jonesborough to Gatlinburg

The road out of Jonesborough isn't the best way to begin a long country ride, and it took a little longer than I expected to get into the mojo of a good ride, but there you go.

Jump onto Highway 11E/321 heading south. About four miles later, the four-lane releases itself into nice pastureland, where there are some mountains, small country roads, and an old flea market. It's good, not great, but every so often there are intriguing points of interest—such as what lies a few miles ahead in the town of Greeneville. You'll have to ride through the ugliness of Highway 321 to reach the **Andrew Johnson National Historic Center** (College at Depot St., 423/638-3551, www.nps.gov/anjo).

Johnson, who came to Greeneville at 17, lived in the home here between 1851 and 1874, and he became president after the death of Abraham Lincoln. Despite history's verdict that he was a marginal president, my take is that the impeachment was based on politics, not cause, and Johnson deserves credit for working his way up from being a tailor to becoming president. He was also the only Southern senator to remain in Congress at the outbreak of the Civil War, managed to withstand the politically motivated attack, and loved the nation enough to become the only former president to return and serve in the U.S. Senate.

Good things come to those who wait, and they'll come when you exit Greeneville. Within a few miles, you'll get into some fancy countryside, with barns and hills and bales of hay. Since 321 is sparsely traveled, the freedom to be alone is wonderful, and it is enhanced when you cross the Olucktucknee River to find a modern country store and gas station on the other side. When you stop for gas and a break, you'll almost certainly talk to locals who will see your bike and ask "where you been" and "where you headed."

For now, you're going onto a great road, where you'll spot the first of many "See Rock City" signs. As you ride along, you may feel blessed that you're out alone in the country. Several miles ahead, you'll find Parrottsville, where side streets are named after birds (Cockatoo Avenue, Canary Drive, Bluebird Circle, and so on), and a small market is available if you need a sandwich or a cracker. Leaving town across the Valentine Bridge, you'll press on through increasingly familiar scenery before being taken aback by the clutter of Newport, which, aside from a Cracker Barrel just past I-40, you can bypass to continue on 321 South toward Cosby.

After the flare-up of Newport, you are back into the wide-open spaces again, in sight of the Smoky Mountains and 1950s-era signs still pitching hillbilly souvenirs, cabins for rent, and cheap tourist attractions. The other advantage is the distinct California feel that arrives in the greenery of the approaching mountains, and the Yosemite-like sweeps and turns in the valleys. Just past the **Smoky Mountain Visitors Center** (423/487-2800), where you can stop to pick up some Gatlinburg brochures and coupons and see a display of a still and jars of moonshine, 321 takes a sharp right—and so should you.

The road rides along the periphery of the northwest corner of Great Smoky Mountains National Park, and it reveals just a hint of what you'll see in the next few days. It's private, narrow, calming, and a pleasure to ride—but eventually, the road becomes four lanes, and you'll know that you're getting close to the center of Gatlinburg, just in time to rest your bike and yourself.

Gatlinburg Primer

Fudge shops and wax museums didn't create Gatlinburg. It's here because the Smoky Mountains are here, and the part that has been preserved is part of the most visited national park in America. Why not? There are more varieties of trees here than in all of the European continent. There are animals found here that are found no place else on earth. The elevations range from a modest 840 feet to an impressive 6,643 feet along the Appalachian mountain chain that runs clear up to Canada. In this one park are ecosystems that include wetlands, grassy balds, spruce forests, cove hardwoods, and the only remaining old growth forest east of the Mississippi.

That's why it's hard to believe that, not too long ago, it was getting razed all to hell. But in the mid-1920s, some folks realized clear-cutting and logging were destroying what God had created and started a drive to protect the region. With support from a variety of sources, they managed to raise enough money and public interest to buy about 800 square miles of forest and save it. Soon families that lived here, well out of the way of civilization, were picked up and moved out, taking with them their few possessions, folk tales, and mountain music. In 1940, Franklin D. Roosevelt arrived to dedicate what would become America's most popular national park. Sadly, what FDR giveth, GWB is taking away, as environmental safeguards that protected this and other parks for decades are being overturned for political payback.

See it before it's razed all to hell.

On the Road: Gatlinburg

When you leave town, you'll ride across the Smokies on Highway 441 and see spectacular sites along the way—but now you have to choose between seeing even more spectacular roads or playing hooky by playing tourist. Either way is fine, and some tourist choices are detailed below. For now, however, consider that there are more than 270 miles of roads in the park. That should convince you to plan a perfect day trip starting and ending in Gatlinburg after riding down one of the most popular motorcycling roads in America.

From the center of town, head east on 441 into **Great Smoky Mountains National Park** (865/436-1200, www.nps.gov/grsm). A pullout by the welcome sign makes a great backdrop for you and your bike, and the **Sugarlands Visitors Center** (865/436-1291), about a mile ahead, is a definite first stop. You'll see a wonderfully written and produced film about the history and nature of the park, as well as a topographical map that gives you a miniature sense of what you're about to encounter. Free road maps, a park newspaper, and information on camping, fishing, horseback riding, and ranger-led tours are all available.

The park straddles the Tennessee–North Carolina border and sits diagonally on that line, so directions may not mean much here. Just leave the visitors center and turn right on Little River Road (Hwy. 73) toward Cades Cove. En route, you'll ride immediately into cool forests that slide along the banks, where the rough textures of the rock and wide sweep of clear water lead you down the road.

After 14 miles of this slow, steady, and magical run, you'll reach an intersection where 73 forks right towards Townsend. Skip it for now, and head straight on Laurel Creek Road and into Cades Cove, the valley where the settlers lived before they were resettled. If you time your ride for off-season or quite early in the morning, you'll enjoy a peaceful one-way tour, stopping at the preserved primitive churches and cabins and overlooks along the way. Be warned that in peak season, the single-lane road is packed like an L.A. freeway, and your patience will cool as your bike overheats. But if you can see it in its natural, vehicle-free state, you'll witness a pristine paradise.

After Cades Cove, double back to 73, hang a left, and follow it to 321. A few miles ahead on your left is the Foothills Parkway, which is mostly overlooked by most motorists, although motorcyclists have discovered it's another superb road. It whirs along the Little Tennessee River or rides atop the spine of a mountain chain for 18 miles before it dumps you out at Calderwood Lake. From here, turn left onto 129, and you'll be riding toward your rendezvous with destiny.

Now you've reached what some folks call the **"Tail of the Dragon"** (www.tailofthedragon.com), the start—or finish—of the legendary motorcycling road that offers, for your personal pleasure and amusement, 318 curves in 11 miles. I was so focused on not dying, I lost count after 293. If you suffer from a heart condition, bad back, or are pregnant, do not ride this attraction. Otherwise, gird your loins, check your shocks, and head for the hills. Chances

a roundabout road sign in the Great Smoky Mountains

are you'll ride slowly and sensibly, distracted only by the multiple curves that block your path and the constant drone of a nearby sewing machine factory. This whirring noise is actually the whining, high-pitched, two-stroke scream of sports bikes racing to complete the entire 11 miles in as little as—believe it or not—*10 minutes*. I can't even put on my boots in 10 minutes.

About 1.5 miles over the North Carolina border, at the junction of Tennessee Route 129 and North Carolina Route 28, the ride slithers to a close in Tapoco at the **Deal's Gap Motorcycle Resort** (828/498-2231 or 800/889-5550, www.dealsgap.com). At the general store/hostel here (rooms are $49), every rider in the Southeast congregates, picking up snacks and food and sharing tales of their rides. On the other side of the parking lot, at the "Tree of Shame," are bits of scrap metal salvaged off wrecked bikes, hung here as a caution for others and a backhanded tribute to riders stupid enough to speed.

After reaching Deal's Gap, only the time of day will determine which way you'll ride to return to Gatlinburg. If you have time, you may head off on Route 143 West and see the scenic Cherohala Skyway, or go full bore and make the complete circle tour to return via Highway 441. Otherwise, you can look forward to turning around and revisiting the same roads you rode on the way up. Not a bad deal, Deal's Gap.

Pull It Over: Gatlinburg Highlights
Attractions and Adventures

There are more activities in and around Gatlinburg than there are in the entire rest of the state of Tennessee. Most are along the main strip through the center of town, which is an attraction in itself, and you'll find brochures and info about most in racks at local businesses. My approach was like grazing at a buffet: I looked over the selections and picked the few that interested me most.

White-water rafting is huge here, and about 40 minutes from town via a different leg of the scenic Foothills Parkway is **Rafting in the Smokies** (865/436-5008 or 800/776-7238, www.raftinginthesmokies.com). It has an armada of rafts and guides who navigate the Nantahala, Ocoee, Big Pigeon, and Lower Pigeon rivers—each of which offers different degrees of difficulty. If you haven't done this before, you've probably seen photos suggesting white-water rafting's a 10-mile stretch of exploding bursts of water. In reality, for the most part, the huge, swirling rapids appear only after drifting through a long stretch of placid, calm flats. Even so, the adrenaline shots will provide a thrill you won't soon forget. Here, and at other operations like **River Thunder** (800/408-7238, www.rollingthunderriverco.com); **Wildwater Ltd.** (800/451-

9972, www.wildwaterrrafting.com); and the **Nantahala Outdoor Center** (888/590-9268, www.noc.com), rates hover around $40 for a three-hour excursion, although some offer coupons in their brochures or online.

In the heart of town, half of **Ober Gatlinburg** (1001 Parkway, 865/436-5423, www.obergatlinburg.com, $9.50) is a huge $5.5 million Swiss-made gondola that sweeps up the side of the mountain to provide a generous aerial view of the valleys, national park, and the thousands of chalets pinned against the side of the hills. It's an impressive sight, and the narrator's info en route to the peak is alternately funny and informative. The downside is part two of the attraction, a tourist trap of fudge shops, an ice-skating rink, gift stores, and black bears slumbering inside empty swimming pools.

On the outskirts of Gatlinburg is the crowded city of Pigeon Forge, which brings to mind a trailer park with amusement rides. Its popularity is, in no small measure, due to Dolly Parton, the hometown gal who grew up, grew out, and came back to buy a failing amusement park and rename it **Dollywood** (865/428-9488, www.dollywood.com). Today the park is the state's top tourist attraction, and so impressed was I with Parton's business acumen that I completely forgot about her celebrity persona. The concept of the park is simple and satisfying, with an old-fashioned feel created by flume rides, thrill rides, a general store, the world's largest bald eagle rookery, a chapel that's actually used for Sunday services, and specialty shops like the "craft preservation schools" where artisans pass along their talents by teaching skills such as woodcarving, blacksmithing, and soapmaking.

Shopping

The core of downtown is like nothing else you've seen. Every inch of 441 is occupied by a gift shop, fudge shop, store, attraction, restaurant, motel—or a combination of all six. The three waterways (Roaring Fork, Baskins Creek, and the Little Pigeon River) that intersect town calm things down and make it tolerable. There are too many stores to recommend just a handful, so park your bike and wander up one side of the street and down the other, and find whatever flops your mop.

Blue-Plate Specials

There are a billion chain restaurants in Gatlingburg and Pigeon Forge, but since you already know the items on their menus, you'll need to know what the independents serve: Meat. **Bennett's** (714 River Rd., 865/436-2400) is a huge, rustic restaurant with wood everywhere and readers' choice awards for best ribs, beef, pork, and chicken. Pig out at the endless soup and salad bar. **Howard's Restaurant** (976 Pkwy., 865/436-3600) has been in town since 1946. In addition to being located in a nice creekside setting, it serves items like Southern-fried catfish, trout, a 20-ounce T-bone for two, a 16-ounce signature steak, and gourmet burgers. For basic food and a beer, the **Smoky Mountain Brewery & Restaurant** (1004 Pkwy., 865/436-4200) is designed like a lodge and has a far-flung menu of wood-roasted steaks, pizzas, fresh breads, burgers, and handcrafted beers.

Watering Holes

Gatlinburg's a tourist town, so finding a juke joint in this family destination is tough. Chances are you'll find a bar and brew waiting at most restaurants along 441.

Shut-Eye

Nearly every type of lodging ever created is available in Gatlinburg. There are log cabins, Swiss chalets, motels, hotels, inns, and condos. It's safe to reserve a night at one of the chain hotels below, but if you're traveling in a group and have designs on a chalet or private home to use as a base while you explore the mountains, the best bet is to visit the Chamber of Commerce website (www.gatlinburg.com) for a comprehensive listing of prices, amenities, and locations. If you're based in the center of town, you can park your bike and walk.

Chain Drive
A, B, C, E, G, I, J, L, M, S, U, Y, CC

Chain hotels are in town, or within 10 miles. See cross-reference guide featuring phone numbers and Web addresses on page 514.

On the Road: Gatlinburg to Waynesville

Odds are you already dipped into the park the day before, but now you get to make the 40-mile run up and over the peaks and into North Carolina. There are pullouts and scenic vistas and spur roads and points of interest along the way, so don't anticipate clearing the park quickly. Give yourself at least half a day to fully appreciate the ride east.

As you enter the park, note this good stop: The markets adjacent to the service station—Parkway and Mountain—can provide you with provisions for today and the rest of your stay in Gatlinburg. And note this bad stop: Before you leave town, find the cheapest gas you can and fill up, or else the last-chance Texaco station at the park's entrance will gouge you without shame. Seriously.

Past the first two stops near the entrance—the park sign and the Sugarlands Visitors Center—just keep riding, and, within miles, the Smoky Mountains will welcome you. I know the term "the woods primeval" is thrown out a lot, but I can't help but throw it back in. From the road, you'll see quiet walkways laced into the woods, coaxing you to stop your ride and replace biking boots with hiking boots. The trails are threaded into the forests beside rocks painted with a sheen of algae and glistening water.

Like the trails, the road is not dangerous or demanding. It is perfectly designed to give you the opportunity to park your bike, appreciate nature, take some pictures, and return to the flow of the forest. The woods and water features are right, and the 35 mph limit slows you down long enough to gaze over the valleys and find steep ravines cut into the hills. Along the roadside and throughout the park are flame azaleas, rhododendrons, mountain laurels, fire pinks, trout lilies, yellow trillium, and 1,600 other types of flowers.

With no sheer drops and few switchback curves, the road lacks danger—but makes up for it with an abundance of slow curves and magnificent vistas. Keep in mind this is the most visited park in the U.S, so the key to fully enjoying all of it is knowing when to travel here. If you can ride in a shoulder season, when the roads are relatively empty, it's like visiting Disneyland during a private party.

Soon you'll get the hint you're rising in elevation, because your ears will pop and you'll start to see 500-foot drops off the side of the road. Near mile marker 14, you're at 4,837 feet; and when you get sidetracked at the pullout, you'll see that the road you rode seconds earlier is now more than 300 feet below. About five miles ahead, you rise to 5,046 feet, and you're sitting at the peak of Newfound Gap on the border of Tennessee and North Carolina. Buses and cars and vans are parked here, their passengers swarming the sidewalks and lookout point and pointing out thread-thin roads hundreds of feet below. Some through-hikers may stumble into view, just 371 miles into a six-month, 2,167-mile walk along the Appalachian Trail.

If you travel between late spring and early fall, the extraordinary sights of the gap will actually pale in comparison to what you'll see around the corner at **Clingman's Dome.** Actually, the dome is seven miles away, and the side road—if it's open—is at times even better than what you've already experienced. The rise in elevation, to a peak of 6,634 feet, delivers views that are farther, wider, and more impressive. From here, a half-mile trail will take you to the actual summit, and resting your bike here and relaxing with the views is a zen moment.

Coasting off the mountaintop, the landscape looks as if a sheet has been laid over the earth, and the folds and interlocking fingers of the ground seem quite flimsy and fragile. The rising ride to Newfound Gap takes only a slight amount of effort, and the drop in elevation into North Carolina will take even less. Tap it into neutral, and for mile after mile, all you hear is the steady spin of your tires on pavement. As I released the throttle and let gravity do the work, I realized roads rarely get any better for bikes. Like water flowing down a stream, I'd splash against a curve, wash into the next corner, and drift through the woods. It seemed end-less. As the bike coasted, I went out for a cup of coffee, read a magazine, came back to the bike, and it was still coasting. Few things can lift your spirits like this.

The park ends near the town of Cherokee, and there's the option of stay-ing here if you choose. A better choice, I'd argue, is tacking to the left off 441 and onto the Blue Ridge Parkway for another 26 miles to a far nicer stop in Waynesville. The only things that may stop you are if the BRP is closed, if it's getting dark, or if there's fog settling in. The first one will guarantee you can't ride it, and the second two are extremely hazardous and should convince you to bypass it. If you can go, you'll be on one of best and most scenic roads in America, en route to one of the nicest towns in western North Carolina. If not, head east from Cherokee on U.S. 19 through Maggie Valley for an alter-nate, and also satisfying, 26-mile ride.

Waynesville Primer

Growing up, I watched and read about fictional towns like Beaver Cleaver's Mayfield and Encyclopedia Brown's Idaville, and I always thought I'd want to live in places like that. Now I can just move to Waynesville. It's in the mountains, there's a fantastic and thriving downtown, there are lakes nearby, and wonderful roads lead to wide-open countryside. All of this started with Colonel Robert Love, a Revolutionary War veteran who donated land for the courthouse, jail, and public square. So, why aren't you visiting Loveville? The town's name was a tribute to his commanding officer, General "Mad" Anthony Wayne.

There's something about war and Waynesville that makes them go together. At the end of the Civil War, the last shots east of the Mississippi were fired at

Sulphur Springs, but lacking a satellite dish, no one knew the war had ended nearly a month earlier. After peace broke out, Waynesville residents took up agriculture for a century, shifted to industry after World War II, and in the mid-1990s, merged their town with neighboring Hazelwood to become a tourist destination based on a great climate, improved cultural environment, and the blessings of the Blue Ridge and Smoky Mountains.

On the Road: Waynesville

You've already ridden some of the nation's best roads just to get here, and if it was too late the previous day to ride the Blue Ridge Parkway, head west on 19 through Maggie Valley, and you'll find the entrance that'll lead back into the park. Another option is working your way over toward Hendersonville to sample a section of the Blue Ridge Parkway Run.

In fact, the appeal of Waynesville is having access to the great mountain and forest roads that surround you. Pisgah National Forest is just to the north and the east, Nantahala National Forest is to the south, and the Smoky Mountains are to the west. So, after you walk around downtown, head out of town to the motorcycle museum (below) and ask the locals to point you toward any of a dozen great rides in the area.

All of this will make even more sense if you arrive on a Sunday, when most of the places are closed, the proprietors are locked up in church, and all you can do is ride.

Pull It Over: Waynesville Highlights
Attractions and Adventures

About 15 minutes from Waynesville in Maggie Valley, motorcycle enthusiast Dale Walksler translated his passion for bikes into the significantly impressive **Wheels Through Time Museum** (828/926-6266, www.wheelsthroughtime.com, $12).

The museum features more than 250 rare, running condition antique bikes—30 of them pre-1916—as well as some mouthwatering motorcycle memorabilia. There are commercial, police and military bikes, hill-climbing bikes, racing bikes, Evel Knievel's jump bike, "one-offs," and a display that bridges early motorcycle technology to the advent of the H-D Knucklehead (which Walksler believes is the grandfather of the modern motorcycle). Automobiles get a fair shake, with 1930s classics represented by a 1929 Duesenberg, a 1915 Locomobile, a 1932 Clobes, and Steve McQueen's Cadillacs and Packards.

Shopping

The large spaces that served as department stores in the past are now Waynesville's galleries, boutiques, and sporting goods shops. Merchants have done a great job of bringing their town back, and roaming around downtown should take the better part of half a day, with a return visit for dinner that evening. While you're browsing, drop in at the **Waynesville Book Company** (184 Main St., 828/456-8062). It's one thing to travel to a place; it's another to understand why you're here and what happened before you showed up. To that end, the store's loaded with maps, trail guides, histories, and biographies about the people and events in the area.

Perhaps the best store of them all is the **Mast General Store** (63 Main St., 828/452-2101, www.maststore.com). A sister store of the original in Valle Crucis, this one found a home in a 1930s mercantile and still has the old cabinetry, oiled floors, a mezzanine, and barrels filled with old-fashioned candies. If you need anything—and I mean *anything,* from jams, frying pans, hats, and tents to dulcimers, dusters, gee-haw whimmydiddles, or an idiot stick, you'll find it all here.

Blue-Plate Specials

I've had the good fortune to ride to a lot of towns, and my good fortune improved when I found the restaurants in Waynesville. Give some of these a try: **Nick and Nate's** (111 Main St., 828/452-0027) offers a lunch buffet, as well as hand-tossed pizzas and handcrafted on-tap micros like Sweetwater Georgia Brown and Alley Cat Gaelic Ale.

Everyone knows about **Whitman's Bakery** (18 Main St., 828/456-8354). It's been packed every day since 1945, with customers sidling up to the counter to order sandwiches and pastries to go, while folks with more time order the same to eat in the neat little dining area. Lunch is served from 11 to 3, so time it right to hit the bakery and sandwich shop to order huge hamburgers, hot dogs, tuna melts, hoagies, stacked sandwiches, and daily specials. By the way, the bakery's 100 different breads are absent of premixes and preservatives.

The setting's so nice that its odd prices are so reasonable at **Wildfire** (190 Main St., 828/456-5559). Entrées range $11–16, including items like baconwrapped meatloaf, Maryland lump crab cakes, wild mushroom ravioli, and Asian chicken salads. Serving fine food in a setting that's sharp but not stuffy, this is a great place to relax and wrap up what was likely a full day of riding.

Watering Holes

As in Jonesborough, there's not a lot shakin' after dark, and most folks searching for nightlife ride out of town and into Maggie Valley, where coveted liquor licenses means places stay open past 9 P.M. If you're smart enough not to drink and ride, stay close to your base and drop in at **O'Malleys on Main** (172 Main St., 828/452-4228). It's half pub/half restaurant, with warm and inviting booths where you can order simple but filling fare such as Reubens, shepherd's pie, fish and chips, BLT wraps, barbecue, and chowders. It's open 'til 2 A.M., so you've got plenty of time to quaff a beer or imported ale while tossing darts or shooting a game of pool.

Shut-Eye

Motels and Motor Courts

When the Germans shift from creating super-engineered cars and bikes to running a motel, you can bet they'll do it with precision and cleanliness. That's what the owners do at the extremely clean and biker-friendly **Oak Park Inn** (196 Main St., 828/456-5328, www.oakparkinn-waynesville.com, $65–75), down the street from the shopping village. The 38 units are standard, and some come with a kitchenette—making this a good base for exploring the surrounding country.

Chain Drive

A, E, CC

Chain hotels are in town, or within 10 miles. See cross-reference guide featuring phone numbers and Web addresses on page 514.

Inn-dependence

If you crave privacy and serenity, have deep pockets, and don't mind the drive out of town, the **Yellow House Inn** (Plott Creek Rd. at Oakview Dr., 828/452-0991 or 800/563-1236, www.theyellowhouse.com, $175 and up) may be the best bet. Situated on five acres, the main house sits prominently over a sweeping lawn and offers seven large rooms and suites, with an annex in back with larger condo-style facilities. Innkeepers Donna and Stephen Shea are as supernice as this pleasing refuge.

Resources for Riders

Smoky Mountains Run

Tennessee Travel Information
Tennessee B&B Innkeepers—800/820-8144, www.tennessee-inns.com
Tennessee Road Conditions—800/858-6349
Tennessee State Parks—866/836-6757, www.tnstateparks.com
Tennessee Vacations— 615/741-2159, www.tnvacation.com
Tennessee Weather Conditions (Memphis)—901/544-0399

North Carolina Travel Information
North Carolina Bed & Breakfasts—800/849-5392, www.ncbbi.org
North Carolina Historic Sites—919/733-7862
North Carolina National Forests—828/257-4200,
    www.cs.unca.edu/nfsnc
North Carolina Parks and Recreation—919/733-7275 or 919/733-4181,
    www.ncsparks.net
North Carolina Travel and Tourism—919/733-8372 or 800/847-4862,
    www.visitnc.com

Local and Regional Information
Gatlinburg Chamber of Commerce—865/436-4178,
    www.gatlinburg.com
Great Smoky Mountains National Park—865/436-1200,
    www.nps.gov/grsm
Haywood County Chamber (Waynesville)—828/456-3021,
    www.haywood-nc.com
Historic Jonesborough Visitors Center—423/753-1010,
    www.historicjonesborough.com or www.jonesboroughtn.org
Sugarlands Visitors Center—865/436-1291

Tennessee Motorcycle Shops

Honda of Greeneville—808 Tusculum Blvd., Greeneville, 423/787-9200
Jim's Motorcycle Sales of Johnson City—1120 E. Market St., 423/926-
   5561, www.jimsmotorcyclesales.com
Smith Brothers Harley-Davidson—3518 Bristol Hwy., Johnson City,
   423/283-0422, www.smithbrosharley.com
Volunteer Cycles—103 South Blvd., Sevierville, 865/774-7170,
   www.volunteercycles.com
Yamaha Kawasaki of Johnson City—2804 W. Market St., Johnson City,
   423/926-5561

North Carolina Motorcycle Shops

Gene Lummus Harley-Davidson—82 Locust Dr., Waynesville, 828/454-
   0066, www.genelummush-d.com
Steve's Cycle Center—3302 Dellwood Rd., Waynesville, 828/926-0127
Waynesville Cycle Center—715 U.S. 23-74 Hwy., Waynesville, 828/452-
   5831, www.waynesvillecycle.com

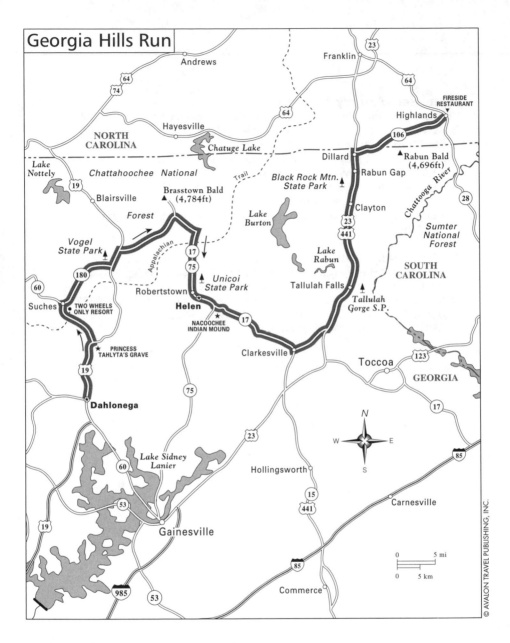

Route: Dahlonega to Helen, via Suches
Distance: Approximately 140 miles; consider four days with stops.
•Day 1—Dahlonega •Days 2–3—Travel/Helen •Day 4—Sidetrip to Highlands
Helmet Laws: In Georgia and North Carolina, helmets are required.

Georgia Hills Run

Dahlonega, Georgia to Helen, Georgia

Consider this a short and sweet research expedition into the mountains of northern Georgia, where the absence of large cities and superhighways have kept most visitors at a distance. Hidden in this region are some of the nation's best motorcycling roads, the gold-mining hometown of a long-forgotten national mint, a rural community resurrected as an Alpine village, and an upscale community perfectly suited as a base to reach even more spectacular paths in the mountains of North Carolina.

Dahlonega Primer

Dahlonega has one of America's saddest and most impressive town histories. In the early 1800s, the village was populated by Cherokee Indians and white settlers, who got along well and created a thriving community together. In addition to owning four million acres, the Cherokees had their own wealth, alphabet, newspaper, government, homes, and cabins, and had even established trade with Europe.

But in 1802, Georgia politicians made an agreement with the federal government. In exchange for trading land that Georgia possessed (which would later be called Mississippi and Alabama), the United States government would take back Cherokee land and give it to Georgia. A deal was struck, but not enforced until something incredible happened in 1828: A hunter searching the woods near Dahlonega discovered 98.46 percent pure gold, kicking off a gold rush that preceded Sutter's Mill by 20 years. Within weeks, 15,000 miners arrived by foot and horseback and wagon.

The meteoric rise in land value caught the attention of Georgia governor Wilson Lumpkin, who began to implement the old agreement and found an ally in President Andrew Jackson, who hated Indians. To prevent the government from seizing their land, Cherokee chief John Ross filed a lawsuit that reached the Supreme Court, which agreed that the Cherokee's land belonged to the Cherokees. The decision didn't affect Jackson, who, in essence, shrugged and asked who the Indians would find to enforce the court's decision.

In 1832, the state of Georgia began to parcel out the land in lotteries to "qualified buyers." Most of the Cherokees, obviously, chose to stay and remained here until 1838 when, foreshadowing the impact of the Third Reich, 16,000 Cherokees, Creeks, and Osage Indians from across the Southeast were rounded up. During the fall and winter, they were dispatched on the infamous and tragic Trail of Tears. On the journey to their new "home" in Oklahoma, 4,000 men, women, and children died.

And the gold? Only a fifth of Dahlonega's gold was ever found, and a federal mint that had operated here folded following the Civil War. After that, the town alternated between periods of boom and bust. Thanks to its roads, preservation, and awareness of its role in America's story, however, Dahlonega is now a enjoying a great moment in history. Start a ride here, and you can enjoy a great moment in Dahlonega.

On the Road: Dahlonega

Tomorrow you'll be on one of America's most exciting motorcycling roads. With that fringe benefit to sleep on, spend some time in the town that happens to be Georgia's most visited historic site. Here are three options to consider.

Swing by the **Visitors Center** (13 S. Park St., 706/864-3711), which has a map that generally pinpoints waterfalls within a 40-mile radius of the town. If this whets your appetite, consult the photo albums, which have both pictures and detailed directions to these stunning falls. Some are hidden off remote roads, so if you go this route, you're embarking on the equivalent of a waterfall safari.

Next option: When miners here heard there was gold in California, they split and left behind approximately 80 percent of Dahlonega's gold. If you have patience and luck, you can still find it in the creeks and hills. There's some information below on how to track it down, and brochures for local mines at the Visitors Center can lead you to gold in them thar hills.

Golden Rules

Aside from my random gold crowns, nose ring, tongue studs, and nipple clips, I don't really care for, or know much about, gold. The guide at the country museum got me wise to gold's malleability, durability, and value. For instance, take a one-ounce cube of gold, and you can pound it out into a sheet that's *1/250,000ths* of an inch thick. Or thin. It sounds more impressive when you visualize slicing a one-inch chunk of gold into a *quarter-million* even pieces. That's the way they do it when they refinish the capitol dome in Atlanta. Every 30 years, a procession of mule-drawn wagons carries 16 ounces of Dahlonega gold to Atlanta, where it's pounded out and laid atop the capitol dome.

The third and closest option is right across the street. In the center of the public square, the 1836 **Dahlonega Courthouse Gold Museum** (706/864-2257) is Georgia's oldest public building. Inside, the city has restored the building and added a museum ($4) that explains Dahlonega's gold-rich, humanity-poor history. What's really cool are the building's hand-formed, hand-fired bricks made from mud that came from Canes Creek. That creek was filled with gold, so if you look closely, you'll see glittering gold specks throughout the building.

Despite the built-in wealth of the walls, locals rarely treated the building with respect. At different points in its history, it housed restaurants, doctors' offices, produce markets, and livestock that rooted through the wooden floors and into the dirt below. When the building was threatened with demolition in the 1960s, the city bought it from the state for a whopping 10 bucks, and it's spent the last several decades treating it right. Ironically, worth more than the gold dust in the walls are the five rare sets of gold coins struck at the long forgotten Dahlonega mint. One set on display is worth $750,000, and an uncirculated mint set of Dahlonega coins sold for a cool *$7 million*. This and other facts about the town and its history are offered by helpful rangers and in an informative 23-minute movie starring local folks and gold miners.

Pull It Over: Dahlonega Highlights
Attractions and Adventures

As I mentioned above, less than 20 percent of Dahlonega's gold was discovered here before the miners headed west with the other 49ers. What does this mean to you as a citizen? It means you can try to find the rest of it. There are two mines: **Consolidated Gold Mines** (706/864-8473, www.consolidatedgoldmine.com) is about a mile outside of town. Head down 250 feet in a massive tunnel network that was part of the largest mine east of the Mississippi, and get a quick education on the engineering and mining techniques used by early miners. The **Crisson Gold Mine** (706/864-6363, www.crissongoldmine.com) is a fourth-generation open-pit gold mine that's waiting for major miners like you to strike it rich.

Appalachian Outfitters (2084 S. Chestatee, 706/867-7116, www.canoe-georgia.com) organizes canoe, kayak, and tube trips on the Chestatee and Etowah rivers. A canoe excursion on the Chestatee costs about $42 for a six-mile, 2.5-hour float down a stretch of river that's returned to its unspoiled, natural state since the heady days of the gold rush. On the Etowah, the route's eight miles, lasts about 3.5 hours, and costs around $52. Short on time? The tubing excursion is a quick 45 minutes.

Shopping

The center of town is the center of commerce, and dozens of shops frame the square. One of the most fun and diverse is the **Dahlonega General Store** (24 Public Sq. S., 706/864-2005). If you're looking for chunks of quartz sliced in half to reveal colored gems inside, if you want a bag of raw peanuts or jar of chow-chow, a cowboy hat, or a five-cent cup of coffee served on the honor system (which apparently works, because there are jars filled with nickels), you'll find it here.

Blue-Plate Specials

For huge food that'll satisfy your appetite through the next fiscal year, walk over to the **Smith House** (84 S. Chestatee St., 706/867-7000). In the basement of a recommended hotel, tank up on Southern fried chicken, baked ham, roast beef, fried okra, candied yams, fresh vegetables, yeast rolls, corn muffins, and desserts in an all-you-can-eat extravaganza.

If you want to fuel up before your ride, stop by the **Mountain Home Café** (125A E. Main St., 706/864-9216). This is a popular meeting place for riders. Want to get an early start? It opens at 5:30 A.M.

The Front Porch (72 Public Sq., 706/864-0124) is, as the name implies, a place where you can picnic on the porch, grazing on barbecue and baked chicken, Brunswick stew, knockwurst, and bratwurst. It's a good place to kick back, and the best view of the town is from the upstairs verandah.

Watering Holes

I love walking around small Southern towns after dark, and Dahlonega's as good as it gets. Wander over to the square, and you'll find a few cool combination bar-and-grills (bars aren't allowed here unless they serve food). If your age is skewed toward your teens, try **Buster's** (438 W. Main St., 706/864-2400), a sports bar that appeals to college students. Beer, of course, is the elixir of choice.

Wylie's (19 N. Chestatee St., 706/867-6324) is a restaurant on the square with a basement pub called Wylie's Down Under. It livens up the town with beer, wine, a full liquor bar, music, and trivia contests.

An upstairs joint is the **Back Porch Oyster Bar** (93 N. Public Sq.), with a tropical Key West feel. On the drinking deck are palm trees, surfboards, and fishing rods, and in addition to wine and pitchers of beer, you can slam back crab, catfish, and raw, steamed, or fried oysters.

If you can't scrounge up any moonshine, a mountain-brewed beer should suffice. At **Caruso's** (19B E. Main St., 706/864-4664), there's the **Dahlonega Brewing Company,** the only microbrewery between here and Atlanta. It brews three beers in-house and serves a total of 16 on tap. Try a pint of each.

The Crimson Moon (24 N. Park St., 706/864-3982, www.thecrimson-moon.com) would have seemed right at home in the '60s. You can hang out in the coffee house and listen to musicians jam on folk, bluegrass, Celtic, blues, country, and gospel tunes. Wines and bottled imports are served.

Shut-Eye

Chain Drive
E, G, L, CC

Chain hotels are in town, or within 10 miles. See cross-reference guide featuring phone numbers and Web addresses on page 514.

Inn-dependence
A few hundred feet from the square is the old and dependable **Smith House** (84 S. Chestatee St., 706/867-7000, www.smithhouse.com, $79 and up). In addition to the aforementioned all-you-can-eat Southern buffet, the hotel offers clean and comfortable rooms, and its proximity to town square makes it a safe bet. I like old hotels like this. It opened in 1884 and has been run by the same family since 1946. There's history in the halls, and a distinct sense of breaking the links to chain hotels. I also like the rates.

On the Road: Dahlonega to Helen

When I ride for hours and hours, I have a lot of time to think. In addition to developing a process of creating viable stem cells from razor stubble, one thought that flew past me in north Georgia was visualizing the state as a person. In my mind, I saw a barefoot kid with buck teeth and overalls, and I don't think I'm far off. Most of the state—including this region—is rural and remote but considerably pleasing. That's what you'll see on your way to Helen.

Before you get started, check your gas, your brakes, and your life insurance. After that, get ready for a road out of Dahlonega that was a favorite for moonshiners anxious to outrun G-men. You'll get this feeling almost immediately when you leave Dahlonega on 19/60 North. The scenic byway is enclosed and quiet and slow, and each curve stretches itself higher into the mountains. You're riding a wide, lazy arc into and over the mountains, although the upcoming million-plus hills and curves will give you and your gears a Jack LaLanne workout.

As the steep grades roll on and on and your ears pop with the change in elevation, your eyes will also adjust to the changes in lighting, which switches from shadows in the canopy roads to brilliant luminescence above an endless procession of Baptist churches.

At the junction where Highways 60 and 19 split, on your right is an Indian burial mound called **Princess Trahlyta's Grave** (yes, this is true), where, it's said, you can leave a stone and bring the princess good fortune in the afterlife. Let's hope it helps you, too. Stay to the left to follow 60 North. It won't be long, as you ride higher into the mountains and leap up and over hills and fly down and around corners, until you smell the crisp aroma of spruce, fir, pine, and burning brake pads.

Relief comes with a pullout at **Dockery Lake,** where you can slip off the road and rest yourself, your brakes, and your bike beside the wide open water. When you return to the business at hand, odds are the sharp curves will slice your speed in half, so you'll hover around 25 mph for several miles.

In the north Georgia woods, you'll careen up and around curves and dodge cars racing downhill, missing your mirror by inches. It's like a high and lonesome Bill Monroe tune, interrupted only by the sound of whining, stinging two-stroke racers flying past.

After crossing a section of the Appalachian Trail and passing Woody Gap, you descend the last few miles toward Suches. It's not a town for motorists, but as the home of the **Two Wheels Only Resort** (706/747-5151, www.twowheels only.com), it manages to seduce motorcyclists.

Sport bikers, trike riders, and random touring bikers gather at the combination hotel and restaurant to discuss where they're going and where they've been. It's a casual feel, more like a hostel, with riders sitting around picnic tables and on old lawn furniture or playing pool inside. The four rooms have queen beds and shared baths, but there are also campsites and a mobile home. Rates range from $12 (camping) to $45 (one bed), and a restaurant here serves breakfast, lunch, and dinner.

A hundred yards past Two Wheels Only, Highway 180 splits off to the right, and Helen is only 37 miles away. But since the road and landscape here are condensed and tangled, it'll still take you a few more hours to ride those 37 miles. For consolation, you're about to enter perhaps the most consistent confluence of righteous motorcycling roads in America.

Just ahead at the **Lake Winfield Scott Recreational Area** is Slaughter Creek, where a posted sign reads: "Sharp Curves Ahead Next Five Miles," which should trigger a sense of inner pleasure as well as the nagging question, "So what did I just pass?" But the sign speaks the truth; the turns ahead will elicit an involuntary mantra of (take your choice) "Oh, my God!," "Holy cow!," "Gee whiz!," and "Motherfu$%#@!" as you leap through an asphalt funhouse that's the blacktop equivalent of a county fair tilt-a-whirl. Sharp turns introduce you to Wolf Pen Gap. At an elevation of 3,260 feet, you're riding near the base of Blood Mountain in **Vogel State Park** (706/745-2628), a 233-acre section of the Chattahoochee National Forest. If you want to base yourself here, there are campsites and cottages and a 20-acre lake.

A continuation of black-topped pretzel twists prevent you from relaxing, and repetitive turns will demand your complete and utter attention. Even without guardrails, one thing you won't need to worry about is dropping hundreds of feet into the gullies or ravines below. The thick stand of pines and oaks above them would break your fall.

The paved punishment concludes at the return of Highways 19/129. Turn left onto the three-lane road and look for photogenic, old-fashioned **Sunrise Country Store & River Cabins** (706/745-5877, www.sunrisecabins.com), on your way toward 180 where the roads get back to what, in north Georgia, passes for normal. Although the magnificent Richard Russell Scenic Byway (Hwy. 348) will appear on your right, think about saving that for a circle tour when you're based in Helen. For now, stick with 180 as the road becomes more peaceful and easy as you ride toward **Brasstown Bald** (706/896-2556). At 4,784 feet, it's Georgia's highest mountain. A three-mile spur road leads to the visitors center, and a half-mile paved walkway leads to a peak that reveals a view of four states.

Soon you'll find Route 75, which drops through the slot and into Helen.

Because you've headed out of the hills, the last several miles lose some of their luster. The road crews here are doing the best they can with what they've got, though. Soon the road reaches Robertstown, where the meandering Chattahoochee River returns to view, dusted with a flotilla of pink inner tubes. These signs of low-budget tourism indicate you're getting close to Helen.

In fact, it's only a few blocks ahead. Have fun.

Helen Primer

In the middle of the north Georgia countryside exists an anomaly: a cute and photogenic Alpine village. Was this the result of generations of Swiss immigrants? No no no…. Before this Kodak moment developed, Helen was merely a rural redneck town where rat-ass pickup trucks parked outside cheap diners and grease-spattered service stations. When did rednecks find the Rhineland? Turn back the clock to 1969, when the city decided what would set Helen apart was a Swiss makeover. It covered up storefronts with chalet facades, ripped up sidewalks and replaced them with cobblestones, hung baskets of flowers from lampposts, and painted German folk symbols and images on the sides of buildings.

Was it effective? Just ask yourself if you'd be staying in Helen if the theme was Birmingham, rather than Bavaria. So, in the end, it's just a gimmick, a folly, a marketing ploy—but it's this kind of weirdness that makes a motorcycle tour memorable.

Bavaria? Zermatt? Salzburg? No, it's Helen, Georgia, which received a Rhineland facelift in the early 1970s. Cleetus, das ist wünderbar!

© NANCY HOWELL

On the Road: Helen

As you've probably discovered, there are few really distinct towns in America—ones that are unique and independent and determined to avoid the soul-killing homogenization that's ruined other towns. Granted, but Helen made an overt attempt to *be* different, it went and done it and it done good.

From Helen, I can recommend taking a 60-plus–mile one-way side trip to Highlands, North Carolina, which is detailed in *Side Trips*. Another option is getting out of town on an incredible day trip without fully retracing the route you took to get here. To take this second excursion, head a mile north on 17 to Robertstown. Highway 17 and 75 are one and the same, and you'll want to watch for Alt. 75, which forks to the left at the inner tube operations. Follow Alt. 75 West until you reach Highway 348, better known as the **Richard Russell Scenic Byway.**

Right away, this is exactly what a scenic byway should be: a great road scribbled across the land, alternately enclosed and quiet, then wide open and wild. You'll be riding about 50 miles one-way on this road, and the two-lane provides you with long, slow, stretching curves followed by steep rises and falls, and every so often, there will be a long straightaway that gives you a chance to catch your breath. Matching the road is the landscape, an amazing compilation of trees and textures, rocks and turns and sinuous twists of asphalt. Every so often, the road narrows and snaps you to attention, and then it expects you to negotiate a tricky corner, after which you'll slam through a canopy and be spat out into a hollow.

There's not much life along the way, just the requisite churches and a small town named Hood. Soon the byway bumps into a T at 180, giving you one of life's great choices: heading east to retrace the ride you took toward Brasstown Bald the day before, or heading west to reach 19/129 for a most incredible, tangled trip south to circle back to Helen. Like every part of your motorcycle tour, the choice is yours.

Pull It Over: Helen Highlights
Attractions and Adventures

Less than three miles northeast of town is **Unicoi State Park** (706/878-2201, www.gastateparks.org). At more than 1,000 acres, this is one of the state's most popular parks, featuring a 53-acre lake and tent and trailer campsites, as well as cottages. Nature lovers will find a full day's worth of diversions, with hiking and mountain-biking trails, fishing, swimming, and canoe rentals available.

A few miles north of Unicoi, in the middle of the Chattahoochee National Forest, is **Anna Ruby Falls** (706-878-3574, $2), a double waterfall created by the confluence of Curtis and York creeks. Fed by underground springs, rain, and snow, Curtis Creek drops 153 feet and York Creek 50 feet to form the twin waterfalls that spring from the rugged cliff face. For the best view, walk up a half-mile footpath to the base of the falls. If you fall in, just keep swimming, and you'll wind up in the Gulf of Mexico.

In Helen, a river runs through it, and that sparked a cool idea: Tube the Hooch. At the headquarters of the **Cool River Tubing Company** (706/878-2665 or 800/896-4595, www.coolrivertubing.com), you shed your clothes, keep on your swimsuit, settle back in an inner tube, and spend between 90 minutes and 2.5 hours floating down your choice of runs on the Chattahoochee River. Down the road, **Helen Tubing** (9917 Hwy. 75 N. Main St., 706/878-1082, www.helentubing.com) has similar inflatables and uses the same river. Its gimmick? Hot pink inner tubes.

Shopping

Who cares about the International Monetary Fund? In Helen, the economy's based on the fudge shop standard. There's a fudge shop for every resident, interspersed with gift shops and clothing shops and art galleries and souvenir stores. It's actually all right to wander around, crossing the bridge in the center of town and heading off down side streets to find some cool junk. One place you'll need your bike to reach is south of town down by the old mill stream: an actual working mill that, since you've probably never seen one, is pretty fascinating.

The **Nora Mill Granary & Country Store** (7107 S. Main St., 800/927-2375, www.noramill.com) has been grinding corn and flour and meal since 1876, and the folks here do a fine job of showcasing and explaining the intricacies of this seemingly simple process. What's more, crock pots contain samples of "Georgia ice cream," otherwise known as white speckled grits, and you can buy small cloth bags filled with mixes for muffins, pancakes, breads, waffles, and cornbread, as well as handmade crafts and other foods you'll want to pack for the road. The setting, along the Chattahoochee River, is peaceful and quiet, making this a nice place to relax while you let them grits settle. By the way, Nora Mill's a member of S.P.O.O.M. (Society for the Preservation of Old Mills). Associate members include Catherine Deneuve, G. Gordon Liddy, Lech Walesa, and Danny Bonaduce.

Across the street, **Nacoochee Village** (706/878-1800, www.nacoochee-village.com) is a collection of shops and attractions, including horse stables for trail rides (706/878-1600); the **Habersham Winery** (770/983-1973, www.habershamwinery.com), which includes a tasting room and views of the barrel and bottling rooms; and a candle company, a soda fountain, gift shops, restaurants, and **Unicoi Outfitters** (706/878-3083, www.unicoioutfitters.com,) which can help you off your bike and into the streams to angle for brown and rainbow trout. Join its Liar's Club and get called up to invitation-only special events and fly-fishing workshops.

When I'm on the road, I love finding small-town markets that seem to carry more merchandise than a warehouse. That's what's in store at **Betty's Country Store** (18 Yonah St., 706/878-2943), a superclean market that has goods and wares ranging from fresh meats in the deli to camping supplies, beer, candy, firewood, wine, candles, cards, walking sticks, steaks, coffee, cheese, cigars, souvenirs, fresh produce, jellies, and God knows what-all.

Unless you're towing a trailer, I doubt you'll manage to load up on all the junk you'd find at the **Flea Market** (9917 Hwy. 75 North/Main St., 706/878-1082). In addition to fresh apples and Kettle Korn, you can buy scrap metal, old stoves, broken buses, pickles, jellies, 58 different kinds of canned goods, and 100-pound bags of peanuts. You can't miss it. These are the same folks who have the pink inner tubes.

Blue-Plate Specials

Taking their lead from the town's theme, many restaurants specialize in German cuisine—if black bread and mashed-up pig intestines qualify for the title. One spot that's designed for tourists but should satisfy you is the **Troll Tavern** (Main St., 706-878-3117, www.trolltavern.com), which, logically, is found under the bridge. Perhaps the most popular restaurant in town, the tavern offers you the treat of sitting by the river to be served the requisite German dishes, as well as chicken, pasta, appetizers, and draught and bottled German beers (Becks, Erdinger, Frankenheimalt, Grolsch, Pilsner Urquell …). *Das ist ein wünderbar Bierkeller, mein Herr.*

For finer fare, the **Nacoochee Grill** (7277 S. Main St., 706/878-8020) is on the south end of town in the Nacoochee Village. The draw here is the live fired grill upon which the chefs are cooking your dinner: big T-bone steaks, frenched double-cut pork chops, full slabs of baby back ribs, grilled grouper or mahi mahi, and Szechuan glazed salmon steak, along with stovetop entrées like cornmeal-dusted trout, roasted duck, veal meatloaf, and, God, I'm hungry.

Watering Holes

There's a lot of German beer floating around, and you'll find it served at nearly every restaurant and steak house in town. At the Troll Tavern, for instance, and at the **Hofbrau Riverfront Hotel** (9001 Main St., 706/878-2248). There's a restaurant (Wiener schnitzel, Hungarian goulash, etc.), but in the Gallery Lounge, you can settle down on a couch, watch the river roll past, and sip on a beer or wine.

For a beer without the oompah, try **Scooter's Nightclub** (8600 N. Main St., 706/878-8048). They call it "Party Central," although the licensing authorities haven't confirmed this. Also on the map is **Big Daddy's American Tavern** (807 Edelweiss St., 706/878-2739).

Shut-Eye

There are more than 2,000 rooms in Helen, available in cabins, hotels, homes, motels, hotels, and campgrounds. The safest bet is any one of the chain hotels listed below. For a more special vacation, of course, choose an inn.

Motels and Motor Courts
If you're traveling in a group, there are dozens of cabin rentals available in town. Your best bet is checking Helen's website for a complete list. One of them at **Nacoochee Village** (7275 S. Main St., 706/878-2300 www .nacoocheevillage.com) has comfortable mountain cabins that are secluded and equipped with kitchens, back porches with rocking chairs, whirlpool tubs, and peace of mind.

Chain Drive
C, E, G, J, L, U, CC

Chain hotels are in town, or within 10 miles. See cross-reference guide featuring phone numbers and Web addresses on page 514.

Inn-dependence
Black Forest Bed & Breakfast (8902 N. Main St., 706/878-3995, www .blackforest-bb.com, $150 and up) is a motel-looking inn, but it goes the extra mile to include in-room whirlpool tubs and fireplaces. A full breakfast is served in the Bavarian dining room, or on an outdoor patio by a waterfall. As if transported from the Alps is the **Alpine Hilltop Haus** (362 Chattahoochee

St., 706/878-2388, www.alpinehilltop.com, $95 and up), an adults-only inn with private baths and fireplaces.

Side Trip: Helen to Highlands, North Carolina

As you ride south out of Helen, turn left on 17. You'll know you're on the right road because after you make that turn, in a pasture on your right is the **Nacoochee Indian Mound.** It's 190 feet long, 150 feet wide, and 20 feet high and contains the remains of an unknown number of Cherokees who lived nearby in their home of Gauxelle, which was visited by DeSoto in 1540.

This is a very short 60-mile ride, but the terminus is a cool little village where roads branch off to the most thrilling hills in western North Carolina. The weird and frustrating part of riding in this region, though, is this: If you decide to follow highways by the numbers, you'll get all sorts of messed up. On this quick trip, Highway 17 and 75 merge and split, then 17 is 115 and briefly 197.... Just remember Clarkesville, Tallulah Gorge, and Highlands, and you'll do OK.

So, stay on 17 and head east toward Clarkesville. As you ride southeast, the two-lane has some nice rolls and drops for several miles, with farms and their accompanying fragrances to keep you company. Take that road to the fringes of Clarkesville, where you'll pass the **Old Clarkesville Mill** (706/839-7500), or what's left of it. The bobbins have stopped bobbing and the looms have been silenced, and in their place stands a huge antiques mall that adjoins a bowling alley. Now take a moment and recall the last time you saw a combination like this. I'll take "never" for $1,000, Alex.

A few miles ahead is Clarkesville's town square, which, because it looks pretty cool, may persuade you to stop. Whenever you're ready, work your way over to Historic 441, the highway that was once the main road between Florida and Michigan. Now it seems to be the main road between nothing and nowheresville. Don't sweat that, hepcats, since the traffic that's moved over to the interstates has left you alone on a two-lane ride through some pleasing rural countryside. There's a lonely and strangely satisfying mood here, and you won't see much but scraggly pines and tractors, stacks of wood, gourds on the ground, and the sincere and gloriously named "Full Faith Tabernacle of the Four Square Holy Experience." This, you may recall, is where Donald and Ivana Trump jumped the broomstick.

As you dart down the blue highway, there's little to do aside from be satisfied knowing you're on your motorcycle and in the midst of a slow, satisfying tour. After about 10 miles, Historic 441 kicks you out onto U.S. 23, a four-lane

Welcome to Highlands!

On the surface, Highlands appears to be an upscale, reserved, and re-mote type of town. This impression was confirmed by a local tourism official who let me know that the local merchants *do not like motor-cyclists* and would prefer not being associated with this book. I took his advice and shied away, but when I arrived in Highlands, this myth was quickly and effectively dispelled by an overly hospitable merchant and others who seemed to have no problem with me or my bike. Unfortunately, I learned this too late to fully appreciate the town. That said, if you travel with friends or plan rallies or rides, I would be grate-ful if you would put Highlands on the map of your next thundering, rumbling road tour.

that cuts through Chattahoochee National Forest. While it doesn't have the beauty of the Smokies, the woodlands make things comfortable as you roll to-ward the day's first real attraction. On your right is **Tallulah Gorge State Park** (706/754-7970, www.gastateparks.org), an attraction since 1819. In fact, it was the most popular attraction in the state between the 1880s and 1912, when the town of Tallulah Falls and the waterfalls here were known as the "Niagara of the South." What changed? When Atlanta started to grow, the city needed more power, and that power came from dams created on the river. A series of dams were constructed, the river dried up, and tourism began moving away. The last straw was when the town of Tallulah Falls burned down in 1932.

They salvaged what they could. Today, the two-mile-long, 1,000-foot-deep crevasse is contained within 2,689 protected acres. While there's a free gorge overlook on the roadside to your right, if you have time and $4, you'll be far more satisfied riding up to the **Jane Hurt Yarn Interpretive Center** via a cool inclined road that's strapped to the side of a mountain. At the center, there are exhibits on the area's ecosystem and the old town's history, as well as a film showing a journey through the gorge.

Each day, the center issues free permits to 100 healthy visitors who are al-lowed to hike to the bottom of the gorge floor. If you gasp for breath when you bend over to adjust your Velcro shoe straps, skip it and just take the short walk on the North Rim Trail to Hawthorne Overlook. From here, you can see the upper gorge, including Tempesta and L'eau d'Or Falls, aka "Water of Gold" (by I. P. Frehley). Walk a little farther, and you'll get down to the tower that Karl Wallenda used while crossing the gorge via tightrope. There's a 341-

step staircase down to Hurricane Falls, which you can see from a suspension bridge swaying 80 feet above the rocky bottom.

Leaving Tallulah, if you had any doubts you were in the South, the innumerable trampolines in every yard around Lakemont will set you straight. The rural scenery, unfortunately, isn't spectacular, and that ailment continues through Mountain City and Dillard. All you have to do now is glance to your right and look for Highway 246/106 East toward Highlands. The road takes you through Sky Valley, a wonderful name that adds some pep to routine scenery. Occasionally, you get a lift from 10-degree grades, while the curves that follow are so soft you can ride with one hand. Be cautious of the mountains to your left, though, since they have a tendency to spit out a stream of gravel and pebbles that can knock your tires out.

Stay with the twists and turns, and soon you'll arrive in Blue Valley, which looks quite a bit like Sky Valley but offers the Osage Mountain Overlook for kicks. As you approach Highlands, the landscape begins to take on the low and fertile look of New England, and the illusion continues when you ride onto a picture-perfect Rockwellian Main Street where upscale shops and upscale shoppers come together. There's every reason to stick around (see *Welcome to Highlands!* sidebar), and you can pick up maps and information about places like Sunset Rock, a rock outcropping that overlooks Highlands and Horse Cove, at the **Highlands Visitors Center** (4th St., 828/526-2112, www.highlandschamber.org).

If you haven't eaten, I highly recommend the **Fireside Restaurant** (163 Main St., 828/526-3636), a large restaurant where the prices are as reasonable as the decor and the menu is impressive. Great Southern cooking and service. After lunch, you'll find what's on the outskirts that matters. For one of the most pleasing rides you can take, head toward the Callusaja Gorge, one of the rare places in America where I actually had to backtrack to see if what I thought I had seen was real. It was, and it was wonderful.

Leaving Highlands on 64 West, you'll enter a narrow string of a road that loves motorcycles. Quick, tight corners and ski-style moguls propel you through the woods to a pullout at Bridal Veil Falls, an interesting, but not overly impressive, waterfall. It's worth a stop to walk behind the fall and see what the back of water looks like.

As you continue on 64, the road gets so narrow you'll think you have to suck in your gut to navigate it. Turn on the power steering as you challenge the corners, then look and listen for **Callusaja Falls.** I snapped a quick mental image as I rode past, but it took nearly a full minute to contemplate what I had seen, and then I had to calculate the dynamics involved in safely turning around on a road that seemed as narrow as a sidewalk. I weighed the risks, considered the benefits, and backtracked before easing my bike onto the narrow shoulder with a view of the falls. Recent rains coupled with the spring thaw were delivering billions of megatons of fresh water over the side of the 250-foot falls, with cascading drops forcing it all to crash into the gulch. Finding it by chance had the same effect on me as if I had I discovered the Lost City of Gold.

Resources for Riders

Georgia Hills Run

Georgia Travel Information

Georgia Department of Tourism—800/847-4842, www.georgia.org
Georgia Road Information—404/635-6800
Georgia State Parks and Historic Sites—404/656-2770 or 800/864-7275,
    www.gastateparks.org

Local and Regional Information

Dahlonega-Lumpkin County Chamber of Commerce—706/864-3711 or
    800/231-5543, www.dahlonega.org
White County (Helen) Chamber of Commerce—706/865-5356,
    www.helenga.org
White County Chamber (Hills Region)— 706/865-5356,
    www.whitecountychamber.org

Georgia Motorcycle Shops

Cain's Custom Cycle—Hwy. 19 N, Dahlonega, 706/864-6124
Custom Cycles of Dahlonega—7101 Hwy. 19 N, Dahlonega, 706/867-
    9691
Gatortail Motorcycles—670 Garnet School Rd., Dahlonega, 706/864-9251

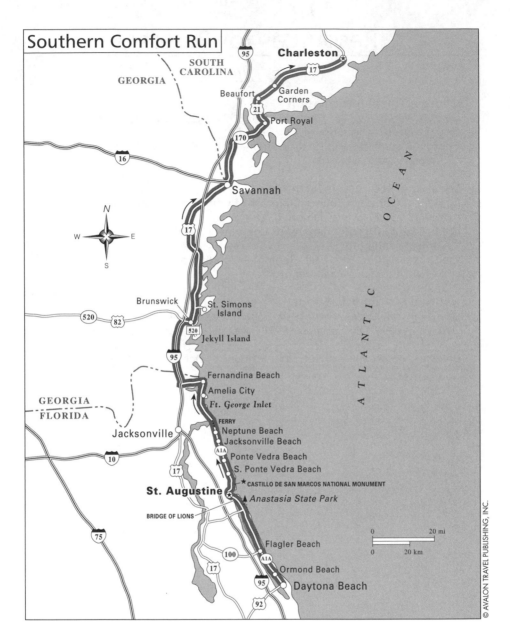

Southern Comfort Run

Route: St. Augustine to Charleston via Amelia Island, Jekyll Island, St. Simons Island, Beaufort

Distance: Approximately 250 miles; consider seven days with stops.

•**Days 1–2—St. Augustine/Daytona Beach** •**Day 3—Travel** •**Days 4–5— Savannah** •**Day 6—Travel/Charleston** •**Day 7 Charleston**

First Leg: St. Augustine to Savannah (150 miles)

Second Leg: Savannah to Charleston (100 miles)

Helmet Laws: In Florida, helmets are not required if you are over 21 and carry a minimum of $10,000 in medical insurance. Georgia requires helmets. South Carolina does not if you are over 21.

Southern Comfort Run

St. Augustine, Florida to Charleston, North Carolina

This run worships the Holy Trinity of the Lower Atlantic's historic walking towns. Ride along the seaside from a historic Spanish colony to Georgia barrier islands to magnolia-scented, mint julep–sipping, well-preserved antebellum towns. Make this run in spring or fall and enjoy perfect riding weather.

St. Augustine Primer

After seeing several dozen "oldest cities," I'd say St. Augustine has earned bragging rights to the title. Even though Spanish explorer Ponce de Leon never actually landed in St. Augustine, and it was 20th-century entrepreneurs who created the Fountain of Youth legend, there are *still* a few dozen reasons to see St. Augustine. When Don Pedro Menendez de Aviles arrived on August 28, 1565, the Feast Day of St. Augustine, he established the first permanent European settlement in North America. With his arrival, he brought European traditions, customs, laws, weights and measures, and city designs to a new continent.

Before settling in, Menendez first had to defeat a French fleet, which he did with the assistance of a well-timed hurricane, and then make peace with the native Timucua Indians who were here to greet him. At the time, they likely attended these early summit meetings thinking, "These Spaniards seem like such nice people...."

English corsairs and freelance pirates attacked and sacked the town several times during the next 150 years, until the Spanish installed a home security system. In 1672, they got wise and started building the Castillo de San Marcos: a squat, sturdy fort that still overlooks Matanzas Bay and the entry into the Atlantic. A flurry of treaties and trades passed the town from Spain to England, then back to Spain, and finally to the United States in the 19th century. The Timucua weren't consulted about any of this.

Traces from these eras remain, but most of what you see took shape during the 1880s. As part of his plan to build railroads and resorts along Florida's east coast, Henry M. Flagler created the magnificent Ponce de Leon Hotel, a short 24-hour rail journey from New York.

What Menendez and Flagler fostered is still present today: the homes, the Castillo de San Marcos, city gates, grand hotels, and cemeteries. This is one of the rare towns that knew better than to raze 500 years of history in favor of a new parking garage. The result: St. Augustine has character and style.

The town boasts great brewpubs, Key West–style bars, horse-drawn carriages, 42 miles of beaches, a first-class marina, fishing charters, hidden alleys and courtyards, and excellent riding weather. And the rest is history.

On the Road: St. Augustine

Few other places in Florida rival St. Augustine as a walking town, but it's also a riding town. Take half a day or longer for a coastal run south to Daytona Beach. Even if it's not Bike Week (roughly the last week of February through the first week of March) or Biketoberfest (first week of October), there's still enough shakin' to keep you entertained.

Remember these directions: Cross the beautiful Bridge of Lions and head south. That's it. Stay on Highway A1A when it veers to the left, and, with the Atlantic Ocean on your side, it's a straight shot down the coast and one of the easiest rides you'll ever make.

At an altitude of six feet above sea level, two-lane A1A takes you along Anastasia Island and 50-odd miles of sandy white beachfront. The county fishing pier, beach ramps, motels, and oyster bars appear in rapid succession.

This is a far gentler ride than the Pacific Coast Highway. Instead of being a few hundred feet above the ocean, you're right beside it, with the Matanzas River creeping along on your right. After passing Highway 206, look to your right for the **Fort Matanzas National Monument** (904/471-0116, www.nps.gov/foma). A short boat ride takes you to the fort (free), which was built in 1740 for the Spaniards' southern defense of St. Augustine.

Bike Week

The spectacle called Bike Week began in Daytona on January 24, 1937, with the running of the first race across three miles of road and beach. Ed Kretz won the race, but the long-distance winner was Bike Week itself.

Although the races were scrubbed in 1942 to save resources for the war effort, fans still arrived to hold an impromptu party called Bike Week. By 1947, when the beach-road races resumed, the party was going at full throttle (no doubt attended by ex-GIs astride surplus military motorcycles). Attendance rose as years passed, but the locals were becoming more leery of bikers. By the late 1980s, fed-up city officials and businesses stepped in and reorganized the chaotic drunken bacchanal into a manageable drunken bacchanal.

Now **Bike Week** (800/854-1234, www.officialbikeweek.com) is a cultural phenomenon that attracts nearly 500,000 riders from around the world. Usually held from the last week of February through the first week of March, festivities revolve around bikes, races, concerts, T-shirts, games, T-shirts, drinking, swap meets, T-shirts, drinking, and contests with some more T-shirts thrown in for good measure.

Seeing a blank space on the fall calendar, October's Biketoberfest premiered in 1992. Although smaller and less threatening than its bigger older brother, Biketoberfest attracts around 100,000 bikers for a last prewinter party.

The road remains the same, always pleasing and with little growth to screw up the view. You'll ride through Marineland (pop. 6), a community as well as a former Old Florida tourist attraction. From here, 15 miles of calm riding take you to Flagler Beach, where the **Pier Restaurant** (215 S. Hwy. A1A, 386/439-3891), at the junction of Highway 100, is the best place on the coast to rest your bike and enjoy an ocean view with breakfast, lunch, or dinner.

There's little else to note, but a world of great riding to savor as you ride south. Savor it now, because 20-odd miles later, after you pass Ormond Beach, you'll enter wide lanes of tourist traffic at Daytona Beach. Stick with it; just past the Ocean Center (a large convention facility) is Main Street. Although the mood is suspiciously quiet when bikers aren't in town, take time to poke around here and the Boardwalk—they're both kinda dirty, but you'd kick yourself if you didn't stop.

Down the Line

Whether you're headed for Bike Week in Daytona or to New England for Laconia or Americade, Amtrak's Auto Train can provide you a 900-mile shortcut. Several years ago, the Auto Train started carrying bikes on its run between Lorton, Virginia (outside Washington, D.C.) and Sanford, Florida (outside Orlando). The Auto Train departs daily at 4:30 P.M. (from either location) and arrives around 9 A.M. the following morning. Provided your vehicle has at least four inches of ground clearance, a 15 x 8 palette can hold up to four bikes, although no trike bikes or sidecars are allowed. Just ride up a four-foot ramp and into a tire-wide groove, and your bike is firmly confined by canvas straps.

Not only will you save a few days and the cost of a hotel room, but the meals on board are served in style (on china and tablecloths); the lounge is open late; and the huge seats can substitute for a bed—although sleepers are available. Rates in coach and first class vary by season and direction. For current rates and reservations, contact Auto Train (800/USA-RAIL or 800/872-7245, www.amtrak.com).

Of the several bars on Main Street, there's one you have to see. Remember how incredible it was to drink your first beer? Well, friend, you can relive yesteryear with a visit to the **Boot Hill Saloon** (310 Main St., 386/258-9506, www.boothillsaloon.com). If you've fantasized about the bar's decor, you won't be disappointed. There are two pool tables and a ceiling cloaked with bras left behind by female patrons, as well as Polaroid pictures taken of same. It's open 'til 3 A.M. daily. As you ride the street, keep an eye open for other Main Street landmarks, including Froggy's, Dirty Harry's, Full Moon Saloon, Bank and Blues, and The Wreck.

The Atlantic Ocean and Boardwalk lie a few blocks east. Changing facilities give you the opportunity to swim, tan, or chill. The Boardwalk is pretty grungy, but its bars and pier keep tourists and, sadly, runaway kids, coming.

Next, head a few blocks south of Main Street to Highway 92 (aka International Speedway Boulevard). Turn right and follow it for several miles, and when you spot the massive race track, pull over at **Daytona USA** (386/947-6530, www.daytonausa.com). Open 9 A.M.–7 P.M. daily, this is the attraction part of the track, and, despite its slant toward cars and not bikes, it's still pretty damn cool.

Admission is $21.50, and the track features interactive displays—after a demonstration by a pit crew, you're challenged to test your skills at cleaning windshields and changing tires. One of the racing movies shown on the 55-foot screen puts you in the driver's seat. Acceleration Alley costs $5 and is a motion simulator ride that puts you behind the wheel for six minutes as you drive the track at virtual speeds of up to 200 mph. If that's not enough to satisfy your mighty motorcycling soul, invest in the pricey but powerful Richard Petty Riding Experience (www.1800bepetty.com, $134). Although you don't get to drive unless you've driven a Petty car at a smaller track, you do ride shotgun in a souped-up heap of metal that hits 170 mph on the Super Stretch. I did it and learned several new ways to shout "motherfu$%#&!" No side windows, just netting, a helmet, three laps, and comp admission to Daytona USA (you're saving $21.50, Gomer). Definitely call ahead for scheduled driving days.

After you wipe that smile off your face, work your way back toward Highway A1A, stopping along Beach Street or Ridgewood Avenue, home to several motorcycle dealers and customizers. When you ride back into St. Augustine and cross the Bridge of Lions once again, you'll get the best view of the city. From the crest of the bridge, you can see yachts moored in the harbor, the bayfront promenade, the plaza, and the fort to your right.

Now all you have to do is park your bike, find a quiet restaurant, or sit by the bayside and find what Ponce de Leon never discovered: eternal youth.

Pull It Over: St. Augustine Highlights
Attractions and Adventures

Flagler College (74 King St., 904/829-6481) was built in 1883 as an extraordinarily luxurious resort known as the Ponce de Leon Hotel. Today, it is a four-year school for some lucky punks. They lead tours here, and if you like history and architecture, you'll find fantastic photo ops around campus.

On the north end of the island, **Anastasia State Recreation Area** (1340-A S. A1A Hwy., 904/461-2000, $3) offers picnic areas, a nature trail that crosses above fragile sand dunes, canoes, sailboarding rentals and instruction, four miles of beachfront, and 139 tent and trailer campsites (904/461-2033 for reservations). The park is open 8 A.M.–sundown daily.

The guys at **Camachee Island Charters** (105 Yacht Club Dr., 904/825-1971, www.camacheeislandsportfishing.com) can arrange charters on 30-plus boats from 20 to 48 feet. Charters typically head out about 50 miles (yowzah!) to reach the Gulf Stream, where you'll troll or fish with live bait for marlin, sailfish, dolphin, wahoo, kingfish, tuna, amberjack, and anything else swimming under your boat. This outfit also arranges night, river, and shark-fishing excursions, as well as tournament charters.

Conch House Sportfishing (57 Comares Ave., 904/829-8646 or 888/463-4742, www.conchhousesportfishing.com) offers private charters for half- and full-day runs; tackle and bait are provided. Seriously consider this place. The Conch House doubles as a pretty active watering hole—especially on weekends, when everyone (including dogs) heads here for outdoor entertainment, drinking, and water sports.

History echoes in the walls of **Castillo de San Marcos** (Bayfront, 904/829-6506, www.nps.gov/casa, $6). Wander around the fort and take a ranger-led tour if possible. There are bastions to climb, cannons to sight, and darkened rooms that once housed prisoners and soldiers. After several rounds of pillaging in the 100 years following the city's founding, the Spanish decided to protect themselves and began construction of the Castillo de San Marcos in 1672. The fort had a dual purpose: to guard the first permanent European settlement in the continental United States and to protect the sea route for Spanish treasure ships returning home. Although never taken by military force, the fortress was ceded to the British—and then back again to the Spanish—before becoming a possession of the United States in 1821. A must-see, the fort is open 8:45 A.M.–4:45 P.M. daily.

Not content to let history create an authentic attraction, a hustler rewrote history in the 1930s by claiming a sulfurous spring here was the Fountain of Youth sought by Ponce de Leon. Suckers have been swallowing that line ever since, and if you don't mind joining their company, the **Fountain of Youth** (11 Magnolia Ave., 904/829-3168 or 800/356-8222, www.fountainof youthflorida.com, $6) awaits. What was on the site was an Indian village as evidenced by the excavated burial grounds of Timucua Indians. When you're here, it's fascinating to consider what America looked like when the Spanish arrived. There were no roads, no cities, no Pilgrims … just Native Americans and a continent that stretched unexplored to the Pacific. Open 9 A.M.–5 P.M. daily.

While no single store stands out along **St. George Street,** this pedestrian boulevard in the heart of the historic district is where most everyone goes. An eclectic collection of shops dot the mall, along with a few bars and restaurants. It's also the gathering site for several historic tours.

Blue-Plate Specials

The independent **Gypsy Cab Company** (828 Anastasia Blvd., 904/824-8244, www.gypsycab.com) does everything right, serving lunch and dinner weekends and just dinner on weekdays. Parking's tight and there may be a wait, but it's worth it. The menu of fish, steak, veal, and chicken dishes changes almost daily and is always good. After trying the Cajun shrimp, call and thank me.

At **Scarlett O'Hara's** (70 Hypolita St., 904/824-6535), the menu is basic—a little of everything—but even a hamburger or red beans and rice seems extra good when eaten on the front porch here. The service is good, prices are fair, and the patio bar is a nice, shady hideout. Scarlett's serves lunch and dinner.

Watering Holes

Tradewinds Lounge (124 Charlotte St., 904/829-9336, www.tradewinds lounge.com) defies the trend of trendy bars; this is the real deal. Here since 1964, this watering hole for locals also attracts a cross-section of tourists, students, dropouts, and beach bums. Weekdays, happy hour runs 5–8 P.M., with live music playing from then until closing. Tradewinds has it all: a full bar, margaritas, rum punch, and, of course, beer. All it's missing is grog.

O. C. White's (118 Avenida Menendez, 904/824-0808) is a restaurant, too, but the patio areas out front are just across from the marina, so it's a great place to have a beer and enjoy the outdoors. Not wild, but perfect for talking and looking.

Yet another restaurant, **A1A Aleworks** (1 King St., 904/829-2977, www.A1Aaleworks.com) is a great place to grab an inexpensive lunch or dinner, and it's usually crowded with a lot of young locals. As the name implies, it's also a great place to grab a cold one (choose from seven micros, as well as domestics) or a drink from the full bar. Upstairs, the balcony seems borrowed from Bourbon Street. Have a drink and watch the yachts sailing in on the bay.

Shut-Eye

St. Augustine has dozens of inns, chain hotels, and moderately priced independent motels—but sometimes that's not enough. Make reservations well in advance, and note that weekday rates are lower than those listed below.

Motels and Motor Courts

The **Monterey Inn** (16 Avenida Menendez, 904/824-4482, www.themontereyinn.com, $59–150) has a great bayside location and clean rooms that overlook yachts at anchor, sailboats skimming past the harbor, horse-drawn carriages, and the fabled Bridge of Lions. Fifty-nine units have double, queen, or king beds, cable TV, phones, plenty of parking, a swimming pool, and AAA discounts on rooms

The **Bayfront Inn** (138 Avenida Menendez, 904/824-1681 or 800/558-3455, www.bayfrontinn.com, $99 and up) is a clean, standard hotel with a nice view and good location (two blocks from the Bridge of Lions). The hotel features a regular array of amenities, including a swimming pool, whirlpool, cable TV, and telephone.

Leaving the city behind, a five-minute ride north on Highway A1A takes you to the beach and a selection of smaller and older motels. The 29-room **Ocean Sands Motor Inn** (3465 Coastal Hwy./N. A1A, 904/824-1112 or 800/609-0888, www.oceansandsinn.com, $79 and up) has a good location and good rates. Rooms come complete with private patios, cable TV, coffee-makers, refrigerators, and microwaves. Bring your own food, and you may never leave.

Chain Drive

A, C, E, G, J, L, S, U, V, Z, BB, CC, DD

Chain hotels are in town, or within 10 miles. See cross-reference guide featuring phone numbers and Web addresses on page 514.

Inn-dependence

The **Casa De La Paz** (22 Avenida Menendez, 904/829-2915 or 800/929-2915, www.casadelapaz.com, $150 weekends) is a bayside Mediterranean Revival home complete with a private courtyard. This inn is more upscale than most—classical music and beverages are provided throughout the day—and one of the more popular accommodations because of its service, location, ambience, and on-site parking. The innkeepers also arrange "soft" adventures (kayaking, sailboating, fishing). Next door, the **Casablanca Inn** (24 Avenida Menendez, 904/829-0928 or 800/826-2626, www.casablancainn.com, $129 and up) features 20 guestrooms (15 with hot tubs) and, therefore, more camaraderie among guests who take advantage of the bayfront verandah and large breakfast. A sister property, the Secret Garden Inn, has three secluded courtyard suites complete with tiled baths, balconies, queen beds, and kitchenettes.

Indulgences

Opened in 1888, the **Casa Monica Hotel** (95 Cordova St., 904/827-1888 or 800/648-1888, www.casamonica.com, $180–249) was vacant by 1932 and became the St. Johns County Courthouse from 1968 to 1997. Hotelier Richard Kessler restored this landmark in the heart of downtown, and once again the Moorish Revival accents of the original are clearly visible throughout, from its 137 rooms and suites (including three-story suites in the towers) to its themed dining room, swimming pool, cafés, and shops. Expect elegance, class, and fun.

On the Road: St. Augustine to Savannah

As you head north out of St. Augustine on San Marco Avenue, you'll pass the St. Augustine School for the Deaf and Blind, where young Ray Charles studied. Take a right at May Street, and, after scaling a steep bridge (look to your right for another fantastic view of the old city), you'll arrive in Vilano Beach, which features a few motels and restaurants. Far more enticing is the return of the Atlantic Ocean.

The road is a combination of country lane and beach road, two lanes of low-key riding right beside the water. This will be your destiny . . . at least for the next 30 miles. Every so often, you'll spy a pullout and steps down to the beach. You'll be hard-pressed to stay on your bike when the waves are right.

By the time you reach South Ponte Vedra Beach, the waves will be hidden by towering walls of vegetation, but if you look closely, you'll see narrow gaps in the brush. If trivial barriers like these don't deter you, prop your bike up on the sandy shoulder and sneak through to find a secluded beach that's close to its natural state.

Within miles, this run comes to a close. Between Daytona and here, you've ridden some of Florida's best uninterrupted shoreline. When you reach Ponte Vedra, Jacksonville Beach, and Neptune Beach, your view is blocked by dense commercial growth. Still, taking Highway A1A is better than riding through Jacksonville, a city that has all the charm of a stomach virus.

After a sharp left after Neptune Beach, A1A weaves up toward the Mayport Naval Station and past a creepy fishing village to reach the **St. Johns River Ferry** (904/241-9969). As if you needed another reason to justify why you ride, sometimes motorcycles are waved to the front of the line. The crossing doesn't take long, but the ferry leaves only once every 30 minutes. The fare for motorcycles is $2.50.

You'll be dropped off at Fort George Island, and within 15 miles, you'll be on a nice pine-rich road that enters the southern end of Amelia Island, the only place in America that has been ruled under eight flags. Fernandina Beach, on the north end, is the only town on the island, and this solitude has made the entire package popular with honeymooners, families, and retirees. You may be tempted to spend an evening here. There are tidy bed-and-breakfasts, large inns, magnificent resorts, and a downtown district with bookstores, restaurants, and unusual stores. Despite this, I'd have preferred this place when moral watchdogs dubbed it a "festering fleshpot," because of its reputation as a hotbed for pirates, brothels, and bawdy ladies.

Highway A1A is called South Fletcher Avenue; from here, turn left at Atlantic Avenue. Stay straight, and after the road becomes Centre Street, you're in the heart of town. It should be around noon, so I suggest lunch at the **Florida House Inn** (22 S. 3rd St., 904/261-3300, www.floridahouseinn.com), the oldest operating inn in the state. The meals here epitomize perfect Southern dining. Around 10 bucks buys you never-ending platters of filling food served at long tables. Follow your meal with a cold one at the **Palace Saloon** (117 Centre St., 904/491-3332), perhaps Florida's most impressive watering hole—half grog shop, half historical museum. The oldest continuously operating bar in Florida, the saloon has kept barkeeps priming the pumps and delivering frosty mugs of beer to sailors, locals, shrimpers, and travelers since 1903.

Having bypassed Jacksonville, you have to head west on A1A to reach I-95 North, where you can make up some time. Within a few miles, you'll be in Georgia, and at Exit 6, just take Highway 17 toward the towns of Brunswick, Jekyll Island, and St. Simons Island, all of which are concentrated at the end of the road. **Jekyll Island** (912/635-3636, www.jekyllisland.com) is accessible via Highway 520, which runs straight into the heart of the resort town. Although you've ridden fewer than 40 miles, you've entered the real South, where the pace is molasses slow. In the 1880s, millionaires like Goodyear, Gould, Pulitzer, Rockefeller, and Morgan paid $125,000 for the island to use as a hunting preserve and family retreat. Today, the getaway is a state park and worth a brief detour.

Return to Highway 17 and work your way through Brunswick and past St. Simons Island (unless you want another detour). Stick with 17 for a slow, rural ride away from the coast and into Savannah, the finest city in the South.

Savannah Primer

If you judged by recent events alone, the most important moments in Savannah's history would be the release of the film *Forrest Gump* and John

Berendt's extraordinary book *Midnight in the Garden of Good and Evil,* about a local murder case. More important than these two events, however, were the actions of James Edward Oglethorpe and General William T. Sherman.

I'll start with Oglethorpe. In February 1733, he led 114 settlers to a high bluff on the Savannah River to create a new colony settled by poor people, soldiers, and foreign Protestants. Although the colony failed when Parliament cut off all funds in 1751, Oglethorpe's planned city of lush squares bordered by beautiful homes survived under the leadership of royal governor James Wright and today puts Savannah in a class by itself.

Then there was Sherman. In late 1864, after Sherman had torched Atlanta, he and his men marched to the sea—and Savannah. Savannahians compared their 10,000 retreating soldiers against Sherman's advancing 70,000 and, displaying a remarkable degree of common sense, decided to surrender. Sherman gave the city of Savannah to President Lincoln as a Christmas present. This act surely endeared him to the locals—about as much as when his soldiers tossed aside tombstones in the Colonial Park Cemetery so they'd have room to pitch their tents.

On the Road: Savannah

If you've never been to the real South, Savannah is a great place to start. In spring (when everyone else is here), the dogwoods and azaleas are in bloom, and the Spanish moss clutches at gnarled oak branches. Inside the ordinary brownstones surrounding the squares, elegance and a sense of tradition reveal themselves in the velvet drapes, cut crystal chandeliers, and oil portraits of long-gone ancestors. Savannah *is* the South.

Just as Daytona worked you up, Savannah will settle you down. Start by circling the fabled squares between Bay Street and Forsyth Park. You are riding within the nation's largest historic district—more than two miles square. It didn't always look like this. Between 1945 and 1950, some idiots demolished more than 950 homes to make room for parking lots. Then some women got wise and bought a single $22,000 house to jump-start the city's preservation movement. You'll pick up this piece of intelligence at the **Savannah Visitors Information Center** (301 Martin Luther King Jr. Blvd., 912/944-0455, www.savannahvisit.com).

The visitors center, a restored train station, is the best place to start learning about what you just saw on your ride. There's a historical movie and museum here ($4 for both), and the center is the departure point for nearly a million tours. The bus tour outperforms the actual tours inside historic

St. Augustine Waterfront

© NANCY HOWELL

houses, since many docents just point at objects and mutter, "This is a mirror from 1794. This is a table from 1812. This DVD player is from 1799 ..." Back on board, the driver's narrative should fill in the blanks for you young whippersnappers.

Make mental notes, and with leads provided by the tour guide, you'll discover a lot of places to visit on your own during the day. For some reason, I prefer seeing this town after dark, although, you obviously want to wander where there's plenty of foot traffic. I find that the streets are less crowded, and the squares more attractive, at night. Get a map and walk over to Monterey Square to see the Mercer House. Forsyth Park, with its glistening fountain and ancient oaks, is a perfect romantic setting if you want to fling some woo. G'wan! Fling that woo!

A notable concentration of nightlife is found a few blocks from the river at the **City Market,** where there may be DJs, live bands, and dancing in the square—but no square dancing. Also check out **Vinnie Van Go-Go's** for New York–style pizza. A few blocks away, down by the riverside, you'll want to park your bike atop Bay Street, since the decline to River Street quickly drops 42 feet. It's not too precipitous a plunge, but the millions of bumpy, rounded paving boulders—once used as ballast on slave ships—make parking and riding tough. As you walk this nine-block stretch of shops, restaurants, bars, and tourist traps, it's hard to conceive that this was once a row of cotton warehouses. Along the way, you may notice a cavernous void amidst the rows of shops. At this site, human misery reached its peak, as newly arrived slaves were sold here to the highest bidder.

Here's a way to see another side of Savannah. If the squares slow you down during the day, you may just want to get on your bike and ride about 18 miles east of Savannah on Highway 80 to **Tybee Island** (800/868-2322, www.tybeevisit.com). It's a nice ride out, past very low and wide salt marshes, with very little to interrupt your view. On Tybee, the **Crab Shack** (40 Estill Hammock, 912/786-9857, www.thecrabshack.com) is "where the elite eat in their bare feet." The Buffett-inspired waterfront restaurant was created during a "bar raising" in the early '80s, and it thrives on beer, live gators, seafood, and music.

Hang out here or ride back to Savannah, where you can check into a hotel, find an inn, or follow Sherman's lead by kicking over a few tombstones and pitching a tent in the cemetery.

Pull It Over: Savannah Highlights
Attractions and Adventures

Full descriptions of most tours—ghosts, historical, *Midnight* book tours are available at the Savannah Visitors Information Center. My luck has been consistently good with **Gray Line Tours** (912/234-8687 or 800/426-2318, www.graylineofsavannah.com.) Like other outfits, they offer a narrated tour through Savannah's historical homes and haunts, and theirs are usually chock full of historical goodness. Tickets range $19–25.

Blue-Plate Specials

If you come to Savannah and don't eat at **Mrs. Wilkes' Dining Room** (107 W. Jones St., 912/232-5997, www.mrswilkes.com), I'll personally track you down and beat you senseless. This is the best food in Savannah and may be the best food in the South (although the Lady & Sons—below—would argue). For about 13 bucks, cash only, it serves everything you need to get fat and happy: huge platters of fried chicken, beef stew, okra, sweet potatoes, cornbread, tea, and banana pudding, all carted to a communal table where you dine with a dozen other visitors. The result is good conversation and great food. Be ready to wait; the line can stretch out the door and down the block. Open for lunch on weekdays only.

The Lady & Sons (102 W. Congress St., 912/233-2600, www.theladyand sons.com) follows in the footsteps of Mrs. Wilkes', serving lunch ($13) and dinner ($17) in a similar buffet style (on weekends as well), but without the communal seating. Locals and travelers contend that this surpasses the quality of Wilkes, and it may. You should definitely try both while you're here. Expect good hearty Southern dishes, with an emphasis on fried chicken and cheese biscuits. One item, hoe cakes, led to popular "Our hoes are complimentary" T-shirts.

Since 1903, locals have been heading to **Clary's Cafe** (404 Abercorn St., 912/233-0402) for down-home cooking and occasional ethnic dishes. Ever since "The Book" came out, tourists have been poking around here, too—this is where Luther, the nut everyone thought was going to poison the town water supply, ate. With the drugstore gone, this is just a restaurant now, and since the food's trailing behind the legend, it may be best for breakfast.

Watering Holes

You wouldn't expect it, but Savannah has a large Irish population (faith and begorrah, Bubba), so pubs are popular. **Six Pence Pub** (245 Bull St., 912/233-3156) features standard pub grub, but it has an atmosphere that'd be just as good even if it served nothing but beer. Live entertainment varies from Irish folk to rock to blues.

On any given night at **Kevin Barry's Pub** (117 W. River St., 912/233-9626), you may find U.S. Marines sharing the bar with businessmen smoking big cigars. Beer is sold by the pint, with an emphasis on the Half and Half (Guinness/Harp). Irish music plays nightly starting at 8:30. There's a $2 cover.

Churchill's Pub (13–17 West Bay St., 912/232-8501, www.thebritish-pub.com) may be the most authentic in Savannah. To complement a full range of draught ales, try the Bubble & Squeak, roast beef and Yorkshire pudding, bangers and mash, and shepherd's pie. A great place to kick back and enjoy pool, darts, drinks, a fireplace, 21 beers and ales on tap, and a rooftop terrace.

A restaurant sits upstairs at the 18th-century mansion known as the **Olde Pink House** (23 Abercorn St., 912/232-4286), but a buried treasure lies below: Planter's Tavern, a low-key basement piano bar with twin fireplaces and Gale Thurmond playing old Johnny Mercer tunes. Her voice, the setting, the comfortable couches ... it's the most pleasingly civilized nightspot in Savannah.

Shut-Eye

Savannah features dozens of chain hotels and a greater number of inns. Book well in advance, because rooms go fast.

Chain Drive
A, C, G, J, K, L, P, S, BB, CC

Chain hotels are in town, or within 10 miles. See cross-reference guide featuring phone numbers and Web addresses on page 514.

Inn-dependence
The generic name of the **Bed & Breakfast Inn** (117 W. Gordon St., 912/238-0518 or 888/238-0518, www.savannahbnb.com, $99–139) suggests a no-frills approach to innkeeping. Surprisingly, the rooms are spacious, the full breakfast hearty, and the location convenient (only a block from Forsyth Park). The **Gaston Gallery** (211 E. Gaston St., 912/238-3294 or 800/671-0716, www.gastongallery.com, $99 and up) is an elegant 19th-century townhouse in the historic district. Some rooms have a balcony, but the entire home enjoys a wide verandah that invites you to pull up a chair and watch the lazy pace of Savannah.

On the Road: Savannah to Charleston

It's a short ride from Savannah to South Carolina. Just find Highway 17 North and ride across the Hugh Talmadge Memorial Bridge and boom—you're there. You're in the lowcountry now, where the road is as flat as a sheet of paper. Highway 17 shoots past marshland for several miles before retreating into the woods with a right turn onto Alt. Route 170.

You'll see signs of the Deep South: hand-lettered posters for bush hoggers, pine forests, and the El Cheapo general store and gas station. But the enjoyment is hard to sustain, because just as you start into a nice run, subdivisions and trailers begin popping up. After passing a trace amount of commercialism, you'll settle back into the South Carolina countryside, as you follow 170 to the northeast toward the town of Beaufort.

The savannahs open up and a few curves appear, along with the requisite Baptist church and adjoining cemetery. Although you're less than a half hour from Savannah, it's intriguing to think of the people who have lived and died here believing that the outside world couldn't penetrate their lifestyle. In this marshland, you soon cross the long, low Broad River Bridge. This spot is scenic in an Everglades sort of way. Just after the bridge, turn right on Route 802 toward Port Royal. There's plenty of nothing to see at first, but then you'll begin to follow the waterfront toward downtown **Beaufort** (800/638-3525, www.beaufortsc.org), which just happens to be South Carolina's second-oldest township. While old antebellum homes and the waterfront provide great photo ops, obvious points of interest are hard to find.

Oddly, the setting gets more Southern the farther north you go. You want Route 280 to U.S. 21 North—you'll find the roads by looking for the greatest concentration of mobile homes and video stores in North America. At the end of U.S. 21, at Gardens Corner, turn right onto two-lane U.S. 17 and let your mind wander. You'll ride this road into the past, complete with gas stations from the '30s; wisteria vines; peaches, tomatoes, and plums sold out of trucks on the roadside; and men in overalls straight out of a Margaret Bourke-White photograph.

Aside from this, there's not a tremendous amount to see here, but all that changes once you roll into Rhett Butler's hometown.

Charleston Primer

Grab a history book and study Charleston. This city is English, Spanish, African, Caribbean, Union, Confederate, old, and young.

Like residents of St. Augustine and Savannah, Charlestonians recognize the irreplaceable value of history, and their town has changed little, at least in the historic district. Despite being a magnet for disaster—bombings, fires, pirates, earthquakes, hurricanes, tornadoes, war—Charleston seems to be content with itself, even when members of the public works department unearth unexploded Civil War shells beneath uprooted pavement.

If you know the South, you've heard about Charleston's fabled "bluebloods," the native Charlestonians who still talk about the Civil War ("the Woh-ah") as if the damned Yankees still controlled Fort Sumter. Yet it is their determination to preserve this epoch that makes this town one of America's top travel destinations.

Although the bluebloods would draw my red blood for saying so, they have General Sherman to thank for this. After he gave Savannah a reprieve, he also bypassed Charleston. Some say this was because Sherman had a soft spot for the city since serving at Fort Moultrie in the 1840s.

Come to think of it, speculating as to why Charleston remains the way it is, is irrelevant. It's here. Enjoy it.

On the Road: Charleston

It goes against a biker's independent spirit to rely on a tour guide for the skinny on a town, but that may be your best bet for understanding Charleston's layered history. The city was shaped by events during the American Revolution, the Civil War, and the Jazz Age (remember the Charleston?), and by Hurricane Hugo, which nearly ripped the place to shreds in 1989.

If you decide to make like the masses and hop on a tour, you'll be fine. They're all right. Most depart from the excellently detailed **Charleston Visitors Center** (375 Meeting St., 843/853-8000 or 800/774-0006). I had good luck with **Gray Line Tours** (843/722-4444 or 800/423-0444). For a generic, Ma and Pa Kettle–style bus tour, the 75-minute ride was surprisingly informative and an easy way to get an overview of the city. The $15 tour passes the standard points of interest for all Charleston tours—such as historic churches, Fort Moultrie, Old Citadel, Battery waterfront, Rainbow Row—but the guides are well read and make it more exciting than your preconceived notions would lead you to believe.

Consider following up this low-pressure tour with another more detailed one. I can't say enough good things about **The Story of Charleston** (843/723-1670, www.tourcharleston.com), which demonstrates the difference between studying with a student and learning from a professor. The walking tour ($15) goes well beyond dates and architecture to illuminate Charleston's religious, sociological, and cultural history, filling in enough blanks to make you dangerous. This company also hosts two other $15 walking tours: the Pirates of Charleston and the Ghosts of Charleston.

Other necessary tours beckon (Fort Sumter, USS *Yorktown*), but the evening is just as important here. As you've guessed, historic Charleston is a great walking town, and every point can be reached on foot within minutes.

The center of activity takes place along Market Street, which would need little alteration to be a Civil War scene. Women weaving intricate baskets sit near the edges of the marketplace; horse-drawn carriages clop past; and street preachers shout for lost souls.

From here, walk a few blocks south. At Vendue Range, turn left and walk past the fountain to the pier, where large porch swings invite you to take a load off. From the end of the pier, you can see Fort Sumter, which looks like a black birthday cake with a flagpole candle. Beyond it lies the Atlantic Ocean.

Having learned the city's layout, walk a few more blocks south to the Battery, which is far more pleasant at dusk. The cannons, mortars, statues, and oak trees all spell "photo op," and the site provides a relaxing place to view the harbor.

Returning toward the nightlife of Market and Meeting streets, get lost as you did in Savannah and St. Augustine. Each "single home" has something different to reveal, from the old carriage stepping stones to the second-floor chandelier-lit "salons" that are cooler and more suitably adorned than any floor below or above. Watch for the barbed iron installed on houses when fears of a slave insurrection spread across the city.

After the sun sets, wander the streets until you find a place to settle back, and then give silent thanks to General Sherman for taking the left fork to Columbia.

Pull It Over: Charleston Highlights
Attractions and Adventures

Tradition holds true at **The Citadel** (171 Moultrie Ave., 843/953-5000), although a few things have changed since 1842 (like women). The best part about a visit here is watching the Dress Parade by the South Carolina Corps of Cadets, which usually takes place Friday afternoons during the school year at 3:45. You don't need a ticket; you don't even need to be a man. Just show up early.

The schooner *Pride* (843/559-9686, www.schoonerpride.com) puts you on the water with style and grace. You can help raise and trim the sails or even take a turn at the wheel. Two-hour cruises cost $20 and typically sail at 2, 4:30, and 7 P.M., with abbreviated sailings in cooler months. Reservations are highly recommended.

You know where the Civil War was fought, but this is where it started—and led to 600,000 casualties in four years. South Carolina had seceded, yet Union forces occupied Fort Sumter at the entrance of Charleston Harbor. The Confederates wanted them out; the Yankees refused; and on April 12, 1861, the Rebels fired from Fort Johnson, sparking a two-day bombardment that resulted in the surrender of Fort Sumter. Of course, the Union wanted its fort back and spent two years pulverizing it with 46,000 shells. The National Park Service maintains the fort, and park rangers are here to answer your questions. **Fort Sumter Tours** (843/722-2628, www.spiritlinecruises.com) depart from City Marina or Patriot's Point. The tour, which costs $13, lasts just over two hours.

It's hard to see everything at the **Charleston Museum** (360 Meeting St., 843/722-2996, www.charlestonmuseum.com, $10), so pick what piques your interest and focus on that. The museum is open 9 A.M.–5 P.M. Monday–Saturday and 1–5 P.M. Sunday. Items on display include muskets, antique fire-fighting equipment, swords, railroads, and a replica of the *Hunley*—the Confederate submarine that sunk the *Housatonic* before it was sunk itself in Charleston Harbor. The real *Hunley* was found in 1995, raised in 2001, and contained some interesting artifacts from the doomed men on board. It's on display (for $10) several miles away at the **Warren Lasch Conservation Center,** which is open only on weekends (archaeologists are exploring it on weekdays). Information is always available at the **Hunley Hotline** (843/744-2186 or 877/448-6539) and at www.hunley.org.

Four ships and 25 aircraft are on display at **Patriot's Point Naval and Maritime Museum** (40 Patriot's Point Rd. via Hwy. 17, 843/884-2727, www.patriotspoint.org). The focal point is the aircraft carrier USS *Yorktown,* which replaced the original after it was sunk at the Battle of Midway. Commissioned on April 15, 1943, the *Yorktown* supported American ground troops in the Philippines at Iwo Jima and Okinawa, and in December 1968, was there to recover the crew of Apollo 8. An admission fee of $14 buys you access to the flight deck, hangar deck, ready rooms, ship's hospital, bridge, and the National Medal of Honor Museum. If you want to take 'er for a spin, here's a tip: I poked around and found the keys under a flowerpot. On deck, you'll see carrier aircraft varying from World War II bombers, fighters, and torpedo planes to modern jets.

The **Charleston Harbor Tour** (843/722-1112, $14) offers a cheap way to get on the bay, and the captain really knows his stuff. The tour (catch it from the foot of Market Street) covers a lot of history you can learn only from the harbor's vantage point. Only problem is, the boat's so dirty I betcha passengers escaping the *Titanic* would have waited for the next one.

Shopping

If you're inspired by the history, architecture, and gentility of this old Southern city, you'll find abundant mementoes of them at the **Historic Charleston Foundation Museum Shop** (108 Meeting St., 843/724-8484). Open daily, the shop carries books, gifts, maps, and other historical items—worth a stop, since the staff will ship your purchases back home.

Given the scarcity of Harley merchandise, it's lucky that the **Harley Shop** (57 S. Market St., 843/722-9472, www.lowcountryharley.com) is filled with motor clothes, gifts, and collectibles.

Tinder Box Internationale (177 Meeting St., 843/853-3720, www.tinderboxcharleston.com) is a cigar shop that boasts the largest selection of domestic and imported cigars in South Carolina, as well as humidors, cutters, estate pipes, tobaccos, and the **Club Habana.** This upstairs martini bar features exotic drinks, coffees, and … cigars! Open until 1 A.M. Monday–Saturday, until midnight on Sunday.

Blue-Plate Specials

Serving lunch and dinner, **Hyman's** (215 Meeting St., 843/723-6000) has been here since 1890. Judging from the lines winding down the sidewalk, it'll be here until 2090. The menu offers oysters, crabs, mussels, steaks, and okra gumbo, as well as 15–25 fish to choose from, cooked any way you like—broiled, fried, Cajun, scampi, steamed, lightly Cajun sautéed, or Caribbean jerk.

Open for lunch and dinner, **Sticky Fingers** (235 Meeting St., 843/853-7427) has been named Charleston's best barbecue joint by several newspapers, magazines, and my stomach. Its ribs are Memphis wet, Memphis dry, Carolina sweet, and Tennessee whiskey. This is standard barbecue fare, but Southern all the way. If you need a few hours to get the barbecue sauce off your fingers, settle down at the Sticky Bar and try to loosen it up with the moisture on a cold glass of beer. If you're truly inspired by the barbecue, you may want to leave with a souvenir shirt: "Come lick our bones."

Watering Holes

Numerous great clubs dot the historic district, so consider this the short list. **Tommy Condon's** (60 Church St., 843/577-3818) attracts families during the day, but at night, it's the adults who can't get enough British beer and live Irish sing-along folk music. You can hear their howling down the street. At **The Griffon** (18 Vendue Range, 843/723-1700), you'll find signed money plastered on the walls, people from all over the world, small tables for good conversation, and a low-beamed ceiling for effect.

Shut-Eye

You can't avoid the fact that Charleston's a popular town; it reaches critical mass in the historic district. There are numerous inns here and several chain hotels.

Chain Drive
A, C, F, J, K, L, P, Q, S, BB, CC, DD

Chain hotels are in town, or within 10 miles. See cross-reference guide featuring phone numbers and Web addresses on page 514.

Inn-dependence
If you can swing it, stay at **Two Meeting Street Inn** (2 Meeting St., 843/723-7322, www.twomeetingstreet.com, $175–310), a nationally recognized inn that symbolizes Charlestonian elegance. Rates include continental breakfast and afternoon tea. Stunning inside and out, the mansion features nine spacious bedrooms and a luxurious ambience. G'wan, treat yourself to an afternoon in a rocking chair on the piazza.

Resources for Riders

Southern Comfort Run

Florida Travel Information
Florida Association of RV Parks and Campgrounds—850/562-7151,
    www.floridacamping.com
Florida Association of Small and Historic Lodgings—800/524-1880,
    www.florida-inns.com
Florida Division of Tourism—888/735-2872, www.flausa.com
Florida State Parks—850/245-2157, www.floridastateparks.org
Florida State Parks Camping Reservations—800/326-3521 or 866/422-
    6735, www.reserveamerica.com
Florida Turnpike Conditions—800/749-7453

Georgia Travel Information
Georgia Department of Tourism—800/847-4842, www.georgia.org
Georgia Road Information—404/635-6800
Georgia State Parks and Historic Sites—404/656-2770 or 800/864-7275,
    www.gastateparks.org

South Carolina Travel Information
South Carolina Bed & Breakfast Association—888/599-1234,
    www.southcarolinabedandbreakfast.com
South Carolina Campground Owners Association—803/772-5354 or
    800/344-4518, www.sccamping.com
South Carolina Department of Tourism—803/734-1700 or 800/872-
    3505, www.discoversouthcarolina.com
South Carolina Road Conditions—803/896-9621

Local and Regional Information
Charleston Convention and Visitors Bureau—843/853-8000 or
    800/774-0006, www.charlestoncvb.com
Charleston Weather Bureau—843/744-3207
Jacksonville Weather Service—904/741-4311
St. Augustine Visitor Information Center—904/825-1000,
    www.oldcity.com
St. Johns Visitor and Convention Bureau (St. Augustine)—800/653-
    2489, www.visitoldcity.com
Savannah Convention and Visitors Bureau—912/944-0455 or 877/728-
    2662, www.savannahvisit.com

Florida Motorcycle Shops
Bill Lennon's Cycle World—2630 U.S. 1 S, St. Augustine, 904/797-8955,
    www.billscycleworld.com
BMW Motorcycles of Daytona—118 E. Fairview Ave., Daytona Beach,
    386/257-2269, www.bmwcyclesdaytona.com

*Bruce Rossmeyer's Daytona Harley-Davidson, Destination Daytona, I-95 and U.S. 1, Ormand Beach, 386/671-7100, www.daytonahd.com
Cycle Accessories of Daytona—712 N. Beach St., Daytona Beach, 386/255-4255 or 877/432-9253, www.polarisofdaytona.com
Daytona Fun Machines—450 Ridgewood Ave., Daytona Beach, 386/238-0888, www.daytonafunmachines.com
First City Honda—210 SR 16, St. Augustine, 904/829-6416, www.firstcityhonda.com
Harley-Davidson Augustine—2575 SR 16, St. Augustine, 904/829-8782, www.hollingsworthhd.com
Honda of Jacksonville—8209 Atlantic Blvd., Jacksonville, 904/721-2453, www.hondaofjacksonville.com
Jacksonville Powersports—10290 Atlantic Blvd., Jacksonville, 904/641-5320, www.jacksonvillepowersports.com
Jim Walker Honda-Suzuki-Yamaha—2385 S. Ridgewood Ave., Daytona Beach, 386/761-2411, www.jimwalker.com
Tri-City Cycles—308 S. 2nd St., Flagler Beach, 386/439-3967
U.S. 1 Powersports—2590 U.S. 1 S, St. Augustine, 904/797-3479, www.us1powersports.com

Georgia Motorcycle Shops
Beasley Kawasaki Polaris Motorcycles—4317 Ogeechee Rd., Savannah, 912/234-6446, www.beasleymotorsports.com
Honda-Yamaha of Savannah—11512 Abercorn St., Savannah, 912/927-7070
John's V-Twin Cycles—77 W. Fairmont Ave., Savannah, 912/925-4666
Savannah Harley-Davidson—6 W. Gateway Blvd., Savannah, 912/925-0005, www.rideharley.com

South Carolina Motorcycle Shops
Hilton Head Motorsports—1286 Fording Island Rd., Bluffton, 843/837-3949, www.specialtymotorsports.com
Low Country Harley-Davidson Buell—4405 Dorchester Rd., Charleston, 843/554-1847, www.lowcountryharley.com
Luke's Honda-Kawasaki—1310 N. Main St., Summerville, 843/871-5371
Luke's Kawasaki-Polaris—7001 Rivers Ave., Charleston, 843/572-4541
Southern Scooters—36 Laurel Bay Rd., Beaufort, 843/846-2188
Yamaha of Beaufort—60 Savannah Hwy., Beaufort, 843/525-1711

*the world's largest Harley-Davidson dealership

Tropical Paradise Run

Miami Beach, Florida to Key West, Florida

It's as far south as you can ride in America, but don't expect to run across rednecks, kudzu, and clay roads. Miami Beach is a cosmopolitan city, and the Keys—especially Key West—have managed to hang on to their independent personality despite the efforts of corporations to tame them with generic mega-hotels.

This is a low, level, and not always scenic ride, but if you enjoy sun, snorkeling, scuba diving, and outdoor dining with no dress code, you can't do much better than a wintertime run between Florida's twin cities.

Miami Beach Primer

An insider tip: When you plan your run to Miami, make sure you plan to ride to Miami Beach. Miami is the mainland city, *Miami Beach* is the "Miami" you know, a string of islands separating Biscayne Bay from the Atlantic Ocean. At the southern tip of these islands is South Beach, the revitalized Art Deco District that attracts European jet-setters, fashion models, suave Latin playboys, and a nightclub crowd that'll stay up way past your bedtime.

A hundred years ago, all this was just a mangrove swamp, until some developers got the bright idea to dredge up sand from the ocean floor, pave the swamp, and turn it into a tropical getaway. The idea worked for about three decades

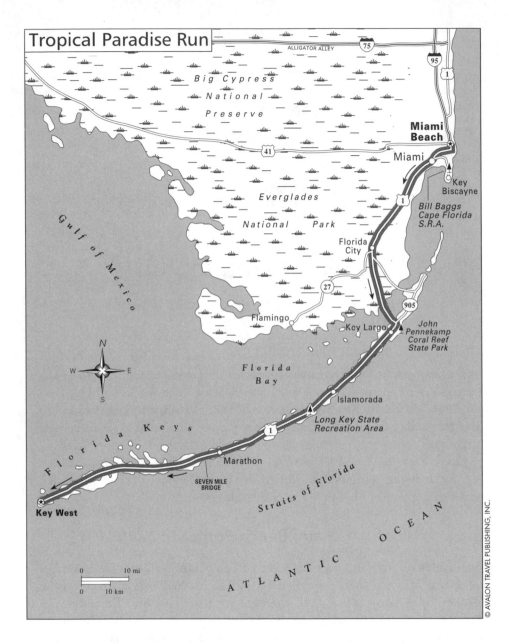

Route: Miami Beach to Key West via Key Largo, Islamorada, Hawk's Cay
Distance: Approximately 150 miles; consider seven days with stops.
•**Days 1–2—Miami** •**Day 3—Travel/Key Largo** •**Day 4—Travel** •**Day 5–6—**
  Key West •**Day 7—Return Trip**
Helmet Laws: Florida does not require helmets if you are over 21 and carry a
  minimum of $10,000 in medical insurance.

What's Art Deco?

If not for art deco, Miami would be just another of Florida's oceanfront cities noted for a crappy collection of condos. Fortunately, back in the 1930s, hoteliers, desperate to lure Northerners to alleviate their great depression, enlisted architects to jazz up staid, boxy buildings. They did so by borrowing accents first unveiled at a Parisian design exhibition a decade earlier. Stealing the shapes they saw used on trains, ocean liners, and automobiles, architects accented new hotels with pylons, spheres, cylinders, and cubes. As a bow to the omnipresent ocean, nautical features, such as portholes and images of seaweed, starfish, and rolling waves were incorporated into the designs. Wraparound windows and glass block became common features. And why the bright colors? Not a deco idea—give credit to *Miami Vice*, which needed a splashier backdrop for Don Johnson.

until September 1926, when the "No-Name Hurricane" hit and burst the land boom that had been sustained throughout the '20s. Afterward, Miami's fortunes rose and fell, taking their most precipitous dive in the 1980s, when Fidel Castro emptied his jails and sent the inmates on a cruise to Florida's sunny shores.

The Mariel Boatlift was the silver bullet that killed Miami tourism. High crime rates and a rapidly aging population sunk the city's image until Crockett and Tubbs arrived. *Miami Vice* depicted Miami Beach as a cosmopolitan, neon-bright tropical city, and the shift was on. Art deco hotels that had fallen out of favor were snapped up by entrepreneurs and turned into chic getaways for European fashion photographers who wanted a sexy, year-round backdrop.

In South Beach, the average age dropped from mid-60s to early 40s in 20 years. Today, cafés crank out Cuban *tinto* day and night, thong-wearing women glide past on in-line skates, and the beach is revitalized annually with powder-soft sands. It's not a great place to actually ride your bike, but it's the best place to kick off a tour down the Florida Keys.

On the Road: Miami Beach

Riding around Miami isn't a great idea—the roads are heavily trafficked, and even when you get somewhere, you're not seeing much. Your best bet is to ride into South Beach and concentrate your efforts there. Most sites are found between 5th Street to the south, 17th Street to the north, Ocean Drive on the east, and Washington Avenue, three blocks to the west. Parking tickets are as prevalent as pierced body parts, so consider locking up at a parking garage.

Ocean Drive is the heart of the Art Deco District, a collection of more than 800 buildings comprising the first 20th-century district to be named to the National Register of Historic Places. If you start here, you can blow off the rest of the day by spreading out a blanket at Lummus Park, the palm-lined stretch of Atlantic Ocean that runs from 5th to 15th streets.

This is Florida's Waikiki. On the wide, white beach, you can hook up with a pickup volleyball game, check out the in-line skaters, and go topless if you're discreet. About a hundred yards west, the cafés and hotels of Ocean Drive make it easy to take a break and chill out in the shade.

When you're ready for a foot tour, you can—and should—slip off the boots, step into sneakers, and invest in a great history lesson. At the **Art Deco District Welcome Center** (1001 Ocean Dr., 305/531-3484), you can rent a 90-minute historical audiotape ($15). It directs you on a walking tour of SoBe that will explain the concept and creation of the buildings of Lincoln Road, Espanola Way, North Beach, and the Art Deco District. The center is open 11 A.M.–6 P.M. daily.

A block north of the Welcome Center, the house at **1144 Ocean Drive** may look familiar if you watched the news the day designer Gianni Versace was killed on the steps. Afterward, the Spanish Mediterranean Amsterdam Palace became an eerie tourist attraction and then, oddly, a private members-only club.

From here, walk two blocks west to Washington Avenue and turn right on 14th Street, and then left on Espanola Way. This was the entertainment district for an old hotel and also where a Miami teenager named Desi Arnaz started beating out a conga rhythm. Today, the Mediterranean Revival buildings contain a row of eclectic shops and a Sunday afternoon flea market. It's a great place to meet locals.

At the next block, Meridian Avenue, turn right and head three blocks to the **Lincoln Road Mall.** Next to Ocean Drive, this is the center of the most activity in Miami Beach, complete with sidewalk cafés, street performers, bookstores, and cigar bars. If you choose the mall over Ocean Drive, the **Van Dyke Cafe** (846 Lincoln Rd., 305/534-3600) features great food, a busy sidewalk café for people-watching, and jazz music up on the second floor seven nights a week. You can't go wrong here.

After that, just saunter back to Ocean Drive and keep an eye out for them thongs.

Pull It Over: Miami and Miami Beach Highlights
Attractions and Adventures

It's a short ride inland from Miami Beach, but the **Venetian Pool** (2701 De Soto Blvd., Coral Gables, 305/460-5356, $6.25) is easily one of Miami's most beautiful havens. Created from a rock quarry in 1923, the stunning community pool conjures visions of an Italian waterfront village. It's a nice ride over and a great place to swim if you hate salt water. Lockers, concessions, showers, and vintage photos round out the perfection of this shaded, quiet retreat. Closed Mondays.

In Miami, before there was fashion, there was fishin'. Head out to the edge of the Gulf Stream and cast a line for sailfish, kingfish, dolphin, snapper, and wahoo. Charters are expensive, averaging about $350–400 for a half day. You may do better on a larger fishing boat, where you'll pay about $35. Don't bother with a fishing license, since the captain's blanket license should cover all passengers. You'll find several boats at the marinas listed below.

Crandon Marina (5420 Crandon Blvd., Key Biscayne, 305/361-1281) offers deep-sea fishing and scuba-diving excursions. **Haulover Marine Center** (15000 Collins Ave., Sunny Isles in North Miami Beach, 305/945-3934) is low on glamour, but high on service, with a bait-and-tackle shop, marine gas station, boat launch, and several deep-sea fishing charters.

Here's a way you can fish out of Miami Beach and save yourself a few hundred bucks. For cheaper excursions, check out the **Reward Fleet** (300 Alton Rd., Miami Beach Marina, 305/372-9470, www.fishingmiami.com), which operates two boats at moderate prices: $35 per person including bait, rod, reel, and tackle.

Far cheaper than fishing is just hanging out on the beach. The water is usually a gorgeous aquamarine, and the sands are soft and white. Lummus Park along Ocean Drive is fantastic, and beaches run north from here for about 20 miles. If these are too crowded, consider heading south to some of these remote and sparsely populated beaches and islands that are uncommonly close to SoBe.

At the far southern end of Key Biscayne, **Bill Baggs Cape Florida State Recreation Area** (1200 S. Crandon Blvd., 305/361-5811, $3) is worth the ride. Open 8 A.M.–sunset daily, the area features boardwalks, a café, picnic shelters, a fishing pier, and the Cape Florida Lighthouse.

North of Bill Baggs and also open 8 A.M.–sunset daily, **Crandon Park** (4000 Crandon Blvd., 305/361-5421, $5) has a marina, golf course, tennis center, ball fields, and a 3.5-mile beach with soft sand and a great view of the Atlantic. Parking is both inexpensive and plentiful.

Vizcaya Museum and Gardens in Miami

© NANCY HOWELL

Just past the tollbooth for the Rickenbacker Causeway, **Sailboards Miami** (Key Biscayne, 305/361-7245, www.sailboardsmiami.com) boasts that for $69, it can teach anyone to windsurf within two hours. It hasn't met my cousin Ricky. Open 10 A.M.–5:30 P.M. daily except Wednesdays.

If you can swing it, summer diving off Miami is as good as it gets. Visibility ranges from 30 to 90 feet, and about five miles offshore, you can explore great natural reefs and "wreckreational" artificial reefs the city created by sinking water towers, tankers, army tanks, a jet, and other recycled structures at depths between 80 and 130 feet. About 150 yards east of South Beach, the world's only underwater margarita bar sits in 20 feet of water. There are too many dive shops to list; you'll be better off checking www.miamidiveoperators.org.

Chicago industrialist James Deering built **Vizcaya Museum and Gardens** (3251 S. Miami Ave., 305/250-9133, www.vizcayamuseum.org, $12), a neoclassical 34-room winter mansion, for a cool $20 million. Vizcaya has entertained the likes of Ronald Reagan, Pope John Paul II, Queen Elizabeth II, Bill Clinton, and Boris Yeltsin—who got drunk and hung naked from a chandelier before he was tasered (that's a joke, comrade). It's a huge house that everyone sees, and it's nice if you like big houses—but the tour verges on boring. Open 9:30 A.M.–4:30 P.M. daily.

Little Havana's **Calle Ocho** (8th St.) is crowded and kind of dirty, but it can seem like an international expedition on a motorcycle. If you puff, the draw here is the cigar shops, where rows of Cubans at wooden benches rip through giant tobacco leaves, cut them with rounded blades, wrap them tightly, and press them in vises. One of the more authentic is **El Credito** (1106 S.W. 8th St., 305/858-4162 or 800/726-9481), which sells *gigantes, supremos, panatelas,* and Churchills to dedicated smokers like Robert De Niro, Rudy Giuliani, and George Hamilton.

Blue-Plate Specials

In South Beach, the **11th Street Diner** (11th St. and Washington Ave., 305/534-6373) serves breakfast, lunch, and dinner in a low-key, working-class setting. Specialties include such classics as meatloaf, burgers, shakes, and blue-plate specials. The 24-hour joint attracts night owls and budget-minded locals who don't need the attitude found at other eateries. The 1948 deco dining car suggests a Miami institution, but it's only been here since 1992.

Fourth-generation landmark **Joe's Stone Crab Restaurant** (11 Washington Ave., 305/673-0365) serves tons of stone crab claws daily, as well as an equal amount of drawn butter, lemon wedges, and mustard sauce. Perhaps the greatest ad headline I've seen: "Before SoBe, Joe Be." Joe's be open for lunch Tuesday–Saturday and dinner daily, but it's closed May–October.

At the 24-hour beachside **News Cafe** (800 Ocean Dr., 305/538-6397), you dine on breakfast, sandwiches, and light appetizers while watching the parade of people pass by. It's a favorite with locals, but tourists are slowly taking over their seats. Still, it's a great setting with great service and a true tropical Miami vibe.

Watering Holes

You may hear a lot about Miami nightlife, but the "hot clubs" drone with the repetitive thump-thump-thump of techno-pop music. Here are some spots that are better for bikers.

In the middle of South Beach, you wouldn't expect to find **Mac's Club Deuce** (222 14th St., 305/673-9537), a dark, dirty, working-class bar where men drink and—believe it or not, supermodels drop in to shoot a game of pool. Now *there's* an idea for a reality show. It sits around the corner from Ocean Drive and within stumbling distance of your hotel.

Opened in 1912, **Tobacco Road** (626 S. Miami Ave., 305/374-1198) holds Miami's oldest liquor license: number 0001! Head west across the bridge from the beach, and you'll find this bar in Miami's downtown (which can look creepy at night). The upstairs Prohibition-era speakeasy is now a stage for local and national blues bands.

South of downtown is hypercool Coconut Grove. At the epicenter is CocoWalk, where you'll find several chain bars and lounges, such as **Hooter's,** and an outdoor bar called **Fat Tuesday** (3015 Grand Ave., 305/441-2992), which serves beer and 190-proof margaritas that have the strength of 10 men.

Shut-Eye

Chain Drive
A, B, C, D, F, H, I, J, K, L, N, O, P, R, S, T, U, X, BB, CC, DD

Chain hotels are in town, or within 10 miles. See cross-reference guide featuring phone numbers and Web addresses on page 514.

Inn-dependence
Miami was reborn on the strength of its hotels, so finding nice digs shouldn't be too hard. Stay on Ocean Drive if you want action. If you want a quiet, out-of-the-way place, check out **Indian Creek Hotel** (2727 Indian Creek Dr., 305/531-2727, www.indiancreekhotel.com, $140–240). With more charm than a teenager's bracelet, the hotel features a Pueblo deco setting, courteous staff, and a secluded oasis of a pool out back.

Indulgences

If your second passion is sailing, hit the high seas with **Florida Yacht Charters** (390 Alton Rd., Miami Beach Marina, 305/532-8600 or 800/537-0050, www.floridayacht.com). After completing a checkout cruise and paperwork, slap down a deposit and take off for the Keys or Bahamas on a catamaran, sailboat, or motor yacht. Charts, lessons, and captains are available if needed.

On the Road: Miami Beach to Key West

Miami is a progressive city (albeit on the politically corrupt side), but it still hasn't progressed to the point of building a scenic highway down to the Keys.

You have two route choices: The Florida Turnpike bypasses a lot of traffic but costs a few bucks to reach Florida City, the step-off point for the Keys. Then there's Highway 1, the one and only road you need to reach Key West (or Maine). You make the call. Although I suggest a straight 120-mile shot to Key West, there are several places to stop for lodging and daytime activities.

On the other hand, towns in between are not that interesting, and the clutter of commercialism is taking its toll.

As you leave Miami, the traffic is horrible at first, but it becomes tolerable after running a gauntlet of urban ugliness. When you reach Florida City, the **Farmer's Market Restaurant** (300 N. Krome Ave., 305/242-0008) provides the perfect kickoff to the Keys. The servers have degrees in Southern hospitality, and the home-cooked food is farm fresh; the place serves breakfast, lunch, and dinner. If you thirst for something other than 100 percent pure Florida golden orange juice, you can find a 100 percent pure Wisconsin beer a few miles south at **Skeeter's Last Chance Saloon** (35800 S. Dixie Hwy./U.S. 1, 305/248-4935). Here since 1945, it's a popular destination for riders and happens to be the northern border of the Conch Republic.

Mile markers that start in Key West at mile marker 0 lead to here, mile marker 127. If you're anxious to get off the main road, take Route 905 and Route 905A, you'll be riding a less-traveled two-lane route that leads to the northern end of Key Largo. Otherwise, you'll ride through a 19-mile buffer zone between mainland America and Key Largo at mile marker 108. You may want to wear full leathers, son, but trust your old man. In the winter, the temperature is just right for riding naked, but otherwise it's too damn hot. I wore shorts, a T-shirt, and sneakers and was still covered with flop sweat.

The speed limit is 55, and the road is as level as a flattop from Floyd's Barber Shop. Along this road, motorcycles pass you so often, your frequent waving will help combat global warming. What's missing here are passing lanes. You can tell by the skid marks that some people can't wait. Be patient and pace yourself, since, as you well know, motorists can be notoriously stupid.

Two miles past a drawbridge at mile marker 106—one of 42 bridges you'll cross to reach Key West—is the **Key Largo Chamber of Commerce and Florida Keys Visitor Center** (305/451-1414 or 800/822-1088, www.keylargo chamber.org). Open 9 A.M.–6 P.M. daily, the center features information on attractions, lodging, and diving excursions—the lifeblood of Key Largo. Most dive centers host snorkeling trips (about $26) and scuba excursions (around $40, equipment extra).

A few miles south on your left is the **John Pennekamp Coral Reef State Park** (mile marker 102.5, 305/451-1202, www.pennekamppark.com), the most active site between Miami and Key West. The only underwater park in America starts a foot offshore and stretches three miles into the Florida Straits. Most Key Largo dive stations come to this underwater preserve to show divers 55 varieties of coral, 500 species of fish, and shipwrecks dating to the 1600s. The park is open 8 A.M.–sunset daily. Admission is $5 per vehicle, $0.50 per person.

Seeking Exile in the Conch Republic?

In the 1980s, invasions in places like Panama and Grenada overshadowed a revolution taking place in South America. To be accurate, it was really the American South.

In April 1982, U.S. Border Patrol agents set up a checkpoint near Skeeter's Last Chance Saloon, close to the northern end of the Florida Keys. Residents of the Keys had to prove their identity before being allowed to travel north or south. It wouldn't have been so bad if the roadblock hadn't affected U.S. 1, the only road to and from Key West.

At Miami's federal courthouse, Key West Mayor Dennis Wardlow requested an injunction to stop the blockade, but he was ignored. He stepped outside and announced to the media that, the next day, the Florida Keys would secede from the Union. And it did. At noon the following day, Wardlow read the proclamation of secession and announced the formation of the new Conch Republic. Then, a minute later, he surrendered his republic to a Navy admiral—and then requested *$1 billion* in aid to rebuild his nation.

The publicity stunt faded away in the mind of the United States government which, by ignoring it, helped establish sovereignty for the Conch Republic under international law. And when the Monroe County Commission approved Resolution No. 124–1994, it gave citizens of the Keys dual citizenship in the United States and the Conch Republic. Is it for real? Consider this:

From the main building, you can book boat tours, snorkeling expeditions, and scuba dives, as well as rent a canoe, kayak, and even swim fins, snorkels, and masks—some with prescription lenses. Or you can skip all this and retreat to one of several shallow swimming areas and use the picnic pavilions or restrooms. If you have the time, experience, and a bathing suit—dive. The water's perfect, and this is where you'll find the oft-pictured underwater *Christ of the Abyss* statue. Allow at least half a day if you dive, less if you don't.

If you're sidetracked by the sea and want to postpone your trip to the end of the line, I highly recommend crashing at the **Largo Lodge** (mile marker 101.7, 305/451-0424 or 800/468-4378, www.largolodge.com, $125 and up), Harriet Stokes's low-key collection of cottages that are locked in the 1940s. Harriet has been here since the mid-1960s, the lodge longer; she's a doll, and this is a

- The Secretary General of the Conch Republic issues "Official Conch Republic Passports," a document also held by the Minister of Internal Security, Supreme Commander of the Armed Forces, Rear Admiral, Prime Minister, and any Conch citizen who requests one.

- The same Secretary General has also traveled throughout the Caribbean carrying no other official documents except his "Diplomatic Passport."

- It's not just the Caribbean that recognizes the Conch Republic. Conchs have used their passports to travel to Germany, Sweden, Cuba, Mexico, France, Spain, Ireland, and Russia.

- The Conch Republic has a very brief foreign policy: "The mitigation of world tension through the exercise of humor."

- Notably, the Conch Republic also has its own flag, a symbolic reminder to the world that everyone is welcome here, regardless of "race, sex, nationality, sex, color, religion, and whether you drink beer, wine, or the hard stuff ..."

Order your own Conch Republic passport (citizen or diplomatic) and other gear at www.conchrepublic.com.

considerable bargain. You and your buddies can rent secluded, house-size units with rattan furniture, kitchenette, large living room, bedroom, and screened porch, all beside an indulgently relaxing bayside setting.

Key Largo offers another sight. The original *African Queen,* next to the Holiday Inn on your left at mile marker 100, is worth a brief, free glance.

At mile marker 86.7, look to your left for a bodacious lobster statue that lures people into a shopping center, but, for your purposes, is better used for a funky Florida snapshot. At the collection of Keys called Islamorada, there's less diving and more fishing. You can pick up information on sportfishing charters at the **Islamorada Visitors Center** (mile marker 82.5, 305/664-9767, www.islamoradachamber.com), open 8 A.M.–5 P.M. daily.

Almost as large as the lobster you saw earlier is the big-ass mermaid on your right at mile marker 82. The restaurant/bar **Lorelei** (305/664-4656), open daily for lunch and dinner, is a gathering spot for Miami riders, and for good reason. Every night, there's a sunset celebration; and every weekend, the backyard band sets the stage for a Frankie and Annette beach movie. There's a restaurant next door, but on a hot day, you'll be just as content having a cold one and dancing the frug.

The Keys start to become more scenic as the road affords longer glimpses of waters that shift from emerald green to azure blue. The commercial growth narrows with the islands, and at times, you're only a few feet from the waterline. If Wyoming is Big Sky country, this is Big Sea country, a liquid Death Valley.

A few miles down on your right, at mile marker 59, the **Dolphin Research Center** (305/289-1121, www.dolphins.org) has welcomed enough stars to outfit the Hollywood Squares. President Carter, Jimmy Buffett, and Arnold Schwarzenegger have all swum with the dolphins here—a $100 experience that requires reservations well in advance. Otherwise, $17 affords admission to look at sea lions and dolphins that stare at you in curiosity. If you book a swim, allow about two hours for your training class and count on roughly 15 minutes in the water, being pushed, pulled, and spun around by friendly dolphins. The center is open 9 A.M.–5 P.M. daily.

From here, the road rolls through Marathon, a crowded island to be endured, and unleashes you to the pleasures of the Seven-Mile Bridge. This impressive span presents you a prime opportunity to soak up vistas stretching far out into the Florida Straits. Remnants of Flagler's original railroad bridge are visible to your right. Enjoy this while you can—once you reach land, the scenery begins to suffer.

At mile marker 4, you cross a final bridge, and you'll have done it—you've ridden as far south as you can ride in America. At the light, Highway 1 turns to the right, passing strip malls, hotels, a Yamaha dealership, and a Harley-Davidson shop before merging with Truman Boulevard, which delivers you to Duval Street—the heart of Key West.

Key West Primer

There are few islands that can match the legends associated with Key West. Before the 1900s, it was associated with pirates, followed in the 1930s by Ernest Hemingway, followed in the 1940s by Harry Truman, followed in the 1970s by balladeer Jimmy Buffett.

Each of these men contributed something to Key West and, in turn, helped erode what had been here before. The publicity surrounding their infatuation with this remote and character-filled retreat opened the floodgates to tourists.

As a result, the island has become a parody of itself in many ways. Trying to get off this three-by-five-mile island without hearing Jimmy Buffett is like trying to square dance in a minefield without losing a limb. His songs drone on longer than Muzak in elevators, and tourists young and old arrive by the thousands to seek Margaritaville, a fictional utopia that exists only in a beer-shrouded fog. These thoughts of paradise have also lured the nouveau riche who have driven the price of real estate beyond reason—to wit, 800-square-foot cottages sell for $400,000.

But all hope is not lost. There are still plenty of characters here who will remain long after the cruise ships set sail and drunken "Parrotheads" return to their cubicles. They'll still be lounging around the Green Parrot or Capt. Tony's or Mallory Square—vagabonds, drifters, and dropouts; writers, artists, and independent thinkers freeing their spirits and feeding their creativity off the Key West streets.

On the Road: Key West

Well, you've made it this far, so now what do you do? There's no best way to see Key West, but here's one way I think is USDA okey-dokey. As corny as it sounds, the $22 **Conch Train Tour** (Mallory Sq., 305/294-5161, www.historictours.com) might be designed for your folks—but for 90 minutes, it gives you a very good historic and geographic overview of the island. Less kitschy is the **Old Town Trolley** (6631 Maloney Ave., 305/296-6688, www.trolleytours.com), which takes a $22, 70-minute tour and can navigate some places the train can't. The advantage here is that you can board and reboard at a dozen stops along the way.

After the tour, head down Duval Street to board a snorkeling, diving, or fishing charter. These half- or full-day excursions usually provide all the equipment you'll need. The charters don't go out too far—they don't need to, since great diving sites surround the island.

At sunset, there's only one place to be. Mallory Square is where everyone congregates, placing the island in danger of flipping right over. Supposedly, the draw is the sunset, but the real show is the street performers, vendors, and local characters hustling for hat money. Fire jugglers, gymnasts, magicians, performing dogs, trained cats, men with pierced nipples carrying iguanas, pot-bellied women in bikinis with pot-bellied pigs in their baskets … they're all here looking for their shot at stardom or a few bucks of your tour money.

Follow up the cheap thrills with dinner at a sidewalk café, and then a late evening doing the "Duval Crawl." There are great bars here, sidewalk stands where you can get a temporary tattoo or a good cigar, secluded courtyards hiding restaurants and martini bars, and, if you look closely ... Margaritaville.

Pull It Over: Key West Highlights
Attractions and Adventures

This "Odditorium" is a kick. At **Ripley's Believe It or Not** (108 Duval St., 305/293-9939), check out shrunken heads, a display of natives eating a crocodile, and a *Birth of Venus* made out of 66 slices of browned toast. You'll especially enjoy the cartoon explaining that one Dan Jaimun of Bangkok locked himself in his room for 22 years because his parents refused to buy him a motorcycle. Idiot—I came out after 21 years.

Key West thrives on aquatic adventures, ranging from glass-bottom boat trips to kayak excursions, snorkeling trips, and scuba dives. The competition means that each group offers roughly the same experience at the same cost, so you'll do better to pick up a handful of fliers at the welcome center and make your own selection.

One outfit I can recommend is **Fury Catamaran** (305/294-8899, www.furycat.com). This huge, steady boat departs from the Hilton Marina to sail out a mile or two for the sunset, serving free champagne, beer, wine, and soda along the way. Prices range $32–40, and Fury also features a slick snorkeling/sunset cruise combination.

Schooner Western Union & Schooner America (Schooner Wharf, 305/292-1766, www.schoonerwesternunion.com) charges $25–59 for cruises aboard the 130-foot *Western Union,* the last tall ship built in Key West. Varnished mahogany decks and canvas sails are part of the appeal; the fact that you can help hoist the sails is part two. Thankfully, there's little Buffetting aboard the boat—the entertainer sings old sea chanties. Beer, wine, and soft drinks are served.

No single tour explains all things Key West, so in addition to the Conch Train, consider filling in the blanks with **Island City Strolls** (305/294-8380, $18). Sharon Wells, the state historian in Key West, is an author and tour guide who knows more about the island than Buffett, Hemingway, and Truman combined. Various tours are available, ranging from architectural tours to writers' residences to the cemetery.

David Sloan is sincere about his job with **Ghost Tours of Key West** (305/294-9255, www.hauntedtours.com), and the fact that he and his henchmen dress like undertakers and drive hearses persuades me to plug this tour.

© GARY MCKECHNIE

Nancy sips on fresh coconut milk in Key West.

I don't believe in spooks, but gee, Wally, I kinda felt sorta creepy when he described the guy who married a corpse (and later consummated his marriage).

Ernest Hemingway moved to the house at 907 Whitehead Street in 1931 and, when he wasn't at Sloppy Joe's, wrote *For Whom the Bell Tolls, To Have and Have Not,* and *A Farewell to Arms* in his second-story writing room. **Hemingway Home** (305/294-1575, www.hemingwayhome.com, $9), is a must-see in Key West, so I'm listing it—even though on my tour, the guide crammed us in a room, ignored our questions, and started talking before we reached the next room. Unless you're a fan, skip it and save yourself the cash.

After years of searching, the late Mel Fisher discovered the circa 1622 wrecks of the *Nuestra Senora de Atocha* and *Santa Margarita,* ships that happened to be carrying a lot of gold and emeralds. Fisher fought the state of Florida for rights to the treasure, and he won. Since he didn't need to cash in all the booty to make himself a multimillionaire, he put some on display at the **Mel Fisher Maritime Museum** (200 Greene St., 305/294-2633, www.melfisher.org, $10). Pay at the door for the chance to ogle a six-pound gold bar, a 77-carat uncut emerald, and loads of treasure. Open 9:30 A.M.–5 P.M. daily.

Key West was President Harry Truman's winter pressure release from Washington. His home on the former naval base, today known as the **Harry S. Truman Little White House** (111 Front St., 305/294-9911, $10), is open 9 A.M.–5 P.M. daily for guided tours through nearly every room. If you're as slick as I am, you can sneak a seat at his desk or at the table where he played poker with his buddies.

a sidewalk in Key West

Shopping

It's leather forever at **Biker's Image** (121 Duval St., 305/292-1328), open 9:30 A.M.–midnight daily and carrying sexy clothes for the womenfolk, manly leathers for mighty men, and shirts, hats, caps, shoes, and thongs aplenty. **Beach Club** (210 Duval St., 305/292-7975) also peddles an assortment of stuff for riders, including backpacks, saddlebags, boots, and jackets. Open 9 A.M.–11:30 P.M. daily.

Blue-Plate Specials

Jimmy Buffet's **Margaritaville** (500 Duval St., 305/292-1435, www.margarita villekw.com) isn't "authentic" Key West, but if you like Buffett, you'll want to check out the offerings: fish sandwiches, yellowfin tuna, Key West pink shrimp, ribs, beer—and margaritas!

Actress Kelly McGillis opened **Kelly's Caribbean Bar & Grill** (301 Whitehead St., 305/293-8484), which serves both lunch and dinner. Lunch centers around sandwiches and salads with a Caribbean twist, and dinner varies from pasta to large steaks to four types of fresh fish. The main draw is outdoor dining in a courtyard or on the upper deck—a great spot to test Kelly's microbrews, Golden Clipper and Havana Red.

Off the beaten path, locals and tourists hang in the **Half Shell Raw Bar** (231 Margaret St., 305/294-7496), a real Key West favorite. Inside the cavernous dockside barn, pig out on raw oysters, chicken, burgers, ribs, crab, lobster, conch, dolphin, grouper, mako, wahoo, and other fish broiled, grilled, blackened, and fried. Beats them damn Fish McNuggets.

Watering Holes

Sloppy Joe's (201 Duval St., 305/294-5717 or 800/437-0333) capitalizes on its connection to Hemingway—he drank and gambled here. This loud and noisy bar is filled with barflies, college kids, and middle-aged tourists who get along well because everyone's drunk. Plan to drink here if you don't have to wake up until noon the next day, although you can find quiet upstairs in the semiprivate speakeasy. You'll find lots of pix and Ernie memorabilia, live entertainment, the requisite T-shirts, and a specialty drink called the Sloppy Rita. You can carouse here daily until 4 A.M.

Captain Tony, namesake of **Capt. Tony's Saloon** (428 Greene St., 305/294-1838, www.capttonyssaloon.com), remains a hard-drinking, woman-chasing, Key West icon known for being Hemingway's fishing guide and for giving Buffett a break by letting him perform in this morgue-turned-bar. Bring a business card or a bra to leave with the rest. Tony stayed true to keeping this a bar, not a tourist attraction, and his rumrunners and pirate's punch prove it. Trivia time: The bar opened the morning after Prohibition ended (November 15, 1933). Open daily 'til 4 A.M.

For a place with a biker name, **Hog's Breath Saloon** (Front and Duval Sts., 305/296-4222 or 800/826-6969, www.hogsbreath.com) is surprisingly tame. Still, you know you're gonna go, so here's what you'll get: entertainment from start to finish, a patio bar, bar food, and a drink called the "Hogarita." Everybody has an angle. Doors close at 2 A.M.

A few blocks from the commercial center, the **Green Parrot Bar** (Southard and Whitehead Sts., 305/294-6133, www.greenparrot.com) is what Key West bars probably looked like before outsiders showed up. It features pinball, pool, locals, and drinking that starts early and lasts late. Open shutters bring in the outdoors, and paraphernalia, including Bahamian art and motorcycle collectibles, make this a sanctuary well away from the cruise-line passengers.

Down and dirtier than dirt, **The Bull** (Caroline and Duval Sts.) has little charm, but it has a great location and an open-air bar that's great day or night. Upstairs, The Whistle places you above the madding crowd that flocks along Duval Street during festivals and most any other night. The rooftop Garden of Eden is opened to naturists who want a tan sans tan lines.

Shut-Eye

Lodging options run from chain hotels to small motels to inns. Don't arrive and try to make a reservation—do it in advance if you can. Two free services to help you out are the **Key West Welcome Center** (3840 N. Roosevelt Blvd., 800/284-4482, www.keywestwelcomecenter.com) and the **Key West Information Center** (1601 N. Roosevelt Blvd., 305/292-5000 or 888/222-5145, www.keywestinfo.com). In addition to offering free assistance to find affordable lodging (no mean feat in a place where rates are skyrocketing), they also make reservations for diving, snorkeling, sailing, and other activities.

Motels and Motor Courts

Before large resorts shoved their way in, there were quiet motels around Key West. Several still exist, although their in-season rates are seriously inflated. Beware. You'll find numerous other (perhaps better) options via the visitors center, but here are a few choices.

The **Blue Marlin Motel** (1320 Simonton St., 305/294-2585 or 800/523-1698, www.bluemarlinmotel.com, $89 off-season, $169 in season), a block off Duval Street and the Atlantic Ocean, has 54 motel-simple rooms with a/c, cable, fridge, and some with kitchenettes. A lush tropical courtyard contains a large heated pool. The **El Rancho Motel** (830 Truman Ave., 305/294-8700 or 800/294-8783, www.elranchokeywest.com, $129–179) is slightly farther from the action but is still a part of "Old Town." Rooms are done in typical motel style but are quite clean and sport a tropical look. The **Key Lodge Motel** (1004 Duval St., 305/296-9915 or 800/845-8384, www.keylodge.com, $99 and up off-season, up to $165 in season) is also well-placed and has 22 ground-level rooms, a pool, a free continental breakfast, and off-street parking.

Chain Drive

A, C, D, I, J, K, L, N, S, T, AA, DD

Chain hotels are in town, or within 10 miles. See cross-reference guide featuring phone numbers and Web addresses on page 514.

Inn-dependence

First there's the **Island City House** (411 William St., 305/294-5702 or 800/634-8230, www.islandcityhouse.com, $125 and up), a nice, laid-back inn consisting of three large buildings hidden within a tropical garden. A pool and free continental breakfast complement the large and comfortable rooms, and it's quite secluded for being in the heart of town. Look for the alligator at the bottom of the pool.

The **Center Court Historic Inn & Cottages** (915 Center St., 305/296-9292 or 800/797-8787, www.centercourtkw.com, $158 and up for an inn room, $188 and up for a deckside efficiency) is between Duval and Simonton streets, just off U.S. 1. The two-block street makes this an oasis, with just 17 Caribbean-style rooms arranged in the Cistern House, Honeymoon Hideaway, The Cottage, and the Family House. A heated pool, spa, exercise pavilion, tropical garden, and sun decks have raised prices. Group riders may want to check out the cottages.

Indulgences

About 20 miles north of Key West is an island retreat that'll dissolve a lifetime of stress (and savings) in less than five minutes. **Little Palm Island** (Little Torch Key, 305/872-2524 or 800/343-8567, www.littlepalmisland.com) is reached by a retro Chris Craft that delivers you to a Fantasy Island setting of spacious thatched-roof tiki huts, a secluded pool, tropical gardens, and a white sandy beach. A sunset dinner on the beach is pure, undiluted paradise. Although activities are available, if you can afford to do absolutely nothing, there's no better place not to do it than here. What's the catch? The privilege will cost you as much as a grand a night. And that's a freakin' huge catch.

Resources for Riders

Tropical Paradise Run

Florida Travel Information
Florida Association of RV Parks and Campgrounds—850/562-7151,
   www.floridacamping.com
Florida Association of Small and Historic Lodgings—800/524-1880,
   www.florida-inns.com
Florida Division of Tourism—888/735-2872, www.flausa.com
Florida State Parks—850/245-2157, www.floridastateparks.org
Florida State Parks Camping Reservations—800/326-3521 or 866/422-
   6735, www.reserveamerica.com
Florida Turnpike Conditions—800/749-7453

Local and Regional Information
Florida Keys and Key West—800/352-5397, www.fla-keys.com
Greater Miami Convention & Visitors Bureau—305/539-3063 or
   800/283-2707, www.miamiandbeaches.com
Key Largo Chamber of Commerce—305/451-4747 or 800/822-1088,
   www.keylargo.org
Key West Visitors Bureau—305/294-2587 or 800/527-8539,
   www.keywestchamber.org
Key West Welcome Center—800/284-4482,
   www.keywestwelcomecenter.com
Miami Beach Visitor Information—305/672-1270,
   www.miamibeachchamber.com
Miami Weather Service—305/229-4522

Florida Motorcycle Shops
Florida Key Cycle—2222 N. Roosevelt Blvd., Key West, 305/296-8600
Harley-Davidson of Miami South—17631 S. Dixie Hwy., Miami,
   305/235-4023, www.harleymiami.com
Horne's Harley-Davidson—1113 Truman Ave., Key West, 305/294-3032
M. D. Custom Cycles—99150 Overseas Hwy., Key Largo, 305/451-3606
Motoport USA—1200 N.W. 57th Ave., Miami, 305/264-4433,
   www.motoportusa.com
Peterson's Harley-Davidson of Miami—19400 N.W. 2nd Ave., Miami,
   305/651-4811, www.miamiharley.com
Riva Motorsports—3671 N. Dixie Hwy., Miami, 305/651-7753, www
   .rivamotorsports.com
Southwest Cycle—8966 S.W. 40th St., Miami, 305/226-9542

Blues Cruise

Memphis, Tennessee to New Orleans, Louisiana

This ride is unusual in its theme, following a single purpose—to immerse you in the birthplace of American music. In Memphis, you have as much chance of avoiding the music of Elvis as you do missing Jimmy Buffett tunes in Key West. When you ride Highway 61 into the vast emptiness known as the Mississippi Delta, you'll understand how this landscape nurtured the blues. And New Orleans? Well, that's a whole different story ....

You can concentrate on music, not frostbite, by riding anytime between March and November.

Memphis Primer

I could talk about Hernando de Soto and paddle wheelers and King Cotton, and all of it would be relevant to Memphis. But the city's history, like that of Vicksburg and New Orleans, is detailed in hundreds of books. Being definitive is impossible, so I'll limit my comments to this: You need only know that Memphis gave birth to the blues, then later to its wild sibling, rock 'n' roll. The city set the bar so high—achieving so much so quickly—that the town seemed weary for years, but it's pouring on the steam again. I seriously doubt that it can score a hat trick by creating another musical genre, but I hope Memphis proves me wrong.

Tired or not, Memphis is one of the most intriguing cities in America. In

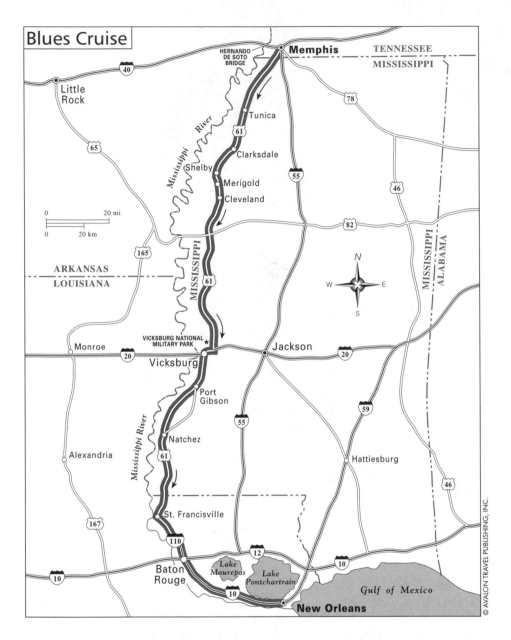

Route: Memphis to New Orleans via Tunica, Clarksdale, Vicksburg, Natchez Trace Parkway, St. Francisville

Distance: Approximately 480 miles; consider seven days with stops.

•**Days 1–2—Memphis** •**Day 3—Travel** •**Day 4—Vicksburg** •**Day 5—Travel** •**Days 6–7—New Orleans**

First Leg: Memphis to Vicksburg (226 miles)

Second Leg: Vicksburg to New Orleans (253 miles)

Helmet Laws: Tennessee and Mississippi require helmets. Optional in Louisiana if over 18 with proof of $10,000 of medical insurance.

addition to the larger-than-life influences of Elvis and W. C. Handy, Memphis offers simpler pleasures like fabulous barbecue joints and places like A. Schwab, where you can still buy celluloid collars and voodoo supplies. *American Heritage* magazine named Memphis a "Great American Place" in 1998. The city may be living on past glories, but who has a problem with that?

On the Road: Memphis

Because I love music, I could spend weeks here hitting great record stores and talking to older Memphians. If you have limited time, I'd suggest that you build a day around Elvis and an evening around the blues.

Memphis's streets are confusing, but if you ignore all but a few roads, you'll see nearly everything worth seeing. From the riverfront, look for Union Avenue, which shoots inland. Take this road, and when you reach Marshall Avenue, look to your left and you'll see a small red brick building. Stop here, because this is where rock 'n' roll was born.

Sun Studio (706 Union Ave., 901/521-0664 or 800/441 6249, www.sun-studio.com) was Sam Phillips's labor of love. When he wasn't recording weddings and political speeches, he was looking for unique black voices from the farms and fields surrounding Memphis. In the back of his mind, he was thinking about finding "a white man with a black man's voice."

On July 18, 1953, 18-year-old Elvis Presley dropped by Sam's "Memphis Recording Service" and paid $3.98 to record "My Happiness." A year later, on July 5, 1954, Phillips asked Elvis to jam with guitarist Scotty Moore and bassist Bill Black. That evening the trio changed history by blending hillbilly and blues to create rock 'n' roll. Not bad for a night's work.

The tour ($9.50) is fascinating not just because of Elvis, but because of "Rocket 88," "Great Balls of Fire," "Blue Suede Shoes," and other break-through songs recorded here in a burst of talent by such artists as Carl Perkins, Johnny Cash, Roy Orbison, and Jerry Lee Lewis. Thank God it's still a recording studio. You can even record your own songs here, karaoke-style ($30 per CD), or, if you're good and passionate, reserve the entire studio for an evening recording session for $75 an hour, with a two-hour minimum. Before you leave, check out the upstairs museum, gift shop, and the picture of Elvis on his 1956 KH Flathead Sportster.

From Sun, head up Union and turn right on Highway 51, aka Bellevue Boulevard. A few miles up on your left is a bike shop that deserves special mention. **Super Cycle** (620 Bellevue Blvd. S., 901/725-5991) sells sexy customized Harleys, parts, accessories, and collectibles. Elvis loved cruising the

Elvis and His Music

Before his fall, Elvis was passionate about his life and his music. Consider this generous tribute to his predecessors from a 1956 interview:

The colored folks been singing and playing it just like I'm doing now, man, for more years than I know. They played it like that in the shanties and in their juke joints, and nobody paid it no mind until I goosed it up. I got it from them. Down in Tupelo, Mississippi, I used to hear Arthur Crudup bang his box the way I do now and I said that if I ever got to the place where I could feel all old Arthur felt, I'd be a music man like nobody ever saw.

night streets of Memphis on his customized motorcycles—bikes souped up right here. Lew and Ronnie Elliott still service Elvis's bikes at Graceland and love talking motorcycles—and they're both as funny and hospitable as you'd expect two good ol' Memphis boys to be. The shop is open 8:30 A.M.–6 P.M. Tuesday–Friday, 8 A.M.– P.M. Saturday.

Now that you've primed yourself with Elvis lore, it's time for the payoff. Ride several miles south on 51 and look to your right for the parking lot for **Graceland** (3763 Elvis Presley Blvd., 901/332-3322 or 800/238-2000, www.elvis-presley.com). The only bad part about being here is that Elvis's image is everywhere, which makes the rest of us look like a race of Elephant Men.

For $27, the "Platinum Tour" takes you through the mansion, the Elvis museum, the auto and motorcycle museum, a movie, and his airplanes and tour bus. The tour is very streamlined: You buy a ticket, stand in line, get a headset and a taped tour, get on a bus, cross the street, and tour the house and museum. Aside from feeling like a herded cow, it's all pretty cool. In 1957, the Presleys moved to this 14-acre, $100,000 estate, where Elvis commenced two decades of all-night parties, recording sessions, and big food that ended when he got everything he wanted but not a thing that he needed.

Take time in the house, in the museum, and especially at Meditation Gardens, where Elvis is buried beside his father and mother. When you return to Graceland Plaza, check out the auto museum, where you'll see his Honda 300 (from Al's Cycle Shop on Summer Avenue), a cool Honda chopper, and his membership cards to the American Motorcyclist Association and Memphis Motorcycle Club.

There's far more of Elvis's Memphis to see—his first home at Lauderdale Courts (185 Winchester, #328), which have been cleaned up and turned into high-class condos; and Humes High (659 Manassas), where he first appeared onstage in a school talent show—but you also need to see Beale Street. The transition is eased by the hypercool Elvis statue on Beale near Main Street. This is Elvis as the Hillbilly Cat, replacing the circa 1970s Elvis, whose crotch was polished to a shiny gold by the fondling hands of female fans.

Time Beale Street for the afternoon and again for later that night. This was, and still is, the entertainment center of Memphis. When the town was segregated, the whites didn't know what they were missing. Blacks had turned this into a commercial district with tailors (birthplace of the Zoot Suit), bars, banks, insurance companies, newspapers, beauty parlors, and medical and dental offices. At night, the music would start.

In 1905, W. C. Handy was playing at PeeWee's Saloon when he was commissioned by E. H. Crump, a mayoral candidate, to write a campaign song. Handy recalled the stark music of the Delta singers, used his formal training to complement it with rich instrumentation, and *voila!*—the blues were born with "Mr. Crump" (soon to be known as "Memphis Blues"). Handy later wrote "St. Louis Blues" and "Beale Street Blues."

To honor W. C. Handy, the city has moved his shack to the corner of Beale and 4th streets. The **W. C. Handy House and Museum** (901/522-1556, $2) is open 10 A.M.–5 P.M. Tuesday–Saturday. When you see the simplicity of his home, you'll know that genius comes from within.

During the day, there are few places to hit on Beale Street, but **A. Schwab** (163 Beale St., 901/523-9782) is an essential stop. It was established here in 1876, and I doubt the inventory has changed much since: celluloid collars, bloomers, lye soap, skeleton keys, and my favorite—voodoo potions, candles, and soaps. A gentleman named "Sonny Boy" has cornered the market on a full range of customized voodoo soaps designed for specific purposes. Buy a few bars and scrub up with "Pay Me Now," "Drive Away Evil," "Come to Me," or, the best-seller for litigants, "Win My Lawsuit Court Case."

At night, Beale Street becomes a completely different place. Street musicians play anywhere and everywhere, and blues, rock, and jazz blow the doors off juke joints and nightclubs.

Go ahead. Get all shook up.

Pull It Over: Memphis Highlights
Attractions and Adventures

When you think of Memphis and music, Elvis comes first and the blues come second, and few people recall that, for one brief, shining moment, there was

Elvis and His Bikes

Lew Elliott, owner of Supercycle, a Memphis bike shop, never took a picture with Elvis; he thought it wasn't right for a businessman to ask for a picture with a customer. Elliott recalls:

Elvis was real easy to get along with. He always was a gentleman the whole damn time, and he made the other guys the same way. They'd come in, and not one of them would sit on a motorcycle unless they asked—including him. Never ever. He would always ask, "Can I sit on this one?"

When he'd come in, the ladies at the building across the street would see his trike and know he was here. Elvis was sitting on the windowsill when one of 'em came over and asked my brother Ronnie, "Is that Elvis?" He said, "I don't know what his name is. He's just delivering Pepsis." Then Elvis says, "Yeah, how many cases do you want, anyway?" Ronnie said, "I don't know, you'll have to check it." That's when Elvis started laughing and said, "Yeah, c'mon over. I'm Elvis."

Stax—aka *Soulsville USA*. The **Stax Museum of American Soul Music** (926 E. McLemore Ave., 901/942-SOUL or 901/942-7685, www.soulsville.com, $9) is presented perfectly to introduce Stax to novices, while pleasing real fans with 2,000 artifacts, rare videos, and insights into the rise and demise of the recording studio. Built atop the empty lot that was once its home, the experience begins with an introductory film and is followed by an explanation of the genre's gospel roots (highlighted by an actual black church) and goes on to play the music and tell the story of artists like the Bar Kays, Otis Redding, Rufus Thomas, Wilson Pickett, the Staple Singers, Booker T., and Isaac Hayes—whose 1972 "Superfly" Cadillac is the pimpest-looking museum display I've ever laid eyes on. 9 A.M.–4 P.M. Monday–Saturday, 1–4 P.M. Sunday.

The **Center for Southern Folklore** (123 S. Main St., 901/525-3655, www.southernfolklore.com) combines a nonprofit museum of Southern folk art with a beer and coffee bar and a stage for local bluesmen like Blind Mississippi Morris. Grab a book, settle back, and dig it the most. 11 A.M.–5 P.M. Monday–Saturday, with evening concerts by schedule, beginning around 7 A.M. and lasting 'til all hours.

The **Gibson Beale Street Showcase** (145 Lt. George Lee Ave., 901/543-0800, www.gibsonshowcase.com, $10 tour) features a 45-minute tour that leads visitors through a guitar factory to see how a block of wood is cut, lathed, bound, painted, buffed, and tuned before rockers like Pete Townshend smash them to bits. After the tour, walk across the street to the **Smithsonian Rock n' Soul Museum** (191 Beale St., 901/205-2533, www.memphisrocknsoul.org, $9) for a self-guided tour that features a 15-minute video celebrating local musicians, 100 songs on portable MP3 players to tune into while looking at displays on artists, and showcases with assorted artifacts and memorabilia, including Al Green's choir robe and lyric sheets from Elvis.

The chance to drop by different religious services is one of the perks of touring. At the **Full Gospel Tabernacle** (787 Hale Rd., 901/396-9192), worship while you dance and sing along with the Reverend Al Green. *The* Al Green. Pay a visit on Sunday at 11 A.M. Ride four lights south of Graceland, turn right on Hale Road, and it's a half mile down.

The **National Civil Rights Museum** (450 Mulberry St., 901/521-9699, www.civilrightsmuseum.org, $11) is in the old Lorraine Hotel, where Martin Luther King Jr. died. Visiting this place is like making a pilgrimage to the Dakota, where John Lennon was killed. This museum is cluttered with displays, so you'll only be able to skim it. Sit on the bus and feel what it was like to be told to "move to the back," and take time to see Dr. King's room the way it was left on April 4, 1968. It's a world-class venue, with legends such as Nelson Mandela, Bill Clinton, Sidney Poitier, and Bono making the trek here to receive the foundation's Freedom Award. The museum is open 9 A.M.–5 P.M. Monday–Saturday, 1–5 P.M. Sunday, closed Tuesday.

Shopping

While a teenager, Elvis couldn't afford many records, so he spent hours and hours at **Poplar Tunes** (308 Poplar Ave., 901/525-6348) listening to platters by white crooners, hillbilly singers, and black R&B artists—later putting this mix on his own albums. In 1954, "Pop Tunes" was the first store in the world to carry an Elvis record. He returned the favor by dropping in often to sign autographs. Great shirts here, too.

Malcolm Anthony, proprietor of **Memphis Music** (149 Beale St., 901/526-5047, www.memphismusicstore.com), is a self-proclaimed doctor—a "bluesologist," he says—and carries a mighty collection of music books and blues and gospel CDs by artists like Fats Waller, Mighty Clouds of Joy, and Little Charlie and the Nightcats. The good doctor also carries movie posters, such as the one for *Beale Street Mama*—which boasted an "all-colored cast!" Great stuff peddled by a nice guy.

Blue-Plate Specials

Memphis is known for barbecue, and **Cozy Corner** (745 N. Pkwy, 901/527-9158) is a local fave, serving lunch and dinner Tuesday–Saturday. Raymond Robinson Jr. runs this chicken-and-ribs joint, which attracts blacks, whites, blue- and white-collar workers, and celebrities like B. B. King, Robert Duvall, and Hank Williams, Jr. Get a slab of two, four, or six ribs with coleslaw, bread, and beans or barbecue spaghetti. Have mercy!

I'd been to Memphis a dozen times before I learned about **Charlie Vergos Rendezvous** (52 S. 2nd St., 901/523-2746). I don't blame myself, since it's hidden out of sight in a basement down General Washburn Alley in the heart of town. When you discover it for yourself, you enter a huge subterranean pork parlor where memorabilia and celebrity photos clutter the walls. A huge bar's going, and white-shirted/black-tied servers are hustling all over the joint, hauling platters of rubbed ribs, mustard-based coleslaw, pork shoulder sandwiches, lamb riblets, and chicken to diners spread out in a dozen dining rooms. A classic since 1948.

Thanks to Chef Bonnie Mack, the **Blues City Cafe** (138 Beale St., 901/526-3637) is a legend. Diners drop by for Mack's mean mess of ribs, steaks, shrimp, catfish, tamales, liquors, beer, and burgers. Serving lunch and dinner, this greasy spoon sports cheap Formica tables and office chairs; there's a bar and stage next door. Good food, plus great ad copy: "The Best Meal on Beale" and "Put Some South in Your Mouth."

Slapping down down-home diner food since 1919, the **Arcade Restaurant** (540 S. Main St., 901/526-5757) is the kind of place where waitresses tell you, "If you need anything, just holler." Just a few blocks from Beale Street, the Arcade serves up basic home-cooked food that fills the bill: hamburgers, butter pasta, squash, baked apples, and stuffed bell peppers, as well as Elvis's favorite: fried peanut butter and 'nanner sammiches.

Watering Holes

Along Beale Street, take your pick from a great concentration of nightclubs within walking distance of downtown. Also consider **B. B. King's Blues Club** (143 Beale St., 901/524-5464, www.bbkingclubs.com), a restaurant that borders on a juke joint. Lots of B. B.'s ("Blues Boy's") gold records are on display, along with guitars from Keith Richards, Memphis Slim, and Stevie Ray Vaughn. The stage hosts blues acts, of course, and there's live music every single night. Oh, yeah. There's also a full bar and lots of beer.

A cavernous Irish joint, **Silky O'Sullivan's** (183 Beale St., 901/522-9596) jumps at night, with imports on tap (Guinness, Fosters, Bass, Newcastle, Harp), a full liquor bar, and a 30-year-old house secret called "the Diver"—a gallon pitcher that contains a little of everything. After you finish the $18 concoction, call a taxi, stumble back to your room, or go to the hospital.

Shut-Eye

On most trips, I try to avoid downtown areas, but in Memphis, most attractions are downtown, down by the riverside. Finding a chain here isn't a problem. One in particular deserves extra attention: the **Residence Inn** (110 Monroe Ave., 901/523-2528, $125). Converted from an old apartment building, the rooms are superspacious, with complete kitchens, large living rooms, and plenty of room to sleep. Putting it over the top is its location (downtown), extraordinary hospitality, and a monumental complimentary breakfast buffet.

Chain Drive
A, C, D, E, G, H, J, K, L, P, Q, S, O, T, U, W, X, BB, CC, DD

Chain hotels are in town, or within 10 miles. See cross-reference guide featuring phone numbers and Web addresses on page 514.

Indulgences

If you can swing it, stay at the legendary **Peabody** (149 Union Ave., 901/529-4000, www.peabodymemphis.com, $210–280). Fancified like the rest of Memphis probably used to be, the hotel features plenty of class in its deluxe rooms and suites. The ducks march at 11 A.M. and 5 P.M. Right across from The Peabody, the generic **Holiday Inn Select** (160 Union Ave., 901/525-5491 or 888/300-5491, $169 and up) has covered parking. In midtown, a few miles from downtown, the **French Quarter Suites** (2144 Madison Ave., 901/728-4000 or 800/843-0353, $99–119) are a good option right next to Overton Square, another site for Memphis nightlife. Some rooms have king beds, and all have double-size whirlpool tubs.

On the Road: Memphis to Vicksburg

Before leaving Memphis, take a few minutes to set off on a tour to the western United States. The Mississippi River flows past Memphis, so after you've crossed the Hernando De Soto Bridge into Arkansas, you've ridden to the other side of the continent in less than 10 minutes. Take Front Street to Adams, turn left, and keep going. It's an impressive sight, considering the mighty Mississippi is 2,350 miles long, receives water from 300 rivers, drains 1.25 million square miles of the nation, and dumps enough sand, gravel, and mud near its mouth daily to fill a freight train 150 miles long. Just like my bathtub.

When you return to Memphis, take 2nd Street south, pass the National Civil Rights Museum, and watch for Highway 61. After about 15 miles of congestion, the road clears up and you enter one of the most unusual regions of the country, the Mississippi Delta.

Almost instantly, the buildings disappear and the farmland commences. The landscape is completely flat, the only structures of prominence are the repetitive billboards for Tunica's casinos followed by billboards for pawnshops. With so little to look at, the sight of the casinos on the horizon may tempt you, but it'd be more fun to spend the money you'd lose here on a trip to Las Vegas. Tunica is like a comet; it flares up and disappears quickly.

Five miles south of Tunica, Highway 61 goes two-lane, but the scenery doesn't change. This is about the time you'll understand why Muddy Waters and John Lee Hooker started singing the blues here—there was nothing else to do.

About 60 miles south of Memphis, watch for the sign to Clarksdale where 61 splits from 49. Veer to the right and follow the signs to the Delta Blues Museum. On your ride through this old town, you'll turn right at the inter-section (DeSoto) where Robert Johnson supposedly sold his soul to become a great guitar player. That's just one of the stories relayed within the surprisingly impressive, must-see **Delta Blues Museum** (1 Blues Alley, 662/627-6820, www.deltabluesmuseum.org). Open 9 A.M.–5 P.M. Monday–Saturday, the free museum is also a research facility and a library of the blues. It's stocked with CDs, books, magazines, vintage photos, more books, one of B. B. King's gui-tars, exhibits on juke joints and harmonicas, a map showing the birthplace of famous blues musicians, and a most impressive exhibit of Muddy Waters's log cabin. If you don't understand the blues, check out the display on who owes a debt to this local creation: John Lennon, Keith Richards, Bob Dylan, Eric Clapton.… It also impressed Led Zeppelin's Robert Plant and Jimmy Page, who dropped by the museum and had their picture taken for the local paper.

On Highway 61, you're back to the flatlands of the Delta. There's nothing to see, but it's strangely calming out here. The wind is powerful, because there's nothing to stop it but you, and the only distraction is your radio—if you have one—which you can tune to WNIX (1330 AM) out of Greeneville. Set the throttle and cruise, listening to the static sound of old '50s and '60s doo-wop, rock, and R&B records—the perfect soundtrack for this stretch of the ride.

Shelby is the next town of any size, full of future blues musicians. After Shelby is Merigold, where the center of commerce is a crawfish cooler, and then there's the metropolis of Cleveland, a good place to buy a tractor. In the town of Shaw, you may see some cows, which vary the scenery slightly, but then it returns to the Delta again.

Although I make this ride sound slow and empty—and geographically, it is—it took a few weeks of reflection to realize that it was one of my favorite rides. Why? Because this isn't the same shaded back road or wide-open desert. This is different, and it is real.

As you ride the final 80 miles to Vicksburg, stopping at any of the plentiful food and fuel stores, you'll have time to think about the despair and the hope that permeate this area. Despite the lack of culture, at least as most of us define it, the people here have developed their own. Their culture, more than opera or ballet or Broadway, spoke to young people around the world—who, in turn, channeled the music into a social and political force that changed the way we live. And it all started right here. In towns like Panther Burn and Nitta Yuma and Hushpekena.

Suddenly, the Delta doesn't seem so empty anymore.

Vicksburg Primer

How valuable was Vicksburg to the Union? President Lincoln observed that "Vicksburg is the key. The war can never be brought to a close unless that key is in our pocket." Ulysses Grant took Lincoln at his word, and the Siege of Vicksburg began.

That's what this sleepy town on the banks of the Mississippi is still known for. Originally, Grant tried to ford the Mississippi River and conquer the city, but bluffs 200 feet high stopped him cold. Grant wanted Vicksburg, so he moved downriver and crossed to Port Gibson, worked his way to Jackson, and came up behind Vicksburg to shell and starve the city into surrender.

When the siege began on May 18, 1863, citizens went underground, hastily digging caves to escape the bombing. Known as the "cave people," they were reduced to eating rats, but they surfaced when the siege finally ended on July 4, and Grant nearly received the "unconditional surrender" he had requested. Five days later, Grant captured Port Hudson, and the commerce of the Mississippi River belonged to the Union.

Vicksburg still looks as if it's seen better days, but the people here practice Southern hospitality without thinking of it as a cliché.

On the Road: Vicksburg

Vicksburg is the perfect-size riding and walking town. Park in the historic downtown district, and you can hoof it nearly anywhere. When you want to ride, saddle up and head out for a great run through the military park. One nice thing about Vicksburg is that you can see most of it in a day and not think you're missing too much.

To get an idea of what happened here in 1863, before you go to the park, go see *Vanishing Glory,* which is shown at the **Vicksburg Battlefield Museum** (4139 I-20 Frontage Rd., 601/638-6500, www.vicksburgbattle-fieldmuseum.com). Also on display here is a 2,500-miniature soldier army that recreates the battles and the siege, the world's largest collection of Civil War gunboat models, and an assortment of maps, clothing, photos, and relics.

The slide show gives you an overview of the battle and prepares you for the **Vicksburg National Military Park** (3201 Clay St., 601/636-0583, www.nps.gov/vick), open 8 A.M.–5 P.M. daily. To get there, head east on Clay Street (Hwy. 80) for about 10 blocks and look for the plaques, markers, and cannons announcing it on your left.

In the visitors center, you can view an 18-minute film and exhibits on the "cave people," along with the usual collection of Civil War books (with an obvious emphasis on the heroic battles here). If your bike has a cassette player, invest in a taped tour that will fill in the blanks as you ride.

The roughly circular road passes 1,300 monuments, of which the Illinois Monument is most impressive. To avoid glorifying the war, the memorial's builders created a model of Rome's Pantheon, and inside listed the names of the Union soldiers who died here.

In light of what happened on these grounds, it seems sacrilegious to tell you this is a great motorcycle road, with nice twists and dynamite blacktop single lanes, but it is. Now back to the war. At the *Cairo,* you'll see the remnants of the Union ironclad sunk in 1862 and raised 100 years later. Next door, within the 40-acre cemetery, are the burial sites of 17,000 Union soldiers who were reburied here with honor after the war. The Confederate dead rest in a city cemetery.

If you're a Civil War buff, continue the ride and return to the entrance; otherwise, from the cemetery, you can skip out a side exit and return to town. It should be lunchtime now, and there's only one place to eat, Walnut Hills (see *Blue Plate Specials*).

Downtown lies just a few blocks away, but ride over to the **Old Courthouse** (1008 Cherry St., 601/636-0741, www.oldcourthouse.org, $5). You'll see ex-

Blues Cruise

hibits that cover the Civil War and more, since locals contributed a lot from personal collections. The most disturbing artifact is from an administrator's sale on December 29, 1842: "Selling church pew, town lot, and at the same time and place, selling 160 Negroes consisting of men, women and children. Also horses and mules." Incredible.

Humanity got its turn in the Vicksburg newspaper that taunted the seemingly impotent General Grant. On July 2, the paper claimed he'd never take over the city. Two days later, Grant and his Union troops were in town and released the suspended paper, having added their own editorial advising the Rebels to respect their Yankee guests.

After you reach Washington Street, take about an hour to drop in at places like the Corner Drug Store, and then stick around. The beautiful Mississippi River is calming, and places to socialize at night are few. Besides, why should you be in a hurry to leave? This is an adventure.

Pull It Over: Vicksburg Highlights
Attractions and Adventures

Joseph Gerache, proprietor of the **Corner Drug Store** (1123 Washington St., 601/636-2756), is a born salesman and, according to his business card, also an apothecary, bon vivant, collector par excellence, entrepreneur, and *raconteur avec savoir faire*. He's also a collector. His drugstore is crammed with moonshine whiskey jugs, Civil War shells, projectiles and cannonballs, rifles, shotguns, quack medical curiosities, and potions like Dr. Sanford's Liver Invigorator and Indian Chief Kidney and Liver Tonic.

Blue-Plate Specials

Walnut Hills (1214 Adams St., 601/638-4910, www.walnuthillsms.com), serving lunch and dinner, is like Mrs. Wilkes's in Savannah. Settle down at a round table, where a lazy Susan the size of a satellite dish holds the finest in all-you-can-eat road food: fried chicken, rice and gravy, fried corn, purple hull peas, green beans, mustard greens, okra, coleslaw, and more. It's good eating, but you'll have to remember to adjust your bike's springs afterward.

Watering Holes

Like other towns along the Mississippi, Vicksburg has built casinos. If you like crowds and drinks and intrusive video-game noises, waste your time at

⊣ 253 ⊢

Harrah's (800/843-2343), **Ameristar** (601/638-1000 or 800/700-7770), **Isle of Capri** (800/946-4753), or **Rainbow** (800/503-377). Otherwise, settle down with some friendly locals back at Walnut Hills.

Shut-Eye

Motels and Motor Courts
The **Battlefield Inn** (4137 I-20 N. Frontage Rd., 601/638-5811 or 800/359-9363, www.battlefieldinn.org, $65–75) is a sure bet. Locally owned, it offers clean rooms, two free cocktails per person per night, and a full Southern breakfast for one low price. Now *that's* Southern hospitality.

Chain Drive
A, C, E, G, I, Q, Z, CC

Chain hotels are in town, or within 10 miles. See cross-reference guide featuring phone numbers and Web addresses on page 514.

Inn-dependence
In Vicksburg, even prices at the fancy places are fairly reasonable. **The Corners Mansion,** (601 Klein St., 601/636-7421 or 800/444-7421, www.the-corners.com, $90–130) lets you sleep in the main house or the former slave quarters. Either is great, but the massive rooms on the top floor afford a great view of the Mississippi River.

Across the street, **Cedar Grove Mansion** (2200 Oak St., 601/636-1000 or 800/862-1300, www.cedargroveinn.com, $100–190) is *Gone-with-the-Wind* fancy, with sumptuous furnishings and a sprawling estate to calm you down. The dining room is usually packed with Vicksburg society, and the piano bar is a nice spot to sip a mint julep.

On the Road: Vicksburg to New Orleans

Riding out of Vicksburg on Washington, watch for the Mississippi River Overlook, a quick stop where you can take a picture of you and your bike that'll stay on your desk for years. Follow Highway 61/I-20 to Exit 1B, which puts you back on 61 South toward Natchez. You'll notice a marked difference in this leg of the trip. Instead of fertile plains, the road is bordered by trees and gas stations, warehouses, and manufacturing plants. After about five miles, the growth stops and the scenery changes to small houses, oak trees, and kudzu.

It's an uneventful ride to Port Gibson, the small town that Grant said "was too beautiful to burn." Once you hit the canopy of trees and see some of the antebellum homes of this true Southern town, you'll understand why Grant put the matches away.

Two miles south of Port Gibson, watch for the entrance to the **Natchez Trace Parkway** (www.nps.gov/natr) on your right. The parkway began as a path used by animals and Native Americans and then, in the late 1700s, became the way home for traders who had taken the Mississippi downstream, but who didn't have the muscle or machinery to get back. One of Franklin Roosevelt's public works projects, it doesn't match the Blue Ridge Parkway for beauty, but it's still a nice ride through the woods.

Expect lots of bikes on the road, mostly on weekends, when local riders hit this for a good run. If you grew up in the South, you'll recognize the smell of these woods—as familiar to us as the scent of maple syrup to a Vermonter.

Every so often, a pleasant field appears, and at Coles Creek, mile marker 17.5, there's a shaded picnic area and restrooms. Watch for the entrance to Emerald Mound, mile marker 10.3, the second-largest temple mound in America and worth a stop for the nice view from the top.

About two miles south of the mound, the parkway slides you back onto Highway 61 toward Natchez. This stretch is not nearly as scenic as what you left—it's mostly a collection of flea markets and radiator shops.

Follow the signs into the historic district, and you'll be riding toward the Mississippi River. The overlook is as impressive as any I've seen; step into a gazebo, and you can look for miles upstream and down.

Natchez is a city where time seems to have stopped a few minutes before Lee surrendered at Appomattox. You get a sense of this at the **Visitors Reception Center** (640 S. Canal, 601/446-6345 or 800/647-6724, www.natchez.ms.us), which provides an introductory movie ($2) and sponsors tours that drive past antebellum homes.

You'll find a slice of Americana in Natchez at a restaurant called **Mammy's Cupboard** (555 Hwy. 61, 601/445-8957). Opened in 1940, the place fulfills every man's dream by ushering diners in beneath the bustle of a 28-foot-tall woman's skirt. The huge roadside art is funky, but hours are short: Open for lunch 11 A.M.–2 P.M. Tuesday–Saturday.

When you leave Natchez, Highway 61 returns to its slow and lonely character, getting narrower, shadier, and more verdant. There are few things to note here, although the razor wire atop the Wilkinson County Correctional Center looks beautiful in the last rays of daylight.

With little else to see, settle in and enjoy the ride. At the junction of 61 and

24 in Woodville, there are three gas stations and a grocery store, but not much to the town.

A few miles south puts you in Louisiana; the road becomes nicer, offering wide pullouts and more forest. Within minutes, you'll reach St. Francisville—where I'd recommend that you just follow the signs to the historic district. One of those towns where everything seems to be just right, it's a perfect place to ride your bike and get lost in neighborhoods. The streets are wide, the homes are pretty, and outdoor cafés coax you to stop. Take advantage of the opportunity, because after this, when you get back on Highway 61, the road begins to fizzle out as you approach Baton Rouge.

I try desperately to keep you off the interstates in this book, and I seek spiritual and psychological counseling when I fail. I needed therapy for this next recommendation: Because Baton Rouge is a mess of urban hillbilly density, it's far easier to detour onto I-110 to I-10 for the final leg into New Orleans.

It's not really a bad ride, although traffic begins to build about 10 miles outside the city. Stick with it and in a few minutes, *laissez les bons temps rouler!*

New Orleans Primer

We all know that nature did its worst to destroy New Orleans in August 2005. Downtown and other low-lying areas took a catastrophic hit, but the French Quarter—where most of the attractions, lodging, and dining highlighted in this section are found—seemed to make it through relatively unscathed. That said, call in advance and see how the Crescent City is shaping up. Based on the *joie de vivre* of its residents, I'll bet the good times in New Orleans will be rolling again.

Early New Orleans must have been a pretty amazing place. Why else would colonists—English, French, and German citizens, political exiles, and criminals—stick around, despite storms, yellow fever, insects, snakes, alligators, and flooding? Even if I lived in Monte Carlo, I'd pack it up after the first chigger bite.

Most stayed because they had been duped into coming here and didn't have a way back. The French later improved conditions with lavish displays of wealth (coupled with corruption and graft), and the city's notorious reputation for decadence and immorality increased.

Things got even more confusing in 1763. A war treaty forced France to surrender everything east of the Mississippi River to the English, but King Louis XV had already given New Orleans to Spain on the sly. The Spanish arrived; the early French settlers (Creoles) rebelled and were defeated; and the Spanish thrived. The Creoles stuck to their language and social customs and later convinced Napoleon to regain their city. He did, but then sold it to Thomas Jefferson through the Louisiana Purchase in 1803.

There you have it. New Orleans is populated with the ghosts of French settlers, Spanish explorers, British soldiers, African slaves, and Caribbean immigrants, as well as modern-day hustlers, gamblers, artists, musicians, dancers, and riverboat captains who wring maximum pleasure out of each day.

On the Road: New Orleans

While Memphis rocks, New Orleans jazzes things up. You'll hear jazz played in the streets, in the clubs, in courtyards, and at funerals. It is everywhere, all the time—like Muzak, but good.

Unfortunately, New Orleans is not a riding town. Park your bike (and lock it), and then take tours of the French Quarter and the Garden District to get an overview of the city before you descend into it alone later or the following day. I've had good luck with Gray Line Tours in several cities, and this is another one.

The town is far too large for me to cover in depth here. If you want to delve deep into it, stay a week and invest in volumes of travel guides. For now, I can only suggest an approach to the French Quarter.

Start early. Very. Hitting the streets by 7 A.M. gives you control of the city before the buses arrive. You'll actually find a seat at the **Cafe Du Monde** (813 Decatur St., 504/587-0833, www.cafedumonde.com), open 24 hours a day. It's been here since 1862, and as more than a century of customers can attest, it's the place to relax over a café au lait and hot beignet. Then wipe the sugar off your lips and head a few blocks east to the **French Market** (504/522-2621, www.frenchmarket.org). Since 1791, this is where locals have shopped for essentials, which today includes turtle shells, gator on a stick, dried snakes, and voodoo potions. Unfortunately, a lot of crappy new stuff has crept into the market, but it's still a cool place to meet some locals and maybe find a good buy.

Double back to Jackson Square (across from the Cafe Du Monde). The **New Orleans Hospitality Center** (529 St. Ann St., 504/566-5661), on the south side of the square, is the place to load up on literature and maps. Take a break in Jackson Square and watch artists, street performers, and musicians set up on the sidewalks as the morning progresses. Or take off into the French Quarter and let yourself go. Go anywhere and see everything you can in this 90-square-block historic district, keeping in mind that Chartres, Dauphne, and Royal streets are longer (hence more diverse) than other avenues in the area.

The French Quarter represents the third try at establishing the city—fires in 1788 and 1794 razed the original buildings. Although it attracts tourists, it isn't solely a tourist attraction. More than 7,000 people live and work here, and the Vieux Carré Commission keeps tabs on preserving the architecture. You'll pass antique galleries, private apartments, guesthouses, gift shops, cheap dives, legendary nightclubs and restaurants, con men, pickpockets, and prostitutes. Watch your wallet, chief. And your zipper.

When you return here after dark, Bourbon Street, like Memphis's Beale Street, is a different world. Fats Domino, Irma Thomas, Wynton Marsalis, and Harry Connick Jr. all call New Orleans home, and there's always a chance of hearing them at a local club if you know where to look. **Tipitina's** (501 Napoleon Ave., 504/895-8477, www.tipitinas.com), perhaps best known for appearances by the Neville Brothers, serves up live R&B, jazz, Cajun, reggae, and rock seven days a week. The most famous jazz venue of all, however, is **Preservation Hall** (726 St. Peter St., 504/522-2841 or 888/946-JAZZ www.preservationhall.com, $8 cover). This place strikes up late-night jam sessions in a crowded, poorly lit room where you can dig an ever-changing ensemble of genuine jazz masters. Open daily 8 P.M.–midnight.

Beyond this, experience—more than words—describes the area best. If you're ready to get looped, you're in luck. With no closing laws, bars can stay open night and day—a distinction that may explain why New Orleans has the third-highest alcohol consumption rate in America.

Pull It Over: New Orleans Highlights
Attractions and Adventures

In a macabre mood? A high water table necessitated "Lestat-of-the-art" above-ground tombs, which are often elaborate, highly photogenic, and historically informative. Half museum, half mausoleum, the city's 42 bone orchards include several historic cities of the dead: Greenwood, Oddfellows Rest, St. Louis Number One and Number Two, and Cypress Grove. You can invest in a guided tour (recommended) or pick up a brochure with cemetery locations at the Jackson Square Louisiana Visitors Center or at the **New Orleans Visitors Center** (529 St. Ann St.).

Burial may be an art form in New Orleans, but so is living it up. Blaine Kern, known in New Orleans as "Mr. Mardi Gras," has filled a cluster of warehouses with colorful giant heads, floats, and figures to create a photographer's playground. Across the river in Algiers at **Blaine Kern's Mardi Gras World** (233 Newton St., 504/361-7821 or 800/362-8213, www.mardigrasworld.com, $15), learn the origins of Mardi Gras, how a Krewe commissions a float, and the safest way to pick up a doubloon (step on it first to avoid broken fingers). Park your bike, and you've got some big-headed backdrops. To get here, you can scam a free 30-minute Mississippi River excursion by hopping aboard the Canal Street Ferry, next to the New Orleans Aquarium near Jackson Square.

Gray Line Tours (504/569-1401 or 800/535-7786, www.graylinenew orleans.com) offers tours of nearly every area at nearly every price range (starting around $18) and leave on foot or in a van or bus. As ordinary as these tourist tours seem, they are excellent ways to get an instant education and sense of history—otherwise, you're just looking at buildings and drunk college kids. Tours hit the French Quarter, Garden District, cemeteries, swamps and bayous, and the Mississippi River cruises.

In addition to Gray Line's, several swamp tours are available outside the city. The trick here is finding a certified Cajun who can make the difference between an adventure and a travelogue at the senior center. Out in Westwego, about 20 minutes southwest of the city, Captain Jerome V. Dupré of **Chacahoula Swamp Tours** (504/436-2640, $22) is the real deal—a Cajun whose ancestors arrived in the Louisiana wetlands in 1785. Dressed in faded overalls and a shapeless coonskin hat, Dupré loves the swamps, and you'll like him.

The *Higgins Boat,* the landing craft developed by New Orleanian Andrew Higgins to get soldiers ashore on D-Day, sparked historian Stephen Ambrose to create the **National D-Day Museum** (945 Magazine St., 504/527-6012, www.ddaymuseum.org, $14). A wealth of World War II memorabilia, oral histories from the men who were there and at Iwo Jima and other battles, and an Academy Award–winning film, *D-Day Remembered,* make this a historically vital stop.

Shopping

Shop 'til you drop on **Magazine Street,** considered the "Antique Attic of New Orleans," a six-mile stretch of antiques shops, java huts, galleries, bakeries, bistros, bookshops, health food stores, music shops, newsstands, pawnshops, and secondhand stores. As one shopkeeper put it, "If you can't find it on Magazine Street, you can't find it anywhere." True, but when I couldn't find inner peace here, I had to head to Tibet. For a full rundown on the hundreds of stores here, check www.magazinestreet.com.

Blue-Plate Specials

In Creole cooking, most meals include oysters, redfish, flounder, crawfish ("mudbugs"), catfish, snapper, crab, shrimp, spices, or jambalaya—a stewlike mix of tomatoes, rice, ham, shrimp, chicken, celery, onions, and seasonings. Po'boys are crispy sandwiches stuffed with fried oysters, roast beef, softshell crabs, or other ingredients. Gumbo is a thick soup prepared with chicken, shrimp, okra, or anything else. New Orleans boasts hundreds of great restaurants, so consider those listed below as a very limited endorsement.

A cheap place to snag chicken andouille gumbo and hot french bread, the **Gumbo Shop** (630 St. Peters St., 504/525-1486) serves traditional Creole cuisine for lunch and dinner.

Ralph Brennan's Red Fish Grill (115 Bourbon St., 504/598-1200) is a casual seafood restaurant in the heart of the French Quarter. After sampling the barbecue shrimp po'boy and sweet potato catfish, check out the oyster bar. Then have another po'boy.

Croissant d'Or (617 Ursulines, 504/524-4663) is a little hole in the wall, but it's popular with locals who drop in for a quick sandwich or pastry or to hang out on the patio. A good place to stop if you're on the run—or want to keep lunch under five bucks.

Camellia Grill (626 S. Carrollton Ave., 504/866-9573), a local diner famous for its breakfasts and pecan waffles, opened its doors in 1946. At lunch, burgers are big and messy, and at dinner, the specials always change. For insomniacs, it's one of the Big Easy's popular night dining destinations.

Watering Holes

New Orleans has more clubs than a deck of cards. Here are a few—but not the only ones—to hit. **Johnny White's Bar** (720 Bourbon St., 504/524-4909) is a bar for riders, as evidenced by the line of bikes in the street. It's been open since 1967—never closing and still cranking 24 hours a day. Hang out at the back bar, which was salvaged from an old whorehouse.

At **Pat O'Brien's** (718 St. Peter St., 504/525-4823 or 800/597-4823, www.patobriens.com), here since 1933, you'll be hanging out with frat boys and conventioneers—but when you're nice and looped, you'll all join in a sing-along on the dueling piano patio bar. Then again, you can just chill out with a Hurricane by the flaming fountain. No cover, no time.

What can a nationally known act do for a club? When it was the Neville Brothers or Professor Longhair, it could make the place a hot spot. They did it here, and in addition to its original location, **Tipitina's** (501 Napoleon Ave., 504/895-8477, www.tipitinas.com) has two other clubs in New Orleans, including one in the French Quarter, with live music every night varying from blues to rock, jazz to Cajun/Zydeco. Cover charge varies.

Shut-Eye

Major hotel chains are represented throughout New Orleans, although staying in a Garden District bed-and-breakfast can be a more memorable experience. A reservation service can save you time and money. For inns, try **Bed & Breakfast, Inc.** (504/488-4640 or 800/729-4640, www.historiclodging.com), which can point you to about 20 local bed-and-breakfasts. For hotels, there's a nationwide service at 800/964-6835 or www.hotels.com that can work a deal for you. Each of these services can find you rooms cheaper than you'd find by yourself.

Chain Drive
A, B, C, D, E, F, G, H, I, J, K, L, N, O, P, Q, S, T, U, V, X, AA, BB, CC, DD

Chain hotels are in town, or within 10 miles. See cross-reference guide featuring phone numbers and Web addresses on page 514.

Inn-dependence
A nice, quiet retreat, the **Beau Sejour** (1930 Napoleon Ave., 504/897-3746 or 888/897-9398, www.beausejourbandb.com, $120–180) has a tropical setting matched by Southern hospitality. Kim and Gil Gagnon's home is in a great neighborhood near the St. Charles streetcar. Rooms are actually suites.

Indulgences

It's a ride out of town into a part of Louisiana that conjures up *Deliverance,* but if you want to witness a different culture, stay the night in a plantation out by the bayous. Keep in mind that most are far out in the country, so stock up on food and gas, and definitely stay off these unmarked roads after dark. **Nottoway Plantation** (30970 Hwy. 405, White Castle, 225/545-2730, www.nottoway.com, $160–300), billed as the largest in the South, was a 7,000-acre sugar plantation for years after its completion in 1859. You can stay in a spacious main house suite or the rustic outbuildings. The most elaborate plantation is **Oak Alley** (3645 Hwy. 18, Vacherie, 225/265-2151 or 800/463-7140, www.oakalleyplantation.com, $115–145), where the entrance is lined with 28 ancient oaks. Although the main house is unavailable to guests, the fully equipped cottages are delightful, and the toasty breakfast beignets are the best.

Side Trips

Louisiana, Mississippi, and Tennessee

Louisiana
Highways 31, 182
Breaux Bridge, St. Martinville, Louisiana
Come on don to de baYO, cher, and pass a good time! In bayou country, start just east of Lafayette in Breaux Bridge on Highway 31. Fill
your tank with crawfish etouffée at Mulate's, and then work it off
by doing a Cajun two-step to Beau Soilleau's fiddle. Follow Highway
182 South along Bayou Teche's curvaceous banks, moss-covered live
oaks, and magnificent plantation homes.

Mississippi
Highway 35, Natchez Trace Parkway
Sturgis, Mississippi
With no commercial traffic on Natchez Trace Parkway, you can enjoy
a leisurely ride through Mississippi. Veer east on Highway 12 near
Kosciusko and head into Sturgis, a quaint town and unlikely home of
Benchmark Works, a vintage BMW motorcycle museum that you do
not want to miss.

Tennessee
Highways 165, 143, Cherohala Skyway
Telico Plains, Tennessee
Take Highway 165 out of town as it follows along the Telico River and
then ascends to meet Highway 143, becoming the truly awesome
Cherohala Skyway. At an elevation averaging more than 4,000 feet,
this flawless, serpentine roadway crosses and sweeps around rocky
summits for more than 45 miles. It offers breathtaking vistas of the
Nantahala and Cherokee national forests.

Contributed by Darryl M. Lodato

Resources for Riders

Blues Cruise

Tennessee Travel Information
Tennessee B&B Innkeepers—800/820-8144, www.tennessee-inns.com
Tennessee Road Conditions—800/858-6349
Tennessee State Parks—866/836-6757, www.tnstateparks.com
Tennessee Vacations— 615/741-2159, www.tnvacation.com
Tennessee Weather Conditions (Memphis)—901/544-0399

Mississippi Travel Information
Mississippi B&B Association—601/437-2843, www.missbab.com
Mississippi Department of Tourism—866/733-6477,
    www.visitmississippi.org
Mississippi State Parks—800/467-2757, www.mdwfp.com

Louisiana Travel Information
Louisiana Office of Tourism—225/342-8119, www.louisianatravel.com
Louisiana State Parks—225/342-8111 or 888/677-1400,
    www.crt.state.la.us/crt/parks
Professional Innkeepers Association of New Orleans—www.bbnola.com

Local and Regional Information
Memphis Visitors Bureau—901/543-5300 or 800/873-6282,
    www.memphistravel.com
New Orleans Visitors Information—504/246-5666 or 800/672-6124,
    www.neworleanscvb.com
Vicksburg Visitors Bureau—601/636-9421 or 800/221-3536,
    www.vicksburgcvb.org

Tennessee Motorcycle Shops
Al's Cycle Shop—3155 Summer Ave., Memphis, 901/324-3767,
    www.alscycle.com
Bellevue Suzuki-Kawasaki—2319 Elvis Presley Blvd., Memphis, 901/774-
    1870
Bumpus Harley-Davidson—2160 Whitten Rd., Memphis, 901/372-1121,
    www.bumpusharleydavidson.com
Honda-Yamaha of Memphis—6174 Mt. Moriah, Memphis, 901/345-
    0088, www.memphiscycles.com
Super Cycle—624 S. Bellevue Blvd., Memphis, 901/725-5991

Mississippi Motorcycle Shops
Cycle Service Plus—2607 E. Hwy. 80, Pearl, 601/939-5077
Harley-Davidson of Jackson—326 Carriage House Dr., Jackson, 601/372-5770, www.bumpusharleydavidson.com
Jackson Honda-Yamaha—113 Briarwood Dr., Jackson, 601/362-6492, www.northjacksonhondayamaha.com
Sevier's Outdoors (Honda-Yamaha)—580 Hwy. 27, Vicksburg, 601/636-2722
Vicksburg Kawasaki-Suzuki—1670 Hwy. 61 N, Vicksburg, 601/630-9490

Louisiana Motorcycle Shops
Boyce Honda—3011 N. I-10 Service Rd., Metairie, 504/837-6100
Cycle Center—3011 Loyola Dr., Kenner, 504/461-0011
Harley-Davidson of New Orleans—1208 Lafayette St., Gretna, 504/362-4004, www.hdno.com

Ozark Mountain Run

Hot Springs, Arkansas to Eureka Springs, Arkansas

This ride reaches north across mountains and hills from the thermal baths of central Arkansas to one of the nation's most impressive resort towns. Nearly 100 percent undiluted natural beauty along a scenic highway reveals a new perspective on a misunderstood state. Gamblers fill up Hot Springs during the January–April racing season, while it and Eureka Springs are shaking from Memorial Day through the end of summer. For best results, look for a riding window on either side of these peak seasons.

Hot Springs Primer

Only about 40 towns across the nation can lay claim to being a president's boyhood home, and Hot Springs happens to be one of those places. Oddly, however, the legend of Bill Clinton plays only a supporting role in this historic town—a town created because it rained in these hills 4,400 years ago. True fact, friend. A thousand years before King Tut was wrapped up, a flood of rainwater fell in the hills here. So, as Jesus was turning tables in the temple and John was signing the Magna Carta, that rainwater seeped 8,000 feet into the earth, and it has since been percolating to the surface. Originally, the Quapaw Indians treasured the heated, mineral-rich waters in what they called the Valley of the Vapors, but when naturalist William Dunbar and chemist George Hunter stumbled across the "Hot Springs of the Washita," white

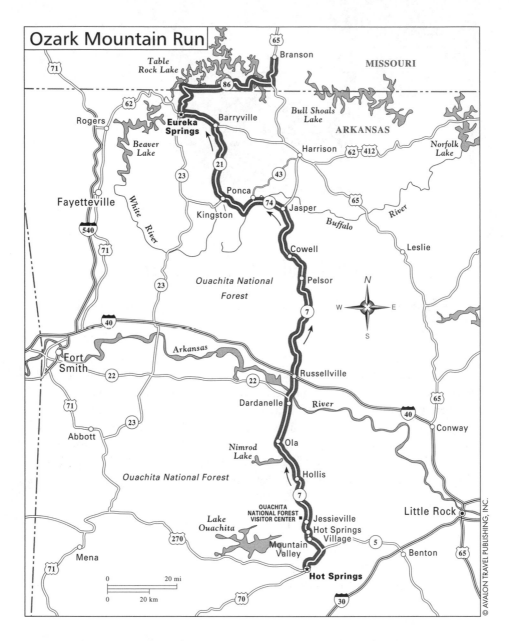

Route: Hot Springs to Eureka Springs via Ola, Russellville, Pelsor, Jasper, Ponca, Hunstville

Distance: Approximately 210 miles; consider six days with stops.

•**Days 1–2—Hot Springs** • **Day 3—Travel** •**Days 4–5—Eureka Springs** •**Day 6—Side trip to Branson**

Helmet Laws: In Arkansas, helmets are optional if 21 or older.

Water, Water Everywhere

Wherever I go, I find it fascinating that when I reach a place known for a *thing*, whether it's sunflower seeds or burlap sacks, some locals seem to know every infinitesimal speck of knowledge *about* that thing. In Hot Springs, that thing is water. The man at Mountain Valley imparted some of his wisdom to me, telling me that like Donald Trump, pure water has no taste. He told me how the water here percolates up through rock formations to carry with it 47 parts per million (ppm) of calcium, 130 ppm of bicarbonate, 4.9 ppm of magnesium, 4 ppm of sodium, 1 ppm of potassium, and an alkaline (CaCo3) level of 190. He said there are trace amounts of enriched and purified silica and a radon level of 43.3 picocuries per liter. At its deepest point, the water's boiling at 3,200 degrees but cools down to a relatively tepid 143 degrees at the surface. It was like talking to Rain Man.

To see what all this means, there are 47 "hot springs" in town and for a free sample, park at the thermal water station Hill-Wheatley Plaza on Central Avenue by the NPS Administration Building (two other "jug fountains" are on Reserve Street and on Bathhouse Row). If you have a thermos, use it otherwise buy an empty jug at the shop across the street and tap into the fountain that splashes out 4,400-year-old water that tastes morning fresh.

entrepreneurs began thinking of ways to get rid of the Quapaw. By 1818, the tribe had been "treated" out of its land. By 1854, the first bathhouse opened and set the stage for a town that would be centered around spas, bathhouses, and casinos.

In a touch of poetic justice, just as the Quapaw didn't have any luck resisting the white settlers, the settlers' ancestors didn't have much luck resisting a tribe of moral crusaders who, by the mid-1960s, had preached and moaned the town's illegal but accepted casinos out of business. That and a simultaneous crackdown on prostitution pretty much screwed the city's economy, and the town languished for a few decades until the National Park Service acquired and began to restore the old bathhouses in the 1980s. That's when residents looked around and realized that their historic hometown could be revived—so that's what they did, and that's why you're here.

On the Road: Hot Springs

What most impresses me about Hot Springs is that much of the town is a national park—and I'm not talking about a sprawling wooded area on the outskirts of town. If you walk down one side of Central Avenue past the historic bathhouses, you're in the Hot Springs National Park. But when you cross the street to visit a gift shop or check into a historic hotel, you've entered the *town* of Hot Springs. It's weird and very pleasing. Every town should have its own national park.

But Bill Clinton, bathhouses, and history alone don't make a great town. You also need the surrounding lakes, the wooded roads lacing through the Ouachita Mountains of Central Arkansas, the extraordinarily nice people, and the racing at Oaklawn Park, which runs at full gallop from the end of January through April. The heart of the old city is easy to navigate, and new growth is relegated to the outskirts so riding or walking is a pleasure.

While it's tempting to take off and get lost on some back roads, there's enough to see in town and on the ride north that you can park your bike and get some satisfaction as a street walker in the historic district. The first part of really seeing the town is soaking in the architecture on **Central Avenue.** It all looks like a movie set and reflects an unusual montage of styles, from Gilded Age hotels to Miami deco apartments to Grecian temples, built to please a cross-section of resort guests (which apparently included ancient Greeks). The focal point of it all is the stunning lineup of eight bathhouses.

A century ago, these were opulent retreats where guests would take the waters, plunge into hot tubs, work out in then-state-of-the-art gymnasiums, and

It's rare when a town can claim to be a president's childhood home —which undoubtedly explains the care and artistry that went into this stunning display.

relax in sun-filled solariums. To see how your ancestors vacationed, visit the restored and ornate **Fordyce Bathhouse** (369 Central Ave., 501/624-2701, www.nps.gov/hosp), where a museum turns back the clock 100 years through films, archival photos, exercise equipment, chiropody and mechano therapy rooms, a gymnasium, and immaculately restored tile baths. Incidentally, an antiquated sign that cautions, "Do Not Urinate in Vapors," provided me with a new and improved personal moral code.

Between Fordyce and the neighboring Maurice Bathhouse, a set of stairs leads to a half-mile-long promenade—impressive when it was built in the 1880s and still impressive today. Running parallel to Central Avenue, this is where spa guests would stroll and show off their direct-from-St.-Louis peacock finery, which you can also do in your chaps.

Placed on the crest of a hill, the walkway elevates you above the town for some great photo ops of Central Avenue and historic downtown. After the promenade, mount up for a steep ride to Mountaintop View Road. The shaded incline begins near the historic Arlington Hotel and rises like a vertical go-kart track to the 1,256-foot peak of Hot Springs Mountain. Along the way, there are several pullouts and overlooks for souvenir photos, with the **Hot Springs Mountain Tower** (501/623-6035) providing aerial reconnaissance for as far as 140 miles.

At the base of the mountain, you have free rein to tour the shops of downtown, tear off on a country run, lay down some cash on a thoroughbred at Oaklawn, or peel off your boots and soak your feet in the steaming hot mineral waters of the main spring. But please . . . do not urinate in the vapors.

Pull It Over: Hot Springs Highlights
Attractions and Adventures

Because President Clinton chose Little Rock (an hour east) as the location for his presidential library, there's hardly any historical reference to him in his own hometown. One site that makes a feeble effort is his childhood home at **1011 Park Avenue** (which is the northern end of Central), just a small white house on a hill where Clinton lived from 1954 to 1961. Only a wooden marker notes that a famous American lived here once. You'll see it on your ride north.

To experience what kept the Quapaw here for so long, soak yourself at the **Buckstaff Baths** (509 Central Ave., 501/623-2308, buckstaffbaths.com). Here since 1912, this is the oldest operating bathhouse in America. You can kick back and sweat it out with thermal mineral baths, hot packs, steam cabinets, Swedish massages, or an oddly soothing sitz bath. A second option is the **Hot Springs Health Spa** (501 Spring St., 501/321-9664, www.hshealth-spa.com), a family and co-ed "thermal bathing facility." There are numerous ways to erode stress here, such as whirlpool tubs, waterfall pools, steam and sauna rooms, bubble rooms, and massages.

A few miles from the historic district is Hot Springs's other leading attraction, **Oaklawn Park** (2705 Central Ave., 800/625-5296, www.oaklawn.com), which has been the center of thoroughbred racing since 1904. In season, bettors swarm the town to make some easy money while also establishing Hot Springs's first peak season. The rest of the year, you can sit here and bet on simulcast races across the nation.

At the opposite end of the adrenaline spectrum is **Garvan Woodland Gardens** (500 Arkridge Rd., 501/262-9300 or 800/366-4664, www.garvan-gardens.org, $7), about four miles out of town. It may not sound exciting, and, to be sure, it's not. But come here to sustain the same feeling you get when you ride through a remote country road. Park your bike and walk along 210 acres of quiet trails intersected by bridges, pavilions, lakes, bird sanctuaries, and waterfalls. Consider this a dumping ground for the stress you've carried since leaving the office.

After race season, summertime marks the second wave of tourism, when a lot of people head for the water. On Lake Hamilton, you can take a narrated paddleboat cruise aboard the ***Belle of Hot Springs*** (5200 Central Ave., 501/525-4438, www.belleriverboat.com, $12). More unusual is a **National Park Duck Tour** (418 Central Ave, 501/321-2911, www.rideaduck.com), a 75-minute historic tour aboard an amphibious vehicle. Leaving from the center of town, you drive over to the shores of Lake Hamilton—then down the boat launch ramp and smack dab into the water. Cool.

Fifteen miles from town, 40,000-acre Lake Ouachita lends its name to **Lake Ouachita State Park** (5451 Mountain Pine Rd., Mountain Pine, 501/767-9366). Created by the Blakely Mountain Dam, the lake was named one of the cleanest in America, and it's a favored destination for locals who come here to swim, ski, dive, boat, and fish. Along the 975 miles of shoreline, you'll find campgrounds and cabins, picnic areas, walking trails, swimming areas, and a marina with boat rentals, bait, and supplies. From Hot Springs, head three miles west on U.S. 270, then 12 miles north on Route 227.

Shopping

The premier bottler in Hot Springs's history is **Mountain Valley Water** (150 Central Ave., 501/623-6671 or 800/643-1501, www.mountainvalleyspring.com). It's been here since 1871 and has maintained a store that's partially a museum, with postcards, old signs and bottles, and a historical review of how Mountain Valley franchisers would open up the Starbucks of their day. In the lobby, a painting of Spanish explorer Hernando De Soto shows him receiving a jug of healing waters from the friendly natives in the spring of 1542, but he died that June, so I doubt the waters were really that healing. In the 1950s, though, after his heart attack, Eisenhower's doctors told him to drink Mountain Valley water—he did, and he was kicking around more than a decade later. To understand the appeal of bottled water, stop by and "quaff the elixir."

Nearly every town has a leather shop, and here it's the **National Park Outfitters** (364 Central Ave., 501/624-5207), which carries biker stuff like vests, jackets, gloves, headgear, saddlebags, hats, and sunglasses. **Cheyenne Trading** (412 Central Ave., 501/321-0267) also carries buckskin boots and Native American souvenirs and feathers.

If you're lured into the woods or onto the lakes, you can find all the gear you need at **Trader Bill's Outdoor Sports** (1530 Albert Pike, 501/623-8403). Backed by the state's largest selection of fishing tackle, it also carries beer, ice, live bait, and hunting supplies.

Blue-Plate Specials

Bill Clinton's favorite Hot Springs diner is **McClard's Bar-B-Q** (505 Albert Pike Ave., 501/623-9665, www.mcclards.com). When you arrive at this small cinder-block building, you'll be "honey"ed and "sugar"ed to bits. Sit in a booth at a scuffed Formica table and compete with a full house of locals shoveling in pulled pork and ribs and chicken and cole slaw and iced tea. I prefer a different style of barbecue, but if you're here, why not give it a try? Say … didn't Clinton's diet lead to a quadruple bypass?

There's more variety of home cooking at **Granny's Kitchen** (362 Central Ave., 501/624-6183), with the matronly proprietor fixing up comfort foods like meat loaf, liver and onions, and pork chops, each for about eight bucks. Breakfast includes a typical lineup of eggs, sausage, hash browns, oatmeal, and cinnamon rolls.

The town's best breakfast may be at the **Colonial Pancake and Waffle House** (11 Central Ave., 501/624-9273). It's been here since 1962 and looks exactly like the places where you ate when you were still ordering off the kids' menu. It offers thick china, small booths and tables, and a range of buttermilk, buckwheat, and blueberry pancakes, as well as waffles served plain, malted, pecan, buckwheat, buckwheat pecan, and the senior-favorite oat bran. Don't forget eggs, hash browns, prunes, and sliced bananas and milk.

For a deli dinner, **Maggie's Pickle Café** (414 Central Ave., 501/318-1866) is across from the Quapaw Baths and offers a quick-fix menu of hot dogs, chili, chili dogs, burgers, sandwiches, coffee, and—dig this—fried dill pickles. Bon appétit.

Watering Holes

If you're not grabbing a drink at the track, choose from a few saloons within walking distance at the heart of the historic district. Try **Schapiro's** (510 Central Ave., 501/624-5500), with blues jams, $1 draft and margarita specials, and a full American menu.

When the rallies roll into town, riders roll over to **Lucky's** (711 Central Ave., 501/622-2570), a basic bar where everyone can grab some pizza and a cold one.

Shut-Eye

Motels and Motor Courts

Does a rider sleep in the woods? At **Lake Ouachita State Park** (5451 Mountain Pine Rd., 800/264-2441 for cabin reservations), you can rent two- and three-bedroom cabins with fireplaces, as well as A-frame cabins that sleep up to six people. All are fully equipped, and some are lakefront. The park also has 112 campsites.

Chain Drive

A, B, C, E, G, J, L, M, S, CC, DD

Chain hotels are in town, or within 10 miles. See cross-reference guide featuring phone numbers and Web addresses on page 514.

Inn-dependence

A towering testament to the original glory days of Hot Springs is the **Arlington Hotel** (239 Central Ave., 501/623-7771 or 800/643-1502, www.arlingtonhotel.com, $98 and up). In addition to the best location of any hotel (across from the main spring and national park), the old-fashioned lobby, grand dining room, spa, and the uncommonly spacious and homelike guestrooms will put you at ease. Rates begin easy, but watch out—they can peak sharply. Historic footnote: Room 443 is the Al Capone Suite, the crook's favorite hideout when he was in town.

On the Road: Hot Springs to Eureka Springs

First, a confession. As a Florida native, I envisioned Arkansas as a state filled with hillbillies and rednecks with crewcuts. My postride opinion is that Arkansas—at least the northwest sector containing Scenic 7—contains the perfect mix of friendly folks, great roads, historic towns, and unbelievable terrain. This ride through the hills of Arkansas will set you firmly on the four-square path to righteous riding—now let me hear an amen!

As you ride north on Central Avenue, aside from a few neat old motor courts that are now dilapidated, the junk side of town is brief. Just past Bill Clinton's boyhood home, the road drops and curves, and the fun begins. You'll need to watch when Route 7 makes a sharp left near a gas station a few miles out of town. Soon you'll be riding through Mountain Valley, home of the water empire; and about a dozen miles later, you're in a new community called Hot Springs Village, which marks the point where the scenery becomes more beautiful. Part of the beauty lies in the roadside rock stands, which accent the route with displays of fire red, glacier green, and brilliant cobalt-colored chunks of glass.

On your left in Jessieville is the **Ouachita National Forest Visitor Information Center** (501/984-5313), well worth a stop to pick up brochures on the road, flora, and fauna you'll soon see. This is the entrance point of the Scenic 7 Byway, and you'll know this because the air is slightly spicy, the pines are more tightly packed, and there's a massive sign announcing "Entering Scenic 7 Byway." Here are some things you should know about the woods: You're entering a 1.8 million-acre forest that stretches from the center of Arkansas to southeast Oklahoma; it was created in 1907 by Teddy Roosevelt, which makes it the oldest national forest in the South; and the French spelling was created from the Indian word "washita," which means "good hunting grounds." Got it? You may proceed.

Instantly, the road becomes sublime. There are slow drops and casual S-curves and streams, like Bear Creek and the LaFavre River, which create a slow and peaceful introduction to the woodlands. Fifteen miles later, with its single gas pump, the Hollis Country Store assures you that you're entering the country and the hills ahead aren't terrifyingly tall—they're just the right size to give you a cheap thrill.

It gets even better. About five miles past Nimrod Lake, you'll climb great hills, and from the ridgeline, the vistas open up on sunken valleys and a porous landscape is sprinkled with mirrorlike lakes. As if in a balloon, you're drifting along the road and able to see the land far below. A few miles later and, hello!, you're in Ola, where the twisting road leads to a neat little town. Since the glitch in the ride's just ahead, this may be a good place to take a break.

Between Ola and Dardanelle and Russellville, there's not a lot of scenery, and the traffic will drive you nuts. Stick with it, and once you've passed over I-40, you'll be back in the pines and see a good sign. It reads: "Caution: Steep Curves and Sharp Drops for Next 63 Miles." Get ready for fall.

There are big drops, and as civilization recedes in your mirrors, dirt roads into the woods disappear toward what could be grand plantations, but odds are they're probably doublewides on cinder blocks. In the Piney Creeks Wildlife Area of the Ozark National Forest, the roads become narrower and higher, and about the time your ears pop, you're at Moccasin Gap and passing a tourist trap called Booger Hollow. About seven miles south of the town of Pelsor, there's a perfectly placed rest stop and overlook for photos, although reducing about 500 square miles of the majestic Ozarks into a 4x6-inch image won't even begin to do them justice.

Then the road returns to a mix of turns and sweeps and pastures and clearings, jumping up over a hill and falling down the other side into more banked corners. Past the town of Cowell and approaching Jasper, the scenery switches to broken-down shacks and cottages that are attractive in the sense that they reveal another aspect of America. The road begins to ascend again to reach the Hog Heaven Scenic Overlook, and they're right, it is scenic and wonderful. As you reflect on all the power lifting your bike's been doing, you should know it's about to let you down on a precipitous road that clings tenaciously to the side of the mountain. Let gravity do the work, because you'll fall nearly four miles to reach the highly recommended **Cliff House Restaurant** (870/446-2292). I've eaten at a lot of diners, but this one is superclean, serves some of the best home cooking in the South, and provides an incredible widescreen view of the valley and mountains. If you'd like to save the rest of the ride until daybreak, there's a just-as-clean motel (rates $50 and up) on the ground floor. Open mid-March to October.

Back on the road, you can give the gas a break as a seven-degree drop shoots you down a hill for the last three miles into the town of Jasper, where there are several shops and restaurants around the town square. Just outside Jasper, turn off Channel 7 and tune into 74 West. There's nothing demanding or dangerous right away, but the keen, steep road slices into a place called Low Gap, which has a general store, a cemetery, and the nearly hidden entrance to the **Buffalo National River** (870/449-4311, www.nps.gov/buff), the oldest national river in America. If you have the guts to ride to it, there's a pockmarked gravel road leading down to the river at the Steel Creek entrance to your right.

You'll know you've found it when you see towering limestone buttes more akin to the Dakotas.

Just slightly north of 74 off 43 is Ponca, worth a brief detour since it leads into a gorge. If your schedule allows an overnight, or if you just want to get some gas and snacks, there's an outfitter and lodge here, **RiverWind Lodge & Cabins** (800/221-5514, www.buffaloriver.com), which arranges trail rides, floating trips, and hot air balloon rides. What kept me on the road was the feeling that things were going to get a whole lot better. And they did.

Back on 74 came the highlight of the ride: great straights where I pumped up the speed, followed by extremely steep drops and similarly steep ascents. More than that, though, were changes in landscapes that—and I loved this—changed from a North Carolina feel at Ponca to scenes of Vermont countryside and pastures at the Elk Refuge, followed by glimpses of central California's grasslands and then traces of a Wyoming prairie. Incredibly, there were four or five ecosystems and landscapes to savor within 10 miles. It was so absolutely stunning, I wished I'd been born twins to enjoy it all even more.

On 74 in the town of Kingston, Route 21 shoots north. Take it—there's hardly a lick of traffic for miles. Instead, you receive the benefit of valleys that release you into wide-open plains, giving you that pure feeling of riding without concerns or cares. As part of these pastoral scenes, every so often you roll over a creek and into a town, where a ramshackle general store reminds you once again that you're on a motorcycle adventure. When you reach Highway 62, head west at Berryville, the final way station before the home stretch into Eureka Springs, one of the most unusual towns you'll have the pleasure to visit.

Eureka Springs Primer

There's something unusual about Eureka Springs, and it's not just knowing that it's in the Boston Mountains of the Ozark Plateau—the only chain that runs east and west. And it's not just realizing that the mountains seem so high only because the valleys are so low, or that the word "Ozarks" comes from *"aux arcs,"* a modification of the French words "of trees" *(aux arbres)*. What's so un-usual is that in a town of about 2,500 people, there are more than 50 bed-and-breakfasts, a passion play, a historic railroad, two grand hotels, several dozen massage therapists, a sanctuary for abused bears and tigers, a Native American site, and one of the 20th century's leading examples of architecture.

Like Hot Springs, mineral water helped create this town. Visionaries thought they could attract wealthy travelers by hinting that the natural springs could heal the blind. Their efforts paid off in the 1800s and continue today, despite fires that burned down the town three times. It also got a boost from some famous residents, such as Robert Ripley, who featured aspects of the town in several of his *Believe It or Not!* comics, and from Carrie Nation, the nutjob zealot who used a bible as an excuse and a hatchet for efficiency when she smashed up saloons.

Residents aren't sent to Eureka Springs in a corporate transfer, and you don't stumble across it either. People are here because they seek it out and want to be here. And that quest has brought an unusual assemblage of old hippies, rednecks, gays, seniors, artists, and punks to create an unusually cosmopolitan community. As in most extraordinary places, the National Register of Historic Places has a presence here—in fact, the *entire downtown* is on the Register.

There are hundreds of miles of wonderful roads surrounding the town and countless Victorian homes and cottages tucked into the angled hills beside the steep and narrow streets. But one of the more incredible aspects of it all is that, unlike in other small towns destroyed by their popularity, a local points out that Eureka Springs "aggressively fought the Bransonization of the town." To that end, a strong planning commission, historical association, and preservationists have kept things just right for you.

On the Road: Eureka Springs

I guarantee that you'll make time to park your bike and wander around the village, but I suggest you start your day with a well-balanced breakfast and a sharp little loop that'll get you out into the countryside for a couple of hours. Highway 62 West (Van Buren Ave.) leads out of town, and there's only a slight buffer between you and the surrounding countryside that you'll reach relatively quickly via some steep, curving roads. Your first destination is **Thorncrown Chapel** (12968 Hwy. 62, 479/253-7401, www.thorncrown.com), which may not mean much to you now, but will soon become unforgettable. About two miles from town, you'll see the entrance hidden in a break in the woods on your right, and you'll see the chapel hidden in the woods themselves. Why is this sanctuary so sacred and revered?

Well, in 2000, members of the American Institute of Architecture ranked Thorncrown Chapel the fourth-best building design of the 20th century—placing it immediately behind Frank Lloyd Wright's Fallingwater and New York's Chrysler and Seagram's buildings. After local resident Jim Reed had a vision, he recruited architect E. Fay Jones of Fayetteville to create the 48-foot-tall wood and glass chapel. Yes, it's just a tiny church in the forest in the Ozarks, but when you see it camouflaged within the 50-foot-tall trees and enter the chapel and *really* look at the organic design that blends it into the land, you'll understand why it's earned such respect. The subtleties of the design reveal themselves a little at a time. A crown of thorns is created by a lattice work of 2x4 beams, 10 tons of pane glass make the modest chapel seem as large as a cathedral, and at night, interior crosses are reflected infinitely into the branches of trees.

Back on 62 West, there's another spiritual center ahead, accessible down a hard-packed dirt road. The **Blue Springs Heritage Center** (479/253-9244, www.bluespringheritage.com, $7.25) was created for peace, reflection, and remembrance at a Native American site where 10,000-year-old artifacts have been discovered, and where tribes like the Osage and Cherokees gathered in 1839 when forced from their homes on the Trail of Tears. A natural spring circulating 38 million gallons of water a day creates the White River, which loops around the grounds to create a 250-acre peninsula.

After the town of Busch, turn right on 187, where few things are as pleasing as twisting the throttle and leaping back onto the road, sweeping around corners, and passing log cabins and antiquated attractions like **Dinosaur World** (501/253-8113), which, based on the chipped and fading concrete dinosaurs, was constructed in either the 1950s or the Mesozoic Era. A few miles ahead, you enter Beaver, where the road makes a wide arc and whirls around the perimeter of Beaver Lake. If you were smart enough to read this in advance, you knew to pack a lunch and your trunks so you could enjoy the swimming beach and picnic pavilions. A few hundred yards farther, the **Beaver Dam** (yes, that's right) is impressive and has a pullout midway, where you can park by the No Parking sign, snap some pictures, and peer over the side. After the dam, the road commences to twist and turn until it merges again with 62 to meet the same crooked and steep hills you rode up earlier. You'll recognize Thorncrown Chapel, now on your left, and ride the last few miles to town, where you can count on a good rubdown from a local masseuse.

Pull It Over: Eureka Springs Highlights
Attractions and Adventures

Built into the side of the hill, downtown seems to flow off the mountain. This makes it neat to photograph, but tricky to park a bike on. Once you're settled, you'll see that for such a compact place, there's a hell of a lot to see. More than in Manhattan, I'd claim. There are only two real streets downtown, Main and

A rescued tiger takes a cat nap at the inspiring Turpentine Creek Wildlife Refuge.

Spring, with Center splitting up and off Main to create another street of cool shops frequented by thousands of riders and shoppers who will find at least one thing they like.

While you may be tempted to ride your bike everywhere, here's an option that'll save a little gas and your parking space: Spend $3.50 on a day pass ($4.50 for two days) and see the surrounding area via the **Eureka Springs Transit System** (479/253-9572, www.eurekatrolley.com). There are several rates and routes around town, and you can board at stops in town and on the outskirts to expand your range. This isn't a historical tour, but you may want to take the one it offers, which is mundane but informative. Departing from the visitors center on Highway 62, the hourlong, $7.50 tour will feed you the intelligence you need to begin to understand the history and diversity of Eureka Springs.

After the historic tour, ride seven miles south on Highway 23 to the don't-miss **Turpentine Creek Wildlife Refuge** (479/253-5841, www.tigers.tc, $15). An admirable family, the Smiths, rescued their first lion in 1978 and have spent the time since saving even more abused tigers and bears. Working from donations and admissions, they've created a retirement home for gorgeous animals, like the tiger that a car dealer bought for commercials and then locked in a cage in a dark warehouse for years. Sad tales like this are countered by the pure respect the volunteer staff has for the animals. It's a great ride to the preserve, and if you can spare some cash for their efforts, I'm sure the Smiths, tigers, and bears would appreciate it.

Since 1968, travelers have been attending the **Great Passion Play** (935

Shotgun Weddings

Some Ozark hillbillies used to get married at the barrel of a shotgun, but today in Eureka Springs, things are slightly more refined. There are several small wedding chapels in the heart of town, but the Marryin' Sam that caught my attention was Jan Ortiz of **All About Love** (470/253-2526 or 888/568-3020, www.eureka-net.com/weddings). She set up shop at the East Mountain Gazebo, with a stunning view of the valley and the historic Crescent Hotel on the opposite hill. When Nance and I showed up, we watched the conclusion of a wedding ceremony and thought it was a fluke—and then looked back at a line of cars carrying an assortment of brides and grooms ready to get hitched. Every 10 minutes, a couple would get out of their car (or pickup), say their vows, sign some papers, pay 40 bucks, and get on their way to a happy, productive, and fruitful life. Get a license, call Jan, and you can do the same.

Passion Play Rd., 800/882-7529, www.greatpassionplay.com), which features a cast of hundreds recreating the trial, execution, resurrection, and ascension of Christ. Believers may want to make a day of it on a Holy Land tour to watch actors recreate biblical stories and personalities, visit a bible museum containing more than 6,000 bibles in 625 languages, and stare at the massive 67-foot-tall Christ of the Ozarks. This is the largest Christ statue in America, one that theologians believe is far taller than the actual son of God.

Shopping

Pretty much everything you can shop for—cats, quilts, dulcimers, pipes, hats, loads of leather, and a few thousand other items—are all on sale in the 170-plus stores here. For riders, **Emerald Forest** (31 Spring St., 479/253-6959) carries sport and adventure clothing, some cool Indian-beaded leather jackets, and other high-quality clothes. The competition is the **Nelson Leather Company** (34 Spring St., 479/253-7162), which carries an impressive lineup of fringed jackets with Indian beading, as well as watches, canes, bullwhips, and local crafts like hardwood cutting boards, knives, hats, masks, togs, and cowhide purses. The **White River Tobacco Company** (99 Spring St., 479/253-5350) is a "work-free smoke place" that carries the sort of tobacco items you once hid in a cigar box under your dorm room bed.

There are a variety of tobacco blends, ashtrays, pipes, hookahs, and novelties, like the cell phone flask to sneak into a game. While you're tripping down memory lane, consider **East by West** (9 Center St., 479/253-6016), a Haight-Ashbury-style freak shop with tie-dyed shirts and assorted Deadhead junk. And hookahs.

Blue-Plate Specials

Main Street Café (9 S. Main St., 479/253-7374) will load you up with basic breakfast items like omelettes, hash browns, grits, and toast that'll hold you until lunchtime—when you can waddle over to **Food, Beer and Bull** (45 Spring St., 479/253-7141), a sidewalk café that draws in bikers like bikers to a sidewalk café. It has only eight tables, but that's all you need to sit back, people-watch, and dine on pizza, subs, calzones, salads, and beer sold by the bottle and bucket.

Seeing as it's attached to a chain hotel, I was astounded to find damn good Southern cooking at **Myrtie Mae's** (207 W. Van Buren/Hwy. 62), 479/253-9768). Oh, pappy, them vittles was some of the best I ever ate. Fried chicken and the rest of the home-cooked stuff—muffins, desserts, soups, mashed potatoes—were just right. Real food in the real South.

The **Cottage Inn** (450 W. Van Buren/Hwy. 62, 479/253-5282) is different in a good way. It's a motor court, as well as a cozy Mediterranean restaurant created in an old home. Linda Hager studied and traveled throughout Europe, and she brought back dishes and recipes and wines from Greece, Spain, France, and Italy. If you're a casual gourmet, you'll find the service and setting here fine and relaxing.

Watering Holes

In addition to having mostly everything, Eureka has even more in the way of cool pubs and clubs in the center of town. **Eureka Live** (35 1/2 N. Main St., 479/253-7020) is a basement bar local fave, where you can get your groove on to rock 'n' roll and order up well drinks and draft specials.

Chelsea's Corner Café and Bar (10 Mountain St., 479/253-6723, www.chelseaspub.com) is the town's quasi-Irish pub. It serves American food and has four imports on tap, plus domestic bottle beers, and live music inside or on the enclosed deck.

One of the biggest and most popular games in town is the **Pied Piper Pub** (82 Armstrong St., 479/363-9976), where there's fab food and good entertainment seven days a week "from mid-day to mid-nite." There's a full bar and big beer list with selections from Mexico, Holland, Ireland, Britain, Australia, and Arkansas. Hang out on the deck and take in the town.

Shut-Eye

Motels and Motor Courts
Yet another thing to love about Eureka Springs is the variety of lodging, which includes old-fashioned mom-and-pop motels. As always, check the local website listed in the Resources section first for a complete listing, but for now here are a few to consider.

The **Cottage Inn** (450 W. Van Buren/Hwy. 62 W, 479/253-5282, www.cottage inneurekaspgs.com, $65–75) was built in 1937 as a tourist court. Linda Hager restored the comfortable individual cabins with modern conveniences, including whirlpool tubs, to create a quiet and private retreat close to town.

A 12-minute walk from downtown, the **Joy Motel** (216 W. Van Buren, 479/253-9568 or 877/569-7667, www.thejoymotel.com, $38 base rate, $125 peak rate) is a typical motel that brags it has the town's largest swimming pool, serves a continental breakfast with homemade breads, provides two queen or full beds, and even goes to the trouble of hanging its sheets on the line to dry. Top that, Ritz-Carlton! Four miles from the village at **Bluebird Lodge & Cottages** (5830 Hwy. 62 W, 479/253-6028 or 800/286-4469, www.bluebird-lodgeandcottages.com, $45–65, $125 for cottages), the sheets aren't air-dried, but the rooms are large (if basic), with a queen or king bed, whirlpool tub, and private balcony. Their cottages are down a country lane and come with a king bed, double whirlpool tub, fireplace, kitchen, and private balcony. **New Orleans Hotel** (63 Spring St., 479/253-8630 or 800/243-8630, $99 and up) is a large, old-fashioned place where the rooms look a little south of 1960 (it opened in 1892), but the heart of town location and lower rates may help you decide it's worth it.

Chain Drive
There are several chain hotels in Eureka Springs, but I can personally recommend the **Best Western** (479/253-9551, $69–99) at the junction of 62 and 23. Rooms are larger than usual, there's plenty of parking, it's clean as a whistle, and the breakfast will increase your body's mass each morning. Nice, nice, nice. Others include: C, E, L, Q, CC, DD.

Please see the cross-reference guide featuring phone numbers and Web addresses on page 514.

Inn-dependence

If you favor grand hotels instead, you're also in luck. The **Crescent Hotel and Spa** (75 Prospect Ave., 479/253-9766 or 800/342-9766, www.crescent-hotel.com, $99–169 premium room, $159–239 specialty suite) is a fantastically ornate place, one that every visitor wants to see. You can sense the history when you enter the lobby of the "Grand Old Lady of the Ozarks," here since 1886. Considering its popularity, the rates seem reasonable. Closer to the center of town—actually it *is* the center of town—is the 1905 **Basin Park Hotel** (12 Spring St., 479/253-7837 or 800/643-4972, www.basinpark.com, $89–132 premium room, $199–239 specialty suite), owned by the same folks as the Crescent. Rooms here are not overly elaborate but should satisfy.

Side Trip: Branson

Based on its reputation, Branson was one of the last places I would have wanted to visit. Based on experience, I can't wait to go back.

Branson is a perfect 50-mile, one-hour road trip away from Eureka Springs, and when I heard Ann-Margret was appearing on stage with Andy Williams, I got on the bike and rolled like thunder. Keep in mind, if you plan to catch an evening show, you may be better off staying the night in Branson than riding the pitch-black roads after dark. Don't sweat it—rooms there start as low as $29.

When you leave Eureka Springs on Route 23, the two-lane highway is alternately slow and bending and pitched and dropping, although nothing is too severe. After the town of Oak Hill, the speed drops to a slow 25 mph, and then real slow, lazy curves take you through the hills toward Missouri. There's something nice about this countryside, and I figured it's the fact that it's very remote and very gentle. When you ride between hills, you drop out of view and get a few moments of privacy. Watch for Highway 86 and head east, after which there's a small town every so often, and the land starts to look like some Tyrolean setting of pastures and grazing cattle. Sometimes there'll be an uncommonly long straight, and then, to make up for it, you'll be slapped into a series of curves that'll bounce you and your bike around like a pinball machine.

When 86 meets 13, hang a long, loping right toward the town of Blue Eye, and where the road Ts above it, hang a left to follow 86 the rest of the way toward U.S. 65. Along the way, it's a thoroughly enjoyable ride through the countryside, and after you cross the Long Creek Arm of Table Rock Lake, it's only a few more country-perfect miles until Highway 86 dead-ends at U.S. 65, 10 miles south of Branson. The shows I saw there—Andy Williams and sex kitten Ann-Margret, the Sons of the Pioneers, Jim Stafford, the Roy Rogers Museum, Silver Dollar City—were absolutely dynamite. Although it's been branded as a hillbilly Las Vegas, if you can deal with the traffic and adjust your attitude, the payoff is a town where working-class folks can spend a little cash and have a hell of a lot of fun.

To see what's shaking in Branson, call 417/334-4084 or 800/214-3661 or visit www.explorebranson.com.

Resources for Riders

Ozark Mountain Run

Arkansas Travel Information
Arkansas Department of Parks —800/628-8725,
   www.arkansasparks.com
Arkansas Game & Fish Commission—501/223-6300 or 800/364-4263,
   www.agfc.com
Arkansas Road Conditions—501/569-2374 or 800/245-1672,
   www.ahtd.state.ar.us
Arkansas State Parks—888/287-2757, www.arkansasstateparks.com
Arkansas Travel and Tourism—501/682-7777 or 800/628-8725, www
   .arkansas.com
Bed and Breakfast Association of Arkansas
   www.bedandbreakfastarkansas.com

Local and Regional Information
Eureka Springs Chamber of Commerce—479/253-8737 or 800/638-
   7352, www.eurekaspringschamber.com
Hot Springs Convention and Visitors Bureau—501/321-2277 or
   800/543-2284, www.hotsprings.org
Ouchita National Forest—501/321-5202, www.fs.fed.us/oonf

Arkansas Motorcycle Shops
Greeson Kawasaki—2695 Airport Rd., Hot Springs, 501/767-2771,
   www.gogreeson.com
Honda of Russellville—3633 Bernice Ave. (Hwy. 7 & 7T), Russellville,
   479/968-2233 or 866/466-3219, www.hondaofrussellville.com
John's Honda—111 Carl Dr., Hot Springs, 501/623-1495,
   www.johnshonda.com
Jones Harley-Davidson Buell—4446 Central Ave., Hot Springs, 501/525-
   7468, www.jonesharley.com
Lanny's Cycle World—2205 Albert Pike Rd., Hot Springs, 501/623-2483
Roger's Cycle—1534 Albert Pike Rd., Hot Springs, 501/623-2121
Yamaha Sportscenter—619 Albert Pike Rd., Hot Springs, 501/624-5414

Wisconsin Thumb Run

Milwaukee, Wisconsin to Door County, Wisconsin

Milwaukee makes a rough start to this run, but if you ride a Harley and don't come here, you'll have hell to pay at your next poker run, since this is where Harley-Davidson was born and reborn. As you follow the curve of Lake Michigan, you'll escape the din of the city and find yourself in a Nordic slice of America. Bear in mind that Wisconsin weather (especially on the northern peninsula) can change quickly—even in summer. Pack for two seasons.

Milwaukee Primer

Bratwurst. Beer. Baseball. Blue-collar workers. Most Americans have a pretty good idea what makes Milwaukee tick. We learned about it by watching beer commercials, face-painting cheeseheads, and Fonzie on TV.

But the 600,000-plus citizens here don't see themselves as beer-guzzling Norwegian-, German-, and Polish-Americans. They see their city as a smaller, friendlier version of Chicago, and their museums, galleries, and ethnic festivals offer proof that they are, in fact, patrons of the arts and proud of their cultural diversity.

This may all be true, but chances are you won't appreciate any of it. You'll be here just long enough to see a brewery, catch a ball game, eat some bratwurst, and go watch the blue-collar workers stick a hydraulic lifter on a new Harley engine.

Dat's a purdy good day dere den, eh?

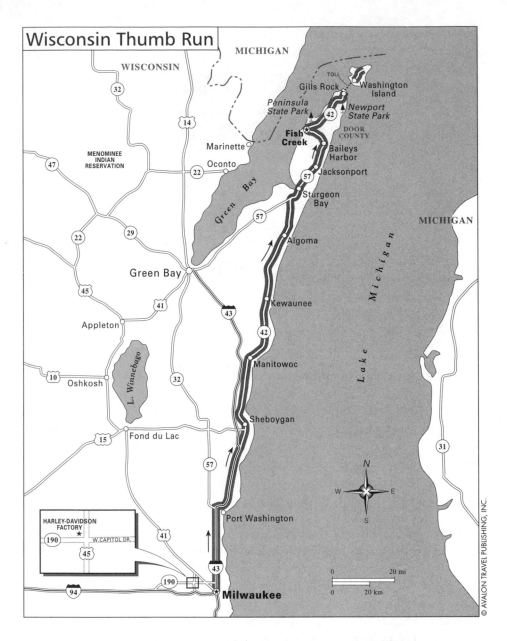

Route: Milwaukee to Door County via Port Washington, Sheboygan, Manitowoc, Two Rivers

Distance: Approximately 175 miles; consider four days with stops.
•**Day 1**—Milwaukee •**Day 2**—Milwaukee/Travel •**Days 3–4**—Door County

First Leg: Milwaukee to Fish Creek (175 miles)

Helmet Laws: Wisconsin does not require helmets.

On the Road: Milwaukee

It's hard to find a great ride inside a metropolitan area, but in exotic cities like Miami and Las Vegas, you just have to go for it. Milwaukee certainly isn't exotic, but an act of Congress mandates it as a stop for Harley riders.

Despite the interstates and some less-than-attractive neighborhoods, it's fairly easy to get around on your bike and see a few sights. If you truly detest city riding, blow out of town before nightfall to more peaceful environs.

Either way, the day should begin in the suburb of Wauwatosa with a free tour of **Harley-Davidson's Capitol Drive Powertrain Operations** (11700 W. Capitol Dr., 414/535-3666 or 877/883-1450). Sportster and Buell engines take shape here (the new V-Rod comes out of Kansas City). Tour days and times vary greatly by season; call in advance. Take I-94 west out of town and turn north onto I-45. There are no directional signs to the plant, so watch for Capitol Drive, where you exit, and then double back beneath the overpass. The factory entrance is on your right.

Although they claim there's a museum here, in reality there are just a few bikes, signage, and archival pictures. What's on the horizon, though, is a $95 million museum complex, café, and rally park that'll occupy a 20-acre site downtown. In late 2004, city officials approved the deal, but, until the complex appears, you'll have to satisfy yourself with things like the 14-inch Hamilton lathe, "the oldest existing asset in powertrain operations." To its credit, the "museum" does spark intrigue through diagrams showing the hundreds of parts (hydraulic lifters and guides, cylinder push rods, cams, oil pump, rocker pump, connector rod, etc.) designed to create motion out of fuel and air, "a chrome and black miracle."

See displays of flatheads, panheads, knuckleheads, and shovelheads, as well as H-D photos and memorabilia solicited for the archives. And you know how H-D merchandise is as scarce as Starbucks coffee? Well, the folks here thoughtfully sell pens, T-shirts, mugs, bandannas, and caps.

Even though the final product takes shape in York, Pennsylvania, and the Twin Cam 88 engines are made eight miles north on Pilgrim Road, the XL engines for H-D and Buell are born here. The hourlong tours, which fill up quickly, begin with a 10-minute video explaining the origins, history, and plans of the company. After the video, you'll don safety glasses and headphones for a tour of the factory floor, individual work stations, and the Genuine Parts Manufacturing plant, which produces more than 1,300 parts for older Harleys (including a kick starter for a 1916 model).

Both gifted mechanics and the mechanically illiterate will be impressed by the detail and ingenuity displayed here. My toolkit consists of a hammer and a spoon, so it floors me that early machinists, without the benefit of a computer and a case of gin, could create anything that moved, but they did.

When you leave H-D (with a few component pieces shoved down your trousers), you may be inspired to see what else Milwaukee's known for: breweries. About 80 of them were here in the 1880s, but most have faded away. For a visit to a stupendous macrobrewery, ride over to the **Miller Brewing Company** (4251 W. State St., 414/931-2337, www.millerbrewing.com). The free 50-minute tour (hours vary; call ahead) includes a walk through the packaging line and shipping centers, brew house, museum, and historic caves. Memories should come flooding back of your college party days, if you and your buddies ever ponied up enough cash for a half million cases of beer, that is. Yes, a *half million cases* are stacked in the shipping center. There are also giant brew kettles, high-speed bottling lines, and best of all, free frosty samples served in the cozy saloon at the Miller Inn.

Milwaukee hasn't forgotten its brewing roots, and microbrewery tours are equally popular. Opened in 1985, **Sprecher Brewery** (701 W. Glendale Ave., 414/964-2739, www.sprecherbrewery.com, $3) has one of the more popular tours. Five miles north of downtown, it brews traditional beers and gourmet sodas and wraps up its tours with samples of any 14 beers (Black Bavarian, Pub Brown Ale, Irish Stout, Russian Imperial Stout …) served amid oompah music in an indoor Oktoberfest-style beer garden tent. Tour times vary, so call in advance for reservations. Part of the admission fee goes to charity.

Opened in 1987 with a total output of 60 barrels, the **Lakefront Brewery** (1872 N. Commerce St., 414/372-8800, www.lakefrontbrewery.com, $5) now cranks out handcrafted beer in traditional and innovative styles. Depending on the season, it brews up pilsners, stein beer, cherry beer, pumpkin beer, ales, coffee stout, and root beer. Tours are Friday at 3 P.M., and Saturday at 1, 2, and 3 P.M. Admission includes a free pint glass and two 8-ounce shots of beer.

Provided you're not looped by now, wrap up the day the way the locals do: digging into a bratwurst, sitting in the stands at a game, hanging out in the historic Third Ward or on Water Street, or dancing a polka at an ethnic fest.

Pull It Over: Milwaukee Highlights
Attractions and Adventures

Milwaukee is a fascinatingly diverse city. If you visit nearly any time between June and September, you're sure to hit one of the several massive ethnic festivals that take place at the lakefront Henry W. Maier Park. Each fest revels in the music, games, and foods of a foreign land: Asia, Mexico, Germany, Ireland, Africa, Poland, Italy, and so on. The biggest blowout of all is Summerfest (414/273-3378 or 800/273-3378, www.summerfest.com), the largest music festival in the world, with national acts appearing on a dozen stages.

In this town, the most popular outdoor activity is watching one of several professional teams. If you ride in on game day, you may want to join the fans of the **Milwaukee Brewers** baseball (414/902-4000 or 800/933-7890, www.milwaukeebrewers.com). Tickets range $5–35. The **Milwaukee Bucks** basketball team (414/227-0500, www.bucks.com) are also in town, or you can go puck yourself at a **Milwaukee Admirals** AHL hockey game (414/227-0550, www.milwaukeeadmirals.com).

Hungry after the game? Swing by **Usinger's Famous Sausage** (1030 N. Old World 3rd St., 414/276-9100) to buy a string of meat shoved in a thin, edible sheath. Mmmmm, boy! Cranking out the meat since 1880, Usinger's boasts more than 75 varieties sold in its turn-of-the-20th-century store. It may seem silly, but it *is* part of the city's history.

Blue-Plate Specials

Harley isn't the only Milwaukee institution. According to Glenn Fieber, step-son of the original Solly, "people from all over, everywhere" check into **Solly's Coffee Shop** (4629 N. Port Washington Rd., 414/332-8808) before checking into their hotels. Since 1936, locals and savvy travelers have been traveling a few minutes from downtown and settling in at Solly's twin horseshoe counters, where Milwaukee waitresses serve up hearty breakfasts, buttery sirloin burgers, and hand-scooped malts served in a steel can.

The oldest lunch counter in Milwaukee is at **Real Chili** (1625 W. Wells St., 414/342-6955). This independent purveyor of chili has been here since 1931, serving celebrities, pro ball players, politicians, and on-the-road travelers. Subs, tacos, chili dogs, and chili served over spaghetti and beans come in mild, medium, and hot. If you need a beer to take the sting out, head to its second location at 419 East Wells Street.

In the heart of downtown on the revitalized Riverwalk, **Rock Bottom** (740 N. Plankinton Ave., 414/276-3030) is a hoppin' spot, especially on the Milwaukee River waterside patio, where most people dine during good weather. Open for lunch and dinner, it's a good place to hang out, and its five microbrews, brick-oven pizzas, prime top sirloin, pork chops, and short ribs put it over the top—although the setting edges out the food.

Part dining, part cruise, and 100 percent satisfying is **Edelweiss Cruise Lines** (1110 N. Old World 3rd St., 414/272-DOCK or 414/272-3625, www.edelweisscruise.com), which runs leisurely two-hour dinner cruises along the river, and then into the harbor on Lake Michigan. The pace is slow, the scenery ever-changing, and the opportunity to see the city from a nautical perch extraordinary. Downside: the cost. Prices range from $48 (seafood buffet) to $72 (table service) to $100 (all-inclusive and full bar).

Watering Holes

Milwaukee's too large a city to ride around looking for a place to party, so you might want to settle down near the greatest concentration of nightspots. Along Water Street between State and Knapp, you'll find a number of worthy choices. This is the short list below, and you may want to virtual bar-hop with members of the **Water Street Tavern Association** (www.onwaterstreet.com), which represents more than a dozen pubs, bars, taverns, and wing joints, all of which are showcased on the website.

Water Street Brewery (1101 N. Water St., 414/272-1195, www.waterstreet-brewery.com) is a pub-style micro that serves 10 varieties of its own brews, plus an assortment of other micros. In addition to beer, it offers an extensive menu of fish, steaks, ribs, pizza, nachos, and other bar food. A big-screen TV comes out for big sports events.

McGillycuddy's (1135 N. Water St., 414/278-8888, www.mcgillycuddys-milwaukee.com) is the largest pub on the block. It combines the best elements of an Irish pub with an American sports bar, serving Guinness on tap, other Brit ales, and Irish stew. Order a mug and settle down on the huge patio.

Flannery's Bar (425 E. Wells St., 414/278-8586, www.flannerysmilwaukee.com) has live jazz and blues and makes it all sound better by serving $2.50 pints of Guinness, Harp, Bass, and Foster's until midnight.

Looking like a gentlemen's club, the **Oak Barrel** (1211 N. Water St., 414/224-0535) features more than 100 varieties of single malt scotch, double barrel bourbon, imported beer, microbrews, and martinis. If you're not too drunk, you can throw darts and shoot a game of pool. Maybe throw darts at the pool table.

Shut-Eye

Motels and Motor Courts

Downtown, the **Astor Hotel** (924 E. Juneau Ave., 414/271-4220 or 800/558-0200, www.theastorhotel.com, $79 off-season, $99 in season) is one of two remaining buildings in Milwaukee that was designed to serve as apartment house/transient hotel room combinations.

Chain Drive
A, B, C, D, E, G, H, J, L, Q, T, U, W, X, CC

Chain hotels are in town, or within 10 miles. See cross-reference guide featuring phone numbers and Web addresses on page 514.

Indulgences

In historic old cities like Milwaukee, Gilded Age hotels are plentiful. If your life has been leading to a Harley tour and you really want to live it up, the **Pfister Hotel** (424 E. Wisconsin, 414/271-8222 or 800/558-8222, www.the pfisterhotel.com, $189 and up peak season) has been a local legend since it opened in 1893. The lobby is elegant, and the rooms follow suit—celebs and sports stars stay here when they're in town.

On the Road: Milwaukee to Door County

Considering from whence you came, you'll be amazed that a single tank of gas can deliver you to such a bucolic setting. Leaving on I-43 North, it takes about 10 miles to shake the Milwaukee dirt off your boots. There's not much between Milwaukee and Exit 306, which you should take east to reach Route 32 for a four-mile run to Port Washington.

There's no reason to stay very long, but the harbor is picture-perfect, and Franklin Street features blocks of interesting stores on the shores of Lake Michigan. It'll take about an hour, slightly longer if you drop in at **Harry's Restaurant** (128 N. Franklin St., 262/284-2861), which serves breakfast, lunch, and dinner. Here since the '50s, this is where most travelers stop for home-cooked hot beef sandwiches, mashed potatoes, chicken and rice soup, pork chop sandwiches, and lake perch. Up the street, **Port Antiques** (314 N. Franklin St., 262/284-5520), open 10 A.M.–5 P.M. daily, carries a strong collection of nautical antiques, hunting and fishing pieces, and 19th-century matted maps.

When you leave Port Washington, follow the lakeshore north and return to I-43 for an uneventful ride to Exit 120 for Highway OK (yes, it's actually "OK") toward Sheboygan. From here, you'll reach Highway LS, the lakeshore run that'll take you north. After a brief flirtation with farmland, you'll be in the city. It's a little hard to navigate here, so you may have to ask directions to 15th Avenue, which eventually turns into Highway LS north of town.

If you didn't eat at Harry's, when you reach the intersection of 15th and Geele, turn left and stop at the **Charcoal Inn** (1637 Geele Ave., 920/458-1147), a corner diner where prices are as small as the dining room. A pork chop sandwich or bratwurst goes for about three bucks, a chocolate sundae for about two. Homemade soups and hand-dipped shakes round out the menu. Serves breakfast, lunch, and dinner.

After lunch, you'll make the great escape into Wisconsin farm country by taking LS North to Highway XX, where you'll turn right toward Manitowoc on Highway 42, and then on to Two Rivers. It was here in 1881 that Ed Berners, my nominee for a Nobel Prize in desserts, put chocolate sauce on a young girl's ice cream, and the ice cream sundae was born.

The original site where the sundae was invented is long gone, but the historical society compensates with the **Washington House** (1622 Jefferson St. just a block off Hwy. 42, 920/793-2490). The restored saloon now houses Berners' Ice Cream Parlor, the town visitors center, and a museum. Docents claim the rare murals in the upstairs ballroom make it the "Sistine Chapel of Two Rivers." It's still early, but the pope has yet to proclaim the Sistine Chapel the "Washington House of the Vatican."

This is the last gasp of city living you'll be subjected to, since the road becomes even more placid as you ride through small villages like Kewaunee and Algoma and past longer and more luxurious expanses of Lake Michigan shoreline.

Following Algoma, Highway S takes you into dairy country for a gentle, easy ride straight to Sturgeon Bay, the portal to Door County. The combination of the fresh country air, reliable views of Lake Michigan, and the unhurried pace of it all is extremely satisfying, although you—like me—may be annoyed by other riders' lack of civility.

Whether it's the proliferation of Harleys, I'm not sure, but in Wisconsin, the part of riders' brains that controls basic motor skills (like waving) has atrophied. No matter how many times you wave, they will not wave back. Remember: Goofus never waves; Gallant always waves. Always.

You'll bypass Sturgeon Bay as you enter Door County, crossing a canal and then veering off to follow Highway 57 North on the eastern shoreline. It's a quieting ride as you pass through Jacksonport and work your way up to Baileys Harbor, where there are a few restaurants and inns.

I'd suggest pushing on to the more active community of Fish Creek, which, judging from the proliferation of flowers, picket fences, and cottage shops, must have been charm school valedictorian. From Baileys Harbor, turn west on Highway F and follow it past pristine farmland, cherry trees, and apple orchards until you roll into one of the most beautiful towns in Door County.

Door County Primer

This part of Wisconsin combines Cape Cod with the Berkshires. The "thumb" of the state is about 75 miles long and 10 miles wide, and its limestone base makes for fertile farmland. Door County produces 95 percent of Wisconsin's cherries and about 40 percent of its apple crop, giving the roads a pink and white hue when the blossoms spring to life.

Fish Creek, arguably the most popular destination on the peninsula, began with Asa Thorp, who arrived in 1854 to make his fortune. Building the first pier north of Green Bay, he began selling cordwood to fuel the steamers that plied Lake Michigan. Thorp increased his land holdings and then built a lodge for steamship passengers, charging $7.50 a week. When the Wisconsin legislature bought the land to create Peninsula State Park, the sawmills stopped, the small farms reverted to forests again, and tourism took the lead.

In 2000, the nearby town of Ephraim was selected by *National Geographic* as one of the best small-town escapes in America, the only Wisconsin town to win that recognition.

Which is the why you're here.

On the Road: Door County

The best part about basing yourself in Fish Creek is that you have easy access to most things worth seeing. Provided you were smart enough not to ride in peak tourist season, you're just a few minutes from peaceful country settings.

Point your bike in any direction, and a trace of your lost idealism will return. As you venture out in the countryside, you'll find that people here actually live on farms and actually make fresh foods. You'll see this as you pass signs tempting you with fresh fruit jams and jellies, cherries, applesauce, fish, fudge, cheese, milk, custard, and cakes.

It's easy to take a roughly circular ride around the county, but before leaving Fish Creek, wander around the village for a few hours. At the western tip of Main Street lies a small park offering an unobstructed view of Green Bay and its islands. Doubling back via Cottage Row and Spruce Street, you'll circle the block to arrive at a small marina. After that, drop in at any number of shops, many of which were converted from old motor courts.

When you do leave town via Highway 42 North, the first detour is at

the broad waters of Green Bay near the "tip of the thumb" in Door County, Wisconsin

© NANCY HOWELL

3,700-acre **Peninsula State Park** (920/868-3258, www.wiparks.net). After being cooped up for the winter, golfers tee up, couples kayak, and families bike and hike over every trail. Admission to the park costs $10, $5 with Wisconsin tags, but it's free if you don't stop. I'm not talking about crashing the gate, I just mean there's an honor system and just not stopping as you ride through. Shore Road is fantastic for motorcycles, with small breaks in the tree line to expose the wide waters of Green Bay and provide you a place to pull over. Shore Road rolls by the 1868 Eagle Bluff Lighthouse and then Eagle Tower, a 75-foot observation platform that offers a superb view of the park, bay, and neighboring villages. Don't be a wimp. It's worth the climb.

The road exits onto Highway 42 three miles north of Fish Creek, and simply by turning left, you'll be riding toward Door County's most picturesque town, Ephraim, founded in 1853 as a Moravian religious community. Today, the steeples of Moravian and Lutheran churches reveal the town's spiritual values and love of natural beauty. Slow down to take in all you see: handsome clapboard inns, sailboats at anchor, horse-drawn carriages, and white sand beaches.

Though Ephraim has no true commercial district, everyone stops at **Wilson's Restaurant and Ice Cream Parlor** (9990 Water St., 920/854-2041). Here since 1906, this authentic family-owned diner serves fantastic hamburgers, soups, sandwiches, milkshakes, and sundaes (thanks, Ed Berners!). Don't miss this preserved look at Americana, and consider investing in the boat-rental concessions across the street.

From Ephraim, follow Highway 42 to its northernmost point. The road is serene, traipsing through the villages of Sister Bay, then Ellison Bay (check out the Pioneer Store, 920/854-2805) and past meadows and marshes to reach Gills Rock and its passenger ferry landing. You've reached the top of the thumb now, but if you continue riding east, 42 leads to one of the most incredible half-mile stretches of road I've seen. If you're riding in a group, get ready for some picture-taking as you hit a winding, canopied road with some great moguls. The ride is as subtle as a Swiss cough drop, and you'll wish only for more land to keep the road going.

Alas, you've reached the end of the world. Here in Northport, the vehicle ferry is waiting if you'd like to leave the peninsula and sail north to **Washington Island** (920/847-2546 or 800/223-2094, www.wisferry.com). On a motorcycle, you'll pay $13 for the round-trip ($10 for an extra passenger). Washington is the largest of Door County's islands and the oldest Icelandic community in the United States—but, of course, you knew that. Crossings of the "Straits of Death's Door" (named for the treacherous currents and unpredictable waves) are safer than in the early days, I hope. When you reach the island, you'll find a pastoral setting, restaurants, shops, and more than 100 miles of country roads.

You'll have to backtrack on Highway 42 to head south, detouring onto Highway NP if you want to see the **Newport State Park U.S. Bird Refuge** (920/854-2500), or continuing to Ellison Bay. There, Mink River Road descends toward Rowley's Bay and Highway ZZ drops farther south until it connects with Highway 57 and then Highway Q back down to Bailey's Harbor.

In other words, explore. When you're riding through Door County, there's no way to get lost.

And there's so much to find.

Pull It Over: Door County Highlights
Attractions and Adventures

In Door County, you're surrounded by water on three sides, making water sports the natural pastime. **Stiletto Catamaran Sailing Cruises** (South Shore Pier, Ephraim, 920/854-7245, www.stilettosailingcruises.com) offers seven sailings daily, with shorter daytime cruises (75 minutes, $18.95) and longer sunset cruises (two hours, $25). On a clear day, go for the sunset cruise—it's incredible.

If you don't see any ice floes, consider hitting the water. Boat-rental rates at **South Shore Pier Boat Rentals** (Ephraim, 920/854-4324) range from $74 for two hours on a 21-foot deluxe pontoon boat to $261 for an all-day excursion on a 25-foot pontoon boat (gas extra). Split the cost with fellow riders, and you've got your own sunset cruise. Traveling solo? Wave runners cost $65 per hour (gas included).

Hubbard Brothers Charters (10919 Bay Shore Dr., Sister Bay, 920/854-2113) began as a family business in the 1920s and remains one of the more reasonably priced fishing charters I've found. The $50 cost of the six-passenger charter includes a captain, poles, and tackle for a half-day excursion; you'll need to spring for the bait, refreshments, and fishing license ($10 for two days). Cash only, no cards. It's important to wear warm clothes and shoes, and know that these tough bastards don't cancel for rough seas, rains, or high winds. Say, you ever listened to "The Wreck of the *Edmund Fitzgerald*"?

Like the Hubbards, **Capt. Paul's Charter Fishing** (921 Cottage Rd., Gills Rock, 920/854-4614) claims to be the longest-running charter in the state and offers four-hour trips in search of salmon and brown trout. The novelty here is that you are always fishing. Whenever someone snags a fish, you rotate to the next rod. The *Lady Linda,* a 32-footer, has a six-passenger capacity. Bait and tackle are included in the $58 fee; the fishing license is not.

Shake out your sea legs and head to the **American Folklore Theatre** (920/854-6117, www.folkloretheatre.com) for an $12 evening performance held in Peninsula State Park's outdoor amphitheater. If you can endure the mosquitoes, you'll enjoy watching actors and musicians perform folk tales in a folksy setting—although the novelty can wear off before the last bow.

Shopping

Siobhan's (9431 Spruce St., Fish Creek, 920/868-3353) is a small shop with some epicurean pleasures: a nice selection of California and European wines, as well as champagnes, liquors, cheeses, cognacs, and single malt scotches. A few cigars round out this small shop's inventory.

Blue-Plate Specials

As long as you're in Door County, you may want to invest your appetite in a fish boil. Several lodges, resorts, and restaurants host them, including: **Leathen Smith Lodge & Marina** (1640 Memorial Rd., Sturgeon Bay, 920/743-5555), **Square Rigger Galley** (6332 Hwy. 57, Jacksonport, 920/823-2408), **Viking Grille** (12029 Hwy. 42, Ellison Bay, 920/854-2998), **Wagon Trail Resort** (1041 Hwy. ZZ, Ellison Bay, 920/854-2385), and **White Gull Inn** (4225 Main St., Fish Creek, 920/868-3517). Call ahead, since some require reservations or can arrange a private cookout for your group.

What the Bejeezus is a Fish Boil?

When I heard about the outbreak of fish boils in Door County, I placed a call to the surgeon general. Then someone helped me get wise. Fish boils are a staple of the Door County diet. Here's what happens, although I'm still not sure why.

Basically, it's a cookout. The process dates back to the days of Scandinavian settlers and lumberjacks who tossed fresh whitefish into a pot of salted water, then added onions and potatoes, stacked flaming boards around the pot, and let the damn thing cook over a boiling fire. The same thing happens today at restaurants throughout Door County.

When everything is cooked to what people here call "perfection," the chef completes the ritual. The pièce de résistance, the "boil over," comes when they toss kerosene over the flaming boards to spark a conflagration. This accomplishes multiple objectives: It boils the oils off the fish meat; it indicates that dinner is ready; and it singes the eyebrows off anyone who stands too close to the pot.

For food that doesn't bubble up from a boiling cauldron of water, try breakfast, lunch, or dinner at **The Cookery** (Main St., Fish Creek, 920/868-3634, www.cookeryfishcreek.com), serving everything you want, done just right. Five breakfast specials start at $3.95. At dinnertime, it loads you up on baked chicken, roast pork loin, stuffed pork chops, perch platters, and meat loaf.

Watering Holes

Here since the 1930s, the **Bayside Tavern** (Main St., Fish Creek, 920/868-3441) is the only local hangout in town. It features a large curved bar, small tables, and the world-famous Bayside Coffee, a potent, flaming, liquor-filled concoction. For grub, sample Smilin' Bob's Bar Room Chili. Bob whips up the spices at home, and they're such a secret that even the cooks don't know the recipe.

Shut-Eye

If you travel in season, you would be foolish—yes, damn foolish—not to reserve a room at one of Door County's many motels, hotels, condos, resorts, cabins, or campgrounds. For help finding one that fits your needs, call 800/527-3529 or www.doorcounty.com.

Motels and Motor Courts
Fish Creek Motel & Cottage (Fish Creek, 920/868-3448, www.fishcreek-motel.com) is a combination of modern motel rooms and original rooms with soothing woodland views. Clean and neat, it promises "free bikes," but I'm certain it doesn't mean motorcycles.

The **Edgewater Cottages** (4144 Route 42, Fish Creek, 920/868-3551) doesn't have much going for it by way of furnishings, but the log cabins and clapboard cottages are Bonnie-and-Clyde-hideout cool and provide a nice view of the cove. The rooms are quiet and comfortable, and some have kitchenettes.

Cedar Court (9429 Cedar St., Fish Creek, 920/868-3361, motel rooms $69 and up off-season, $89 in season; specialty rooms $98–128) gives you larger lodgings, since this is really a compound with guesthouses and a pool in back. One block from the bay and the shopping area, Cedar Court offers standard amenities in each room and whirlpool tubs in the choice ones.

Indulgences

One place that fills up months in advance is the fabled **White Gull Inn** (4225 Main St., Fish Creek, 920/868-3517, www.whitegullinn.com, $145–265). Each room or suite has a porch or deck, fireplace, TV/VCR, and space to spread out. If you're riding with a group, the Lundberg Guest House ($425) sleeps eight. The inn also features a full restaurant.

A few miles away in Ephraim, the **Eagle Harbor Inn** (9914 Water St., Ephraim, 920/854-2121 or 800/324-5427, www.eagleharbor.com, rooms $96 and up in season, suites $165–199) rests on five peaceful acres across from the bay. This quiet resort offers breakfast and nice landscaping. Suites, which sleep up to six, have a whirlpool tub, fireplace, kitchen, CD/TV/VCR, and private deck.

In the heart of the village, most rooms at the summers-only **Ephraim Inn** (9994 Pioneer Ln., Ephraim, 920/854-4515, www.theephraiminn.com, $110–195) afford great views of the harbor and tiered green bluffs. A continental breakfast is included.

Resources for Riders

Wisconsin Thumb Run

Wisconsin Travel Information
Wisconsin Association of Campground Owners—608/582-2092 or
800/843-1821, www.wisconsincampgrounds.com
Wisconsin Department of Tourism—800/432-8747,
www.travelwisconsin.com
Wisconsin Innkeepers Association—www.lodging-wi.com
Wisconsin Road Conditions—800/762-3947
Wisconsin State Parks—608/266-2181, www.wiparks.net
Wisconsin State Parks Reservations—888/947-2757,
www.reserveamerica.com

Local and Regional Information
Door County Chamber of Commerce—920/743-4456 or 800/527-3529,
www.doorcounty.com
Ephraim Information Center—920/854-4989,
www.ephraim-doorcounty.com
Fish Creek Information Center—920/868-2316 or 800/577-1880
Greater Milwaukee Convention & Visitors Bureau—414/273-7222 or
800/554-1448, www.milwaukee.org
Milwaukee Weather Information—414/744-8000 or 414/936-1212
Washington Island Chamber of Commerce—920/847-2179,
www.washingtonislandchamber.com

Wisconsin Motorcycle Shops
Corse's Superbikes—700 E. Milan, Saukville, 262/284-2725,
www.corsessuperbikes.com
Hal's Harley-Davidson-Buell—1925 S. Mooreland Rd., New Berlin,
262/860-2060 or 800/966-4443, www.halshd.com
House of Harley-Davidson—6221 W. Layton Ave., Milwaukee, 414/282-
2211, www.houseofharley.com
Milwaukee Harley-Davidson/Buell—11310 Silver Spring Dr., Milwaukee,
414/461-4444, www.milwaukeeharley.com
Route 43 Harley-Davidson—3736 S. Taylor Dr., Sheboygan, 920/458-
0777, www.route43hd.com
Sheboygan Yamaha—N7402 Hwy. 42, Sheboygan Falls, 920/565-2213,
www.sheboyganyamaha.com
Southeast Sales (BMW, Triumph, Honda, Kawasaki)—6930 N. 76th St.,
Milwaukee, 414/463-2540, www.southeastsales.com
Stock's Harley-Davidson Motorcycles—3206 Menasha Ave., Manitowoc,
920/684-0237, www.stockshd.com
Suburban Harley-Davidson/Buell—139 N. Main St., Thiensville, 262/242-
2464, www.suburbanharley.com

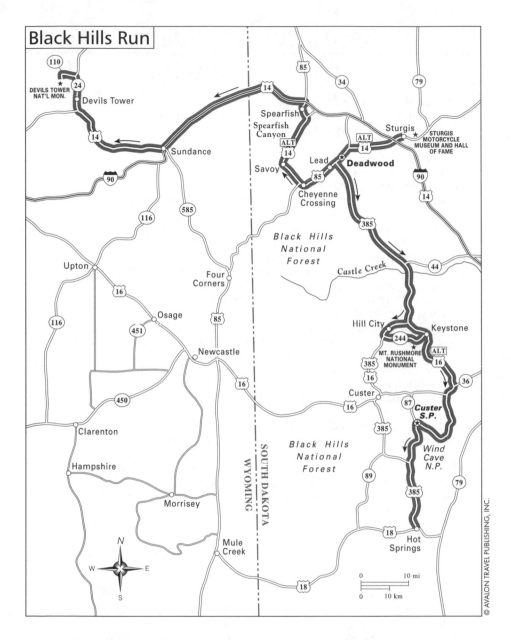

Route: Deadwood to Custer State Park via Devils Tower, Sturgis, Hot Springs, Mount Rushmore, Iron Mountain Road

Distance: Approximately 160 miles (with side trips); consider four days with stops.

•Day 1—Deadwood/Devils Tower •Day 2—Travel/Sturgis/Mount Rushmore •Days 3–4—Custer State Park/Hot Springs

First Leg: Deadwood to Custer State Park

Helmet Laws: South Dakota does not require helmets.

Black Hills Run

*Deadwood, South Dakota to Custer State Park,
South Dakota*

Thanks to the Sturgis Rally, South Dakota attracts its share of motorcycle travelers, but there's more to the state than a single week in August. In the Black Hills, you will see things that teach you the West isn't a location but a lifestyle. There are towering structures and wide-open spaces, caves and fossil beds, natural beauty and a desire to preserve it. And when you travel during shoulder season (May or September), the roads are wide open and free.

Deadwood Primer

Gold was the key. When word got out that there was gold in Deadwood, tent cities were erected, and the boom was on.

Folks here are still searching for gold, but now they do it in the small-stakes casinos. The casinos have turned Deadwood into a town of contradictions, but since the entire town's on the National Historic Register, it's still the nicest place to base yourself before exploring the Black Hills.

Prior to 1989, this small town's Main Street was lined with restaurants and independent businesses. Then low-stakes gambling—uh, *gaming*—was introduced. Old inventory and displays were out; computerized slots were in. Ask the locals, and they admit that gambling seemed like a great idea at first, but most of them miss their old hometown.

One fortunate event that helped turn the clock back and enhance the future was the HBO series that premiered in 2004. *Deadwood* focuses on the town's more explosive days, when you took a gamble just by walking into one of the frontier saloons. The popularity of the series—which showcases the violent power struggle between camp settlers and new arrivals—has created another surge in Deadwood's history.

The pioneer feel is displayed in the facades of buildings and, at first glance, everything seems perfect. The brick streets are clean, the people content ... but then come those damned contradictions. At a casino called Chinatown, you listen to American rock classics, dine in a Mexican cantina, and stare at a London taxi. It is Vegas flashy without the energy.

It's not depressing, just out of sync.

On the Road: Deadwood

There are things to see in Deadwood, but the roads are more appealing. Then again, if you're a Kevin Costner fan, you may never want to leave.

Costner, whose acting style follows his early role as a corpse in *The Big Chill,* opened the Midnight Star casino, displaying nearly every costume, prop, and script he ever touched.

More intriguing than Costner memorabilia is a ride out to Devil's Tower via Spearfish Canyon. You won't need a passport to ride into Wyoming; just take Route 85 out of Deadwood toward the town of Lead (pronounced "leed"). The road isn't too attractive, but stay on it—it gradually improves.

About eight miles from Lead at the junction of Routes 85 and 14A, turn right and take a break at the **Cheyenne Crossing Store** (605/584-3510). Open 7:30 A.M.–7:30 P.M. daily, this is one of those old-fashioned combination café/lodge/souvenir stand/beer stop/bait shop/filling stations. I tried to sell them on expanding their inventory to include plutonium, beetle larvae, and chimpanzees.

Although Spearfish Canyon is a national scenic byway, the scenery isn't so fantastic. It does let you explore some backcountry, though. Spearfish Creek runs along a curving road, and when the road narrows, the ride gets more interesting. At the town of Savoy, you'll find a fancy restaurant, cultural center, and resort—too fancy for these parts. Keep heading north through the canyon, and the road ascends and descends rapidly, with other riders springing up in the oncoming lanes.

When you've completed the canyon, 14A takes you through the clean streets of Spearfish and onto I-90 West. You have 50-plus miles to ride before reaching **Devils Tower,** (307/467-5283, www.nps.gov/deto), the icon that haunted

Richard Dreyfuss in *Close Encounters* (FYI: Ginger Grant's the icon that still haunts me). For now, the road is low-key, and when you reach Highway 14, head north and be prepared to slow down behind campers who got up a little earlier than you did. The landscape alternates between lush pine forests and open plains, but it's an easy ride to reach Highway 24, which you take north, veering off at 110.

From the road, you'll see the 1,267-foot Devil's Tower monument thrusting into the sky. Numerous pullouts afford views. If you enter, you'll pay $3 per passenger (free if you sprung for a money-saving annual National Parks Pass) and gain access to a steeply inclined three-mile road that leads to a museum, bookstore, and 1.3-mile paved trail surrounding the tower.

What formed this monolith? The Kiowa Indians believed eight children were playing when suddenly, the lone boy among them turned into a bear. The girls climbed onto a talking tree stump and, as the bear tried to kill them, the stump rose so high that the girls turned into the stars of the Big Dipper. The long gashes on the tower are claw marks from the homicidal boy/bear. I spoke to my imaginary geologist friend, Hank, who confirmed that this is what happened.

After circling the tower, backtrack to Spearfish Canyon, then to Deadwood for a night at the casinos and another loving look at Kevin Costner's quiver.

Pull It Over: Deadwood Highlights
Attractions and Adventures

Three cemetery plots a short ride from Main Street should gain your attention at Mount Moriah. Wild Bill Hickok, Calamity Jane, and local character Potato Creek Johnny are buried here. If Hickok's head wound hadn't killed him, the procession up this steep grade would've. Wild Bill's faithful following drop packs of "aces and eights" by his tombstone. Admission is $2.

If you're planning a heist, target some of the displays at **Nelson's Garage Car and Motorcycle Museum** (629 Main St., 605/578-1909, free) at the Celebrity Hotel. Stashed here are Evel Knievel's helmet and jumpsuit, James Bond's suit from *Diamonds Are Forever,* Sylvester Stallone's Ducati Paso 750 Limited, Steve McQueen's '66 Triumph 650, Harleys owned by Peter Fonda and Ann-Margret, Clint Eastwood's Trans Am, and Paul McCartney's '73 Honda 125. Ship them to me care of my publisher.

No snapshots here—these are actually nice photographs at **Woody's Wild West Portrait Emporium** (641 Main St., 605/578-3807, www.woodyswild-west.com). I know there are a lot of vintage photo places, but this one's better,

Sturgis Rally and Races

Why in the world do riders head to the barren landscape of South Dakota? Because of a rally started in August 1938 by Indian (brand of motorcycle) motorcycle dealer J. C. "Pappy" Hoel. Back then, nine riders raced on a half-mile dirt track for a $500 purse, followed by crowd-pleasing stunts, such as head-on collisions with cars, board wall crashes, and ramp-jumping. From this, the Jackpine Gypsies Motorcycle Club was born, and the rally was proclaimed the Black Hills Motorcycle Classic.

After World War II, the rally and race drew up to 5,000 people and 150 competitors. By the 1960s, the Sturgis Chamber of Commerce had begun to take part by hosting barbecues in the park and awarding prizes to the rally queen, oldest rider, best-dressed couple, and the longest-distance traveler. During the rally's 45th anniversary, the governor proclaimed "Pappy Hoel Week" to honor its founder, and attendance peaked at 30,000.

The big leap came during the 50th anniversary rally, when as many as 400,000 riders flocked to Sturgis. In 1991, the event was renamed the **Sturgis Rally and Races** (605/720-0800, www.sturgismotorcycle rally.com) and became (promoters wished) a "family event." In reality, it is a wild drinking, riding, racing party where inhibitions are checked at the door. In 2004, what started as a down-home event attracted more than half a million riders, making it the biggest outdoor event in America.

since the large studio features 25 settings and nearly 1,000 costume combinations that allow women to dress in their bordello finest and men to become cardsharps and gunslingers. Another advantage is that riders can bring in their bikes for a Western-style shot. Open daily, hours vary.

Blue-Plate Specials

It's hard to find great food and a normal restaurant in Deadwood, since you have to navigate a casino to do it. Up and down Main Street, you'll find home cooking and ethnic eateries, but only one stands out.

On the second floor of the Midnight Star, **Jake's** (677 Main St., 605/578-1555) serves lunch and dinner. Expect fine dining in a nice atmosphere, with entrées like rack of lamb, steaks, and Cajun seafood. High rollers (a relative term in Deadwood) dine here. The third-floor sports bar is less fancy and less expensive.

Watering Holes

Casinos have cornered the market, but there are a few joints to check out. Friendly barkeeps at **Oyster Bay** (628 Main St., 605/578-3136) may persuade you to sample the $2 "oyster shooter" concoction, created with an oyster, beer, Worcestershire sauce, tabasco, cocktail sauce, salt and pepper, and other stuff I'm running tests on. If that grabs you, try Walk the Plank: seven oyster shooters increasing in potency until you're over the edge. The beer and oyster bar attracts riders and regulars folks from around the world.

Not the saloon where Wild Bill was blown away (that was across the street at #622), the **Old Style Saloon #10** (657 Main St., 605/578-3346, www .saloon10.com) does have his "death chair" (look over the door after you enter). The place feels authentic, with sawdust on the floor (used by saloonkeepers to camouflage dropped gold dust), an 1870s atmosphere, and a full liquor bar. If you draw Hickock's hand in the casino next door, don't worry, be happy: You've just won $250. But watch your back.

Shut-Eye

An organization called **Black Hills Central Reservations** (800/529-0105, www.blackhillsvacations.com) can arrange rooms, adventures, and activities—and also takes a 5 percent fee. Most hotels in Deadwood are along Main Street, and all have a casino attached.

Among the better choices is the **Franklin Hotel** (700 Main St., 605/578-2241 or 800/688-1876, www.historicfranklinhotel.com, $97–109), the grande dame of Deadwood. Undergoing restoration since 1989, the Franklin has large rooms that make up for the lack of fine furniture, and the owner's celebrity friends (Tom Brokaw, Mary Hart, Jann Wenner, et al.) don't seem to mind. Rates are reasonable, except during rallies, when you won't find a room. There's a motor court across the street, but try to stay in the main hotel, which has a dining room and Durty Nelly's Irish Pub. Down the street, the **Bullock Hotel** (633 Main St., 605/578-1745 or 800/336-1876, www.heartofdeadwood.com, $95–159) boasts the nicest rooms. Well decorated, they are separated from the noise of the casino and include king or queen beds, shower baths, and some whirlpools. A restaurant, casino, and full liquor bar downstairs mean that you can stay in for the night. The **Celebrity Hotel** (629 Main St., 605/578-1909 or 888/399-1886, $89–139), also where you'll find the motorcycle museum, features clean, functional rooms with a fridge, a TV, and a patio deck that lets you enjoy the weather if it's nice.

Chain Drive
A, C, E, L, CC

Chain hotels are in town, or within 10 miles. See cross-reference guide featuring phone numbers and Web addresses on page 514.

On the Road: Deadwood to Custer State Park

This next leg is like taking four rides in one. You could take a few days to do this, but here's one way to do it all at once if you wish.

From Deadwood, take 14A a short 14 miles to Sturgis. Yes, Sturgis. When the rally's not here, there's little to see. Downtown is depressing, although you can salvage a good feeling at the **Sturgis Motorcycle Museum and Hall of Fame,** (999 Main St., 605/347-2001, www.sturgismuseum.com, $3, weekdays 9 A.M–5 P.M., weekends 11 A.M.–3 P.M.). The museum showcases a jaw-dropping fleet of American and imported bikes in a chronological collection including an '09 Exelsior Auto Cycle, '11 Flying Merkel, '15 Harley-Davidson Boardtrack Racer, '28 Calthorpe, '34 Crocker Racer, '48 Royal Enfield Flying Flea, a '52 Vincent Black Shadow, and dozens of others. If you have a museum quality motorcycle you wouldn't mind having displayed for a year, give them a call. When you leave Sturgis, return past Deadwood and follow Highway 385 South. Along the way, you'll see signs reading "X marks the spot. Think." These are posted after riders lose their challenge with tight turns. Think.

Still, it's hard to resist accelerating into this steeplechase for bikes. The road spins up, then down, then around every terrain ever invented. The landscape alternates between boondocks, fields, and meadows, with an occasional general store popping up on the roadside.

After the turnoff to Rapid City (skip it), the road returns to its unpredictable layout, taking you down hills and whipping around corners and past Pactola Lake, a picturesque spot with pullouts for photos and a National Forest information center on the opposite side.

When you reach Hill City, turn left onto Route 16 and follow it six miles toward Keystone. Exit at Highway 16A and ride through cluttered Keystone, more touristy than anyplace you've seen.

From here, follow SR 244 toward **Mount Rushmore National Memorial**

(605/574-2523, www.nps.gov/moru), open 8 A.M.–10 P.M. daily. You cannot deny the thrill when that first face peeks through the trees. Although you can go to the main parking lot ($8 for an annual pass), you can save some cash by watching for the "no-fee parking area" to your right, just beneath the summit. From here, you'll be at Gutzon Borglum's studio, where steps lead to the monument.

Once you scale the steps, the crust of cynicism dissolves and lost idealism returns. This is not a cheap postcard, this is a 3-D testament to an experiment with democracy and the leadership of four great men. A $56 million renovation (using no tax dollars, just donations) created a restaurant, a massive gift shop, an amphitheater you'll return to that evening, a theater, and exhibit hall featuring original models and sketches, firsthand accounts of the construction, and an inspiring explanation of why these presidents were chosen for the honor (respectively, they symbolize the founding, development, growth, and preservation of the country). Instead of watching the faces with everyone else, find a quiet spot to sit and reflect on the massive undertaking.

Only if you feel comfortable riding supernaturally dark roads, make plans to return here at dusk (usually around 8 P.M. in the summertime) for a first-class presentation. At around 8:30, patriotic music plays in the amphitheater, and at 9, a ranger takes the stage to answer questions and explain the lighting ceremony. A short documentary is shown, and when the national anthem plays and the audience sings along, the faces are illuminated. As if you needed encouragement, this will make you proud to be an American.

When you leave Mount Rushmore, get ready for one incredible road. Peter Norbeck, the South Dakota senator and governor who was instrumental in the creation of Mount Rushmore, the Needles Highway, and the preservation of Custer State Park, rode on horseback to map out Iron Mountain Road. The result is a magnificent motorcycle run.

Turn south onto Highway 16A, and the test-track tight turns begin adding alternating stretches of canopy roads, great countryside, 15-mph switchbacks, and the occasional "pigtail bridge," an ingenious invention that spans steep climbs within a short stretch.

This road is not for sissies. The turns throw you around like Nature Boy Rick Flair and pumps up your left leg to maximum density with all the shifting. This is a red-hot, helluva fun road.

Occasionally, it settles down to a nice ride through the forest, and then it rocks and rolls you over the countryside and into nearly vertical ascensions. You'll get an upper-body workout tackling these turns. Since the landscape hasn't been violated, even as you're being tossed around like a rag doll, your spirits will lift.

It's a long ride to Custer State Park, but when you turn right and follow Highway 16A to the park entrance, you'll enter the park equivalent of Iron Mountain Road, a place filled with adventure, excitement, and natural beauty.

Custer State Park Primer

Doomed General George A. Custer led a scientific army expedition into the Black Hills in 1874. Although his team found gold, Custer seemed more interested in the area's natural beauty. Fortune seekers weren't so magnanimous. They arrived in droves, and their presence took a toll on the area's wildlife.

By 1913, the South Dakota legislature created a state game reserve in the southern Black Hills, where they would replenish the wildlife population with bison, pronghorn, elk, bighorn sheep, and mountain goats. Governor Peter Norbeck envisioned a 73,000-acre showcase for the area's spectacular resources. With that, the reserve became Custer State Park, which has all the appeal of Yellowstone and Yosemite, yet on a manageable level. It's as close to a perfect park as you'll ever find.

On the Road: Custer State Park

I'll start with a warning: You may be tempted to sign on for the Buffalo Jeep Safari—but based on experience, I say you'll see just as much, if not more, by riding your bike south on the Highway 87 section of the 18-mile Wildlife Loop Road.

From the State Game Lodge, turn left and follow Highway 16A West past meadows and creeks until you reach Highway 87, and then head south toward Hot Springs. This is one of the top 10 rides you can make—provided you're not impaled by a buffalo. Get your camera ready: Chances are you'll spy enough wildlife to fill an ark while riding a road that twists like a knot.

If someone charged you with the task to build a road, this would be it. As you pass the Blue Bell Lodge and general store and cross French Creek, you couldn't ask for a better ride, complete with peaks and valleys. It narrows and most likely will put you in the midst of a buffalo herd. It's safer to be in a car when these 2,000-pound beasts are around, but you don't have that option. If they're blocking the road, wait patiently. Do not try to approach them. Although they appear to be as slow and stupid as paint-sniffing monkeys, they

The buffalo roam near the Wilderness Loop at Custer State Park.

can hit you at 30 mph and pierce you like a pincushion. Still, these damned beasts are fascinating.

Farther on, you'll hear a high-pitched chirping. A glimpse of a single prairie dog will suddenly reveal thousands of these creatures standing sentinel atop their holes or scattering like rats in front of traffic. You can spot the local drivers: They're the ones speeding through here, popping a few prairie dogs. If you're lucky and your vision is good, you may also see bighorn sheep, mountain goats, elk, deer, burros, coyotes, falcons, mountain lions, and bobcats—animals too big for the locals to kill.

When you reach the end of Highway 87, follow Highway 385 South and detour to the loop road that takes you to **Wind Cave National Park** (605/745-4600, www.nps.gov/wica). Beneath one square mile of earth lie 83 miles of tunnels. For $8 (or $20 if you're an adventurous psychopath eager to take the Wild Cave Tour, a strenuous four-hour caving class), you'll join a two-hour tour. If you've never been in a cave before, it's frightening at first, then you think you'll die, then you think about earthquakes, then you're fine, and then the passages get narrow and the ranger turns out the lights and you're frightened again.

Although there are no grand stalactites or stalagmites or waterfalls, the cave is interesting and cool (a constant 53°F). The fact that the ranger carries barf and waste bags tells you this tour isn't for everyone. Avoid it if you're claustrophobic.

When you're back on the road, ride south on 385 to Hot Springs, an ordinary old town with one interesting site about a mile out of town. The **Mammoth Site** (605/745-6017, www.mammothsite.com, $6.75) seems as if it would be a tourist trap, but once you're inside, it's like walking into an archaeological dig. About

26,000 years ago, a spring-fed sinkhole formed, and dozens of mammoths that had dropped by for a drink dropped in and couldn't get out. In the 1970s, when a developer started to clear the land, diggers found bones, and a tourist attraction was born. Archaeologists dig only in July, but it's fascinating to see this bone orchard. Outside of a Beverly Hills plastic surgeon's office, it's the only display of fossilized mammoths in America. The site is open 8 A.M.–7 P.M. daily.

When you're ready to roll, return via the same roads, but when you reach Custer State Park again, watch for the eastern side of the Wildlife Loop Road and take that back to the State Game Lodge (or wherever you're staying) to complete the circle. And watch out for them prairie dogs.

Pull It Over: Custer State Park Highlights
Attractions and Adventures

To explore the park itself, rent a mount from **Blue Bell Stables** (605/255-4571). Horseback rides last from one hour ($18) to a full day ($125), with two-hour ($30) and half-day ($75) options in between. Do this in South Dakota, and you'll be a cowboy, my friend.

The Needles, also known as Highway 87 North, comes fully equipped with narrow granite tunnels and hairpin turns. The name comes from the long, slender granite spires that border the road. The 14-mile thrill leads through rugged Black Hills to Sylvan Lake.

Although it's outside the park, it's worth seeing what will become the largest sculpture ever created. **Crazy Horse** (on Hwy. 385, 605/673-4681, www.crazyhorse.org, $4) is open daybreak–dusk. Right now, only the face is complete because, out of respect for the subject, sculptor Korczak Ziolkowski turned down federal money. Why Crazy Horse? Ziolkowski admired the martyr (he was stabbed in the back under a flag of truce by a U.S. soldier), and he sympathized with Crazy Horse and his people, who endured a string of broken treaties. Ziolkowski is dead now; his family continues his work.

Shopping

Each lodge at Custer has a general store nearby, but the oversized **Coolidge General Store** near the State Game Lodge gets my vote for best store in a state park. Minnesota shipbuilders built it in 1927 to accommodate the tourists and reporters who accompanied President Coolidge on his visit. Check out the ceiling and you'll see the hull of a ship turned upside down. Of course, the smaller general stores are perfect places to stop while you're out for a pleasure ride.

Blue-Plate Specials

As in Yellowstone, you can grab snacks and quick meals at snack bars and general stores in the park. For sit-down meals, there are also dining rooms where you can order breakfast, lunch, and dinner: the **Tatanka Dining Room** at the Blue Bell Lodge (605/255-4535), the **Legion Lake Dining Room** at the Legion Lake Resort (605/255-4521), and the **Lakota Dining Room** at the Sylvan Lake Resort (605/574-2561). The nicest location may be the **Pheasant Dining Room** (605/255-4541) at the State Game Lodge. Comfortable and rustic, the restaurant serves buffalo, salmon, trout, steak, chicken, and pheasant, and the service is excellent. Reservations are a smart idea at any park restaurant.

Shut-Eye

The park makes a great day trip, but staying here is even better. For reservations at any lodge, call 800/658-3530. Rates vary widely according to season and type of accommodation (cabin, hotel, or lodge).

It's easy to see why Calvin Coolidge extended his stay at **State Game Lodge and Resort** ($75–99) from three weeks to three months. The idyllic front porch overlooks a sweeping lawn; there's an artist in residence; and, like the park, it is not so large as to be overpowering. The lodge features cool creekside cabins, along with hotel rooms, a small wooden church, and the Coolidge General Store nearby.

At an elevation of 6,250 feet, **Sylvan Lake Resort** ($95 and up) overlooks a picturesque mountain lake and offers cabins, lodge rooms, and a lounge. You'll need to run the Needles Highway to reach your room. Not a bad deal. **Blue Bell Lodge** ($105 and up) is a cowboy resort with cabins, a general store, gas station, campground, and laundry. Trail rides and cookouts leave from here. The least flashy of the lodges, **Legion Lake Resort** ($90 and up) rents cabins that are complemented by a restaurant, gift shop, grocery store, and sport-boat rentals on the lake. For campsite reservations, call 800/710-2267.

Side Trips

Minnesota and Nebraska

Minnesota
Highway 16

River roads usually provide the most satisfaction for riders. In Southeast Minnesota, Highway 16 follows the lead of the Root River. Between La Crescent and Dexter, the road surface is silky, while the surrounding rough bluffs beg bikers to stop and take souvenir pix. Keep an eye open for Spring Valley, which delivers on a full slate of narrows and twists.

Highway 14

Escape the breakneck I-90 traffic en route to the Sturgis Rally and take a casual cruise on Highway 14 through Minnesota. Riding north and parallel to the interstate, the advantage is a tour of small Minnesota towns and farms. If you've got the energy, stay on Highway 14 all the way through South Dakota, and you'll arrive in jam-packed Wall.

Contributed by Sharon Haak

Nebraska
U.S. 385

North of Alliance on U.S. 385 is Carhenge—an astronomically correct automobile replica of Stonehenge. Sculptor Jim Reinders designed the structure as a memorial to his dad, who once farmed this land. The bodies of 38 granite gray cars were placed in a circle 96 feet in diameter, planted trunk-down in five-foot-deep pits, while others were welded at their front bumpers to form arches. Carhenge is open 24/7 year-round.

Contributed by John M. Flora

Resources for Riders

Black Hills Run

South Dakota Travel Information
Bed & Breakfast Innkeepers of South Dakota—888/500-4667,
  www.soutdakotabb.com
South Dakota Department of Tourism—605/733-3301 or 800/732-
  5682, www.travelsd.com
South Dakota Road Conditions—605/773-3571
South Dakota State Parks—800/710-2267, www.campsd.com

Local and Regional Information
Black Hills, Badlands & Lakes Association—605/355-3600,
  www.blackhillsbadlands.com
Custer State Park—605/255-4515 or 800/710-2267,
  www.custerresorts.com
Custer State Park Resort Company—605/255-4772 or 800/658-3530,
  www.custerresorts.com
Deadwood Chamber of Commerce—605/578-1876 or 800/999-1876,
  www.deadwood.org

South Dakota Motorcycle Shops
Black Hills Harley-Davidson—141 E. Omaha, Rapid City, 605/347-2056
  or 800/458-1485, www.sturgishd.com
Black Hills Powersports—3005 Beale St., Rapid City, 605/342-5500 or
  888/642-5505, www.blackhillspowersports.com
Petersen Motors—422 S. Fort St., Pierre, 605/224-4242,
  www.petersenmotorcycles.com
Sturgis Yamaha-BMW-Suzuki—2879 Vanoker Rd., Sturgis, 605/347-2636

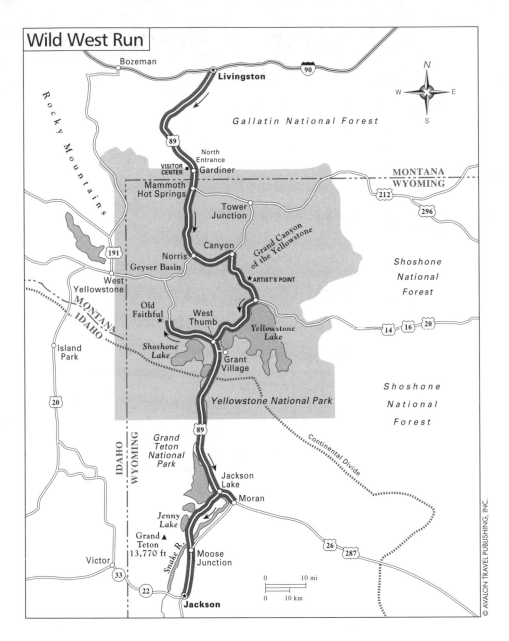

Wild West Run

Route: Livingston to Jackson via Yellowstone National Park, Grand Teton National Park

Distance: Approximately 210 miles; consider six days with stops.
- •**Day 1—Livingston** •**Day 2—Livingston/Travel** •**Days 3–4—Yellowstone** •**Day 5—Travel/Jackson** •**Day 6—Jackson**

First Leg: Livingston to South Yellowstone (125 miles)

Second Leg: Yellowstone to Jackson (82 miles)

Helmet Laws: Montana and Wyoming do not require helmets.

Wild West Run

Livingston, Montana to Jackson, Wyoming

This tour may be the best run in the West. It begins in an authentic Western town, traverses a kaleidoscope of natural wonders, and comes to a close in another Western town—one with a nice twist.

The roads are not challenging in themselves, but the ride is unforgettable: It offers the most magnificent scenery and wildlife in America. You can avoid harsh weather and tourists by riding in May or September.

Livingston Primer

Everything was going fine in Clark City until the Northern Pacific Railroad decided to relocate its line. That's when 500 people, six general stores, two hotels, and 30 saloons wound up in nearby Livingston. In 1872, when Congress established Yellowstone, the completion of the park branch of the Northern Pacific brought Livingston new business.

The town profited from the railroad and mining; in the 1880s, cattle, sheep, and grain became the major economic forces. Livingston hasn't grown much since then, although there's a distinct difference today. The town's year-round population of about 7,500 swells when part-time residents arrive to take advantage of the spells of good weather. Folks who call Livingston home at least part of the year include celebs like Jeff Bridges, Tom Brokaw, Meg Ryan, Dennis Quaid, and Peter Fonda. The veneer here may be pioneer, but the town's soul is sophisticated.

On the Road: Livingston

There are some great loop roads outside of town (ask for directions at the Chamber of Commerce), but it'll be hard to pull yourself away from the anachronism that is Livingston—the town is locked in the 1940s, which means that your senses won't be assaulted by franchises and chain stores when you arrive. Their absence makes wandering around downtown as satisfying as any ride.

On the surface, Livingston seems to be an ordinary Western town filled with rustic cowpokes. Dig a little deeper, and you'll detect the town's sophistication, perhaps casually revealed in an art gallery, nice restaurant, or conversation with a rancher who probably carries more money than the Federal Reserve.

So, park your bike and look around. For now, the road can wait.

Pull It Over: Livingston Highlights
Attractions and Adventures

The great outdoors is big around Livingston, and several outfitters can take you to it. **River Services Ltd.** (4 Mount Baldy Dr., 406/222-3746, www.riverservices.com) coordinates boat and gear rentals, white-water rafting trips, scenic floats, fishing excursions, rowing instruction, overnight kayak tours, canoe floats, and fishing guides—at a low, low, no charge to you.

Here, as elsewhere in Montana, fly-fishing is big, and it all culminates at the **International Flyfishing Museum** (215 E. Lewis St., 406/222-9369, www.fedflyfishers.org or www.livingstonmuseums.org, $3). The old Lincoln School was turned into an enclave of sculptures, watercolors, and exhibits showcasing the lure and lures of the sport. The museum also offers free fly-casting and tying lessons. What's so hot about fly-fishing? Practitioners claim it's more rewarding because you get away from 200-horsepower boat engines and into the rhythms of nature.

If your visit to the museum has inspired you, head to **Dan Bailey's Fly Shop** (209 W. Park St., 406/222-1673 or 800/356-4052, www.danbailey.com). One of the most famous names in the sport has owned one of the most comprehensive stores in town since 1938, and it's packed to the gills with everything you need and hundreds of things you don't. How many times have you lost sleep wondering where you could find strung schlappen, hackle capes, and bumblebee popper foam? You'll rest easy after a visit here, open 8 A.M.–6 P.M. Monday–Saturday. Bailey's also organizes daylong fishing excursions for $300–350. Since I only had three dollars, they gave me a four-minute session.

A more urban pleasure awaits you at the **Livingston Depot** (200 W. Park St., 406/222-2300, $3), a museum within a beautiful restoration of the Northern Pacific passenger depot. Open May–September, it features exhibits on Western life and art shows, and it hosts annual events, such as railroad swap meets. Check out the building's ornate brickwork and lion's-head accents.

Shopping

Gil's Got It (207 W. Park St., 406/222-0112), open 9 A.M.–5 P.M. daily, carries everything you used to crave when your parents were lugging you around the country in the backseat of the Buick. Here since 1914, it survives by selling straw cowboy hats, popguns, and wallets with cowboys on them. Hip.

You really need to look into this one: Customize one of the teepees available from **White Buffalo Lodges** (522 E. Park St., 406/222-7390, www.whitebuffalolodges.com), and you've got it made. Choose Sioux, Cheyenne, Blackfoot, or Crow style, and dress it out with custom paintings based on traditional designs, stories, medicine symbols, and animals. Kits range from $570 (for two kids) to a $2,000 teepee that sleeps eight adults and includes a liner, poles, carrying bag, rope, door cover, willow lacing pins, and stakes. If you can figure out how to haul one on your bike, imagine how freakin' cool it'd be setting one up on a Great Plains road trip.

Pardner, if you collect Old West memorabilia, mosey on by the **Cowboy Connection** (110 1/2 N. Main St., 406/222-0272, www.thecowboyconnection.com). Stocked items include gambling mementoes, antique Colts and Winchesters, saddles, chaps, spurs and bits, Stetsons, artwork, bronzes, boots, frock coats, knives, and shotguns.

Blue-Plate Specials

For several reasons, I'd rank **Martin's Cafe** (108 W. Park St., 406/222-2110) among America's top diners: Ranchers, cowboys, and working folks eat breakfast, lunch, and dinner here seven days a week; it made its debut in 1902 as the beanery for Northern Pacific passengers; and it serves chicken-fried steak, fried chicken, burgers, onion rings, and banana, coconut, and chocolate cream pies. Is it popular? Check out the well-worn counters, where decades of elbows have rubbed the green Formica clean.

At the corner of 8th and Park, **Mark's In and Out** is a drive-in where you can fuel up on the four food groups: burgers, hot dogs, onion rings, and milkshakes. Clean as a whistle, Mark's service and prices are straight out of the

1950s—fitting, considering it opened in 1954. Burgers and cheeseburgers are $0.99. If you don't mind bypass surgery, order a mess of Cadillac fries with gravy, chili, or cheese sauce.

Filled with local characters who hang out at the bar (open 'til 2 A.M.), **The Stockman** (118 N. Main St., 406/222-8455) also serves lunch and dinner to folks who believe that this small restaurant's got the best steaks in town. Weekends are packed, so try to go on a weeknight for a hand-cut top sirloin, New York strip, or rib eye. Bring cash—credit cards aren't accepted.

The best thing about the **The Sport** (114 S. Main St., 406/222-9500, www.thesportmontana.com) is that it's not a sports restaurant. The original opened in 1909, when the popular sports were hunting and fishing, and women weren't allowed in until the late 1940s. This must-see restaurant has an authentic Old West atmosphere with mounted heads and archival newspapers. The menu advertises burgers, ribs, wings, seafood, homemade soups, chicken sandwiches, and Montana ranch steaks. The real sports bar, Sports Next Door, is the place to go if you've got a wager with Pete Rose and have to catch a game.

Watering Holes

I drink only to excess, so I had a hard time staying out of Livingston's bars. Each has the feel of a Western roadhouse: bartenders who can be sassy or sympathetic, and enough smoke to trigger the oxygen masks. They're all over downtown Livingston, but here are a few standouts.

The bar at the Murray Hotel, **Swingin' Door Saloon** (201 W. Park St., 406/222-9816), features two pool tables, seven beers on tap, a full liquor bar, live rockabilly bands, and lots of energy. If you stepped into a time machine and were transported back to the '40s, you'd see just what awaits you at **The Mint** (102 N. Main St., 406/222-0361). Break out the booze and have a ball. There used to be a brothel upstairs at the **Whiskey Creek Saloon and Casino** (110 N. Main St., 406/222-0665), but no more—if there were, the ladies on call would be pushing 100. The bar still attracts locals who come early and stay late.

Shut-Eye

Not a motel, but a legend, the **Murray Hotel** (201 W. Park St., 406/222-1350, www.murrayhotel.com, $72–129) premiered in 1904 and has since greatly enlarged its pleasant rooms while retaining the touches of an old-fashioned hotel.

Check out the washbasins in the rooms, rocking chairs in hallway alcoves, and desk clerks who double as elevator operators. But be prepared—noise from the bar and nearby trains may keep you up at night.

Chain Drive
A, C, G, CC

Chain hotels are in town, or within 10 miles. See cross-reference guide featuring phone numbers and Web addresses on page 514.

On the Road: Livingston to Yellowstone

It's a straight 55-mile shot to Yellowstone National Park via Paradise Valley, but the ride doesn't compare to the park itself. When you do get out of Livingston, the land starts to look larger, a portent of things to come. The country ride brings mountains to your left and hills to your right, but it takes a while to notice that there is nothing out here; you are so swept up with the emptiness, you don't notice the absence of homes, stores, and billboards. The Yellowstone River shows up, brushing against the road and then retreating toward the mountains. For now, you have only to enjoy the sun and the mountains, pausing if you wish at a roadside chapel and rest stop about 30 miles south of Livingston. Later, the river starts picking up steam, rolling and boiling and churning along as it flows north. The road tries to match its energy,

In Yellowstone you'll share the road with buffalo and bears. Without a zoom lens to capture the grizzly bear, Nancy went in for a closer shot. I took refuge in a stranger's car.

adding some curves and descents. This all builds up to your farewell to mighty Montana—a state that needs no improvement.

When you reach Gardiner, you'll find restaurants, motels, and service stations, but if you don't need them, roll around the corner to a great photo op. The Roosevelt Arch says more than the words inscribed on it: "Yellowstone National Park. For the Benefit and Enjoyment of the People. Created by Act of Congress March 1, 1872."

Unless you have a National Parks Pass (a $50 investment that gets you into every national park for one year), you'll pay $15 to enter Yellowstone (www.nps.gov/yell). The pass is valid for the Grand Tetons as well. Even though you may have seen the park in elementary school filmstrips, you've never seen anything like the real thing.

Yellowstone Primer

Instead of its history, consider what makes up Yellowstone National Park: steaming geysers, crystalline lakes, thundering waterfalls, and panoramic vistas sprawled across two million acres of volcanic plateaus. This was the world's first national park and accounts for 60 percent of the world's active geysers. The Lower Falls on the Yellowstone River are nearly twice as high as Niagara's. The land rises in elevation from 5,282 feet at Reese Creek to 11,358 feet at Eagle Peaks Summit. Yellowstone is home to 12 tree species,

Animal Sense

Riding a bike through Yellowstone poses an element of danger. Seriously. People in cars can shield themselves from bears and bison, but you can't. Here are some tips that may save your life:

• Give animals plenty of space when they are crossing the road.
• If one animal crosses the road, wait to see if another is following before proceeding.
• Don't try to entice any animal with food.
• If you see an animal and wish to stop, try to park in an established turnout, not in the middle of the road.
• If you're shooting photographs, don't try to get closer to the animals. For a good shot, use a telephoto lens.

more than 80 types of wildflowers, 58 mammal species, and 290 species of birds.

Yellowstone contains five "countries." Mammoth Country, a thermal area in the northwest, is home to elk, bison, hot springs, and limestone terraces. Geyser Country, in the southwest, encompasses Old Faithful, fumaroles, mud pots, and hot pools. Lake Country, in the southeast, is habitat to native cut-throat trout, osprey, and bald eagles, as well as moose, bison, and bears, which wander the 100-mile shoreline of Yellowstone Lake. Roosevelt Country, in the northeast, recaptures the Old West, and Canyon Country comprises the Lower Falls, Hayden Valley, and the Grand Canyon of the Yellowstone. Free ranger-led programs, sightseeing tours, fishing, boating, horseback riding, and more than 1,210 miles of marked hiking trails all conspire to help you explore the park.

Believe it or not, all of this takes up less than 4 percent of the park itself. The rest is wilderness. And it's there for you and your bike.

On the Road: Yellowstone

Why do I love Yellowstone? Let me count the ways.... Commercial trucks are prohibited, it has more wildlife than a hundred zoos, it fulfills every image I had formed about it, and it delivers what the government intended when it protected these lands in 1872.

The road from Tower Junction to Canyon Junction over Dunraven Pass in the northeast corner is the first to close and last to open when snow hits, so there's a good chance you won't be able to ride it. If it's open, terrific; if not, start at the park's northwest section and head south, soaking in the views as you climb rapidly over 6,200 feet. Dealing with the campers who clog the road is discouraging at first, but soon you'll cross the 45th parallel, which marks the midway point between the equator and the North Pole. For some reason, at this point, you'll calm down.

Your first stop should be the **Albright Visitors Center** to talk to a park ranger, get maps, and check on programs. From 1896 to 1916, this was the site of Fort Yellowstone, where the U.S. Army protected the park from poachers, vandals, robbers, and anyone or anything that threatened the preserve and its early tourists. Today's rangers can help you decide how and where to allot your time. Be selective in what you see if you're on a schedule.

Follow the road south to Mammoth Hot Springs, which builds tier upon tier of cascading terraced stone. These are interesting not only for their beauty, but also because, despite clearly visible warning signs, some idiots have scalded or burned themselves to death by walking out on and falling through the fragile layer of minerals.

Soon you'll smell a familiar aroma. This is no kitchen cleanser; it's the trees emanating the original pine-fresh scent. The geological wreckage of mountains is omnipresent, and when you approach Swan Lake Flat, you're on top of the world. If you ride in the late spring, you may share my fortune and see a grizzly and her cubs—an experience that made me appreciate nature and wish my bike had automatic door locks. Moments like this remind you that, despite the roads here, this is wilderness, and it doesn't belong to you, it belongs to the animals. Respect them.

Riding on, you'll spot the glacial green waters of North Twin Lakes and, past the Gibbon River, buffaloes grazing, which may cause gridlock. Steer clear of these brutes. They're big enough to wreck a Humvee and could easily disintegrate a bike.

Near the Norris to Canyon Road in the middle of the figure 8, the Norris and Firehole River Geyser Basins feature the largest display of geysers. Steamboat Geyser, at Norris, is the world's tallest, with infrequent, unpredictable eruptions that reach 400 feet. Next, head east on the middle road toward Canyon Village. The landscape isn't impressive here, but if you head straight until you reach the Grand Canyon of Yellowstone you won't mind the break. The 24-mile-long canyon sneaks up on you, and once in full view, it is majestic. At 800–1,200 feet deep and 1,500–4,000 feet wide, it is marked by rainbow-hued cliffs of orange, yellow, pink, white, and tan.

At first, you can only hear 308-foot-high Lower Falls, and then it appears through the trees and takes your breath away. You've reached a geological crossroads, where hot springs have weakened the rock and spout into the river to create an unusual confluence of waterfalls, cliffs, canyon, and geysers.

Down the road, a bridge crosses to Artist's Point on the opposite side of the canyon. When you get back on the road, the ride improves as the road follows the river's course and the frostbite on your fingers tells you you're reaching higher elevations. There's something in the air … bubbling, churning, sulfurous mud boils that smell worse than the awards ceremony at a baked bean festival.

Depending on where you're staying, you could wrap up a long day by resting at the Lake Lodge or the Lake Yellowstone Hotel (see *Shut-Eye*) or continuing the journey to Old Faithful. Either way, Yellowstone Lake opens up on your left. After miles and miles of riding, you could swear this lake would come to a close, but it has more stamina than you do. Big enough to create its own weather, the lake is a large crater formed by a volcano and filled by glaciers about 12,000 years ago.

Even after the lake is blocked by lush forests for miles, you round the corner … and it's still there. Eventually, you'll adopt it as your riding buddy and hope it continues. After about 45 minutes, half of its 100 miles of shoreline finally come to a close, and you're alone again as you ride to the West Thumb Geyser Basin. This is where you'll find the Fishing Cone, so named because fishermen caught trout from the frigid lake and cooked them still on the hook in the cone's boiling waters.

Between here and Old Faithful, a long 17 miles away, the thrill of the road depends on the weather. When the snow is packed up high on the sides, it's like being in a bobsled race, with the road rising and falling like the Roman Empire. There's not a lot to see, but this may be the best stretch for motorcycle travelers.

If you've timed it right, by the time you reach the exit to Old Faithful, you won't have long to wait before seeing the geyser blow. Approximately every 79 minutes, thousands of gallons of thundering, hissing, steaming water blast into the sky. An American icon, it's worth seeing. The benches close to the Old Faithful Inn (see *Shut-Eye*) may afford the best view.

From here, you can double back and commence your trip south, or check into whichever lodge you were smart enough to book in advance.

Pull It Over: Yellowstone Highlights
Attractions and Adventures

Yellowstone is less like a park than a country. Seven full-service gas stations and four auto repair shops function within the park. *Yellowstone Today,* a free newspaper available at visitors centers and at the entrance, carries seasonal news and current information about park facilities and programs.

The powers that be have also developed a complete retinue of tours and adventures, although prices are getting jacked for these and lodging to compensate for an orgy of federal spending. Check the park's website (listed in *Resources for Riders*) for complete details on choices such as the **Old West Cookout** ($52), **Stagecoach Adventure** ($9), various guided tours ($9–52), horseback trail rides (one hour, $32; two hours, $52), guided fishing trips ($140 for two hours with longer excursions available), power-boat rental ($30 per hour), and photo safaris ($55, offered June–September). The **Firehole Basin Adventure** is a three-hour, $25 tour that leads to the geyser basin near Old Faithful, where you'll learn about the geothermal features of the area. The **Teton Vista Rendezvous** ($51) is a daylong tour through the southern park and down to Grand Teton National Park, which you'll ride through later.

For complete details and reservations, call 307/344-7311 or visit www.travel-yellowstone.com.

Blue-Plate Specials

Snack bars, delis, cafeterias, fast food joints, and grocery stores can be found throughout Yellowstone, but don't travel after dark for dinner. Mammoth Hot Springs Hotel, Old Faithful Inn, Grant Village, Canyon Lodge, and Lake Yellowstone Hotel have dining rooms (also serving breakfast and lunch). Dinner menus include prime ribs, steak, seafood, and chicken; reservations are strongly recommended. Grant Village and Roosevelt Lodge feature family-style restaurants. If you've got a hankering for cowboy cuisine, an Old West Dinner Cookout leaves from Roosevelt Lodge. You'll ride on horseback through Pleasant Valley to reach a clearing where there's a hearty dinner of steak, corn, coleslaw, cornbread muffins, homemade Roosevelt beans, watermelon, and apple crisp. For dining or cookout reservations, call 307/344-7311 or contact any lodging front desk, dining room, or activities desk.

Shut-Eye

An iconic classic, the **Old Faithful Inn** ($86 shared bath, $204 upscale room) is your best bet. Built in the winter of 1903–1904 with local logs and stones, it features a towering lobby with a 500-ton stone fireplace and a handcrafted clock made of copper, wood, and wrought iron. This stunningly beautiful hotel offers a nice dining room, fast food restaurant, gift shop, and the Bear Pit Lounge. The inn shares a general store and service station with the **Old Faithful Snow Lodge and Cabins,** which opened in 1998 and charges around $170, while the Old Faithful Lodge Cabins fetch from $88 to $128.

If you decide to ignore me and travel during peak summer tourist season, I cannot overemphasize the importance of making reservations well in advance by calling 307/344-7311 or checking www.travelyellowstone.com. Lodging options range from rustic cabins to fine hotels, but because of the park's remoteness, few rooms have phones, and none have televisions. Request a private bath if that's important to you. Among your in-park choices are those listed below.

Completed in the 1930s, **Mammoth Hot Springs Hotel and Cabins** ($70–107) offers hotel rooms and cabins with and without private baths.

A classic historic hotel, **Lake Yellowstone Hotel and Cabins** opened in

1891 and has been restored to the grandeur it enjoyed during the 1920s. The original wicker furniture has even been returned to service. The sun room, a sitting area designed for relaxation and conversation, affords wonderful views of the lake and is also a good place to relax with a cocktail and listen to the piano or chamber music in the evening. Choices range from deluxe historically renovated hotel rooms to more moderately priced annex rooms. Rooms are the most luxurious (and expensive) at $189–204, but annex rooms are more affordable at $132 and cabins even more so at around $107.

You'll also find lodges and cabins (with and without baths) at the **Lake Lodge** ($65–128), **Canyon Lodge** ($66–153), and **Roosevelt Lodge** ($62–101), as well as 1,400 campsites ($18 per night). The motel-like **Grant Village** ($123) sits at the west thumb of Yellowstone.

On the Road: Yellowstone to Jackson

When you slip out of Yellowstone via Highway 89, you'll notice little to distinguish Yellowstone from **Grand Teton National Park** (307/739-3399 or 307/739-3600, www.nps.gov/grte). In the pristine wilderness between Yellowstone and the Grand Tetons, you'll enjoy a quieting ride, interrupted only by the **Flagg Ranch Resort** (307/543-2861 or 800/443-2311, www.flagg ranch.com). If the overpowering scenery of the area wrestles you to a halt, you can rest easy here with camping and lodges, as well as food and fuel.

Just past Flagg Ranch, the vistas have received a booster shot of scenery. In 1929, more than 500 square miles were set aside to preserve and protect the land around the Teton Range; that area was expanded in 1950 when John D. Rockefeller Jr. donated adjacent lands. Incidentally, you can also thank the Rockefellers for purchasing land needed for Acadia National Park and the area around Woodstock, Vermont. I'm sure they'd appreciate a lovely bundt cake.

There's only one way to experience this park on a bike, and that's via the Jenny Lake Loop. Actually, the first body of water you'll see is Jackson Lake, which deserves a dozen rolls of film and a 10-hour miniseries. The lake mirrors the mountains, and the result is a surreal, colorful blend of green waters, white mountain peaks, and blue sky. As the mountain chain recedes in the distance, the peaks appear uniform in height and shape, a clue why French trappers called them Les Trois Tetons (The Three Breasts) which, oddly enough, was a malady suffered by my great-aunt Agnes.

Four miles later, the road has risen in elevation to place you midway between the lake and the towering peaks. There is a museum, store, and gas station at

cruising past the Grand Tetons south of Yellowstone

Colter Village, but you may be so inspired by the visuals that you'll just stick with the road. The mountain chain stays with you as you rocket toward Grand Teton (13,770 feet), the largest mountain in the chain.

In addition to seeing these most incredible peaks, you get to ride Alpine runs, then pine-bordered roads and quick drops, where the valley floor opens and the road dives right into it. The road is seemingly custom-designed with bikes in mind, and after riding it, you'll probably need a cigarette—even if you don't smoke.

Where the road Ts, turn right into vast emptiness, and you are in Jackson Hole, the 48-mile-long valley that actually begins just south of the Yellowstone entrance. It seems like a lonely, deserted land, but just wait, cowboy. A few miles south, and you'll be in the nicest town in the West.

Jackson Primer

Trailblazers have made their mark on this town. The territory was named Jackson's Hole (later Jackson Hole) after trapper David E. Jackson. Prior to Jackson's arrival, however, there were summer residents: the Shoshone, Crow, Blackfoot, and Gros Ventre tribes.

With six trapping trails converging at Jackson Hole, it became a popular fur trading area, but around 1845, the trade—not to mention the animals—was in decline. For the next 40 years, the isolated area lay dormant, until the Hayden Expeditions arrived in 1871 and 1878 and introduced the region to the rest of the country. Yellowstone was formed and big game hunters, foreign royalty, and East Coast "dudes" started showing up.

After the town was founded in 1921, cattle ranching took hold. Nearly a century later, this mix of hardworking locals and affluent outsiders still typifies the town, though tourism and skiing have long since supplanted ranching. Less than 3 percent of Teton County is privately owned; the rest is contained within Grand Teton National Park, the Bridger-Teton National Forest, and the National Elk Refuge.

It's hard to imagine a more perfect town.

On the Road: Jackson

You can't disguise it. Jackson is a cowboy Carmel. There's lots of money here, generated by tourism and movie executives who invest part of their time and fortunes here.

As in Montana, great rides await you on the outskirts of town, but wandering around Jackson is damned fun. Everything here centers around the town square, marked by the famed Antler Arches. Gathered each year by Boy Scouts who scour the nearby National Elks Refuge, most antlers are auctioned off on the third Saturday in May to western export houses, regional craftspeople, and Asian druggists that believe that powdered elk horn works faster than Viagra. It doesn't. Trust me.

Wooden sidewalks lead you through numerous shops, bars, restaurants, and galleries. Take an afternoon, find some places on your own, check out a few listed below, and enjoy a pocket of civility in an otherwise harsh world.

Now git along, lil' dogie.

Pull It Over: Jackson Highlights
Attractions and Adventures

White-water rafting is the warm-weather equivalent of Jackson's winter ski season. Most excursions run the same rapids and charge about the same rate (from around $45). Some trips combine white-water and scenic float trips with the majestic Grand Tetons as a backdrop. Ask if trips include breakfast and/or lunch, and if overnight rafting/camping trips (roughly $150) are offered.

I haven't done them all, so you'll have to make the call on selecting the best white-water rafting outfitters. Avoid ones advertising high casualty rates. Try **Charlie Sands Wild Water River Trips** (307/733-4410 or 800/358-8184, www.sandswhitewater.com), **Dave Hansen Whitewater** (307/733-6295 or 800/732-6295, www.davehansenwhitewater.com), **Jackson Hole Whitewater** (307/733-1007 or 800/648-2602 or 888/700-7238, www.jhwhitewater.com),

Lewis & Clark Expeditions (307/733-4022 or 800/824-5375, www.lewisand-clarkexpeds.com), and **Mad River Boat Trips** (307/733-6203 or 800/458-7238, www.mad-river.com).

Two miles north of Jackson on Highway 89 is the **National Museum of Wildlife Art** (307/733-5771, www.wildlifeart.org, $8). You want to see this: the premier collection of wildlife art in America, from prehistoric carvings to art by mound dwellers to the sculptures and paintings of historic and contemporary Western American artists like W. R. Leigh, C. M. Russell, and Robert Bateman. In all, the museum showcases more than 2,000 paintings, sculptures, photographs, and works on paper by more than 100 wildlife artists. No unicorns and rainbows here—this is fine art that could turn a condo into a lodge.

Shopping

Sure, you can buy a hat off the rack, but you'd end up looking like a dude. The nationally known **Jackson Hole Hat Company** (245 N. Glenwood, 307/733-7687, www.jhhatco.com) can make you a custom-made beaver felt hat at cowboy prices. Not cheap, but it's an American original. If you like leather (and I'm sure you do), you gotta see the collection at **Hideout** (40 Center St., 307/733-2422), packed with hand-painted custom clothing, moccasins, boots, chaps, Native American headdresses, flying helmets, and leather jackets with fringe and studs and buckles and zip-out linings and body armor…. Having a nicotine fit? Head to **Tobacco Row** (120 N. Cache, 307/733-4385) and check out the cigars, pipe tobacco, and hand-carved pipes.

Blue-Plate Specials

Whether they're cowboys or corporate execs, locals fuel up on breakfast and lunch at **Jedediah's** (135 E. Broadway, 307/733-5671). Breakfasts are big, with inexpensive sourjack pancakes, Teton taters, eggs, waffles, and bacon. Afterward, you'll be waddling, but you'll have no regrets.

Bubba's BBQ (515 W. Broadway, 307/733-2288) serves breakfast, lunch, and dinner for you meat-eating mammals. The basic, pretty inexpensive grub includes ribs, chicken, pork, sandwiches, baked beans, coleslaw, and corn on the cob.

Snake River Grill (84 E. Broadway, 307/733-0557, www.snakerivergrill.com) was named Jackson's best restaurant by *Wine Spectator,* so you can't expect the place to be diner cheap. For some, though, the premium has a payoff. The Grill serves only fresh fish and free-range veal and chicken, as well as more than 200 wines, plus ports and single-malt scotches. In this casual Western setting, you can order Chilean sea bass, venison chops, double-center-cut pork chops, and a bunch of other stuff I love to eat when somebody else is buying.

Watering Holes

The **Million Dollar Cowboy Bar** (25 N. Cache, 307/733-2207, www.mil-liondollarcowboybar.com) is the absolute coolest bar you'll ever see. From the cutout stagecoach in the chandelier diorama to the saddle seats at the bar, from the chiseled faces of the patrons to the Western swing bands who lure the wallflowers out on the dance floor, this place has got it all. And the patrons aren't just drugstore cowboys. On weekends, ranchers who sowed their wild oats here 50 years ago return, their faces filled with more character than you'd find in a dozen Louis L'Amour novels.

Attached to the fancy Wort Hotel, the **Silverdollar Saloon** (50 N. Glenwood, 307/733-2190 or 800/322-2727) accents the decor (actual silver dollars are embedded in the bar) with saws, antlers, and saddles. The saloon serves wines, microbrews, and bar food. I list it because it's popular, but it seems contrived fun to me. Open 11:30 A.M.–11 P.M. daily.

Just north of town, the **Log Cabin Saloon** (475 N. Cache, 307/733-7525) is a theme-free roadhouse open 'til 2, which makes it a safe haven for locals who want to get some relief from the 3.2 million tourists who've descended from Yellowstone.

Shut-Eye

For such a small town, Jackson offers many options for bunking down. A central number for the **Town Square Inns** (800/483-8667, www.town squareinns.com) puts you in touch with four reasonably priced, generic, and clean motels.

Motels and Motor Courts

The **Cowboy Village Resort** (120 S. Flat Creek Dr., 307/733-3121 or 800/962-4988, www.townsquareinns.com, $98 and up shoulder season) rents great little air-conditioned cabins equipped with combinations of queen beds, sofa sleepers, kitchenettes, TVs, tub/showers, covered decks, and barbecue grills. It also throws in a continental breakfast.

Chain Drive
A, E, Q, S, CC

Chain hotels are in town, or within 10 miles. See cross-reference guide featuring phone numbers and Web addresses on page 514.

Inn-dependence
The **Parkway Inn** (125 N. Jackson, 307/733-3143 or 800/247-8390, www.parkwayinn.com) borders on a motel, but the rooms are large and clean; it sits a few blocks outside the rush of town square; it feeds you a good breakfast; and the pool and hot tub are just right after a day on the road. If you arrive preseason (April–May), you'll pay around $99—in the summer, double that. Ka-ching!

Indulgences

Read this only if you think you may want to park your bike for a week and rough it on the saddle of a real horse. Dude ranches and trail rides are a cottage industry (actually, a bunkhouse industry) within 20 miles of here, and while I can't attest to any of these, check 'em out if you'd like to live the life of Hoss.

Among them are **Triangle X Ranch** (307/733-2183, www.trianglex.com), **Gros Ventre River Ranch** (307/733-4138, www.grosventreriverranch.com), **Rancho Alegre Lodge** (307/733-7988, www.ranchoalegre.com), and the **Red Rock Ranch** (307/733-6288, www.theredrockranch.com). Most dude ranches include one or a variety of activities, including trail rides, fly-fishing, swimming, horseback riding, float trips, pack trips, cookouts, hunting, square dancing, hiking, scenic tours, photography, breaking stock, and shoeing horses. Lodging will usually be in log cabins. Prices aren't inexpensive, but they may be a bargain for what you get and how many people you can crowd into a group rate. Plus, at most ranches, you get your own horse and a chance to ride like the Lone Ranger. Hi-yo!

Resources for Riders

Wild West Run

Montana Travel Information
Montana Bed & Breakfast Association—www.mtbba.com
Montana Camping Reservations—877/444-6777, www.reserveusa.com
Montana Fish, Wildlife, and Parks—404/444-2535,
  www.fwp.state.mt.us
Montana Road Conditions—800/226-7623
Travel Montana—800/847-4868, www.visitmt.com

Wyoming Travel Information
Wyoming Game and Fish—307/777-4600, http://gf.state.wy.us
Wyoming Homestay and Outdoor Adventures—307/359-1289,
  www.wyomingbnb-ranchrec.com
Wyoming Road Conditions—307/772-0824
Wyoming State Parks Camping Reservations—877/996-7275,
  www.wyo-park.com
Wyoming State Parks and Historic Sites—307/777-6323,
  www.wyobest.org
Wyoming Tourism—307/777-7777 or 800/225-5996,
  www.wyomingtourism.org
Wyoming Weather—307/635-9901 or 307/857-3827

Local and Regional Information
Jackson Hole Area Chamber of Commerce—307/733-3316,
  www.jacksonholechamber.com
Jackson Hole Central Reservations— 888/838-6606,
  www.jacksonholewy.com
Livingston Chamber of Commerce—406/222-0850,
  www.yellowstonechamber.com
Yellowstone Activities and Reservations—307/344-7311,
  www.travelyellowstone.com
Yellowstone National Park Visitors Services—307/344-2107,
  www.nps.gov/yell

Montana Motorcycle Shops
Alpine Yamaha—301 N. Main St., Livingston, 406/222-1211
Yellowstone Harley-Davidson—540 Alaska Frontage Rd., Belgrade,
  406/388-7684, www.yellowstoneharley.com

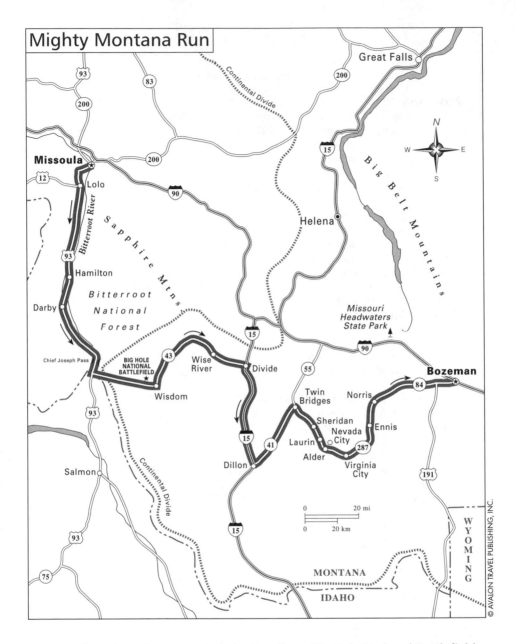

Route: Missoula to Bozeman via Lolo, Hamilton, Big Hole National Battlefield, Divide, Dillon, Sheridan, Nevada City, Virginia City, Ennis, Norris

Distance: Approximately 335 miles; consider four days with stops.

•Day 1—Missoula •Day 2—Travel •Day 3—Dillon/Travel •Day 4—Bozeman

First Leg: Missoula to Dillon (210 miles)

Second Leg: Dillon to Bozeman (123 miles)

Helmet Laws: Montana does not require helmets.

Mighty Montana Run

Missoula, Montana to Bozeman, Montana

This is a grand ride: large in scope, large in scenery, and large in memories. Montana bursts with mountains, rivers, ghost towns, and saloons; Montanans project a refreshing self-reliance and strength of character. The essence of the state is palpable on this journey. May and September are good times to ride.

Missoula Primer

Geographically, this is the perfect setting for a town. The Flathead Indians called the area Nemissodatakoo, meaning "by or near the cold, chilling waters." It's an apt moniker, considering that four trout-rich rivers—Rock Creek, Blackfoot, Lower Clark Fork, and Bitterroot—converge here. Lewis and Clark passed through this way in the early 1800s, but the first permanent settlement, Hellgate Village, wasn't established until 1860. Four miles from Missoula's current location, the town limits encompassed the flour and sawmills. When the railroad came to town, townspeople ditched Hellgate and changed the name to Missoula.

Missoula offers a great way to get used to Montana and is a great starting point. The third-largest city in Montana, Missoula is easy to tour. It also reveals reasons to love this state: no sales tax, saloons and roadhouses that still have character, and a citizenry made up of a pleasing mix of university students, artists, and regular folks. *American Heritage* named Missoula a "Great American Place" in 1999.

On the Road: Missoula

Don't expect to ride into Missoula and stay indoors. The town is surrounded by some of the most pristine country and abundant waters in America. That's why fly-fishing is as popular here as jai alai is in Miami and purse-snatching is in Central Park.

The road south is a fine ride, but first spend a few hours wandering around downtown, the heart of the city, where independent merchants, junk shops, and watering holes haven't changed much in half a century. Ride Reserve and Higgins, the main thoroughfares, and you'll think you're in a 1950s time warp. On Saturday morning, local farmers and craftspeople set up shop on side streets to sell their plants, handcrafted rugs, jewelry, and weavings. The University of Montana is also near downtown as are bookstores, cool, dark saloons, and the historic and eye-popping art deco **Wilma Theatre** (131 S. Higgins Ave., 406/728-2521, www.thewilma.com), which hosts concerts and shows current and classic flicks.

Pull It Over: Missoula Highlights
Attractions and Adventures

At the **Smokejumpers Center** (5765 W. Broadway/U.S. 10, 406/329-4934, www.smokejumpers.com), brave bastards learn how to skydive behind fire lines in the remote wilderness and fight forest fires. Open 8:30 A.M.–5:30 P.M. daily in season, the center features free tours, videos, a lookout tower, and exhibits showing the history and training requirements for these crazy asses. If riding across the country isn't exciting enough, they're always looking to recruit new members....

It's easy to be cynical when you're wearing more leather than a cow, but the **Carousel for Missoula** (1 Caras Park, 406/549-8382, www.carrousel.com) is interesting. Chuck Kaparich wanted to give the community a carousel, so he carved four horses. Others got in on the act and donated time to carving mirror frames, gargoyles, and horses to create the first fully hand-carved carousel since the Depression. It's a Charles Kuralt moment when you see that the horses—with names like Bud, Cannonball, Hardhat, and Sweet Sue—have been "adopted" by local families. Open 11 A.M. daily. Admission is a mere $0.50.

Montana rivers and streams teem with trout: rainbows, cutthroats, browns, and brook. Guides can take you to where the fish are; most head out about 60 miles to find a favorite fishing spot. Some gear can be rented, licenses and other items must be purchased, and a tip is never included in prices that start at $350 for a day's outing for one or two anglers. Fishing trips are offered

miles of big sky and pristine road in the Treasure State

© NANCY HOWELL

by **Missoulian Angler** (401 S. Orange St., 406/728-7766 or 800/824-2450, www.missoulianangler.com) and **Grizzly Hackle** (215 W. Front St., 406/721-8996 or 800/297-8996, www.grizzlyhackle.com).

Montana's stretches of wilderness are so vast, it looks like a foreign world to those of us who live in towns and cities. In addition to exploring this relatively pristine frontier on your bike, you may want to see it from other angles by walking in the footsteps of America's greatest explorers. **Lewis and Clark Trail Adventures** (912 E. Broadway, 406/728-7609 or 800/366-6246, www.trailadventures.com) offers white-water trips, including overnights, where all meals, tents, camping, and rafting gear are provided.

If you'd rather climb every mountain, **Trailhead Mountain Sports** (221 E. Front St., 406/543-6966, www.trailheadmontana.net) rents gear for camping, climbing, kayak, and canoe excursions. Not a bad start for novices.

The fastest-growing wildlife conservation center in the country, **Rocky Mountain Elk Foundation** (2291 W. Broadway, 406/523-4545 or 800/225-5355, www.rmef.org) works to preserve more than 2.4 million acres of elk country by hosting exhibits, talks, and displays of stuffed dead elk. An inspirational stop for outdoors enthusiasts. Summer hours are 8 A.M.–6 P.M. Monday–Friday, 9 A.M.–6 P.M. weekends.

Blue-Plate Specials

A Northwestern-style downtown restaurant, **Iron Horse** (501 N. Higgins Ave., 406/728-8866) has a good vibe with college students and mature people.

Lunch and dinner fare includes steaks, quesadillas, hamburgers, and pub food. Pitchers of cold beer are particularly enjoyable at the sidewalk café. This is a good place to hang out, since the bar's open 'til 2.

It was at the **Double Front Cafe** (122 W. Alder, 406/543-6264) where I ordered a chicken and an egg just to see which would come first. It sold its first chicken in the 1930s, and the current owners have been plucking and frying here since 1961. You can order burgers and seafood in the restaurant, but the big deal is the $6 chicken dinner, chased by a glass of pop. Check out the full bar in the basement, and then go back upstairs and get some more chicken. A Missoula legend.

Not overly impressive, **Doc's Gourmet Sandwich Shop** (214 Higgins Ave., 406/542-7414) is just a nice retro diner serving breakfast and lunch. The menu includes soups, burgers, and a concoction known as "hangover stew," which is potato corn chowder with an active ingredient of green chiles.

Watering Holes

Drop in any bar along Higgins, and you'll find a hole in the wall filled with cowboys and mountain men and a distinct personality. Here are a few to try.

Enter the **Oxford** (337 N. Higgins Ave., 406/549-0117), and you fall into a Steinbeck novel. It's been here since the 1880s and in its present location since the '40s, and it's open 24 hours a day. Step inside to a full liquor bar, an interior unchanged since the Depression, gun displays, a card room in back, pool tables, and a revolving lineup of local characters—although the guy who thought he was a leprechaun passed away in 2004. **Charlie B's** (428 N. Higgins Ave., 406/549-3589) stays open 'til 2. As you enter, notice the wall of photos of regular patrons and, when your eyes get accustomed to the dark, check out the elk heads, pool tables, and mountain men.

The Rhino (158 Ryman St., 406/721-6061) has a slightly less impressive lineage (it's been around only since 1988), but it compensates by having 50 beers on tap. What's more, the beer flows through a beer engine, which uses air instead of CO_2 to make the cask-kegged beer smoother and creamier—exactly the way they poured it in the Old West (before cowboys would go in the street and kill each other).

Shut-Eye

Most of Missoula's best lodging choices are chain hotels.

Chain Drive
A, C, E, L, Q, BB, CC, DD

Chain hotels are in town, or within 10 miles. See cross-reference guide featuring phone numbers and Web addresses on page 514.

Inn-dependence

Goldsmith's (809 E. Front St., 406/728-1585 or 866/666-9945, www.goldsmithsinn.com, $79–144) is connected to a riverfront restaurant, which is actually a plus, since it has a great patio deck overlooking the Clark Fork River. There are plainly furnished rooms and large suites at reasonable prices.

On the Road: Missoula to Dillon

As you leave Missoula, Montana doesn't assault your senses. It just grows on you until you realize there is no other state quite so attractive, no great outdoors quite so great. As Missoula recedes in your mirrors, the sky ahead opens and draws you forward.

Highway 93, a wide four-lane road, sweeps you up and over Missoula toward Lolo, then south through the Bitterroot Valley toward Hamilton. The road opens into a straightaway and, spotting mountains far on the horizon, you get your first inkling of how large this trip will be.

The stretches of emptiness are long. When they are interrupted, it's usually by Montana businesses, such as the Antler Creation Gallery and the wood carver who claims he can carve you a nice made-to-order totem pole. I ordered one that looks like Marcia Brady.

Hamilton appears after you cross the Bitterroot River, offering several opportunities for gas and food. The **Coffee Cup Cafe** (500 S. 1st St./Hwy. 93, 406/363-3822) serves great home cooking and mighty tasty pies and cakes that'll push you back into husky pants.

After Hamilton, the road is effortless. The slow curves don't ask much, and thus begins a perfect combination of scenery and landscape, although the fires of 2000 took out thousands of acres of forest, which are now struggling to return. The road widens and gives you room to breathe and think. Sheep graze in the fields, and as you roll past small towns like Darby, you're witness to the American West without the pretense. Only about 900,000 people live in Montana, an average of six people per square mile, and the land reflects this pioneering spirit.

About 25 miles south of Hamilton, the road narrows and the riding becomes more challenging. As you enter the backcountry and head toward the Bitterroot River, the road leads through the valley and to the **Sula Country Store** (7060 U.S. 93 S, 406/821-3364, www.bitterroot-montana.com), "one of

on the Kawasaki outside of Dillon, Montana

the cleanest and friendliest stops you'll make." This is a possible stop if you'd like to explore the expansive backcountry of the Bitterroot National Forest. Add to this cabins, gas, a diner, fishing licenses, and a nice front porch to kick back on, and there's every reason to stop and do absolutely nothing.

Civilization lies behind you and for the next 13 miles, you'll see every vision the name Montana brings to mind. The road wraps around mountains, swings into 25-mph curves, and propels you into snowcapped elevations. Keep one eye on the gravel and the other on the vistas that appear as you top this mountain chain. Pine trees puncture the snow cover, and when you reach the Lost Trail Pass at 7,014 feet, you're on top of the world.

This is only the beginning. On Highway 43 at the Montana/Idaho border, turn left to reach Chief Joseph Pass (7,241 feet) and cross the Continental Divide. Great descents, pristine woodlands, and the first of hundreds of miles of split-rail fencing follow. You're not riding through some puny East Coast farm country now. You're into something far greater. This is big.

Although the entrance to **Big Hole National Battlefield** (406/689-3155, www.nps.gov/biho) isn't well marked, it's the only detour for miles, so you should be able to spot it on your left. It's as sad a place as I've seen, and here's why: In the summer of 1877, five bands of Nez Perce had fled Oregon and Idaho to escape the U.S. Army and General Oliver Howard, who were trying to round them up and put them on a reservation. They outmaneuvered the army in nearly a dozen battles across 1,200 miles, but when they made it here, Colonel John Gibbon's Seventh U.S. Infantry attacked their sleeping camp on August 9 and 10, 1877, killing warriors, women, and children. Despite the surprise attack, the Nez Perce managed to kill or wound nearly 70 soldiers and drive them back.

The Nez Perce beat the army again at Canyon Creek but surrendered in October 1877, at Bear Paw Battlefield. Nez Perce civil leader Chief Joseph had had enough. He told Colonel Nelson Miles, "Hear me, chiefs. I am tired; my heart is sick and sad. From where the sun now stands, I will fight no more forever."

In my opinion, this reflects the very worst of American history. And while I shouldn't feel personally responsible for what happened here, I sure felt bad.

When you leave the center, the breadth of the land you see becomes phenomenal. There is enough earth here to build new planets. You're in the Big Hole Valley, riding at an average elevation of 1.2 miles. Even though the horizons are empty, the view is more inspiring and far more beautiful than you can comprehend.

A few miles later, when you ride into Wisdom (pop. 78), you'll encounter something else to file in your growing collection of "on the road" stories. Pull into the **Big Hole Crossing Restaurant** (406/689-3800), and you've entered an anomaly. The restaurant is no Montana greasy spoon. They serve up damn good food here and have as backdrop a toasty fireplace, an art gallery, and a clothing store where handcrafted dresses sell for as much as $250 and cool leather jackets for $1,000. If you're on a liquid diet, next door is **Antler's Saloon** (406/689-9393), where cowboys shoot stick and locals work out with 16-ounce weights. The decorative touches, antlers, and guns recall an early roadhouse. I expect that by now, the sights have tempted you to become a part-time Montanan. Don't. If you're not ready to "earn your spurs," leave the state to the people who belong here, those who endure its hardships and deserve its rewards.

If your mind can handle it, the road and landscape following Wisdom improve exponentially. The Great Plains lay themselves out beneath your wheels, sunlight falls in large shafts on the valleys below, and the landscape grows so large that even grazing horses look as insignificant as Shetland ponies. You're in the "Land of 10,000 Haystacks." By the time you're through riding, only reconstructive surgery will be able to erase the smile from your face.

Amid the straights and curves and low sloping hills, something is missing: This great land is uncluttered by houses, billboards, factories, gas stations, and strip malls. There is nothing but land and the road, which, when you get down to it, is really all you need.

The ride's grandeur sustains itself as you cruise alongside the Wise River, taking 40-mph turns as the water churns and boils on your left. In the town of Wise River, the good news is that on your right, you'll find a scenic byway

rounding the corner on the Lost Trail Pass, near the Montana/Idaho border

© NANCY HOWELL

that slices through 3.3-million acre Beaverhead Deerlodge National Forest—the area where Sacajewea met Lewis and Clark in 1805. The bad news is that the road's seldom open because of impassable snows. If it's open, go off on a tear and enjoy what one local says is the most beautiful scenery in the region, filled with coniferous forests of lodgepole pine and Douglas fir. Caution: The entire road's not paved; there are sections of gravel to contend with.

Odds are, though, that you'll keep plowing on toward Divide, where you'll find **Blue Moon** (406/267-3339), a mile off I-15 in Divide. The gas station and saloon is filled with friendly locals, and odds are you'll want to stop and have one for the road. Afterward, when you head south on the lonesome interstate, it's worth noting that this may be the only federal highway that you can ride without seeing any other car, truck, or bike.

You'll ride 38 miles to reach Dillon, not because there's anything to do there, but because it gives you a place to sleep and prepare for the next day's ride.

Dillon Primer

Dillon had an impressive start. It was born when the Utah and Northern Railroad was headed toward Butte in 1880, but the railroad stopped when it reached rancher Richard Deacon's spread. He wouldn't let the line continue until a group of businessmen raised enough cash to buy him out. While the railroad stalled during the winter of 1880–1881, the town site was named after railroad president Sidney Dillon.

That's really all you need to know. Dillon also enjoyed a gold boom that went bust, and today the town relies on agriculture. There's not much else shaking here. Not much at all.

On the Road: Dillon

Thumb through this book, and you won't find another town like Dillon. Usually even if there's nothing to see in a town, there's something to talk about. Not here. I won't belabor the point. There are a few chain motels, a grain silo, a quiet downtown, University of Montana-Western and, most important, a Dairy Queen. If you want to know more, stop by **Dillon Visitors Information Services** (10 W. Reeder, 406/683-5511).

Pull It Over: Dillon Highlights
Shut-Eye

Chain Drive
A, C, CC

Chain hotels are in town, or within 10 miles. See cross-reference guide featuring phone numbers and Web addresses on page 514.

Inn-dependence
The **Centennial Inn** (122 S. Washington St., 406/683-4454, www.bmt.net /~centenn, $89) is the saving grace of Dillon. If you stay here, you'll be handled with care by Jean James, a very gracious innkeeper. This is the way travel should be. You roll into town and check into a clean and comfortable room. Although the pace is slow in Dillon, there are stories here if you look. For instance, the James family also owns a 3,000-acre ranch and runs the horrifically named hunting/fishing guide service Bloody Dick Outfitters (T-shirt, anyone?). They also oversee the Dillon Junior Fiddle League, which has represented Montana in Japan, New York City, and elsewhere in the United States. In the evening, the James family likes to sit around and jam on their fiddles and guitars. This is what makes travel great: meeting nice people who make good down-home music.

On the Road: Dillon to Bozeman

Leaving Dillon on Route 41 North takes you right back to the prairie and photo ops with a Rocky Mountain backdrop. The landscape varies little, so just let your mind wander until you've gone about 25 miles to Twin Bridges, as close to not being a town as any town I've seen. The road forks here; turn onto Highway 287 toward Virginia City.

About now, you'll notice a few things: The fierce wind smacks your body as it pours over the plains; every pickup you've passed since Missoula has a dog in back (I believe they come standard with Montana trucks); and there is so much of nothing around you, it's really something.

Sheridan fizzles to a close and merges with the prairie as you head out of town. About five miles later, you'll pass Robber's Roost on your right, where desperadoes, rustlers, and Enron execs came to plan their heists. Beyond that, random towns crop up when nothing else is around, such as Laurin, Ruby Valley, and Alder, each of which grows progressively dirtier and more lonesome.

The landscape rapidly changes into mining country. The ground is gritty with sagebrush and mean brown creeks that penetrate the deadwood. This is the perfect setting for **Nevada City,** a strange shambles of a place that's half ghost town, half museum. There's a hotel here worthy of *Gunsmoke,* a saloon where you can bring your own drinks, and a complete town hidden beyond the streetfront buildings. Check out the darkened music hall and find nickelodeons, fortune telling machines, and the "famous and obnoxious horn machine" stashed inside. In the village, they've saved everything from outhouses to stores stocked with unopened merchandise.

A hundred years ago and a few miles north of Nevada City, six discouraged prospectors stopped to pan for enough gold to buy tobacco. Within three years, the Alder Gulch gave up $30 million in gold and **Virginia City** (406/843-5555 or 800/829-2969, www.virginiacitychamber.com) was born. It's a more modern town than Nevada City, but the term is relative, since Virginia City is still a frontier town as well. It does have a few great shops and restaurants, such as the **Roadmaster Grille** (126 W. Wallace, 406/843-5234), displaying old Buicks on hoists. Stop here for a great burger and shake and sit in a booth created from split cars.

Without embellishing, I can say the road to Ennis is as magnificent a road as you'll ever ride. As you climb into the hills, the glorious country is at your feet, and when you reach an overlook hundreds of feet above the Madison Valley, it will dazzle and humble you with mountains, rounded hills, broad beams of sunlight, and far more beauty than your mind can take in. Thank whatever gods you believe in for their handiwork.

Descending from the promontory is a kick and, if you're traveling with others, take time to stage a few photographs here. I did, and it's the one I treasure most. When you reach Ennis, turn left on Highway 287 toward Norris. Unlike in Washington, the scenery here never falters. Ride toward the brink of a cliff and look down the shaft of a long, empty valley where shadows of clouds smudge the ground. When you reach Norris and the junction of 84, turn right, and the terrain takes you back into hill country. The low, flat road gives you instant twists beside the fantastic Madison River.

Anglers wade in the waters here, and the canyon turnouts are perfect for resting your bike, peeling off your boots, and cooling yourself with a walk into the river. Try this, and when you shut off your bike and listen to the silence, I defy you to imagine a more beautiful country.

As you continue into Bozeman, the land turns into farmland. Hear the wind pouring over your helmet and the engine's low-pitched, pulsing hum.

Combined with Montana, it is a symphony.

Bozeman Primer

Others arrived before Lewis and Clark, but those two were the first to generate a written description of the valley, in 1805 and 1806. Decades later, when gold was discovered, Bozeman Trail became the chosen path west—and then east, when the prospectors returned here to create the town in 1864.

By 1883, the Northern Pacific Railroad had completed its line through the town, and Montana Agricultural College held its first classes in 1893. With settlers arriving from around the country, Bozeman developed a unique local heritage. Today, the town has eight historical districts and more than 40 properties listed on the National Register of Historic Sites.

While the outskirts of town look suspiciously like everyplace else, the heart of downtown still has a 1940s flavor, with 10-gallon hats, pointy-toed boots, drugstore cowboys, and antiquated signage at stores like Western Drug and Big Bair's Western Wear.

Mosey on down and check 'em out.

On the Road: Bozeman

As in Missoula, the road has been so generous that it's satisfying to stay in town and see what's shakin'. Main Street is the main part of town, more compact than Missoula's. Just a few hours up and down the street will acquaint you with the more interesting shops. Beyond that, just take it easy in the Old West.

Pull It Over: Bozeman Highlights
Attractions and Adventures

If you've never been fly-fishing, there's no better place to start than right here. What does it take to take up this sport? Money, mostly. Guides charge $250–350 for a day of fishing, but as you learned in Missoula, that doesn't include gratuities, a license, or equipment. In most shops, you can rent a rod, reel, and waders, but you have to buy gear and flies—unless you've got some plastered on your visor. Most excursions depart at 8:30 A.M. and return about nine hours later. Bear in mind that this is catch and release—you're fishing for the fun of it (if you think spending 300 bucks is fun). The shops below also arrange trips and guides.

Opened in 1944, **Powder Horn** (35 E. Main St., 406/587-7373) is sacred ground for sports enthusiasts, featuring books, rods, reels, clothing, boots, rifles, shotguns, shells, and cooking supplies. It also represents 20–30 local guides—not college students—who know where to go. Working with novice to serious fly fishers, **Bozeman Angler** (23 E. Main St., 406/587-9111 or 800/886-9111, www.bozemanangler.com) offers walk/wade or float trips on the Yellowstone, Beaverhead, Gallatin, Madison, and Missouri rivers. A few miles outside of Bozeman in the town of Belgrade, Dave Warwood at **Bridger Outfitters** (15100 Rocky Mountain Rd., Belgrade, 406/388-4463, www.bridgeroutfitters.com) can arrange a half-day horseback ride, a full day with sack lunch, or a full-on adventure that lasts four days and three nights and features overnight camps, cattle drives, horseback rides, and fishing in backcountry lakes and streams. Does he know his stuff? He grew up in the business his great-granddad started almost 100 years ago.

The biggest draw in Bozeman, the **Museum of the Rockies** (600 W. Kagy Blvd., 406/994-3466, www.museumoftherockies.org, $8 museum, $3 planetarium) is a great source of data that center around dinosaur fossils unearthed by local legend Jack Horner. I'm glad I came here. I was investing my money in coprolite until I learned that it's just fossilized dinosaur crap. On display are fake dinosaurs, CAT-scanned dinosaur eggs that reveal embryos, skulls of a triceratops and tyrannosaurus, and thoughtful exhibits on Native Americans and Lewis and Clark. Combined, the flood of information will wear your brain down quickly, so take in only the exhibits that catch your interest. Open 9 A.M.–5 P.M. Monday–Saturday, 12:30–5 P.M. Sunday.

The free **Gallatin County Pioneer Museum** (317 W. Main St., 406/522-8122, www.pioneermuseum.org) pays tribute to the history of Bozeman and the pioneers who settled in the Gallatin Valley. Take a look at the travels of your spiritual ancestors, Lewis and Clark, who are honored in this old jail at

taking a break on the Kawasaki overlooking Gallatin Valley, Montana

© NANCY HOWELL

the L&C library. Other exhibits include an 1870s log cabin, American Indian exhibits, a sheriff's room with a hanging gallows, a whiskey still, and more than 11,000 archival photos from the early days of the town.

Blue-Plate Specials

Serving lunch and dinner, **Boodles** (215 E. Main St., 406/587-2901) features a refined but not stuffy setting, a bar where you can smoke cigars, and food so good it's hard to believe. Excellent servers help you navigate through the wines and meals, and they never rush you—this is the perfect place for a leisurely dinner. When you're done, head to the full bar, a popular hangout.

Looie's Down Under (101 E. Main St., 406/522-8814) rivals the setting of Boodles, but in a basement. A nice retreat, Looie's features such entrées as lamb shank, blackened salmon, sea bass, and sushi.

The **Western Cafe** (443 E. Main St., 406/587-0436) opens at 5 A.M.—just in time to serve early rising regulars tins of fresh-baked cinnamon rolls and pies. When lunch rolls around, it rolls out the T-bone steaks, chicken-fried steaks, homemade soups and stews, and dinner rolls. The only drawback? There's just not enough time to eat it all—closing time's 4 P.M.

Watering Holes

Famous for its hats, **Rocking R Bar** (211 E. Main St., 406/587-9355) at its best is just a funky watering hole that keeps a full bar going for students, locals, and tourists. It's cool in a smelly, smoke-filled way, but I imagine oxygen masks deploy when things get too bad. Open daily 'til 2 A.M.

If you wear boots even when you aren't riding, you may feel at home at **Crystal Bar** (123 E. Main St., 406/587-2888), open 8 A.M.–2 A.M. daily. This country cowboy bar opens a second-floor rooftop beer garden in the summertime. Year-round, you'll find a few pool tables and lots of beer—and it's clean.

The clientele changes throughout the day at **The Cannery** (43 W. Main St., 406/586-0270), from doctors and lawyers after work, to college students after class, to real people later at night. Open 11 A.M.–2 A.M. daily, this joint features sassy bartenders and a pool table attached to the ceiling.

Shut-Eye

Motels and Motor Courts
The **Lewis and Clark** (824 W. Main St., 406/586-3341 or 800/332-7666, www.lewisandclarkmotel.net, $79 and up) probably saw its best days in the '60s—it still boasts a "dining room, coffee shop, and lounge." Still, the rooms are clean, large, and have two queen beds.

Chain Drive
A, C, E, I, L, Q, U, CC

Most chain hotels are on 7th Avenue and, since they're fairly close to the downtown district, may be your best option. See cross-reference guide featuring phone numbers and Web addresses on page 514.

Inn-dependence
The nicest inn, century-old **Voss Inn** (319 S. Wilson, 406/587-0982, www.bozeman-vossinn.com, $120 and up in season), features spacious rooms (sans TVs). They're kinda frilly, but some rooms are masculine, with king beds. Morning brings a full breakfast in your room or the parlor.

Resources for Riders

Mighty Montana Run

Montana Travel Information
Montana Bed & Breakfast Association—800/453-8870,
www.mtbba.com
Montana Camping Reservations—877/444-6777, www.reserveusa.com
Montana Fish, Wildlife and Parks—406/444-2535,
www.fwp.state.mt.us
Montana Road and Weather Conditions—800/226-ROAD
   (800/226-7623)
Travel Montana—800/847-4868, www.visitmt.com

Local and Regional Information
Bozeman Chamber of Commerce—406/586-5421,
   www.bozemanchamber.com
Bozeman Visitors Bureau— 406/586-5421 or 800/228-4224,
   www.bozemancvb.visitmt.com
Dillon Visitors Information Services—406/683-5511,
www.bmt.net/~chamber
Missoula Chamber of Commerce—406/543-6623,
   www.missoulachamber.com
Missoula Convention and Visitors Bureau—800/526-3465,
   www.missoulacvb.org
Missoula Road Conditions—406/728-8553
Missoula Weather—406/329-4840

Montana Motorcycle Shops
Adventure Cycle—201 E. Helena St., Dillon, 406/683-2205
Al's Cycle—619 Hwy. 93 S, Hamilton, 406/363-3433
Big Sky BMW Kawasaki—1804B North Ave. W, Missoula, 406/728-5341,
   www.bigskybmwkawasaki.com
Five Valley Honda-Yamaha—5900 U.S. Hwy. 93 S, Missoula, 406/251-
5900
Mountain Motorsports and Marine—620 Hwy. 93 S, Hamilton,
406/363-4493
Team Bozeman Polaris/Kawasaki/Yamaha—403 N. 7th Ave.,
Bozeman, 406/587-4671 or 800/830-4671, www.team-bozeman.com
Yellowstone Harley-Davidson— 18 W. Main St., Bozeman, 406/586-
   3139; and 540 Alaska Frontage Rd., Belgrade, 406/388-7684 or
   877/388-7684, www.yellowstoneharley.com

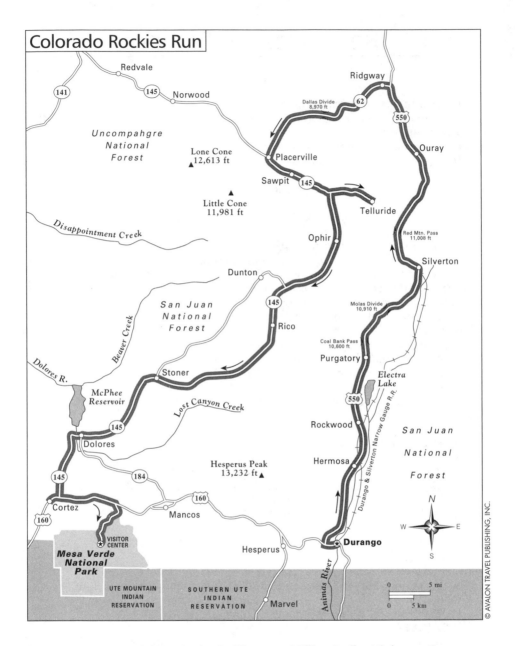

Colorado Rockies Run

Route: Durango to Mesa Verde via Silverton, Million Dollar Highway, Ouray, Telluride

Distance: Approximately 200 miles; consider five days with stops.

•Day 1—Durango •Day 2—Durango/Travel •Day 3—Telluride •Day 4—Telluride/Travel •Day 5—Mesa Verde

First Leg: Durango to Telluride (120 miles)

Second Leg: Telluride to Mesa Verde (80 miles)

Helmet Laws: Colorado does not require helmets.

Colorado Rockies Run

Durango, Colorado to Mesa Verde National Park, Colorado

This ride won't take very long, but it will last a lifetime. Every Colorado beer commercial is evoked here. Feast your senses on waterfalls, switchbacks with sheer drops, frontier towns in no hurry to leave the 19th century, and a mysterious village frozen in time. You'll ride across mountain passes at 11,000 feet, with the option of renting a Jeep to ride past 13,000 ... if you don't mind a collapsed lung. Ride in early or late summer for prime weather and less traffic.

Durango Primer

After the Anasazi vanished and the Utes, Navajo, and Spanish came and went, Durango was born by way of the rails.

With the San Juan Mountains overflowing with gold and silver, the folks at the Denver and Rio Grande Railroad had a brainstorm. In 1879, they established the town of Durango as the base point for their railway. The tracks were completed by 1882, and by the time the line stopped in the 1960s, about $300 million worth of gold and silver had been removed from the hills.

Durango was a wealthy town at the turn of the 20th century and, judging by the architecture, still looks well-off today. But it's not just money that makes this town rich. Its natural setting on the Animas River and the town's proximity to cool, lush forests and broad, powerful mountains both play a role. But its greatest asset is arguably its people. Their hospitality and lack of pretense make Philadelphians look like street thugs.

On the Road: Durango

Since the impending ride will satisfy your thirst for adventure, you might as well hang out downtown while you're in Durango or, if you have a day to invest, board a steam train for a real cliffhanger.

If you stay in town, the epicenter of activity stretches between 5th and 12th along Main Avenue. A showroom's worth of motorcycles typically sit at an angle along the curb, because this is an Old West walking town that hasn't lost its flavor. Here, the independent merchants, local saloons, and historic buildings give Durango an edge that ordinary cities surrendered when mall developers flashed their cash.

Along Main Avenue, you'll find leather and saddle shops, newsstands, old photo shops, a one-of-a-kind hatmaker, and one of the best melodramas in the West. After strolling Main Avenue, don't leave town by bike. Not yet. Seriously consider a run on the **Durango-Silverton Narrow Gauge Railway** (479 Main Ave., 970/247-2733 or 888/872-4607, www.durangotrain.com). Back in the 1880s, about the time the Rolling Stones released their first wax cylinder, mining in Silverton was going full steam. The best way to get the goods down to Durango was via this narrow gauge railway.

If you think the San Juan Skyway is gonna be tricky on an 800-pound bike, surrender the job to the engineer of a circa 1923, 50-ton, coal-fired steam train as he creeps it along the cliffs of the Animas River Gorge. When you enter the mountainous terrain and peer 400 feet straight down, you'll understand why cruising at 10 mph makes sense.

The locomotive chuffs along the canyon for about 3.5 hours, rising from 6,512 feet in Durango to 9,288 feet in Silverton (a town you'll see later on your bike, even if you don't take the rail). The layover in town lasts only two hours—enough time to eat, down a beer, and buy a rubber tomahawk. If you've never ridden a steam train and get a kick out of historic modes of transportation, it's worth the $62 you'll pay for the nine-hour round-trip (passage in a parlor car costs $109). Reservations are recommended. Touring the museum and the railyard costs $5 if you took the train, $10 if not.

Back in Durango, rest up and get ready for an old-fashioned evening listening to a honky-tonk pianist at the Diamond Belle Saloon or booing the villain at the melodrama. When you're in Durango, this sure as shootin' beats a night at a sports bar.

Pull It Over: Durango Highlights
Attractions and Adventures

When you've got a river in your backyard, you'd be a dope not to use it. As in many towns in the West, outfitters in Durango wring maximum use out of the mighty Animas. From serene to extreme, the river runs offered by **Outlaw Rivers and Jeep Tours** (690 Main Ave., 970/259-1800, www.outlawtours.com) last from two hours ($30) to full day ($65)—and then it adds Jeep rentals ($100 daily) and Jeep and Hummer tours to ghost towns and mining districts to the mix. **Durango Rivertrippers** (720 Main Ave., 970/259-0289 or 800/292-2885, www.durangorivertrippers.com) provides local folklore and wildlife observation from $25 (two hours) to $35 (half day).

Trimble Hot Springs (6475 CR 203, 970/247-0111, www.trimblehotsprings.com) doesn't qualify as a water adventure, since white water appears only when someone does a cannonball, but you can ease them saddle-sore muscles here. The spa features Olympic pools, massages, herbal wraps, and waters at 85°F, 102°F, and 108°F. Open 8 A.M.–11 P.M. daily.

When you see the sublime setting of the airstrip at the **Durango Soaring Club** (27290 U.S. 550 three miles north of Durango, 970/247-9037, www.soardurango.com), you may never want to leave the ground. When you do, you'll soar to 9,500 feet before popping off from the tow plane and soaking up tremendous views of the San Juan Mountains, as far away as 100 miles, and see the Animas River snake through the valley. If you're in a pack, your friends will be nearly as content sunning themselves on the observation deck. Weight limit 260 pounds, reservations suggested. Flights cost $85 (25 minutes) and up.

Shopping

Long before trendsetters beatified cigars, **Hall's Brothers Smoke Shop** (113 W. College Dr., 970/247-9115 or 800/742-7606, www.durangosmokeshop.com) was smoking. Claiming to be the "tobacconist to the Four Corners," Hall's stocks many cigars, Zippo lighters, and risqué postcards.

Thomas and Melissa Barnes are experts at making custom hats and saddles, which they do with great skill and care at the accurately named **Durango Custom Hats and Saddles** (563 Main Ave., 970/259-5900 or 800/895-7098). After you've had your head examined, it'll take Thomas a few months to create a hat you'll own for a lifetime. Motorcycle seats, too, are a specialty—and for about $650, he'll measure your seat, get your input, and go to work to create a custom saddle displaying anything that can be carved, tooled, or stamped on it. Unicorns and rainbows not permitted.

Blue-Plate Specials

Francisco's Restaurante y Cantina (619 Main Ave., 970/247-4098) is a local favorite for its homemade soups, great Mexican food, impressive wine list, and full bar, where margaritas are a specialty and locals gather to watch the big game. Expect a long wait if you travel in season. Serves lunch and dinner.

The **Ore House** (147 E. College Dr., 970/247-5707), in a rustic miner's shed, is a great setting for an evening retreat. The chefs start with pan-fried steaks and work their way up to chateaubriand; in between, they whip up center-cut bacon-wrapped filets stuffed with king crabmeat, steak ranchero, and the Ore House grub steak. Eat dinner here and annoy a vegetarian.

Inside a renovated Ford tractor showroom, the **Steamworks Brewing Company** (801 E. 2nd Ave., 970/259-9200, www.steamworksbrewing.com) draws local college students and a smattering of tourists for lunch, dinner, and five regular and three seasonal microbrews. The style is basic, with corrugated tin walls, copper vats, and smooth concrete floors. Oh yeah, the food: Mexican, chicken, pastas, sandwiches, and pizza. The patio deck is great for all this, plus a cold one and conversation.

The **Durango Diner** (957 Main Ave., 970/247-9889, www.durango-diner.com) is a local landmark, and it keeps going thanks to its no-frills meals. Beyond serving breakfast all day, it spices up the menu with its trademark green chili, southwest salsa, and enchilada sauces—sold here and across the country. If you're afraid you'll run out of gas on the San Juan Skyway, stop here first.

Watering Holes

You cannot *not* have a good time at the **Diamond Belle Saloon** (in the Strater Hotel, 699 Main Ave.). This corner bar, locked in the 1880s, boasts a full line of drinks, from beer to bourbon. From the flocked wallpaper to the honky-tonk piano player to the nude painting to the sign that suggests "work is the curse of the drinking classes," this is one of the best bets for bikers I've seen. Chances are you'll meet people from around the world. The only thing missing here is Festus. Open 11 A.M.–midnight daily.

If you're driven by thirst, check out **Lady Falconburgs** (640 Main Ave., 970/382-9664), open 11 A.M.–2 A.M. daily. The rathskeller-style interior isn't that impressive (the basement of a shopping mall), but the establishment pours 100 types of bottled beer, 38 beers on tap, and serves a five buck sampler.

Players Sports Bar & Grill (652 Main Ave., 970/259-6120) features four pool tables, an extra bar in back, 30 bottled beers, five on tap, and a full liquor bar. It calls itself a sports bar—true, if holding a pool cue makes you an athlete. Open daily 'til 2 A.M.

If your nights aren't fueled by beer, amuse yourself with the **Diamond Circle Melodrama** (at the Strater Hotel, 699 Main Ave., 970/247-3400, www.diamondcirclemelodrama.com), an authentic melodrama where the acting is stuck in the 1800s. The rapid-fire action makes it hard to follow at first, but once you catch on, it's completely entertaining. Stick around for the vaudeville sketches that follow the show. In peak summer seasons, the curtain rises at 8 P.M. Monday–Saturday. Tickets go for $20.

Shut-Eye

The city operates a central reservations line (800/525-8855, www.durango.org) for lodging, activities, and the Durango-Silverton train. Most chain hotels are north of downtown on Main Avenue.

Chain Drive
A, C, E, G, L, S, U, X, CC, DD

Chain hotels are in town, or within 10 miles. See cross-reference guide featuring phone numbers and Web addresses on page 514.

Inn-dependence
A block off the main drag, Kirk Komick and his mom, Diane Wildfang(!), run both the **Leland House** and **Rochester Hotel** (721 E. 2nd Ave., 970/385-1920 or 800/664-1920, www.rochesterhotel.com., $149). Both offer superb rooms. I liked the Rochester for its Western film–themed rooms and mighty manly decor (some with kitchens), huge breakfast, fresh coffee and tea, and the fact that it used to be a bordello. Yowzah! Then again, both give you the comfort of an inn with the conveniences of a hotel.

A larger and more expensive choice is the magnificent **Strater Hotel** (699 Main Ave., 970/247-4431 or 800/247-4431, www.strater.com, $169 and up in summer). Built in 1887, it's one of the nicest restored hotels you'll have the pleasure of finding. The antiques are real, the restoration flawless, and the saloon and melodrama (see *Watering Holes*) will add flavor to your tour. Not only are the 93 rooms large and quiet, the elegant Gilded Age accoutrements throughout the lobby will turn you into a frontier high roller. Western novelist Louis L'Amour loved room 222—he said the ragtime music from the bar below gave him inspiration for his plots and characters.

On the Road: Durango to Telluride

Before you saddle up for the San Juan Skyway, heed the advice offered by local riders: Plan to stay longer than you expect; be aware that at night, it gets supernaturally dark; be careful of gravel on mountain corners; and watch for wildlife. Although I suggest Telluride as the first overnight, you'll ride through other intriguing towns where you can stay the night without disappointment.

When you leave via 550 North, the road rises slightly as you enter the San Juan National Forest. Soon you are surrounded by nothing but Colorado, where the purple mountains' majesty will elicit enough "Oh, my God!"s to start a new religion. After Cascade Creek, it gets trickier, but you will fear no mountain, even as you ride over 10,000 feet into thin air. If you parked your bike and trotted 50 feet, you'd be panting like a dog.

When you reach the Colbank Pass Summit at 10,640 feet, you may think you've hit the highest height—but you haven't. There's much more to come, but for now observe the waterfalls, great timber, Alpine meadows, and switchbacks that open the trapdoor into valleys below and then rise again to 10,910

rolling down Colorado curves on the Otto Mears's Million-Dollar Highway

Riding at High Elevations

When you ride in the mountains, for the first few nights you may experience symptoms that accompany reduced amounts of oxygen: insomnia and headaches. By staying in good physical condition, you'll have better reserves to cope with the change in altitude. Still, if you'll be residing or riding at elevations over 6,000 feet, it's wise to gradually adapt to physical activities over several days.

feet at Molas Pass. If you wanted to go underground, you wouldn't need the FBI's help. You'd just camp out here.

Ride with caution: What follows are miles of steep grade, yet only a two-foot-high guardrail stands between you and eternity. When you reach the overlook outside of Silverton, make sure your seatback's in its upright position for the final approach.

Silverton (elevation 9,318 feet), the terminus for the narrow gauge steam train, is a Victorian mining town that dates to 1874. As you cruise into town, the information center lies on the right (open 9 A.M.–5 P.M. daily), followed by a small village of gift shops, bakeries, small hotels, and markets. The same is found on notorious Blair Street, where bordellos once thrived. If you never rode the Durango train, listen for its cacophonous grand arrival, and then roam around town. Drop by **Handlebars** (117 13th St., 970/387-5395), a combination bar and paraphernalia-cluttered restaurant, where you can order up big food for lunch or dinner, or a big brew.

Succeeding Silverton is a fantastic ride on Otto Mears's "Million-Dollar Highway." Roadside creeks flow outside rainbow-wide curves. Be careful here, since both the air and the road thin, and there's no margin for error in the mountains—especially when you approach Red Mountain Pass. At 11,075 feet, this is the highest pass on your journey.

From here, it's back to Monaco riding, with more twists than a Hitchcock film. Some of the sharpest banked curves are right here, and the road becomes confused, not knowing which way it's supposed to turn. The repetitive corners give way to high canyon walls and valley overlooks that will remain with you for years, especially as you approach the "Switzerland of America"—the town of Ouray (elevation 7,706), an optional overnight. For lodging information, check with the **Ouray Chamber of Commerce** (970/325-4746 or 800/228-1876, www.ouraycolorado.com).

Like Silverton, Ouray (you-RAY) made and lost its fortunes through

*an impressive road
warning sign high in the
Rockies along the San
Juan Skyway, south
of Ouray*

mining. Whether you stay overnight or not, don't miss **Box Canyon Falls**
(970/325-7080). If you venture across the steel grating ($5 fee) to get close to
the falls within this narrow gorge, the spring runoff thunders and throws the
full weight of its freezing waters on you.

Ouray also has Jeep tours and rentals that peel you off your bike and thrust
you into the country and up to the stratosphere, with trails climbing past
13,000 feet. **Colorado West Jeep Rentals** (701 Main St., 970/325-4014 or
800/648-5337, www.coloradowesttours.com) and **Switzerland of America Jeep
Rentals** (226 7th Ave., 970/325-4484 or 800/432-5337, www.soajeep.com)
rent Wranglers and Cherokees for half- and full-day excursions. Most riders,
though, seem to prefer to leave the driving to guides who know area history
and the right roads to reach fields of wildflowers, mining districts, waterfalls,
and Alpine meadows. Either way, with a Jeep, you can explore ghost towns,
old mining camps, and gold mines in and around Ouray. Bring warm clothes,
food, a camera, and around $50 (tours) to $130 (on your own).

If your body's aching after a long ride, head to Ouray's main attraction,
the **Hot Springs Pool** (970/325-7073), where you'll pay $8 to soak in waters
ranging from pleasantly warm to a muscle-melting 106°F.

The most important must-see is the **Bachelor-Syracuse mine tour**
(970/325-0220, www.bachelorsyracuse.com). Take 550 North to Country
Road 14, and then turn right and follow a gravel road to the mine entrance.
Save room for food—the cowboys here cook killer breakfasts and lunches.
After boarding a rickety mine car, you'll head 3,350 feet through a cool
(55°F), CAT scan–style tunnel eight feet wide by eight feet tall. It's eerie

as hell riding along the veins of gold and silver, and it's even worse when the guide turns out the lights. Guides will provide a historical perspective to give you an in-depth and painless education on the hazards faced by Western miners. Don't miss it.

The second leg down to Telluride is easier than the first, starting atop a plateau that gives way to a valley floor. When you reach Ridgway, turn left at Highway 62. The landscape grows larger and more impressive, and the consistently nice road affords several photo ops. This is not a road to be hurried through. This is slow-paced cowboy country; chances are you'll be tempted to unscrew the footpegs and string up some stirrups instead. The curves, neither dangerous nor demanding, lead easily to Route 145, which turns south on the western side of the San Juan Skyway.

The road rides through vapid Placerville, into a canyon, and then beside red rock cliffs and into the Uncompahgre National Forest. Sixteen miles after your reach 145, Telluride comes into view as you stare in awe at staggering Bear Mountain Pass, a zigzag, motorcycle-destroying road that scales the mountainside beside a gushing river.

A great introduction, and the follow-up will not disappoint.

Telluride Primer

Telluride has a mighty strange history, friend. The nomadic Utes arrived in the Telluride Valley searching for elk, deer, and mountain sheep, and then they split. The Spanish arrived in the 1700s searching for an overland route to the Pacific Coast, but they didn't stay either. The settler who decided to stick it out was a man with a reason to stay: prospector John Fallon.

Fallon staked his claim above the town in 1875, registered the Sheridan Mine, and then struck it rich with zinc, lead, copper, iron, silver, and gold. This was the Silicon Valley of the 1870s, drawing fortune-seekers from around the world: Finns, Swedes, Irish, French, Italians, Germans, and Chinese. Unlike the millionaire geeks in California, these boys had gambling halls, saloons, brothels, and friends like Butch Cassidy, who arrived to plan his first heist at the San Miguel Valley Bank in June 1889.

When the mining boom collapsed, the town suffered a slow decline, approaching ghost-town status in the 1960s. That's when a few resolute citizens realized that "white gold" (aka snow) could save their town. With a few shakes of entrepreneurial spirit, they transformed Telluride into a ski resort.

The result will keep you satisfied. There are hippies trying to re-create the halcyon days of Haight-Ashbury (minus the nuisance of personal hygiene), art galleries, a surplus of natural beauty, and handsome young ski bums who make life worth living for middle-aged women and comparably depressing for middle-aged men. And then there is money, lots of it, imported by recent transplants and celebrity residents.

Beneath it all, however, this is an ordinary mountain town. There are small markets and a hardware store; the "Free Box," where the needy or greedy filch donated surplus; and a calendar of festivals, from the Telluride Airmen's Rendezvous to the Bluegrass Festival to the legendary Telluride Film Festival.

It's a great little town. Have fun.

On the Road: Telluride

You entered a valley when you entered Telluride, so a pleasure ride isn't worth the effort—at least, not on a bike. There are ways to get around and experience the town, most of which you can do fairly easily.

I'd suggest starting before 9 A.M., when the morning light bathes the mountains in a rich gold, and the streets are perfectly deserted for photos. After grabbing a breakfast with the locals at Sofio's, walk over to the gondola on the south end of Oak Street. When it's not hauling skiers in winter, it hauls sightseers in summer. And it's free.

Wait for an empty car and start your 30-minute round-trip. From this vantage point, the aerial views of the town and mountains grow increasingly more majestic—but wait for the return ride to take photos, when ski or bike racks won't block your view. There are two stops along the way, the first at Sophia Station (just under 11,000 feet), the second at Mountain Village (9,545 feet), a picturesque yet oddly artificial affluent neighborhood. Return for a nighttime ride to enjoy equally magical views.

When you return to town, roam on foot. Don't pressure yourself. Just savor the mountain air and views and the fact that you're not in an office.

Pull It Over: Telluride Highlights
Attractions and Adventures

You can wander around searching for individual outfitters and rental companies, or you can save some shoe leather by stopping at **Telluride Adventures** (150 W. Colorado Ave., 970/728-4477 or 800/828-7547, www.telluride sports.com). Since 1972, it's been a one-stop shop for all things outdoors: fly-fishing, white-water rafting, hiking excursions, glider rides, horseback riding, and kayaking. Prices range from $15 (mountain bike rental) to $65 (paddleboat rental)—although prices for guided excursions are much higher.

Roudy, the town character, offers "gentle horses for gentle people, fast horses for fast people, and for people who don't like to ride, horses that don't like to be rode." Choices at **Riding with Roudy** (off Hwy. 145—call for directions, 970/728-9611, www.ridewithroudy.com) include a variety of trail rides starting at roughly $30 an hour, as well as dinner rides ($60) and custom pack trips. If you ride, ride with Roudy. He's good company.

Telluride Outside (121 W. Colorado Ave., 970/728-3895 or 800/831-6230, www.tellurideoutside.com) is a full-service provider of fly-fishing and float trips, white-water rafting, ballooning, and Jeep tours.

Shopping

If you haven't already invested in a custom hat from Thomas Barnes in Durango, I'm sure Steve King, proprietor of **Bounty Hunter** (226 Colorado St., 970/728-0256), would like to take a crack at your skull. He's created custom hats for Ted Nugent, Madeleine Albright, the Clintons, and other people who can easily afford his customized beaver-skin hats, boots, belt buckles, $3,500 hand-burned deerskin jackets, and $4,200 beaded jackets. He can re-create your favorite riding jacket with new leather and beaded eagle designs. Now, if you can figure out how to put this on your company's expense account, you've got it made.

A cool little neighborhood spirits shop, **Telluride Liquors & Wine Shop** (219 W. Colorado Ave., 970/728-3380) features about 450 wines—100 in the wine cellar—and 250 bottled beers, as well as a small humidor with a good selection of cee-gars. Its counterpart and competition is **Telluride Bottle Works** (129 W. San Juan Ave., 970/728-5553), which has delivery service, a wider selection, and lower prices.

Now that most antiques shops claim that *Flintstones* jars are collectibles, it's great to find a place like **Telluride Antique Market** (324 W. Colorado Ave., 970/728-4323), which sells quality antiques, such as silver-plated Indian prints, cheesecake calendars, art deco items, and old travel posters and prints.

Blue-Plate Specials

Perhaps the best place to grab an early breakfast, **Sofio's** (110 E. Colorado Ave., 970/728-4882) looks like a typical Mexican restaurant and is a favorite with locals who gather for big portions of eggs, pancakes, sausages, omelettes, and waffles made with fresh ingredients. Sofio's also serves dinner.

Open for lunch and dinner, **Eagles Bar & Grill** (100 W. Colorado Ave., 970/728-0886) is one of the town's more active restaurants at night. The creative spins on Mexican, pasta, pizza, seafood, chicken, ribs, and steak entrées may be the reason, or the corner location, or the casual interior, or the full bar … whatever it is, it works.

Noticing a dearth of affordable dining options, **Smugglers Brewpub and Grille** (225 S. Pine St., 970/728-0919) opened in 1998 and gained an instant following for its 10 on-site microbrews, ribs steeped in barbecue sauce, drunken chicken breasts, Philly cheesesteak sandwiches, and an interior created from an old miner's warehouse. Open for lunch and dinner, this casual, laid-back joint is a great place to grab a brew on the patio.

If you're on a writer's budget, you'll be pleased with **Baked in Telluride** (127 S. Fir St., 970/728-4775), serving breakfast, lunch, and dinner. You can grab a baked breakfast, slice of pizza, deli sandwich, soda pop, or big salad. Nothing fancy, but the food's real groovy.

Watering Holes

There are two authentic hangouts in Telluride. **Last Dollar Saloon** (100 E. Colorado Ave., 970/728-4800) is one of them. "The Buck" comes complete with hardwood floors, brick walls, tin ceiling, pool table, full liquor bar, bottled beers, and a few on tap. Can't do much better when you want a main-street view and a place to meet real people.

O'Bannon's Irish Pub (121 S. Fir St., 970/728-6139) is the other authentic hangout. This one's a small, loud basement bar with $4 pints of Harp, Bass, and Guinness, a pool table, a jukebox, a well-worn bar, and a ceiling draped with flags of Ireland.

One of the town's original drinking establishments, **Sheridan Bar** (231 W. Colorado Ave., 970/728-3911) is open 3 P.M.–2 A.M. daily. It has a more manufactured feel, but you may not notice because of the tin ceiling, upright piano, long bar, and mighty cool pool hall in back.

Shut-Eye

Aside from chain hotels, lodging options abound in Telluride; rates peak during winter and are higher in summer than in spring and fall. **Resort Quest of Telluride** (800/538-7754, www.telluridelodging.com) books inns, condos, hotels, and homes. Rates aren't cheap, but if you're traveling with a group, its houses may be an option. The town's own service, **Telluride Central**

Reservations (970/728-3041 or 88/TELLURIDE—888/355-8743, www.visittelluride.com) handles lodging, too, as well as air service, performance tickets, and activities. Keep in mind that some accommodations require two-night minimum weekend stays, and prices rise during special event weekends like the Film and Bluegrass festivals.

Inn-dependence
The **New Sheridan Hotel** (231 W. Colorado Ave., 970/728-4351 or 800/200-1891, www.newsheridan.com, $120–240) is one of the town's best bets. It was built in 1891 and has since gotten itself gussied up with 32 spacious, tasteful rooms and suites with nice furniture and spa tubs. There are also a few condo-style suites. The full breakfast, library, and fitness room are impressive, but what puts it over the top are the two rooftop hot tubs with spectacular mountain views.

On the Road: Telluride to Mesa Verde

The overwhelming beauty of this run will either inspire you or cause cardiac arrhythmia. Leave Telluride via West Colorado and turn left after the service station on Route 145. You're back on the San Juan Skyway now, gearing up for scenery you cannot imagine.

Within minutes, you're riding into the mountains for a view of wildflowers, lakes, cliffs, and valleys slung between jagged mountain peaks. The road curves, drops, dives, and twists, taking your bike down into portions of these valleys like an elevator falling down a shaft.

This section of highway is where all your Colorado visions come together. The curves are not difficult, but the overwhelming combination of colors and textures is hard to fathom. Drink in multiple shades of green from the rail-straight pines, fields of brilliant wildflowers, black-and-white mountains, and surreal blue skies.

The road is reluctant to become routine, and the surge of energy it triggers may spark you to goose it—but watch your speed, since some curves can be deceptively tight. You'll cross the 10,000-foot plateau once again and see tundra and meadows before descending to 8,827 feet into the town of Rico, where there's not much except a gas station.

After Rico, the road transforms into an ordinary ride through the country. It may not be as inspiring as the earlier run, but when you consider the alternative—bending paperclips in an office or sitting in city traffic—you should have no complaints.

Ride past red rocks and, before you know it, you've reached the Colorado Plateau between the San Juan Mountains and Sonoran Desert. When you reach the end of Route 145, turn left onto Route 160 East toward Durango. As you ride toward Mesa Verde, look to your left; about 40 miles away, you'll see the mountains you conquered a few hours earlier.

From here, it's only seven miles to Mesa Verde National Park, although if you opt to stay the night at Far View Lodge (the park's only indoor lodging option), you have another 15 miles to go.

Whether or not you stay inside the park, get ready for the grand finale of your nearly circular run. After springing for the $10 fee (free if you carry a $50 annual National Parks Pass), you'll ride a road that rises like a phoenix, with fantastically sharp ascents that open up to endless views of the desert plains.

Four miles later, the Morefield Campground has a launderette and café, as well as the park's only option for gas. The road continues with curves similar to those of the Pacific Coast Highway, with each corner opening up to an ocean of earth. Once you've risen to the top of the mesa, take everything you recognize—and then erase it from your databank. That is what you'll see—absolutely nothing. The emptiness lasts for mile after mile, with the only constant being the shifting, braking, and cornering you'll undertake to reach the visitors center.

Now the mystery begins.

Mesa Verde Primer

Mesa Verde is a strange and mysterious place. Take the tales of ghost ships and the Lost Colony, multiply them by a hundred, and you still won't even begin to understand Mesa Verde.

The "Ancestral Puebloans" (the term now preferred over the previously common "Anasazi") settled here, carving homes into the cliffs. They were hunters, traders, artisans, and farmers, and this area was the heart of their civilization for nearly 800 years.

They built stone villages on mesa tops and cliff dwellings within canyon walls, and they created elaborate stoneworks, ceremonial kivas, intricately designed pottery, and four-story housing structures. Then, around 1300 A.D., the inhabitants of Mesa Verde packed it up. No one knows what they left with, but they left behind crops and personal belongings. Since they had no written records, to this day no one knows for sure why they left.

Their very existence remained a mystery until 1888, when ranchers Richard Wetherill and Charles Mason rode through the area to round up stray cattle.

On Mesa Verde

I saw a little city of stone asleep—that village sat looking down into the canyon with the calmness of eternity, preserved with the dry air and almost perpetual sunlight, like a fly in amber, guarded by the cliffs and the river and the desert.

Willa Cather on Mesa Verde

That's when Wetherill saw Cliff Palace hidden within the canyon. A few years later, amateur archaeologist Gustaf Nordenskiold arrived from Sweden to document the dwellings and sites.

What's intriguing is that there are mysteries that remain to this day. Even though the park and services aren't on the level of Yellowstone or Yosemite, Mesa Verde was still selected the world's number-one historic monument by readers of *Condé Nast Traveler* in 1998—ranking ahead of even the Vatican! In 1978, UNESCO, a United Nations organization, named the park a World Heritage Cultural Site, and Mesa Verde was also the first park dedicated to the preservation of cultural resources. While it doesn't feature the multitude of services you can find in Durango and Telluride, it's a logical and fascinating archaeological place to wrap up your San Juan Skyway run.

On the Road: Mesa Verde

Unless you're an anthropologist or Indiana Jones, there's only one way to see—and really understand—Mesa Verde: Take one of the tours departing from the Far View Lodge and Morefield Campground. Unless you are willing to marinate your head in the intelligence of trained guides, you'll simply be looking at a map and struggling to comprehend more than 4,000 identified sites and ruins. Although the ride around the park's juniper- and piñon-dotted landscape is pleasing, it's just not worth traveling solo—and more difficult from mid-September–mid-May, when not all services and tours are available.

Start at the Far View Visitor Center and arrange a special ranger-led tour ($2.75) to either Cliff Palace, Balcony House, or Long House, since demand restricts guests to one site per day. Hold off on touring the museum—it will make more sense once you've taken a half- or full-day tour.

On just the half-day bus/walking excursion, I learned more in three hours than I did in three years of high school. Anyway, the first sites you see are ordinary, but the stories and structures become increasingly more fascinating. Starting with the ruins of a simple kiva (ceremonial room), you'll eventually reach Spruce Tree House, an elaborate structure of 130 rooms and eight kivas that you can walk to and, in some sections, through. Keep in mind that with ingenious hand and toe-holds carved directly into the cliffs, many of these structures were accessible only by scaling cliff walls—so you can assume that cross-eyed and knocked-kneed children probably didn't live very long. You also have to walk a half mile down to reach it, although it seems like two miles coming back up. Wear comfortable shoes and carry your own drinking water—none is available at any site.

I can't even begin to explain what you'll see and learn here—just swing by the Far View Visitor Center, sign up for a tour, and dig information out of the rangers. When you're done, plan to return to some of the places you missed, such as the visitors center and Chapin Mesa Museum (open 8 A.M.–6:30 P.M. daily), where dioramas and exhibits on pottery, jewelry, tools, weapons, and beadwork will fill in some of the blanks. The park also has well-stocked bookstores as well as inexpensive and informative pamphlets on specific sites.

Pull It Over: Mesa Verde Highlights
Attractions and Adventures

The entire park is a historic site, with guided bus tours departing from **Morefield Campground** and **Far View Lodge** (800/449-2288). Half-day tours ($39) leave at 8:30 A.M. from Morefield and at 9 A.M. and 1 P.M. from Far View. Make reservations, especially in season.

Adjacent to the Chapin Mesa Museum, Spruce Tree Terrace sells silver jewelry, etched and painted pottery, and sand paintings. There is also a shop at the Far View Visitor Center. At various times throughout the summer, Native Americans hold handicraft fairs and demonstrations in the park.

Blue-Plate Specials

There are few places to eat at Mesa Verde. Snack bars and cafeteria-style restaurants at Far View and Spruce Tree are adequate if you're not agile enough to kill and skin a rabbit with an *atl atl*. If you can swing it, the **Metate Room** at Far View Motor Lodge is the park's signature restaurant. No corn dogs here—load up on roast turkey, chicken *escalante*, Rocky Mountain trout, broiled salmon, lamb chops, or buffalo fajitas. The Southwestern-style dining room has a huge wall of windows revealing the mesas and finger canyons, so the views are almost as good as the cuisine.

Shut-Eye

If you don't stay in the park, the town of Cortez, 10 miles west, has loads of chain hotels. Durango is 36 miles east of the park entrance station on Highway 160. The park offers two options. The exterior of the top-of-the-line **Far View Lodge** ($111–128) is 1970s ugly, and the interior is generic hotel, but you get a balcony with stunning views from a 2,000-foot plateau. The **Morefield Campground** ($20 tent, $25 full hookups), a popular spot if you don't mind roughing it, has 435 campsites with picnic tables, grills, and benches, as well as a grocery store, showers, and a laundry. Reservations for either can be made by calling 970/564-4313 or 800/449-2288.

Chain Drive
A, C, E, G, L, CC, DD

Chain hotels are in the nearby town of Cortez. See cross-reference guide featuring phone numbers and Web addresses on page 514.

Resources for Riders

Colorado Rockies Run

Colorado Travel Information
Bed & Breakfast Innkeepers of Colorado—800/265-7696,
 www.innsofcolorado.org
Colorado Division of Wildlife—303/297-1192 or 303/291-7534,
 www.wildlife.state.co.us
Colorado Road and Weather Conditions—303/639-1111 or instate
 877/315-7623, www.cotrip.org
Colorado State Parks Reservations—303/470-1144 or 800/678-2267,
 www.parks.state.co.us
Colorado Travel and Tourism—800/265-6723, www.colorado.com
Distinctive Inns of Colorado—303/665-0974 or 800/866-0621,
 www.bedandbreakfastinns.org

Local and Regional Information
Durango Area Chamber Resort Association—970/247-0312 or 800/525-
 8855, www.durango.org
Mesa Verde National Park—970/529-4465 or 800/449-2288,
 www.visitmesaverde.com or www.nps.gov/meve
Silverton Chamber of Commerce—970/387-5654 or 800/752-4494,
 www.silverton.org
Telluride Chamber of Commerce—970/728-3041,
 www.visittelluride.com
Telluride Visitor Services— 888/353-5473, www.telluride.com

Colorado Motorcycle Shops
Fun Center Suzuki-Kawasaki—50 Animas View Dr., Durango, 970/259-
 1070, www.funcentercycles.com
Gene Patton Motor Company—2120 S. Broadway, Cortez,
 970/565-9322
Handlebar Cycle—346 S. Camino Del Rio, Durango, 970/247-0845
Ridgway Motorsports—566 Hwy. 62, Ridgway, 970/626-5112

Land of Enchantment Run

Taos, New Mexico to Santa Fe, New Mexico

You'll take a short ride along the "High Road" to Santa Fe, as well as a loop around the Enchanted Circle, a stretch punctuated by the creativity of Southwestern art. If you believe in the power of energy fields, this ride may give you a boost. Look for perfect riding weather and relatively quiet roads in late summer or early fall.

Taos Primer

I'll give Taos credit. Its ad campaign is so effective, there's hardly a person in America who doesn't know about this town of 6,200. The short, soft name conjures images of bronzed Native Americans skillfully creating silver necklaces, copper bracelets, and turquoise rings. This isn't so much a compliment as it is an observation that Taos has created more out of less than any city I can recall.

When you talk to locals and ask what it is about Taos, they eventually admit, "The mountain either speaks to you or it doesn't." They're referring to Taos Mountain, which, some say, controls the lives of all who enter its domain: "If the mountain likes you, you must return. If you displease the mountain, it will banish you forever." Apparently, I'm not a mountain man.

Anyway, when you're here, you're in the Sangre de Cristo Mountains, where Native Americans arrived more than 1,000 years ago, followed by Spanish

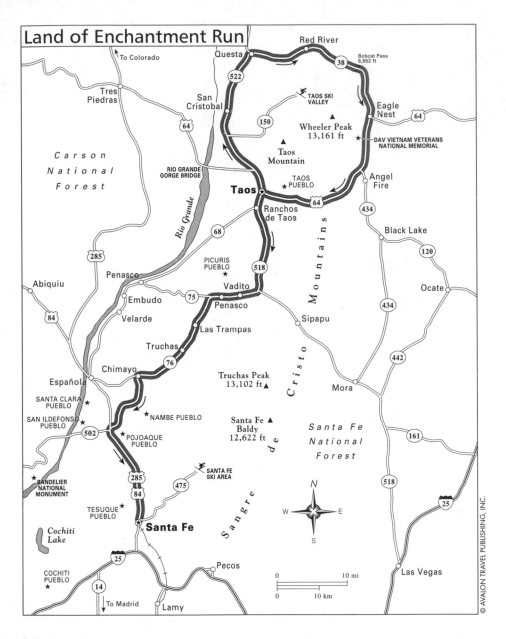

Land of Enchantment Run

Route: Taos to Santa Fe via the Enchanted Circle, Red River, Eagle Nest, High Road, Peñasco, Madrid

Distance: 80-plus miles; allow three days.

•**Day 1**—Taos/Enchanted Circle •**Day 2**—Travel •**Day 3**—Santa Fe

Helmet Laws: New Mexico does not require helmets.

colonists, who introduced the wheel, iron, horses, cattle, and disease. They were followed centuries later by French-Canadian trappers, and then, in 1898, by two artists whose wagon broke down. Apparently, the two pleased the mountain, because they stuck around and turned Taos into an artist's colony.

On the Road: Taos

Though an artist's colony, Taos leans toward a monochromatic palette of brown and gray, mud, and less-than-attractive streets. The city promotes the galleries and museums of Taos Plaza as well as the nearby Taos Pueblo. Each is worth seeing, but even more intriguing is the 84-mile loop known as the Enchanted Circle. I've come to realize that New Mexico gives some attractions positive reinforcement to boost their self-esteem—the circle isn't as enchanting as it is a good ride with some nice views.

You can hit the Taos Pueblo before or after your ride, which begins by taking Highway 64 (Kit Carson Road) North. At the junction of Highway 522, turn left on 64 and ride for seven miles to reach the Rio Grande Gorge Bridge, the "second largest suspension bridge on a national highway in America." (Everybody's got an angle.) Rest your bike, walk across the bridge, and look down into the gorgeous gorge 650 feet below.

Head back on 64 to take Highway 522 North on a clockwise run around the circle. It takes only a few miles to get into the groove; the plains create a surreal landscape, where clouds hover near the ground (or vice versa) and the valley stretches for miles. There are mile markers along the roadside, and at mile marker 10 in San Cristobal is the D. H. Lawrence Ranch, a gift to the writer from Mabel Dodge Luhan.

Six miles later, the winds and the views pick up as you enter Carson National Forest. When you reach Questa, turn right at the stoplight at Highway 38 and head east into a forest of spruce, Douglas fir, and ponderosa pine. If you're ever on a quiz show, remember that spruce trees have square needles and fir trees have flat needles, and you'll be just fine.

Beyond the trees, the road jazzes things up. Although the terrain's not Alpine and the Red River here is just a stream, the many curves and the rising elevation do expect you to pay attention. By the time you reach the town of Red River, you've climbed 8,750 feet into the hills and haven't broken a sweat.

Things have certainly changed here since the old days. Back then, there was only one hospital, and the town's doctor was its only patient. Then he died, so they tore the hospital down. Today, the town is full of pizza places, Mexican

San Geronimo Church in Taos

© LARRY MESSIN/TAOS COUNTY CHAMBER OF COMMERCE

restaurants, trout fishing guides, and a few hotels and lodges—most here for the winter ski season.

The next 17 miles jack up the excitement. The road rises sharply and reveals a fantastic view of the valley below. At times, it can be close to frightening; other times, it's just really scary. Suddenly, the trees aren't over your head but falling away below as you cross Bobcat Pass at 9,852 feet and gun it into a series of steep grades and equally steep drops. Look to your right and you'll spot Wheeler Peak, which, at 13,161 feet, is the highest point in New Mexico.

Once you've tamed Bobcat Pass, you can pick up speed—at least until you reach a valley overlook that's perfect for yet another memorable motorcycle photo. From here, the road is simple and empty until you reach the intersection of 38 and 64. Just past your fairing is Eagle Nest Lake, which you'll ride beside shortly. At the corner on your left lies a gas station/convenience store where you can buy everything from liquor to groceries, and where the clerks are as friendly as diner waitresses.

The town of Eagle Nest is to your left, and if you didn't grab a bite in Red River, there are some restaurants here. Otherwise, turn right and you're riding down Highway 64, the last road you need to return to Taos. Although desert states like New Mexico don't have much water, they do have reservoirs like Eagle Nest Lake. In a state park, it was created by the largest privately built dam in the United States.

You'll ride beside the waterfront for several miles, and there's no reason to stop, except for the **DAV Vietnam Veterans National Memorial.** David Westphall died in Vietnam in 1968, and his father created this site as a memorial to him and the 13 soldiers who died with him. Whether you're a vet or not, it's worth a moment to pay your respects to the soldiers and to the father who didn't forget.

Pass the winter resort town of Angel Fire and stay on Highway 64 for a heart-pumping ride. Almost immediately, you're into the sharpest and most consistent series of rises and twists along the circle. This beautiful ride takes you on winding roads, slows you down to 20 mph, and weaves back and forth as you reenter Carson National Forest.

For several miles, the road is hyperactive. Development is scant (a plus), trees plentiful, and turns tight. When you return to Taos County, the road becomes less curvy and cabins start cropping up along the river's edge and, as in Vermont, you'll find crafters making a living in the middle of nowhere.

After this, the road returns to normal and you ride back into the heart of Taos. Walk around the plaza and see a museum—or blow it off, get back on your bike, and do the whole ride counterclockwise.

Pull It Over: Taos Highlights
Attractions and Adventures

A clearinghouse for outdoor adventures, **Taos Mountain Outfitters** (114 S. Taos Plaza, 505/758-9292, www.taosmountainoutfitters.com) sells outdoor gear, but as a sideline, it can help you arrange mountain climbing lessons and excursions, white-water rafting, and hiking trips.

Van Beacham is a fourth-generation New Mexican who's carved out a nice niche—taking serious anglers on a trip called Solitary Anglers. The retreat emphasizes year-round fly-fishing, without the crowds. Find him at **Los Rios Anglers** (125 W. Plaza Dr., 505/758-2798 or 800/748-1707, www.losrios.com). Charging rates of about $250 for one person to $350 for three people for a full day, he and his guides work with beginners and seasoned casters. Rod, reel, and wader rentals are available. If you're curious about the appeal of fly-fishing, this is where you can get the answer.

Since 1350, Taos Indians have lived in and near **Taos Pueblo** (505/758-1028, www.taospueblo.com). Talk about rent control—this is the largest pueblo structure in America, a five-story creation of mud and straw, where residents still bake bread in outdoor domed ovens and sell the requisite baskets, pottery, jewelry, moccasins, and drums. Call in advance for a schedule of religious ceremonies, such as the Turtle Dance, Buffalo Dance, and Deer Dance. The pueblo is open for tours ($10) 8 A.M.–4:30 P.M. daily. They also generate extra cash through pictures. Remember: If you take photos, you're stealing the souls of the residents, but this minor transgression is overlooked if you slip them $5 for still photos and $10 for a video. Either way, be courteous and ask their permission first.

Shopping

If you're on the lookout for a leather jacket, you may want to postpone your purchase until you can come to **Overland Sheepskin Company** (three miles north of Taos Plaza on Hwy. 522, 505/758-8820, www.overland.com).

The folks at **Taos Drums** (Hwy. 68, 505/758-3796 or 800/424-3786, www.taosdrums.com) make and paint log, ceremonial, and hand drums out of rawhide and indigenous materials. They've been "Caretaker of the Drum" since 1951 and claim to have the world's largest selection of Indian drums. You can't beat that. Free drumming sessions and tours of the workshop are offered at 11 A.M. and 2 P.M. Monday–Friday. This can be an inspirational stop. I was inspired to become "Caretaker of the Sousaphone."

If you're a doctor, optometrist, or medicine man, check out the old quack machines and medical instruments at **Maison Faurie Antiquities** (1 McCarthy Plaza, 505/758-8545). The owner's a hoot (he's a Frenchman!) and the weird junk he has here is cool—and pretty expensive.

After awhile, all Southwestern art starts to look the same to me. The difference at **Blue Rain Gallery** (117 S. Taos Plaza, 505/751-0066 or 800/414-4893, www.blueraingallery.com) is that the selection here is big enough to be different: baskets, sculptures, kachinas, glass, paintings, bronze, jewelry, photography, pueblo pottery, and blankets. The focus here is on the work of young Native American artists who "depict their native culture with elegant style and creative awareness." Not a bad mission statement. Open 10 A.M.–6 P.M. Monday–Saturday.

Blue-Plate Specials

The food's fancy and the setting's casual at the **Trading Post Cafe** (4179 Hwy. 68, 505/758-5089). Dig into crispy garlic pork loin chop, Creole pepper shrimp, or Sonoma lamb chops—and send me your leftovers. **El Taoseño** (819 S. Santa Fe Rd., 505/758-4142) is a locals' hangout for breakfast, lunch, and dinner. The menu features steaks, fish, Mexican, and Mexican-American offerings.

Michael's Kitchen (304 Paseo del Pueblo Norte, 505/758-4178) has been cooking since 1974, whipping up chopped steaks smothered with gravy, onions, and potatoes, chicken-fried steak, mammoth pork chops, fried chicken, trout, and Spanish dishes. Opens at 7 A.M., closes at 8:30 P.M., and serves all foods all day long. Can't beat that.

Watering Holes

At **Eske's Brew Pub and Eatery** (106 des Georges Ln., 505/758-1517, www.eskesbrewpub.com), the menu is strange (burritos, bangers and mash, nachos), but its New Mexican wines and nine varieties of beer on tap are fresh, unfiltered, and unpasteurized. In a 1920s flat-roofed adobe home, this outdoor pub is a good spot to discuss the day's ride.

In the oldest building in Taos, locals are groovin' to live blues, salsa, and nuevo Latino music at the **Alley Cantina** (121 Teresina Ln., 505/758-2121, www.alleycantina.com). Just off the plaza, this popular watering hole lets you hang out with locals (always good) and keep an eye open for the ghost of Teresina Bent, the daughter of the first territorial governor.

The **Adobe Bar** (125 Paseo Del Pueblo Norte, 505/758-1977, at the Taos Inn, www.taosinn.com) is a hangout for locals and visiting artists and musicians. Tune into the most diverse playlist you can find. Every day, you'll find musicians playing country, folk, Western swing, flamenco, bluegrass, alternative country, gospel, Celtic, world, and native folk songs. You'll get a real sense of Taos by hanging out at this eclectic gathering spot—called "the living room of Taos" by locals.

Shut-Eye

Taos has a handful of chain hotels but more inns. **The Taos Association of B&B Inns** (505/758-4246 or 800/939-2215, www.taos-bandb-inns.com) represents 30 inns with rates from $70 to a honking big $325.

Motels and Motor Courts
El Pueblo Lodge (412 Paseo del Pueblo Norte, 505/758-8700 or 800/433-9612, www.elpueblolodge.com, $55 and up) is an adobe-style collection of motel and condo rooms within walking distance of the plaza. The setting is secluded and private, with a thick adobe wall concealing a heated swimming pool and hot tub. Rooms are just rooms, but a light breakfast and reasonable rates set this place apart.

Sun God Lodge (919 Paseo del Pueblo Sur, 505/758-3162 or 800/821-2437, www.sungodlodge.com, $65 one-bedroom in season, $119 two-bedroom in season) is farther away (1.5 miles south of the plaza), but you can justify the difference in distance. The God has 45 rooms and four kitchenettes, a hot tub, laundry facilities, picnic and barbecue areas, and six decked-out suites.

Chain Drive
A, E, S, U, CC

Chain hotels are in town, or within 10 miles. See cross-reference guide featuring phone numbers and Web addresses on page 514.

Inn-dependence
Casa Benavides (137 Kit Carson Rd., 505/758-1772 or 800/552-1772, www.taos-casabenavides.com, $89 and up) features Southwestern-style rooms with fireplaces, VCRs, antique furnishings, large beds, and room to spread out. If you want to get out of Taos and back to nature, ride six miles to **Taos Creek Cabins** (Rte. 1, 505/758-4715 or 800/580-5434, www.taoscreekcabins.com, $70–120), where a stream flows below the mountain decks and you'll capture views of Carson National Forest. Some cabins accommodate up to four people and include full kitchens, baths, glass-front woodstoves, large living rooms, and decks. So, whaddya think about that, Davy? Davy Crockett?

On the Road: Taos to Santa Fe

Instead of taking Highway 68 to Española and heading south, take the more exciting and life-affirming "High Road" to Santa Fe. You'll thank yourself repeatedly.

Leave Taos via Highway 68. Once you reach the outskirts of town, the plains open and the cliffs on the horizon look as insignificant as termite mounds. The road introduces some nice rises, and soon the scenery starts looking larger than life. The Rio Grande Gorge is in the distance, a monstrous gash in the earth; and over your right shoulder, the landscape—with a dusting of snow—looks like the label on a Nestlé bar. This is one mighty view.

Hang a left onto Route 518 and let the joy begin. This first stretch is 16 miles of mountain riding. Stick with it, and in less than a mile you'll see on your right the remains of a torreon, one of the round lookout towers that ranchers used for protection against nomads. Historic churches dot the landscape, but even more divine is the entrance into Carson National Forest for an exciting run toward Route 76. Run, forest, run.

Although the towns are poor, the roads are rich with daring corners and a splendid emptiness that gives you room to think. Everything here is scenic and natural—although there are so many icons of sliding trucks, you'll think you're part of a convoy. You may even consider investing in a seatbelt.

Take the road past Vadito (nothing here) six more miles to Peñasco, which looks like a major metropolitan area compared to everything else you've just seen. There are a few restaurants and a gas station, so fuel up with food and fuel if you need it.

From here, take Route 76 South toward the towns of Las Trampas and then Truchas, a ghost town that hasn't given up the ghost. The road is great and the landscape as inspiring as any O'Keeffe painting. Keep watching, because that's all you can do for the next 35 miles until you reach Chimayo. Settle back and reward yourself with a good ride.

It gets tricky around here. Highways aren't always marked, and most roads have Spanish names that many Anglos have a hard time deciphering. Look for the entrance to 98 (aka Juan Medina Road) and head south. After the sporadic craft shops, haciendas, and restaurants comes a wild road.

Roads 518 and 76 were just a prologue to this stretch. The road, which leads into 503, is like Nolan Ryan—it throws you curves when you don't expect it. Then there are the moguls, the series of quick rises and falls that would be great in winter if you could lash some skis to your tires. Take advantage of this road. Treat it like a beast. Once you've mastered turns that switch directions when you crest a hill, it'll start to slow down into some graceful bends as it works its way toward U.S. 84/285 north of Santa Fe.

Compared to your recent past, the road into Santa Fe is less than thrilling, but there's something to watch for: Camel Rock. I've seen rocks that look like things, but this rock really looks like a camel. Sadly, its hump was trampled into dust by generations of hyperactive climbing kids.

Hump-bustin' little bastards.

Santa Fe Primer

La Villa Real de la Santa Fe de San Francisco de Asis, aka Santa Fe, has seen its fair share of conquistadores. It's been the capital city of Spain, Mexico, the Territory of New Mexico, and New Mexico itself.

Francisco Coronado showed up in 1540 searching for gold, but he eventually gave up and left for Mexico. Priests started digging for souls instead of gold, and missions began springing up alongside the Native American pueblos. Not willing to accept defeat, more Spanish explorers returned to hunt for gold, and the country's capital moved around a few times before settling here in 1610.

Then Mexico overthrew the Spanish here in 1821, and Santa Fe became a commercial center. Apparently, the Americans who showed up with goods to sell liked the city, because they figured out a way to get it away from the Mexicans in 1846. The Americans didn't have it long, though, because in 1861, the Confederates took over—but I'm pretty sure the Americans got it back later.

Today, Santa Fe is a large town that looks small, a historic community where everything is adobe, a religious town where faith lies somewhere between Christianity and Native American spirituality. There's not much beyond the historic district, but that alone is worth the trip.

And you don't have to please no damn mountain.

On the Road: Santa Fe

If you're wondering if your future holds a good ride through Santa Fe, consider Will Rogers's thoughts on the matter: "Whoever designed the streets in Santa Fe must have been drunk and riding backwards on a mule." That said, when you're in the historic downtown section, look at Santa Fe as a condensed walking town with enough authenticity to make you feel as if you're not being ripped off. Even though the tourists look touristy, there are also hippies and Native Americans surrounding the plaza, probably the best place to hang out and watch people.

Although the city doesn't legislate interiors, it does have a say in "culturally appropriate exteriors." If it's Spanish, Native American, or early American Mexican architecture, then it's OK. This isn't a recent bureaucratic decision. In the early 1900s, artists thought Santa Fe had begun to look as uniform as other American towns, with new citizens bringing in Gothic, Romanesque, Queen Anne, and Italianate architecture from the Midwest. So they did something about it.

As in Charleston or Savannah, you can ride around the historic section and stare at buildings from your bike, but until you have a point of reference, it won't mean a thing. When you've finished getting an insider's view, wander around and check out hidden courtyards and church interiors. Roam the plaza, where Native Americans sell jewelry and pottery on blankets. If you travel with a camera, be sure to ask before taking their picture—and then have 10 bucks ready to pay them for the privilege. You may do better with a postcard.

Since any tour takes only a couple of hours, allow an afternoon for a ride down the Turquoise Trail. To reach it, take Highway 84-285 out of Santa Fe to I-25 and then exit at 278A onto Highway 14 South toward Albuquerque.

It's always satisfying when an interstate doubles as a scenic road, and I-25 is just that, so when it leads to 14, the transition is seamless. Well, almost.

One of the first points of interest is the now shuttered New Mexico State Penitentiary. You'll ride past it and into roads that aren't as curvy as those in Napa Valley, but they seem to reflect a similar landscape. After passing 44A, the mountains seem rounder and the trees are of uniform height and shape.

This ride doesn't expect much from you. Just enjoy the afternoon, since there's not much to see—except Madrid. Picture the Waltons, except poorer, and you can visualize this place. It's a strange old town, once thriving with coal mines, the sort that appears out of nowhere with the Madrid Country Store, art galleries, a bookstore, a bed-and-breakfast, a coffee shop, and the must-see **Mine Shaft Tavern** (505/473-0743)—which, judging by the rows of motorcycles, appears to be popular with riders. I imagine it serves miners, too.

Stay in Madrid or keep riding down past Golden, then to Highway 536, and turn right for a $3 ride up to **Sandia Crest** (505/243-0605, www.turquoise-trail.org), elevation 10,678 feet. The view from "High Point on the Turquoise Trail," as from other high points, is tremendous. A restaurant and observation platform sit at the peak, and the views are all yours.

After descending the peak, head back on the Turquoise Trail. The road is extremely easy but never mundane. It'll test your reflexes but doesn't expect you to be a motocross rider. The other advantage is that it seems lightly traveled; out here in the middle of nowhere, it's just you, desert cactus, and the world. Perfect.

Pull It Over: Santa Fe Highlights
Attractions and Adventures

Dig this: On the Ninth Day of Novena, the nuns at Loretto Chapel prayed to Joseph to create a way to get to the choir loft. Well, wouldn't you know it, a carpenter leading a donkey appeared and he got busy creating the "Miraculous Staircase": two 360-degree spirals in a staircase built without a central supporting rod! Then he left without a word! Even though historians know the fix-it man was a French master carpenter and not Joseph, the faithful don't let that interfere with a good story. Pay $2 to tour the **Loretto Chapel** (207 Old Santa Fe Trail, 505/982-0092, www.lorettochapel.com).

More than 80 paintings, watercolors, drawings, pastels, and sculptures created by O'Keeffe between 1914 and 1982 are on exhibit at the relatively new **Georgia O'Keeffe Museum** (217 Johnson St., 505/995-0785 or 505/946-1000, www.okeeffemuseum.org, $8). Schedules vary, although it's open daily in summer. If you ride and are inspired by the beauty of New Mexico, you're seeing O'Keeffe's vision. She felt she belonged here to paint the ragweed and scraggly maples and cow skulls. "That was my country," she said. "Terrible winds and a wonderful emptiness." I feel that way after I eat cabbage.

The "A Boot About" tour elevates you from a tourist to a student of history. When the two hours are over, you'll understand in detail what was shakin' around Santa Fe during the last 500 years. The $10 tour departs at 9:45 A.M. and 1:45 P.M. from the **Hotel St. Francis** (309 W. San Francisco St., 505/988-2774, www.abootabout.com).

If the history of Native Americans and ancient tribes intrigues you, **Outback Tours** (505/820-9375 or 888/772-3274, www.outbacktours.com, $65–96) takes you out of the city and into the countryside on a variety of tours to Bandelier National Monument to explore Anasazi ruins, to the Jemez volcano, and to O'Keeffe country, land of red rock canyons and O'Keeffe's Ghost Ranch. Other tours leading to remote mesas, juniper, and pine forests cover fossil safaris, history, and geology.

Several white-water rafting operations run out of Santa Fe—although the water's out of town. Most feature half- and full-day white-water rafting, as well as overnight trips, fly-fishing, canoe trips, and kayak instruction. Among the many operators, the **New Wave Rafting Company** (505/984-1444 or 800/984-1444, www.newwaverafting.com) has been paddling since 1980. It offers tame trips, as well as ones that navigate the Racecourse, which is five miles of white-water, and the Taos Box, 16 miles of wilderness gorge. Ask for current prices and whether your excursion includes lunch and gear.

Blue-Plate Specials

The Razatos family has been on the plaza since 1918, and their old-fashioned diner is infused with their character. Serving breakfast, lunch, and dinner, **Plaza Restaurant** (54 Lincoln Ave., 505/982-1664) is packed with locals who dine on standard diner meals (meat loaf, hot turkey sandwiches, burritos). I like the signage that marks a family restaurant. If you have a complaint, they list numbers for the police chief, mayor, governor, and president. You're also reminded not to talk back or fidget, and to keep your elbows off the table, be nice, and say thank you.

If you think that eating at small joints is the most memorable part of a good ride, ride about five miles north to the **Bobcat Bite** (420 Old Las Vegas Hwy., 505/983-5319). The Bobcat's received applause for the best cheap eats in town and praise for its green chili cheeseburgers. Don't expect to spread out: Seating capacity's about 18, and you often have to wait for a seat.

Horseman's Haven (6500 Cerrillos Rd., 505/471-5420) has been all in the family since the 1960s, whipping up breakfasts, burgers, burritos, chili, and authentic Mexican dishes. Yes, the sweat will pop out of your head almost as if you were dancing the bossa nova with Ann-Margret.

I love the theme of the **Cowgirl BBQ & Western Grill** (319 S. Guadulupe St., 505/982-2565), and the food has worked its magic on me, too: mesquite smoked barbecue ribs, chicken and brisket, grilled salmon soft tacos, jerk chicken, monster T-bones, and made-from-scratch *chiles rellenos*. The dozen draft beers, ales, and full bar are best savored on the deck. Check out the portrait library of honorees from the National Cowgirl Hall of Fame and walls crammed with memorabilia celebrating the American Cowgirl.

Watering Holes

Although not a "biker" bar, **Evangelo's** (200 W. San Francisco St., 505/982-9014) plays the blues and caters to bikers. If you arrive on your bike, it waives the cover—even when there's a band. The place features four pool tables, a downstairs bar, 150 kinds of beer, and a cool and comfortable look that mixes the South Pacific and Mediterranean. Right on the plaza.

El Farol (808 Canyon Rd., 505/983-9912, www.elfarolsf.com) is a restaurant, but the draw is the bar, where you can listen to local musicians playing hot Spanish music, blues, country and western, Mexican flamenco, or rock—the format changes each night. Arrive after 10 P.M., when things start to cook—and then go home and display your newfound flamenco dancing skills.

San Francisco Street Bar and Grill (50 E. San Francisco St., 505/982-2044) serves food (its hamburgers have been featured in *Esquire* and the *New York Times*), but you'll want to concentrate on the 14 wines, soft ice margaritas, tequilas, sangrias, spirits, and draft beer.

Shut-Eye

You can make one call to find a variety of places in Santa Fe. **Santa Fe Detours** (505/986-0038 or 800/338-6877, www.sfdetours.com) is a reservation service for hotels, motels, inns, horse rides, river runs, and rail trips.

Chain Drive
A, C, D, I, L, P, Q, S, T, X, U, W, BB, CC, DD

Chain hotels are in town, or within 10 miles. See cross-reference guide featuring phone numbers and Web addresses on page 514.

Indulgences

If you can swing this one, more power to ya. The **El Dorado Hotel** (309 W. San Francisco St., 505/988-4455 or 800/955-4455, www.eldoradohotel.com, $269–299) is a grand Southwest hotel that fits Santa Fe perfectly. Spoil yourself silly with butler service (really), balconies, rooftop swimming, a whirlpool, and exercise rooms. It also takes reservations for the Inns of Santa Fe (three smaller properties within walking distance), which let you use the facilities here.

Resources for Riders

Land of Enchantment Run

New Mexico Travel Information
Highway Hotline—800/432-4269
New Mexico Bed & Breakfast Association—800/661-6649,
  www.nmbba.org
New Mexico Department of Tourism—800/733-6396,
  www.newmexico.org
New Mexico State Parks and Recreation—505/476-3355 or 888/
  NMPARKS (888/667-2757), www.emnrd.state.nm.us/nmparks

Local and Regional Information
Santa Fe County Chamber of Commerce—505/988-3279,
  www.santafechamber.com
Santa Fe Visitors Bureau—505/983-7317 or 800/777-2489,
  www.santafe.org
Santa Fe Weather Information—505/827-9300
Taos Visitors Center—505/758-3873 or 800/732-8267,
  www.taoschamber.com
Taos Reservations and Recreation—800/732-8267, www.taosguide.com

New Mexico Motorcycle Shops
Bobby J's Yamaha Inc.—4724 Menaul Blvd., Albuquerque,
  505/884-3013
Centaur Cycles (BMW)—452 Jemez Rd., Santa Fe, 505/471-5481
Chick's Harley-Davidson/Buell—5000 Alameda Blvd. NE, Albuquerque,
  505/856-1600, www.chickshd.com
Dave's Custom Cycle—214 Paseo Del Pueblo Sur, Taos, 800/968-3556,
  www.davescustomcycle.com
Motorsports—6919 Montgomery Blvd., Albuquerque, 505/884-9000
R & S Kawasaki-Suzuki—9601 Lomas Blvd. NE, Albuquerque, 505/292-
  6692, www.teamrands.com

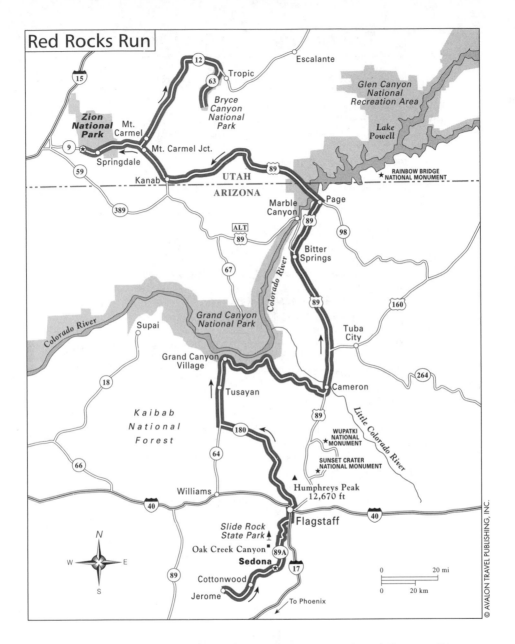

Red Rocks Run

Route: Sedona to Zion via Oak Creek Canyon, Tusayan, Grand Canyon, Page, Bryce Canyon

Distance: Approximately 365 miles; consider six days with stops.

•Day 1—Sedona •Day 2—Travel •Day 3—Grand Canyon •Day 4—Travel •Day 5—Page/Travel •Day 6—Zion National Park

First Leg: Sedona to Grand Canyon (110 miles)

Second Leg: Grand Canyon to Page/Lake Powell (143 miles)

Third Leg: Page/Lake Powell to Zion National Park (112 miles)

Helmet Laws: Arizona and Utah do not require helmets.

Red Rocks Run

Sedona, Arizona to Zion National Park, Utah

Over the next several days, you'll find that just as the Calistoga–Sausalito–Carmel run is a perfect showcase for California towns and roads, Sedona–Grand Canyon–Zion is the right blend for Arizona and Utah. With the exception of Sedona, the roads are not very challenging, but you may not mind too much. The vast openness of this part of the country is intriguing in its own way. The riding weather in early fall is ideal.

Sedona Primer

Sedona. A beautiful name for a beautiful place. But would you feel the same way if you rode into Schnebly Station? That was the first name proposed by settler T. Carl Schnebly when he wanted to establish a post office here in the early 1900s. When the postmaster decided the name was too long for a cancellation stamp, the honor went to Carl's Pennsylvania Dutch wife, Sedona.

Turn back the clock, and you'll see that it's taken nature about 350 million years to make Sedona what it is today. No standard-issue brown and gray rocks here. Sedona's fire-red buttes and mesas, spires, and pinnacles are the result of a prehistoric sea's washing over, and receding from, the area seven times. The cyclic sea coverings left behind a patina of iron oxide.

First settled around A.D. 700, the area was home to the Sinaguans, who stuck around until 1066, when a volcano blew. They left, and the Anasazi arrived to take advantage of the recently fertilized soil and introduce modern amenities like multistoried pueblos and burglar-proof homes. Low doorways forced intruders to crouch upon entering, so the vigilant Anasazi homeowner could bash their brains out.

No one knows why the Anasazi left in the 1300s. In the 1500s, Spanish explorers came looking for gold and didn't find any, so they left, too. Prospectors, pioneers, and trappers began to arrive in the early 1800s and got along fine with the new tribes here, until the white man began fencing off Native American hunting grounds. By 1872, the American army had heard enough complaining and shoved the Native Americans off their land.

Despite the injustice, Native Americans are well represented throughout Sedona. Today, this is a major cultural center, with dozens of artists, actors, writers, and musicians gaining their inspiration from the beauty outside their doors. New Age disciples also congregate here, claiming Cathedral Rock is Sedona's most powerful female "vortex"—an electromagnetic energy force rising from within the earth. If you believe, you may find balance in health, relationships, work, and money.

Chances are you'll spend the majority of your time in Uptown Sedona, the older commercial district, or take a quick run down Oak Creek Canyon. There's nearly nothing you'd want to do indoors except sleep and eat, which makes this a natural for motorcycle travelers.

Wherever you ride, the roads will be right.

On the Road: Sedona

It's been said that God created the Grand Canyon, but he lives in Sedona.

Sedona *is* divine. When you arrive, you'll see that the physical beauty combines the mountains of Vermont, the rocks of California, and the clay of Georgia's back roads. If it looks at all familiar, that's because you may have seen a similar landscape from Pathfinder's mission to Mars.

There's a lot to see on surrounding roads. Perhaps the most popular stop for motorcycle travelers is 24 miles away in Jerome, an old mining town and now a weird destination. From Sedona, the ride's not that nice, but if you didn't go there, your friends might beat you with sticks.

From Uptown Sedona, South Highway/West Highway 89A is a wide four-lane road that passes franchise restaurants and rides away from the red rocks—which look outstanding in your mirrors. The road remains the same until you reach Cottonwood, where you turn left at the gas station in Clarkdale and

resting by the red rocks in Sedona, Arizona

© NANCY HOWELL

begin your steep ascent. It's another four miles up the mountain, where the landscape was borrowed from a Saturday-morning cowboy matinee.

Next to Taos, Jerome has done the best job of creating something out of nothing. In its heyday as a copper mining community, it was the third-largest city in Arizona. Now there's no gas station or grocery, no doctor or pharmacy, and the bank is an ATM. It won't matter to you after you park your bike with all the others outside the **Spirit Room** (144 Main St., 928/634-8809) and consider yourself at home.

This joint has become the base for riders making their way to high mountain country, low desert, red rocks, and canyons in an easy one-day ride. No fighting, no country music, no pointy boots, just a watering hole for riders who appreciate the lack of a cover, $2 brews, and Bloody Marys that can hurt you. You can add to the bar's collection of graffiti or donate a bra (if you wear one).

Farther down on Main Street, **Paul and Jerry's** (928/634-2603) has been a saloon since 1887. Today, it serves beer and has a full bar and three pool tables in back. **Mile High** (309 Main St., 928/634-5094), built in 1899, is one of a few restaurants serving standard hamburgers, enchiladas, soups, and appetizers.

Unless you've got a mighty deep hankering for a drink, Jerome should take only a few hours. When you return to Sedona, you'll be tempted to examine the red rock monoliths that contrast beautifully with the green of piñon, juniper, and cypress trees. Pick up a Sedona map that identifies the monoliths, which are named for their appearance: Cathedral, Courthouse, Snoopy, Elephant.... You'll have to find the local off-color favorite on your own.

Since you'll be running down Oak Creek Canyon on your way north, head down Highway 179 to Chapel Road and turn left to reach the **Chapel of the Holy Cross** (928/282-4069). A labor of love, the chapel was purposely designed to appear like part of the rock formation. From its summit, you have an unobstructed view of Courthouse Butte, Bell Rock, and the Two Nuns. Time this for late afternoon. and you'll be here to witness one of the most spectacular sunsets in the country.

Afterward, the town is yours to explore. Wander around uptown or go deeper into the desert on a Jeep tour. Sedona is a great town—you shouldn't cheat yourself.

Pull It Over: Sedona Highlights
Attractions and Adventures

The term "great outdoors" doesn't do justice to Sedona. It's greater than that—but inaccessible to touring bikes. Other modes of transportation—rental Jeeps, guided tours, and hot air balloons—can be almost as much fun, though. Most ground-based tours take you on rugged and historic trails leading to off-the-beaten-path canyons and mountains.

Ride with a guide on **Sedona Red Rock Jeep Tours** (270 N. Hwy. 89A, 520/282-6826 or 800/848-7728, www.redrockjeep.com). Choose from an introductory vortex tour to a horseback ride. Everyone needs a gimmick, and **Pink Jeep Tours** (204 N. Hwy./W. Hwy. 89A, 928/282-5000 or 800/873-3662, www.pinkjeep.com) has chosen color. These folks offer tours ranging from a $40, 90-minute Canyon West ride to the $65 Ancient Ruin ride. The 2.5-hour trip heads to a Sinaguan Indian cliff dwelling, where a guide points out and explains the rock art. Roughriders can try the Broken Arrow run, which offers two hours of heavy-duty 4x4-ing.

A Day in the West (252 N. Hwy. 89A, 928/282-4320 or 800/973-3662, www.adayinthewest.com) has an array of tours. Photo tours, Jeep tours, horseback rides, and chuck-wagon trips are planned by guides "who've been riding these trails so long, there's red dust in their veins." Prices range from $45 for the pioneer trail ride to $145 for a Jeep/horseback/Western dinner.

Although it's mighty 'spensive and you won't see the rocks up close, **Northern Light Balloon Expeditions** (928/282-2274 or 800/230-6222, www.northernlightballoon.com) offers the most peaceful way to see them—provided you can shake yourself awake for the sunrise flight. These folks will pick you up at your place and get you worked up for an hour flight ($180), but the entire experience lasts up to four hours because of the inflation and postflight lunch. The payoff for the early day is that you'll feast on a brilliant palette of colors found only in nature. And Sedona.

If you're looking for a concentration of Southwestern art, you'll find it uptown or at **Tlaquepaque** (tah-lah-ca-POK-ee), on Highway 179 at the bridge, open 10 A.M.–5 P.M. daily. Modeled after a Mexican village, the shopping district spreads out and rambles through shaded courtyards and ivy-covered walls.

Blue-Plate Specials

It looks like a hole in the wall, but at **Cowboy Club Grille & Spirits** (241 N. Hwy. 89A, 928/282-4200), "high desert cuisine" goes hand in hand with Old West tradition and hospitality. Try the rattlesnake(!), pistachio-crusted halibut, buttermilk fried chicken, or buffalo(!) sirloin, low in fat, high in protein. The bar is great, too. Its margaritas are legendary, and the Prickly Pear is made with real cactus juice. The prices are fair here, and the service excellent. Cowboy is open for lunch and dinner. Oh, and the Cowboy Artists of America was founded here.

I usually wake up before breakfast, so it was a boon to find the **Coffee Pot Restaurant** (2050 W. Hwy. 89A, 928/282-6626), which can create—upon request and with no help from confederates—101 types of omelettes. I ordered one with pencil shavings, string, and gravel and got the hell beat out of me. Here since the 1950s, the Coffee Pot is the place for locals (and celebrities) and anyone who wants a hearty breakfast or lunch.

Shut-Eye

For a complete listing of more than 20 bed-and-breakfast inns that are inspected and approved by the Sedona Bed & Breakfast Guild, check 800/915-4442 or www.bbsedona.net. The **Sedona Chamber of Commerce** (928/282-7722, www.sedonachamber.com) is a good source of information on the many cabins of Oak Creek Canyon.

Motels and Motor Courts
The **Sedona Motel** (218 Hwy. 179, 928/282-7187, www.thesedonamotel.com, $80–120) is just over a half mile from the town center and offers 16 rooms with microwaves, coffee makers, and mini-fridges.

La Vista Motel (500 N. Hwy. 89A, 928/282-7301 or 800/896-7301, www.lavistamotel.com, $59 and up) is one of the most economical choices.

Don't expect luxury from this family-owned motel, but for a clean room close to everything, it's a fine place to bunk down.

Chain Drive
A, C, E, J, K, L, S, T, CC

Chain hotels are in town, or within 10 miles. See cross-reference guide featuring phone numbers and Web addresses on page 514.

Inn-dependence
The **Creekside Inn** (99 Copper Cliffs Dr., 928/282-4992 or 800/390-8621, www.creeksideinn.net, $175–275) rests—coincidentally—right beside Oak Creek. Although the setting is wild, the inn is not—it's Victorian, with swank guestrooms featuring jetted tubs and a furnished garden patio. This is the place for husband and wife riders who've paid off the mortgage.

Indulgences

If you're traveling in a pack or need room to spread out, **Junipine** (8351 N. Hwy. 89A, 928/282-3375 or 800/742-7463, www.junipine.com, $215–360) features one-bedroom, two-bedroom, and creekside cottages—all in the heart of Oak Creek Canyon. The cottages contain a fully equipped kitchen, private deck, living room, and two fireplaces. The secluded, wooded setting may make it hard to break away.

On the Road: Sedona to the Grand Canyon

If you couldn't resist temptation, you may have already ridden up this road. Not a bad idea, because it's definitely worth a second look. The beginning of this run is a perfect goodbye to Sedona, since it is just as beautiful, albeit in a lush, more verdant way.

The topography changes immediately as Highway 89A slides into Oak Creek Canyon. From your seat, you command a vantage point not enjoyed by motorists. The canyon appears on your right, so close to the guardrail it seems much deeper than it actually is. The railing is low enough to flip you over the side if you're not careful.

So far, this gentle ride doesn't demand a lot, except that you pay attention to nature. Just when you didn't think it could get better, it does, with red rocks on one side and a canopy road on the other. You're descending into the canyon now and approaching **Slide Rock State Park** (928/282-3034), a slippery run down the rocks that's worth a stop if you have a bathing suit in your bags. Admission is $10 per vehicle in the summer, $8 off-season.

Continuing north, you'll pass small motels and creekside cabins; gradually, the red rocks give way to white granite formations that look like El Capitan in miniature. Soon you begin your ascent into hearty pine forests, riding up to 6,000 feet and facing some exciting 20-mph twisties. You can see the challenge ahead when you look straight up and see the Babel-esque road winding overhead. This is a very nice road and slightly safer thanks to a sprawling chain-link fence that keeps the mountain from falling on top of you.

At 7,000 feet, pull off at Oak Creek Vista, a great place for a picture, with the creek flowing 1,500 feet below. Joining you will be about 30 Native Americans who sell silver and turquoise jewelry and other handcrafted artwork.

Just as you're getting used to the curves, the road turns into a level pine forest and Oak Creek Canyon Road surrenders to I-17. A few miles ahead is I-40, but bypass it in favor of Highway 180, a two-lane that forks to the left and takes you on a roughly 30-mile tour of pine forests and mountains. You are riding in proximity to Humphrey's Peak, which, at 12,633 feet, is the highest point in Arizona. As the road skims along its base, you have the privilege of continuing the same pine forest run that's become a part of your life. You won't face the challenge of switchbacks, nor will you suffer from the hypnotizing effects of straights either. Instead, the road is marked by slow, meandering curves that glide across a fairly level landscape. As soon as you've grown accustomed to the richness and verdant green of the forest, nature decides to change the scene. You start dropping slowly and imperceptibly as you cruise into the high desert. As you ride steadily along 180, you'll ride across another 20 miles of desert and sagebrush before reaching the junction of Highway 64, which you'll take north.

Even though the road is flat, you may have the same gut feeling I did: that you're riding on the crest of an abnormally large mountain. In reality, you are. The Kaibab Plateau is a low, rounded mountain, and while you still have 30 more miles before hitting Grand Canyon, the ease and solitude of the landscape grant abundant time to relax and think. At mile marker 196, the land rises slightly and the plains spread out before you. On a clear day, you can see the Grand Canyon, just a black streak from here.

There's little to note between here and there, just straight riding until you reach the growing village of Tusayan—and your destination.

Grand Canyon Primer

Each time a magazine or TV program does a "Best of America" piece, you can bet you'll see an image of the Grand Canyon. For good reason. It's large, it's beautiful in an empty sort of way, and, as a national park, it belongs to you.

Back in 1530, though, it belonged to Don Lopez de Cardenas, a captain in Coronado's expedition. It was de Cardenas who discovered the Grand Canyon—which was news to the Indians who were already here.

Fast forward to the 20th century. The Grand Canyon was named a national monument in 1908 and a national park in 1919. The reasons are clear: This canyon is far larger than anything you can imagine. When you stand at the rim and look down, you're seeing only a fraction of the entire canyon. The dimensions are staggering. Measured by river course, the chasm is 277 miles long and up to 18 miles wide, and has an average depth of one mile. It took six million years (give or take a few hours) to cut the Grand Canyon, and nature is not finished yet. Rain, snow, heat, frost, and wind are still sculpting new shapes, bluffs, and buttes. The reed-thin creek at the bottom is the Colorado River, which averages 300 feet wide and up to 100 feet deep. This sliver of water is the erosive force that carved the canyon.

Try to avoid a summer tour. Grand Canyon Village is packed, and no vehicles—not even your faithful mount—are allowed on Western Drive. The road is open only mid-October–mid-March. This and dense traffic detract from the experience. See it in autumn and in the morning, before the high sun washes out its colors. If you have the wherewithal, see it via mule train, helicopter, or raft.

the Grand Canyon from the Watch Tower overlook

© NANCY HOWELL

On the Road: The Grand Canyon

Unless you start with an aerial tour, your first stop should be the park's visitors center. Here you can get a map of the park showing the best overlooks, watch an introductory film, and see a very large-scale model of the canyon that, in proportion, would make you as thin as a paper match.

If you can swing it (because it *is* pricey), invest in a helicopter tour that will define the canyon. Flying lower and slower than an airplane (although no one can fly beneath the rim), you'll cross the 18-mile-wide canyon twice at 100 mph and receive the benefit of the pilot's narrative. Among the stories guides tell is the tale of Louis Boucher. When a settler encroached on Boucher by establishing a homestead two miles away, the silver miner retreated into the Grand Canyon for a little privacy.

Whether you see the canyon from a helicopter, airplane, or mule, or just by standing on its edge, the Colorado River is a squirt-gun stream, and an 8,000-square-foot boulder appears no larger than a pebble. The canyon's architecture is far larger than you can comprehend. You can take pictures until you pass out, but unless you blow them up to actual size, they won't begin to reflect the breadth, width, depth, and grandeur of the canyon.

When you enter the park on your bike ($20) and tour the canyon rim, you'll find that the roads aren't designed for motorcycles and aren't exciting until you get to the vista points. When you do look over the side, however, what you'll see is Sedona in reverse. Every red rock is sucked down into the earth, and the heroic hole loses all sense of dimension.

The view is different from each overlook, although one thing remains the same: the sight of tourists gathering at the same protective barricade. Be bold. You can walk about 30 feet to either side and usually find a secluded spot where the view is just as nice and you can find a promontory to sit on. If you have time—and you should allow some—arrive near dusk and head down the Western Road to watch the canyon moon rise and the shadows fall like the sweep of the second hand.

Perhaps the most spectacular view is several miles east in Desert View. Climbing the 70-foot Watch Tower, built in 1932 as an observation station, places you a total of 7,522 feet above sea level. Of all the vista points at the Grand Canyon, this is definitely worth a stop, and the pictures are priceless.

Pull It Over: Grand Canyon Highlights
Attractions and Adventures

Grand Canyon: The Hidden Secrets is a must-see. For 10 bucks, catch it at the **IMAX Theater** (Hwy. 64, Tusayan, 928/638-2203, www.grandcanyonimax-theatre.com). The film captures great views of the canyon, offers a historical perspective, and earns your undying respect for the one-armed stuntman who portrays explorer William Powell shooting the rapids on the Colorado. How he didn't paddle in circles, I'll never know. Some scenes in this film are so scary, you'd swear you're in the raft yourself. Outside, the tourist information center and gift shops are a convenient stop.

There are abundant fun and freakishly expensive opportunities to kick up your adrenaline. Helicopter and airplane tours are the most popular. If you do only one, choose the helicopter; they fly lower and slower than airplanes. Both depart from the Grand Canyon Airport, fly similar routes, and cost about the same. **Grand Canyon Helicopters** (928/638-2764 or 800/541-4537, www.grandcanyonhelicoptersaz.com) offers flights 8 A.M.–6 P.M. daily during summer, 9 A.M.–5 P.M. daily during winter. Cost is $145 for 25–30 minutes, $205 for 45–50 minutes. **Papillon Grand Canyon Helicopters** (928/638-2419 or 800/528-2418, www.papillon.com) flies 9 A.M.–4 P.M. daily and charges $109 for 25–30 minutes, $169 for 45–50 minutes. **Air Star Helicopters** (702/262-7199 or 866/689-8687, www.airstar.com) also offers flights 9 A.M.–5 P.M. daily, charging $139 for 25–30 minutes, $199 for 45–50 minutes.

If you don't trust helicopters, opt for an airplane tour. **Grand Canyon Airlines** (928/638-2359 or 866/ 235-9422, www.grandcanyonairlines.com) takes you up on a twin-engine Otter for one of the longest (45–50 minutes), most complete air routes permitted over the canyon. Operating since 1927, the Otters fly more slowly than other planes, and their high wings and panoramic windows are designed for aerial sightseeing. Flights cost $89. **Air Grand Canyon** (928/638-2686, 800/247-4726, www.airgrandcanyon.com) offers 30- to 40-minute flights for $74, 50–60 minutes for $89, and 90 minutes for $174. The longer flights fly over the western canyon, so you can see waterfalls and the Native American village.

If you'd rather be on the river than up in the air, choose from nearly 20 Colorado River outfitters, who take either gentle cruises down the river or hair-raising, coronary-busting, life-threatening races through the rapids. Some are one-day affairs, most go overnight or longer. The best source for information on these companies is the **Grand Canyon River Trip Information Center** (928/638-7843 or 800/959-9164, www.nps.gov/grca). The center also provides updates on which launch dates have been cancelled. Rafting is popular enough to recommend reservations up to six months in advance.

Less thrilling than a raft ride, **Grand Canyon Mule Trips** (303/297-2757, www.xanterra.com) nevertheless can be fun and save your feet. On one-day trips to Plateau Point ($120), you'll spend about six hours in the saddle, or you can be bold and take an overnight to Phantom Ranch ($338). The ranch is not luxurious, but you get a stew or steak dinner. Cabins include bunk beds and showers. Both are physically rigorous trips. There's a weight limit of 200 pounds, and prices can go lower if more people ride.

Outside the park, the center of Grand Canyon commerce lies in the **Tusayan General Store** (Hwy. 64, Tusayan, 928/638-2854). This grocery store serves double duty as a post office and gift shop.

Blue-Plate Specials

Choices are limited, but **El Tovar Hotel** has a fine dining restaurant. Get the full rundown on this and other Grand Canyon choices by calling 928/638-2631. In Tusayan, the **Canyon Star** (inside the Grand Hotel, 928/638-3333) serves big food, such as hand-carved steaks and turkey, and features a large salad bar. The entertainment (folk singers or Native American dancers) doesn't cost you a dime.

Shut-Eye

For general Grand Canyon information, call 928/638-7888. More than 2,000 rooms are available in Tusayan and Grand Canyon Village, and the park has several campgrounds. **Mather Campground** (800/365-2267, $15) features full amenities, a store, and showers, and takes reservations. Sites at **Desert View** (928/638-7851, $10), are available on a first-come, first-served basis, but organized groups of 9–40 people may make reservations ($2 per person, plus $2.50 per campsite). Facilities include restrooms and picnic tables, but no showers. Have fun, Stinky.

Grand Canyon National Park Lodges (303/297-2757, www.xanterra.com) features the most prized lodging options, and reservations can be made two years in advance; same-day reservations are taken at 928/638-2631. The 78-room **El Tovar** ($123–285) is the most expensive and most beautiful lodge, although only four suites have a view of the canyon. Opened in 1905, the precursor to Yosemite's Ahwahnee features a stone-and-timber design, concierge and room service, and fine dining at the on-site restaurant. Less than 40 steps from the

Company Snapshot: Yamaha

While Suzuki started with spinning looms, Yamaha took a more sensible approach: It made reed organs. The company started in 1887, but the first bike didn't appear until 1954—a 125cc single-cylinder two-stroke based on a German DKW model. The YAI (aka the Red Dragonfly) was a success and sparked the introduction of a larger 175cc, twin-cylinder model. By 1959, the five-speed YDSI was in stores, followed in the 1960s by more powerful bikes, until in 1973, the company's production surpassed one million bikes. Now just look at 'em.

rim, it also includes a gift shop and small general store. Other less attractive options include **Maswik Lodge,** which is a quarter mile from the canyon's edge and features cabins ($66) and motel-style rooms with two queen beds and a full bath ($77–119). The **Bright Angel** starts at $49 and accelerates to $240, and the ugly-ass **Thunderbird and Kachina Lodges** range $123–133.

Several chain hotels and suites lie along Highway 64 in Tusayan. There are two safe choices run by the same company. The **Grand Hotel** (928/638-3333 or 888/634-7263, www.gcanyon.com, $70–138) styles itself after an Old West national park resort, but is housed in a new and attractive building. The rooms are large and comfortable, and at night, it features Western entertainment and Native American dancers. It has a great restaurant, too. At its sister property, the **Grand Canyon Suites** (520/638-3100 or 888/538-5353, www.gcanyon.com, $139 and up), every room is a suite with a king and a fold-out double bed, microwave, and wet bar. Suites are named after Western legends, such as Wild Bill, Zane Grey, Wyatt Earp, and Route 66.

Chain Drive
A, Y, S

Chain hotels are in town, or within 10 miles. See cross-reference guide featuring phone numbers and Web addresses on page 514.

On the Road: Grand Canyon to Page

When you head east on 64, cruising along the South Rim, you'll see a little more of the Grand Canyon. The ride starts out gently, with pine forests on both sides and, occasionally, a turnout where you can pull over for one last, less crowded look. After Navajo Point, you'll pass the Watch Tower and then depart the park by the East Rim.

The road is nice and wide, and the way it's laid out, you can cruise into curves low and slow. The landscape can be deceptive, because when you leave the Grand Canyon, you assume the views are behind you, but you still have enough elevation to afford glimpses into tributaries. The natural beauty is interrupted only by the self-derogating signs of roadside Navajo trinket stands: "Nice Indian behind you! Chief sez turn back now! Chief love you!" Sad.

Like the highway through Death Valley, Highway 64 is breathtaking in its desolation—that is, until you reach Highway 89 at Cameron. Turn left (north) and ride a few hundred yards to a good fuel and food stop. The **Cameron Trading Post** (928/679-2231 or 800/338-7385, www.cameron-tradingpost.com) is a miniempire with a motel, artwork, fudge, gas, moccasins, cowboy hats, ponchos, rugs, replica weapons, jackets, and $400 Indian headdresses. Other than that economic anomaly, prices are fair here, and the merchandise is of surprisingly good quality. Get gas here—the next leg across the Navajo reservation is relatively empty. Speaking of empties, if you need evidence of the alcohol problem on reservations, just look at the roadside, where beer bottles bloom like sagebrush.

There's scant scenery as it's typically defined, but you'll feel satisfaction observing a different way of life. No suburbs or neighborhood beautification programs here, just old trailers that come complete with horse and truck.

Things pick up about 34 miles south of Page, where great red cliffs rise on the horizon. About 10 miles later, near Bitter Springs, you'll start to ride right into them. They are majestic and overpowering, and as you ride directly down the throat of one of these giants, the road turns and you ascend to one of the most amazing vistas on the trip. Stop here and take a long look. A gorgeous gorge opens up far below, and a plain spreads out for hundreds of miles. When you saddle up again, around the corner is yet another fantastic sight: You're riding through a red cavern. Although it's only a few hundred yards long, the walls dwarf you and create a memorable motorcycling moment.

After twisting your bike through canyon walls, you'll encounter mile after mile of nothing but plains at 6,000 feet, and cliffs rising higher. The desert floor is red and white and brown and yellow and speckled with sagebrush. Ride it at sunset, when the light reaches out to the farthest points on the horizon and over the wonderful buttes that dwarf manmade smokestacks. It sounds strange, but seeing this endless vista makes you feel as if you're part of infinity.

Allow time to let this scene fix itself in your mind. After that, you can turn to Page.

Page Primer

The Navajos thought that this barren land was a bewitched place, where the trees had died of fear. They didn't care too much after 1956, when they swapped 24 square miles of this land with the government for a larger tract in Utah.

Back then, Page was just a construction camp for workers building the nearby Glen Canyon Dam. When they weren't busy, workers applied their engineering skills to the sand and rock and turned this into a frontier town of metal structures.

Page was incorporated in 1975, and in the last quarter century or so, this slow-paced town of about 8,000 has become a base for water sports on Lake Powell, which now fingers its way up into Utah. There's not much to see here unless you plan on fishing, skiing, or sitting on a houseboat. Page is the hub of the "Grand Circle," though, and from here you can opt to continue the final 115 miles to Zion or 133 miles to Bryce Canyon, or go off script and ride the 235 miles to Mesa Verde National Park (see the *Colorado Rockies Run* chapter).

On the Road: Page

Page is too new to be of great interest, but if you stay over, ride down to the visitors center at the **Glen Canyon Dam** (928/608-6404) for a tour of the dam and displays on geology, water, turbines, and dams. By any measure this is a damn big dam. At 1,560 feet across, 710 feet high, and 300 feet thick at the bottom, it holds back the force of a 186-mile-long lake. Bear in mind that the dam only scratches the surface of the 1.25 million-acre **Glen Canyon National Recreation Area** (928/608-6200, www.nps.gov/glca).

Since the roads here are relatively ordinary, you may be better off cruising on Lake Powell. To see every nook and inlet on the lake, you'd travel nearly 2,000 miles—nearly the width of America—and see blue waters lapping at cliffs, buttes, and gentle sands where the color of the canyon changes as evening shadows fall. The easiest way to get on the water is through the **Lake Powell Resorts & Marinas** (800/528-6154, www.lakepowell.com), which has cornered the market on water sports. Five miles north of Glen Canyon Dam on Highway 89, it's the recreation area's largest marina and lodging facility, with gift shops, campgrounds, RV park, laundry, showers, and a service station. From here, you can rent houseboats, powerboats, personal watercraft, and assorted water toys, or arrange a fishing excursion for bass, catfish, bluegill, crappie, trout, and walleye. Float down below the dam, where the cold waters are a favorite spot for trophy trout.

Remember: Dam. Good fishing.

Pull It Over: Page Highlights
Attractions and Adventures

It's not an adventure per se, but **Stix Bait and Tackle** (5 Lake Powell Blvd., 928/645-2891) is Page's favorite fishing spot. Locals congregate here before dawn to swap fish stories and plan their fishing strategies. The store has everything: licenses, tackle, sporting goods, rod and reel rental, guide referral, groceries, snacks, pop, beer, liquor, coolers, ice, bait (live, plastic, or frozen), fresh anchovies, coffee, and doughnuts.

Colorado River Adventure (outfitters store at 50 S. Lake Powell Blvd., 928/645-3279 or 800/528-6154, www.lakepowell.com) offers a calming half-day cruise ($62) into historical canyons first navigated by Major John Wesley Powell. Guides are part pilot, part historian as they explain ancient Anasazi petroglyphs. Bring a wide-brimmed hat, tennis shoes, a bathing suit, and a camera. A bus will drive you to the base of Glen Canyon Dam for the cruise, and then pick you up at Lee's Ferry for the one-hour trip back to Page. On some summer trips, a lunch buffet is served.

For a full list of activities or to make reservations for water sports on Lake Powell, call the **Wahweap Reservations Service** (800/528-6154, www.lakepowell.com).

Blue-Plate Specials

Serving big food for lunch and dinner, **Ken's Old West** (718 Vista, 928/645-5160) is appropriately accented with miner's lamps, sturdy wooden beams, and an old upright piano. Entrées include thick meat—steaks and barbecue ribs. The backroom bar and dance floor make it one of Page's few nightspots.

Finding an authentic, unpretentious '50s diner is a rarity, so don't miss **R. D.'s Drive-In** (143 Lake Powell Blvd., 928/645-2791). Settle in a booth and pretend you're Fonzie. Open for breakfast, lunch, and dinner, R. D.'s serves all the good and occasionally greasy foods your parents fed you on road trips (before you heard about cholesterol), including flavorburst cones, chili, burritos, shakes, fries, and the "famous" R. D. burger. Good food, cheap.

Whiners, crybabies, penny pinchers, and complainers are barred from the **Dam Bar & Grille** (644 N. Navajo, 928/645-2161, www.damplaza.com), a restaurant/saloon serving dinner and the self-proclaimed "best bar by a dam site." The huge dining room serves all the basic food groups, including porterhouse steak, king crab, ribs, dirty Sonoran chicken, and pastas.

Watering Holes

Next door to the Dam Bar, the **Gunsmoke Saloon** (644 N. Navajo, 928/645-2161) features a large rectangular bar, 10 wide-screen TVs, four beers on tap, a fireplace, dance floor, billiards, and darts.

Shut-Eye

Page has several chain hotels, so take your pick. The **Wahweap Lodge** (520/645-2433, www.visitlakepowell.com, $159–169) features 250 hotel-like rooms, a restaurant, a convenience store, and a gift shop, along with boat rentals, boat tours, and marina services.

Chain Drive
A, C, D, E, G, L, Q, S, CC

Chain hotels are in town, or within 10 miles. See cross-reference guide featuring phone numbers and Web addresses on page 514.

On the Road: Page to Zion National Park

As you rode north from the Grand Canyon, you may have noticed colorful examples of geological rioting. During the last 10 million years, rock compressions, deformations, and uplifts created Grand, Zion, and Bryce Canyons, as well as cliffs that change color from chocolate to vermilion, white, gray, and pink as you drive north.

On your ride to Zion, you'll be cruising through the Vermilion Cliffs, which begin with scattered sagebrush and grazing cattle. About eight miles out of Page, you enter Utah. The rocks begin to turn white and take on new shapes; the forces of wind, water, and erosion have applied a different finish to these cliffs.

After this, the scenery dissipates, and the long, straight roads change little in elevation until you reach a section of Grande Escalante (Grand Staircase), 18 miles into Utah. Arches striped red, brown, and white dot the landscape, and you'll spot caves that'll tempt you to park your bike and go look for Injun Joe.

The lull in scenery reasserts itself, and the lack of visual activity may break your concentration, but stay focused (the roadside monuments for dead motorists may rouse you). About 50 miles from Page, you'll see Kanab in the distance. Although folks in Page speak of Kanab with a reverence usually reserved for the Holy Trinity, there's not much here, save for an interesting roadside diner.

Houston's Trails End Restaurant (32 E. Center, 435/644-2488) is a great place to pull over and rest your bike. Thankfully, this is no chain restaurant, just an authentic slice of America, where you can get a cowboy breakfast, sandwiches, and home-cooked lunches and dinners.

You're not far from Zion National Park, and Highway 89 continues winding across the plains. Foreshadowing what's to come, the cliffs add more swirls and colors to their composition, as if from a watercolor painting. Embedded in the coral pink rocks are designs suggesting knotted rope, tire marks, and the pattern you see when you stir cake batter.

When you reach Mount Carmel Junction, where 89 veers sharply north, you'll likely be tempted to detour 60 miles to Bryce Canyon. If so, you'll find an ordinary road, a few valleys, and a town called Orderville, where there's a rock shop, then another rock shop, and across the street—a rock shop. A little farther along on the left, there's a rock shop. The road is easy, and the view is simple after seeing Sedona and the Grand Canyon. When you reach Bryce itself by following Highway 12 East toward Tropic, you'll know at first glance it was worth the ride. Not so much red as orange, the landscape beckons with short rock tunnels and arches; after these, you ride on a wide-open plain with mesas.

At Highway 12, turn right and you'll see **Ruby's Inn** (435/834-5341, www.rubysinn.com), a small town disguised as a gas station/hotel/restaurant/rodeo arena/store. Not a bad place to stay if you're tired of riding. A few miles more, and you're at **Bryce Canyon National Park** (435/834-5322, www.nps.gov/brca). Twenty bucks takes you and your bike to overlooks to see the fabled "hoodoos," pillars of red rock created about 60 million years ago in a prehistoric lake. If time is short, the first five pullouts should give you a sense of the park fairly quickly.

If you forsake Bryce, take Highway 9 into Zion National Park. For roughly four miles, you get a few twists and curves, and the speed limit drops to 30 mph—slowing not for curves, but for cows. A few miles later, you'll reach the east gate of Zion National Park. Although you may have booked a room at Zion Lodge, more likely your night's rest awaits in Springdale, a few miles beyond the southern exit. Either way, you'll get a small taste of Zion—enough to inspire you to feast on the park once you've settled down.

Zion Primer

It's no small praise that, even when compared to Yosemite and the Grand Canyon, Zion exudes a stronger sense of nature. Here, you and your bike make immediate contact with the environment. Zion National Park contains less than one-tenth of 1 percent of Utah's land area, but more than 70 percent of the state's native plant species. Within its 229 square miles are plateaus, canyons, waterfalls, creeks, and narrows. Differences in elevation, sunlight, water, and temperature have created microenvironments that nurture hanging gardens, forested side canyons, and isolated mesas. It is altogether a beautiful place.

If you're wondering where "Zion" came from, credit the Mormons, who borrowed the Hebrew word for "a place of safety or refuge" to name the area in the 1860s. Today, Zion is a refuge for 2.5 million visitors a year, meaning you should ride well before or after the summer peak. From Easter weekend to October, shuttles—not motorcycles—take park guests from Springdale into the far reaches of the park at the Temple of Sinawava. Only hikers, bicyclists, shuttle vehicles, and overnight lodge guests are allowed on the Zion Canyon Scenic Drive, although the rest of the park is open for riding.

With that in mind, accept this advice: Cash in your 401(k), build a log cabin, live here, and be happy.

On the Road: Zion

What can I say about the perfect blend of road and land? Once you enter Zion ($10), you have nearly free rein to ride and gorge yourself on the impressive and endless views. From the east gate, the Checkerboard Mesa appears just as its name implies. Unlike at other national parks, you have the freedom to park your bike and stride up rippled, textured rocks.

Around each copper-colored curve are rocks with fantastic shapes and variegated swirls ranging from dark red to light orange to pink and white. This wonderful ride connects 15-mph switchbacks with the magnificent motorcycle-friendly Zion-Mount Carmel Tunnel. Too small for large motor homes, this tunnel offers one of the best biking experiences you'll ever have. As if a cosmic drill punched through the mile-long mountain, the passage loses daylight on both ends before you're halfway through. The adrenaline rush continues when you exit and see another mile or two of switchbacks ahead, the first of which propels you into the presence of a natural amphitheater created inside a cliff at least a quarter mile wide. On these curves, beware the low retaining wall that's just high enough to snag a footpeg and toss you over the side.

You can't help but gun it past the 35-mph limit when you realize that the best LeMans roads aren't in Monte Carlo, but right here. The seven-mile Zion Park Scenic Drive is great if you can ride through, but, again, it's open only to shuttle buses Easter weekend–October. Whether on a shuttle or on your cycle, head north, and you'll pass the Zion Lodge; keep going, and eventually you'll reach Angels Landing, Weeping Rock, and the Temple of Sinawava.

Plan to pull over frequently—around each bend, another perfect photo beckons. To really give you a sense of the park, rangers offer programs and lead guided hikes from May through September, which will get you beyond the implied barriers and into places like The Narrows, rock passages that are 60–100 million years old and tower 1,500 feet overhead. You've come this far, chicky-babe. Don't blow it.

Pull It Over: Zion Highlights
Attractions and Adventures

For a basic understanding of what you'll see, there's a free orientation film shown in the park's Zion Human History Museum auditorium on the hour and half hour throughout the day. Another option is the film *Zion Canyon: Treasure of the Gods,* an impressive—although often fictionalized—introduction to the park. Shows are 11 A.M.–7 P.M. daily on the hour at **Zion Canyon Theatre** (145 Zion Park Blvd., 435/772-2400, www.zioncanyontheatre.com). Tickets are $8. Few things can do justice to the beauty of this park, but this large-format film comes close. You'll travel back to meet the ancient Anasazi and experience what it's like to be a rock climber.

The average tourist heads down the scenic drive, walks down a sidewalk, sees some steps, and turns around. Zion boasts the best canyons in the world, most of which are hidden behind the hills. Get off your bike and allow time to see what everyone else is missing.

The first stop you should consider making before wandering into the wilderness on your own is the **Zion Adventure Company** (36 Lion Blvd., Springdale, 435/772-1001, www.zionadventures.com), which (for $16) provides the maps and gear you'll need to hike through the Narrows. Donning a drysuit and carrying provisions and a walking stick, you'll trudge through thigh- to waist-deep water and enter silent, sublime passages. The signature Zion experience, it may whet your appetite for its Jeep tours and rock climbing classes.

If you'd rather let a horse do the walking, **Canyon Trail Rides** (Zion Lodge, 435/679-8665, www.canyonrides.com) offers one-hour ($30) and half-day ($55) tours through the park. If you really want to test your mettle and leave your bike behind, it also offers the **Red Rock Ride** (www.redrockride.com), which is for the strong, the mighty, and the affluent. The seven-day trip costs a whopping $1,795 and includes all meals, hot showers, tents, and beds. This is no sissy trip. You'll ride the old trails used by cattle rustlers, Butch Cassidy and the Sundance Kid, and see Bryce Canyon, the Grand Canyon, and Zion National Park. Of course, you need to have riding experience—and motorcycle time doesn't count.

It's hard to capture nature's intricate beauty with a disposable camera, so Michael Fatali has done the work for you. Lugging his camera to canyons and mountains you don't even know exist, he has spent weeks looking for the perfect shot. His efforts show in the colorful, passionate photographs on display at **Fatali Gallery** (868 Zion Park Blvd., 435/772-2422, www.fatali.com). With the right light, shadow, and surreal natural colors, ordinary objects take on a different and far more interesting visage.

Blue-Plate Specials

The **Bit and Spur Restaurant and Saloon** (1212 Zion Park Blvd., 435/772-3498) claims to be one of the best Mexican restaurants in Utah, but it's hard to judge, since it's so packed, it's hard to get inside to eat the food. Serving dinner daily and breakfasts on weekends, the eatery uses locally grown produce in traditional Mexican favorites, and it pours a great selection of Utah microbrews like Whip Tail Ale, Frogs Legs, Slick Rock Red Lager, and the Mormon favorite, Polygamy Porter—why have just one? To top it off, the restaurant features a garden patio, billiards, and sports TV.

Zion Pizza and Noodle Company (868 Zion Park Blvd., 435/772-3815, www.zionpizzanoodle.com), in an old church, serves lunch and dinner. Along with creative pasta dishes, salads, and Utah microbrews (Wasatch and Squatters), the menu features specialties like Thai chicken pizza and hot and spicy Southwestern burrito pizza. A back porch patio and front porch deck are perfect when the weather is right, and it usually is.

Shut-Eye

Xanterra (303/297-2757 or 888/297-2757, www.xanterra.com) is the corporation that runs lodging operations at several parks: Grand Canyon, Bryce Canyon, Zion, and Furnace Creek and Stovepipe Wells in Death Valley. Make advance reservations through Xanterra or same-day reservations at the lodge itself.

The only place to stay inside the park, **Zion Lodge** (435/772-3213 for same-day booking, 303/297-2757 or 888/297-2757 for advance booking, www .zionlodge.com, $129 and up) was designed in the 1920s, destroyed in 1966 by a fire, and rebuilt without the classic rustic design and historic appearance.

The oversight was corrected in 1990, and now it looks as it should—an outdoors lodge in the heart of beautiful country. With 120 rooms and a restaurant, the lodge often fills up, so don't be disappointed if you can't get in.

Springdale lodging is surprisingly diverse. The **Zion Park Inn** (1215 Zion Park Blvd., 435/772-3200, www.zionparkinn.com, $99) is a link in the Best Western chain, but it's very nice in a small town where conveniences are hard to come by. The inn features a pool, hot tub, gift shop, guest laundry, state liquor store, large and comfortable rooms, and a terrific restaurant, the Switchback Grille. Slightly more upscale, yet surprisingly reasonable, is the **Desert Pearl Inn** (407 Zion Park Blvd., 435/772-8888 or 888/828-0898, $118 and up). Swank, cathedral-ceiling rooms come with a TV, fridge, and microwave; outside are a waterfall and sparkling blue pool. The rooms are not quite suites, but with growth hormones, they would be. Old-fashioned and reasonable describes the **Pioneer Lodge** (838 Zion Park Blvd., 435/772-3233, 888/772-3233, www.pioneerlodge.com, $79 and up). It gives you what you want, if you just want a bed, a pool, and a neat old motel diner that claims to be the "home of home-cooked cooking."

Resources for Riders

Red Rocks Run

Arizona Travel Information
Arizona Association of Bed & Breakfast Inns—800/752-1912, www
.arizona-bed-breakfast.com
Arizona Road Conditions—888/411-7623
Arizona State Parks—602/542-4174, www.pr.state.az.us
Arizona Travel Center—866/275-5816 or 888/520-3433,
www.arizonaguide.com

Utah Travel Information
Bed & Breakfast Inns of Utah— www.bbiu.org
Utah Road Conditions—800/492-2400
Utah State Parks—801/538-7220 or 800/322-3770,
www.stateparks.utah.gov
Utah Travel Council—801/538-1030 or 800/200-1160, www.utah.com

Local and Regional Information
Grand Canyon Chamber of Commerce—928/638-2901,
www.grandcanyonchamber.com
Grand Canyon Road and Weather Conditions—888/411-7623
Grand Canyon Switchboard—928/638-7888, www.nps.gov/grca
Grand Canyon Visitors Center—928/638-7644
Page/Lake Powell Chamber of Commerce—928/645-2741 or 888/261-
7243, www.pagelakepowellchamber.org
Sedona-Oak Creek Canyon Chamber of Commerce—928/282-7722 or
800/288-7336, www.sedonachamber.com
Zion Canyon Information—435/772-3256, www.nps.gov/zion
Zion Canyon Visitors Bureau—435/772-3757 or 888/518-7070,
www.zionpark.com

Arizona Motorcycle Shops
Big Joe's Cycles—7911-C N. Hwy. 89, Flagstaff, 928/774-4662
Grand Canyon Harley-Davidson—I-40 at Exit 185, Belmont, 928/774-
3896, www.grandcanyonhd.com
Northland Motorsports—4308 E. Rte. 66, Flagstaff 928/526-7959,
www.northlandmotorsports.com
Outdoor Sports Lake Powell—861 Vista Ave., Page, 928/645-8141
Sedona Motorcycles—1575 W. Hwy. 89A, Sedona, 928/282-1093,
www.sedonamotorcycles.com

Sawtooth Range Run

Boise, Idaho to McCall, Idaho

Remote and expansive plains usher you into sometimes intricate yet always scenic low-mountain riding. Start with a wide-open ride custom-designed to relieve stress and cleanse your mind, and then cruise across the charcoal-black cinders of an ancient lava bed. After rolling into a valley retreat favored by cowboys, skiers, and America's most powerful people, ride out on a final run combining the majesty of wild rivers and scenic byways.

If you're heading to Idaho specifically for this ride, odds are a major road will lead you toward Boise. It's a nice city, but doubtful one that you'd explore on a motorcycle, so look at your map and consider following a roundabout route from here and into the heart of Idaho via a meandering and extremely pleasing 232-mile run.

On the Road: Boise to Ketchum/Sun Valley

There's not a scenic way to exit Boise, but in a state of only 1.4 million residents, even the interstates are relatively empty. It's much faster to reach the junction of U.S. 20 at Mountain Home by taking I-84 East, but a better alternative is adopting the "Marv Albert pain before pleasure" principle. This means you'll confront some congestion, but there'll be some plenty good stuff on the horizon.

Set your coordinates and depart Boise via I-84 West, riding toward the suburb

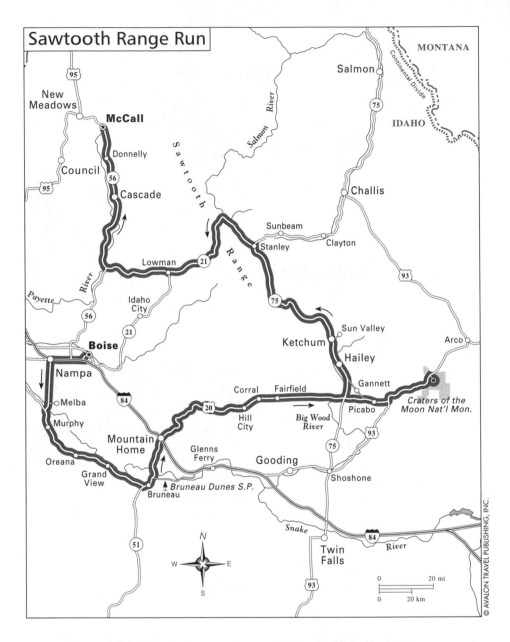

Sawtooth Range Run

Route: Boise to McCall via Nampa, Bruneau, Mountain Home, Ketchum, Stanley, Banks, Cascade

Distance: Approximately 450 miles; consider six days with stops.

•Day 1—Boise •Day 2—Travel •Days 3–4—Ketchum •Day 5—Travel •Day 6—McCall

First Leg: Boise to Ketchum (235 miles)

Second Leg: Ketchum to McCall (215 miles)

Helmet Laws: In Idaho, helmets are optional if over 18.

of Nampa, where Route 45 drops due south toward Melba. Only about 30 minutes into the ride, you'll reach the outskirts of Melba, where the residue of urban traffic dissolves. In this farm country, the hills and valleys are the Gem State's finest welcoming committee.

If you were watching television on September 8, 1974, the sight of Snake River should ring some bells. This is the river Evel Kneivel planned to clear aboard a rocket-powered motorcycle called X-2 Skycycle. Although Evel had trouble crossing the river from his launch pad near Twin Falls, thanks to a well-placed bridge, you'll have no difficulty whatsoever.

More impressive than memories of Kneivel's jump is the terrain Snake River helped create. Where Route 45 joins Route 78, the landscape is slowly washed clear of everything, including the constricting sights of strip malls, stores, and city traffic. Free of all this, you can gun it and pour yourself into the wind, taking advantage of the highway where speed limit signs should include the promise "100 percent satisfaction guaranteed."

The town of Murphy is here ... and gone, memorable if only for a nice dip that hugs both the summit and plummet of a hill. By the time I rode to Oreana, the land had worked its magic on me. I looked at the road leading to the horizon and, for the first time in my life, I had a new appreciation for an old song. As I watched the world through the windscreen, Woody Guthrie's endless skyway and ribbon of highway were no longer just lines from "This Land Is Your Land"—they were very real and had become part of my ride.

Riding into a sparse desert region, I entered one of my favorite environments. As a solo rider, I find that deserts invariably match my mood and desire for privacy; and while this stretch gave me enough curves to keep me alert, at times I rode upon straights that pierced the land for as much as six arrow-true miles. And when the road turned and decided to sneak up on Snake River, it revealed the nice high walls of the canyon. The 19 miles between Grand View and Bruneau are a perfect mixture of riding, a weird confluence of mountains and desert and fertile farmlands irrigated by 300-yard long sprinkler systems poised above the fields.

In addition to the scenery (or lack of it), what also impressed me about 78 was its speed. There were few towns and no switchbacks, and since I had rarely seen any cops, there was a near absence of speed controls—so 78 became a very fast road. If you've ever considered setting a land speed record, forget the Salt Flats and come to Idaho.

Near Bruneau, 78 swings to the north, where it wants you to cross Snake River and roll onto Highway 51. Don't go yet. Stay on 78 for two more miles to **Bruneau Dunes State Park** (208/366-7919). When you enter the park, a winding road leads to the park office, which has information on what's ahead. Until you get there, here's the skinny: It's a five-mile run to the end of the trail, and along the way are 12,000-year-old soot-colored dunes, one of which—at 470 feet—is the largest single-structured sand dune in North America. Unlike the dunes of Florence, Oregon, though, there are no dune buggies here—but there are lake, marsh, desert, prairie, and dune habitats to explore. If you decide to bunk down at the campground or cabins here and stay the night, the popular Bruneau Dunes Observatory has a collection of telescopes that'll help you see into the clear country skies.

Returning to Highway 51, the road spans Snake River (take that, Evel) and points you north toward Mountain Home. Here the highway is marked with periodic "open range" signs that I'm sure refer to livestock, but I took them as a sign that it also means free-range motorcycling.

On this open road, the lure of the landscape will find you twisting the throttle (no, that's not a euphemism) to rocket down the road. The intensity of the ride may be tempered if you're lapped by one of the jets screaming back to the neighboring Mountain Home Air Force Base. Aside from the random jet, there is nothing—nothing—here except the flat, endless prairie and the strip of asphalt that divides it. The emptiness continues until you hit a touch of density in and around Mountain Home, after which you squeeze under I-84 and work your way toward U.S. 20 East, at which point you're bound for glory. For an alternative route, swing east on 84 toward Twin Falls, near the center of the Great Rift. This 635-square mile geological phenomenon across the Snake River Plain makes up the earth's plumbing system; it's a series of fissures, spatter cones, and lava tubes from 60 lava flows and 25 volcanic events.

When you're back on U.S. 20 once again, the road ahead is clean and spare. You may spy a home every 10 miles or so, and when a curve does appear, its arc is so long and slow that you may think you're still on a straight. Rolling on toward an area called Tollgate, you can look around and realize this desert was once the floor of an ancient ocean, as shifting sands and the trails of long-evaporated streams lead off to the horizon. So, you can you see it all, as the road elevates you above the landscape and presents wonderful aerial views of the ride ahead.

There's not much shaking in Hill City or Corral or Fairfield, save for the random gypsy wagon parked in the middle of a field. The hills are snug and low and packed tightly together to create repetitive, easy corners. Creeks and ravines intersect the land, and wonderful scenes that were new to me appeared, like the random woodchucks that crept toward the road before dashing away from the growl of my bike.

Highway 20 becomes increasingly more alluring, not thanks to any magnificent formations but really to the lack of them. This lasts for about 20 miles until you reach the junction of Highway 75 and well beyond it. Trust me—after the months you've spent planning and then waiting for the office clock to tick down to the zero hour, wonderful emptiness like this is what you need.

Depending on your schedule, you may want to invest time to ride over to an unusual parcel of real estate. To see it, pass 75 for now and stick with 20 toward Picabo. Along the way, there is almost omnipresent desolation. To your right, the southern horizon is flat and endless. From horizon to horizon, you will not see a living soul; and clouds probably 50 miles away look quite strange and surreal, since there is nothing at all to break the view. Gradually, scrub brush and desert sand are replaced by black lava rock, and off in the distance at about 2 o'clock, there's an ancient volcano that looks as if it coughed up this very ground.

The manmade views here are limited to a few service stations, homes, and ranching supply stores. But nature delivers towering formations lacerated by rocks piercing through the grass, and more beds of crisp black lava tell you you've reached the entrance of the mysterious **Craters of the Moon National Monument** (208/527-3257, www.nps.gov/crmo). Before heading down the loop road, stop at the visitors center, where you can get a basic education on what happened here. In short: Several times during the past several thousand years, a parallel line of fissures in the area erupted through volcanic buttes and cones to spread a flow of lava that cooled into either pahoehoe (pa-HOY-hoy), a ropelike lava, or "Aa (AH-ah), a rough, jagged rock. No one was here to see the last eruption 2,000 years ago, but you can check out old volcanoes and see where lava beds created caves that you can explore.

So unusual is this area that Apollo XIV astronauts came here to study geology when training for their moon mission to get a sense of what the moon's surface would look like. So, in a sense, for the next few hours, your bike will become a lunar rover.

There are several stops on the seven-mile loop, such as Big Craters, Devils Orchard, and an extinct 6,181-foot tall volcano called Inferno Cone. Since you're already just a few hundred feet from the summit, you can hike to the top fairly quickly and easily, although the pebblelike consistency of the black gravel contrasts with the steep 14-degree grade of the hill. When you reach what you thought was the summit, you'll see another plateau ahead. To a chorus of crunching rocks, swift winds, and your own chuffing breath, you pass several peaks before reaching the final one, where the reward is a view well worth the effort. There is no crater left here, just a few flat boulders and a lone tree that draws your eyes to the east, where another extinct volcano rests far, far, far away. On a quiet day, you may be the only fool on the hill. Alone in private, you can scan the entire world. If you've ever considered meditation, there's no better place where you can reflect on your ride and your life.

Back down the hill, the loop road leads to other overlooks and then to the enticing "lava tubes"—caves hidden beneath a crust of lava. It may be tempting, but if you're alone or lack the right gear, such as a hardhat and lantern, heed the warning signs that remind you help may be a long time coming. And if you're wondering if you'll be able to leave the park with a few lumps of lava—the answer is no. Every year a few truckloads of rock are pilfered from the park, and for kicks some jerks even chip souvenir chunks off delicate formations. Please, what erupts in Idaho should stay in Idaho. So take pictures, and file away mental images, but leave the lava alone if you want to avoid a $250 fine.

Now you have the pleasure of backtracking to Highway 75, one of the nicest roads in Idaho, which takes you to Ketchum and beyond. Rather than riding 20 all the way, watch for a spur road to the right just past Picabo that'll take you northwest on Gannett Road (Route 23) toward Bellevue and Hailey. At 75, head north toward Hailey, where today's downtown bears little resemblance to the Hailey of yesteryear. What changed? Bruce Willis. He and Demi Moore moved here to raise their kids, and even though they split, they still love the town and have shown it by investing in places like a theater and **The Mint** (116 S. Main St., 208/788-6468, www.clubbruno.com), a Willis-owned bar.

From here, it's just another 10 prairie-rich miles to Ketchum and Sun Valley, one of the leading "lucky break" stories of the 20th century.

Ketchum/Sun Valley Primer

Ketchum's always had a penchant for wealth. The town was originally known as Leadville back in 1879, when prospectors came here to rip gold, silver, and lead ore out of the mines—but only after they had ripped the Tukudeka Indians from their land. After the tribes were gone and the mines were spent, Basque sheepherders from Spain showed up and roamed through town, guiding the flocks through the crossroads of Wood Valley.

Aside from silver and sheep and a stab at creating a spa from local hot springs, Ketchum didn't really catch on until 1936. That's when Averell Harriman, the chairman of the Union Pacific Railroad (and later Secretary of Commerce under Harry Truman), sent Austrian Count Felix Schaffgotsch on a mission to find one place in America that could rival European ski resorts

magnificent desolation, as seen from the top of Inferno Cone, an extinct volcano at Craters of the Moon National Monument

© NANCY HOWELL

such as St. Moritz. After several months of scouting, the Count was getting ready to wire Harriman the news that he had failed when an Idaho rep of the railroad directed him to the old mining town of Ketchum. Fewer than 100 people lived here then, but the site was perfect.

Backed by his fortune and connections, Harriman bought the 4,300-acre Brass Ranch and, just 11 months and five days after the count hit town, millionaire socialites from the east and stars from Hollywood hit Sun Valley. The blend of money and celebrity worked and today's Ketchum was born. Within a few years, this was known as the "American Shangri-La." In 1941, Glenn Miller came here to film *Sun Valley Serenade* with Sonja Henie. Clark Gable, Robert Kennedy, Ginger Rogers, and Lucille Ball were frequent guests. Even he-man Gary Cooper came by to go duck hunting with pal Ernest Hemingway, who liked shooting ducks. Hemingway shot himself here in 1961 and is buried in the last row of the Ketchum Cemetery on Route 75.

The popularity of this hole-in-the-wall resort has seldom abated. Power players from Washington and Hollywood have made this a favored retreat, and the power surges each summer when investment banker Herbert A. Allen Jr. hosts CEOs and CFOs from leading entertainment, technology, communications, and computing companies at a Sun Valley retreat.

After Allen's guests jet out, longer-term residents stick around, including Tom Hanks, Julie Andrews, Dennis Miller, John Kerry, Robin Williams, Clint Eastwood, Bill Gates, Demi Moore, Arnold Schwarzenegger, Christopher Guest, Jamie Lee Curtis, Oprah Winfrey, and Bruce Willis. Fortunately, prices on basic goods and lodging are still reasonable—just don't plan on buying a home and settling down.

Why not? Reveals a local: "The billionaires are pushing out the millionaires."

On the Road: Ketchum/Sun Valley

The surrounding area has more than enough to keep you occupied for a day—perhaps even a few years, if you bump into Oprah and she wants to marry and support you. If you're here for one day, though, half the day will keep you grounded, and the other half will have you heading for the hills.

If I were in your boots, I'd start at the **Visitors Center** (251 Washington St., 800/634-3347, www.visitsunvalley.com), which has a library's worth of brochures and information on the local area, as well as maps and guides for sites on the outskirts of town and across Idaho. Then take your pick. If you look, you'll see mountains all around you. Odds are you've arrived in the summer, which is even more crowded than in winter. What's cool, though, is that even in the summertime, the ski lift still clips along to the top of Bald Mountain. What does that mean to you? Listen closely, Pedro: While you can't get your bike to the top of the peak, you can get a *bicycle* there.

There are several rental shops in Ketchum, and one of the oldest (since 1948) and largest is **Sturtevants** (340 N. Main St., 208/726-4501 or 800/252-9534, www.sturtos.com). Provided you're not the size of Billy or Benny McCrary, for about $20 you can rent a sturdy cross-country mountain bike and ride the high-speed quad lift to the top of Bald Mountain. There are two lift stations; one at River Run, and the other pitching up farther north at Warm Springs. Slap your bicycle on a rack, take a 10-minute ride to the peak, and hop off at Lookout Lodge, where you can grab a light lunch at the grill and settle back with some outstanding views of the surrounding Pioneer and Sawtooth ranges. After living in the moment for a moment, spend the next hour riding down from 9,000 feet, burning off lunch as you navigate foot-wide trails carved out by animals and motocross riders.

I can understand if the thought of riding a bicycle down a steep hill strikes fear into your heart, so here's an alternative: Jump off the mountain. *Oui, monsieur, c'est ci bon.* It's expensive ($195), but when the weather's right, you can sign up for a tandem paragliding leap with **Fly Sun Valley** (160 W. 4th St., 208/726-3332, www.flysunvalley.com). After you run and jump off the side of Bald Mountain, you'll swirl through the air for as long as an hour before swooping in for an approach at a nearby parking lot or soccer field. And your friends on the bicycles? Those poor bastards are still pedaling.

Pull It Over: Ketchum Highlights
Attractions and Adventures

If you're active, there are enough outdoor adventures to keep you occupied for well over a week. If you want to hit a few of the trails in the Wood River Valley but don't want to destroy your cruiser on the rough roads, check out **Mountain Thunder Motorsports** (345 Lewis St., 208/726-4221, www.mountain thundermotorsports.com). It rents new and used street bikes, dirt bikes, ATVs, and snowmobiles for half and full days. Call ahead.

For a one-horsepower ride, James Super's **Super Outfitter Adventures** (208/788-7731, www.sunvalleyoutfitter.com) leads trail rides on 20 different trails within Sun Valley that last from half a day to a full day. Once the wilderness whets your appetite, you may want to stick around for its overnight camping and combination fly-fishing trips. And if that really lights your campfire, ask about its annual horse-drawn wagon train trip.

There are more than 40 miles of hiking trails within a five-mile radius of Ketchum: Fox Creek, Adams Gulch, Trail Creek, and others at Sun Valley. They're all free and maps are available at the **Ketchum Ranger Station** (206 Sun Valley Rd., 208/622-5371).

Sun Valley (www.sunvalley.com) is a full-service resort, meaning it offers outdoor adventures as well. Two that may do it for you are **guided trail rides** on Dollar Mountain (208/622-2387) and skeet shooting at its **Gun Club** (208/622-2111). Rent one of the Beretta shotguns and try trap, double trap, wobbletrap, and duck tower shooting. Smack a few clay pigeons, and you've got yourself a dinner. Good eatin'.

Shopping

Shopping is a significant part of life in Ketchum, with about 20 square blocks of stores, galleries, thrift stores, and restaurants to see. I didn't hit all of them, but the few that I did visit seemed pretty all right, and one was quite above average. That one was the **Images of Nature Gallery** (371 N. Main St., 208/727-1836 or 888/339-1836, www.mangelsen.com), an outlet for some of the most stunning wildlife photography I've ever seen. A former wildlife biologist, Thomas Mangelsen, found himself out in the wilderness for so long that he started looking at animals through a camera. After a few years, his amazing images of lions, moose, bears, eagles, polar bears, and gorillas had attracted an audience, and most any portrait he sells would look great in a den, office, lounge, sauna, bathroom, bomb shelter, or closet. Check out his website if you don't believe me. G'wan, do it, and tell me "Catch of the Day" isn't one of the most well-timed shots ever. For a comprehensive listing of galleries in town, pick up a **Sun Valley Gallery Association** guide (208/726-5512, www.svgalleries.org).

At heart, this is a tourist destination, and that means someone *has* to sell T-shirts. Here, the store is **Main Strip Ts** (240 Main St., 208/726-9543). Along with T-shirts and sweats, it also sells baseball caps, stickers, and other Ketchum and Sun Valley souvenirs.

A jim-dandy bookstore (and a bookstore *can* be jim-dandy, damn it) is **Iconoclast Books** (211 N. Main St., 208/726-1654, www.iconoclast-books.com). If you fall ass-over-teakettle for Idaho, odds are you'll want to peruse the new and used volumes here. They provide great historical and photographic references of the state and, most important, the areas you'll explore. It's not just regional guides, either—there are volumes on philosophy, art, history, and literature, as well as collectible first editions.

If you're staying in a cabin or efficiency and need groceries or beer, two great in-town markets can help. On Main Street, **Williams Market** (100 N. Main St., 208/726-3771) has everything you need and is open late. Around the corner is **Atkinson's Market** (4th and Leadville, 208/726-5668), which also has a full-service deli and drugstore.

Blue-Plate Specials

Ketchum is an important part of a well-balanced diet. There are some great restaurants here, and despite the money in the pockets of many locals, prices at most places felt pretty fair to me.

Looking upscale is the affordable **Sawtooth Club** (231 N. Main St., 208/726-5233), which opens into a cool bar, with the dining area on the second floor. It puts a creative spin on basic dishes to create supergood chicken Senegalese, mesquite-grilled steaks, chops, ribs, and wood-grilled duck and lamb. Food so nice, I ate here twice.

Completely starving, I dined at **The Kneadery** (260 Leadville Ave., 208/726-9462) and fully expected to finish just a single sandwich. I couldn't. It was way big, as were the massive home-style breakfasts that were defeating other diners. The portions are large and the prices medium, and the Rocky Mountain lodge look went a long way to please this rider.

If you just need food as fuel, a downtown staple is the **Main Street Café** (210 N. Main St., 208/725-5482), which serves the usual suspects: hot dogs, chili and cheese, mozzarella sticks, wings, nachos, and ice cream.

Watering Holes

You've probably realized that Ketchum has just about everything you need. At night, it has even more. Every bar and saloon in sight is built for locals, and they all have at least two things in common: a real good vibe and a moose head on the wall. Even if you don't imbibe, these are some good places to hang out with locals—and each saloon complements its drinks with an impressive menu.

The **Sawtooth Club** is a wonderful restaurant, but there's an even better bar and lounge downstairs. Fat, padded armchairs and couches around a fireplace make it seem like combination dorm room/gentlemen's club.

A few doors down, **Whiskey Jacques** (251 N. Main St., 208/726-5297) is part restaurant (pizzas, burgers, quesadillas) and part legendary bar. Perhaps the main gathering place in town, it appeals to folks who want to watch eight satellite televisions and a 61-inch big screen, shoot pool, hear live music, and pick up drinks at the full bar.

Stumble across the street to **The Roosevelt Tavern,** another restaurant whose twin is a lounge. A Western theme is the obvious choice, accented by a sign asking what is now so very clear: "24 hours in a day, 24 beers in a case. Coincidence? I think not." Count on at least 10 beers on tap, 15 brands in bottles, and specialty martinis. In good weather, head on upstairs—way up—to the roof to drink a brew under clear Ketchum skies.

The Casino (351 Main St., 208/726-3200) isn't a place where you'd really gamble, but you can bet on it. Here since 1936, it's had decades to become what it is: a place with three pool tables, a long, long bar, $2 Pabst on tap, and some micros.

The Pioneer Saloon (308 N. Main St., 208/726-3139) is just that. Once a place where mountain men and frontiersmen hung out and conducted business over a drink and a handshake, it still has an authentic saloon-style atmosphere. The restaurant's fancy, although the lounge and bar are where you'd want to relax at the end of the day.

Shut-Eye

You shouldn't have any trouble finding a place to bunk down. Even if everything's full in Ketchum, you have two options: Lodging's available and less expensive 10 miles south in Hailey and 15 miles south in Bellevue. In addition to motels, in Ketchum you're surrounded by the Sawtooth National Recreational Area—which is government-owned land, so camping's free in the wilderness (although not at serviced campsites).

Motels and Motor Courts

Here and throughout Idaho, a *free* service that'll save you the trouble of finding the right lodging is the McCall-based www.inidaho.com. For rates and references to hotels, cabins, condos, and inns, call 800/844-3246 or check www.inidaho.com. It also creates packages that combine lodging with outdoor adventures such as rafting and trail rides.

Chain Drive

A, B

Chain hotels are in town, or within 10 miles. See cross-reference guide featuring phone numbers and Web addresses on page 514.

On the Road: Ketchum/Sun Valley to McCall

Somewhat challenging and almost always picturesque, the trip north will put you in the midst of some tricky riding and the beauty of four scenic routes.

As you get started on the Sawtooth Scenic Byway (aka Route 75), the often elaborate homes and condos of Ketchum will fill the roadside. Some are delicately and expertly constructed for CEOs and CFOs, while other older shacks look like shop-class projects after the kids got hold of a case of wood glue. The residences gradually taper off and disappear and are replaced by wooden structures known locally as spruce, aspen, fir, ponderosa, and lodgepole pine.

If you plan on camping or spending more time in the region, about eight miles north of Ketchum, just past the Big Wood River, is the headquarters of the **Sawtooth National Recreational Area** (208/727-5013 or 208/727-5000, www.fs.fed.us/r4/sawtooth), a great stop for information. There's a steady incline to the road, and while it's not a dramatic ascent, what it delivers for the next 20 miles is the money shot. As you ride, the breadth and width of land are sensational, with straights stretched taut across the plains. As this rekindles memories of the road from Boise, you'll run into steeper drives that haul you into the heart of the Sawtooth Mountains.

Now it's Miller Time. If viewed from space, the road ahead would appear to be scribbling back and forth like a seismograph needle during an earthquake. Now you get to take full advantage of it. For several miles, your attention will switch from the road to the drops to the curves, and as you navigate these jigsaw ridges and twisted corners, you may be looking at high-elevation pine trees still sugar-coated with snow. Eventually, you'll reach the road to the **Galena**

Sun Valley

You already know the story of Sun Valley, but what's it all about? Basically, it's accepted as "America's First Destination Resort," and it may well be. It's also something of an artificial city that has everything a real city does. Just a short walk east of downtown Ketchum, **Sun Valley** (208/622-2001 or 800/786-8259, www.sunvalley.com) is centered around the main hotel that was built in 1936, and at the lodge are a few restaurants, a sports lounge, and a circular heated pool that looks hedonistic when it's steaming in the cool months. There's a vintage six-lane bowling alley in the basement, and behind the lodge is an ice-skating rink where Olympic skaters practice during the day and appear in a popular, free ice show each Saturday in the summer. On the second floor, Room 206 was Ernest Hemingway's favorite and where he wrote *For Whom The Bell Tolls*.

Down a winding sidewalk, a mock Alpine village features more of the resort's dozen stores, 13 restaurants, and five bars, as well as a theater where, each afternoon at 5, you can watch *Sun Valley Serenade*, filmed here in 1941. Elsewhere, you'll find a shooting club, trail rides, ski lifts, and golf.

It's a neat little operation, and the best part of it all is that it's not so expensive. Travel between seasons and you can get one of its 500 rooms for less than a hundred bucks.

Lodge (208/726-4010, www.galenalodge.com), an old resort that's managed to survive and become a landmark destination.

Racing another five miles and several hundred feet higher into the atmosphere, you'll tackle six-degree grades to reach the 8,701-foot summit at Galena Pass. Two miles ahead, your reward is reaching one of the nation's finest overlooks. More than a mile below and shooting clear to the northern horizon is Sawtooth Valley. I'd argue that scenes like this have appeared on too many postcards, calendars, and inspirational bookmarks, but the real-life sight of this hallowed ground drives home the absolute beauty we're blessed with in America. Quite a while passed as I contemplated this vision, and even though the miniscule images I collected on camera will never do it justice, I hope they add something to my new calendar of postcard-sized inspirational bookmarks.

After meditating, you and your bike fall down the mountain, rolling around corners that lead to Smiley Creek, an out-of-place place marked by the **Smiley Creek Lodge** (208/774-3547), a store and restaurant and lodge that offers cabins and teepees. Now there's nothing between you and the town of Stanley. Really, there's nothing. Around you, it's a Cinemascope view of the world, with nothing for more than 20 miles except flat-open land stretched across the earth, tacked down by mountains on the horizon. Just south of Stanley, though, on the laserbeam straight near mile marker 174, look for the pullout where you can park and look around. Do this and shut off the bike. With pure silence as a soundtrack, tune into the sound of the wind and birds you can hear, but which may seem lost in the emptiness. Around you is an almost complete circle of the mountains, which pulls your view from side to side to see the sharp peaks of the Sawtooth Range and then to the Salmon River that leaps into view, kept at a distance behind a crisscrossed timber fence.

Only a mile ahead at the junction of 75 and 21 is the town of Stanley. Stanley gets an unusual amount of attention, roughly as much as Chicago, but when you ride in, you may wonder why. It's quite desolate and quite strange, and even though it's as small as a residential subdivision, there are tens of thousands of travelers who join Stanley's 100 residents for backcountry hiking, rock climbing, white-water rafting, and all the things outdoor adventurers do outdoors. If this style of solitude appeals to you, the **Mountain Village Resort** (800/843-5475, www.mountainvillage.com) anchors a combination market, service station, motel, and restaurant, all run by the same family. Make use of the gas pumps—there won't be any for quite a while.

Having completed the Sawtooth Scenic Byway, you'll head west on 21, which puts you on the Ponderosa Pine Scenic Route, the habitat of eagles, osprey, heron, elk, deer, bear, and fox. For several miles, though, scenic is just a rumor. Routine views and mile after mile of straight riding through a low-key forest sets the tone as you enter what could be grazing land where nothing's grazing. As on the ride out of Ketchum, though, things are happening behind the scenes. You are in the Salmon-Challis National Forest on a plateau that's slowly and surely increasing in elevation. The lack of traffic may trigger the part of your brain that says "ride faster," and if you do, you'll quicken your arrival to Banner Summit, at an elevation of 7,200 feet.

Although there are no open views from the summit, what did draw my attention were the snow drifts that, I learned, had shut the road down only a few days earlier. Keep in mind this was in late May. The weather here can get squirrelly, and had the gates been down to block my path, I'd have been forced to double back to Ketchum. To be safe, call the **Idaho Transportation Department's Road Reports** (888/432-7623) to check road closures.

As you ride, on your left is the Sawtooth Wilderness Area and its 217,000 acres of ponderosa pine and steelhead fishing. On the right is the Challis National Forest, gateway to the 2.3-million-acre Frank Church River of No Return Wilderness Area, where there are fewer roads than anywhere else in the Lower 48. Nearly 40 miles out of Stanley, the mountains become steeper and more angular, and the South Fork of the Payette River introduces itself and decides to stay with you for the next 50 miles to Banks. It's a great riding partner, sticking with you when it narrows to a mere stream just a few feet from the road, and still hanging around when it switches to furious rapids in a chasm far below.

The cliffs and low mountains, jackstraw pines, and loneliness of the ride continue for 20 more miles to Lowman, which is a town like Stanley's a town. You've ridden 120 miles now, and although 21 makes a buttonhook to the south at Lowman, veer to the right to follow a new part of the route, the Wildlife Canyon Scenic Byway. For quite a stretch, this is a paved pep pill, with 25-mph curves and fast ascents that bring to mind the Scottish Highlands, as the lanes reach higher and the canyons plummet deeper. Signs warn you to watch for hikers and falling rocks, and with the pitch of the terrain, you'd expect to see falling hikers. Seriously, what you watch for are not huge boulders that'll knock you off your bike, but the hundred small chunks of gravel that'll knock your bike off you.

Curves start shaking fast and furious here because—as you've probably learned—the roads that always seem right are the ones that follow the free-form flow of a wild river. It's true in the Smoky Mountains, in Arizona, and right here. The Payette River leads through remote country, even more remote than what you challenged south of Stanley.

The land changes again, with green swaths created where the Payette meets another creek, and civilization comes back near Garden Valley, with its churches and sporadic log cabins. After 10 miles of this high-test scenery, the byway spits you out at Route 55 and the town of Banks. Although you'll be heading north, just a few hundred yards south is the kind of diner that you've frequented from Acadia to San Simeon. The **Banks Country Store and Café** (208/793-2617) has been here since 1915, serving its first guests slightly more than a decade after the invention of Ford's motorcar. With nearly a century of experience, it's learned its lessons well. When you stop for lunch (no gas), you can recall the beauty of the ride so far and enjoy the freedom of feasting on a Big Bubba burger at a table by the river.

Turning true north once again, you've reached the fourth of the day's scenic runs: the Payette River National Scenic Byway. Like Cash's ring of fire, you're going down, down, down, swallowed by the gravity of the river in the heart of a gorge. There's not much to look at, but there's so much to see. An old swinging bridge and the pullout where you can stop and listen to the crushing sounds of the river. The pine forest layered through here in a nice wooded ride within the Boise National Forest. The river and a railroad track on the far bank following you around curves and across bridges and into the backcountry.

This joy continues for miles and slowly gives way to flatlands near Smiths Ferry, where the **Cougar Mountain Lodge** (208/382-4464), a convenient market and bar and motel, appears out of thin air. Surrounding you is the Round Valley, an area that takes on a Swiss, rather than Scottish, visage—which is important because it gives me the rare opportunity to use the word "visage." The thin river that you recall from earlier is now the wide North Fork of the Payette, seen across the pastures far to your left. The ground is coated with sandbars, driftwood, and rocks, and a waterfall appears as you close in on the start of a four-mile stretch of S-curves and vertical mountain slopes that make you feel somewhat vulnerable until you reach a safe pocket of civilization in Cascade. I'm sure there are things here besides the retro Chief Hotel sign, but that's all I remember about it.

North of town, the swift and sharp road darts through the center of hills and beside a lake. Horses graze and trot on the plains, but they're enjoying the outdoors only half as much as you. The wide-ranging range is split by the Gold Fork River, where you'll see the entirety of Donnelly and its little red schoolhouse before graduating, 13 miles later, to the second-most popular tourist destination in Idaho.

Last call for McCall.

McCall Primer

Like nearly every area in the nation, the Long Valley region of Idaho was populated by Native Americans; in this case, the Shoshone, Bannock, and Nez Perce tribes. Eventually, as Chief Joseph of the Nez Perce was pursued into submission, there was a void to fill. So, in 1891, on the shores of Payette Lake, homesteader Tom McCall arrived in the area that would become his namesake. Thanks to help from more than 30,000 Chinese workers, the Warren and Marshall Mountain Mining District fueled the area's economy, with McCall's Brown Tie and Lumber Company hiring the bulk of the town's citizens. Naturally, the twin industries sparked a loose and open society highlighted by lakeside whorehouses, dance halls, and casinos. Sadly, they are gone now, but their effects lasted for decades. Guns were finally banned from local bars only in the early 1980s.

The arrival of the Tamarack Resort, about 15 miles south, helped sustain McCall's appeal—and today, the town is the second-most popular resort destination in the state, which begs the question: Why is it so small? I cannot tell you.

On the Road: McCall

As I hinted above, the center of town is about the size of a walnut, and there may not be much to hold your interest—but after a great ride up here, you may be satisfied just walking around town. Another option is cruising up the west shore of Payette Lake on Warren Wagon Road, en route for a circle tour up and around the lake. Pick up a map at the visitors center, and you'll see that, near the terminus of the loop, a scenic overlook on a peninsula is accessible via Scenic Drive.

If you do walk around town, you'll be surprised to find you can cover the whole thing on foot in a few hours, tops. In the center of town, you're at the south end of the lake. A few blocks west is the **Manchester Ice and Event Center** (200 E. Lake St., 208/634-3570), an impressive facility that occupies a good chunk of prime real estate and is open for ice hockey, curling, and skating.

From here on out, the day is yours.

Pull It Over: McCall Highlights
Attractions and Adventures

McCall is within the **Payette National Forest** (208/634-0700), a massive parcel of land that contains more than 2,100 miles of trails, 2,500 miles of roads, 15,000 miles of streams and rivers, and 30 campgrounds. Within the national forest on the eastern and northern shores of the lake is the **Ponderosa State Park** (208/634-2164), the peninsula that leads to the scenic overlook.

The park is on the shores of Payette Lake, a 5,377-acre playground that's nearly two miles wide, more than six miles long, and as much as 300 feet deep. With that in mind, you'd be missing a lot if you didn't check in with **Cheap Thrills Rentals** (303 N. 3rd/Hwy. 55, 208/634-7472 or 800/831-1025, www.cheapthrillsrentals.com). It rents boats, wave runners, and water tow-toys that'll get you cooled off while heating things up in the middle of the lake.

Shopping

With so little ground to cover, there are just a few places to hit. One, in my opinion, was a pretty cool shop called the **Granite Mountain Nature Gallery** (317 E. Lake St., 208/634-1111), in the small McCall Mall. Dennis DeLaet is passionate and tuned in to his one-of-a-kind fossils of starfish and trilobytes and plants, and what's so cool about all this is the age of these things: between 40 million and 500 million years old. He also peddles shadowboxes of butterflies and butterfly wings (made in Mexico—illegal here), as well as displays of some of the creepiest-ass insects I've ever seen, including the cave spider, a grossly overgrown arachnid nearly 10 inches in diameter.

Aside from the standard gift shops in town, **McCall Drug** (1001 2nd St., 208/634-2433) may look suspiciously familiar if you can recall drugstores from the 1950s. This place encompasses everything, including a pharmacy, toys, a record store, office supplies, a bookshop, a candy counter, and a soda fountain that serves huckleberry milkshakes. Dig the nostalgic Johnson's Toasted Nut display case with a rotating pan.

Blue-Plate Specials

A few miles from town on the west side of the lake is **Lardo's** (600 W. Lake St., 208/634-8191), a big, barnlike restaurant and saloon where locals hang out. The name, by the way, stems from the tale of an overturned wagon that dumped out a shipment of fat here. The entrées, though, are more appetizing, with the menu listing "old-time spaghetti" (whatever that means), as well as assorted configurations of the "famous" Lardo Burger and fries. After dinner, you may find yourself hanging out at the bar.

The Mill (326 N. 3rd St./Hwy. 55, 208/634-7683) seems to be the center of McCall's social circle. It's usually the first place locals recommend, although you may have to visit the bank before dining. You enter what feels like an old mine and arrive at a circular fireplace where chairs, some made from old ski lifts, provide a comfortable place to hang out and go to work on a drink. The low-ceiling dining room's down another mine shaft, where you sit down to a big dinner of Western beef: strip steak, ribeye, tenderloin, porterhouse, and prime rib. Connected to the restaurant, **Beside the Mill** is a sports bar with seven televisions, cocktails, specialty drinks, pool, and darts.

Watering Holes

In addition to hunkering down at the warm bars of Lardo's and The Mill, the local brewpub is the self-explanatory **McCall Brewing Company** (807 N. 3rd St., 208/634-3309), where cowboys, blue collars, and mountain men hang out and watch sports to the accompaniment of the pub's eight brewed beers. To temper the alcohol content, the kitchen whips up burgers, sandwiches, prime rib, and sirloin. Dine inside or grab some basic grub on the rooftop beer garden.

Shut-Eye

When in Idaho, consider checking with www.inidaho.com, 800/844-3246. It can give you rates and references to hotels, cabins, condos, and inns here in McCall and throughout the state.

Motels and Motor Courts
One of the smartest-looking motor courts I've seen is the **Brundage Bungalows** (1005 W. Lake St., 208/634-2344 or 800/643-2009, www.brundage vacations.com, $99 peak season). The rooms are across the street from Payette Lake and have that cool old-fashioned knotty pine or log interior. Some have fireplaces and some have a kitchen or kitchenette—but all are really cool. The same folks also rent rooms at the Brundage Inn and Brundage Motel. The larger cabins sleep as many as six.

Chain Drive
A, L, CC

Chain hotels are in town, or within 10 miles. See cross-reference guide featuring phone numbers and Web addresses on page 514.

Inn-dependence
Opened in 1904, the **Hotel McCall** (1101 N. 3rd St., 208/634-8105 or 866/800-1183, www.mccall-idchamber.org, $60–125 and up) is close to an inn—it's the largest hotel in town and sits within a few feet of Payette Lake. In addition to a clean, old-fashioned feel in its 34 rooms, there's a library, lounge, and the Epicurean, the in-house restaurant that serves award-winning beef Wellington, chicken and crawfish crêpes, rack of lamb, and New York strip.

Resources for Riders

Sawtooth Range Run

Idaho Travel Information
Idaho Outfitters and Guides Association—208/342-1919 or
    800/49-IDAHO (800/494-3246), www.ioga.org
Idaho Parks and Recreation—208/334-4199, www.idahoparks.org
Idaho Road Reports—888/432-7623
Idaho Travel—208/334-2470, www.visitid.org
Idaho Vacation and Travel Assistance—800/844-3246,
    www.inidaho.com

Local and Regional Information
Boise Convention and Visitors Bureau, 208/344-7777 or 800/635-5240,
    www.boise.org
Ketchum Visitors Center—800/634-3347, www.visitsunvalley.com
McCall Chamber of Commerce—208/634-7631 or 800/260-5130,
    www.mccall-idchamber.org
Payette National Forest—208/634-0700
Sawtooth National Recreation Area —208/727-5013,
    www.fs.fed.us/r4/sawtooth
Stanley Ranger Station—208/774-3000
Stanley-Sawtooth Chamber of Commerce—208/774-3411 or
    800/878-7950, www.stanleycc.org

Idaho Motorcycle Shops
Big Dog Motorcycle Boise—1450 S. Maple Grove Rd., 208/323-4636
Boise Cycle—9621 Ustick Rd., Boise, 208/375-9431,
    www.boisecycle.com
Cycle Nuts & Bolts Harley-Davidson—3602 W. Chinden Blvd., Boise,
    208/331-2938 or 800/666-4644, www.cyclenuts.com
Easy Rider Performance Cycle—4545 W. Chinden Blvd., Boise,
    208/376-4664
Hinson Power Sports—13924 Hwy. 55, McCall, 208/634-7007,
    www.hinsonpowersports.com
Meridian Cycles—7015 W. Fairview Ave., Boise, 208/375-7563
Mountain Thunder Motor Sports—345 Lewis St., Ketchum, 208/726-
    4221, www.mountainthundermotorsports.com
Stan's Motorcycles—2909 S. Curtis Rd., Boise, 208/562-0400

Washington State Run

Seattle, Washington to Port Townsend, Washington

Washington is a big state with more than its share of natural beauty. The mountains are snowcapped even in summer, and the glacier lakes, bays, and islands are more striking than any postcard you've seen.

Unlike other rides described in this book, this tour has no perfect beginning point. The downside of Washington is that many of its back roads are poorly marked, and blue highways are often clogged with local traffic and logging trucks. Additional drawbacks include the small window of warm riding time (summer), perpetual rains west of the Cascades, and towns either too small or too large to enhance a ride. Consider this an introduction to a state too vast to condense in a single chapter.

On the Road: Seattle to La Conner

From Seattle, you can ride to Mount Rainier, Mount St. Helens, or the Olympic National Forest, but there's never a perfect combination of roads and walking towns within reach. On the other hand, you can get a good glimpse of the Washington countryside by leaving the Seattle area en route to some small towns.

I-90 out of Seattle reveals why this state is so popular. Even the federal highway is scenic. The road extricates you from city traffic and suddenly, you're riding a wide, flowing road past lakes and mountains—and then, when

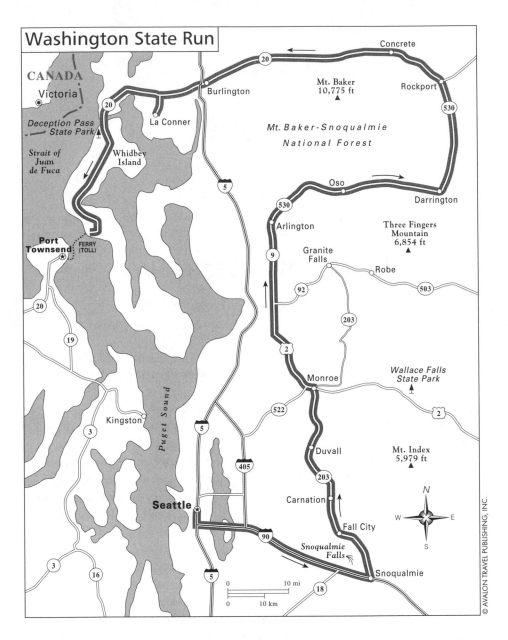

Washington State Run

CANADA
Victoria

Deception Pass State Park

Strait of Juan de Fuca

Whidbey Island

Port Townsend · FERRY (TOLL)

Burlington

La Conner

20

Concrete

Mt. Baker
10,775 ft ▲

Rockport

530

Mt. Baker-Snoqualmie
National Forest

Oso

Darrington

530

Arlington

Three Fingers
Mountain
6,854 ft ▲

Granite
Falls

Robe

9

92

503

203

2

Monroe

Wallace Falls
State Park

2

522

Duvall

Mt. Index
5,979 ft ▲

203

Carnation

5

Kingston

Puget Sound

405

3

Seattle

N
W   E
S

90

Fall City

Snoqualmie
Falls

5

3

16

5

18

Snoqualmie

0   10 mi
0   10 km

20

19

20

© AVALON TRAVEL PUBLISHING, INC.

Route: Seattle to Port Townsend via Snoqualmie, Fall City, Carnation, Duvall, Monroe, Arlington, Darrington, Whidbey Island

Distance: Approximately 245 miles; consider four days with stops.

•Day 1—Seattle/Travel •Day 2—La Conner •Day 3—La Conner/Travel •Day 4—Port Townsend

First Leg: Seattle to La Conner (196 miles)

Second Leg: La Conner to Port Townsend (46 miles)

Helmet Laws: Washington requires helmets.

you reach the exit for Snoqualmie, into even more desolate countryside. If you ever watched the cult favorite *Twin Peaks,* you'll recognize the speck known as Snoqualmie by its main attraction: Snoqualmie Falls. Follow the signs to the village and ride to the **Salish Lodge** (425/888-2556 or 800/272-5474, www.salishlodge.com, $189 and up off-season).

Outside the lodge, park at the adjacent parking area and walk to the gazebo, a great spot for watching and hearing the thunderous waters. At 270 feet, Snoqualmie is 100 feet higher than Niagara and kicks out spray for hundreds of yards. Be sure to pack a lunch, and then settle at a picnic table or, if you have time and a healthy heart, take the half-mile trail that winds down to the riverbanks. Add the fragrance and brilliance of the flowers and the sounds of nature and this is a must-see. If you can swing the price for a room, the lodge may be a good place to start—or stop. The spa here combines the styles of Asia and the Pacific Northwest. Fireplace-equipped rooms are indulgent, and the setting is a visual tranquilizer.

If you're ready to move on, the falls are a perfect introduction to a road that runs briefly through a dynamite combination of woods, rivers, and hills. Canopy roads give way to country roads, and soon you reach the junction of Route 203 at Fall City. Turn right onto 203 or, if you ride another hundred yards past the bridge, you may elect to make a stop at the **Last Frontier Saloon** (425/222-5640). Here since 1941, it's the only place I've seen where the bartender I met seemed more gassed than the barflies.

When you return to 203, head north toward Carnation and Monroe. The two-lane road is level and winds slightly on the way to Carnation, a nice small town, but what comes next is more appealing. On your way out, you'll cross a bridge and then enter green fields and great valleys, a subtle version of Vermont's Route 100.

After riding through Duvall, you'll reach Monroe, which is also a small town but features a few restaurants and pubs. Although maps show 203 continuing north to Granite Falls, the road actually ends here, and unless you're Ernest T. Bass or a logger, you won't be able to navigate the unmarked mountain roads. Instead, you'll have to bite the bullet and ride Highway 2 West, which navigates dense growth before freeing you into miles of farmland and then dumping you onto Highway 9 North. This isn't a great road, but the Mountain Loop Road to Darrington usually is not an option, since there's a long section of gravel (or late snows) that makes it impassable. Option B takes you up to Arlington, where the ride gets nice in a hurry.

Get onto Route 530 toward Darrington, a short 25 miles away. This is what you've been waiting for. Instantly, the road gets better and wider, and you're riding between Washington majestic mountains. The smells are hearty; the grass is plump. Tufts of clouds stuffed between the summits slowly tug at their granite mooring, break free, and drift away. Even in early summer, slivers of snow from the peaks pierce into the woods below.

Past the town of Oso, pull off alongside the creek, and everything is perfect—with the glaring exception of clear-cut forests that have scarred the mountaintops.

Then comes Darrington. Stay on Route 530 North through the Mount Baker-Snoqualmie National Forest for another great moment in motorcycling. After every slow corner comes a magnificent run through a tunnel of 50-foot straight-as-nails pines. This wonderful road runs beside and over the Sauk River, not terribly far from the dense urban traffic surrounding Seattle and Puget Sound.

The woods continue on both sides and the air is fresh. At mile marker 60, the river, woods, and mountains converge, and the twisty roads drop you past meadows, moss, and an almost fluorescent green landscape.

When you reach Highway 20 at Rockport (there's a gas station here), turn left. Around here, natural beauty takes a backseat to small towns like Concrete and larger ones like Sedro Woolley. Be prepared for a decent, though not breathtaking, ride. Once you cross beneath I-5, the mood of the road switches instantly from commercial to agricultural.

Farmland stretches from horizon to horizon. When you reach the turnoff to La Conner, ride on over to tulip town.

The Roozengaarde Gardens sit outside La Conner. La Conner exports more tulip bulbs than Holland.

La Conner Primer

A town built on a trading post, shipping industry, canneries, and farms, La Conner ultimately became a retreat for artists and writers. On a point of land inaccessible by rail, folks had to make an effort to reach it. Not much has changed since then. Commercial development hit Skagit County, but distance has preserved La Conner. It remains a waterfront community relatively unaffected by the explosion of technology and music a few hours south in Seattle. Victorian-era buildings are still in use more than a hundred years later; pleasure boats are moored in the Swinomish Channel; and countless acres of fields burst into a rainbow each April when the tulips are in bloom. In fact, La Conner claims to export more tulip bulbs than the whole of Holland.

On the Road: La Conner

At first glance, it doesn't seem as if La Conner would be intriguing or popular. But it is, and here's why.

In addition to hosting springtime's omnipresent tulips, the town has reinvented itself as an artists' colony. There are galleries and pubs and antique shops and restaurants in one condensed area, so you can park your bike and easily explore everything on foot. La Conner's other advantage is its location. Equidistant from Seattle and Vancouver, the town is invaded every Friday by weekenders from both cities.

This is the kind of town I prefer on a ride—not so large you think you've missed something, and not so small you go stir-crazy. You can ride past the flower fields on the way out of town, but first just park your bike and walk down to 1st Street.

This could fill an afternoon and give you a place to relax at night. Notice the street window artwork displays: Based on nature, most wood carvings, glassware, and paintings include grizzly bears, eagles, wolves, or a combination of the three.

The chamber of commerce offers tours of historic homes, and whale-watching cruises are available, but you don't really need to do anything. Just enjoy the town at a leisurely pace, give yourself time to relax, ride across the Rainbow Bridge once or twice, and then just kick back and watch the flowers grow.

Pull It Over: La Conner Highlights
Shopping

Jon Peterson's got a limited market, but if you collect antique fishing tackle, pay a visit to **Plug Ugly** (313 E. Morris St., 360/466-1212). Open 11 A.M.–5 P.M. Thursday–Sunday, this place sells duck decoys and marine gear as well.

Good thing La Conner has a well-stocked grocery store like **Pioneer Market** (416 Morris St., 360/466-0188). This way, you can stock up on road food and supplies before you go. Even better, it's open 'til 10 every night.

Blue-Plate Specials

On the outskirts of town just off Highway 20, **The Farmhouse Restaurant** (13724 La Conner-Whitney Rd., 360/466-4411) serves old-fashioned big road food for breakfast, lunch, and dinner. Within this cavernous restaurant, you can get platters filled with steak, ham, chicken 'n' dumplings, grilled pork chops, hot turkey sandwiches, pies, and cakes. After dinner here, I puffed up to 438 pounds.

Not only is **La Conner Brewing Company** (117 S. 1st St., 360/466-1415, www.laconnerbrewing.com) a warm and intimate little restaurant serving wood-fired pizzas, soups, wings, quesadillas, and salads for lunch and dinner. It also has a great and active bar serving wines, ales, lagers, porters, stouts, pilsners, and dopple bocks. Can you believe it? Dopple bocks!

La Conner Seafood and Prime Rib House (614 1st St., 360/466-4014) is a traditional waterfront hangout open for lunch and dinner. Using only fish and meat, this restaurant has created about 100 different dishes—firecracker prawns, shrimp-smothered red snapper, Cajun prime rib, and more.

Watering Holes

If the Brewing Company's too tidy, **La Conner Pub** (702 S. 1st St., 360/466-9932) is the alternative. This blue-collar bar has two pool tables, some old guys, a few young'uns, bottled and tap beers, and a full bar open until at least 1 A.M. Why there's a family restaurant attached is beyond me.

Shut-Eye

La Conner offers relatively limited lodging choices, most of them inns. Motels and chains are more than 10 miles east or west of town. Contact

Company Snapshot: Kawasaki

Shozo Kawasaki got a head start on other motorcycling manufacturers, but he did it by way of steamships, helicopters, bridges, trains, and robots. Founded in 1878, Kawasaki Heavy Industries built its reputation by building big things—including aircraft during World War II. Post-World War II production, however, required a new product centered around its new small, lightweight engines. The Meguro Manufacturing Company, Japan's oldest motorcycle company, made frames that were a perfect fit for Kawasaki's engines, so Kawasaki bought the company. By 1961, it was producing a line of bikes ranging from 50 to 500 ccs.

Kawasaki didn't begin to crack the American market until 1965. When it opened its U.S. headquarters in an old meat warehouse in Chicago, it had no customers and no distributors, but that didn't stop it from selling a small, two-stroke bike called the Omega. It seemed to click, so Kawasaki built the Samurai and Avenger, a pair of rotary valve twins. In 1969 came the 500cc Mach III two-stroke triple, followed in 1973 by the four-cylinder 900cc Z1. Kawasaki was a player.

the **La Conner Chamber of Commerce** (360/466-4778 or 888/642-9284, www.laconner-chamber.com) for additional recommendations.

Inn-dependence

The **Wild Iris Inn** (117–121 Maple Ave., 360/466-1400, www.wildiris.com, $109–189) has 20 large rooms—12 with hot tubs—and provides a full breakfast. More basic, the **La Conner Country Inn** (107 S. 2nd St., 360/466-3101, www.laconnerlodging.com, $95–120) provides its guests generic, motel-like rooms (some with king beds). The homemade breakfast is included.

On the Road: La Conner to Port Townsend

When you're ready to leave La Conner behind, look for Morris Street, which bypasses Highway 20. This short detour will take you to a patch of beautiful farmland. Less than a half mile from town, Morris Street zigzags and turns into Chilberg; once you've ridden past Best Road, start looking for Beaver Marsh Road. Turn left here and cruise down a few more miles to **Roozengaarde**

(15867 Beaver Marsh Rd., 360/424-8531), a small garden of multicolored tulips that will give you an idea of what the fields look like when they're in bloom. Though it's an excellent photo op, remember not to ride your bike over the flower beds. Open 9 A.M.–5 P.M. Monday–Saturday. Admission is free.

When you leave, follow Beaver Marsh to your right and then take another right at McLean Road, where, if you need some supplies, you can stop in at the **Evergreen Grocery Store** (16016 McLean Rd., 360/424-4377). After you pick up supplies, head a few blocks more to Avon-Allen Road, where you'll hang a left to wind back up on Highway 20—the last number you'll have to think about for the next several days.

With the Washington breeze in your face, you'll pass sporadic mountains and a few commercial enterprises before turning left to follow 20 toward Whidbey Island. The island's just about a dozen miles away and marks the entrance to the Olympic Peninsula. Once you make this turn, images from rides past will flash into mind; the start of this ride is comparable to the Berkshires, Yosemite, and the Blue Ridge Parkway.

On your right, you'll see glacier lakes that look frigid even at the height of summer. Near mile marker 43, watch for Pass Lake and a pullout where, if you're riding in a group, you can get a shot with the lake and mountain as a backdrop.

This level of scenery continues for several miles, bringing to mind the look of a 1940s *Field and Stream* magazine. Ahead, the Straits of Juan De Fuca can be seen to the right, but one of the most impressive sights of the trip arrives as you round the corner and approach Deception Pass. Where the Canoe Pass and Deception Pass bridges span a huge gorge, the vista is breathtaking. At the bottom, blue-green water rushes to the sea, and you'll spy massive trees washed ashore like twigs. It's a larger-than-life scene, and crossing this span is more thrilling than running the Golden Gate.

On the opposite side of the 976-foot bridge are restrooms, a parking area, and a trail that you should walk down even if you have a heart condition, gout, and a wooden leg. The views around each bend in the trail are fantastic, and the pine forest scents are reminiscent of a Christmas tree farm.

Less than a mile later, consider pulling into the free, 4,128-acre **Deception Pass State Park** (360/675-2417 or 360/675-7277, www.parks.wa.gov). Built primarily by the Civilian Conservation Corps in the 1930s, this marine and camping park boasts 30 miles of hiking trails, 19 miles of saltwater shoreline, three freshwater lakes, 246 campsites, freshwater swimming, fishing, and canoeing. The old-growth forest is sprinkled with cedar, spruce, yew, apple, and cherry trees, as well as fields of foxglove, lupines, rhododendron, and roses.

Due to the temperate climate here, wildlife thrives, and there's a strong chance you'll spy bald eagles in flight.

Now, I hate to have to break this to you, but following this spectacular introduction to Whidbey Island, the scenery fizzles. From here to Port Townsend, the landscape is pockmarked by random development, so even after you get your mojo going on a good run, it withers out when you encounter trailer parks and hideous commercial sprawl.

From south of Coupeville, all you need to do is watch for the turnoff to the **Port Townsend Ferry** (206/464-6400). For about $4, you and your machine can take a 30-minute sea cruise to one of the nicest towns on the peninsula.

Port Townsend Primer

Before Port Townsend was infected with quaintness, it was a real town—a real get-drunk-in-the-bar-get-laid-upstairs kind of town. A century ago, Port Townsend was home to 40 saloons and 17 brothels (the most prosperous of which was adjacent to City Hall). A writer visiting town remarked that the "stench of whiskey permeates Port Townsend to a depth of nine feet"—although no one knows how he measured it, and I lost the scent at four feet.

It was an affluent town that accommodated a thriving maritime port and the consulates of 17 countries. As in other resurrected cities, a period of decline was eased by the arrival of hippies in the 1970s. From the luxury of their smoke-filled VW buses, artists and writers emerged and fueled a creative spark that sustains itself today. The hippies grew up and learned business and restored old homes, and rich Californians came in and bought the homes and turned them into inns. And the town was turned around.

Oddly, citizens seem to take obsessive pride in the movie *An Officer and a Gentleman,* filmed here in the early '80s. If someone from Port Townsend were ever elected pope, you can bet the new pontiff would call himself Pope Zack Mayo in honor of Richard Gere's character. The film has become a religion.

What you'll see today is a tight-knit community that combines new money, young hippies, established businesses, and trendy shops in Woodstock-era ambience.

Far out.

On the Road: Port Townsend

Port Townsend poses a dilemma. If you check the map, **Olympic National Park** (360/565-3130, www.nps.gov/olym) seems so close, and a ferry trip to Victoria, British Columbia, looks tempting. I chose to hang out in town for several reasons. A trip to Victoria makes for a very long day—the ferry trip lasts several hours, and reaching the boat takes about as long. Olympic National Park didn't pan out either because, after riding halfway there, I realized that the road was beating me into submission with slow-moving traffic and a disturbing lack of scenery. Port Townsend calmed me down and kept me entertained. I was content. But if your schedule affords you more time, give them both a try.

Port Townsend is a great walking town, and the people are friendly. If you hang around town, definitely stop at **Bergstrom's Antique and Classic Autos** (809 Washington St., 360/385-5061). Based on the building's exterior, you wouldn't expect to find much, but inside you'll see motorcycle stuff, a '47 Cushman scooter, a '53 Triumph, and a '35 Cadillac, plus garage memorabilia, hubcaps, lighters, and technical manuals representing a fleet of antique cars.

A short ride away lies **Fort Worden State Park** (360/344-4431 or 360/344-4400, www.olympus.net/fortworden), which is where they filmed ... *An Officer and a Gentleman!* The base is closed now, which makes it even more intriguing to ride through. It looks like Fort Knox after Goldfinger's ladies sprayed the soldiers with knockout gas. There are parade grounds, officers' quarters, gun batteries, an artillery museum, a natural history museum, a theater, and a performing arts center, as well as nice shoreline beside the frigid waters of the straits. If you're traveling with a large group, you can reserve lodging space in some of the older, renovated barracks and officers' quarters.

With a decent map, you'll likely find some nearby back roads to satisfy your desire to explore, and you shouldn't miss the stretch of restaurants and stores in the section of town known as uptown Port Townsend, which is higher up the bluff. Aside from that, just appreciate the broad waters of the Straits of Juan De Fuca and the magnificence of Port Townsend Bay.

Pull It Over: Port Townsend Highlights
Attractions and Adventures

If you don't mind devoting touring time to a movie, you may as well do it at the restored **Rose Theatre,** (235 Taylor St., 360/385-1089, www.rose theatre.com). Show tickets cost $7. Buy some licorice and Necco wafers at the counter, and then sit back and listen to owner/preservationist Rocky Friedman introduce and explain the upcoming film—just the way it should be.

A center for maritime education, the **Wooden Boat Foundation** (Cupola House, Port Hudson, 360/385-3628, www.woodenboat.org) offers several courses—each of which will get you on the water. You can learn to sail a large wooden ship, sail a small wooden boat, or rent a rowboat and explore on your own. If you appreciate fine craftsmanship and tales of the sea, hang out at the chandlery and talk boats.

You cannot avoid fly-fishing in the Northwest. Do not even try. The folks at **Port Townsend Angler** (940 Water St., 360/379-3763, www.ptangler.com) have all the gear and arrange guides for fishing in streams and on the Sound. They claim this as the best spot for wild steelhead fishing in the lower 48. But it's an expensive hobby: A full day of fly-fishing for two will cost around $250, and gear will tack on another $35. Too much? A McFish sandwich costs two bucks.

Shopping

Joe Euro runs **Wine Seller** (940 Water St., 360/385-7673 or 888/286-7674, www.winespt.com), the oldest wine shop on the peninsula. Open 10:30 A.M.– 6 P.M. daily, the small shop features an array of wines (including generic "cheap white" and "cheap red" wines), plus cigars, gourmet cheese, smoked salmon, and free back issues of *Wine Spectator.*

Blue-Plate Specials

Silverwater Cafe (237 Taylor St., 360/385-6448, www.silverwatercafe .com), serving lunch and dinner, features creative spins on fresh seafood, meat, and vegetarian entrées. The meals are upscale, but the clientele casual—an unusual mix, but it works here. In its quiet corner location, you can dine in peace.

Also open for lunch and dinner, **Waterfront Pizza** (951 Water St., 360/385-6629) sells takeout by the slice downstairs, and the upstairs dining room serves pizza that keeps the locals coming back.

Watering Holes

Waterstreet Brewing and Ale House (639 Water St., 360/379-6438, www.waterstreetbrewing.com) sits on the site of the old Town Tavern and features an 1800s bar, three pool tables, two fireplaces, and a dozen beers on tap (six of them brewed right here).

Sirens (823 Water St., 360/379-1100), open 'til 2 A.M., is a real hipster's hootenanny, with local musicians playing jazz, blues, or rock to a packed bar full of their neighbors. The back porch looks out over the bay, making it a great spot to work on a pitcher of beer.

More coffeehouse than bar, **Upstage** (923 Washington St., 360/385-2216) pours wine and draft microbrews. An eclectic entertainment calendar changes nightly, featuring everything from open mike to blues to swing.

Shut-Eye

Surprisingly remote, Port Townsend does not have any chain hotels. It does, however, have plenty of inns. Check with the **Port Townsend Visitors Center** (360/385-2722 or 888/365-6978, www.ptguide.com) for the full slate, and consider this list just the tip of the iceberg.

Inn-dependence
The **Quimper Inn** (1306 Franklin St., 360/385-1060 or 800/557-1060, www.quimperinn.com, $98–165 year-round), a large 1888 home, rests on a hill overlooking Port Townsend. Elegant without the clutter. Kick back on the second-story terrace or relax in the living room and talk to innkeeper Ron Ramage about his Porsche collection and rebuilt trio of Triumphs. The **Palace Hotel** (1004 Water St., 360/385-0773 or 800/962-0741, www.palace hotelopt.com, $59–229) is a nicely restored 1889 hotel on the town's main drag. Large rooms and suites (ask for a private bath) sport an Old West look.

Resources for Riders

Washington State Run

Washington Travel Information
Washington State Ferries—206/464-6400, www.wsdot.wa.gov/ferries
Washington State Parks—360/902-8844 or 888/226-7688,
    www.parks.wa.gov
Washington State Road Conditions—800/695-7623
Washington State Tourism—800/544-1800,
    www.experiencewashington.com

Local and Regional Information
La Conner Chamber of Commerce—360/466-4778 or 888/642-9284,
    www.laconnerchamber.com
Mt. Baker-Snoqualmie National Forest—425/775-9702 or 800/627-
    0062, www.fs.fed.us/r6/mbs
Olympic Peninsula—360/437-0120, www.olympicpeninsula.org
Olympic Peninsula Bed & Breakfast Association—www.opbba.com
Port Townsend Visitors Center—360/385-2722 or 888/365-6978,
    www.ptguide.com
Whidbey Island Information—www.visitwhidbey.com

Washington Motorcycle Shops
Bellevue Kawasaki—14004 N.E. 20th St., Bellevue, 425/641-5040
Bellevue Suzuki-Ducati-Polaris—13029 N.E. 20th St., Bellevue, 425/882-
    4300, www.eastsidemotosports.com
Everett Powersports—215 S.W. Everett Mall Way, Everett, 423/437-
    4545, www.everettpowersports.com
I-90 Motorsports—200 N.E. Gilman Blvd., Issaquah, 425/391-4490,
    www.I-90motorsports.com
Port Townsend Honda—3059 Sims Way W., Port Townsend, 360/385-
    4559
Renton Motorcycle Co.—900 Lind Ave., Renton, 425/226-4320,
    www.rmcmotorsports.com

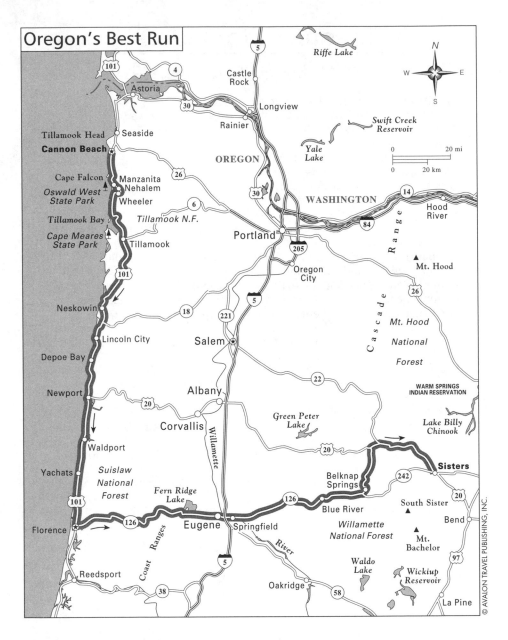

Oregon's Best Run

Route: Cannon Beach to Sisters via Manzanita, Tillamook, Lincoln City, Newport, Florence, Eugene, Vida, Santiam Pass

Distance: Approximately 325 miles; consider seven days with stops.

•**Days 1–2—Cannon Beach** •**Day 3—Travel** •**Day 4—Florence** •**Day 5—Travel** •**Days 6–7—Sisters**

First Leg: Cannon Beach to Florence (160 miles)

Second Leg: Florence to Sisters (165 miles)

Helmet Laws: Oregon requires helmets.

Oregon's Best Run

Cannon Beach, Oregon to Sisters, Oregon

Incredible coastal scenery, preserved courtesy of a visionary governor, creates a ceaselessly awe-inspiring tour. Begin in a beachside community that could serve as the model for future coastal towns, and then enjoy the finest 160-mile stretch of two-lane you may ever ride. Stop in an old town with character that's enveloped within a larger town lacking the same; hang around for an adrenaline-pumping, mind-blowing dune buggy attack on the sand; then head east, where the forests, falls, and mountains herald your arrival in a new Old West village.

Cannon Beach Primer

There are several dozen communities along Oregon's coast, and whether it was a river, a ravine, or a forest, each needed something to root the town as it grew. In Cannon Beach, it was a rock. Granted, it is not your ordinary rock. First of all, Haystack Rock really looks like a stack of hay. Second, it happens to be 235 feet tall, which makes it the third-largest coastal monolith in the world.

In addition to this icon, which you may have already seen on countless postcards and calendars, consider the origin of the town's name. In 1846, the U.S. Navy schooner *Shark* was pulling out of the Columbia River into the Pacific Ocean. After waves tore the ship to shreds, a section of the deck with a cannon and capstan on it floated down the coast and came to rest on a stretch of shore that would become known as Cannon Beach. Glad it wasn't the poop deck.

Also ranking high in the town's history is the Lewis and Clark Expedition. Cannon Beach was the farthest south the explorers traveled, venturing here for an overnight in 1806 when they heard they could carve some blubber off a dead whale. And that's it. A shipwreck, a rock, and a rotting whale anchored the town long enough for it to evolve into a natural preserve that some folks consider a mini-Carmel. It has art galleries, bistros, bookstores, kites, sandcastle contests, tide pools, hiking trails, natural sanctuaries, and a migration of tufted puffins that flock to Haystack Rock each year to lay their eggs.

That's been enough to see Cannon Beach through its sesquicentennial—and it should keep you satisfied for a few days.

On the Road: Cannon Beach

Cannon Beach is a place where you go to avoid having to go to your room. Each minute you're here, outdoors is where you want to be. To get outdoors, Hemlock is the street you'll need to know, since it's the main coastal route that leads to and through the center of town. With it, you can ride north to Ecola State Park or south to the beach, or stop in the middle and see the town. And it's worth seeing. After I get done cleaning out my gutters, I'm going to get started on building a beachside community of 1,600 people, and I'll use Cannon Beach as a blueprint. It's not so large as to be impersonal, or too small to be dull. Another bonus is that no building here is more than three stories tall, a far different architectural principle than you'll find on coastlines in Florida and California. In Oregon, the ocean is for everyone.

That said, the best way to see the best of Cannon Beach is to check out the attractions and adventures below.

Pull It Over: Cannon Beach Highlights
Attractions and Adventures

When I asked at the visitors center how someone would spend a perfect couple of days in Cannon Beach, I was sure they were wrong telling me to just head to **Ecola State Park** (503/436-2844 or 800/551-6949) and the tide pools at Haystack Rock. Then I went.

From the center of town, the road north connects with a fork that leads right onto Ecola Park Road and into the woods. Accustomed to Florida scrub pines, I had never seen anything like what was ahead: an old-growth rainforest where the trees were a near-luminescent green, which, when mixed with the fog and mist and the moisture, seemed strangely prehistoric. Riding this land of the lost in the midst of a stalled storm when the midday sun was hidden by rolling clouds was an exciting and, to be honest, eerie experience. The warped road passes massive trees and a forest bed of ferns before it reaches the ranger station, where you'll pay $3 for the day. What you'll see in a few minutes is worth that and far more.

From the parking area, a walkway leads to a lookout point, where you'll savor a vision that will last a lifetime, especially if you've never had the privilege of seeing the Pacific Ocean. The ocean is massive and awe-inspiring, with views seeming to last for billions of miles. To the south, several miles of arched shoreline are swept by an infinite series of waves. To the west, a column of curving rocks slips into the ocean like a dragon's tail. To the north, an inlet dips into shore and springs out again, directing your view to the Tillamook Rock Lighthouse, perched on a rock 12 miles offshore. Construction began in 1879 and took two years and the lives of a few workers before it went into service. Decommissioned in 1957, in 1980 it became—can you believe this—a columbarium! Twice a year, cremated ashes are flown out and deposited for an eternity at sea.

Sublime and weird things like this aren't all Ecola gives you. From the parking area, the Tillamook Head trail is an eight-mile walk to Seaside, while the Clatsop Loop Trail is a short, two-mile hiking path that connects Ecola Point to Indian Beach, following a path blazed by members of the Lewis and Clark Expedition. Elk graze in the meadows, eagles and falcons catch the currents, and in winter and summer, more than 20,000 gray whales pass by in the midst of a 12,000-mile migration. The spiritual effect of it all is ceaseless, magical, and a miracle. You'll be pleased to hear that you can look forward to 160 miles more of this on your journey south.

Descending from the hill, ride south again to the second stop: **Haystack Rock.** There are parking areas along Hemlock, although if you're staying at a beachside lodge, you'll just walk along the shore to reach it. What will you see when you're there? Tufted puffins, possibly. The chunky, pelagic seabird lives on land only when it's time to nest, hanging out here from the end of April to late July. Bring binoculars to spot the squat black body, white face, bright orange bill, and tufts of feathers above the eyes of the bird sailors call the "sea parrot." Sharing a piece of the rock with the puffins are pigeons, guillemots, cormorants, and seagulls, whose leisure time is occasionally interrupted by eagles, who swoop to the ground, isolate a gull like fighter pilots peel off bombers, and take it down.

It's unusual to admit there's pleasure in looking at a rock, but there is, although you may need the assistance of a ranger to understand what you're looking at. During the summer, volunteers are on the beach to host **Haystack Rock Awareness Programs** (503/436-1581, ext. 108) and explain the intricate ecosystem that supports dozens of creatures living in tide pools left by the receding ocean. Look closely, and in the shallows you'll see limpets, barnacles, starfish, hermit crabs, sea sculpins, and anemones. Be careful where you walk, and leave the creatures where they are.

If you have a hard time leaving the beach, plan to come back later. The oldest business in town is **Sea Ranch Stables** (415 Fir St., 503 436-2815, www.searanch.com). Here since 1927, it rents horses for daytime group rides between mid-May and Labor Day that follow the Ecola Creek to Chapman Point and south to Haystack Rock. When there's a low tide, moonlight rides are offered.

Shopping

Remember this while you visit Oregon: There's no sales tax. Keep this in mind when you buy food or souvenirs or a new bike. While you're in Cannon Beach, your best investment is walking around Hemlock Street. Granted, this delivers all the things a tacky tourist town should (taffy kitchens, T-shirt shops), but there are also places like **Mariner Market** (138 N. Hemlock, 503/436-2442). Sidewalk benches are reserved for Democrats or Republicans, and aisles are inventoried with beer, deli meals, tide charts, videos, groceries, ready-made and ready-to-be-prepared foods, and everything you'd need for a beachside cookout.

As you'll discover, the history and images of Oregon's coast, roads, and lighthouses is fascinating, and you can find good regional research materials at the library or at the **Cannon Beach Book Company** (130 N. Hemlock St., 503/436-1301).

Cannon Beach has earned a reputation as an artists' colony and, judging by many of the galleries here, I'd tend to agree. Not knowing your taste in art, I'd suggest you pay a preride virtual visit to see some of the extraordinary paintings, ceramics, oils, acrylics, and woodcarvings online via the **Cannon Beach Gallery Group** (www.cbgallerygroup.com).

I doubt you'll shout "Surf's up!" when it's bleak and drizzly and Oregon gray, but think how cool it'd be to tell your friends that you did. So whether you're a Gidget or a Grommet, you can shred a tube on a tri-skeg stick rented from **Cannon Beach Surf** (1088 S. Hemlock St., 503/436-0475, www.cannonbeachsurf.com). It offers lessons and rent wetsuits, skim boards, and boogie boards.

Blue-Plate Specials

Even though Cannon Beach features several great restaurants, think about dining at an open-air café: the beach. Bonfires are allowed, and at the Mariner Market you can stock up on hot dogs, marshmallows, corn, and everything else you'd need for a cookout and live it up at your personal make-shift oceanside restaurant. You don't even need a permit—all you need are matches. Just keep your fire at least 25 feet from wooden seawalls, beach grass, or driftwood, and don't wait for the tide to extinguish the flames when you're done. Do it yourself.

If the weather craps out and you're locked in your room, **Fultano's Pizza** (220 N. Hemlock, 503/436-9717) delivers traditional and gourmet pizza hot—steam lines drawn on the boxes attest to this. Its dining room, too, is an option.

The Lumberyard (264 3rd St., 503/436-0285) is a big Pacific Northwest–style restaurant where locals gather around the bar to draw on the 10 beers (some brewed here) served on tap in pint glasses. Diners settle into natural wood booths and dine on rotisserie-grilled chicken, pork loin, pot pie, turkey meat loaf, barbecue pork, oven-roasted pizzas, and plank salmon made in the open kitchen. It's also a great place to drop in for a nightcap. Big and clean and neat.

Before leaving town, load up at the **Pig 'N Pancake,** (223 S. Hemlock St., 503/436-2851). There are 35 varieties of breakfast here, something Einstein hypothesized in 1905. The kind of diner you look for when touring, it also offers homemade soups, chowders, and desserts, including some made from family recipes.

Watering Holes

For a small town, Cannon Beach has more than enough places to plan for the upcoming ride or take a break after riding over to the coast. One very good thing is that these places all seem to have a good vibe. Here are two of them. The grandpappy of most is **Bill's Tavern and Brewhouse** (188 Hemlock St., 503/436-2202), which opened as a café in 1923. The local gathering spot is in the heart of town, where you and your buddies can grab a booth and feast on hamburgers, fried oyster burgers, albacore, cod, and seafood stew. Along with beers made right here, there are about a dozen beers on tap in the warm, inviting bar.

The **Warren House** (3301 S. Hemlock St., 503/436-1130) is a smokehouse that serves burgers and steaks, which you can wash down with beers brewed here. The beer garden has an ocean view.

Shut-Eye

Although there are no chain hotels in Cannon Beach, there's something better: old-fashioned motor courts.

Motels and Motor Courts

Like most things, Cannon Beach does lodging well as well—although rates can double between winter and summer, so get ready to dig deep. There are condos, inns, and places like the triplex of **The Waves, Argonauta Inn,** and **White Heron Lodge,** (503/436-2205 or 800/822-2468, www.thewaves motel.com, $109 and up peak season). Under one owner, they occupy several sites and present a combination of choices that range from motel rooms to suites to home-style accommodations that have kitchens, fireplaces, and hot tubs. Rates can double for the homes and they may require a two-night minimum.

The **McBee Motel Cottages,** (888 S. Hemlock St., 503/436-1392 or 800/436-4107, www.mcbeecottages.com, $45 off-season, up to $115 in season) are a throwback to the days when folks would take motoring trips down the coast. Fitting, I guess, since the McBee opened in 1941. Just steps from the beach, the cottages are cozy, some units feature fireplaces and kitchens, and all have old-fashioned touches to complete the effect.

Chain Drive
A, C, L, CC

Chain hotels are eight miles north of Cannon Beach in Seaside. See cross-reference guide featuring phone numbers and Web addresses on page 514.

Inn-dependence
Stephanie Inn (2740 S. Pacific off Hemlock St., 503/436-2221 or 800/633-3466, www.stephanieinn.com, $189 and up) has a sissy name, but its 50 rooms are very large, well-appointed, and in high demand. Right on the ocean, this is very much like a lodge, with fresh cookies offered and the Chart Room open for afternoon wine socials and evening drinks. In its casually elegant dining room, it serves a four-course supper that sells out quickly. If you miss it, return for the breakfast buffet that's beyond belief.

On the Road: Cannon Beach to Florence

. . . and we have a winner. Of all the rides I've taken since 1974, this day's tour down Oregon's coast really did it for me. With no frame of reference to go on, nearly every turn delivered more than I thought was possible. I owe this to Oswald West (see sidebar) and U.S. 101. When planning most rides, I'd research alternate byways and look for other routes just in case the road fizzled out. This was different. The combination of Oregon's coast and U.S. 101 delivered mile after mile. In hindsight, though, I did err. I thought the first five miles were the finest "first five" I'd ever seen. It turned out that the first 20 miles (followed by the remaining 140) were truly great. Here's how your day will unfold.

Hemlock Street rolls out of Cannon Beach and slides into U.S. 101 about three miles south of town. Immediately the friendly scent of the pines joins you on a journey that adds close-up views of ravines, rainforests, and the Pacific on a winding stretch of two-lane traffic. The road has an old-fashioned feel to it—diners and motor courts would be right at home. Although they were absent, what did appear before me was a magnificent tunnel punched directly through the center of a mountain. It looked like one Wile E. Coyote would have painted on the side of a hill. It didn't seem real, but it is, and it is overwhelming.

Even at 45 mph, you won't ever feel rushed, because here and for the rest of the ride, there are frequent pullouts giving speeding cars the option to pass you. In these initial 10 miles, you set a pattern for the entire trek: You ride

a tunnel near the starting point of my favorite one-day ride south of Cannon Beach

Oswald West

It's a shame politicians these days have little interest or desire in creating something for the people. For inspiration, they should ride the Oregon Coast and think of Oswald West. I learned about West at the magnificent lookout point south of Cannon Beach, where a plaque offered a glimpse of his life and a reminder of what public service makes possible. He was described as a charismatic and intelligent man, with "a keen sense of humanity and an open mind." Tired of corruption in government but undaunted by a lack of funds and influential friends, he rode on horseback to campaign in small communities across the state. He ran to make a difference, and he won.

As you ride, you're experiencing one of the greatest achievements of "Governor Oz", as another plaque here attests: "If sight of sand and sky and sea has given respite from your daily cares, then pause to thank Oswald West, former governor of Oregon, 1911–1915. By his foresight, nearly 400 miles of the ocean shore were set aside for public use, from the Columbia River on the north to the California border on the south."

All hail the great and powerful Oz.

beside the ocean until the road weaves to the east, and that's when you enter the rainforests, where the trees and trunks and ferns are the same iridescent green that you found at Ecola. Past Necarney Creek, you'll enter the **Oswald West State Park,** and a few miles farther south, you can roll off to a pullout to see one of America's most marvelous overlooks. I'd like to say this panorama is picture-perfect, but a thousand pictures wouldn't even begin to convey how wonderful this is.

As a flatland Floridian, I've always held a sea-level view of the sea. Now I was hundreds of feet above the shoreline that opened up majestic views of the coast to the north and south, the endless waves flying past rocks and onto the curving beach. I stayed awhile to enjoy the free show, gave a silent thank-you, and then resumed the ride south. At 1,661 feet, upcoming Neahkahnie Mountain is one of the highest points along the coast. A seven-degree grade around its base follows, and the pleasure of the path increases as you ride. Things change slightly when you pass Manzanita and then enter Nehalem, where you'll wonder when things changed. Suddenly you're aware it's not the coast any more; you're in a valley surrounded by forests, rivers, and farmlands. If magically changing views like these don't do it for you, just stop your bike right now and take a bus home.

You'll cross the Nehalem River to enter Wheeler (pop. 330), where there's a visitors center and some antiques shops, and not much more than that. Afterward, as you ride to and through Rockaway Beach and Farview, the scenery suffers slightly, but you stick with it because you have no choice, and your gut tells you that soon you'll clear it to the coast. Personally, I admire the tenacity of residents in these small towns who stuck with it through financial hardships and are building communities to be proud of. One subtle yet intriguing feature that'll hold your attention is that each of these ordinary towns has a certain presence and personality. A prime example is the town of Garibaldi where, in the middle of extraordinary emptiness, is a monumental smokestack standing long after the lumber mill it served vanished into history.

Today, the smokestack towers over estuaries that rise and fall with the tide, so during the day, you'll ride beside a sea of mud as you cruise into the town of Tillamook, the "Land of Cheese, Trees, and Ocean Breeze." Yet another place I knew nothing about. When I arrived my gut instinct was to race through it and stay on a self-imposed schedule. But at the town's visitors center I was instructed to go next door to **Tillamook Cheese** (4175 U.S. 101, 503/815-1300 or 800/542-7290, www.tillamookcheese.com). Even though I really didn't want to see a cheese factory, I went, and I was honestly glad I did.

Inside, a self-guided tour leads to an observation platform where you watch a squad of Oompa-Loompa-like cheesemakers at belts and slicers and rollers, turning single 40-pound blocks of cheese into forty symmetrically sliced one-pound units, while across the hall, workers are whipping up and packaging ice cream. It was yet another of the day's surprises. I watched this for far longer than my doctor would have allowed before heading downstairs to a restaurant for a grilled cheese sandwich and double scoop of some of the freshest, most pure ice cream I've ever tasted. A weirdly intriguing stop. I now see it was a reminder to lose the schedule and allow the day to reveal itself.

There are three ways to go from here. The first is staying on U.S. 101 and continuing the ride south. Or you can take the Three Capes Loop Road detour to the coast, which will present a bag full of scenery while adding only an additional 10 miles before reconnecting with U.S. 101. The third is mixing up the two with half a loop that'll take you to the coast and the Cape Meares Lighthouse and back to Tillamook. That was my choice.

Turning right on 3rd Avenue, which is also the Netarts Highway, I rode west where, I'm reluctant to say, the aroma of cow crap was a welcoming reminder I was back in the country. Dairy country, no less—hence all the cheese. A few miles down, Bay Ocean Road shoots off a subtle fork to the right, over a river, and into a road slipped into place beside Tillamook Bay. The fact I was now riding north on my journey south was at first disconcerting and then comforting, a fresh reminder that it was indeed the journey and not the destination.

At low tide the view of moist, soot-colored mud lasted for several miles until I reached a junction at Crab Harbor, where the road led to the left and a sign warned "rough roads for the next five miles." How true. The rough gravel road on this Alpine pitch managed to rattle my shocks and shock my rattles. Then a short, narrow bridge opened up a view of the coast and that compelled me to ride on toward the lighthouse.

The opening to **Cape Meares State Park** (503/842-3182) is on your right, and the road to the summit, with its pitch, gravel, and twists, creates a hat trick of good riding. From the parking area, it's a short walk to Oregon's shortest lighthouse. Built in 1890, the 38-foot beacon sits 232 feet above the waves. The other attraction here, the Octopus Tree, is a multitrunked Sitka spruce that's an equal distance through the woods in the opposite direction. Better than both, I thought, were the overlooks above inlets that have been carved into the cliffs through millions of years. Waves continued to flood in with the tide and small waterfalls poured over the ledges.

Back on the loop toward Netarts, where the Pacific Ocean was in sight, the high-pitched roads perfect for riding. Netarts itself offered a gas station and then it was back to the two-land forest run that brought back memories from a few hours earlier. At a junction immediately south of town, you can turn left and follow the Netarts Highway back to Tillamook. If you take the right fork, you'll whip into Whiskey Creek Road, which zips past Cape Lookout and eventually Cape Kiwanda before merging again with U.S. 101 just past Pacific City. If I'm lucky enough to be reincarnated as myself, I'll take that route next time around.

I made the loop back to Tillamook to catch the **Tillamook Air Museum** (6030 Hangar Rd., 503/842-1130, www.tillamookair.com). Even Stevie Wonder couldn't miss this place. On the east side of U.S. 101, this is the largest clear-span wooden structure in the world: a massive hangar built in 1943 to house U.S. Navy blimps searching for Japanese submarines. Nearly 200 feet tall and 1,072 feet long, it encloses enough space for six football fields. Today, it's a museum housing more than 30 historic aircraft, including a great assortment of World War II warbirds. Nearly as large is **Munson Falls,** which you'll find about six miles south. Tucked out of sight nearly two miles off the main road, it's worth the effort to reach it. The 319-foot waterfall springs out of a mossy cliff and is the highest in the coast range. Amazingly, everything you've seen today has been within 50 miles of Cannon Beach, and there's another hundred to go.

There is much desolation in this area, but even though you're on Oregon's main coastal highway, there is little to distract you from enjoying the tour. There are mountains and pines spiked on the hills, and rhododendrons may be in bloom. You'll pass homes of people you'll never meet on a road you'll never forget, and you'll witness scenes that are new to you but destined to become part of you. Deep in the woods now, then south of Neskowin, where the ocean appears again, completely undisturbed—it's perhaps the longest stretch of coastline I've seen that hadn't been destroyed by development. When you enter Siuslaw National Forest, the scenery isn't thrown at you. Instead, the well-placed pullouts, small towns, farms, valleys, hills, beaches, and bays appear for you at perfectly timed intervals.

Civilization returns in Lincoln City, where you cross the 45th parallel. Back at home, tell your friends you rode across the midway point between the equator and the North Pole, and they'll be impressed. Past the city, there's not much privacy until Depoe Bay, after which you'll be dipping into the woods and the water.

Pullouts sewn onto the shores of the ocean allow you to park your bike and spy lighthouses, such as Oregon's tallest, a 93-foot-tall model flashing out at Yaquina Head, followed four miles south by the Yaquina Bay lighthouse by the bridge. As you ride through Alsea and Waldport and contemplate the end of the line in Florence, you'll reflect on the ride and may agree that it's been most excellent. For a grand finale, it's about to get even better.

After Yachats (ya-HOTS) is one of the coolest views I've ever seen: the road spinning around a curve, shooting up an incline, and hugging the side of a cliff into extreme elevations. It spun and snapped and popped across the land, and that good riding lasted for a dozen miles and beyond, all the way past the **Heceta Head Lighthouse** (541/997-3851 or 866/547-3696, www.hecetalighthouse.com), the most photographed on the Pacific Coast. Built in 1894, this light sends out a glow that can be seen 20 miles away. If you can swing it, a bed-and-breakfast is in the old lighthouse keeper's cottage. I couldn't swing it, so I pressed on another mile to **Sea Lion Caves** (U.S. 101, 541/547-3111, www.sealioncaves.com, $8).

This is the way old tourist attractions were created: Someone would find a natural phenomenon, buy the land, and sell tickets. That's what happened in 1932, 40 years after William Cox discovered sea lions in the world's largest sea cave. From the gift shop, walk down to an overlook, where, a hundred yards below, approximately a hundred Steller's sea lions are sunbathing on a flat

The Heceta Head Lighthouse as seen from Sea Lion Caves on Highway 101 is a testament to the overwhelming beauty of the Oregon coastline.

© NANCY HOWELL

rock, their chorus of yawps and aarps sounding like a frat house after a kegger. From here, an elevator within the mountain lowers you 180 feet into the world's largest sea cave, a massive hollow where sea lions surge in with the sea and doze atop the basalt rock formations. The sound of the water adds to the impressive sight of the two-acre, 125-foot-tall domed cavern.

After passing the seals, the road swoops down from the cliffs to the dunes for the final 10 miles into Florence. A most memorable ride has come to a close.

Florence Primer

Several hundred years before I got the idea to explore Oregon's coastline, the Spanish were doing it from the sea, creating maps as they cruised along the coast. English explorer Captain James Cook, who was used to driving on the left side of the road, headed over in 1778 to make some maps of his own. Watching this from shore were the Siuslaws who, like nearly every tribe in America, were displaced when white settlers showed up.

By 1900, 300 residents were making a living in this remote community by either logging, fishing, working in a sawmill, saloon, newspaper, cannery, or general store. One enterprising resident, who was making a killing by opening a ferry service across the Siuslaw River, was likely quite furious when the picturesque Siuslaw River Bridge opened in 1936.

By accident or design, the original village—today called Old Town—was preserved on a bend in the river and has been revitalized with shops, restaurants, galleries, and gift shops. Without this important asset, odds are you'd see Florence as just another generic village. But it's here, as is another vital attraction, the **Oregon Dunes National Recreation Area.** There are 38,000 acres of sand mountains here, and if that doesn't sound like much then just you wait.

On the Road: Florence

The previous day's ride may still have you buzzing, and it's tempting to consider zipping 11 miles north back up the coast around Heceta Head or, perhaps riding south along the Pacific for an enjoyable thousand-mile run down to San Diego.

If you just want to experience Florence, though, you can fill up the better part of the day with just two activities: shopping and sand dunes.

The former is pedestrian but satisfying, a low-key, laid-back approach that won't take much out of you. The latter is one of the most outlandish adventures you'll ever experience, kind of like plunging a syringe of adrenaline into the middle of your heart.

Have a nice day.

Pull It Over: Florence Highlights
Attractions and Adventures

I've had the good fortune to do a lot of cool stuff (motorcycling across America included), but I've rarely, if ever, done anything quite as cool as heading to the Oregon Dunes National Recreational Area and hitting the sands with Darin of **Sand Dunes Frontier** (83690 U.S. 101, 541/997-3544, www.sanddunes-frontier.com). I thought a dune buggy ride would include going to a clambake with Frankie and Annette and Moondog, and I also thought I'd drive the dune buggy myself. Thankfully, I've never been so wrong.

Arriving early (and off-season), I was the only passenger, trussed up in a net of harnesses. We rode slowly through the woods, and since I thought *that* was the ride, I was creating excuses to bail. Then we reached the edge of the forest, and I saw Oregon's most unusual landscape. It wasn't simply a patch of shoreline between us and the ocean, it was immense towers of sand as high as 300 feet that stretched about 40 miles north and south. Darin gunned the engine, and the huge tires bit into the sand and sent us on a 50-degree ascent to the peak of a dune that I knew would propel us into the unknown or on a collision course with another driver racing up the opposite side. My death grip threatened to crush the metal cage around me, but at the peak, in a split second

the classic 1936 Siuslaw River Bridge in Florence

Darin triggered a small handbrake that slapped the tail parallel with the seam at the top of the dune. We raced on, the dune buggy slipping over the side, but clinging like a knife in the sand. For the next 30 minutes, I was driven like a maniac to peaks and then down dangerous hills and, at one monumental moment, around the 60-degree basin of a Daytona 500-style bowl called the NASCAR berm. All of this helped me achieve a higher level of consciousness.

Perhaps a large part of my fascination with the ride was being here when there was no one else on the dunes, which made it seem like driving on the moon. In peak season, as many as 3,000 dune buggies and ATVs clog the sands each weekend. So get there early, invest $20, tie yourself down, and experience the motorized equivalent of a heart paddle.

A sedative about three miles south of the bridge is **Jessie M. Honeyman Memorial State Park** (800/452-5687). Created by the CCC in the 1930s, this 500-acre park has three freshwater lakes, with swimming and canoeing on 85-acre Lake Woahink. There are picnic pavilions, guided kayak tours, and a campground with 191 tent sites available for around $25 a night.

Shopping

As you ride into town, there's a buffer zone of new development that surrounds the real and unique shopping village of Old Town. Tucked beneath the bridge on the banks of the Siuslaw River, there are several blocks of stores and gadget and gift shops and restaurants you can see after you park your bike. Part of the appeal is the layout itself, with old buildings recycled for today. The drawback is that after a national magazine ranked Florence as one of the best places to retire, merchants hoping to capitalize on the momentum rushed in and ended up selling an identical inventory of junk.

An exception is the **Sticks & Stone Gallery** (1368 Bay St., 541/997-3196). If you've avoided wildlife art galleries because you've seen too many paintings of mustangs galloping across the plain, this place offers a cure. There are twigs made into lamps, metallic trout leaping in a metal stream, schools of wooden salmon, driftwood eagles, and tigers painted on bird's-eye maple, as well as fish, frogs, and pheasants etched, carved, and painted in a variety of mediums.

Blue-Plate Specials

Oregon often amazed me, and it did it yet again with the **Waterfront Depot** (1252 Bay St., 541/902-9100). Roughly the size of a small home, the old train depot is now the setting for an Irish bar (which explains the Peter O'Toole/ Richard Burton poster), as well as a fantastic restaurant based on an international tapas menu. For less than 10 bucks, you can mix and match entrées like crab-encrusted halibut, jambalaya pasta, and wild coho salmon. For a great experience, wait for a window seat overlooking the river.

Basic but popular meals are served at **Mo's** (1436 Bay St., 541/997-2185). Right on the river, the interior has the look and feel of a Howard Johnson's, circa 1950. That's a compliment, too, since it's packed with regular folk ordering seafood basics like clam strips, popcorn scallops, albacore tuna melts, and chowders. In addition to adding beer to the batter, Mo's also pours it into empty frosted mugs.

If you're craving home-away-from-home cooking, ride about two miles south of the bridge to **Morgan's Country Kitchen** (85020 U.S. 101, 541/997-6991). Serving down-home cooking since the 1950s, Morgan's is still at it with breakfast and lunch dishes like biscuits and sausage gravy, pecan waffles, roast beef, and chicken-fried steak.

In the heart of Old Town is the popular **Firehouse Restaurant** (1263 Bay St., 541/997-2800). Ribs, steaks, sirloin, "Code 3" burgers, salmon, halibut, sandwiches, and pasta cover most of the bases—and sidewalk dining and a lounge will take you the rest of the way home.

Watering Holes

Beachcomber Tavern (1355 Bay St., 541/997-6357) seriously exemplifies its name. A tavern since 1936, this really looks and feels like one of those places where people who like to drink, drink. It helps the cause by opening at 9 A.M., serving pub food and things like deep-fried prawns and Cajun-grilled oysters, and running a full bar. The local favorite.

Shut-Eye

Motels and Motor Courts

There's abundant quality lodging in Florence, and three great old-fashioned choices—two of which are within easy walking distance of Old Town. The **River House Motel** (1202 Bay St., 541/997-3933 or 888/824-2454, www .riverhouseflorence.com, $80 and up) is the best-placed place of all—less than a hundred yards from Old Town. Rooms have two queens or a king, and some have terraces to watch the drawbridge and fishing boats.

South of the Sisulaw is the **Ocean Breeze Motel** (85165 U.S. 101, 541/997-2642 or 888/226-9611, www.oceanbreezemotel.com, $75 and up in season). Although its appearance harkens back several decades, it seems quite modern, thanks to its meticulously clean rooms, each with a queen or two.

A block from the river and a short walk to Old Town, the **Lighthouse Inn** (155 U.S. 101, 541/997-3221, $65 and up) has that cool old knotty pine look going its way. Queen and king beds are offered, some rooms include sleeper sofas to add another couple to the mix, and family suites sleep five.

The **Old Town Inn** (170 U.S. 101, 541/997-7131 or 800-570-8738, www.old-town-inn.com, $71 and up) is a large complex a few blocks north of Old Town. Rooms are clean and basic—just like the rates.

Chain Drive
A, G, L

Chain hotels are in town, or within 10 miles. See cross-reference guide featuring phone numbers and Web addresses on page 514.

On the Road: Florence to Sisters

It's hard to leave Florence behind, because this also means saying so long to the Pacific Ocean and U.S. 101. On the north end of town, Highway 126 shoots straight toward the heart of Oregon, and as the waves wave goodbye, you ride into an area of river and grass. A railroad trestle spans the river and heads into the woods for God knows where, and when that passes, you look around and see a living life-insurance calendar of rivers, hills, forest, and wide-open landscape.

Within 15 miles, you'll pass the Siuslaw River and reach the low hills and a canopy road that could pass for the Berkshires of Massachusetts. Ahead is nothing but green and the road and a tunnel drawing you farther into the ride. There's something cool about tunnels like this, and it's not just the temperature. The echo makes your bike sound 10 times more powerful and muscular. Two lanes lead into more hills, and when you reach Mapleton, split off to the right for a stretch of dips and nice, though not extraordinary, roads. After the Siuslaw National Forest eases up, there are 40 miles of wide country riding ahead. Wide lanes and slow traffic announce the metropolis of Eugene and, as you can guess, the town doesn't offer a speck of the enjoyment you've received from the casual cruise. It's sluggish riding from about 10 miles before Eugene to about six miles past it. In fact, now's a good time to enjoy intermission....

And we're back. We hope you enjoyed your visit to Eugene, and after you pass Springfield and enter the McKenzie State River Recreation Area, you can start to look forward to 100 miles of overwhelming Oregon riding. With the return of two-lane roads and the absence of city traffic, you'll notice a distinct change in mood. Your mood will be lighter when you enter countryside accented by Christmas tree farms and groves of hazelnut trees (locals call them "filberts"). Then there are the signs of rural living: small homes that occupy many acres of land, the antithesis of urban life.

The McKenzie Valley is really great and the road, of course, is just as nice. Meandering and lazy, it's bordered with ivy and wildflowers as it follows the course of the McKenzie River all the way to a neat dam that powers the town of Leaburg. Just past the town, an old wooden bridge named after racing legend Barney Oldfield crosses the Leaburg canal, but I don't know why. Vignettes like this—finding a nice little river and a walking path on its banks—are still nice discoveries.

A short distance east, the same flowing creek leads to one of the nicest covered bridges I've seen. Lane County's Goodpasture Bridge was built in 1938 and is one of the most photographed covered bridges in Oregon. Considering the spiritual vibe of this ride, its Gothic-style louvered windows and carpentry seem fitting. From here, you may notice an unusual sensation as you ride, and I realized this as the lanes seemed to mimic the river. When the river was in sight, the road matched its mood, seeming to curve more sharply where I saw rapids, and smoothing out when the river rolled out of view.

It was one of those moments when all I had to do was hold the throttle and drift into a glide track. My bike followed the flow of the river while I looked ahead to find and negotiate every curve. Overall, the riding was effortless.

You ride past Nimrod, Finn Rock, and Blue River, and the road never fails. Before Belknap Springs, **Harbick's Country Store** (541/822-3575) is a well-stocked service station, restaurant, and motel that's worth a stop, since there's precious little ahead in terms of conveniences. About six miles east, good weather may give you the opportunity to follow Highway 242—the McKenzie Pass Scenic Byway—for 38 miles to Sisters. Most months, though, the road is impassable because of heavy snows that clog the Cascades. If you can take it here, you can take it anywhere—at least across the McKenzie Pass, which runs through one of the state's most recent lava flows. Recent, in this case, is 3,000 years ago. At the top of the 5,325-foot pass, the Dee Wright Memorial is a CCC-built lava rock observatory with trails to follow, and Proxy Falls is an ethereal wonder; a pair of horsetail falls just a short walk from the road.

The more likely option between November and June is sticking with the road ahead, and that's a damn fine option. You'll ride a scenic arc north through the Willamette National Forest. Guiding the way are enormous Douglas firs, standing like the honor guard as you roll down the blacktop. It's a magnificent experience to be heralded into the woods this way. About a dozen miles up the road is the entrance for Koosah Falls, and a half mile later are the entrance and parking area for Sahalie Falls. Park here at Sahalie and get ready for a magnificent spectacle. Down a short wooded path, you'll hear thundering waters that draw your eyes ahead to the Sahalie (Chinook for "heaven"), and when you reach the falls, you'll marvel at a torrent of water rocketing over a short cliff. It all seems more incredible and more gorgeous when combined with the mossy green rocks and trees surrounding you in the canyon. Take the time to walk the loop trail beside the frothing, tumbling white-water cascades and you'll discover Koosah ("sky") about a 15-minute nature walk away. There are few things you'll see in your life that rival finding a nice waterfall while on a forest run like this.

Back on the road, you may want to make another stop a mile or so on at Clear Lake, the headwaters of the McKenzie River. The "lake born of fire" got its start 3,000 years ago, when lava from Sand Mountain reached the river and backed up water to form the lake. The water's cold as hell, and you can't swim in it, but canoeing, fishing and boating are available, and the absence of motorized boats helps keep things clear. How clear? Look into the water, and 120 feet below the surface, you'll see the remainder of tall trees submerged when the lake was formed.

Three miles north is Highway 20, which can be ignored, as can Highway 22. As a matter of fact, ignore every other damn highway as 126 attacks the Cascades, taking you up and over Santiam Pass at 4,817 feet. The higher elevations inject clean air into your lungs and carburetors and deliver soothing views of firs and mountain hemlock, lodgepole and ponderosa pines as you ride into the high desert. It's soothing because, unlike on most mountain roads, nothing is dangerous or drastic. In fact, it's quite quiet and peaceful and calming as you snatch glimpses of the horizon across the Mount Washington Wilderness, with snowcapped mountains and miles of forests.

Take it easy, and when the road falls away to the south, you can look forward to spending the night with Sisters.

Sisters Primer

I wouldn't call Sisters's theme Wild West. It's more like Mild West. I'll explain why in a minute. First, though, I can tell you its history includes visits by Indians and fur traders and soldiers who established soon-to-be-abandoned Fort Polk in the 1860s. In the 1880s, Sisters became a supply center for sheep shipments passing through, and after that, lumber took the lead until the 1960s, when the last mill closed.

Then, just as they did in Helen, Georgia (and at about the same time, too), some folks in Sisters decided to come up with a new look for the town. But it wasn't the city council that requested the facelift. It was the owners of the Black Butte Ranch, a new local resort. It offered merchants a generous sum if they'd slap up an Old West facade over their storefronts, and most went along with the scheme. The plan worked, and by the early 1970s, the city passed a resolution that future construction would have an 1880s frontier theme. Surprisingly, it all works. When you mosey around town, you aren't wondering why Sisters looks the way it does. It just does. As to why it's named this way, look to the three mountain peaks visible from town. From north to south, the "sisters" are Faith, Hope, and Charity.

Footnote: After I came home, I recalled the energy of the town. The citizens there generated such an unusual and active vibe, I assumed there were at least 20,000 residents making it all work. On the contrary. Fewer than 1,100 people are driving Sisters' mojo. And they're doing it all for you.

You go, Sisters.

On the Road: Sisters

Although there's an all right ride out of town that will take you north to Mount Hood, in comparison to what you've already experienced, much of it's fairly routine. If you eventually have to ride north, however, within the 145-mile ride to Mount Hood and up to the Columbia River Gorge, you'll ride through the Deschutes and Mount Hood national forests to reach the communities of Hood River and The Dalles. Of this, I'd estimate that around 65 percent of it is decent riding in hills, on promontories, in canyons, and by rivers.

Since Sisters is the end of the line for this chapter, however, I'll suggest a day wandering around downtown. It may not take a full day, but from cowboy boots to fine art, the stores here can occupy a good part of the day. If you get done early, the city of Bend is only 20 miles south.

Pull It Over: Sisters Highlights
Attractions and Adventures

In addition to the annual **Sisters Rodeo** (541/549-0121 or 800/827-7522, www.sistersrodeo.com), held in early June, there's a wad of adrenaline pumping in the great outdoors. If you don't mind swapping your bike for a boat, **Destination Wilderness** (541/549-1336 or 800/423-8868, www.wildernesstrips.com) is an outfitter that also plans adventures on the McKenzie, Clakamas, Umpqua, and Salmon rivers—and all over Oregon, for that matter. The streams here are filled with rainfall and melting snow from above 10,000 feet, so the waters are crystal-clear. You'll run Class II and III rapids on trips that last from half a day ($60) to two full days ($280) and include all your gear, food, and transportation. If you'd rather fish, it can gear you up for fly- and spin-casting excursions.

Shopping

Wandering around Sisters is an all right experience since, in addition to the standard retinue of ordinary inventory, there's some pretty cool stuff as well. As always, you'll be hard-pressed to find junk small enough to put on your bike, but if there's something you really dig, consider shipping it home. Some of the big stuff's at **Sisters Log Furniture** (140 W. Cascade St., 541/549-8191, www.sisterslogfurniture.com), where chainsaw-carved cowboys and bears and big wooden beds are sold alongside Western-themed metal and horseshoe art, paintings, rugs, and jewelry.

Doc Holliday's Trading Post (291 W. Cascade St., 541/549-1506) was one of my favorites, thanks to a full library of books on Western characters (Calamity Jane, Annie Oakley, Buffalo Bill, George Custer, et al.) sharing equal space with tomes on American Indian legends like Chief Joseph, Sitting

Bull, and Geronimo. You'll also find merchandise like cowboy hats, moccasins, headbands, furs, and powder loaders.

Oregon is such an overlooked state, it's good to find a place like the **Oregon Store** (271 W. Cascade, 541/549-6700, www.theoregonstore.com). Across Oregon are craftspeople, artists, and manufacturers creating the merchandise you'll find here—and it's pretty cool stuff, like knives, saddle blankets, myrtlewood bowls, Oregon jams, syrups, stoneground flour, Native American robes, and Immigrant American T-shirts.

When an artist really makes it, that's really something. One who's done very well, thank you, is **Lorenzo Ghiglieri.** You may not know his name, but look who does: Ronald Reagan, Pope John Paul II, Tiger Woods, Al Gore, Mikhail Gorbachev, and Queen Elizabeth, who have received his commissioned pieces. Like Remington, he's a sketch artist, oil painter, and sculptor who has a fascination with the West, as seen in pieces that focus on buffalo, cattle, elk, horses, explorers, bears, and Indians. His impressive statue *Victorious Flight* is an eagle carrying an American flag, and it would make a great gift to me. You may run across Lorenzo working at his gallery in Sisters (103 E. Hood, 541/549-8751 or 877/551-4441, www.art-lorenzo.com).

For mostly everything else, there's **Sisters Drugstore** (211 Cascade Ave., 541/549-6221). The corner drugstore carries household goods, specialty foods, wine, gifts, and T-shirts, and has a pharmacy.

Blue-Plate Specials

When in Sisters, you must order up some big food at a big restaurant. **The Gallery** (171 W. Cascade, 541/549-2631). A favorite with locals and tourists, it serves old-fashioned family-style food like pork chops and meat loaf and soups, soft rolls, homemade pies, and cinnamon rolls. If you're riding early, it opens at 6 A.M. Friendly and filling. A full bar and lounge are in back.

Another place with an Old West theme is **Bronco Billy's Ranch Grill** (190 E. Cascade, 541/549-7427). It specializes in ribs, but it's not a rib joint—there are burgers, sirloin, tacos, pork bowls, chicken, and more. Housed in an old hotel, former rooms upstairs can be reserved for private dining. As at The Gallery, there's a jumping bar here.

A chain I'd like to see on my street is **Soba** (291 E. Cascades, 541/549-8499, www.eatsoba.com), an Asian counter-service bistro where you can get really good Thai, Japanese, Korean, Vietnamese, and Chinese food cooked over a wok and served fast and cheap—main dishes are only about seven bucks. I thought I was back in college.

Watering Holes

As mentioned above, you may do best by looking for nightlife at The Gallery or Bronco Billy's Saloon. They're already a hit with locals, and you're bound to fit right in at these joints where the clientele seem pretty loose and friendly.

Shut-Eye

Motels and Motor Courts
One of the sweetest motor courts I've run across is the **Sisters Motor Lodge** (511 W. Cascade St., 541/549-2551, www.sistersmotorlodge.com, $89 and up for rooms, $195 for extended-stay suites). Built in 1942, it's become a national historic landmark and each room has handmade quilts, cable TV, and fully stocked kitchenettes. The in-town location is conveniently close, yet perfectly secluded.

Chain Drive
A, CC

Chain hotels are in town, or within 10 miles. See cross-reference guide featuring phone numbers and Web addresses on page 514.

Inn-dependence
One of the best built and well-run B&Bs I've stayed at is the **Blue Spruce Bed & Breakfast** (444 S. Spruce, 541/549-9644 or 888/328-9644, www.blue sprucebandb.com, $125). About four blocks from downtown, the house was built as an inn, so rooms are large, with fireplaces. The beds are soft, the bathrooms have hot tubs and towel warmers, the den is massive, and your breakfast is as large as a water tower.

Indulgences

If the artificial Old West theme of the town seems real to you, then you may be inclined to wander over to **Long Hollow Ranch** (71105 Holmes Rd., 541/923-1901 or 877/923-1901, www.lhranch.com). This is a working cattle ranch where you'll work with wranglers, explore the ranch on horseback, dine on home-cooked meals, fish in the reservoirs, practicing roping, or hanging around the yard pitching horseshoes—just as they did in the Wild West.

Resources for Riders

Oregon's Best Run

Oregon Travel Information
Central Oregon Visitors Association—800/800-8334,
  www.visitcentraloregon.com
Oregon Department of Transportation—888/275-6368
Oregon Dunes NRA—877/444-6777, www.reserveusa.com
Oregon Lighthouse Society—541/259-4778,
  www.oregonlighthousesociety.org
Oregon Parks and Recreation—800/551-6949,
  www.oregonstateparks.com
Oregon Road Conditions—800/977-6368
Willamette Forest Headquarters—541/225-6300

Local and Regional Information
Cannon Beach Chamber of Commerce—503/436-2623,
  www.cannonbeach.org
Cannon Beach Weather Information—503/861-2722
Florence Chamber of Commerce—541/997-3128 or 800/524-4864,
  www.florencechamber.com or www.oldtownflorence.com
Lane County 541/484-5307 or 800/547-5445,
  www.travellanecounty.org
McKenzie River Chamber of Commerce (Leaburg)—541/896-3330
Sisters Chamber of Commerce—541/549-0251,
  www.sisterschamber.com

Oregon Motorcycle Shops
Cascade Motorcycle—4065 W. 11th Ave., Eugene, 541/344-5177
Cycle Sports—555 River Rd., 541/607-9000, www.cyclesports.net
Florence Polaris—U.S. 101 and S. Jetty St., 541/997-0518
Florence Yamaha—2130 Hwy. 126, Florence, 541/997-1157,
  www.florenceyamaha.com
North Coast Motorcycles—240 S. Roosevelt Dr., Seaside, 503/717-8700,
  www.northcoastmotorcycles.com
Pro Cycle—2101 W. 10th Ave., Eugene, 541/688-9543, www.procycle.us

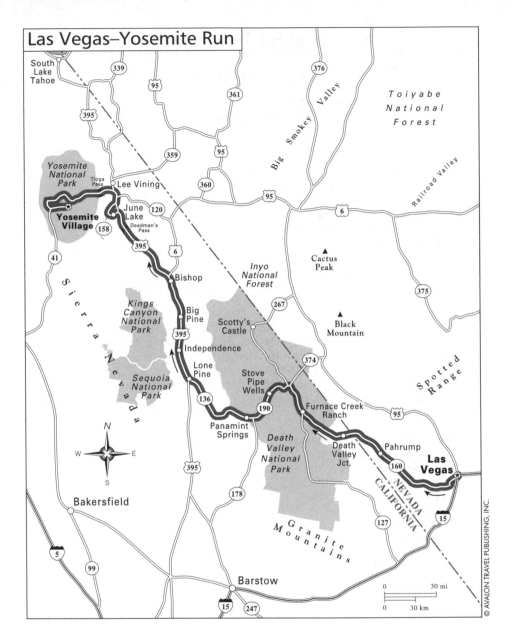

Route: Las Vegas to Yosemite via Death Valley, Lone Pine, Bishop, Lee Vining

Distance: Approximately 450 miles; consider six days with stops, add two days for optional Lake Tahoe run.

- **Days 1–2—Las Vegas** • **Day 3—Travel** • **Day 4—Lone Pine/Travel** • **Days 5–6—Yosemite**

First Leg: Las Vegas to Lone Pine (240 miles)

Second Leg: Lone Pine to Yosemite Village (200 miles)

Optional Third Leg: Yosemite Village to Lake Tahoe (200 miles)

Helmet Laws: Both Nevada and California require helmets.

Las Vegas–Yosemite Run

Las Vegas, Nevada to Yosemite National Park, California

Of all the runs profiled in this book, this is the most exciting, frightening, grueling, exhilarating, fascinating, inspiring, and humbling.

From the materialistic and surreal city of Las Vegas, the mood descends to the stark landscape of Death Valley. What follows are arguably the grandest vistas in America at Yosemite and, if you desire, the clear and clean waters of Lake Tahoe—a treasure to see on a spring or fall run. This ride will test your mettle and reward your efforts.

Las Vegas Primer

Las Vegas is a town steeped in excess. From multibillion-dollar themed hotels to less-than-discreet prostitution, Las Vegas is where the circus came to town—and never left.

A little more than half a century ago, it was a way station in the middle of nowhere—until the Mafia saw an untapped oasis of cash. You know the rest: Sammy and Frankie and Dean begat Elvis and Engelbert and Wayne, and then the stakes were raised, and old hotels were blown up and corporations muscled in to build casinos disguised as hotels. In the late 1990s, when the local convention bureau needed to fill more beds, it decided to position Las Vegas as a great family getaway, but no one bought that lie, so it retooled the party line. More recently, it has admitted it's a place where you can do all the kinds of things that you would never dare tell your wife, husband, children, employer, coworkers, priest, minister, rabbi, carwash attendant, caddy, convenience store clerk, produce manager, or a complete stranger.

So, accept that Vegas is crowded, expensive, noisy, profane, and no place for kids (unless you're teaching them about escort services and loan sharking). If you're an adult who's prepared for a juiced-up, high-tension, all-night bacchanal, however, it can be the fuel for a long and winding journey.

Just save enough money for gas.

On the Road: Las Vegas

It's impossible to condense and define Las Vegas, especially for motorcycle travelers. You can ride your bike anywhere in the country and be content with yourself, your thoughts, and a few possessions stuffed in the saddlebags. A millisecond after you ride into Vegas, you're swept up in an orgy of greed and desire. Pray that it dissipates when you leave town, or you'll be the most miserable sumbitch on the road.

This concludes the warning. From here, it's a pleasant surprise to find that most employees are hospitable and the roads easy to navigate. The city is laid out roughly like a grid, with Las Vegas Boulevard the main north–south artery. A section of this street is "The Strip," where you're most likely to spend your time and money. The magnet for tourists and conventioneers, it is where hotels are destroyed and rebuilt, phoenixlike, as billion-dollar resorts.

The farther north you go, the less impressed you'll be, unless you're looking for the preresort vintage Vegas. Fremont Street has been retooled as an enclosed pedestrian mall where chain-smoking seniors on gambling junkets try to score bad food at cheap buffets. In their favorite casinos, marathon slot-machine players press buttons in a sad choreography, looking like research monkeys awaiting banana-flavored pellets.

The stakes are raised as you ride south and pass the Sahara, Stratosphere, Stardust, Flamingo, Aladdin, and Circus Circus casinos. When you reach the Strip, you'll enter a universe of world-class hotels and high rollers. Yet there's a certain sameness to every venue: the ringing bells of an electronic arcade, the absence of windows and clocks, and VIP status applied not on the basis of your worth as a person, but on your value as a loser. And that concludes the rant.

To be fair, you should experience Vegas for yourself. You won't be harassed by bums or hustlers, since casinos don't want them cutting in on their racket. Besides, it is not all gambling. It's a playground for adults, a place where you

Gettin' Hitched

Tying the knot in Vegas is either a romantic or pathetic amalgam of hormones, love, and kitsch. More than 70 wedding chapels (including ones themed for *Star Trek* and Graceland) operate in town, and if you want to get married (please, not to someone you just met through an escort service), the only requirement is a $55 license, which you can get at the seven-day-a-week **Clark County Courthouse** (200 S. 3rd St., 702/455-3156).

can feel the same freedom you experience on your bike—although a bike will never give you the clap.

Pull It Over: Las Vegas Highlights
Casinos

Larger and louder than life, the most impressive casinos are found along the Strip. Each is a community unto itself, with a distinct theme, headlining acts, guestrooms, restaurants, pools, and abundant services. Rates vary wildly—often daily—especially if there's a major convention in town, and suites naturally cost more. Rather than listing rates, then, I recommend you call in advance or check the travel section of your newspaper for discounted prices on Vegas rooms. Sunday through Thursday is a better time to look for discounts (unless a convention's in town). Even if you don't stay at a hotel, ask about the hotel's headliner—a very big draw here.

Luxor (3900 Las Vegas Blvd., 702/262-4000, 800/288-1000 for room reservations, or 800/557-7428 for show reservations, www.luxor.com) sports an Egyptian theme and a pyramid out front. You'll see its spotlight at night. Clean up NYC, multiply it by 10, and you have **New York New York** (3790 Las Vegas Blvd., 702/740-6969, 800/693-6763 for room and show reservations, www.nynyhotelcasino.com). A subtle Hollywood theme sifts through the **MGM Grand** (3799 Las Vegas Blvd., 702/891-1111, 800/929-1111 for room and show reservations, www.mgmgrand.com), just a very large hotel with big shows and special events—including prizefights.

The Mirage (3400 Las Vegas Blvd., 702/791-7111 or 800/627-6667 room reservations, 800/963-9634 show reservations, www.mirage.com, was the home to Siegfried and Roy, who kept their "Secret Garden" filled with exotic animals and dolphins. Their show has been replaced by a Cirque du Soleil extravaganza based on the music of The Beatles—and you know that can't be bad.

At **Treasure Island** (3300 Las Vegas Blvd., 702/894-7111, 800/944-7444 for room reservations, or 800/392-1999 for show reservations, www.treasure-island.com), the big show is Cirque du Soleil's *Mystère.* Oh, the pirate theme? That walked the plank in favor of burlesque and sex at the Tangerine Lounge.

An old favorite that attracts families, **Circus Circus** (2880 Las Vegas Blvd., 702/734-0410 or 800/634-3450 for room reservations, www.circuscircus.com) is not dirty, not clean. Theoretically, there's a French Riviera theme at the **Monte Carlo** (3770 Las Vegas Blvd., 702/730-7777 or 800/311-8999 for room and show reservations, www.monte-carlo.com), which is home to popular Vegas headliner Lance Burton, Master Magician! **Caesars Palace** (3570 Las Vegas Blvd., 702/731-7110 or 800/634-6001 for room and show reservations, www.caesars.com) is one of the city's traditional favorites and the place where you can enjoy Elton John and endure Celine Dion. I'd give the waitresses here my vote for best costumes. They's sexy.

Excalibur (3850 Las Vegas Blvd., 702/597-7777, 800/937-7777 for room reservations, or 800/933-1334 for show reservations, www.excaliburcasino.com) has a medieval castle theme. Why not? A mixture of the tropical and mystical and upscale chic, **Mandalay Bay** (3950 Las Vegas Blvd., 702/632-7777 or 877/632-7000 for room and show reservations, www.mandalaybay.com) features a House of Blues, stage shows, and off-off-off-Broadway productions.

The mighty large **Venetian** (3355 Las Vegas Blvd., 702/414-1000 or 888/283-6423, www.venetian.com) materialized in June 1999 where the Sands once stood. The Italian-themed resort of more than 4,000 suites gets raves on the swank-o-meter and credit for hosting "Art of the Motorcycle." Oh, the theme: It's Italian Renaissance, sprinkled with a dash of porn. The nightclub Vivid is a tribute to the porn production company that gave rise to, among other objects, the career of Jenna Jameson.

Attractions and Adventures

If you'd like to experience skydiving and live to tell about it, **Flyaway Indoor Skydiving** (200 Convention Center Dr., 702/731-4768, www.flyawayindoorskydiving.com) offers a one-hour program for $50 where you don skydiving clothes and step out over a monstrous bathroom blow dryer. No parachute, no worries. About 70 miles north of Vegas, the **Las Vegas Skydiving Center** (Mesquite Airport, 702/877-1010) shows you the city at 120 mph. It picks you up in Vegas, and after a 20-minute lesson and brief flight, you and the instructor you're strapped to will jump and free-fall for 45–50 seconds. The memory will last a lifetime—or until you hit the ground—whichever comes first. Either way, you pay a steep $179.

In the flamboyant tradition of Gorgeous George and '70s Elvis, Liberace epitomized the vanity of Vegas. The performer's **Liberace Museum** (1775 E. Tropicana, 702/798-5595, www.liberace.org, $12.50) showcases some surprising exhibits that may appeal to riders: an Excalibur car covered with rhinestones, a customized Bradley GT, a Rolls-Royce Phantom V Landau limousine (one of only seven, this one dons the license tag "88 Keys"), as well as a custom rhinestone-covered Stutz Bearcat with a matching rhinestone-covered toolkit. The museum is open 10 A.M.–5 P.M. Monday–Saturday, 1–5 P.M. Sunday.

The accessory branch of Las Vegas H-D/Buell, the **Harley-Davidson Shop** (4th and Fremont, 702/383-1010, www.lvhd.com) carries the requisite overdone clothing, parts, and souvenirs. A bulletin board announces motorcycle-related products and services.

One of the best things that's ever happened in my life was being invited to a class at **Freddie Spencer's High Performance Riding School** (702/643-1099 or 888/672-7219, www.fastfreddie.com). It's like shooting 18 holes with Arnold Palmer. Spencer, a three-time World Grand Prix champion (and the youngest ever), trains riders on superspeedy Honda CBR600F4s. After getting decked out in full leathers, you ride a few blocks to the Las Vegas Motor Speedway and spend two or three days learning to ride fast. Very, very fast. Even if you're content cruising along at a casual clip, the principles you learn here for braking, cornering, and accelerating can be used on country roads and city highways. In the meantime, scraping your knee along the asphalt at the speed of light is one of life's greatest moments—if you've got the cash.

Blue-Plate Specials

Hundreds of restaurants line the Strip, both inside and outside the resort casinos. Surprisingly, the quality indoors is actually pretty good, and choices range from quick snacks to very elaborate meals. In fact, Vegas is gaining a reputation as a fine-dining capital, with dozens of celebrity chefs showing up to open high-end restaurants. For your purposes, however, here's a lower-end choice.

If you think that no one understands your passion for bikes, you'll find a sympathetic ear at **Harley-Davidson Cafe** (3725 Las Vegas Blvd., 702/740-4555, www.harley-davidsoncafe.com). The café boasts plenty of parking out back, while the inside looks like an assembly line. Gleaming Harleys ride up and around the room, passing before a large map of Route 66 and a giant American flag created from red, white, and blue chains. What else? Oh, yeah. Food.

Shut-Eye

As Las Vegas turns into a convention clearinghouse, many of the 135,000 rooms are booked months in advance. Make reservations as early as you can—perhaps as part of a gambling package, which will knock the rates down considerably. If not, you'll probably pay a premium to stay in a trashy hotel. Keep in mind that staying at a casino hotel can be soul-rattling after a peaceful desert ride. The local convention bureau has opened a hotel hotline, 877/VISIT-LV (877/847-4858), and a website, www.visitlasvegas.com. Another nationwide reservation service that covers Las Vegas may help find you a room and save you some money: 800/96-HOTEL (800/964-6835) or www.hotels.com.

Motels and Motor Courts
OK, so they're not really motels, but here are a few places I really like. For peace and quiet without a premium, **La Quinta** (3970 S. Paradise Rd., 702/796-9000, $75–85) is a bargain and includes continental breakfast. Just a few blocks from the action, it also has a pool. Even cheaper is the **Golden Gate Hotel and Casino** (1 Fremont St., 702/385-1906 or 800/426-1906, www.goldengatecasino.net, $60). It offers cable, a free newspaper, and not much else besides a restaurant that's served 25 million giant shrimp cocktails since 1959. The **Hard Rock Hotel** (4455 Paradise Rd., 702/693-5000 or 800/473-7625, www.hardrockhotel.com) hits the jackpot with great accents like Flying V door handles, a Beatles display case, and an H-D Hardtail Springer owned by Motley Crüe's Nikki Sixx. It's more inviting than the darkened casinos, but rates here leap around like Pete Townshend, so call ahead. The on-site restaurant is another reason to stay here—it displays one of Elvis's jumpsuits and Roy Orbison's Electra-Glide.

Chain Drive
A, C, D, E, F, G, H, I, J, L, N, P, Q, S, U, X, Y, CC, DD

Chain hotels are in town, or within 10 miles. See cross-reference guide featuring phone numbers and Web addresses on page 514.

On the Road: Las Vegas to Lone Pine

Of all the rides you'll make in America, this one will require the greatest degree of guts. It demands that your bike be in peak condition, that your nerves be sure, and that you are ready to face the challenge of fierce, twisting curves in the Inyo Mountains and the barren loneliness of Death Valley.

Leaving Las Vegas on Route 159 West, it'll take a half hour to shake the Vegas glitter off your bike, just about the time you'll reach Red Rock Canyon, a magnificent sight and, if you ride the loop, one that affords possible views of bighorn sheep, gray foxes, and wild burros. Otherwise, head south toward Blue Diamond and Highway Route 160, and then west to Pahrump; follow a shortcut to Route 127 North, then to Route 190, which leads west across Death Valley.

Immediately, the road is a lonely stretch. There are no twists, no turns, just rolling desert. The road wakes up near Spring Mountain Ranch State Park, giving you curves to compensate.

Pahrump is just a lump of a town—an embryonic L.A. that spreads across the sands. Friendly clerks staff the well-stocked Mobil station (Hwys. 160 and 372), but here you wouldn't be surprised to see Kubrick's cavemen tossing bones into the sky. Instead of turning south to reach 190 via Shoshone, head a few miles north of Pahrump, where an alternate route (Belle Vista Road) cuts west to Death Valley Junction. Take it.

After four miles of twisties and 15 miles of straightaway, the big, empty desert starts to look like the Grand Canyon (minus the canyon). Roughly an hour later, you're at the intersection of 190 and 127, poised for your ride across Death Valley. Definitely stop for a look (or an overnight) at the strange and fascinating **Amargosa Opera House and Hotel** (760/852-4441, www.amargosa-opera-house.com, $45–60). Built by the Pacific Coast Borax Company in the 1920s, the combination office space and hotel had fallen into disrepair by 1967. Then New York dancer Marta Becket drove through, had a flat tire, and fell in love with its desolation. She bought the forlorn complex and now rents rooms. As if that's not enough, on Mondays and Saturdays from October to May, Marta and friend Tom Willett still perform a ballet and mime revue in the adjacent opera house. Now that's entertainment! No phones, no television, no food (a restaurant's seven miles away), but a place for some well-deserved rest before the upcoming ride.

Things get mighty strange here, sheriff. If you've ever judged times to reach distant points, don't expect to do it here. The land is so flat, it'll take 20 minutes to reach an object you can see halfway to the horizon.

Mile after mile, this lasts. You're riding across the Amargosa Range, passing 20 Mule Team Canyon. If you're interested, before Zabriskie Point a one-way, 2.7-mile dirt loop road detours south again through the canyon and brings you back to the highway. Then nothing is something. A four-star resort, in fact. In an area where a snack machine could win the award for finest restaurant, **Furnace Creek Resort** (760/786-2345, www .furnacecreekresort.com) is a mystery. You can stay the night in below-sea-level luxury, go horseback riding, or take a break on the verandah and view the upcoming 104-mile challenge. If you want to play golf on the lowest golf course in the world, the one here is 214 feet *below sea level.* Despite its existence in exile, the resort is popular and the rates prove it: from $265 at the inn and $128 at the ranch. Reserve in advance if you think you'll stay. If not, get ready for a most incredible ride.

A few miles down the road, there's a gas station that will gouge you on gas, but fill 'er up again. You're about to start a heart-stopping ride.

As you start to descend into the valley, you'll see into the future. Car headlights can be seen from 10 miles away, and about 20 miles outside of Furnace Creek, the absence of life echoes around you. You may experience a most humbling and spiritual moment here. After running a satisfying series of mountain curves, you take a wide, sweeping left and then 3, 2, 1 ... you've fallen hundreds of feet below sea level and are riding in the basin of Death Valley.

Picture yourself, a black speck alone in a place as flat and desolate as any on earth. Solo riders especially will feel the emotional deprivation of this silent world. If your bike is finely tuned, stop and experience the mystical solitude. It is as memorable as any experience you will have on the road.

When you turn your attention back to riding, the quiet continues until you reach **Stovepipe Wells** (760/786-2387, www.stovepipewells.com). It has an elevation of five feet, but don't let anyone sell you lift tickets. If you're tired of riding, Stovepipe offers an Einstein-smart option. It has 83 motel rooms, an RV park, gas, a general store, swimming pool, and saloon. A welcome sight, rooms here go for an affordable $63–103.

Between here and the next oasis, you'll ride through the antivalley, some of the most harrowing and dangerous dips and twists you'll encounter. Six-degree grades and serious shifts in terrain roll on for miles at a time. Minus any guardrails, a moment's distraction can easily turn your bike into scrap metal, but if you stay focused, this ride is rich in adventure. Accelerating drops let you click into neutral and speed through twists at 60 mph, propelling you into valleys where the emptiness is sublime in its beauty. Realize that this is the same desert you may have flown over countless times, but now it is a planet you've tamed beneath your tires.

When you reach **Panamint Springs Resort** (775/482-7680, www.deathvalley.com, $65–94), you have another excuse to stay the night in a 15-room motel and reminisce about the ride. You may have doubted your resolve or the belief you could find beauty in this wasteland, but by now, the desert has spoken to you. Chances are you'll be keyed up for the last 48-mile leg to Lone Pine.

From Panamint Springs, you're riding the backbone of a mountain range, with sheer drops on your side and no barriers to break your fall. What you will find are infinite reasons to stop and shoot photos. Father Crowley Vista Point (elev. 4,000 feet) is a good bet, and I doubt you'll be hassled by oncoming traffic when you park your bike in the middle of the road. Look for the intersection of Highway 136 North, take it to reach U.S. 395, and turn north for a well-deserved rest in the historic Hollywood cowboy town of Lone Pine.

Yippeeiyay.

Lone Pine Primer

Lone Pine (elev. 3,700 feet, pop. 2,060), the first town of any size west of Death Valley, flares up for a few blocks and then disappears back into the sand. Lexicographers believe the phrase "blink and you'll miss it" was coined here.

But there's more to Lone Pine than meets the eye. If you're old enough to recall matinee cowboys falling off cliffs, only to return the following week, you'll have already seen Lone Pine. If you frequent antique shows, looking for a Hopalong Cassidy lunch box or Roy Rogers guitar, you'll have Lone Pine to thank.

More than 300 Westerns were filmed here, from serial episodes to full-length features. Capitalizing on this unique history, each October the Lone Pine Film Festival draws a few surviving stars of Hollywood's Old West movies.

Even if you were born too late to recall Lash LaRue and the Cisco Kid, being in Lone Pine and at the gateway to Mount Whitney is a purely American experience. After Death Valley, you deserve it.

On the Road: Lone Pine

One stoplight, three blocks, and years of history. It's enough for an interesting ride, primarily because of the Whitney Portal, a long and winding road to the majestic mountain. After defeating Death Valley, you may want to take a break from mountain roads, but if not, you can take a curvaceous 12-mile run to the base of Mount Whitney, California's highest peak (elev. 14,495).

Otherwise, stay a while in Lone Pine. After all, stopping in small towns

back on the Whitney Portal which leads to Mount Whitney, California's highest peak (elev. 14,495 feet)

offers some of the most enjoyable moments of a ride. If you're ready to rest, you can see downtown in about 25 minutes—a half hour if you take your time. One must-see is at the lone stoplight. The **Indian Trading Post** (137 S. Main St., 760/876-4641) was a favorite stop for stars such as Edward G. Robinson, Jack Palance, Errol Flynn, Chuck Connors, Maureen O'Hara, Gary Cooper, and Barbara Stanwyck, who scribbled their names on the walls and window frames while shooting in town. Today, the walls are a priceless piece of Americana.

After the mountain and the town, there's not much else to do but settle back at the diner, grab a beer at the saloon (yes!), do your laundry, and, if you share my good fortune, see a real live prospector walking down the street with his pickaxe and shovel.

Pull It Over: Lone Pine Highlights
Attractions and Adventures

You're surrounded by natural beauty, and there are two places to visit to take full advantage of this. **Mount Whitney Ranger Station** (640 S. Main St., 760/876-6200, www.fs.fed.us/r5/inyo) issues the wilderness permits you'll need to enter the Whitney Portal area. There's no charge, but if you want to camp here ($6–14), you'll need to make arrangements well in advance. A mile south of Lone Pine, at the junction of 395 and 136, the **Interagency Office** (760/876-6222) stocks information about Death Valley, Mount Whitney, the Inyo National Forest, and other natural parks and sights.

Blue-Plate Specials

Besides a few pizza places and Mexican diners, eateries in Lone Pine are few, but it's easy to find some good USDA-approved road food if you know where to look. The largest joint in town is the **Mt. Whitney Restaurant** (227 S. Main St., 760/876-5751). Here since the 1930s, the family-owned diner offers—dig this—venison, buffalo, ostrich, and veggie burgers. Ask politely, and maybe they'll make you a real one with beef. Open from morning to evening, it's popular with riders thanks to the pool tables, pinball, beer and wine, and football on a 50-inch TV. Open 24 hours for breakfast, lunch, and dinner, the **High Sierra Café** (446 S. Main St., 760/876-5796) serves breakfast anytime, beer and wine later on, and entrées include American favorites like chicken-fried steak and chopped sirloin with mushrooms and grilled onions.

Watering Holes

One of the most enjoyable bars you'll find in America, **Jake's Saloon** (119 N. Main St., 760/876-5765) is open daily 'til midnight. It's the home of the "notorious" Alabama Hills Gang, a loose affiliation of local characters who hold shoot-outs the second and fourth Saturday nights May–September—or whenever they feel like it. They suggest you be ready for anything. Even when guns aren't blazing, the bar is a perfect place to settle down after your Death Valley run and crack your thirst with a cold beer.

Shut-Eye

Motels and Motor Courts
For a small town, Lone Pine offers more than adequate lodging choices. In the middle of town, the **Dow Villa Motel** (310 S. Main St., 760/876-5521 or 800/824-9317, www.dowvillamotel.com, $38–115) features clean rooms, a pool, outdoor spa, and rooms with TVs, VCRs, king and queen beds, and mini-fridges. Be sure to check out the John Wayne exhibit in the den, which includes a poker table from a movie he shot here. At the south end of town, the **Comfort Inn** (1920 S. Main St. at the junction of 395 and 136, 760/876-8700, www.comfortinn.com, $48) is as clean as can be, with larger than normal rooms and a nice view of Mount Whitney (in back) and the Alabama Hills (in front). Rooms feature two queen beds, bathtubs, mini-fridges, and microwaves.

Chain Drive
A, C

Chain hotels are in town, or within 10 miles. See cross-reference guide featuring phone numbers and Web addresses on page 514.

On the Road: Lone Pine to Yosemite Village

Aside from the monumental wall of wind, the ride north is easy—at least until you turn onto Highway 120 to reach Yosemite. That's when you may want to call your stunt double.

For now, the road out of Lone Pine stays true to form: impressive mountains and straight runs. Fourteen miles later, bypass Independence, and then slow down through well-patrolled Big Pine. Forty miles from here, Bishop's oasis of green lawns, trees, golf courses, and restaurants may entice you to stop.

When you continue north, the ride becomes comfortable as you blaze down the road with the Sierra Nevada on your left and the Inyo Mountains on your right. Be thankful you've been freed from the confines of a car: The spicy fragrance of the desert is just as bracing as the chill of the mountain air. You're in the groove now, with another 120 miles of motorcycle-friendly road to ride. Forget the canopy lanes of New England; the wide-open road places you in God's Country.

After passing sprawling Lake Crowley on your right, the road rises forever, ascending to 7,000 feet and Sherwin Summit, and then, miles later, Deadman's Pass, at 8,036 feet. The desert has been replaced by rich, green California forest. If you have time to prolong your ride and acquire other indelible images, turn left onto Highway 158 for the June Lake Loop. Most motorists bypass it, but it's worth the detour for motorcycle travelers.

The Bear Facts

Although lead poisoning killed off California grizzlies in the 1920s (they were shot), other bears are still sniffing out food in Yosemite Village. They can easily tear a car to shreds when searching out uncovered food, so when you leave your bike, take anything perishable with you. Better yet, leave items in your room. If you're camping, invest in bear-proof containers. Maybe buy one large enough to sleep in.

A small creek running on your right soon spills into one of the most beautiful mountain lakes you'll encounter, and the combination of road, forest, lake, and sky is as picturesque as Switzerland's Lake Lausanne. This is a ski resort town, so the off-season traffic is lighter and makes it easy to stop for coffee in the small lakefront village.

On the road again, you'll cruise quietly past snowcapped mountains, log cabins, and waterfalls until, suddenly, you'll notice an eerie silence. There is an absence of movement and people, and the landscape has an unusual science fiction design. See it for yourself. Weird.

Highway 158 connects back with 395, so turn left and ride to Lee Vining, a nice town with a few motels and restaurants. If you're scared of heights or aren't prepared for the demanding two-hour, 74-mile push to Yosemite Village, you should stop here. Really. You'll also be stopped when 120 closes following the first big snowstorm after November 1. Otherwise, turn left onto 120 and, after about a quarter mile, you'll see on your left the **Tioga Gas Mart** (22 Vista Point Dr., 760/647-1088). The supermarket-size Mobil station lets you stock up on food and supplies for Yosemite. If the weather's nippy, now's the time to get comfortable in a survival suit before heading for the mountains.

Already at 8,000 feet, you'll head up a steep grade on your way to the even higher Tioga Pass (elevation 9,941 feet). Muscle-flexing turns are rampant for the first several miles, and the road demands attention. At the ranger station, pay $10 per vehicle and $10 per passenger (unless you've purchased a $50 National Parks Pass) and enter the mother of the mother of all national parks. The simple and helpful park pamphlet will be tempting to look at, but chances are you'll be focused on wilderness scenery that'll leave your jaw on your gas tank.

The two-lane road is fairly wide, and a collection of slow curves and pine forests soon gives way to boulders and cliffs. Guardrails are few and drops precipitous, so be on your best biking behavior. You'll be sucked into several tunnels and spat out to glimpse coming attractions in the distance, but unusually noticeable are the textures you can distinguish. Wood, rock, water, or light, everything appears—if this makes any sense—to be better than nature.

Speeds can reach 60 mph on straights and drop to 20 mph on tight curves, and even though you could make the trip from Lee Vining in two hours, allow an extra hour just to stop at turnouts, shoot pictures, or savor the visual feast of twisting roads and the golden glow of autumn leaves.

About 55 miles into this leg, you'll reach Highway 41. Turn left and follow the signs to Yosemite Village. It is bigger and better than anything you can imagine.

Yosemite Primer

Yosemite conjures thousands of images and raises expectations to dizzying heights. You'd think it would fail to deliver, but it doesn't. It is just as beautiful, wild, tame, rich, and sublime as you'd expect.

It's tempting to think the rest of America would look like this if we hadn't beat Mother Nature into submission, but there is only one Yosemite. Initially set aside by President Lincoln in 1864, Yosemite Valley and the Mariposa Grove of giant sequoias were to be "held for public use, resort, and recreation … inalienable for all time."

In 1890, an act of Congress preserved 1,170 square miles of forests, fields, valleys, and streams equal in size to Rhode Island. Today, it is traversed by 263 miles of roads and 840 miles of hiking trails and is home to 240 species of birds, 80 species of mammals, and 1,400 species of flowering plants.

The park is as bold and as beautiful as America. Enjoy it.

On the Road: Yosemite

While you could take your bike and explore the park on your own, I suggest you start by putting yourself in the hands of Yosemite's park rangers. They are knowledgeable and courteous and will likely be able to answer every question you have.

Although it's high cheese, the tram tour (or bus tour in cold weather) is the best way to see Yosemite Valley, the most visited section of the park. The tour also stops at Bridal Veil Falls, Half Dome, and monumental El Capitan.

While the size of the high granite edifice may not impress you at first, look closely until you spot a pinpoint dabbed on the mountain, and you'll get an instant education in proportion. That is a mountain climber. Focus on the parsley sprigs ticked in slivers of rock. Those are pine trees you are looking at, and they are at least 80 feet tall. Soak this in, and respect for those pin-headed climbers increases.

The tour takes you by lush meadows that make up only 20 percent of the park but support 80 percent of its flowers. Information like this flows without restriction—tour guides think they're at a *Jeopardy!* audition and freely fling out data on botany, geology, and forestry. The tour lasts two hours, after which you'll have plenty of time to ride back to the highlights, this time with knowledge about what you're seeing.

Exploring on your own may be the most rewarding experience of Yosemite. At Curry Village and Yosemite Village, you can fill up a backpack with water, snacks, camera, and film, and the park is yours. Hiking trails, which range from easy to grueling, deliver you to impressive sights, such as giant boulders and trees as wide as Cadillacs. The woods are welcoming in their solitude and open your senses to every movement, sound, and fragrance. Rustling leaves recall a rushing stream, flaked bark peels off the gnarled trunks of cedar trees, acorns drop, and pine cones fall with a soft splat.

Stopping to feel the environment is akin to slowing down on a great ride and far more satisfying. Allow time to rest when you want, where you want, and realize that the "real world" is hundreds of miles away, your office even farther. If you absolutely have to do something, check the lodges for listings of daily events, such as fishing, photography classes, and nature talks.

When night falls, the sky looks more white than black, since stars can be counted by the millions. It's been only two days since leaving Las Vegas. There, the city demanded you stay up late. Here, the rewards of Yosemite are offered when you rise early and take advantage of another day in paradise.

Pull It Over: Yosemite Highlights
Attractions and Adventures

If you plan to fish at Yosemite, you need a fishing license, available at the Sport Shop in Yosemite Valley, the Wawona Store, and the Tuolumne Meadows Store. If you want to take the first step toward tackling El Capitan, sign up for climbing lessons by calling the **Mountaineering School** (209/372-8344).

Several sightseeing tours are available; call 209/372-1240 for details on each. The most popular is the introductory **Valley Floor Tour** ($20.50), which lasts two hours

Company Snapshot: Suzuki

Before World War II, Michio Suzuki was hoping to diversify his manufacturing base from spinning looms to vehicles. It wasn't until June 1952, however, that the company entered the motorcycle market with a 36cc single-cylinder two-stroke called Power Free. The bike's innovations (such as a double-sprocket gear system, like today's moped) earned the company a financial boost from the patent office, which Suzuki used to develop Power Free's two-speed transmission and, later, a 60cc version called the Diamond Free. It followed this in 1954 with Colleda CO, a relatively massive 90cc single-cylinder four-stroke. So, if you're thinking of starting your own motorcycle factory, be encouraged. The genesis of the 180-mph Hayabusa was a little spinning-loom factory in Hamamatsu.

and travels 26 miles through the heart of Yosemite. The **Glacier Point Tour** is $29.50. A full day's adventure, the **Grand Tour** ($55 plus optional $8 lunch) winds through Glacier Point and Mariposa Grove, site of the famous giant sequoias. Each tour is led by a park ranger who knows more than is natural about the park.

Yosemite's "downtown" is Yosemite Village, complete with post office, groceteria, pizza parlor, deli, auditorium, museum, cemetery, a few hotels, and the Ansel Adams Gallery, which features works for sale by Adams and other wildlife photographers. At the visitors center station, you can sign up for photo courses or ranger-led activities, check road conditions, or buy some books. Over at Curry Village, there are gift shops, a tour center, bike rentals, and snack shops.

Blue-Plate Specials

After a day of grazing on picnic grub or at concession stands, experience lunch or dinner at the **Ahwahnee** hotel (209/372-1489). At the original Western lodge, the setting is extraordinary. The big food and flawless service match the design and character of this massive room. Call me, and I'll join you.

Shut-Eye

Yosemite used to reach peak popularity between Memorial Day and Labor Day; today, stretch that from April to the end of November. Make reservations as far in advance as possible. For hotel reservations within the park, call 559/252-4848 (Fresno), www.yosemitepark.com; for campground reservations, call 800/436-7275.

The park boasts a range of facilities, from dirt-cheap rustic to over-the-top indulgent. In the heart of the park, Yosemite's fabled **Ahwahnee** (209/372-1407, $326) tops the price list. One of the most beautiful inns in America, it was built in 1927 and is breathtaking in design, superb in service. You'll find character and tradition in the grand fireplace, massive timbers, Great Room, and baronial dining room. Reserve one of 123 rooms, at eyebrow-arching prices, as far in advance as possible. Other choices offer greater variety at a wider price range, such as private baths, cabins, or canvas tents. Choose from the motel-style **Yosemite Lodge** (about $115–161), **Wawona Hotel** ($115–170), or Curry Village tents and cabins ($69–108).

Side Trip: Yosemite to Lake Tahoe

The road so far has been rich in both kindness and treachery. If you think it's been more of the latter, leave Yosemite Village on 120 West and head for home. Otherwise, get ready for another adventurous 200-mile run, returning via 120 East to 395 and on to Lake Tahoe. Warning: Make this a daytime ride, since the tight curves can be dangerous after dark.

Even if you never ride another mile, you'll have experienced the most complicated blend of riding in terms of terrain, scenery, sociology, psychology, and climate. And there's more to come.

About three miles north of Lee Vining, Mono Lake reveals itself from a highway vista. Now drying out like a Miami retiree as folks in Los Angeles drain the lake for their lawns and bathwater, the exposed white sands are a curiously surreal landscape.

Six miles later, you're at 7,000 feet and climbing, with the vast Mono Basin in the distance on your right. This run soon places you back in a desert landscape, a curious fact when you cruise past 7,700 feet and look back to see Yosemite's Tioga Pass. The altitude also introduces winds that can kick your tires out from under you. Keep a low profile, Bugsy.

It's difficult to fathom that these changes are occurring during one incredible journey. And to prove its power, nature will once again change environments on you. After you cross the Conway Summit at 8,138 feet, the desert leaves the stage and you enter California ranch country. Small cow towns come into view. Scan the horizons and you may spy snow falling in one section, clear blue skies in another, rain in a third. It is altogether impossible to absorb the varying expressions of nature that surround you, but you don't really need to. Just file this information away under Memorable Motorcycle Run.

Past Bridgeport, the slow winding roads get their act straightened out and whisk you into Devil Gate's Summit, at 7,500 feet. This will sharpen your senses for the impending pinball run, but for now, the hills are low and rolling and fun.

Although you've already defeated the toughest terrain, you now face Walker Creek Canyon. After 10 miles of tranquility, the winding roads snatch you back into the challenge of rushing water, boulders, pine needles, and fallen trees. As you catch fleeting glimpses of red rocks and black rocks and sand, you'll be making mental notes to thank the highway engineers and sign up for the Sierra Club.

When the canyon breathes its last, you'll enter the tiny town of Walker, where nothing seems to be living, and then Coleville (pop. 43), which makes Walker look like Chicago. The next town, Topaz, is your cue to look for Highway 89; if it's open, it will be on your left.

For a minor road, 89 is amazingly beautiful. Three miles into it, you climb to 6,000 feet and enter a fertile valley rich with fields of pines and sagebrush.

You have no choice but to keep riding, and you won't be disappointed. The higher you ride—and you will—the more spectacular the view. As your attorney, I advise you to stop at the peak and look back over the valley. It is an image that will stay with you for a long, long time. You can look for miles down the valley's breadth, and with keen eyesight you may make out stacks of logs that are, in fact, remote cabins locked within the breeches of behemoth mountain walls.

No picture can do it justice; only your memory will capture the scope of this incredible vista. Desert, snow, mountains, valleys.... From here, you are ruler of the world, in command of all that you survey. It is as inspiring as it is humbling.

You are nearing Monitor Pass at a mighty 8,300 feet, and the imminent descent is a gift to enjoy. Drop it into neutral and rest your engine for several miles as you glide your bike into easy curves and experience the decline of western mountain ranges.

Continue on 89 toward Markleeville, 32 miles south of Lake Tahoe. You may stop for several reasons: If the sun is setting, the mountains you just crossed will look like a Maxfield Parrish landscape painted with pinks, violets, blues, and crimson—and you certainly should avoid the upcoming roads at night. The **Cutthroat Saloon** (14830 Hwy. 89, 530/694-2150) offers another good reason. It's quite popular with riders because of the Western Victorian decor, the adjoining Wolf Creek restaurant, and the ladies' underwear pinned on the ceiling. Maybe you'll find something in your size. I did.

From here, the road is pleasing and predictable and leads to South Lake Tahoe. The city's population, 21,000, is why you're riding to the less populated northern shore, although you will find motels, hotels, and cabins here.

Highway 28 along the west shore gives you a final burst of excitement. Unlike most lakefront roads that blend into the shoreline, this one has dangerously high cliffs, Jordache-tight switchbacks, and eye-popping glimpses of Lake Tahoe from inlets and Alpine vistas. In a way, this heart-throbbing run is the natural counterpoint to the artificial fun of Las Vegas.

Shut-Eye

Chain Drive
A, E, G, H, J, Q, S, Y, CC, DD

Countless cabins and cottages surround the lake, as well as a number of chains. See cross-reference guide featuring phone numbers and Web addresses on page 514.

Resources for Riders

Las Vegas–Yosemite Run

Nevada Travel Information
Nevada Road Conditions—702/486-3116
Nevada State Parks—775/687-4370, www.state.nv.us/stparks
Nevada Tourism—800/638-2328, www.travelnevada.com

California Travel Information
California Association of Bed & Breakfast Inns—www.cabbi.com
California Division of Tourism—916/444-4429 or 800/862-2543,
    www.gocalif.ca.gov
California Road Conditions—916/445-7623 or 800/427-7623
California Road and Weather Information—916/979-3051
California State Parks—916/653-6995, www.parks.ca.gov

Local and Regional Information
Lake Tahoe Central Reservations Service—530/583-3494 or 888/434-
    1262, www.mytahoevacation.com
Lake Tahoe Forecast and Road Conditions—530/542-4636, ext. 3
Las Vegas Chamber of Commerce—702/735-1616, www.lvchamber.com
Las Vegas Visitors Information Center—702/892-0711,
    www.vegasfreedom.com
Lone Pine Chamber of Commerce—760/876-4444 or 877/253-8981,
    www.lonepinechamber.org
Yosemite Information—209/372-0200, www.yosemite.com or
    www.nps.gov/yose
Yosemite Road Service—209/372-0200, ext. 1

Nevada Motorcycle Shops
Desert Motorsports—3535 W. Tropicana Ave., Las Vegas, 702/795-
    2000, www.desertmotorsports.com
Kawasaki of Las Vegas—3850 N. Rancho Dr., Las Vegas, 702/656-1955,
    www.kawasakioflasvegas.com
Las Vegas Harley-Davidson/Buell—2495 E. Sahara Ave., Las Vegas,
    702/431-8500, www.lvhd.com
Motorcycle City—4260 Boulder Ave., Las Vegas, 702/451-1121,
    www.azmotorsports.com

California Motorcycle Shop
Golden State Cycle—174 S. Main St., Bishop, 760/872-1570,
    www.goldenstatecycle.com

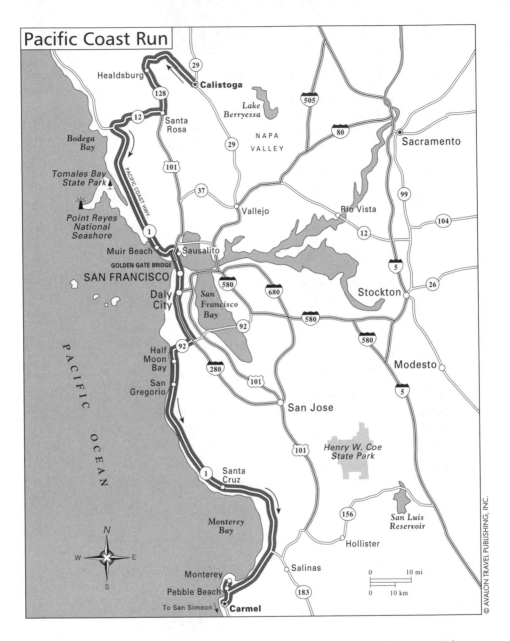

Pacific Coast Run

Route: Calistoga to Carmel via Sausalito, Monterey, Big Sur, Pacific Coast Highway
Distance: Approximately 300 miles; consider 10 days with stops.
•**Days 1–2—Calistoga/Napa Valley** •**Day 3—Travel** •**Days 4–5—Sausalito/
San Francisco** •**Day 6—Travel** •**Days 7–8—Carmel/Monterey** •**Day 9—
Travel** •**Day 10—San Simeon**
First Leg: Calistoga to Sausalito (80 miles)
Second Leg: Sausalito to Carmel (120 miles)
Optional Third Leg: Carmel to San Simeon (112 miles)
Helmet Laws: California requires helmets.

Pacific Coast Run

Calistoga, California to Carmel, California

As evidenced by the ride through Death Valley, Lone Pine, and Yosemite, eastern California was designed by God specifically for motorcyclists. He did a pretty good job on the West Coast as well. Napa Valley is the closest you'll come to riding along Mediterranean roads, unless you ship your bike to Piraeus. Although the region is marked by affluence, you don't have to be rich—the roads are free. From the luxury of Calistoga's spas to the pure beauty of the San Francisco skyline, from Carmel's fantasy architecture to the dream world of Hearst Castle, this run features short rides on roads that are just right. What's more, the journey from valley to hill to coastal highway creates a satisfying blend of environments, especially during late summer or fall.

Calistoga Primer

Some motorcycle travelers make a critical error when visiting Napa Valley by staying in the valley's namesake, Napa. Far more appealing is the town of Calistoga. As your advance team, let me tell you why you need to stay here.

Several thousand years ago, a volcano named Mt. Konocti erupted 20 miles away and plopped about five feet of ash on the valley floor. Around the 1500s, the Wappo Indians realized the ash had mixed with the naturally heated mineral water and started bathing in the mud and water. They finished up with a sweat wrap, and they felt good. Damn good. The Wappos called the valley Tu-la-ha-lu-si ("Oven Place").

When Sam Brannan, California's first Gold Rush millionaire, arrived here in the 1860s, he saw the potential for a resort spa town. At a promotional supper, he proclaimed that this would be the "Calistoga of Sarafornia!" The slip became a marketing ploy, and Calistoga was born. Sorry, Wappos. Riding the wealth of the mines and the natural hot springs, Brannan's community became the central point for a railroad serving the upper valley, and it sustained itself through the turn of century, past World War II, and into a new millennium without losing its appeal.

As in Brannan's day, Calistoga appears to be riding the crest of a prosperous wave again. Spas and businesses that were closed in the early 1990s are thriving now. The film *Sideways* impressed an already intense subculture of San Francisco wine sippers, who flock to town for vineyard runs and body wraps. But if you see 'em, don't even mention merlot. More important, motorcycle travelers park up and down Lincoln Avenue, frequenting small saloons and planning sorties into the surrounding mountain roads. One of the state's more pleasing towns, it is the perfect starting point for this journey.

On the Road: Calistoga

The best towns to visit are those where you can ride in, park for free, and check out the town on foot. Calistoga is just such a place and one of the best motorcycle towns you'll ever find—especially if you like drinking wine and having someone upgrade the condition of your muscles to happy. From Dr. Wilkinson's Hot Springs and Mud Baths to the fine restaurants, this is the Old West with a 21st-century facelift.

Unfortunately, you'll have to wait to see all that it offers, because the roads of this region are so damn tempting, you'll be hard-pressed to sit still.

The number of riding options rivals that of vineyards here. The Greek Peloponnese, Swiss Alps, and Italian Dolomites are all here for your pleasure. Within minutes, you can take comfort in roads as curvaceous as Marilyn Monroe, traverse hills that are soft and low, ride over green creeks and past drooping brown trees and pumpkin patches and groves bursting with almonds, avocadoes, and black walnuts. Not only will your ride be visually exciting, it will be redolent with the fresh, fragrant aroma of nut trees, strawberries, grapes, and flowering plants.

It is a thrilling experience to be here, where the outdoors are treasured, not tamed. You should see all of this and travel beyond the hills, but also consider a manageable trip to the region north of Napa Valley.

Although the larger wineries are in the southern Napa Valley, head north on Highway 29 (aka Silverado Trail), on the east side of the valley. Turn left on Tubbs Lane, and then right at Highway 128. Soon you're on twisting canopy roads that offer some of the finest motorcycle riding in the country. Motorcycles springing up and over the hills look like ants on a mound, but be careful when the afternoon sun and shadows play tricks on the pavement.

Head north, and you'll ride into Alexander Valley. Although there are no major towns, you must stop in Healdsburg at the strangely well-stocked **Jimtown General Store** (6706 Hwy. 128, 707/433-1212, www.jimtown.com). Think back a few decades—your childhood is right here: Mary Jane candies, bubble-gum cigars, Chinese finger traps, whoopee cushions, old toys from the '40s and '50s, a convenient deli, and, if your name is Jim, a chance at immortality by signing the autograph hound.

From here, you can head farther north, south, east, or west to explore other valley back roads. Like those around New Hope, Pennsylvania, all roads lead to a great ride.

Pull It Over: Calistoga Highlights
Attractions and Adventures

If you want a spa treatment without feeling obligated to stay at a resort, you have two options; both have stood the test of time. Established by town founder Sam Brannan in 1871, **Indian Springs** (1712 Lincoln Ave., 707/942-4913, www.indianspringscalistoga.com) is the oldest continuously operating thermal pool and spa in California. Spread across 16 acres of volcanic ash are mud baths, thermal geysers, massages, and a mineral pool. Yowzah! **Dr. Wilkinson's Hot Springs** (1507 Lincoln Ave., 707/942-4102, www.drwilkinson.com) was founded in 1951 by Doc Wilkinson. Aside from a great name and continuous family ownership, the spa features mud baths, mineral whirlpools, steam rooms, facials, and an indoor mineral pool.

One of the main reasons you're here is because of the more than 150 wineries in this region. You can get information and directions to all of them by making a few calls, doing a little pretrip online research, or stopping at the **Chamber of Commerce** (1458 Lincoln Ave #9, 707/942-6333) for maps and discount coupons to wineries and spas. The hunt is well worth it since the roads to the vineyards are unusually seductive. For more information contact the **Napa Valley Vintners Association** (707/963-3388,

What's in a Mud Bath?

You know how you can get achy after 10 hours in the saddle? A mud bath will loosen you up faster than an Ex-Lax smoothie. A mud bath is a mixture of heated mineral water and volcanic ash and/or peat moss. After you settle into this gloop, the thick mixture heats up to penetrate your body, relax your muscles, and alleviate stress, tensions, aches, and pains. Ten–twelve minutes should be enough, or more if you're really keyed up.

www.napavintners.com), the **Sonoma County Wineries Association** (707/586-3795, www.sonomawine.com), or **Alexander Valley Wine Growers** (888/289-4637, www.alexandervalley.org).

The terrain and mood throughout these valleys is unique in America, and the experience of soaring above it all is as extraordinary as the price ($205) with **Napa Valley Balloons** (707/944-0228 or 800/253-2224, www.napavalleyballoons.com). The steep fee includes breakfast before the launch from the Domaine Chandon Winery and flights of up to two hours. Right in Calistoga is the adequately named **Calistoga Balloons** (707/942-5758 or 888/995-7700, www.calistogaballons.com), which includes breakfast and a flight lasting around an hour. The **Bonaventura Balloon Company** (133 Wall Rd., Napa, 707/944-2822 or 800/359-6272, www.bonaventuraballoons.com) is another option with similar rates (around $200). Each operation adds options for breakfasts, picnics, or champagne brunches. Before deciding on any flight, ask how many passengers share your basket, whether or not you'll be able to help (if you'd like) as part of the crew, and if you can suck in some helium to change your voice.

Ben Sharpsteen made good by becoming an Academy Award–winning animator, producer, and director for Walt Disney. His love for his adopted hometown led to the creation of the surprisingly intriguing **Sharpsteen Museum** (1311 Washington St., 707/942-5911, www.sharpsteen-museum.org). The downtown museum provides a great introduction to Calistoga and the history of upper Napa Valley. With careful detail, its 32-foot diorama depicts 1860s life at the opulent resort. Sam Brannan's cottage is connected to the main museum, which is open 11 A.M.–4 P.M. year-round. Admission is free—but they'd appreciate it if you slipped 'em three bucks.

Not any pricier than Calistoga's spa treatments, this option is just more ... unusual. West of Calistoga at **Osmosis** (209 Bohemian Hwy., Freestone, 707/823-8231, www.osmosis.com), after a Japanese tea ceremony, you strip down to your absolute bare nakedness and settle into a wooden tub filled with antiseptic cedar fiber, rice bran, and 600 active enzymes. An attendant covers you up, and you spend the next 20 minutes in the compost heap, throwing off more sweat than Secretariat. After you're dug up, you're hosed down and invited upstairs for the pièce de résistance—a massage. Surreal, yet fantastically relaxing. The enzyme bath for one is $75; add a massage for a total of $155.

Blue-Plate Specials

Locals agree that one of the best breakfast spots is the **Café Sarafornia** (1413 Lincoln Ave., 707/942-0555). A casual start to an extraordinary day's ride, the breakfasts—scrambles, omelettes, blintzes, crepes, and oat bran pancakes—range a modest $4–8.

Off the beaten path, southeast of Calistoga on Highway 128, the **Corners Cafe and Saloon** (6005 Monticello Rd., Lake Berryessa, 707/258-8138) is the starting line and rest stop for riders embarking on weekend runs. Riders of every racing stripe and model fuel up with breakfast, arrive to play pool or pinball, or sit in the bar and watch the game on a large-screen TV. A great place for breakfast, burgers, and pork chops, as well as the inside scoop on hidden roads.

Perhaps the nicest restaurant in town, **Brannan's Grill** (1374 Lincoln Ave., 707/942-2233, www.brannansgrill.com) serves lunches and dinners that are elegant, simple, and creative. The wide-open dining room and fireplace are settling, and the pace never seems rushed, even when it's packed. The menu changes seasonally, so check its website for current appetizers and entrées.

A low-key local favorite, **Pacifico** (1237 Lincoln Ave., 707/942-4400, www.pacficorestaurant.com) serves traditional Mexican food for lunch and dinner. It wins high marks for its chips, salsa, guacamole, and hand-shaken margaritas. The full bar is a rarity in Napa Valley.

Watering Holes

Open daily 'til 2 A.M., **Susie's** (1365 Lincoln Ave., 707/942-6710) is literally a hole in the wall. Head down a narrow hallway and you end up here, at a cool, dark refuge in the netherworld between "dive" and "joint." Regulars are quick to befriend strangers, and you'll soon settle in at the only pool tables in town. You're also welcome to try your hand at the piano (provided you can play). Happy hour? All day long. The Redwood Empire HOG Chapter dubbed Susie's a biker-friendly bar.

You'll find a microbrewery and full bar at the **Calistoga Inn** (1250 Lincoln Ave., 707/942-4101); a full bar and restaurant at **Stomp** (1457 Lincoln Ave., 707/942-8272); and a full bar all by its lonesome at the **Hydro Bar and Grill** (1403 Lincoln Ave., 707/942-9777). Each features live music, and Hydro pours 20 microbrews on tap.

Shut-Eye

Calistoga is so perfect, you may want to extend your stay by a year or two. Most lodging options include a spa, so plan on at least one massage to complement your visit. **B&B Style** (707/942-2888 or 800/995-8884, www.bandbstyle.com) is a free service with information on more than 250 houses, cottages, and inns in wine country.

Motels and Motor Courts
The **Roman Spa** (1300 Washington St., 707/942-4441, www.romanspahotsprings.com, $135 and up) has ordinary rooms but lush landscaping and a laidback atmosphere. After a ride, you can rest outside in a mineral pool, jet spa pool, or sauna. Its spa services include the standard lineup of mud baths, mineral baths, and massages. Rates here run about 20 percent less off-season.

Chain Drive
A, C, Q, U

Chain hotels are in town, or within 10 miles. See cross-reference guide featuring phone numbers and Web addresses on page 514.

Inn-dependence
One of the most pleasing places you can stay is the **Cottage Grove Inn** (1711 Lincoln Ave., 707/942-8400 or 800/799-2284, www.cottagegrove.com, $325). These luxurious Napa Valley cottages, shaded by towering trees, feature whirlpool tubs, fireplaces, private porches, and distinct themes (fly-fishing, equestrian, Audubon, musical, etc.). The price at Cottage Grove is panic-inducing, but the cottages sleep three, and they *do* include breakfast.... Check them out; you may think it's worth it just to be able to park your bike out front and walk downtown. No loud pipes, please.

On the Road: Calistoga to Sausalito

From Calistoga, you have several options, two of which are quite different. For a fast, ordinary, straight shot, ride west to U.S. 101, and then drive south until you reach Sausalito. Here's the alternative for experienced riders.

Route 12 South (also called Calistoga Rd.) heads about 30 miles due west past Santa Rosa toward Bodega Bay (the setting for Alfred Hitchcock's *The Birds*), and then reaches the Pacific Coast Highway.

Let me warn you: The road to the coast can be wonderful at first, but it soon gives way to city traffic in Santa Rosa, and then to less than spectacular scenery until you reach fabled Highway 1 (aka the Pacific Coast Highway, or PCH). Also, the stretch from Bodega Bay south can be pretty spooky, unless you've replaced your tires with mountain goats. Seriously. Curves are very sharp and safety rails nonexistent, the twists can be hypnotic, and sometimes the road's layout can range from impassable to impossible. But if you're ready, here's what you'll experience.

After you get on Highway 1, the road sweeps east and beyond the view of the coast. To compensate, there are great straightaways, and your path follows the rise and fall of the mountains. You'll ride toward Tomales Bay, a long drink of water, where the rustic cabins of fishermen crop up every few miles.

Scenery remains a constant until you pass Lima. About eight miles later, the run approaches Dogtown, which, despite its elegant moniker, is a simple village that is seven times older than it looks. The road leads into a forest and a brief but most enjoyable series of 20-mph turns and shady, slow twists. A few miles later, as you rumble along the slow, graceful bayside, flecks of water may hiss on your pipes as you follow the curving shoreline on this mighty low road.

When you reach Point Reyes Station, you can follow the path blazed by other bikers and head out to the Point Reyes Lighthouse. It's a popular run for locals, but I didn't get much out of it. If you pass it by, the next big show lies south of Stinson Beach.

The ability to ride from here to U.S. 101 is what separates human from animal. Throw back a few Maalox tablets and get ready to attack the road between here and Muir Beach, a paved funhouse of gravel, dangerously sharp turns, and very steep drops. Maybe it was because I was riding a monster bike, but I often tapped it into first and took turns at a speed exceeded only by tree sloths. For several miles, my mood alternated between excitement and sheer terror. Just about the time I was thinking, "What hell is this?" I was dumped out into level-headed Tamalpais Valley and then onto U.S. 101 for a short, citified ride in Sausalito.

About damn time.

Sausalito Primer

It's almost a cliché to find that a quaint seaside town was once a hotspot for drunken sailors, bawdy saloons, and come one, come all bordellos—but I still get a kick knowing that all this happened in Sausalito. It has the essence of the Cote d'Azur, and the European style is no accident. The town was discovered by Juan Manual de Ayala in 1575 and later became a favored shelter for full-rigged sailing ships from around the world. Today, those ships have been replaced by private yachts.

During World War II, Sausalito was a major shipbuilding site, with Liberty ships, landing craft, and tankers taking shape here. Afterward, the area became a haven for writers and artists—as evidenced by the galleries along Bridgeway Street.

It's an uncommonly exotic town, and I guarantee you'll enjoy it—or my name isn't Orville Redenbacher.

On the Road: Sausalito

You've already enjoyed a ride from the northeast, and later you'll embark on a great ride south. For now, just park your bike and enjoy the town. You'll never tire of the view, which is even more impressive than that of Camden, Maine, where the Appalachians dissolve into the Atlantic.

Sausalito also has plenty of restaurants and galleries and pubs, and if you need even more, simply head over to San Francisco via ferry or the mighty Golden Gate Bridge.

I chose to continue the low-key theme I'd grown accustomed to in Calistoga and decided to stay in town. Not a bad choice. The heart of Sausalito is as foreign as any village along the Mediterranean and evokes the loveliness of the Riviera.

Besides, the views from here rival any in the world, from the San Francisco skyline to the fogbanks rolling over the bay. The only thing missing is the Golden Gate Bridge, hidden from view behind some ill-placed hills.

In town, the Plaza de Vina Del Mar Park has a visitors center and, more prominently, two 14-foot-tall elephant statues created for the Panama-Pacific Exposition of 1915. The architecture defies generic business district, instead blending Victorian, French, Spanish, and Irish accents. Not only are the people friendly and the setting perfect, you'll find the town to be as cosmopolitan and as relaxed as any you'll find as you explore the central district.

This is clearly a town of affluence. As a double-naught spy, I deduced this from the forest of yachts I saw at the marina, a short and pleasant walk from the park. As you roam the town, a few shops are worth exploring in greater detail. The **Venice Gourmet Delicatessen** (625 Bridgeway St., 415/332-3544, www.venicegourmet.com) has been here since 1966 and continues to be the local favorite. The shop is cluttered with copper kettles, baklava, dried sausage, soft drinks, and premium wines.

If you finish making the rounds early, you may opt to visit San Francisco, or head north on Bridgeway to reach Caledonia Street, which is an authentic Sausalito neighborhood.

Then, in the evening, as ferryboats start knocking across the waters, shuttling workers back from San Francisco, you can relax on the promenade or inside a waterfront restaurant and watch the most spectacular city skyline in America come to light.

Pull It Over: Sausalito Highlights
Attractions and Adventures

While an inmate on Alcatraz, I was only able to cruise the bay on my inner tube. Now released, I can cruise to SF cheaply aboard the **Blue and Gold Ferry** (415/773-1188, www.blueandgoldfleet.com). The ships depart Sausalito several times daily ($7.50 one way) for Fisherman's Wharf. From there, you can catch tour boats to Alcatraz. Be sure to make reservations for the $16 trip to the shuttered prison, which includes a cell house audio tour. **Golden Gate Ferry** (415/923-2000) avoids Fisherman's Wharf and goes to the foot of Market Street; fares are $6.15 one way. Sorry, no room for motorcycles.

Mark Reuben Vintage Gallery (34 Princess St., 415/332-8815 or 877/444-3767, www.markreubengallery.com) displays thousands of vintage photographs, many taken from the original negatives. Matted and framed original pictures include those of the Davidson brothers, the Beatles, and Marlon Brando in *The Wild One*. You could spend days in here. Topics cover sports, history, entertainers, political figures, and other photos perfect for the office and home. Shipping's available, and dig this: The store manager was the Harley Queen of York, Pennsylvania.

Blue-Plate Specials

A great way to start the day is at the **Bridgeway Cafe** (633 Bridgeway St., 415/332-3426). With a great view of the city and the bay, this friendly little diner serves all-day breakfasts, lunches, and dinners, and the waitresses are kind and considerate.

When the evening falls, consider **Horizons** (558 Bridgeway St., 415/331-3232). In addition to its rich woods and high ceilings, the wide bay windows and patio dining reveal a breathtaking view of San Francisco. Serving lunch and dinner, the waterfront restaurant features fettuccini jambalaya, five-cheese spinach cannelloni, and lobster tails.

Watering Holes

Two bars in town are among the best I've had the pleasure to discover. At the **No-Name Bar** (757 Bridgeway St., 415/332-1392), there's character in abundance, a fireplace inside, and a garden patio outside. Owner Al Stanfield rides and often makes the 2,000-mile jaunt to Sturgis. His place delivers live jazz on weekends, blues on weekdays, and pub food in the afternoon. Beers and spirits abound in this mighty beautiful bar.

Since the late '60s, **Paterson's** (739 Bridgeway St., 415/332-1264) has been frequented by spirits—and ales and more than 100 kinds of malt whiskey. In fact, it stocks a variety of rums, from $6-a-shot brands to a top-of-the-line Glen Grant for $30 a sip. This place rivals the best British pub and does so with style. During the day, the clientele changes from locals to tourists to commuters to younger locals. Anytime you arrive is the best time to be here. Another plus: Pints are 20-ounce imperials.

Shut-Eye

I'd suggest making every effort to stay the night in Sausalito, but across the bridge in San Francisco exists every chain hotel known to man.

Chain Drive
A, B, C, E, G, H, K, L, N, Q, R, S, T, U, Y, AA, CC, DD

Chain hotels are in town, or within 10 miles. See cross-reference guide featuring phone numbers and Web addresses on page 514.

Inn-dependence
There are four unique and (thankfully) nongeneric hotels in Sausalito. In an area where homes sell for billions of dollars, the rates at all but one are relatively inexpensive. The **Alta Mira** (125 Bulkley Ave., 415/332-1350, $85 and up) has

been around since the '20s and hasn't changed much. On Sausalito's high ground, it's the most moderately priced hotel downtown. Its Mediterranean interior and commanding views of the bay alone are worth the price of admission. The rooms are somewhat small, but the balcony opens them up. The **Casa Madrona Hotel** (801 Bridgeway St., 415/332-0502 or 800/567-9524, www.casamadrona.com, $149 and up in season) opened in 1885. It features single cottages and elevated rooms with perfect bay views. The staff is friendly; the rooms are plush; the gardenlike atmosphere is soothing; and it's all within sight of one of America's largest and loudest cities. Room 315 lets you soak in the tub while watching the city lights. Included in the rate is an evening social hour that affords the opportunity to get looped on some free wine. On the park, **Hotel Sausalito** (16 El Portal, 415/332-0700 or 888/442-0700, www.hotelsausalito.com, $145 and up) is the most European of the four. The rich, warm, gold tones of this hotel perfectly mirror the sunrise over the bay. The hotel offers 16 1920s-style rooms and suites with modern amenities and views of the park or harbor. As the name implies, the **Inn Above Tide** (30 El Portal, 415/332-9535, 800/893-8433, www.innabovetide.com, $265 and up) is on the waterfront. All 30 rooms face the hillside city, although they are more modern than I prefer. You may be lured by the free breakfast and sunset wine and cheese receptions.

On the Road: Sausalito to Carmel

The next leg of the journey revs you up for some spectacular scenery and the unforgettable experience of riding across the Pacific Ocean in less than five minutes.

When you leave Sausalito, take Bridgeway Street and follow it south. Three minutes from the center of town, you'll round the bend and see the twin towers straight ahead. Before you cross the bridge, get in the right lane and watch for a lightly trafficked access loop road that leads to Point Bonita. Taking this road will afford one of the best souvenir photos you'll ever take. Turn right, and a few hundred yards ahead, pull off and pose with your bike—the Golden Gate Bridge, bay, and city behind you help create photos suitable for framing.

When you get back on the road, you'll pay five bucks to cross the bridge, and even though you'd think it would be paid for by now, it's worth it. To your left is the bay, to your right the Pacific Ocean, which will be your traveling companion for the next 100-plus miles.

Navigating through town to reach PCH is a little tricky and trying to explain how to do it can drive a man to drink. The abridged version is this:

After crossing the bridge, veer to the right to reach 19th Avenue (which is also Hwy. 1) and work your way through a tunnel then into residential neighborhoods and toward Daly City. Stay on Highway 1. At I-280, the road splits. Veer left to take 280 farther south to Route 92, where you turn west toward Half Moon Bay. Veer right onto PCH if you want to get right to the coast. Not a bad idea at all.

But after slow city traffic, I wanted to blow out the cobwebs, so I took I-280. Surprisingly, it wasn't bad. The farther from the city you get, the greater the pleasure, as you see buildings and urban sprawl wither away into the natural landscape.

The next surprise was taking 92 West. I was back in the land of curvy roads and nice lakes, and I also passed miles of flower farms—a far sweeter aroma than I sniffed in Amish country.

The road ends at PCH, and from here, it's 100 miles south to the Monterey Peninsula. Unlike PCH north of San Francisco, the road here is fairly flat, straight, and ordinary. Based on the inventory I spied at roadside produce stands, I deduced that the farmers of this fertile region raise artichokes, pumpkins, carrots, hot dogs, and soft drinks.

It's impossible to explain how easy this road is. Flat and smooth, the pleasure is in the tranquility of the environment. This lasts for about 60 coastal miles until you reach the Santa Cruz county line. Thus ends the scenic route.

Unfortunately, you have to run a gauntlet of urban ugliness to reach your final destination. You're in for fast food joints, cheap gas, bike shops, and a crappy highway that lasts for more than 10 miles.

Sadly, the ocean remains hidden behind miles of land, and there's not a damn thing you can do about it except get to one of the most enchanting towns in California. After passing Monterey, look for Ocean Avenue, turn right, and head straight into a dreamscape called Carmel.

Most extraordinary Carmel.

Carmel Primer

Carmel may be the crown jewel in the Monterey Peninsula, one of California's more naturally beautiful regions. The Essalen Indians knew it when they made it their home in A.D. 3,000–500 Next the Ahlone Indians showed up, and they were doing fine until their time started running out in 1542, when Spanish explorer Juan Rodriguez Cabrillo sighted the white sand beach and pine forest. Even though Cabrillo couldn't land because of rough waters, he claimed it for Spain anyway.

an artist in his outdoor studio on 17-Mile Drive near Carmel

Yes, he did. And I've decided that I own the Bahamas.

Several explorers later, in June 1770, Father Junipero Serra, a Spanish governor and a Franciscan priest, proclaimed the area the military and ecclesiastical capital of Alta, California.

With natural beauty and easy access to the ocean, it was obvious people would covet the Monterey Peninsula. Mexico owned it and then surrendered it to the U.S. Navy without a fight. In 1906, refugees from the San Francisco earthquake made it their new home. And in 1916, in Carmel itself, bohemian artists with no architectural training showed up and formed the village on Halloween.

From the town's earliest days, art was in the forefront. When Hugh Comstock's wife asked him to build a separate house for her doll collection, he ended up building 20 whimsical cottages that are still highly prized (and livable) today. While best known as Clint Eastwood's domain (he served as mayor from 1986 to 1988), the town of 4,500 remains true to the original vision of its founding artists and preserves an oasis of art and extraordinary beauty.

On the Road: Carmel

Before you start wandering around the village, you may want to stock up on a half dozen digital cameras and memory cards, since you could easily burn up the spares shooting every picturesque building, alcove, courtyard, and garden throughout the town.

On one street, you may photograph a Swiss village, turn the corner and enter a Spanish *mercado,* and then spy the rounded archways and thatched roof of an English cottage. This is a town that will always be a village. Restrictions prohibit neon signs, street numbers, parking meters, high-rises, plastic plants, and high heels.

Here you have the option of walking a few blocks to the beach, resting at a sidewalk café, or hanging out. The best way to understand the essence of the village is with **Carmel Walks** (831/642-2700, www.carmelwalks.com), which offers two-hour guided tours through secret pathways, courtyards, and side streets, complete with some insider information. Tours ($20) are given at 10 A.M. and 2 P.M. on Saturday, 10 A.M. Tuesday–Friday. Alternatively, you can take a free walking tour with a map provided by the visitors center, which is upstairs between 5th and 6th.

Touring downtown is only the beginning. Off Ocean Drive, for $8.50 you have access to the Carmel Gate of 17-Mile Drive. But, damn it to Sarge, only residents and employees can bring in motorcycles. If you're determined (and you should be, since this is a hyperfun run), **Rent-A-Roadster** (229 Cannery Row, 831/647-1929, www.rent-a-roadster.com) in Monterey rents reproduction 1929 Model As for $30–35 per hour. With the top down and sea winds blowing, it's the next best thing to a bike.

Anyway, after paying the toll, you'll get a map listing points of interest along 17-Mile Drive, and you can drive in and out from various gates around the loop. Theoretically, road signs should direct you on the tour, but they're often hard to follow. Just stick close to the coastline and have your camera ready.

Several points jut into the Pacific, each with turnouts that reveal the sheer beauty of this rugged coastline. At Pescadera Point, white foam wraps around rocks, and at Cypress Point, a lone tree is the inspiration for one of California's signature icons. A little farther, at Bird Rock, the seals and birds bark and caw without pause.

Although you may not have your favorite clubs with you, it'd be a shame to miss **Pebble Beach** (800/654-9300, www.pebblebeach.com). Golfers consider this America's St. Andrews and are charged accordingly: Nonresidents pay a whopping $450(!) for 18 holes. Personally, I'd invest that kind of cash in a troupe of juggling monkeys. Even if you don't golf, it's worth driving through just to see the dynamic shoreline.

You can exit at the Pacific Grove gate to visit a town of bungalows, Victorian homes, and a neat main street. There's something else about this village: Each October, swarms of monarch butterflies return here, just as sure as vultures return to roost in Washington, D.C.

Eventually, the roads and advice of well-intentioned friends will guide you to Monterey and Cannery Row. According to brilliant American writer and native son John Steinbeck, Cannery Row was "a poem, a stink, a grating noise, a quality of light, a tone, a habit, a nostalgia, a dream." Now it's all this, plus some tacky tourist shops. Fisherman's Wharf is part carnival midway, where merchants seem to believe that the world's problems could be solved if everyone ate "chowder in a bun," a concoction that looks suspiciously like a bread bowl full of vomit.

The definitive attraction is the **Monterey Bay Aquarium** (886 Cannery Row, 831/648-4888, www.mbayaq.org, $19.95). More than 100 galleries and exhibits highlight the diverse habitats of the bay, and most are larger than life. In addition to the million-gallon outer bay exhibit, there are whale skeletons, a stingray petting pool, and an otter exhibit (did you know otters have pockets?). If you don't scuba dive, the aquarium is a good substitute, and the outdoor promenade puts you on the 50-yard line of the pounding waves.

From here, you can return to Carmel via 17-Mile Drive or work your way over to PCH and take the Ocean Avenue exit. The village is easily worth a day, or maybe 10 years of walking.

Pull It Over: Carmel Area Highlights
Attractions and Adventures

John Steinbeck was one of our greatest writers, and his favorite topic, America, places his works among the best road-reading material you'll find. The **Steinbeck Center** (1 Main St., Salinas, 831/796-3833, www.steinbeck.org, $11) celebrates the author's life and work. Open 10 A.M.–5 P.M. daily, the center exhibits items taken from the pages of his books, but the focal point is his GMC camper, Rocinante, from *Travels with Charley*—the inspiring cross-country journey he made with his poodle. If you love Steinbeck, you'll love the 30,000-piece archives, which include original manuscripts, oral histories, first editions, and photographs. The center includes a museum store and café.

Hey, Nanook! Wanna see a seal up close? Kayaks are big in this area, and you can rent them for $30 a day from **Adventures by the Sea** (299 Cannery Row, 831/372-1807, www.adventuresbythesea.com). Tours are also available ($45). Also check out **Monterey Bay Kayaks** (693 Del Monte Ave., 831/373-5357 or 800/649-5357, www.montereybaykayaks.com), which charges $30 per day. As you paddle among the harbor seals, you'll also see kelp forests, sea lions, otters, snowy egrets, and tourists. The bay is protected from large swells, so it should be smooth paddling.

Besides the sea, there are ranch lands inland to explore. You can ride trails in Carmel Valley at **Molera Horseback Tours** (831/625-5486 or 800/942-5486, www.molerahorsebacktours.com), which depart from and ride through a 4,800-acre state park and onto the adjacent beach. Rates range from $36 to $59 for 90-minute to 2.5-hour rides. They wind through groves of sycamore and ancient redwood trees, beds of clover and fern, across the Big Sur River, and along the sandy Pacific shore. Rides depart at various times, with a special sunset ride that's magical.

Okey-doke, Icarus, I've got a few aerial adventures as well. Forty-five minutes away in Hollister (where a biker's bacchanal inspired *The Wild One*), **Bay Area Glider Rides** (Hollister Airport, 831/636-3799 or 888/467-6276, www.bayeareagliderrides.com) features sailplane rides from $99. The expensive one-hour trips ($300) will glide you back to Monterey and over the Pacific.

People who call you crazy for riding a motorcycle would bust a vessel if they saw you cavorting with the folks at **Skydive Monterey Bay** (3261 Imjin Rd., 831/384-3483, www.skydivemontereybay.com). After 15–20 minutes of training, you can take a tandem fall. If you're motivated, it offers accelerated free-fall and static-line training programs. Reservations are suggested for the $148 first jump. Pay in advance.

The draw at Laguna Seca, an unusual county park and campground hybrid about 20 minutes northeast of Carmel, is the **Laguna Seca Raceway** (831/648-5111 or 800/327-7322, www.laguna-seca.com). Only one motorcycle race is held here each year, but that may be enough to make it worth a visit. In July, the Superbike World Championship draws SBK and AMA riders to a super showdown.

Shopping

Even though there are stores within stores within stores in Carmel, you can have a good time just window-shopping and then dropping into at least two must-sees. **Wings America** (Dolores and 7th, 831/626-9464, www.wings america.com) presents aviation accent pieces, signed pictures, tropical shirts, aviation scarves, nearly full-size models, and aerodynamically dynamic accessories designed with an aviation theme. Buy a tile from space shuttle *Columbia* for $2,200. Buy several thousand and build your own spacecraft. The same person owns **Boatworks** (Ocean Ave. at Lincoln, 831/626-1870), which is nautical and nice. It sells cool clothes, great steamship posters, ship models, and smaller items. If you made the mistake of ordering the optional boat rack from your bike dealer, you can put it to use with a sleek $28,000 wooden canoe. Both are open 9:30 A.M.–6 P.M. daily.

Blue-Plate Specials

Katy's Place (Mission between 5th and 6th, 831/624-0199, www.katysplace-carmel.com) has one of the largest breakfast and lunch menus in Californi-yi-yay, even offering 10 varieties of eggs Benedict alone. Joining the lineup: blintzes, pancakes, hash, burritos, omelettes, French toast, buckwheat cakes, bacon, sausage, steak, eggs, cereal, bagels, and muffins.

In a cozy cottage with a fireplace, **Em Le's** (Pantiles Court Delores between 5th and 6th, 831/625-6780) is hot at breakfast with French toast, omelettes, pancakes, and fresh OJ (but not the kind that kills you). At lunch, the menu switches to burgers, sandwiches, soups, and salads. In addition to having a soda fountain, it serves beer and wine.

There's a fine Italian restaurant at **Il Fornaio** (Ocean Ave. at Monte Verde, 831/622-5115), but I recommend trying its adjacent bakery for a casual breakfast. This is where the locals go for conversation, coffee, and quiet. It's not fancy, but it smells great, and the rounded, draped room features a fireplace and newspapers.

You'll look like a local if you drop in for breakfast or lunch at the **Tuck Box** (Dolores between Ocean and 7th, 831/624-6365, www.tuckbox.com), a nonlinear fairytale cottage/breakfast nook. Even if you don't eat breakfast, you need to see this place. One of Comstock's original cottages, it seems it's somewhere beyond the looking glass. Here since 1940, it opens at 7 A.M.

Watering Holes

It's hard, but not impossible, while in Carmel to find a place to have a quiet brew and talk with friends. If there's a designated rider, Cannery Row nightspots in Monterey have replaced sardines as the main source of commerce.

A local tradition for food and drink since the '70s, **Jack London's Bar & Grill** (Dolores between 5th and 6th, 831/624-2336) is tucked inside Su Vecino Courtyard. The menu offerings of burgers, calamari, and Mexican dishes are just precursors to a pint in the outdoor setting. Kick back here and take advantage of the full bar, seven TVs, and 10 beers on tap.

Forge in the Forest (5th Ave. and Junipero, 831/624-2233) also has a cool outdoor dining area and an even cooler bar. If you travel in a pack (like the animal you are), set up your summit meeting at the brick-thick 15-foot table. The place is cluttered with antlers, skates, maps, and dozens of restroom signs, which you'll give thanks for after polishing off a Bass or Spaten Pils.

Shut-Eye

About 50 bed-and-breakfasts and hotels dot the peninsula. And even though Carmel reeks of wealth, rates are remarkably reasonable. If everything's booked in town, numerous chain hotels can be found in nearby Monterey.

Chain Drive
A, B, C, E, F, G, L, N, Q, S, U, CC, DD

Chain hotels are in town, or within 10 miles. See cross-reference guide featuring phone numbers and Web addresses on page 514.

Inn-dependence
Tops in my book (and it *is* my book) is **La Playa** (Camino Real and 8th, 831/624-6476 or 800/582-8900, www.laplayahotel.com, $175 and up), a large and gorgeous Mediterranean hotel a few blocks from the ocean. The building's design, character, gardens, pool, and flowers all combine to make this a spectacular choice. A second-floor terrace restaurant and five cottages make it even nicer. Also in the heart of the village, the **Normandy Inn** (Ocean Ave. and Monte Verde, 831/624-3825 or 800/343-3825, www.normandyinncarmel.com, $140 and up) is an excellent choice, with a collection of buildings and cottages connected by shaded courtyards. Large rooms that feature featherbeds and mini-fridges are pricier; some have fireplaces, and all include a continental breakfast. There's also a pool. Trust me, Carmel offers more than enough choices, but the **Seven Gables Inn** (555 Ocean View Blvd., 831/372-4341, www.pginns.com, $175–385), in appealing Pacific Grove, is another nice option. The classic Victorian may seem a far cry from what motorcycle travelers are looking for, but the view from the bay window may be enough to compensate. A full breakfast, four o'clock tea, and a park across the street round out the amenities.

Indulgences

It'll put a mighty dent in your wallet, and your kids may not receive an inheritance, but **Stonepine** (150 E. Carmel Valley Rd., 831/659-2245, www.stonepinecalifornia.com, $275 and up) may provide you with the most memorable evening of your ride. The rates zoom to $1,200 for a massive wing of the house, but that hasn't stopped guests like Bill Gates, Warren Buffett, and Arnold Schwarzenegger from dropping by for a long weekend. On this 330-

acre estate is a majestic 1920 French château home with grand rooms, a large fireplace, and private lounge. The opportunity to rest and dine in such luxury is thoroughly self-indulgent and satisfying. If this is a once-in-a-lifetime stay, you'll thank yourself when you're relaxing by the pool or quiet pond, worlds away from all sounds except those of nature. Bring binoculars, and you may spy Doris Day at her home about a half mile up the hill. Bring an extra helmet, and she may take a ride with you... *que sera, sera.*

Side Trip: Carmel to San Simeon

If you have a fear of heights, consider this ride a pleasant form of aversion therapy. As natural forces continue to pound boulders into pebbles, you'll rise above it all on this 112-mile route that scribbles along the Pacific Ocean. There's a reason why this is one of motorcycle travelers' most favored rides. It combines slow curves, sharp turns, and elevations magnified by the view of mountains and sea.

Watch for the sign south of Carmel: Curves ahead next 74 miles. But unlike the psychologically brutal Stinson Beach/Muir Beach/Tamalpais Valley ride, you can experience these slow curves and broad vistas without fear of death. In other words, this ride doesn't challenge your mortality; it affirms your vitality.

As you ride south, get used to miles of weaving curves that foreshadow upcoming jolts of adrenaline. Make sure your brakes are in working order, because you'll stop often to photograph the handsome cliffs and endless ocean—but watch for loose gravel and unpaved shoulders. This is a sustained pleasure that spikes about 30 miles into the run, when you take your bike across the Bixby Creek Bridge. Get those cameras ready, folks.

Construction on the "Rainbow" started in 1919 and took until 1937 to complete, but it was worth the wait. Thanks to some anonymous engineers and the fact that you wanted to get out of the house, you're riding 260 feet above sea level on a 718-foot race to the other side of the mountain.

After this jolt, the road is like a Chesterfield—it satisfies for the next 20 miles. When you arrive in Big Sur, you may start looking for the commercial district. You won't find it here, Wilma. Big Sur is a decentralized region, where residents enjoy the solitude and don't feel compelled to build city halls and shopping malls. It's why writers and artists come here, and it's where Henry Miller rediscovered his creative spark (while living in an abandoned convict labor camp).

The most active address on this stretch of road is **Nepenthe** (831/667-2345, www.nepenthebigsur.com), a stop as necessary for motorcyclists as breathing.

Hearst Castle

Hearst Castle (805/927-2020 for recorded information or 800/444-4445 for reservations, www.hearstcastle.org, $20) reminds me of my first apartment—except this place has 165 rooms, 30 fireplaces, and 127 acres of gardens. If not for Hearst Castle, San Simeon (pop. 18) would be nothing surrounded by nothing else. But after losing three runs for political office, William Randolph Hearst decided that his bid for immortality would come not through ballots, but through building.

Everything begins at the visitors center, where you buy a ticket for the mansion that includes the National Geographic IMAX movie *Hearst Castle, Building the Dream,* which describes how the castle was designed, built, and decorated. Then you'll board a bus for a long and winding ride to the mansion.

The scale here is off the scale: Guesthouses are the size of overwhelming mansions; the gardens are Edenic; the dining room is royal. A seductive and sensual outdoor pool holds 345,000 gallons of spring water, and a smaller indoor Roman pool contains a paltry 205,000 gallons. Furnishings are equally dazzling, and it's worth noting that Hearst had so much extra stuff stashed in a warehouse that he could have built five more castles. At least, that's what Bob the Tour Guide said.

The home is now owned by the citizens of California. Don't be jealous. They also own San Quentin.

Constructed around land and a log cabin owned by Orson Welles and Rita Hayworth, Nepenthe (Greek for "sorrow banisher") was purchased by the Fassetts and expanded by Rowan Maiden, a disciple of Frank Lloyd Wright. Today, it is a restaurant/overlook where lunch includes such fare as broiled swordfish sandwiches and the famous Ambrosia Burger; sunset dinners focus on steaks and fresh fish. Even if you're not hungry, you must stop here to feast on the view from the terrace, 800 feet above the shoreline. The surf sounds like muffled cannons from this height, yet another magical experience you'll add to your journey.

A quarter mile south, the **Henry Miller Library** is more of an artists' village than a library, but people still stop. Beyond this, PCH gets back into the rugged and exhilarating coastline you've come to love. Within miles, you'll be riding past different environments—ocean, desert, pine forests—each constantly interchanging.

There are few places in the nation more suited to your purpose. Take advantage of turnouts, where you can just park it and watch the water swallow rocks the size of mountains and pound the hell out of monoliths. In some spots, the water seems as clear as the Caribbean, and a few miles later, the coastline disappears into fog.

As you ride south, you'll experience a sense of contentment, knowing that you're six feet closer to the ocean than those poor bastards in the oncoming lane. To reward yourself for this insight, when you reach the town of Gorda, buy yourself a sodee pop at the service station/general store.

When you resume the run, the rises are subtle. At times, the ocean appears without warning, 200 feet down a cliff. Be careful—you'll be contending with riders and drivers who see this as a test track.

The final miles to **Hearst Castle** lose their scenic punch, but I promise that you will look back on this run and agree that this—like your ride across America—was everything you expected it to be. It was dangerous within limits, vast beyond measure, and beautiful beyond description.

Resources for Riders

Pacific Coast Run

California Travel Information
California Association of Bed & Breakfast Inns—www.cabbi.com
California Division of Tourism—916/444-4429 or 800/862-2543,
   www.gocalif.ca.gov
California Road Conditions—916/445-7623 or 800/427-7623
California Road and Weather Information—916/979-3051
California State Parks—916/653-6995, www.parks.ca.gov

Local and Regional Information
Calistoga Chamber of Commerce—707/942-6333 or 866-306-5588,
   www.calistogachamber.com
Carmel Visitors Center—831/624-2522 or 800/550-4333,
   www.carmelcalifornia.org
Monterey Peninsula Visitors Bureau—831/649-1770 or 888/221-1010,
   www.montereyinfo.org
Napa Valley Visitors Bureau—707/226-7459, www.napavalley.com
Pacific Grove Chamber of Commerce—831/373-3304 or 800/656-6650,
   www.pacificgrove.org
Sausalito Chamber of Commerce—415/331-7262, www.sausalito.org
Sonoma County Visitors Bureau—707/996-1090,
   www.sonomacounty.com

California Motorcycle Shops
BMW of San Francisco—1675 Howard St., San Francisco, 415/863-9000,
   www.bmwsf.com
Cycle Stop Honda—511 Abbott St., Salinas, 831/394-8889
Dudley Perkins Harley-Davidson—66 Page St., San Francisco, 415/703-
   9494, www.dpchd.com
Golden Gate Cycles—1540 Pine St., San Francisco, 415/771-4535,
   www.goldengatecycles.com

Golden Gate Harley-Davidson/Buell—7077 Redwood Blvd., Novato, 415/878-4988, www.gghd.com

Jim & Jim's Yamaha—910 Santa Rosa Ave., Santa Rosa, 707/545-1672, www.jjyamaha.com

Magri Motorcycles—1220 Pennsylvania Ave., San Francisco, 415/285-6735

Monterey Peninsula Powersports—1020 Auto Center Pkwy., Seaside, 831/899-7433, www.montereypowersports.com

North Bay Motorsports—2875 Santa Rosa Ave., Santa Rosa, 707/542-5355, www.northbaymotorsports.com

Santa Rosa BMW—800 American Way, Windsor 707/838-9100, www.santarosabmw.com

Santa Rosa Vee Twin—1240 Petaluma Hill Rd., Santa Rosa, 707/523-9696, www.santarosaveetwin.com

Warren's Harley-Davidson—333 N. Main St., Salinas, 831/424-1909, www.warrenshd.com

Yamaha of Salinas—330 Kings St., Salinas, 831/422-3232

Appendix

Top Motorcycle Websites

Great American Motorcycle Tours
www.motorcycleamerica.com
Partner site for this book, with abridged
ride descriptions, photographs, and
links.

Moto-Directory
www.moto-directory.com
Perhaps the best bike site, with roughly
10,000 links to events, rallies, magazines, videos, tours, stolen bike reports,
riding clubs, rental operators, dealers,
and salvage yards.

Motorcycle Roads
www.motorcycleroads.us
Super site with recommendations from
riders on popular and seldom traveled roads across America, viewable
state by state. Links for submitting
your favorites and finding travel resources.

Motorcycle Shopper
www.motorcycleshopper.com
Quick access to clubs, salvage yards, new
and used bikes, parts and shipping,
tours, and feature articles.

Motorcycle-USA
www.motorcycle-usa.com
News, product reviews, bike tests,
photo galleries, classifieds, message
boards, and ride ratings.

*Ronnie Cramer's Motorcycle
Web Index*
http://sepnet.com/cycle
7,500-plus links to manufacturers,
dealers, clothing, racing, tours, and
more.

Trader Online
www.cycletrader.com
The online version of the popular *Trader*
magazines. Search by model, size, year,
price, location, and so on.

Other Motorcycle Sites

American Motorcycle Network
www.americanmotor.com
News and more than 1,000 articles on
events, rallies, and manufacturers.

Motorcycle Accessories Warehouse
800/241-2222
www.accwhse.com
Parts, supplies, and thousands of links
to clothes and closeouts, from goggles
to tank covers.

Motorcycle Online
www.motorcycle.com
Digital motorcycle magazine with
bikes, products, reviews, videos,
clubs, events, how-tos, rides, classifieds, financing, and chats.

Rider Magazine
www.riderreport.com
Links to *Rider, American Rider, Woman Rider,* and *Cruising Rider* magazines and archives.

Sport-Touring
www.sport-touring.net
Central information center for the art of motorcycle touring, with articles, photos, merchandise, accessories, and riders' reviews, reports, and recommendation on great trips.

Selected Manufacturers
Most manufacturers' sites will lead to showrooms, accessories, clothing, riders clubs, FAQs, dealers, and riding products.

BMW
800/831-1117
www.bmwmotorcycles.com

Buell
www.buell.com

Ducati
www.ducati.com

Harley-Davidson
800/CLUB-HOG (800/258-2464)
www.harley-davidson.com

Honda
310/532-9811 or 866/784-1870
www.hondamotorcycle.com

Kawasaki
800/661-7433
www.kawasaki.com

Moto Guzzi
www.motoguzzi.it

Suzuki
800/828-7433
www.suzukicycles.com

Triumph
770/631-9500
www.triumph.co.uk

Victory
www.victory-usa.com

Yamaha
800/889-2624
www.yamaha-motor.com

Selected Motorcycle Organizations
American Motorcyclist Association
800/AMA-JOIN (800/262-5646)
www.ama-cycle.org
If you belong to one motorcycling organization, make it the AMA. The association sponsors thousands of sanctioned events and provides a monthly magazine, trip routing, hotel discounts, and club information for approximately 250,000 members.

Motorcycle Events Association
605/224-9999 or 800/675-4656
www.motorcycleevents.com
Provides information on Daytona, Sturgis, Laconia, Hollister, and other major rallies, as well as charity rides and motorcycle shows.

Motorcycle Industry Council
714/727-4211 or 800/833-3995
www.motorcycles.org
Marketing clearinghouse for motorcycle-related news items and consumer information.

Motorcycle Product News
608/249-0186
www.mpnmag.com
Lists products, distributors, manufacturers, parts, and accessories; primarily used by dealers and rental operators. Password required.

Motorcycle Riders Foundation
202/546-0983 or
800/MRF-JOIN (800/673-5646)
www.mrf.org
Lobbying group for riders' rights, with links.

Motorcycle Safety Foundation
800/446-9227
www.msf-usa.org
Offers safe riding courses throughout the United States; participation can lower your insurance rates. Also features information on rider training and industry contacts.

Selected Riding Clubs
Visit www.motorcycle.com/mo/clubs .html for state-by-state listings.

American Gold Wing Association
www.agwa.com

Blue Knights
207/947-4600 or 877/254-5362
www.blueknights.org
International organization of retired law enforcement officers, with 19,000 members in 541 chapters in 24 countries.

BMW Motorcycle Owners of America
636/394-7277
www.bmwmoa.org

Christian Motorcyclists Association
870/389-6196
www.cmausa.org

Gold Wing Road Riders Association
623/581-2500 or 800/843-9460
www.gwrra.org

Harley Owners Group
800/258-2464
www.hog.com

Honda Riders Club of America
800/847-4722
www.hrca.honda.com

Motorcycle Clubs & Associations
www.moto-directory.com/clubs.asp

Riders of Kawasaki
877/765-2582
www.kawasaki.com

Women on Wheels
800/322-1969
www.womenonwheels.org
Founded in 1982, WOW has more than 75 chapters with more than 3,500 female members.

Selected Rallies

Each year across the country, there are figuratively more than a million rallies of all shapes and sizes. Here are links to some of the largest—visit their websites for upcoming dates. Most rally sites include information on registration, rides, vendors, lodging, histories, and entertainment.

Americade Motorcycle Rally
518/798-7888
www.tourexpo.com
Lake George, New York

Bike Week and Biketoberfest
386/255-0981
www.officialbikeweek.com
Daytona Beach, Florida

Hollister Independence Rally
831/634-0777
www.hollisterrally.com
Hollister, California

Honda Hoot
800/347-1289
www.hondahoot.com
Knoxville, Tennessee

Laconia Rally
603/366-2000
www.laconiamcweek.com
Laconia, New Hampshire

Sturgis Rally and Races
605/720-0800
www.sturgismotorcyclerally.com
Sturgis, South Dakota

Selected National Tour Operators

Adventure Cycle Tours
763/449-4908
www.winternet.com/~act
Offers 16 tours of the Midwest and Canada.

America Harley Tours
310/487-1047
www.ridefree.com
Rides across the West on Harley-Davidsons. Insurance, food, lodging, and road support provided.

Arkansas Cycle Touring and Training
479/665-2202
www.arkansascycle.com
Rides through the Ozarks.

Bob Duffey's Motorcycle & ATV Tours
505/523-1700
www.zianet.com/bobduffey
Ride your own bike on guided tours of southwestern New Mexico.

Freedom Tours
303/823-5731
www.twisty-roads.com
Tours range from a three-day weekend to an eight-day Colorado Rockies run to a 15-day marathon.

Rebel USA Tours
858/292-6200
www.rebelusa.com
Specializes in Harley adventure tours of Baja, national parks, Pacific Coast Highway.

Ride the Dream
505/660-3684
www.ridethedream.com
Tours of the Southwest on Harleys.

Selected National Rental Companies
California Motorcycle Rentals
858/456-9577
www.calif-motorcyclerental.com
Specializes in BMWs; located in La Jolla.

EagleRider Motorcycle Rental
310/536-6777 or 888/900-9901
www.eaglerider.com
Nationwide service renting fully equipped Road Kings, Softails, Fat Boys, and Electra Glides. Locations in America, Mexico, and Europe. Also conducts tours.

Harley Motorcycle Rental
415/456-9910 or 888/812-9253
www.harleymc.com
Located in San Rafael, California.

Motorcycle Rental Resource Page
www.harleys.com/mrrp.html
Rental operators listed by state.

Route 66 Riders Motorcycle Rentals
310/578-0112 or 888/434-4473
www.route66riders.com

Miscellaneous Travel Information
Campground Reservations
877/444-6777
www.reserveusa.com
A one-call-books-all national company that handles reservations for 45,000 campsites at 1,700 national forest campgrounds across America. Does not include national or state parks.

Historic Hotels of America
800/678-8946
www.historichotels.org
Affiliated with the National Trust for Historic Preservation, HHA is a diverse collection of uniquely American lodgings, from rustic inns to elegant hotels. Rates at these member properties may be on the high end, but if you split the costs, you may do all right.

Kampgrounds of America (KOA)
www.koa.com
Information on more than 500 campgrounds nationwide.

Mad Maps
www.madmaps.com
Superb, informative motorcycle maps custom-designed to highlight scenic

roads and popular routes across the country.

MapQuest
www.mapquest.com
Trip planning, route, and mileage information.

National Forest Service
www.fs.fed.us
Links to national forests and campgrounds.

National Park Foundation
888/467-2757
www.nationalparks.org
Partner site of America's national parks, designed to introduce you to the parks and assist in trip planning.

National Park Service
www.nps.gov
Central point for links to parks and recreation, history and culture, nature, science, interpretation, and education.

National Parks Reservations
800/436-7275
http://reservations.nps.gov

Road Conditions
www.usroadconditions.com
Links to information on road conditions in every state.

Road Images
www.pashnit.com
Great road photographs and expert route suggestions.

Road Trip USA
www.roadtripusa.com
Eleven cross-country riding routes to get you off the beaten path and onto preinterstate roads.

Scenic Byways
www.byways.org
A must-visit site detailing thousands of miles of scenic byways and back roads across the nation. Also offers links for trip planning and personal journals.

Sport Fishing Information
800/ASK-FISH (800/275-3474)

State Motorcycle and Helmet Laws
www.amadirectlink.com/legisltn/laws.asp

State and National Park Links
www.llbean.com/parksearch

Travel Information
www.officialtravelguide.com
All-purpose information site with links to state and local convention bureaus that offer info and assistance with lodging, dining, and attractions.

Weather Channel
www.weather.com

Yahoo! Travel
www.yahoo.com/recreation/travel
Starting point for links to books, maps, restaurants, and lodging.

Useful Information

National Parks Pass
Each year, America's National Parks are visited more than 265 million times, a figure totaling more fans and guests than visit NFL games, Disney parks, and Universal Studios attractions combined. If you plan to visit more than one national park, invest in the National Parks Pass. For $50, the pass will provide admission to any national park for a full year. The Golden Eagle Pass offers the same benefits, plus admission to many fee areas of the U.S. Forest Service. How far will your 50 bucks go? As far as 80.7 million acres of park land at 379 national parks, from Acadia in Maine to Zion in Utah, all cared for and explained by more than 20,000 rangers, archaeologists, historians, biologists, architects, laborers, and gardeners.

Food Faves
One of my favorite vocations while riding is finding great roadside diners along the highway or in a village. Two of my favorite American writers are Jane and Michael Stern, who, in addition to writing the classic *Elvis World,* wrote *Eat Your Way Across the USA: 500 Diners, Lobster Shacks, Buffets, Pie Palaces, and Other All-American Eateries.* While my book can lead you to a handful of restaurants, their book is a buffet of great American greasy spoons, hash houses, doughnut shops, cafeterias, and small-town cafés.

Offbeat USA
If your motivation to ride is partially fueled by the chance discovery of kitsch Americana, check out www.roadsideamerica.com. This site is the online guide to offbeat tourist attractions, and it may provide you with some side-trip ideas when you're in the vicinity of places like the Zippo Lighter Visitors Center in Bradford, PA, or the giant advertising statues that still plug businesses across the United States.

Selecting an Organized Tour
As the popularity of motorcycles grows, so does the proliferation of motorcycle tour operators. If you decide to ride on a prearranged trip, there are two constants you'll encounter: You will need a major credit card and a motorcycle endorsement on your license. There are also several variables. For instance, you may or may not need to bring your own bike, helmet, or rain gear.

With these variances, play it smart by asking the "stupid" questions. Ask who covers specific expenses: lodging, meals, tolls, fuel, laundry, tips, insurance. What type of lodging can you expect? Is it a flophouse, campground, or inn? Private bath? Shared rooms? Carrying a passenger will cost extra—how much? As you sift through these questions, also ask if you'll be allowed to break away from the group and meet them later. Is there a guide? A support vehicle? A trained mechanic? Does the ride include overnights, or do you return to the same city each evening?

Make sure that if your ride is cancelled because of inclement weather, your deposit will be refunded (you may want to safeguard your investment by taking out traveler's cancellation insurance).

Chain Hotel Guide

A) *Best Western*
800/528-1234
www.bestwestern.com

B) *Clarion*
800/252-7466
www.choicehotels.com

C) *Comfort Inn*
800/221-2222
www.choicehotels.com

D) *Courtyard by Marriott*
800/321-2211
www.marriott.com

E) *Days Inn*
800/329-7466
www.daysinn.com

F) *Doubletree*
800/222-8733
www.doubletree.com

G) *Econo Lodge*
800/553-2666
www.choicehotels.com

H) *Embassy Suites*
800/362-2779
www.embassy-suites.com

I) *Fairfield Inn*
800/228-2800
www.marriott.com

J) *Hampton Inns*
800/426-7866
www.hampton-inn.com

K) *Hilton*
800/445-8667
www.hilton.com

L) *Holiday Inn*
800/Holiday
(800/465-4329)
www.holiday-inn.com

M) *Howard Johnson*
800/446-4656
www.hojo.com

N) *Hyatt*
800/233-1234
www.hyatt.com

O) *Knights Inn*
800/843-5644
www.knightsinn.com

P) *La Quinta*
800/687-6667
www.laquinta.com

Q) *Motel 6*
800/466-8356
www.motel6.com

R) *Omni Hotels*
800/843-6664
www.omnihotels.com

S) *Quality Inn*
800/228-5151
www.choicehotels.com

T) *Radisson*
800/333-3333
www.radisson.com

U) *Ramada*
800/272-6232
www.ramada.com

V) *Red Carpet Inn*
800/251-1962
www.reservahost.com

W) *Red Roof Inn*
800/843-7663
www.redroof.com

X) *Residence Inn*
800/331-3131
www.mariott.com

Y) *Rodeway*
800/228-2000
www.hotelchoice.com

Z) *Scottish Inns*
800/251-1962
www.reservahost.com

AA) *Sheraton*
800/325-3535
www.sheraton.com

BB) *Sleep Inn*
800/627-5337
www.hotelchoice.com

CC) *Super 8*
800/800-8000
www.super8.com

DD) *Travelodge*
800/578-7878
www.travelodge.com

Index

Accommodations Index

Restaurant Index

Goolrick's: 135
Herr Tavern: 122
J. Bryan's Tap Room: 135
Johnson's Charcoal Beef House: 130
Kings Court Tavern: 130
Leesburg Restaurant: 130
Lincoln Diner: 121
Mighty Midget Kitchen: 130
Olivia's: 121
Plaza Restaurant: 121
The Pub & Restaurant: 122
Spring House Tavern: 122
Tuscarora Mill: 130
2400 Diner: 135

Blue Ridge Parkway Run
Blowing Rock Cafe: 149
Cheeseburgers Grill and Paradise Bar:
  149
Cypress Cellar: 156
Days Gone By: 156
Expressions: 156
Hannah Flannagan's Pub: 157
Knight's Restaurant: 149
Leon's Burger Express: 142
Pandowdy's Restaurant: 144
Snappy Lunch: 144
Speckled Trout Cafe: 149

Smoky Mountains Run
Bennett's: 171
Bistro 105: 164
Cranberry Thistle: 164
Harmony Grocery Store: 164
Howard's Restaurant: 172
Kemosabe's Road House: 164
Main Street Café: 164
Nick and Nate's: 176
O'Malleys on Main: 177
Pizza Parlor: 164
Smoky Mountains Restaurant: 172
Whitman's Bakery: 176
Wildfire: 176

Georgia Hills Run
Back Porch Oyster Bar: 185
Big Daddy's American Tavern: 192
Buster's: 185
Caruso's: 185
Crimson Moon: 185
Fireside Restaurant: 195
Front Porch: 184
Hofbrau Riverfront Hotel: 192
Mountain Home Café: 184
Nacoochee Grill: 191
Scooter's Nightclub: 192
Smith House: 184
Troll Tavern: 191
Wylie's: 185

Southern Comfort Run
A1A Aleworks: 205
Churchill's Pub: 212
Clary's Cafe: 212
Crab Shack: 211
The Griffon: 218
Gypsy Cab Company: 204
Hyman's: 217
Kevin Barry's Pub: 212
The Lady & Sons: 211
Mrs. Wilkes' Dining Room: 211
O.C. White's: 205
Olde Pink House: 212
Pier Restaurant: 201
Scarlett O'Hara's: 205
Six Pence Pub: 212
Sticky Fingers: 218
Tommy Condon's: 218
Vinnie Van Go-Gos: 210

Tropical Paradise Run
The Bull: 237
11th Street Diner: 227
Farmer's Market Restaurant: 229
Green Parrot Bar: 237
Half Shell Raw Bar: 236
Hog's Breath Saloon: 237
Joe's Stone Crab Restaurant: 227

La Conner Seafood and Prime Rib
  House: 430
Monroe: 427
Silverwater Cafe: 435
Sirens: 435
Upstage: 435
Waterfront Pizza: 435
Waterstreet Brewing: 435

Oregon's Best Run
Beachcomber Tavern: 453
Bill's Tavern and Brewhouse: 443
Bronco Billy's Ranch Grill: 459
Firehouse Restaurant: 453
Fultano's Pizza: 443
The Gallery: 459
Harbick's Country Store: 456
The Lumberyard: 443
Mo's: 453
Morgan's Country Kitchen: 453
Pig 'N Pancake: 443
Soba: 459
Tillamook Cheese Factory: 447
Warren House: 443–444
Waterfront Depot: 453

Las Vegas–Yosemite Run
Ahwahnee: 478
Cutthroat Saloon: 480

Harley-Davidson Cafe: 467
High Sierra Cafe: 473
Jake's Saloon: 473
Lee Vining: 475
Mt. Whitney Restaurant: 473
The Strip: 467

Pacific Coast Run
Brannan's Grill: 487
Bridgeway Cafe: 491
Café Sarafornia: 487
Calistoga Inn: 488
Corners Cafe and Saloon: 487
Em Le's: 499
Forge in the Forest: 499
Horizons: 492
Hydro Bar and Grill: 488
Il Fornaio: 499
Jack London's Bar and Grill: 499
Katy's Place: 499
Nepenthe: 501–502
No-Name Bar: 492
Pacifico: 487
Paterson's: 492
Sausalito: 490
Stomp: 488
Susie's: 487
Tuck Box: 499

Acknowledgments

Although I could have easily written this book without anyone's assistance, my publisher wouldn't extend the deadline until 2038. Therefore, I owe a great deal of gratitude to hundreds of people across the country. I would like to acknowledge the assistance of the following folks, listed in order of their favorite Beatle.

John Lennon: John McKechnie, Bud McKechnie, Ian McKechnie, all McKechnies everywhere, Peter Fonda, Cassandra Conyers, Dianna Delling, Donna Galassi, Peg Goldstein, Ken Thompson, Jessica Icenhour, Fred Good, Jana Greenbaum, Chuck Haralson, Ken Grimsley, Lisa Richardson, Jeri Riggs, Lynn Berry, Matt Bolas, Carrie Clark, Trey Hines, Tony Hayden, Chris Jones, Haley Gingles, Greg Lasiewski, Jan Plessner, Robyn McPeters, Tim Buche, Cheryl Smith, Trish Taylor, Hal Williams, Walter Yeldell, Emily Raabe, Cara O'Donnell, Alan Rosenzweig, Barbara Ashley, Janet Dutson, Mary Bennoch, Nick Noyes, Jo Sabel Courtney, John Formichella, Anne Marie Basher, Nancy Arena, Ruth Parsons, Stacey Fox, Philip Magaldi, Charles Hardin, Melody Heltman, Erika Backus, Rich Wittish, Chris Nobles, Melina Martinez, Michelle Revuelta, Josie Gulliksen, Emy Bullard Wilkinson, Beverly Gianna, Jon Jarosh, George Milos, Jezal McNeil, Phil Lampert, Kelly Barbello, Kim Latrielle, Judy Siring, Jay Humphries, Anne Barney, Sandy Smith, Kim Cobb, Tessie Shirwakawa, Aimee Grove, Melanie Ryan, Steve Lewis, Jan Mellor, Jennifer Wess, Kathy Lambert, Dwayne Cassidy, Ron Terry, Erika Yowell, Kathleen New, Scott Gediman, Carol Jones, Sue Mauro, Beth Culbertson, Ron Gardner, Ellen Gillespie, Timothy James Trifeletti .…

Paul McCartney: Jean James, Lin Lee, Susan Albrecht, Patricia Kiderlen, Lynn Dyer, Judith Swain, Suzanne Elder, Phyllis Reller, Karen Baker, Gwen Peterson, Tony Fortier, Ken McNenny, Susan Sullivan, Pepper Massey-Swan, Karen Connelly, Liz Porter, Steve Lewis, Shelly Clark, Jenny Stacy, Susan Belanski, Jack Dunlavy, Phillip Magdali Jr., Paula Tirrito, Steven Skavroneck, Valerie Parker, Joel Frey, Lenore Barkley, Jan Osterman, Howard Gray, Christine DeCuir, Sandy Tucker, Don Sparks, DeRoy Jenson, Ed and Minna Williams, Rennie Ross, Didi Bushnell, Jim Pelletier, Stan Corneil, Chris Mackey, Amy Ballenger, Jeff Ehoodin, Jeff Webster, Nina Kelly, Todd Morgan, Dave Blanford, Nancy Borino, Tom Lyons, Krista Elias, Shannon Mackie-Albert, Rachel Keating, Maureen Oltrogge, Mike Finney, Julia Scott, Sue Bland, Natasha Johnston, Laura Simoes, Wyndham Lewis, Dennis Cianci, Marjie Wright, Karen Hamill, Sue Ellen Peck, Tom Hash, Rick Gunn .…

George Harrison: Rick Wilder, Ken Crouse, Donna Bonnefin, Pettit Gilwee, Keith Walklet, Amy Herzog, Susan Carvalho, Kathy Langley, Kirk Komick, Jennifer Franklin, Mike Pitel, Jody Bernard, Sarah Pitcher, Nancy Brockman, Paul Schreiner, Bev Owens, Billy Dodd, Heather Deville, Joel Howard, Annie Kuehls, Bob and Paula Glass, Troy Duvall, Jeff Lupo, John and Diane Sheiry, Croft Long, Mel Moore, Mark Kayser, Lisa Umiker, Rich Gates, Ray Towells, Julie Smith, Carrie Wilkinson-Tuma, Mike Dorn, Wendy Haase, Jan Dorfler, Mary Cochran, Traci Varner, Dirk Oldenburg, Mark Reese of American Suzuki Motor Corporation, Ty van Hooydonk, Scott Heath, Linda Adams ....

Ringo Starr: Trevor and Regina Aldhurst, Rosemary and Fabrizio Chiarello, Frank and Mary Newton, Mary Beth Hutchinson, Anna Maria Dalton, Karen Hedelt, Emily Case, Pauli Galin, Elmer Thomas, Nancy and Tom Blackford, Karen Suffredini, Mike McGuinn, Susan Williams, Virginia Mure, Ron and Sue Ramage, Leslie Prevish and Joe Hice ....

Pete Best: Every engineer, surveyor, road crew, and chain gang that helped build America's beautiful back roads.

About the Author

© LEE MCKEE

Blessed with the chiseled features of a matinee idol, writer/rider Gary McKechnie is also a Florida native, a fourth-generation motorcyclist, a professional speaker, founder of the Charles Kuralt Travel Society, and is recognized around the world as the Emperor of Masculinity. *Great American Motorcycle Tours* is the winner of the Benjamin Franklin Gold Award and the Lowell Thomas Silver Award. Gary lives in Mount Dora, Florida.